MW01629144

Rrose is a Rrose is a Rrose

GENDER PERFORMANCE IN PHOTOGRAPHY

Rrose is a Rrose is a Rrose

GENDER PERFORMANCE IN PHOTOGRAPHY

JENNIFER BLESSING

with contributions by

JUDITH HALBERSTAM

LYLE ASHTON HARRIS

NANCY SPECTOR

CAROLE-ANNE TYLER

SARAH WILSON

GUGGENHEIM MUSEUM

Rrose is a Rrose is a Rrose:
Gender Performance in Photography
Organized by Jennifer Blessing

Solomon R. Guggenheim Museum, New York
January 17–April 27, 1997

This exhibition is supported in part by
the National Endowment for the Arts

ISBN 0-8109-6901-7 (hardcover)
ISBN 0-89207-185-0 (softcover)

Guggenheim Museum Publications
1071 Fifth Avenue
New York, New York 10128

Hardcover edition distributed by
Harry N. Abrams, Inc.
100 Fifth Avenue
New York, New York 10011

Designed by Bethany Johns Design, New York

Printed in Italy by Sfera

front cover:
Claude Cahun
Self-Portrait, ca. 1928
Gelatin-silver print,
11 13/16 x 9 3/8 inches (30 x 23.8 cm)
Musée des Beaux Arts de Nantes

back cover:
Nan Goldin
Jimmy Paulette and Tabboo! in the bathroom, NYC, 1991
Cibachrome print,
30 x 40 inches (76.2 x 101.6 cm)
Courtesy of the artist and
Matthew Marks Gallery, New York

Contents

Lenders to the Exhibition

Timothy Baum, New York
Cecil Beaton Archive, Sotheby's London
Galerie Berggruen, Paris
Patrick Breen
Galerie Bugdahn und Kaimer, Düsseldorf
Robert C. Conn, California
The Detroit Institute of Arts
Deutsche Bank AG, Frankfurt
William S. Ehrlich and Ruth Lloyds
Alexandra Epps
M. Anthony and Anne E. Fisher
Fonds Albert-Birot, Paris
Barry Friedman Ltd., New York
Nan Goldin
Howard Greenberg Gallery, New York
Ronnie and Samuel Heyman, New York
Jane B. Holzer
Vivian Horan
Jedermann Collection, N. A.
Joan and Gerald Kimmelman
Kinsey Institute for Research in Sex, Gender, and Reproduction, Inc., Bloomington, Ind.
Margo Leavin Gallery, West Hollywood
Los Angeles County Museum of Art
Christian Marclay
Matthew Marks Gallery, New York
Richard and Ronay Menschel
Carol and Paul Meringoff
Annette Messager
The Metropolitan Museum of Art
Robert Miller Gallery, New York
Musée d'Art Moderne de la Ville de Paris
Musée des Beaux-Arts de Nantes
Musée National d'Art Moderne, Centre Georges Pompidou, Paris
The Museum of Modern Art, New York
National Portrait Gallery, London
Daniel Newburg
Galerie Nierendorf, Berlin
Michael James O'Brien
Parti Communiste Français, Paris
The Philadelphia Museum of Art
REFCO Group, Ltd.
Regen Projects, Los Angeles
G. Rossi, Milan
The Royal Photographic Society, Bath
Beverly and Harris Schoenfeld
Michael Senft, New York
Fisher Stevens
Jack Tilton Gallery, New York
Ubu Gallery, New York
Wooster Gardens, New York

Three lenders who wish to remain anonymous

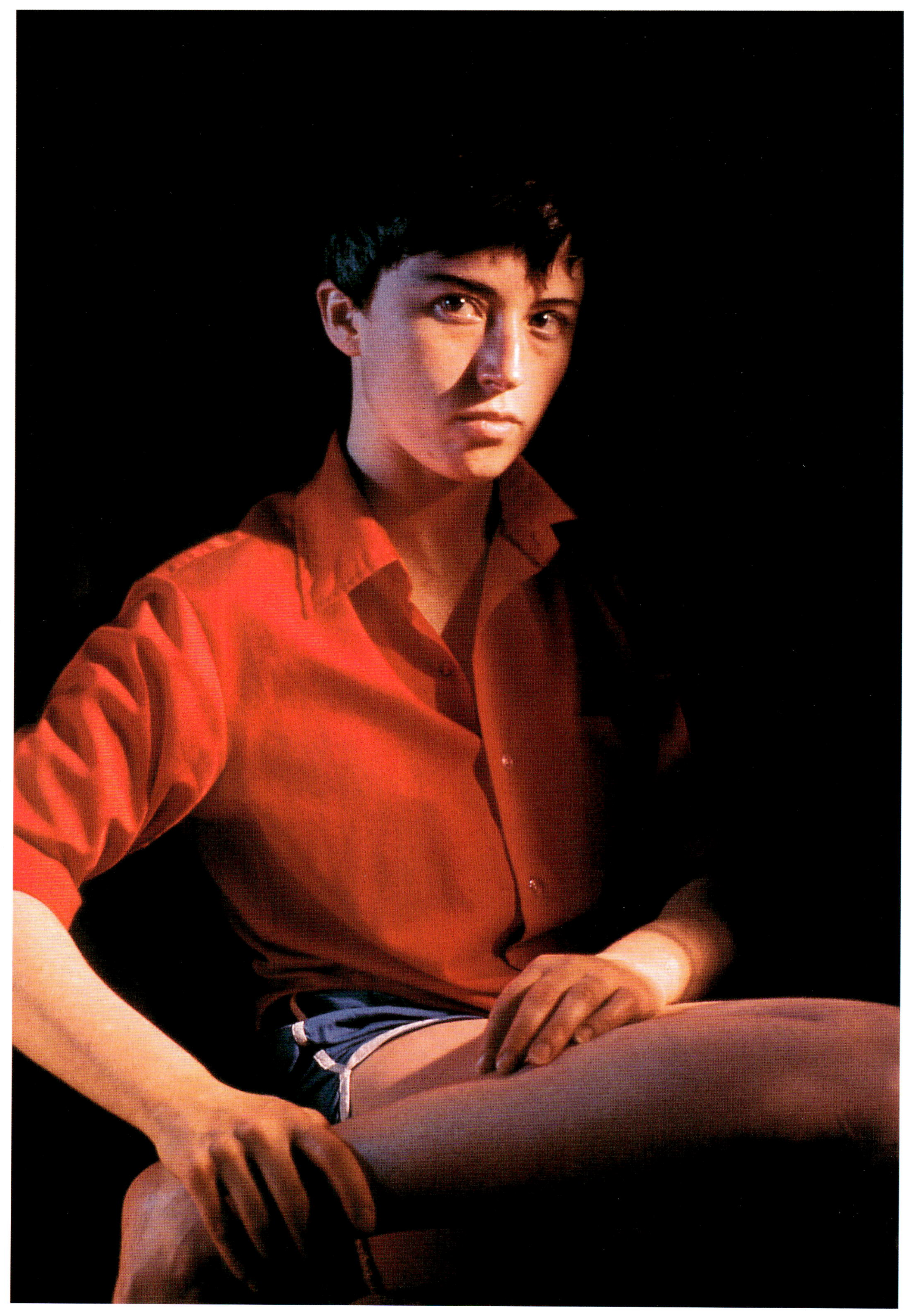

Cindy Sherman
Untitled, #112, 1982
Color photograph, 45 ½ x 30 inches (114.9 x 76.2 cm), ed. 1/10
REFCO Group, Ltd.

J'aime, je n'aime pas ~ **I like, I don't like**

I like: salad, cinnamon, cheese, pimento, marzipan, the smell of new-cut hay (why doesn't someone with a "nose" make such a perfume), roses, peonies, lavender, champagne, loosely held political convictions, Glenn Gould, too-cold beer, flat pillows, toast, Havana cigars, Handel, slow walks, pears, white peaches, cherries, colors, watches, all kinds of writing pens, desserts, unrefined salt, realistic novels, the piano, coffee, Pollock, Twombly, all romantic music, Sartre, Brecht, Verne, Fourier, Eisenstein, trains, Médoc wine, having change, *Bouvard and Pécuchet*, walking in sandals on the lanes of southwest France, the bend of the Adour seen from Doctor L.'s house, the Marx Brothers, the mountains at seven in the morning leaving Salamanca, etc.

I don't like: white Pomeranians, women in slacks, geraniums, strawberries, the harpsichord, Miró, tautologies, animated cartoons, Arthur Rubinstein, villas, the afternoon, Satie, Bartók, Vivaldi, telephoning, children's choruses, Chopin's concertos, Burgundian branles and Renaissance dances, the organ, Marc-Antoine Charpentier, his trumpets and kettledrums, the politico-sexual, scenes, initiatives, fidelity, spontaneity, evenings with people I don't know, etc.

I like, I don't like: this is of no importance to anyone; this, apparently, has no meaning. And yet all this means: *my body is not the same as yours.* Hence, in this anarchic foam of tastes and distastes, a kind of listless blur, gradually appears the figure of a bodily enigma, requiring complicity or irritation. Here begins the intimidation of the body, which obliges others to endure me *liberally*, to remain silent and polite confronted by pleasures or rejections which they do not share.

(A fly bothers me, I kill it: you kill what bothers you. If I had not killed the fly, it would have been *out of pure liberalism:* I am liberal in order not to be a killer.)

—ROLAND BARTHES

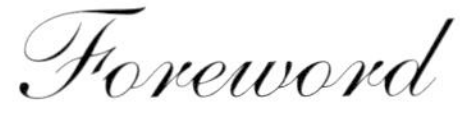

Foreword

THOMAS KRENS

An important milestone in the history of the Guggenheim Museum was reached in 1993, when the Robert Mapplethorpe Foundation made a combined gift of a significant body of photographs and a supporting grant for the future acquisition of Modern and contemporary photography. The gift established photography as a significant part of the Guggenheim's permanent collection, thus offering an additional medium to further the Guggenheim's mission of interpreting the art of this century. In the past few years, the museum has offered a rich selection of photography exhibitions including monographic shows on Robert Mapplethorpe and Joel-Peter Witkin; photography sections within the context of other exhibitions (*The Italian Metamorphosis, 1943–1968*; *Joseph Albers: Glass, Color, and Light*; and *In/sight: African Photographers, 1940 to the Present*); as well as exhibitions organized by other institutions, such as *Photography in Contemporary German Art* (Walker Art Center); *Women on the Edge: Twenty Photographers in Europe, 1919–1939* (J. Paul Getty Museum); and *Dieter Appelt* (Art Institute of Chicago).

As we reach the end of this century, more exhibitions that attempt to synthesize the art and issues of the twentieth century are being organized. The Guggenheim is committed to approaching art as an international and transhistorical phenomenon. The institution has always been strongly linked to Europe; now, responding to changes in contemporary society brought about through advances in transportation and telecommunications, its orientation has become global. *Rrose is a Rrose is a Rrose: Gender Performance in Photography* is the Guggenheim Museum's first photography exhibition to be based on premises that are thematic and theoretical rather than monographic or strictly historical. It traces an issue across the course of the twentieth century and examines its development in several countries.

We are most grateful to the National Endowment for the Arts, a Federal agency, for its early support of *Rrose is a Rrose is a Rrose*. Without its imprimatur, it is unlikely that the research for this project could have been undertaken. Through this support, our audience will be permitted to enjoy the art of many artists whose work has not previously been exhibited at the museum and, in some cases, has never before been shown in the United States.

Guggenheim Museum Assistant Curator Jennifer Blessing proposed this exhibition several years ago. I want to thank her for suggesting this innovative show, and for her diligence and commitment in seeing it through to its splendid realization.

And, finally, this exhibition would not be possible without the artists who created the works and the lenders who were so considerate as to lend them. My gratitude goes to all of the individuals and institutions who so generously contributed to the success of this project.

Acknowledgments

JENNIFER BLESSING

If I have seen further it is by standing on the shoulders of Giants.

— ISAAC NEWTON

This exhibition is the fruit of encouragement from colleagues, without which I might not have pursued the topic. I am grateful to have had the opportunity to present my initial ideas in graduate seminars conducted by Linda Nochlin and Robert Lubar at the Institute of Fine Arts, New York University. In 1993, Guggenheim Museum Associate Curator Nancy Spector first suggested that I propose an exhibition related to my academic work in Surrealism and the theory of masquerade. I thank her for being a source of inspiration and a supportive comrade throughout this project.

At an early stage in its development, the National Endowment for the Arts awarded a grant to *Rrose is a Rrose is a Rrose: Gender Performance in Photography*. Although the various parties who supported the show are unknown to me, I wish I could personally thank each one. This important grant provided the necessary impetus to propel the show from the drawing board to the implementation stage. I feel that I should also thank the NEA on behalf of the people who have told me over the years that they felt the exhibition would speak to their interests and concerns. If, in the final analysis, the exhibition has achieved that result, it will have accomplished one of the goals of the NEA.

Of course, without the support of the museum's director, Thomas Krens, this exhibition would never have become a reality. I am, as ever, grateful for his perspicacity and insight. At crucial moments, I have relied on the support and advice of Lisa Dennison, Curator of Collections and Exhibitions, and Germano Celant, Curator of Contemporary Art.

On behalf of everyone at the museum, I would like to extend my heartfelt gratitude to the exhibition's lenders, who are listed elsewhere in this catalogue. I would particularly like to thank the many private collectors who have so generously lent their important works. It is our great good fortune that they were willing to share their pieces with our visitors.

I would also like to express my appreciation to colleagues and their institutions whose loans made this exhibition possible: Samuel Sachs II, Director, The Detroit Institute of Arts; John Bancroft, Director, and Jennifer Pearson Yamashiro, Associate Curator, Kinsey Institute for Research in Sex, Gender, and Reproduction, Inc., Bloomington, Ind.; Graham Beal, Director, Robert Sobieszek, Curator, and Tim Wride, Assistant Curator, Los Angeles County Museum of Art; Philippe de Montebello, Director, and Maria Morris Hambourg, Curator in Charge, The Metropolitan Museum of Art, New York; Suzanne Pagé, Director, and Gérard Audinet, Curator, Musée d'Art Moderne de la Ville de Paris; Jean Aubert, Director, Musée des Beaux-Arts de Nantes; Germain Viatte, Director, and Alain Sayag, Curator, Musée National d'Art Moderne, Centre de Création Industrielle au Centre Georges Pompidou, Paris; Glenn Lowry, Director, Peter Galassi, Chief Curator, and Virginia Dodier, Study Center Supervisor, The Museum of Modern Art, New York; Terence Pepper, Curator of Photographs Collection, and Paul Cox, Picture Librarian, National Portrait Gallery, London; Anne d'Harnoncourt, Director, Innis Howe Shoemaker, Senior Curator, and Martha Chahroudi Mock, Associate Curator of Photography, The Philadelphia Museum of Art; and Pam Roberts, Curator, The Royal Photographic Society, Bath.

I am deeply appreciative of the galleries from which we borrowed works; they are also listed among the lenders. Frequently, their directors and staff also provided important information and assistance. I am especially grateful for the efforts of Alexandra Rowley, Robert Miller Gallery, New

York; Florian Karsch, Galerie Nierendorf, Berlin; Shaun Caley, Regen Projects, Los Angeles; Adam Boxer, Ubu Gallery, New York; and Brent Sikkema, Wooster Gardens, New York. In the research process, I also benefited from the expertise (and enthusiasm) of other dealers, most particularly Virginia Zabriskie, Zabriskie Gallery, New York and Paris. I must also thank Christian Bouqueret and Marie-Claude Lebon, Galerie Bouqueret-Lebon, Paris; Christine and Isy Brachot, Galerie Christine et Isy Brachot, Brussels and Paris; Martin McGeowin and Andrew Wheatley, Cabinet Gallery, London; Chantal Crousel, Galerie Chantal Crousel, Paris; Ealan Wingate, Gagosian Gallery, New York; Mark Fletcher, formerly Barbara Gladstone Gallery, New York; Rhona Hoffman and Judy Brauner, Rhona Hoffman Gallery, Chicago; Paul Kasmin, Paul Kasmin Gallery, New York; Rudolf Kicken, Galerie Rudolf Kicken, Cologne; Matthew Marks, Andrew Leslie, and Jeffrey Peabody, Matthew Marks Gallery, New York; Janelle Reiring and Tom Heeman, Metro Pictures, New York; Ben Barzune, formerly Metro Pictures; Marcel and David Fleiss, Galerie 1900–2000, Paris; Deborah Irmas, formerly PaceWildensteinMacGill Gallery, Beverly Hills; Eleanor Barefoot, PaceWildensteinMacGill Gallery, New York; Alain Paviot, Galerie Alain Paviot, Paris; and Jack Tilton and Annabella Johnson, Jack Tilton Gallery, New York. Michael Joseph, Janine Antoni's assistant, has been quite helpful on various occasions. I am also grateful for the good offices of Ariane Grigoteit, Deutsche Bank AG; Georges Marchais and Jean-Louis Raach, Parti Communiste Français; and Philippe Garner and Lydia Cresswell-Jones at Sotheby's London.

My research was assisted by various colleagues, to whom I am especially grateful: Jörn Merkert, Director, Berlinische Galerie; Dana Friis-Hansen, Senior Curator, Contemporary Arts Museum, Houston; Julian Cox, Assistant Curator, and Jacklyn Burns, Rights and Reproductions Coordinator, J. Paul Getty Museum, Santa Monica; Erna Haist, Institut für Auslandsbeziehungen, Stuttgart; Didier Schulmann, Chief Curator of Collections, and Nathalie Leleu, Loan Coordinator, Musée National d'Art Moderne, Centre de Création Industrielle au Centre Georges Pompidou, Paris; Paul Schimmel, Chief Curator, Russell Ferguson, Editor, and Connie Butler, Associate Curator/MSW, Museum of Contemporary Art, Los Angeles; Adam Brooks, Curator, REFCO Group, Ltd., Chicago; Ulrich Krempel, Director, Sprengel Museum, Hannover; Peter Boswell, Associate Curator, and Rochelle Steiner, Curatorial Assistant, both formerly Walker Art Center, Minneapolis; and Vincent Fremont, Exclusive Agent, The Andy Warhol Foundation for the Visual Arts, New York. Other individuals who have provided important information and support are: Arlette Albert-Birot, Wayne Baerwaldt, Gaia Battaglioli, Gilberte Brassaï, Eileen Cohen, James Crump, Daniel Filipacchi, Frank Kolodny, Janet Lehr, Anne Radcliffe, Michael and B. Z. Schwartz, Arturo Schwarz, Thomas Walther, and Jack Woody.

Many Guggenheim Museum staff members contributed enormously to the success of this exhibition. At various times, I have greatly relied on the astute aid of Vivien Greene, Curatorial Assistant, who also wrote the bulk of the catalogue biographies. I have benefited from the adept assistance of Exhibition Assistants Josette Lamoureux and Claudia Schmuckli. Other curatorial colleagues whose counsel I have frequently depended upon include Assistant Curators Clare Bell, Matthew Drutt, and J. Fiona Ragheb, and Exhibition Coordinator Jon Ippolito. Heidi Weber, Manager of Government Grants and Research, and Julie Schieffelin, Manager of Foundation and Corporate Giving, both thoughtfully developed grant applications for this project.

Aileen Rosenberg, Assistant Registrar, has ably handled the myriad complex arrangements for the loans to this exhibition. I also thank Suzanne Quigley, Head Registrar for Collections and Exhibitions, for offering assistance at various moments. Gillian McMillan, Conservator, has thoughtfully considered the conditions of the works and how best to present them. Elizabeth Jaff, Assistant Paper Preparator, carefully realized ingenious solutions to various framing issues. Jocelyn Brayshaw, Exhibition Technician, led a wonderful installation crew that included Jack Davidson, Jody Hanson, Matt Schwede, and Bob Seng. Without their expertise, the exhibition presentation would have been diminished. Peter Read, Jr., Production Services Manager/Exhibition Design Coordinator, deftly organized the overall installation arrangements, which included the services of Richard Gombar, Museum Technician. Jocelyn Groom, Exhibition Technician/Administrative Assistant, made numerous helpful contributions to this project in the design stages. Mary Ann Hoag, Lighting Technician, sensitively devised the lighting for the exhibition. I would also like to thank Scott Gutterman, Director of Public Affairs, and Julia Caldwell, Public Affairs Coordinator, for their efforts on behalf of the show.

I am deeply appreciative of the encouragement of Anthony Calnek, Director of Publications, and his skillful realization of this catalogue. Without him it is no understatement to say that this book would likely have remained a figment of my imagination. I am especially grateful for the talents of Elizabeth Levy, Managing Editor, and Melissa Secondino, Production Assistant, who have meticulously controlled the book's production. Edward Weisberger, Editor, and Jennifer Knox White, Associate Editor, lent their editorial acumen to this project, and Keith Mayerson provided invaluable assistance.

My gratitude to Deborah Drier, Project Editor, for her sensitive editing of the essays in this book is profound. Her expertise was essential for this project and her contribution is greatly appreciated.

I am most fortunate to have had the opportunity to work with Bethany Johns, who designed this catalogue as well as the exhibition graphics. She has created a beautiful book, which superbly articulates the intentions of *Rrose is a Rrose is a Rrose.*

This project has been subsidized by the contribution of many interns who have worked, over the past few years, on myriad aspects of the show. These interns include Pamela Burns, Raffaella Cardinali, Alison Engel, Jan-Philipp Frühsorge, Franziska Martin, James McNamara, Jennifer Miller, Lee Ann Pomplas-Bruening, Rajendra Roy, Janice Yang, and Kate Zamet. I am grateful for their assistance, without which I would not have been able to see this project to its fruition.

I am delighted to include the work of catalogue contributors whose efforts are a constant source of inspiration. These authors have brought their unique vision and style to the material and immeasurably enhanced the final product. I want to thank Judith Halberstam, Lyle Ashton Harris, Nancy Spector, Carole-Anne Tyler, and Sarah Wilson for their stimulating insights. I also deeply appreciate my colleagues in the curatorial department, Tracey Bashkoff, Susan Cross, and J. Fiona Ragheb, who contributed additional biographical entries on the artists in the exhibition.

Finally, my deepest thanks go to the artists whose work is in the exhibition. It is ultimately their creativity that has inspired my efforts. Studying their work has been a tremendous pleasure for me, and also a great challenge, because each oeuvre and object has its own logic, which will always on some level defy any discourse (like mine) that attempts to define it. I have benefited enormously from many of the artists' patient responses to my numerous inquiries and their thoughtful comments. I am honored to include their work in this exhibition, and look forward with anticipation to their future endeavors.

To my colleagues, friends, and family, who not only have borne my obsession with this project, but who have actually enjoyed the ride, I give my sincere gratitude and affection, and heartfelt wish that I may be for you in the future that which you have been for me.

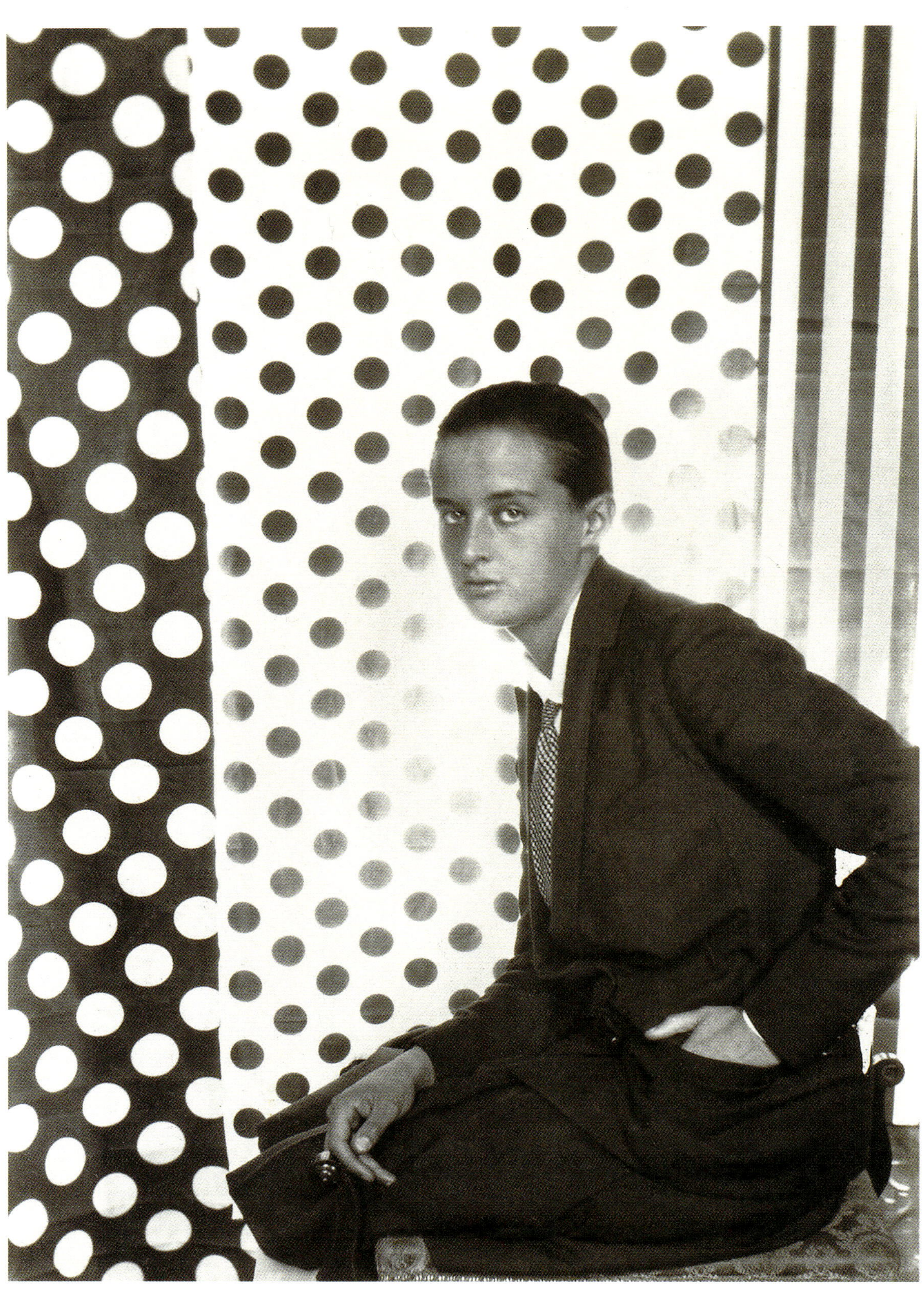

Cecil Beaton
Countess Castega, 1927
Gelatin-silver print, 8 ¼ x 5 ¹³⁄₁₆ inches (21 x 14.5 cm)
Cecil Beaton Archive, Sotheby's London

Introduction

JENNIFER BLESSING

This exhibition and book represent an argument. They are based on a chain of interlocking premises that you, the reader, may choose to follow or not. As in all group shows, there is a willfulness about the selection of works: artists who have never met, who lived at different times, who sought to achieve widely disparate goals are linked together despite their differences. Which is not to say that the selection is arbitrary. Rather, these works, gathered together as they are, shape a narrative of sorts, reflect a story of human existence in the twentieth century.

In skeletal form, the chain of postulates I develop, and which underlie the other contributions to this book, looks like this:[1]

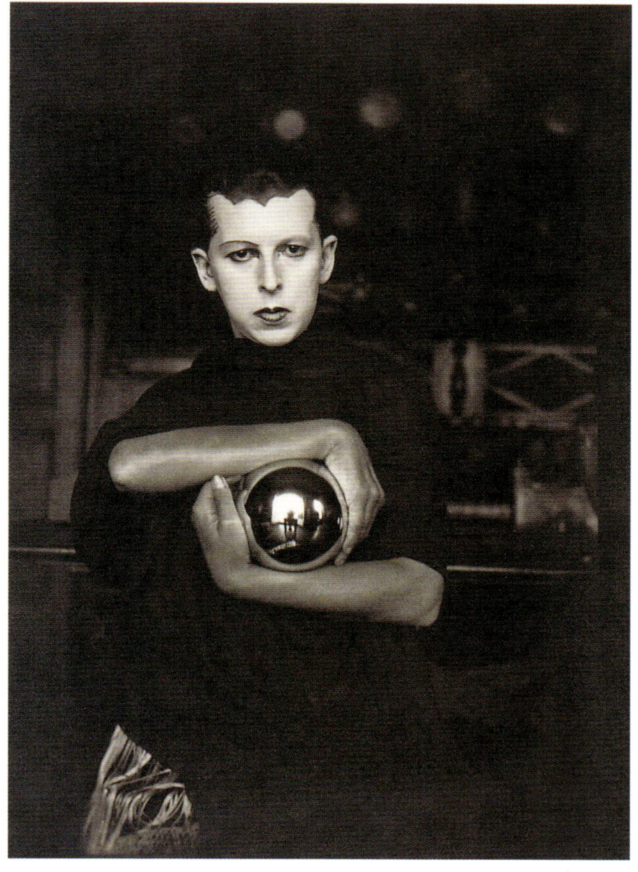

Claude Cahun
Self-Portrait, 1927
Gelatin-silver print,
4⅝ x 3½ inches (11.7 x 8.8 cm)
The Detroit Institute of Arts,
Founders Society Purchase, Albert and Peggy de Salle Charitable Trust and the DeRoy Photographic Acquisition Endowment Fund

A strikingly visible popular interest in gender presentation and sexuality in the 1990s intersects with an explosion in the production of art that takes as it subject the body and its coverings. Books, articles, films, and web sites on cross-dressing, transgenderism, and various sexualities ("lesbian chic," the rehabilitation of bisexuality, and so on) proliferate. Neo-Expressionist painting and language-based Conceptual art of the 1980s is followed, in this decade, by work that focuses on the body as a physical entity and the construction of identity. In this light, Cindy Sherman's feints and disguises seem to herald developments of the 1990s. The contradictory juxtapositions of body parts and vestimentary codes foreground gender play, or "gender trouble."

The 1990s witness an exponential expansion in the growth of academic gay and lesbian studies, much of which is influenced by the provocative new theoretical models of gender construction developed by philosopher Judith Butler. Butler's 1990 book *Gender Trouble: Feminism and the Subversion of Identity* inspires subsequent research in a variety of disciplines, including art history.[2] Queer studies present some of the most stimulating developments in the theoretical understanding of the formation of identity since the 1970s and

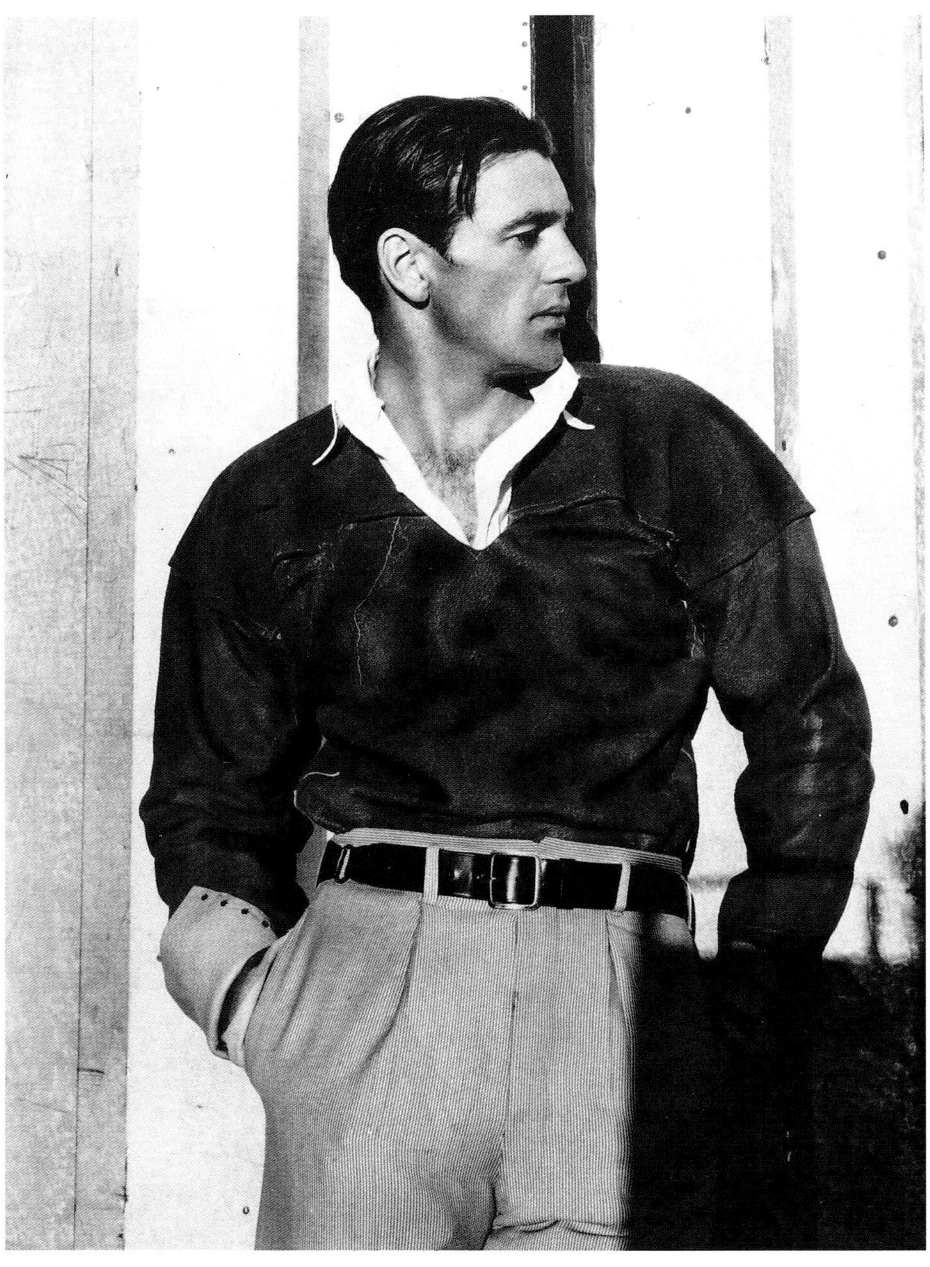

Cecil Beaton
Gary Cooper, 1931
Gelatin-silver print,
12 x 8 15/16 inches (30.5 x 22.7 cm)
Cecil Beaton Archive,
Sotheby's London

1980s work of feminist psychoanalytic and film theorists. These conceptual tools enable fruitful readings of contemporary cultural production—whether fine art or mass media.

When the lens of investigation is widened beyond our contemporary preoccupations, it is clear that now is not the first, nor will it be the last, historical moment in which issues of gender and sexuality hold a particular prominence. Not only do aspects of European art production between the two world wars (notably Dada and its legacy in Surrealism) resemble certain features of contemporary art, but some of the psychoanalytic roots of current gender theory date to the late 1920s and 1930s. Furthermore, a subsequent continuum appears to begin in the late 1960s, proceeding with greater or lesser vitality until the present. The phenomenon of "Sexual Liberation" manifested itself in cultural production, so that performance and body art of the early 1970s resonate in contemporary art. Hypotheses concerning the lacuna of the early postwar period—from 1945 to the mid-1960s—remain to be analyzed.

The medium of photography yields the perfect arena for the play of gender and sexuality. The technological inception of photographic means of reproduction corresponds (not by accident) with the nineteenth-century unfolding of the legacy of the Enlightenment's exaltation of the individual. The rise of mythologies of the self such as psychoanalysis and capitalism coincide with the technological means to reflect each being unto itself, as well as to promote it in the world without. Representing the physicality of the body in contemporary art, photography and other reproductive mediums such as film and video share with sculpture and performance a special relationship with notions of the Real. This exhibition examines the manner in which photography's strong aura of realism and objectivity promotes a fantasy of total gender transformation, or, conversely, allows the articulation of incongruity between the posing body and its assumed costume. The range of photographic representations includes documentary-style portraiture, theatrically constructed self-portraits, and photomontages created from found photographically based materials, with frequent overlaps in technique or method among such categories.

These are the postulates that generate the patterns of *Rrose is a Rrose is a Rrose: Gender Performance in Photography.*[3] In the following essay , I present four narratives that encompass, in roughly chronological order, the works. These are not the only stories that could be told, but rather four ways to look

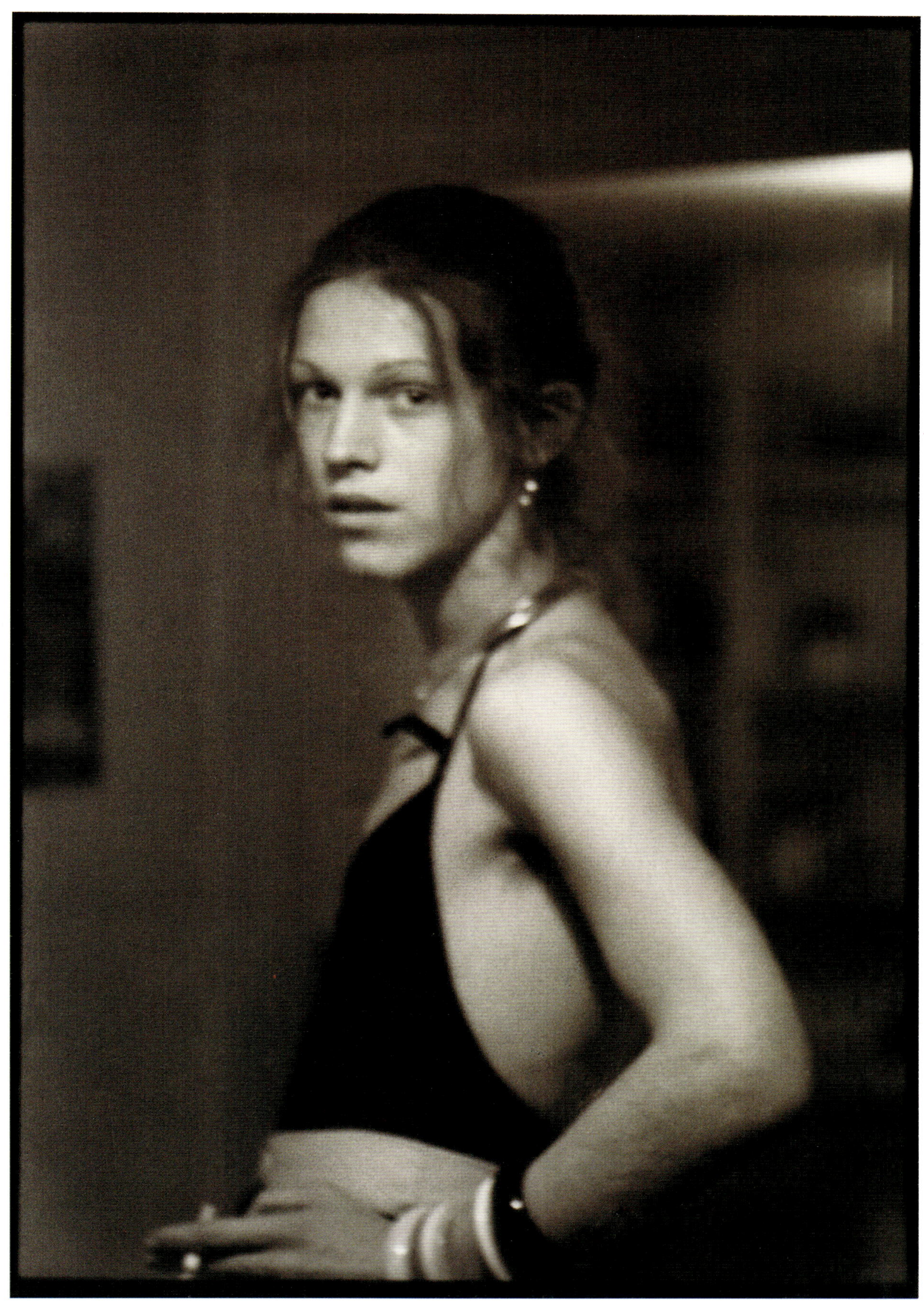

Nan Goldin
David at Grove Street, Boston, 1972
Gelatin-silver print,
20 x 16 inches (50.8 x 40.6 cm)
Courtesy of the artist and
Matthew Marks Gallery,
New York

at the assembled material. They elaborate the premises listed above, providing historical evidence to support the theses, yet they should not be construed as indicating that the artists involved created their works to illustrate a theory, or that the works themselves are reducible to a single issue. Rather, the art is examined as a text, among other texts (literary, historical, theoretical), yet with its own motives and internal logic. Each of my fellow authors elucidates some of the same themes, enriching them through their particular expertise, and, at times, diverging from them in meaningful ways.

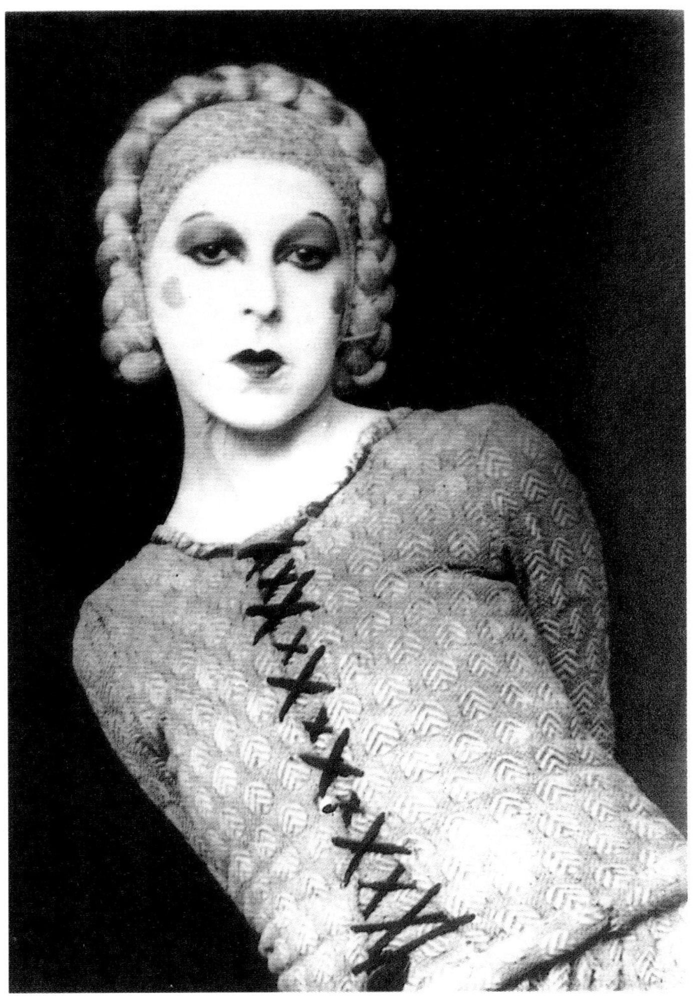

Claude Cahun
Self-Portrait, 1929
Gelatin-silver print,
5½ x 3½ inches (13.9 x 8.8 cm)
Museum Boymans-van
Beuningen, Rotterdam

A Brief Historiography of Gender Theory and a Reminder of the Mystery of Sex

We may not know exactly what sex is;
but we do know that it is mutable,
with the possibility of one sex being changed
into the other sex, that its frontiers are often
uncertain, and that there are many stages
between a complete male and a complete female.
HAVELOCK ELLIS, *The Psychology of Sex*, 1933[4]

With the post-Enlightenment decline of such explanatory systems of human civilization as monarchy and religion, there arose the central discipline concerned with the epistemology of the individual, the science of psychoanalysis. By the end of the nineteenth century, psychoanalysis had organized itself around issues of the sexual body and the development of its behaviors in the mind. Psychoanalytic accounts of the formation of gender identity (and here Sigmund Freud's texts are key) posited masculinity as normative, and femininity as a kind of enigma, an excess or inscrutable other.[5] The period between the two world wars witnessed a burst of publications examining the nature of feminine sexuality and identity, many written by women analysts, whose assimilation into their profession reflected wider changes in the role of women in society.[6] It is not accidental that women were drawn to the question of feminine identity, as the very nature of femininity was part of a larger social debate. The rise of the "new woman," with her call for changes in women's inferior legal status and domestic and public roles, took on particular urgency in this period, in which women demanded the right to vote, modifications in marriage and inheritance laws, access to universities and professions, as well as alterations in dress and comportment. In each case, women sought to have equity with men, which led to ambivalence, and the fear that women were *becoming* men (wearing their clothes, smoking, endangering their reproductive capacities through "unnatural" intellectual pursuits, and so on). It is in this context that the analyst Joan Riviere made her contribution to the debate in the form of a paper entitled "Womanliness as a Masquerade," published in 1929, in which she posited that professional women appear in ultrafeminine attire in order to assuage their male colleagues, who fear their prerogative is imperiled.[7] For Riviere, femininity is constituted in dissembling or the masking of women's masculinity by burying it beneath a veil of decoration. She makes no claims for an inherent femininity, but rather constructs feminine identity as an alienated social performance.

Jacques Lacan resuscitated Riviere's work in a 1958 paper, "The Meaning of the Phallus," which contains a line that has since become a dictum: "I would say that it is in order to be the phallus, that is to say, the signifier of the desire of the Other, that the woman will reject an essential part of her femininity, notably all its attributes through masquerade."[8] In the context of his rereading of Freudian psychoanalysis with linguistics, Lacan maintained that the phallus is a signifier of power; however,

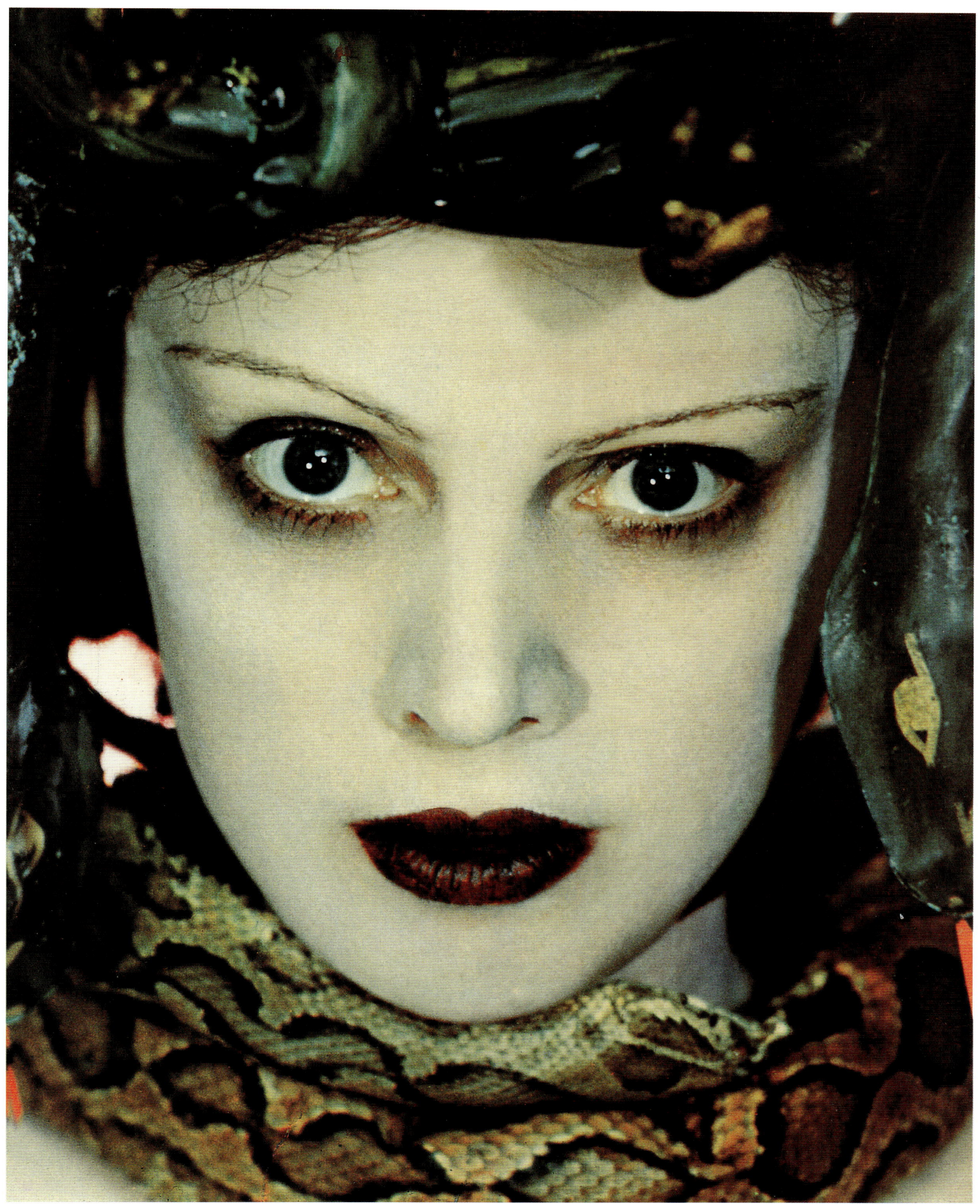

Madame Yevonde
Mrs. Edward Meyer as "Medusa," from the *Goddesses* series, 1935
Vivex color print, 14 5/16 x 11 11/16 inches (36.3 x 29.7 cm)
The Royal Photographic Society, Bath

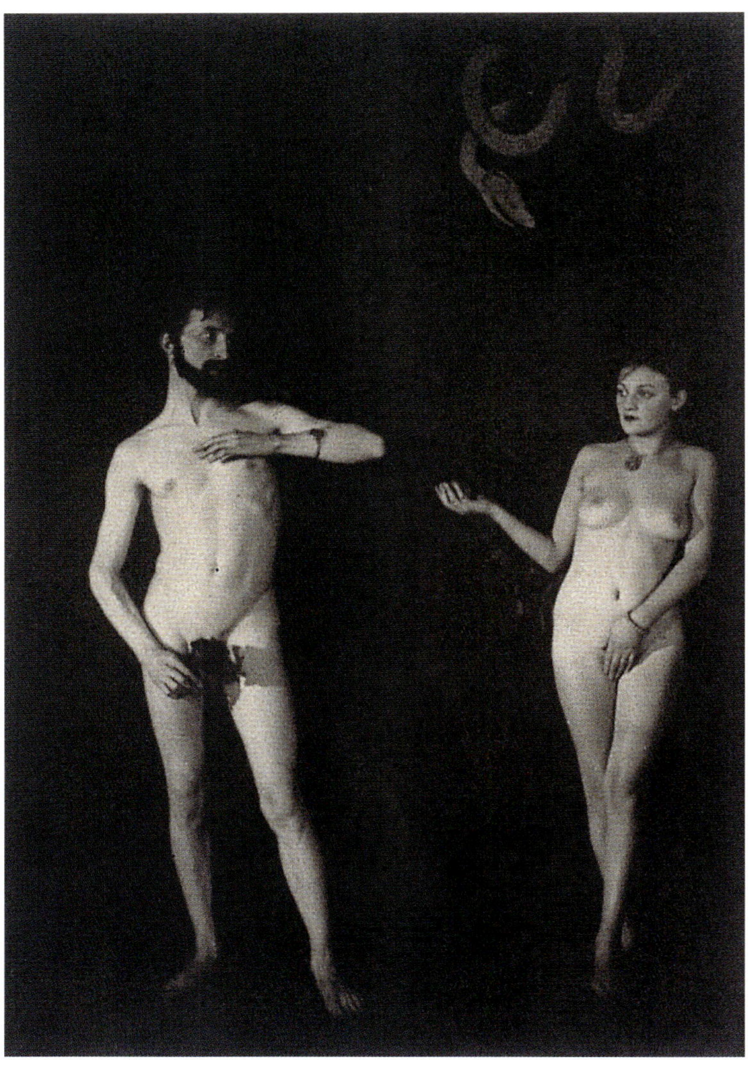

Man Ray
Ciné-sketch: Adam and Eve,
1924–25
Gelatin-silver print,
8¼ x 5½ inches (21 x 14 cm)
Collection of Daniel Newburg

although each subject has a Symbolic relationship to the phallus in the form of "having" it or "appearing" as it (*being* the phallus), no one actually possesses it. Film theorists interested in how identity is constructed diegetically in movies, as well as in the conditions of spectatorship, absorbed Lacan's work into their own. French critics first specifically engaged his reading of Riviere in 1970, British critics in 1975.[9] From the 1970s to the present, Lacanian constructions of femininity as masquerade have been developed and contested in many disciplines, including feminist psychoanalysis, cultural studies, and art criticism.[10]

In the 1990s, theorists have broadened the notion of femininity as masquerade to encompass any gender identity. Like femininity, masculinity is a mythic construction that is perpetuated through the performative repetition of stereotypes of behavior and dress.[11] Gay and lesbian theorists have been especially concerned with the study of various sites in which performances cause "gender trouble," namely female impersonation, cross-dressing, and butch/femme aesthetics. This work convincingly exposes the heterosexist presumptions of earlier theoretically inspired studies, and delineates the range of gender positions (as opposed to a strictly binary dichotomy) as well as their historical diversity. When an interviewer mentioned the simplified reading of Butler's work as indicating that "*all* gender is drag," Butler responded, "Yet I accept the idea that gender is an impersonation, that becoming gendered involves impersonating an ideal that nobody actually inhabits, and that's where I have a certain sympathy with Lacanian discourse."[12]

Accepting as a given that a fixed notion of the concepts "man," "woman," "masculine," and "feminine" is impossible does not mean that each individual can always voluntarily choose to inhabit a position. For example, the feminine masquerade of a female-born subject may involve conformity to social expectation, while, for the same person, a butch presentation may yield a forced self-consciousness in certain contexts because of a socially perceived enunciation of difference. Which is drag? Hypermasculinity and hyperfemininity in a heterosexual situation may be perceived as essentially equivalent to their respective male and female subjects, while cross-dressing is more easily read as a purposeful (or artificial) performance. The hyperbolic representation of gender seems conformist when sex and gender presentation correspond and oppositional when they differ.[13] Yet, as Butler asserts, "There are no direct expressive or causal lines between sex, gender, gender presentation, sexual practice, fantasy and sexuality."[14]

It might seem that, having evacuated these concepts of any essential biological determination, they would become amorphous, free-floating signifiers subject to arbitrarily assigned meaning. Instead, as the works in this exhibition exemplify, myriad codes exist that are, alternately, accepted or manipulated. Throughout history there have been attempts to transcend the notion of binary sexual and gender distinctions through "third sex" concepts such as the androgyne and neologisms such as Eonist, Uranian, invert, Sapphist, or Amazon.[15] The nineteenth-century figure of the androgyne appeared to deny difference, basically annexing "femininity" to masculine precepts.[16] Third-sex terms

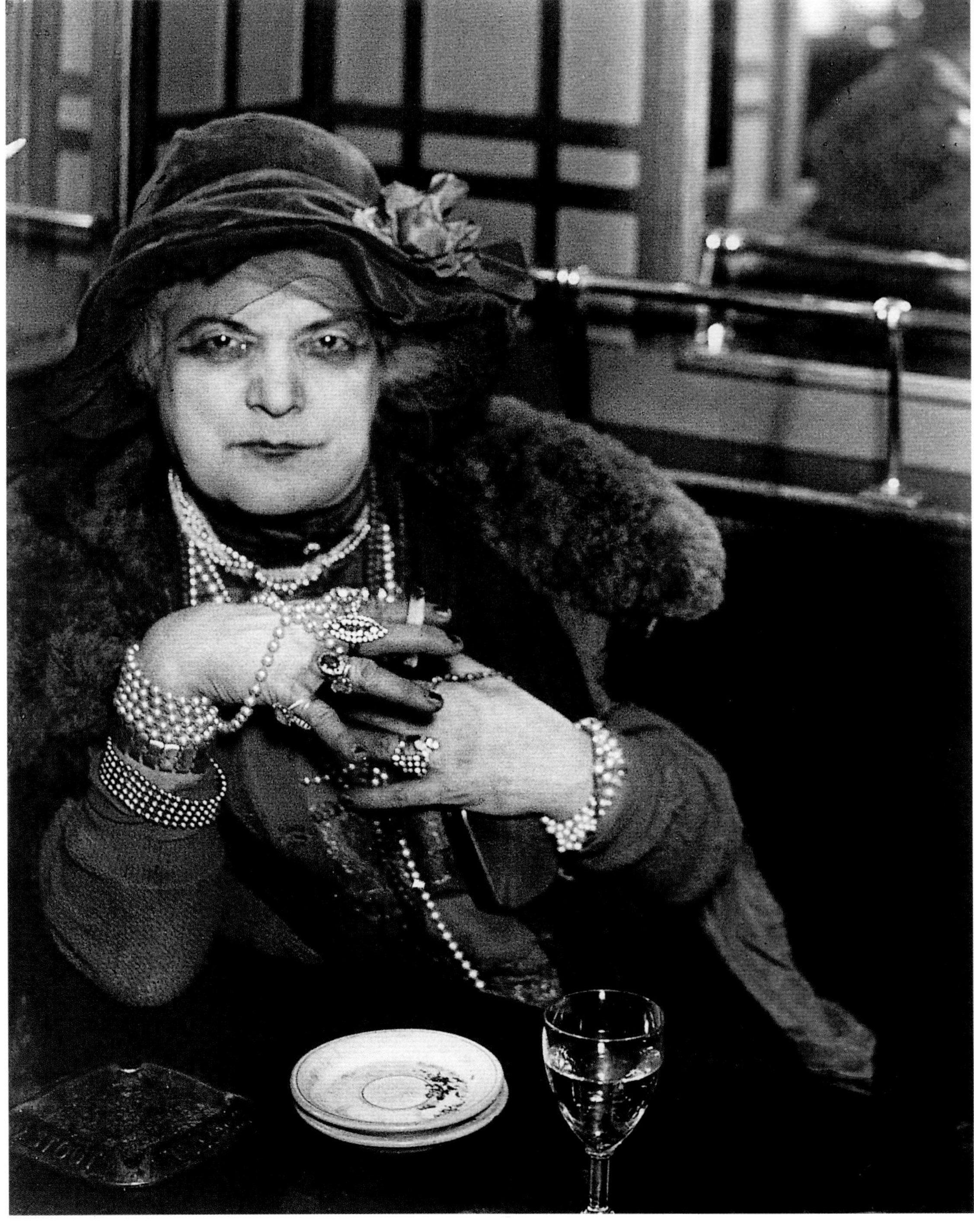

Brassaï
"Bijou" of Montmartre, 1932
Gelatin-silver print,
11⅞ x 9⅛ inches (30.2 x 23.2 cm)
The Museum of Modern Art,
New York,
David H. McAlpin Fund

fix a variety of subjectivities under one banner, on the margins of the "master" binary logic. Current theoretical conceptualizations of identity recognize both the inability to escape the binary system and the desire to corrupt it in a pleasurable way. Occasionally, these pleasures, these troubled genders, are described as ambiguous, yet they seem to be anything but. Mixing gender codes does not so much result in uniform gender blurring, which presupposes a kind of equal distribution of gender effects yielding indeterminability, but rather a variety of specific, readable, and nameable performances. In other words, a gender-ambiguous subject is never invisible; it announces the juxtaposition of codes in one subject.

So where does the pleasure come from? I am reminded of that commonplace of the casual art lover: "I don't know much about art, but I know what I like." Perhaps gender operates in the same way, in that sometimes you don't want to know, you just want to feel.[17] And yet, as any student will tell you, the more you learn, the more your tastes change. In the epigraph that appears at the start of this book, Roland Barthes posits a deceptively simple notion of self that is defined by the peculiar

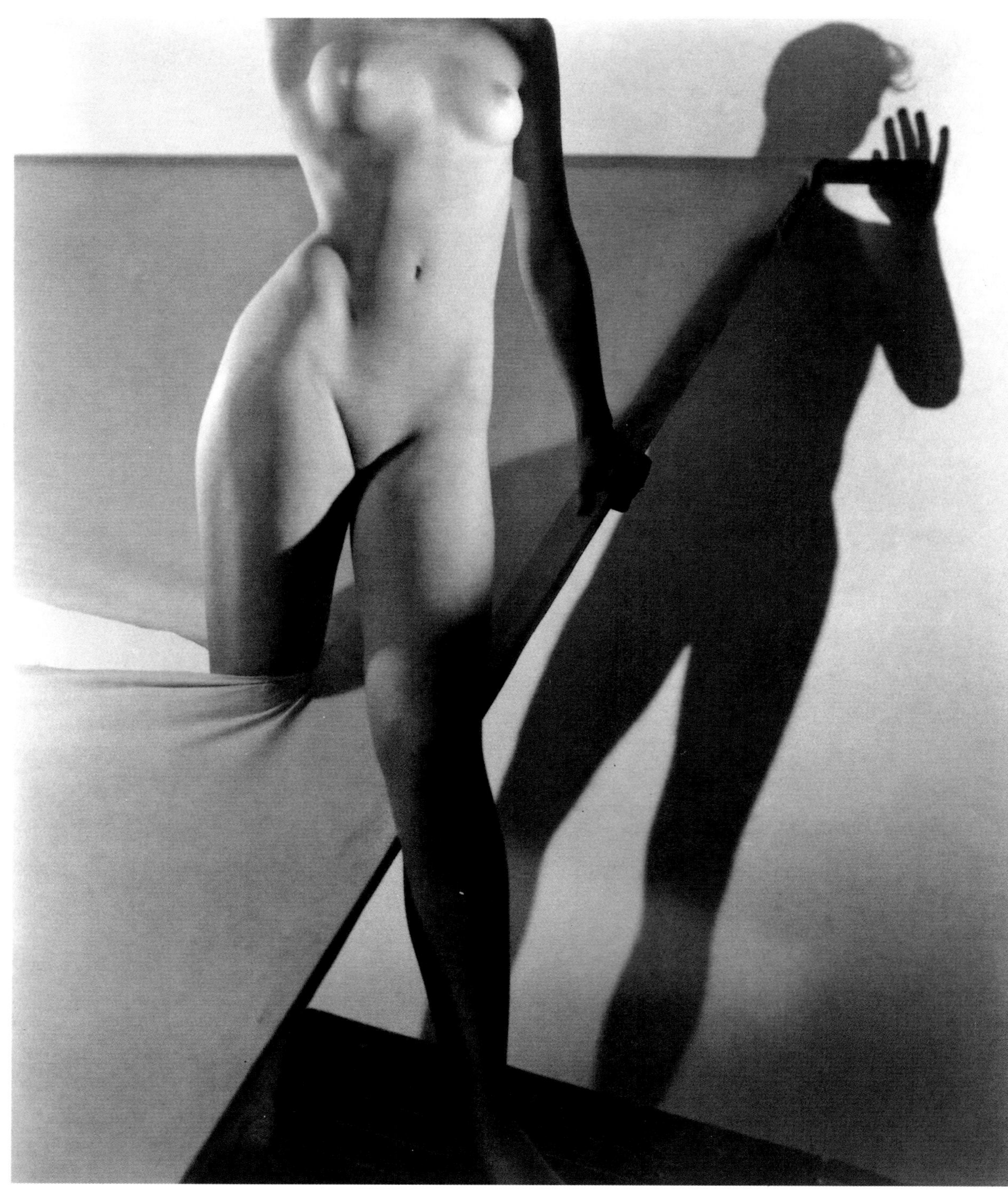

George Platt Lynes
Untitled, ca. 1941
Gelatin-silver print,
9⅛ x 7⅝ inches (23.2 x 19.4 cm)
Courtesy of the Kinsey Institute for Research in Sex, Gender, and Reproduction, Inc., Bloomington, Indiana

accumulation of seemingly inconsequential likes and dislikes, the concatenation of tastes.[18] Each individual can define itself by similarities to and distinctions from others ("I like cherries, too; but unlike him, I like women in slacks. My body is like/unlike his.") The possible reasons for given tastes can always be examined and more or less convincing explanations developed, if you are so inclined. Perhaps one's gender presentation and responses to those of others are determined by how one thinks (consciously/unconsciously) one *ought* to look at a given moment. Here it is a question, to a greater or lesser extent, of my taste, which has been formed by a confluence of factors—environment, knowledge, desire.

In the course of developing this exhibition, an elaborate system of selection criteria emerged, which was modified the more I read, the more I looked, the more I spoke, the more I wrote. At frequent junctures, I questioned the apparent logic or arbitrariness of my choices. I understood why I did not want to include any photographs that are voyeuristic or sensationalistic in a predatory kind

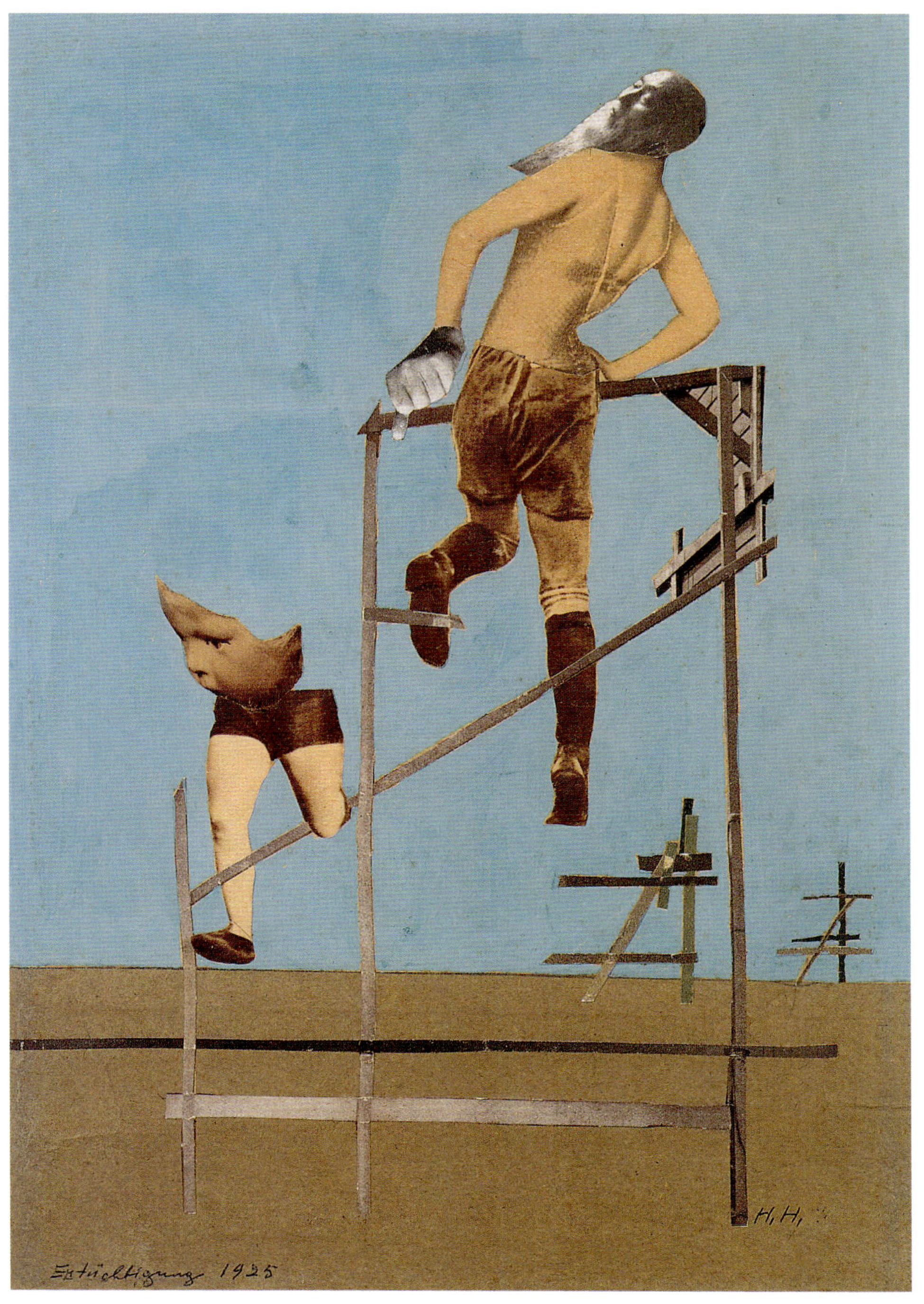

Hannah Höch
Training (Ertüchtigung), 1925
Photomontage,
11 x 7⅜ inches (28 x 18.7 cm)
Galerie Nierendorf, Berlin

of way, but this exclusion broadened to include intimate or sexualized nudity. The result is a group of highly artificed, social images with a remote, lapidary quality that exudes an exhibitionistic self-delight without, for a moment, indicating any gap in the performance, any self-doubt, any sentimentality. How different that is from a quotidian experience of the world, in which your face uncontrollably betrays every emotion, where your heart is worn on your sleeve, and your body is an awkward stranger. These photographs, instead, are images of fantasy—they represent the dream of total control, the icy demeanor of mastery, like a femme fatale preserved on film, the classic phallic woman.

Most of the photographs in this exhibition and book are characterized by direct address—a figure looks directly at the camera, at you, fixing you with its stare. This is not a subject "captured" on film, this is a subject who is capturing you: you are its other, through which it defines itself with a vengeance. This is a world where to perform is to control. It is a world in which you are who you will be, forever. Even when the address is not direct, your presence is acknowledged. The performer is playing to you, smiles and winks at you. There are those who present the picture of seriousness, yet a smirk always remains a split-second away (the moment after the shutter clicks). And there are others who clown, but theirs is a self-absorbed laughter, which you may join if you wish. This spirit of pleasure and play pervades the exhibition, holding a promise of transcendence (not a taunt), a possibility that you, too, are not trapped in a body, that time can be stilled, that you, too, have the phallus that is power.

Notes

1. During the period in which this exhibition was being developed, the Centre Georges Pompidou in Paris presented *fémininmasculin: Le sexe de l'art* (October 24, 1995–February 12, 1996). The premises of one of *fémininmasculin*'s five sections, entitled "Identités & Mascarades" (Identities and masquerades), are somewhat similar to those of *Rrose is a Rrose is a Rrose*. See M.-L. B. [Marie-Laure Bernadac], "II Identités & Mascarades," in *fémininmasculin: Le sexe de l'art*, exh. cat. (Paris: Gallimard/Electa and Centre Georges Pompidou, 1995), pp. 119–21. Furthermore, the form of my introductory exposition has been inspired by the presentation of *fémininmasculin*, where the exhibition's premises were presented in wall labels and the catalogue as a series of postulates. Like the organizers of *fémininmasculin*, I would like to underscore the rhetorical nature of my argument.

   Despite these similarities, however, my approach to the material differs markedly. *Rrose is a Rrose is a Rrose* is more historically oriented than the "Identités & Mascarades" section of *fémininmasculin*, and the theoretical apparatus underpinning the show is distinct as well. The present exhibition focuses exclusively on issues of photographic representation, including the use of "found" photographic reproductions in collage. For a thoughtful critique of the heterosexist bias of *fémininmasculin*, and its focus on literal phallic and vaginal imagery, which receive their apotheosis in metaphorical representations of biological reproduction, see the reviews by Juan Vicente Aliaga, *Frieze* 27 (March–April 1996), pp. 58–59; and Elisabeth Lebovici, "French Lessons," *Artforum* 34, no. 3 (March 1996), pp. 34, 119.

   Of course, other exhibitions and publications have influenced this project, including Jean-François Chevrier and Jean Sagne, "L'Autoportrait comme mise en scène . . . Essai sur l'identité, l'exotisme et les excès photographiques," *Photographies* 4 (April 1984), pp. 47–82 (English-language abstract, "Staging the Self . . . Essay on Identity, Exotism, and the Photographic Excesses," pp. 132–34); and James Lingwood, ed., *Staging the Self: Self-Portrait Photography 1840s–1980s*, exh. cat. (London: National Portrait Gallery; Plymouth, England: Plymouth Arts Centre, 1986).
2. Judith Butler, *Gender Trouble: Feminism and the Subversion of Identity* (New York: Routledge, 1990).
3. I have frequently been asked to parse *Rrose is a Rrose is a Rrose: Gender Performance in Photography*. The descriptive subtitle indicates the theme of the show, photographic representations in which the gender of the subject is highlighted. For those familiar with the literature of gender theory, it calls to mind the work of scholars like Butler and Eve Kosofsky Sedgwick. The flowery title proper reiterates Gertrude Stein's famous motto with an additional *R* intended to recall Marcel Duchamp's feminine alter ego, Rrose Sélavy. The references to Duchamp and Stein allude to the historical basis of the exhibition in between-the-wars Paris. Also, both Duchamp's and Stein's creations have erotic connotations that parallel the gender premises of the exhibition: Rrose Sélavy is pronounced like a dictum, "Eros, c'est la vie"; and Stein's line first appeared in a sensual poem dedicated to Emily Dickinson. Although gender can be conceived as a form of presentation, it is irrevocably tied to sexuality and desire, and thus, to my mind, the happy confluence of meanings.

   In the art-historical literature, Duchamp's drag gesture has been canonized into an act from which all subsequent masquerades are considered derivations. My reference to Stein is intended to complicate that reading, to indicate that Duchamp's gesture is not singular, that there are different types of drag, impersonation, or gender performance, in various contexts and with diverse meanings.
4. Havelock Ellis, *The Psychology of Sex* (New York: Ray Long and Richard R. Smith, 1933), p. 255; quoted in Sandra M. Gilbert and Susan Gubar, *No Man's Land*, vol. 2: *Sex Changes* (New Haven: Yale University Press, 1989), pp. xii–xiii.
5. See, for example, Sigmund Freud, "Femininity, Lecture XXXIII, New Introductory Lectures" (1933), in *The Standard Edition of the Complete Psychological Works of Sigmund Freud*, ed. and trans. James Strachey (London: Hogarth Press, 1953–1974), vol. 22, pp. 112–35; see also "Some Psychical Consequences of the Anatomical Distinction between the Sexes" (1925), in *Standard Edition*, vol. 19, pp. 241–60; and "Female Sexuality" (1931), in *Standard Edition*, vol. 21, pp. 223–43.
6. For a review of the "great debate" over female sexuality, see Juliet Mitchell, "Introduction-I," in Juliet Mitchell and Jacqueline Rose, eds., *Feminine Sexuality: Jacques Lacan and the école freudienne*, trans. Jacqueline Rose, (New York: W. W. Norton, 1982), pp. 20ff.
7. Joan Riviere, "Womanliness as a Masquerade," *International Journal of Psychoanalysis* 10 (1929), pp. 303–13; reprinted in Victor Burgin, James Donald, and Cora Kaplan, eds., *Formations of Fantasy* (New York: Routledge, 1986), pp. 35–44.
8. Jacques Lacan, "The Meaning of the Phallus," reprinted in Mitchell and Rose, eds., *Feminine Sexuality*, p. 84.
9. Stephen Heath, "Joan Riviere and the Masquerade," in Burgin, Donald, and Kaplan, eds., *Formations of Fantasy*, p. 57, cites: "*Morocco* de Josef von Sternberg," *Cahiers du cinéma*, no. 225 (November–December 1970), pp. 5–13; reprinted in Peter Baxter, ed., *Sternberg*, trans. Diana Matias (London: British Film Institute, 1980); and Claire Johnston, "Femininity and the Masquerade: Anne of the Indies," in Claire Johnston and Paul Willemen, eds., *Jacques Tourneur* (Edinburgh: Edinburgh Film Festival, 1975),

pp. 36–44. Perhaps the most influential adoption of Riviere's theory was that by American scholar Mary Ann Doane. See her "Film and the Masquerade: Theorising the Female Spectator," *Screen* 23, nos. 3–4 (September–October 1982), pp. 74–97; reprinted in Doane, *Femmes Fatales: Feminism, Film Theory, Psychoanalysis* (New York: Routledge, 1991), pp. 17–32.

10. The earliest example of the use of Riviere's theory in an art-historical context is probably that of Craig Owens, via Doane. See Owens, "Posing," in Kate Linker, ed., *Difference: On Representation and Sexuality*, exh. cat. (New York: New Museum of Contemporary Art, 1984), pp. 7–17.

11. In "The Meaning of the Phallus," p. 85, Lacan notes that "virile display itself appears as feminine." The Lacanian analyst Eugénie Lemoine-Luccioni explains, "If the penis was the phallus, men would have no need of feathers or ties or medals. . . . Display [*parade*], just like the masquerade, thus betrays a flaw: no one has the phallus." (*La Robe: Essai psychanalytique sur le vêtement* [Paris: Editions du Seuil, 1983], p. 34); cited by Heath, "Joan Riviere and the Masquerade," p. 56.

    Recent publications that examine constructions of masculinity encompassing artistic manifestations include Andrew Perchuk and Helaine Posner, eds., *The Masculine Masquerade: Masculinity and Representation*, exh. cat. (Cambridge, Mass.: MIT List Visual Arts Center and MIT Press, 1995); and Maurice Berger, Brian Wallis, and Simon Watson, eds., *Constructing Masculinity*, with picture essay by Carrie Mae Weems (New York: Routledge, 1995).

12. Liz Kotz, "The Body You Want" (interview with Butler), *Artforum* 31, no. 11 (November 1992), p. 85.

13. For Butler's articulation of the hyperbolic, see "Critically Queer," in Butler, *Bodies that Matter: On the Discursive Limits of "Sex"* (New York: Routledge, 1993), pp. 223–42.

14. Butler, "Imitation and Gender Insubordination," in Diana Fuss, ed., *Inside/Out: Lesbian Theories, Gay Theories* (New York: Routledge, 1991), p. 25.

15. "Eonist," named for the eighteenth-century Chevalier d'Eon de Beaumont, is Havelock Ellis's term for the transvestite. "Uranian" and "invert" are late nineteenth-century terms indicating the homosexual subject, the first used in literary circles, the second derived from the psychopathology of Richard von Krafft-Ebing and others. Sapphist and Amazon suggested the lesbian. All of these neologisms indicate a disturbance in language, in the sense that the contestation of names and their significations are manifestations of a society's inability to agree on meaning. Note, for example, the changing connotations in the twentieth century for girl, gal, Mrs./Miss/Ms.; gay, homosexual, queer; or negro, black, African American. It is not a coincidence that the names and identifications of people demanding rights and political visibility inhabit this field of contested language, or that the marginalized should attempt to replace words that are derogatorily coded and to reinvest those words with positive meaning. Marginalization itself is manifested, and created, through an inability to name an identity because it appears to resist a master (named or implicit) logic.

16. See Kari Weil, *Androgyny and the Denial of Difference* (Charlottesville: University Press of Virginia, 1992).

17. "I'm not sure that anybody knows how to account for their sexual practices, and if they were able to account for their sexual practices, they probably wouldn't be interested in them anymore." (Butler, "The Body You Want," p. 86.)

18. *Roland Barthes by Roland Barthes* (1975), trans. Richard Howard (Berkeley: University of California Press, 1994), pp. 116–17.

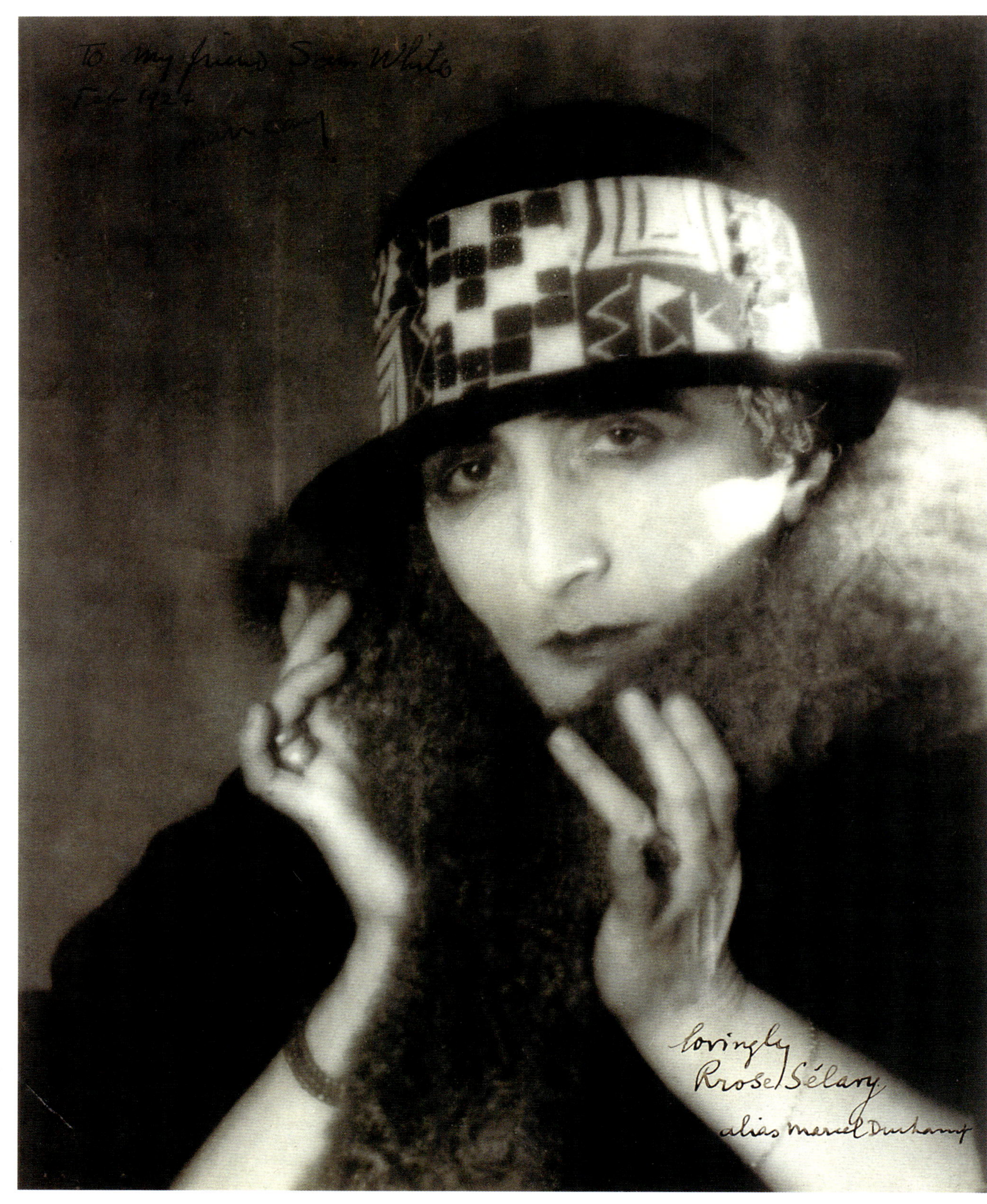

Man Ray

Marcel Duchamp as Rrose Sélavy, 1920–21
Gelatin-silver print, 8 1/2 x 6 13/16 inches (21.6 x 17.3 cm)
The Philadelphia Museum of Art, Samuel S. White III and Vera White Collection

Rrose is a Rrose is a Rrose

JENNIFER BLESSING

Gender Performance in Photography

1. Some European Photography Between the Two World Wars

Rose is a rose is a rose is a rose.
Loveliness extreme.
Extra gaiters.
Loveliness extreme.
Sweetest ice-cream.
GERTRUDE STEIN, "Sacred Emily," 1913[1]

What I do recollect is this. I collect black and white. From the standpoint of white all color is color. From the standpoint of black. Black is white. White is black. Black is black. White is black. White and black is black and white. What I recollect when I am there is that words are not birds. How easily I feel thin. Birds do not. So I replace birds with tin-foil. Silver is thin.
Life and letters of Marcel Duchamp
GERTRUDE STEIN, "Next: Life and Letters of Marcel Duchamp," 1920[2]

Rrose Sélavy born in 1920 in N.Y. Jewish name? change of sex—Rose being the most "ugly" name for my personal taste and Sélavy the easy play on words That's life.
MARCEL DUCHAMP, handwritten note, undated[3]

My intention was always to get away from myself, though I knew perfectly well that I was using myself. Call it a little game between "I" and "me."
MARCEL DUCHAMP, interview, 1962[4]

Dada Dandies (1919–30)[5]

Rrose Sélavy first appeared in 1920 as the author of various Dada artworks, which she signed.[6] Shortly thereafter, Man Ray photographed Marcel Duchamp in drag as Rrose. A version of these photos was mounted on a Rigaud perfume bottle as part of the packaging for a line of "eau de voilette," called "Belle Haleine," in a playful punning reference to the beautiful Helen of Troy. Rrose Sélavy thus became the spokesperson for the Belle Haleine brand of perfume.

This gesture bubbles with double entendres and inside jokes, manifesting a typical Dadaist delight in and yet ironic disdain for mass culture, in this case advertisements and product marketing. For Rrose is not beautiful, she is not Helen, and she is not a she.[7] Like the phantom Helen in Euripides's account, this Helen is not the "real" Helen, but rather an imposter. She, too, is as

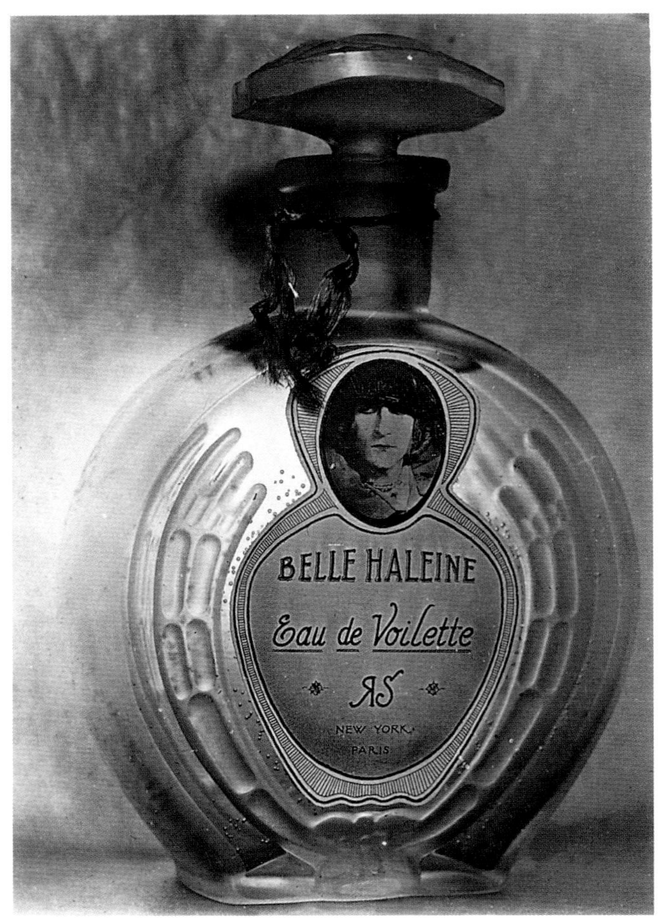

Man Ray
Belle Haleine, Eau de Voilette,
1921 (printed 1930s)
Gelatin-silver print,
4 5/16 x 3 3/8 inches (11 x 8.5 cm)
Collection of Michael Senft,
New York

ephemeral as the breath (*haleine*) of the perfume and as "faked" as the appropriated perfume bottle. Tristan Tzara facetiously pointed to the artificiality of *Belle Haleine, Eau de Voilette*, and, by extension, the fashion system that it parodied, in the journal *New York Dada*, which featured *Belle Haleine* on its cover: "Therefore, Madam, be on your guard and realize that a really dada product is a different thing from a glossy label."[8]

Or is it? Disputing the distinction between reality and illusion—or for that matter binary distinctions of any kind—is a keystone of Duchamp's artistic practice: though insistently devoid of artifice, his readymades are, through a process of selection and naming, transformed into art; and using a scientific system of notation, Duchamp creates "real" technical diagrams of fantabulous machines. Like *11 rue Larrey* (1927), a door hinged between two entryways, Duchamp's objects, not one thing or another, are multivalent. Which is not to say that difference is erased, but rather that one thing is defined by another and is in a constant state of redefinition in relation to its opposites.[9]

The binary system that perhaps most fascinated Duchamp (apart from the game of chess) was the sexual one—male versus female. In works such as *The Bride Stripped Bare by Her Bachelors, Even (The Large Glass)* (1915–23), he created feminine and masculine spheres, charting the uncertain exchange between the two. In *L.H.O.O.Q.* (1919), by drawing a moustache and goatee on a reproduction of the *Mona Lisa*, Duchamp asserted that he had discovered the hidden sexual identity of the portrait sitter.[10] It is in this context that the gender bending of Rrose Sélavy should be seen.

Born in 1887, Duchamp witnessed an explosive increase in consumerism and the advertising intended to foster it, a legacy of the convulsive growth of capitalism in the nineteenth century. The rise of capitalism and industrial rationalization was, in part, responsible for the "Great Masculine Renunciation" of flamboyance and ostentation in favor of the standardization of a more sober and

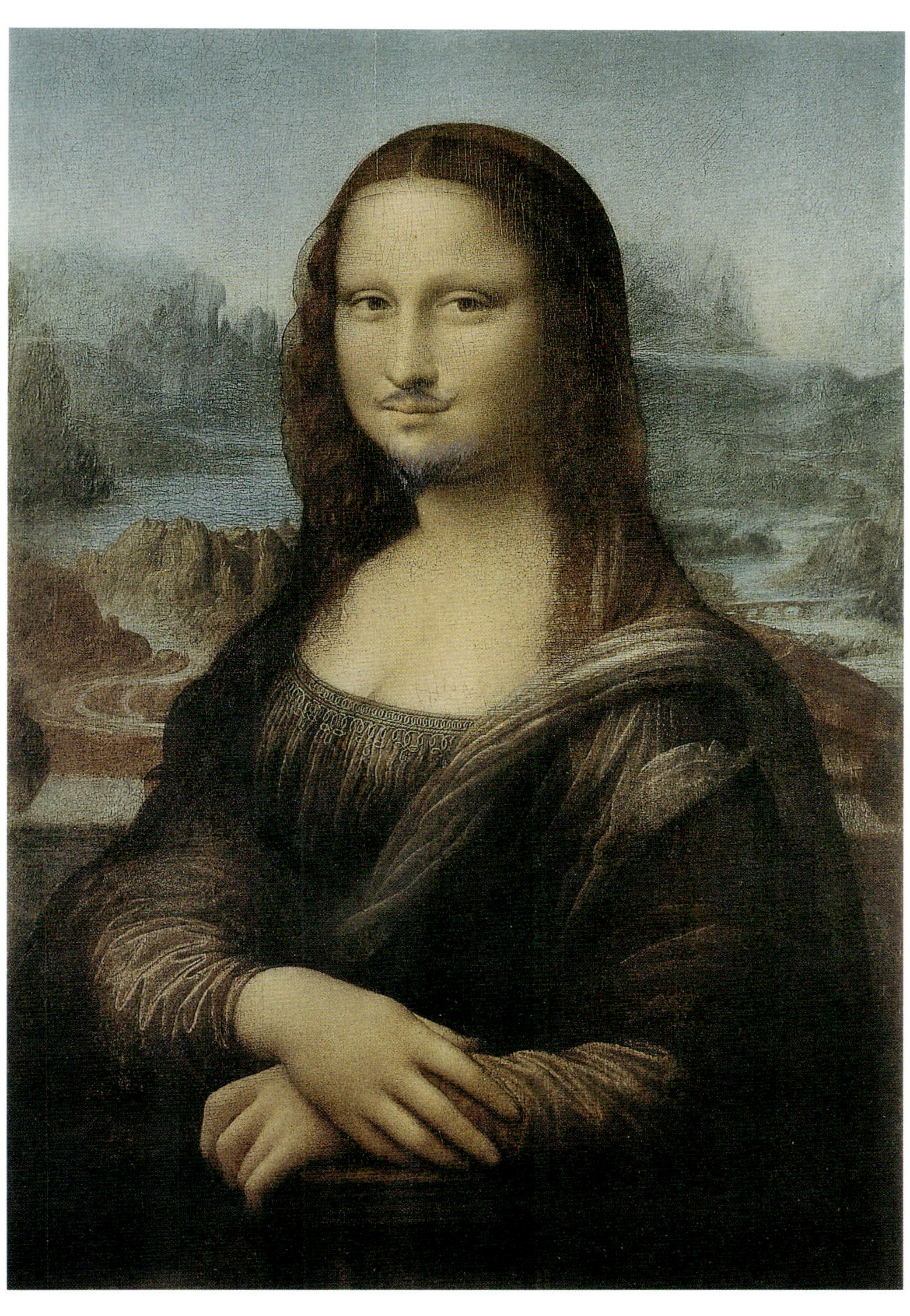

Marcel Duchamp
L.H.O.O.Q., 1919/1930
Pencil on reproduction, 19 x 13 inches (48.3 x 33 cm)
Gift of Louis Aragon to Georges Marchais for the Parti Communiste Français, Paris

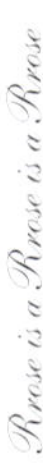

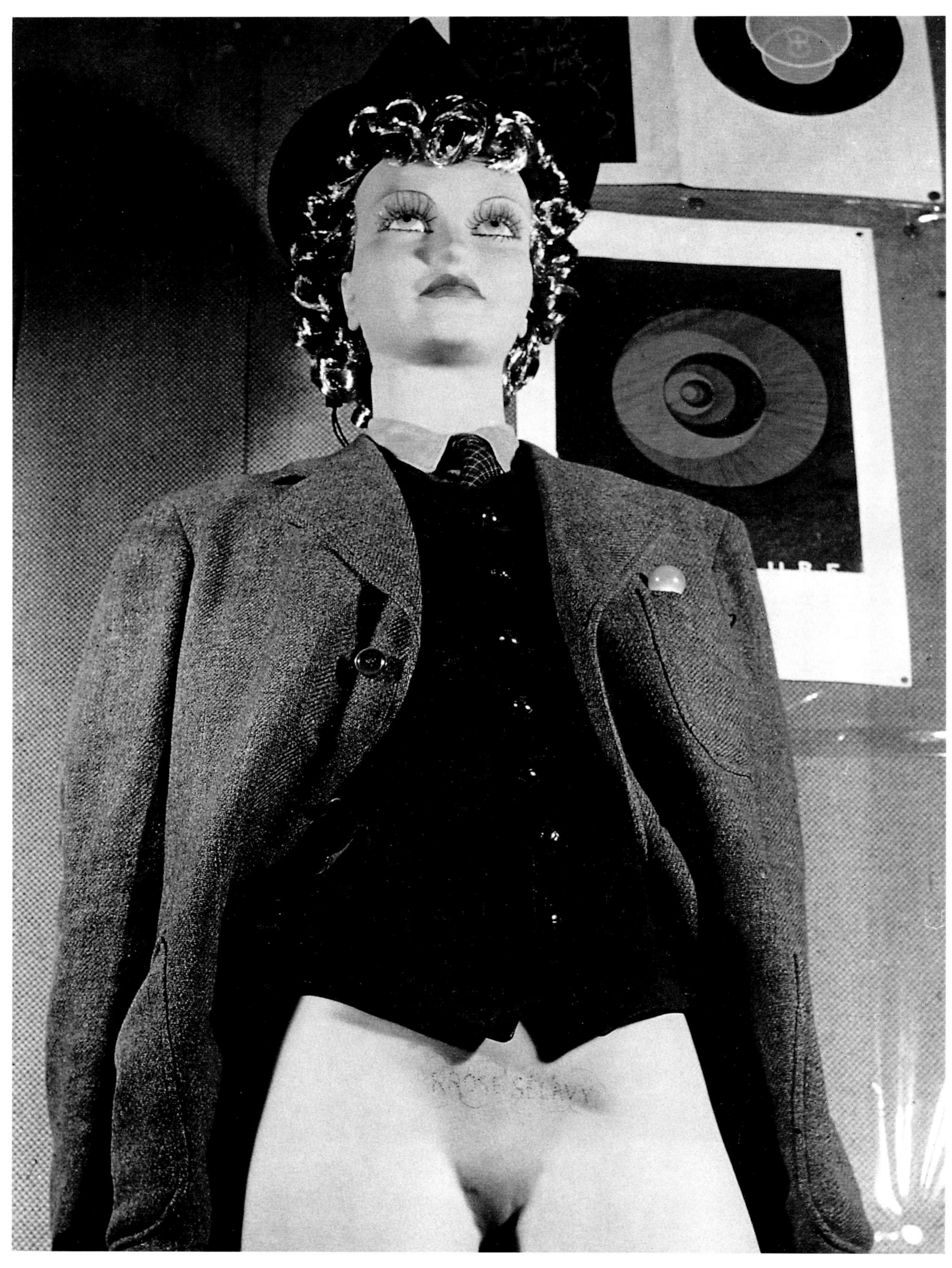

Raoul Ubac
Mannequin by Marcel Duchamp, 1938
Gelatin-silver print, 9⅛ x 6¾ inches (23.2 x 17.2 cm)
Musée d'Art Moderne de la Ville de Paris

circumspect form of male dress. The harshly drawn sexual distinctions of modern masculine and feminine attire—in which male clothing came to reflect moral seriousness and feminine dress remained the sole domain of sensuality and play—are both symptom and cause of an increasing self-consciousness about self-presentation, artifice, and the dividing line between the sexes.[11] In the early twentieth century, while women challenged social strictures by wearing men's clothing or elements thereof, engaging in presumably masculine activities ranging from working outside the home to sports to smoking, men dressed in traditional women's wear in only the most limited circumstances.[12]

Certain stereotypical "ideals" of feminine and masculine dress were perpetuated in mass-media fashion magazines and advertisements. Hannah Höch, one of the early exponents of Dada photomontage, cruised popular magazines in the 1920s, shattering the classically ordered, integrated bodies represented in the magazines into fragments, which she recombined into strange and exotic hybrid personae.[13] Mixing body parts and articles of clothing, Höch created unnaturalistic, fantastical creatures out of the "real" (photographs representing real objects and actual clippings from magazines). While an implicit critique of the "normative" rigidity of advertisements seems apparent in this work, there is also an undeniable playfulness and humor, which suggests Höch's own pleasure in her practice. The titles of the montages made during this period frequently refer to performers and marginalized members of society (tragediennes, vagabonds, lion tamers, clowns, strong men, singers, dancers). Here, Höch follows the traditional identification of artists with actors and circus performers, who represent for them a mutual ostracism due to lack of conformity to society's norms (precursors include Antoine Watteau's players from the commedia dell'arte and the *saltimbanques* of Pablo Picasso's Rose Period paintings). Höch's montage titles metaphorically indicate the social position of category crossers—people who represent ambiguous identities of any kind—which her hybrid subjects present. Like carnival and circus performers, they occupy the liminal space of the freak, in which the unusual is permissible as long as it is circumscribed.[14]

It is the juxtaposition of apparently disparate parts that causes the "gender trouble" in Höch's photomontages, just as it does in the drag performance of Duchamp as Rrose. In one set of photographs of Rrose Sélavy, she holds the fur collar up around her neck in a typically "female" coy gesture. Upon careful inspection, the hands appear too small in relation to the face and are at an impossible angle to the body, but we do not need these clues, since Duchamp has never intended to pass—his playful subversion would not work if we were not in possession of the knowledge that he is a man wearing women's clothes. (In fact, Rrose Sélavy's hands and hat belonged to a female acquaintance, Germaine Everling.) This back-and-forth game is the keystone to Duchamp's work, unfolding across the course of his lifetime. After drawing a moustache on the *Mona Lisa*, making "her" into a "him," in 1965, he "shaves" her, creating a reverse drag. Similarly, a female mannequin is cross-dressed in Duchamp's clothes at the 1938 *Exposition Internationale du Surréalisme*, reversing Rrose's male-to-female drag. In a 1950 letter, Duchamp refers to himself as "*une primadonna à l'envers*" (a prima donna in reverse) and signs himself "Sarah Bernhardt alias Marcel Duchamp."[15] Here, Duchamp performs textual cross-dressing in an unending circuit of identifications: he represents himself as a woman, referring to an actress famous for her own cross-dressed performances. The "prima donna in reverse" makes him a man again, while recalling the artist's own inverted prima donna—the bearded *Mona Lisa* and, by extension, Leonardo's possible hidden portrait of himself as a woman. Leonardo, known as a lover of men, conceives himself as a married woman; Duchamp, a lover of women, shares his identity with a similarly disposed actress.

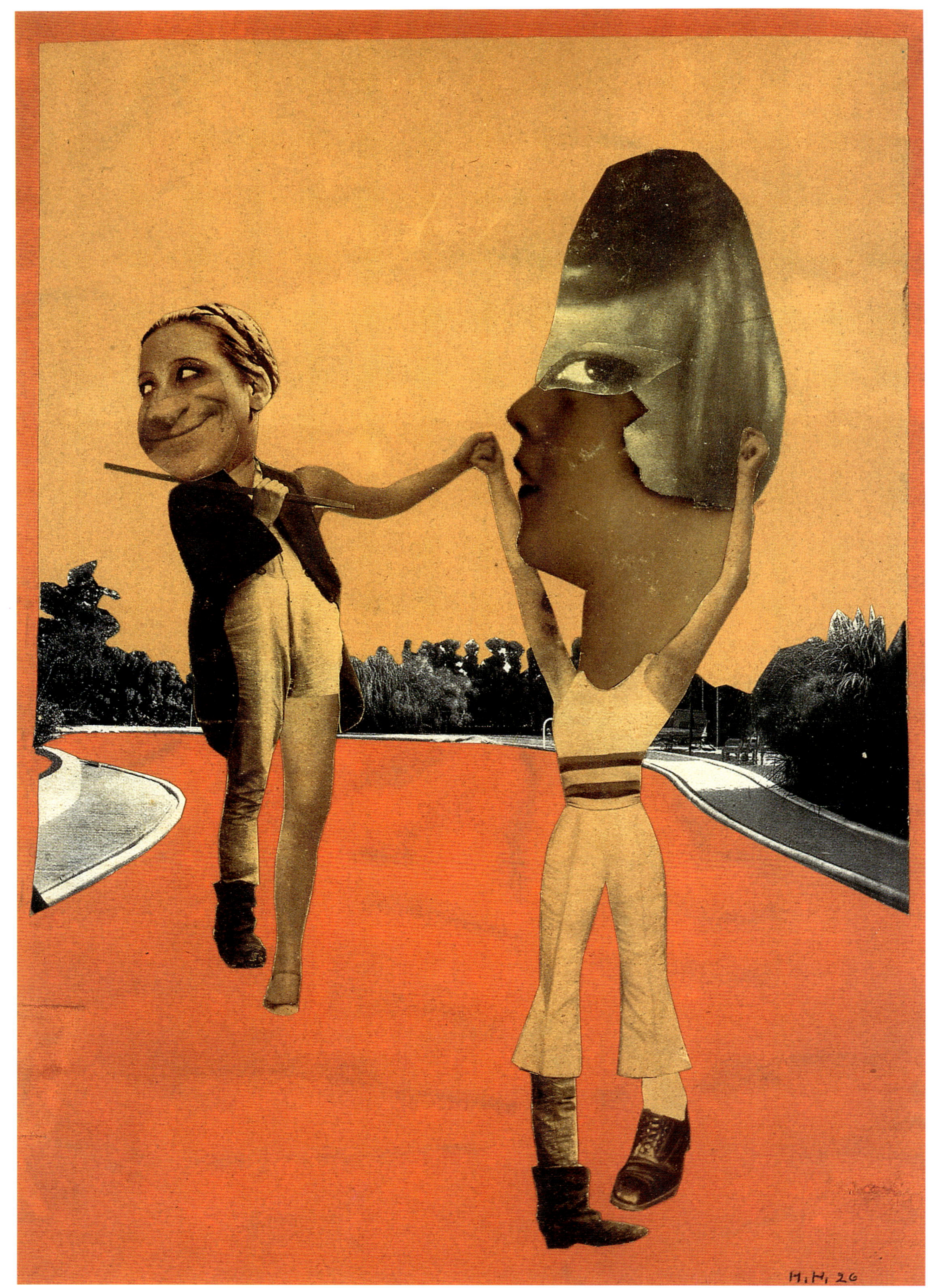

Hannah Höch
Vagabonds (*Vagabunden*), 1926
Photomontage, 12 3/8 x 8 7/8 inches (31.5 x 22.5 cm)
Collection of G. Rossi, Milan

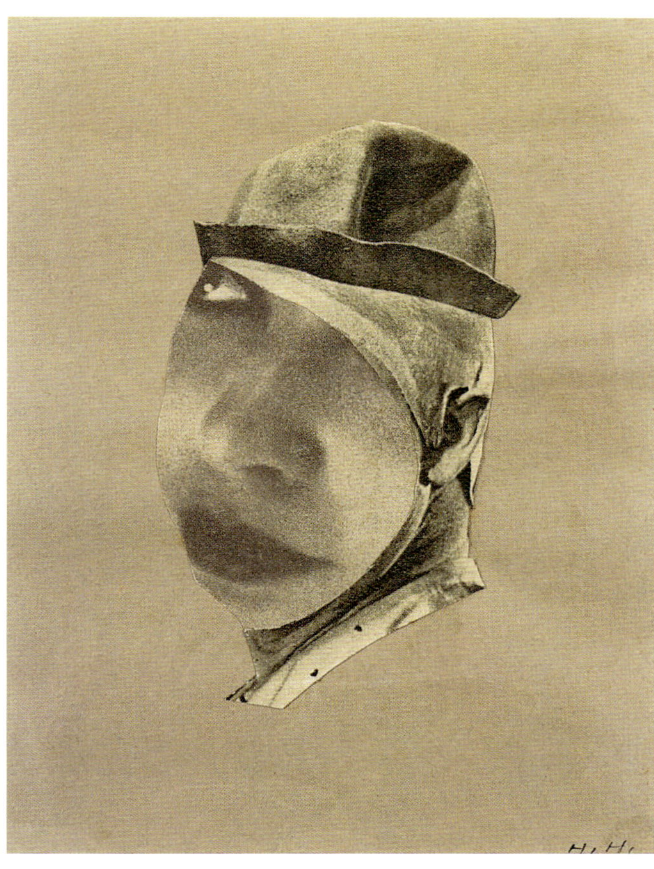

Hannah Höch
Clown, 1924
Photomontage, 4 15/16 x 3 3/4 inches (12.5 x 9.5 cm)
Barry Friedman Ltd., New York

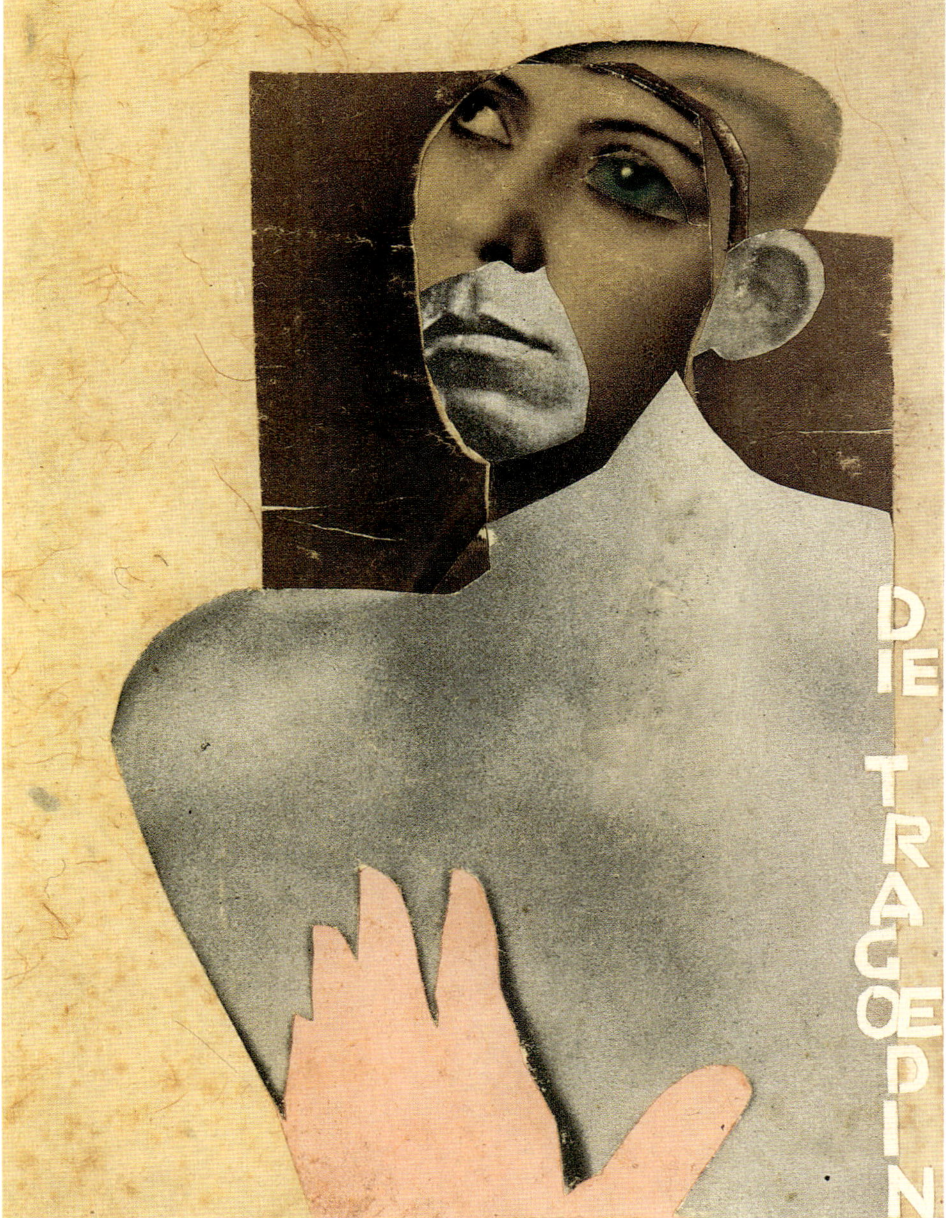

Hannah Höch
The Tragedienne (*Die Tragoedin*), 1924
Photomontage, 6 5/8 x 5 inches (16.8 x 12.8 cm)
Sprengel Museum, Hannover

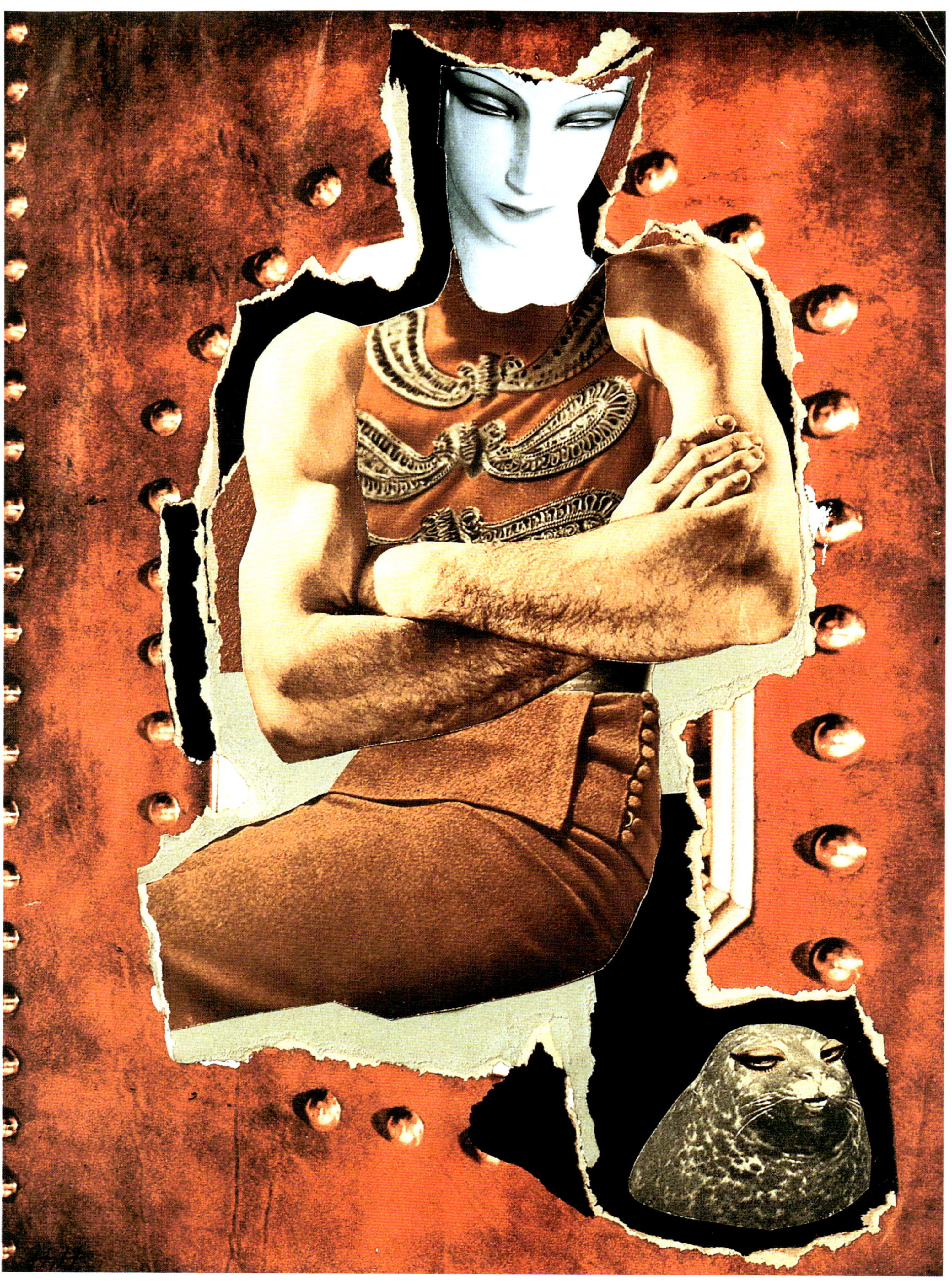

Hannah Höch
Tamer (*Dompteuse*), ca. 1930
Photomontage, 14 x 10¼ inches (35.5 x 26 cm)
Kunsthaus Zürich

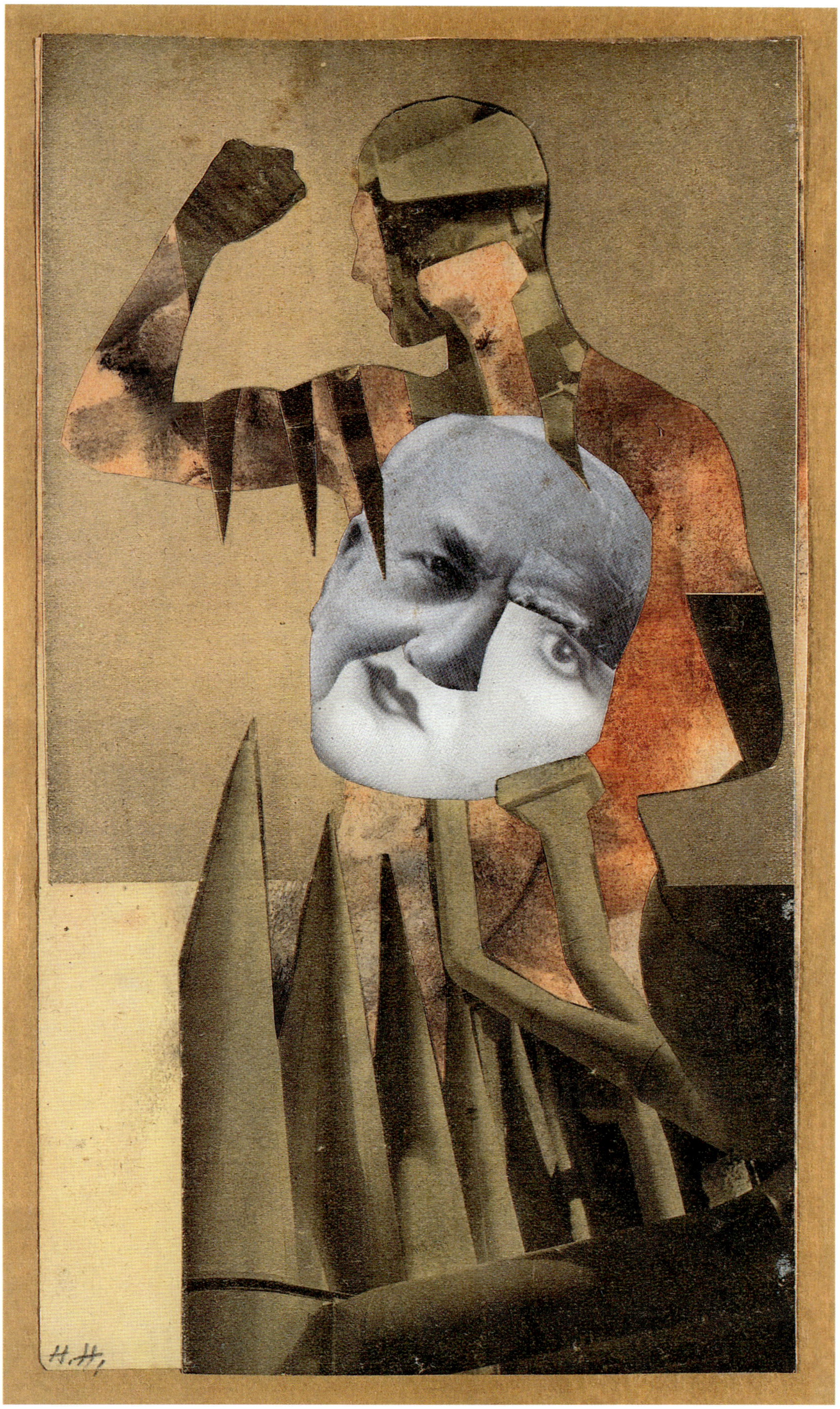

Hannah Höch
The Strong Men (*Die starken Männer*), 1931
Photomontage, 9 5/8 x 5 5/16 inches (24.5 x 13.5 cm)
Institut für Auslandsbeziehungen, Stuttgart

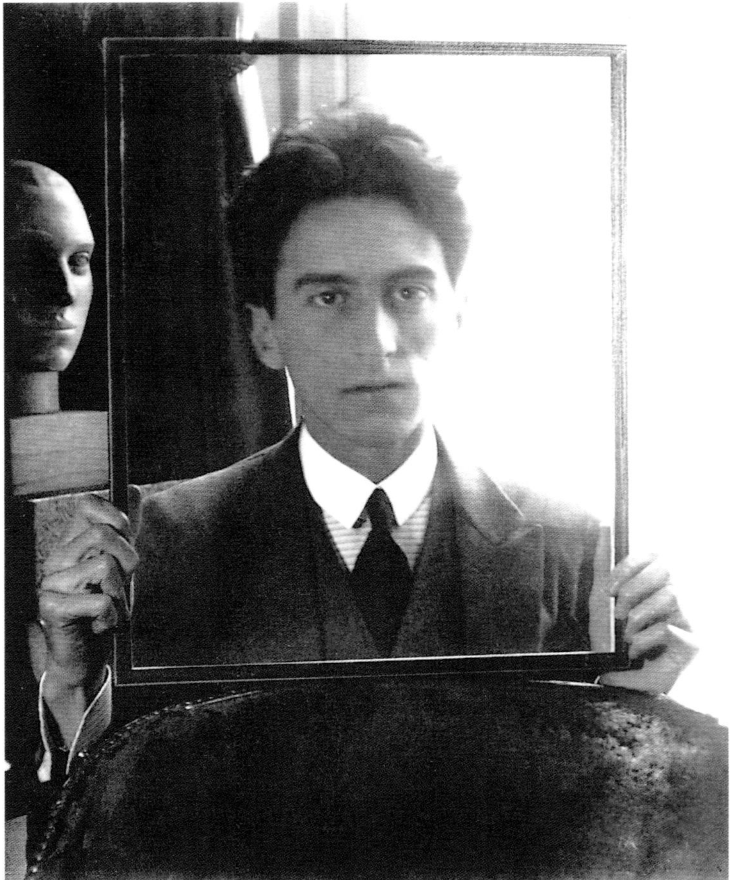

Man Ray
Jean Cocteau, 1922
Gelatin-silver print,
4¾ x 3¾ inches (12.1 x 9.6 cm)
The Metropolitan Museum of Art,
New York, Purchase, Joyce and
Robert Menschel Gift, 1987

Gay Paris (circa 1930)

Man Ray participated in many of these gender games with Duchamp, photographing Rrose Sélavy and pieces signed by her.[16] In his own endeavors, Man Ray became a photographer of women par excellence: his fashion work, portraiture, and more experimental images significantly feature female subjects. Employing the kind of puns favored by his Dada friends Duchamp and Francis Picabia, he would create a female torso that resembled a minotaur; a woman with her head thrown back to suggest the male member; or a nude portrait of a woman with a printing-press handle as surrogate penis. These fetishistic pictures of phallic women—literal representations of women having the phallus and being the phallus—stand out in Man Ray's lavish and glamorous female portraiture. Among his most sumptuous photographs are those of Barbette, the transvestite trapeze artist championed by Jean Cocteau and beloved by Surrealist Paris. This circus performer, born Vander Clyde in Texas, was one of the most beautiful "ladies" in between-the-wars Paris. Barbette's transformation was especially appealing to Cocteau, who was perennially drawn to the theme of metamorphosis in his own work.[17] In writing about the trapeze artist, Cocteau refers to the liminal space of Barbette's public performances as being "in that magic light of the theater, in that club of tricks where the truth no longer has currency, where the natural no longer has any value."[18]

Barbette's fame should be seen in relation to a contemporaneous interest in gender identity, both in the psychoanalytic literature, as well as in more popular writing. Joan Riviere's 1929 article on feminine masquerade,[19] predicated on Freud's notion of the bisexual foundation of identity, was produced in the context of a burgeoning literature on homosexuality, in which cross-dressing was examined as a symptom of "psychopathology."[20] The early twentieth century witnessed the flowering of the nineteenth century's seemingly insatiable interest in the sexual body: the psychomedical construction of identity (and its disruption in madness); its sexual practices, both hetero and homo; and especially its commerce (prostitution).[21]

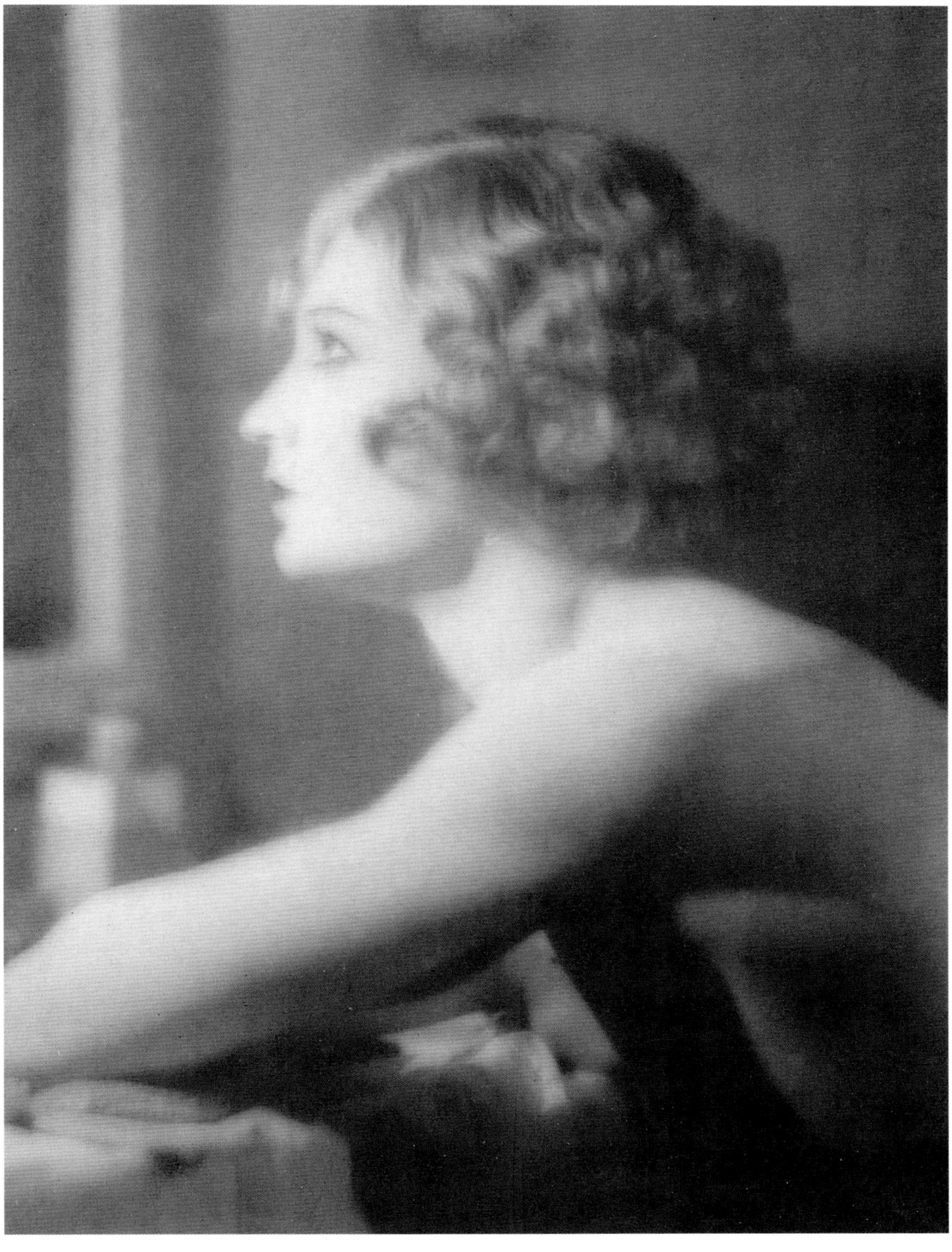

Man Ray
Barbette, 1924
Gelatin-silver print, 7⅞ x 5⅞ inches (20 x 14.9 cm)
Collection of Timothy Baum, New York

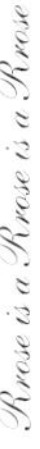

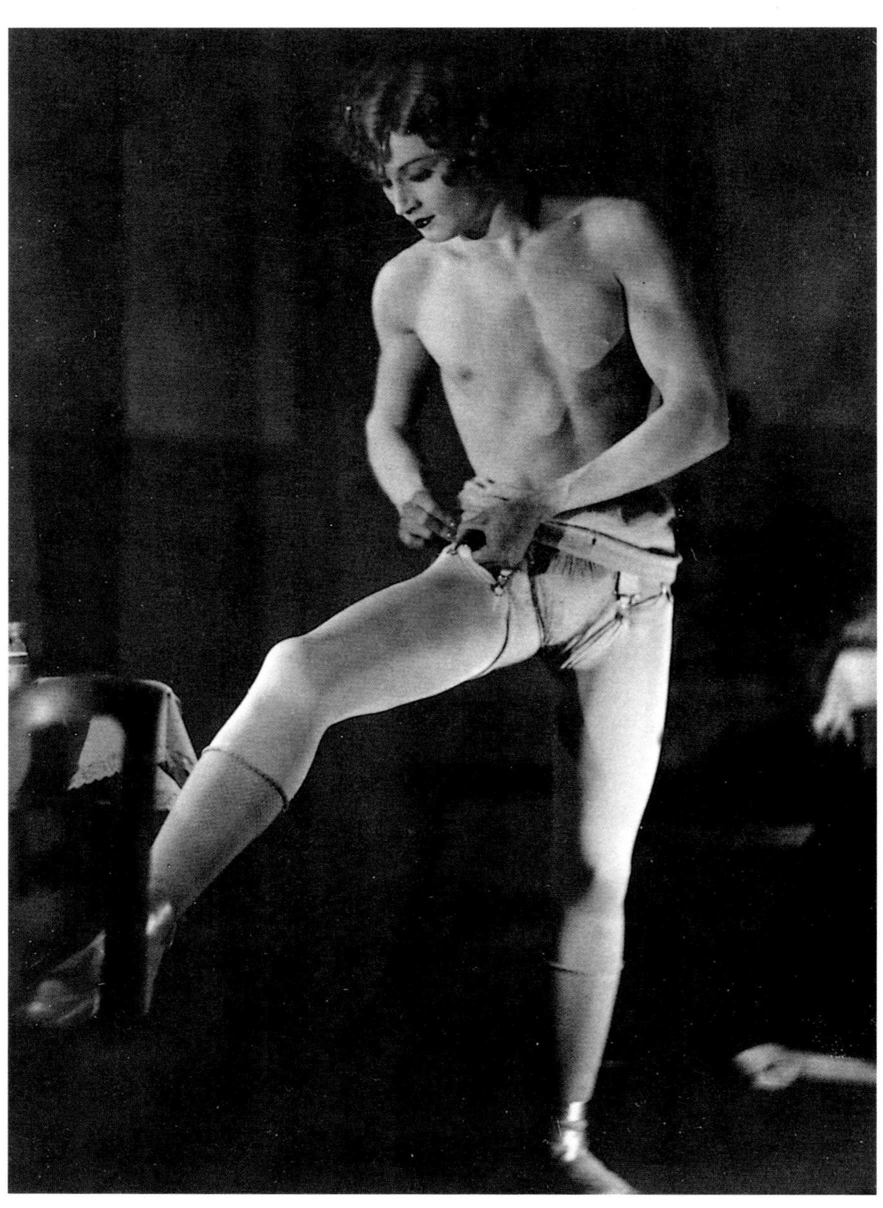

Man Ray
Barbette, ca. 1920s
Gelatin-silver print, 4⅛ x 3 .nches (10.5 x 7.5 cm)
The Metropolitan Museum of Art, New York, Ford Motor Company Collection,
Gift of Ford Motor Company and John C. Waddell, 1987

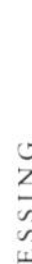

Brassaï's photographs of brothels, gay and lesbian clubs, and masked balls document the sexual activities of early 1930s Parisian nightlife, illustrating the intersection of scientific and popular interest. Like the Surrealists he frequented, Brassaï followed the nineteenth-century realist tradition of the journalistic voyeur-observer, the flaneur who perambulates the city, gathering material in the process. First published in 1933, in his book *Paris de nuit*, Brassaï's photographs are characterized by the voyeur's delight in the unusual and forbidden.[22] In the text accompanying his later edition of photographs from this period, *The Secret Paris of the '30s*, Brassaï's value-laden descriptions indicate the disdain with which he approached these subjects.[23] While he is drawn in by "*les fleurs du mal*"—the transgressive pleasures his "outlaw" subjects enjoy—he also underscores their dangerousness and violence. Yet he was not necessarily unsympathetic to the people in his photographs. They are individualized in tight close-ups and frequently look directly at the camera with a haughty disdain or even a kind of patience, the latter perhaps the result of the cooperation required to get the shot.

In theatrical traditions from the ancients to Shakespeare to the circus, men have frequently appeared as women, and women often performed cross-dressed as men in burlesque shows. At carnival time and at masked balls, sex changes were common. As mentioned above, these diversions from "normal" behavior were sanctioned in certain spaces and at certain times. Yet there is a history of individuals who determined to dress the part they chose whenever they wanted, and whose acts have become the stuff of historical accounts. In the period between the wars, apart from the psychomedical literature, a number of books collecting the stories of these figures were published. The French author O. P. Gilbert's studies spawned English translations and imitators.[24] In all of these works there is a focus on the role of clothing in the fixing (or undoing) of gender identity. The narrator of Virginia Woolf's 1928 novel *Orlando: A Biography* articulates this view of attire when s/he states, "In every human being a vacillation from one sex to the other takes place, and often it is only the clothes that keep the male or female likeness, while underneath the sex is the very opposite of what it is above."[25] Two years after the publication of *Orlando*, Virginia and Leonard Woolf's Hogarth Press, the main publisher of psychoanalytic texts in London, released J. C. Flügel's study *The Psychology of Clothes*, which identified the "Great Masculine Renunciation" of vestimentary finery.[26] Flügel argued that, while it was possible for women to wear men's clothes, men could not breach the gender divide without opprobrium.

Poets throughout history have conceived of social identity as a mask. Certainly, individuals whose lives specifically involve a daily decision about artifice might be especially disposed to such reveries. Anyone who does not automatically fit the expectations of dominant (read patriarchal) society will understand the masquerade of conformity. So it comes as no great surprise that women, who have been schooled from childhood in the arts of makeup and graceful deportment, have chosen to examine gender identity in the twentieth century. Or that some of the most incisive work embodying "gender trouble" between the wars was produced in the context of lesbian relationships (for gay or lesbian subjects, who are put in the position of "passing" or "coming out," are similarly forced to confront their identity). These creations often functioned as love letters, which indicates the pleasures inherent in the production of the work. For example, Höch's gender-blending photomontages were produced during her relationship with Til Brugman (*Clown* is a portrait of Brugman);[27] *Orlando* was created as an act of love for Vita Sackville-West; and Claude Cahun, a writer and photographer associated with the Surrealists, collaborated with her companion, Suzanne Malherbe.

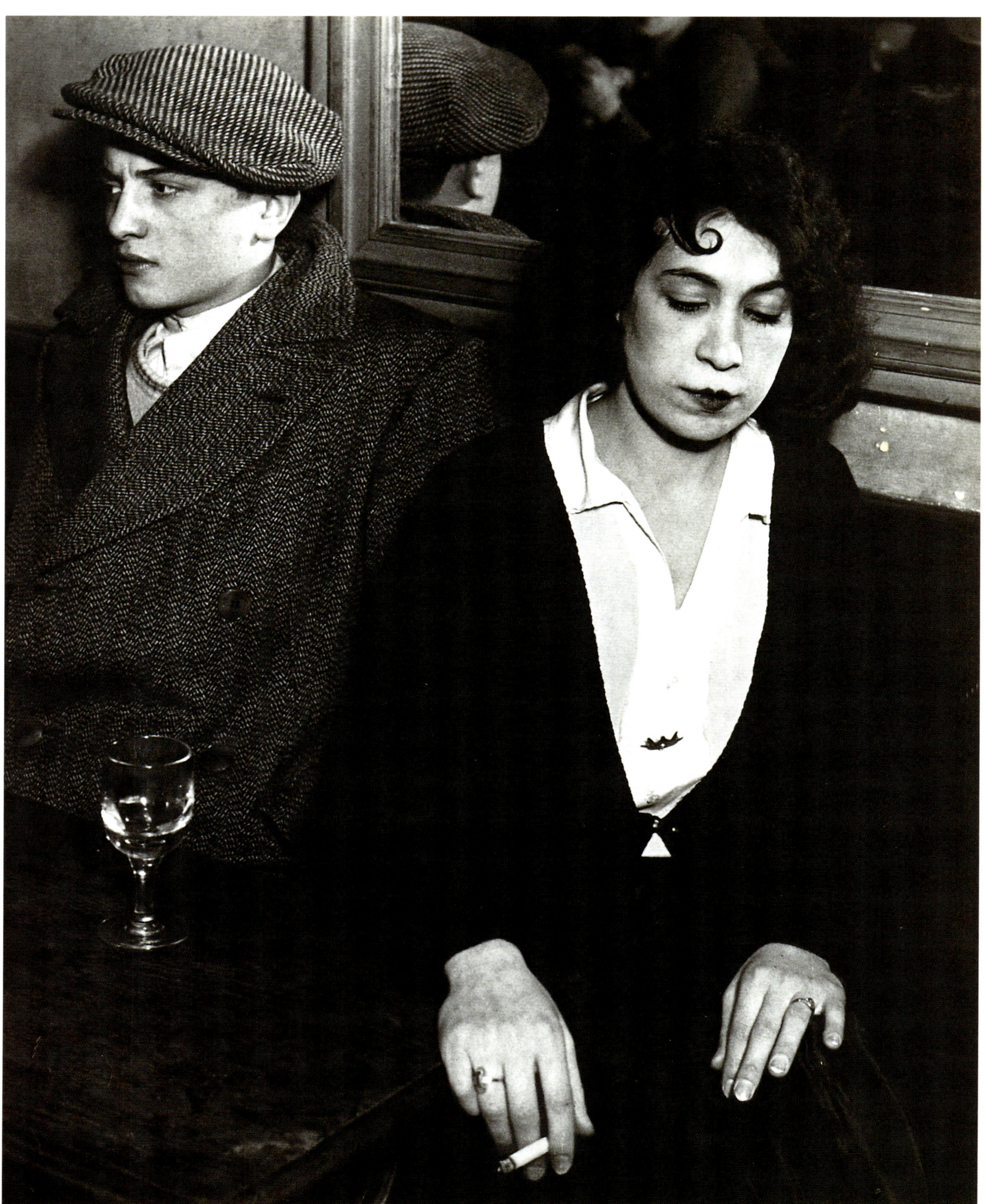

Brassaï
Quarrel, 1932
Gelatin-silver print, 11½ x 9¼ inches (29.2 x 23.5 cm)
The Museum of Modern Art, New York,
David H. McAlpin Fund

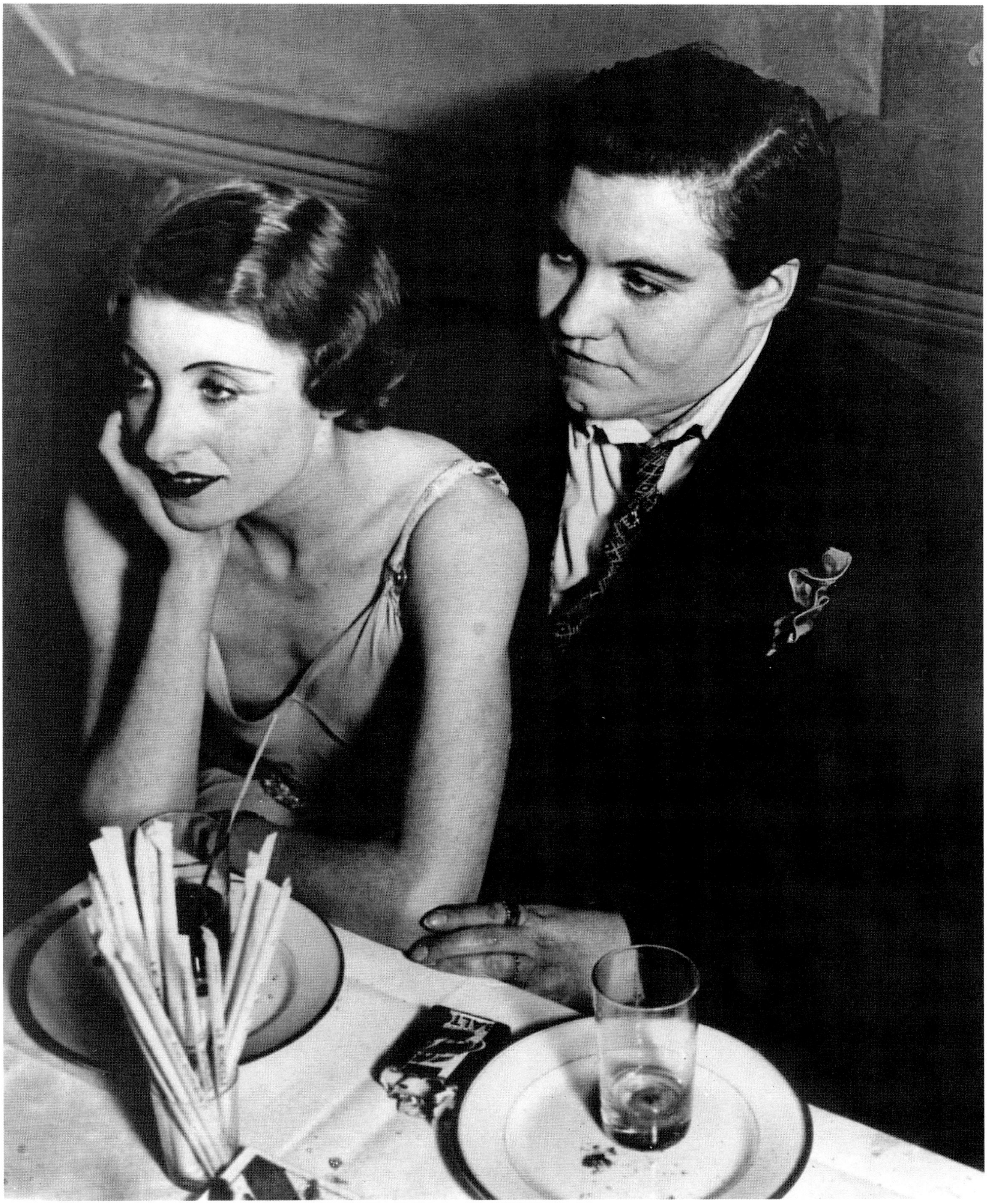

Brassaï

Female Couple, 1932

Gelatin-silver print, 11⅞ x 8⅞ inches (30.2 x 22.6 cm)

The Museum of Modern Art, New York,

David H. McAlpin Fund

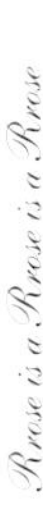

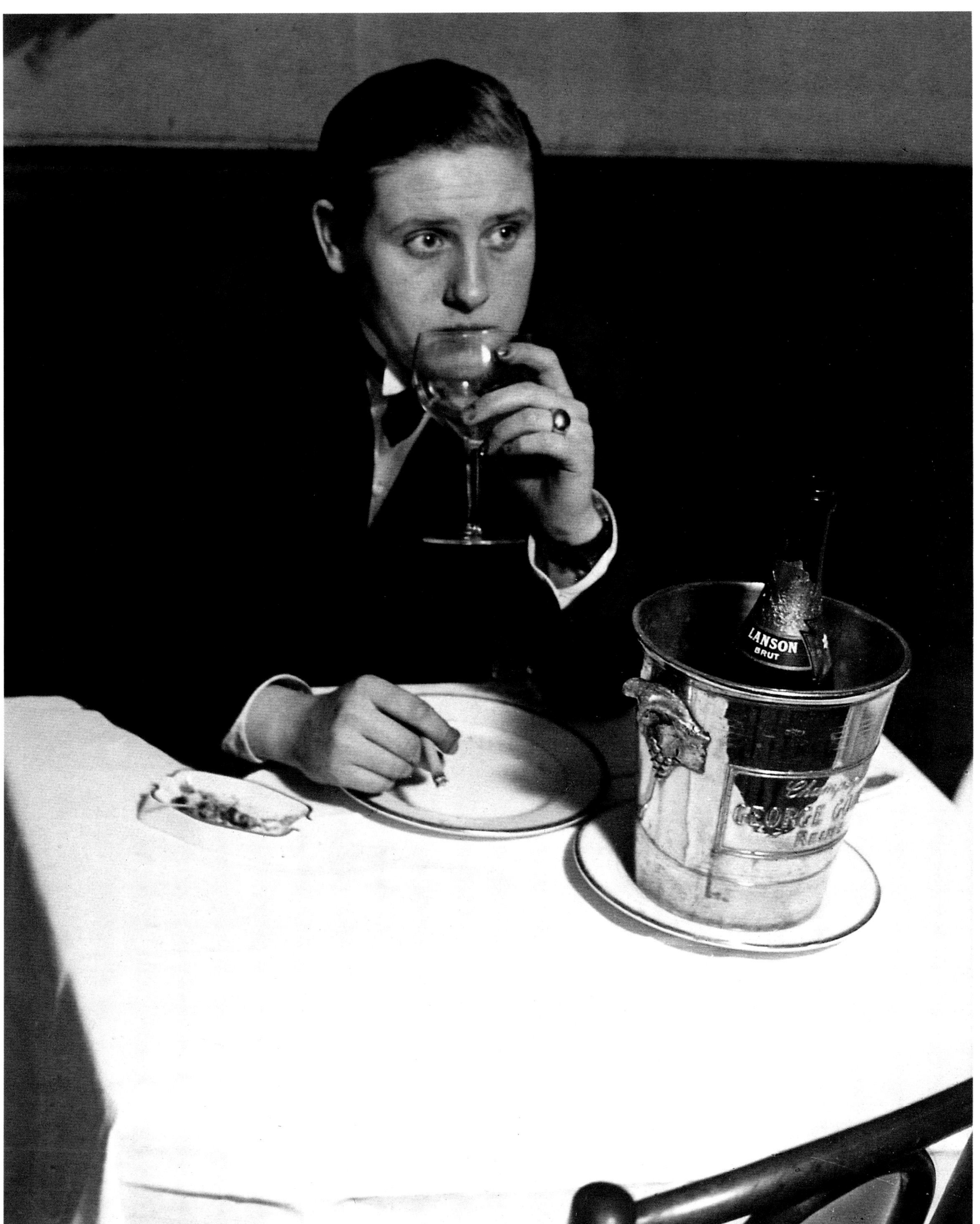

Brassaï
Woman at Le Monocle, Montparnasse, 1933
Gelatin-silver print, 12 x 9½ inches (30.5 x 24.1 cm)
The Museum of Modern Art, New York,
David H. McAlpin Fund

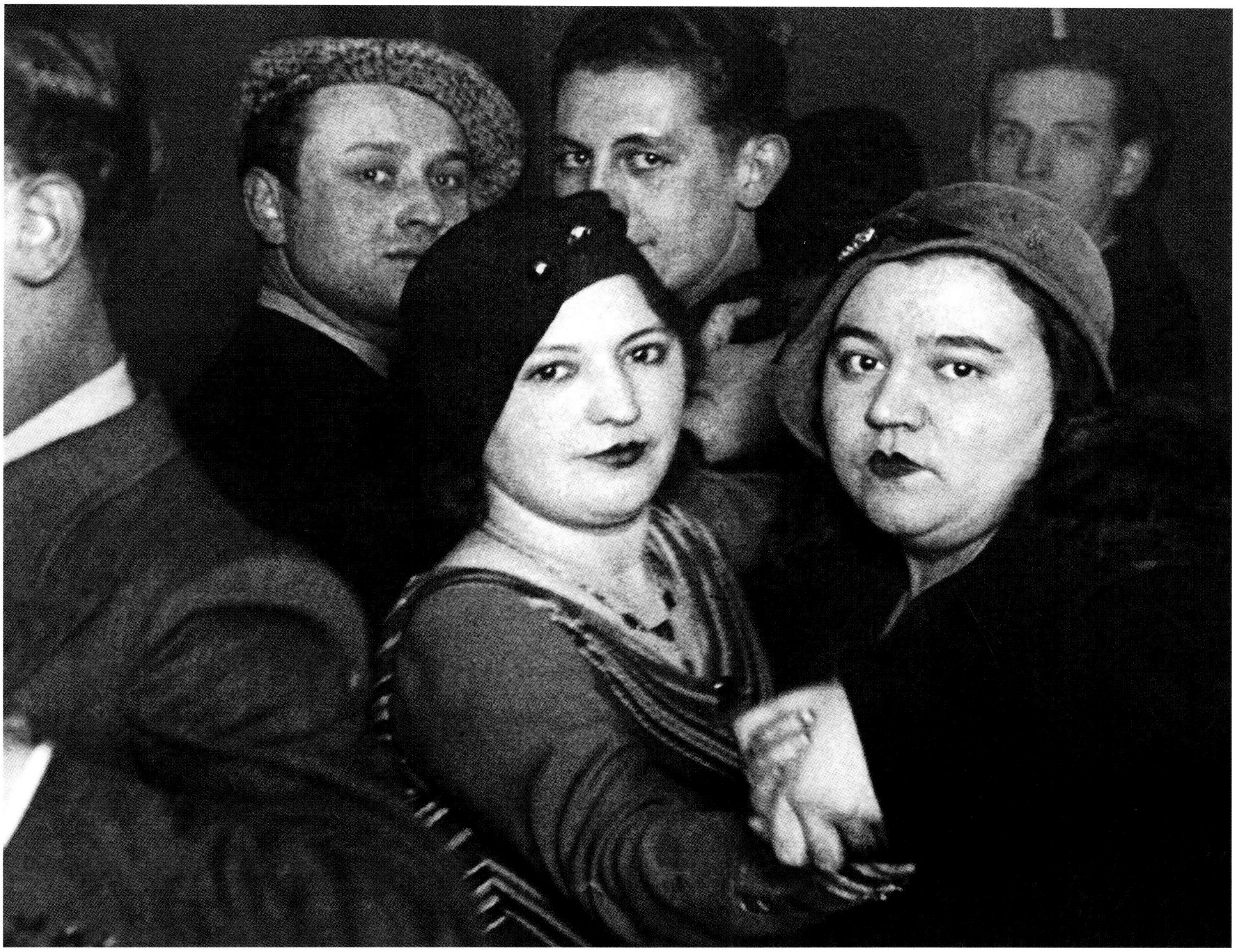

Brassaï

Homosexual Ball, 1933

Gelatin-silver print, 9 ¼ x 11 ⅝ inches (23.5 x 29.5 cm)

The Museum of Modern Art, New York,

Gift of Gilberte Brassaï

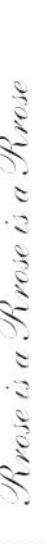

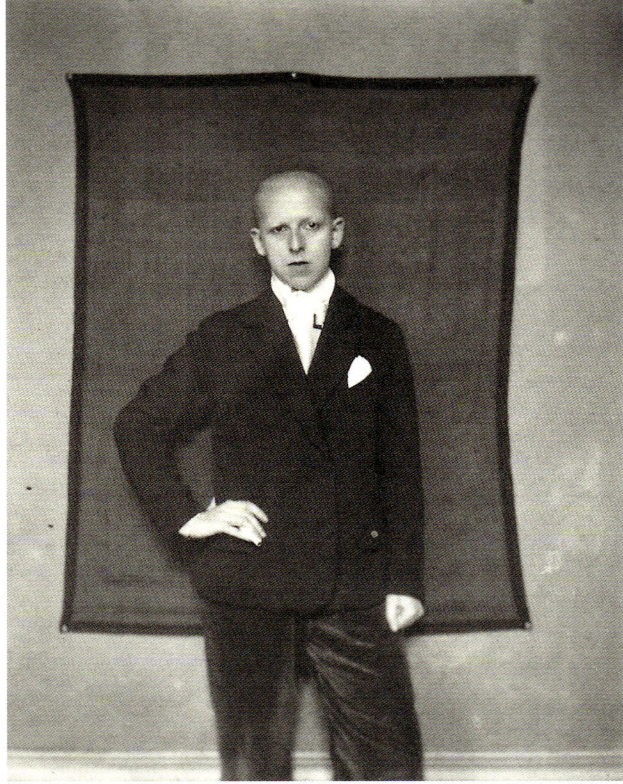

Claude Cahun
Self-Portrait, ca. 1921
Gelatin-silver print, 4 5/16 x 3 1/4 inches (10.9 x 8.2 cm)
Collection of Richard and Ronay Menschel

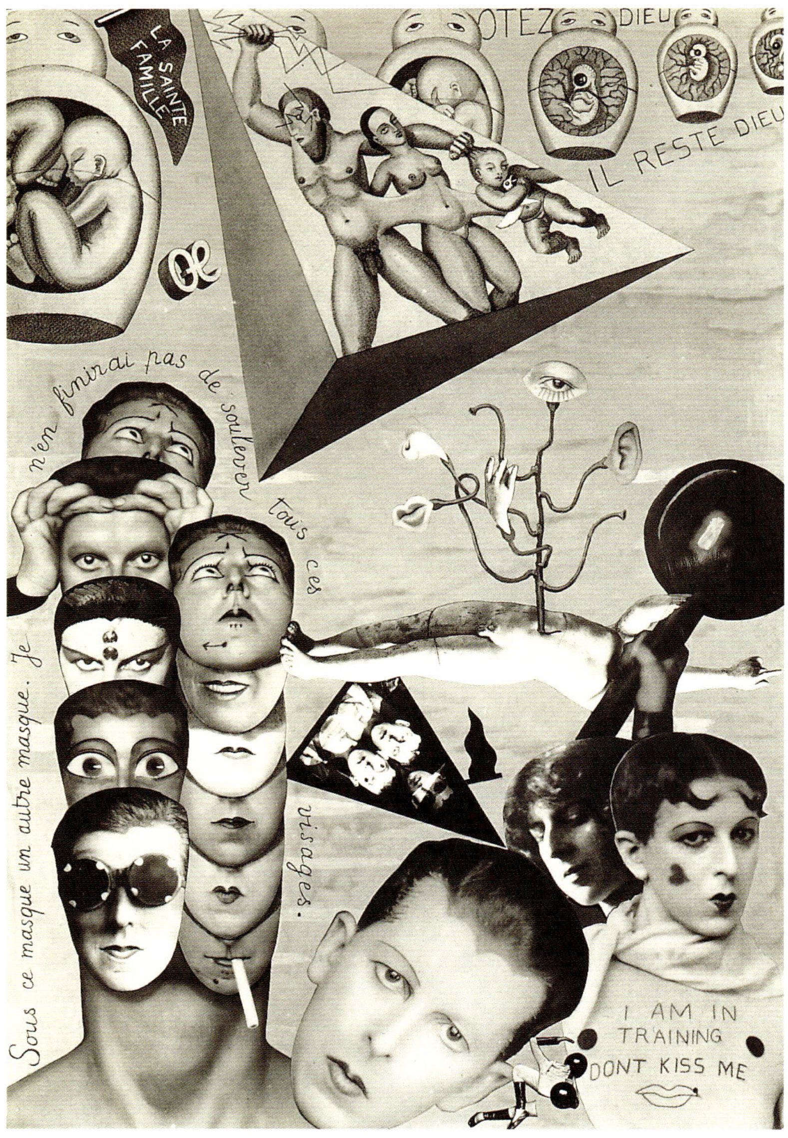

Claude Cahun
I.O.U. (Self-Pride), 1929–30
Gelatin-silver print, 6 x 4 1/8 inches (15.2 x 10.3 cm)
Los Angeles County Museum of Art,
The Collection of Audrey and Sydney Irmas,
Gift of the Irmas Intervivos Trust of June 7, 1982

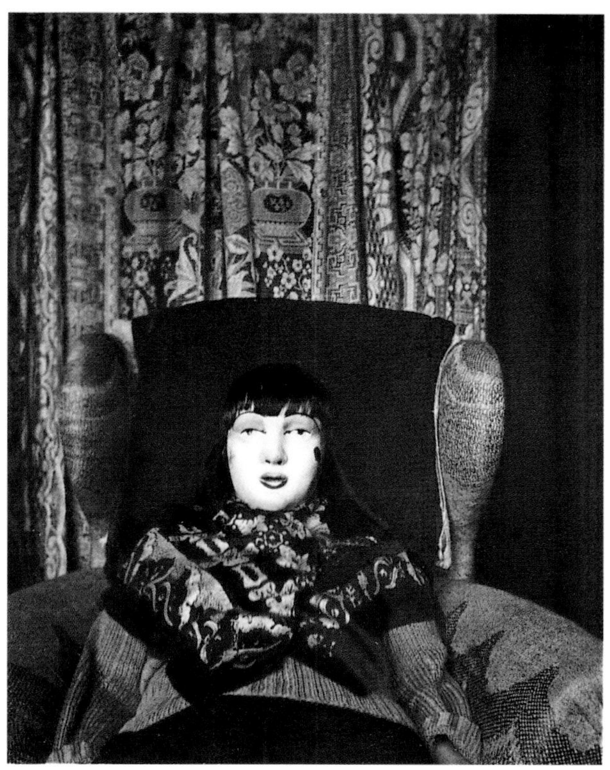

Claude Cahun
Self-Portrait, ca. 1928
Gelatin-silver print,
3 15/16 x 2 15/16 inches (10 x 7.5 cm)
Galerie Berggruen, Paris

Cahun performed both textual and photographic cross-dressing. Born Lucy Schwob, her pseudonymous first name, Claude, is gender ambiguous in French.[28] In her photographic self-portraits, she often appears as a dandy in masculine attire and short hair. In fact, during her lifetime and even today, Cahun has frequently been presumed to be a man on the evidence of her literary as well as artistic pursuits. Cahun was profoundly committed to exploring questions of identity—and her own identity, as woman and as creative person. She was well known for *Les Paris sont ouverts*, her engagé defense of Surrealist practice in the face of Communist criticism; she translated the renowned sexologist Havelock Ellis; and, in her prose poem *Aveux non avenus*, she examined the divided self, continuing the literary legacy of Arthur Rimbaud and the Symbolists, whom she admired and to whom she was linked through her uncle, Marcel Schwob, who was their contemporary.[29] *Aveux non avenus* is illustrated with photomontages Cahun created with Malherbe, who identified herself as Moore.[30] In *I.O.U. (Self-Pride)* (1929–30), which was reproduced as plate X in *Aveux non avenus*, eleven heads, including that of a doll-like Sumerian-style goddess, all of which appear to be Claude, rise on one neck. The resulting lingam shape is surrounded by the words, "Beneath this mask another mask. I will never be done lifting off all these visages."[31] That Cahun saw identity as a masquerade is indicated by the artifice of all her self-portraits, including those in which she literally wears a mask. Like many of the artists in this exhibition, Cahun was involved with the theater. Thus, it is not always clear which of her costumed self-portraits were produced in the context of theatrical productions. The distinction is not, however, consequential because the very nature of portraiture involves the subject's collaboration in its creation. Cahun is the author of her self in these performances, whether theatrical or strictly photographic.

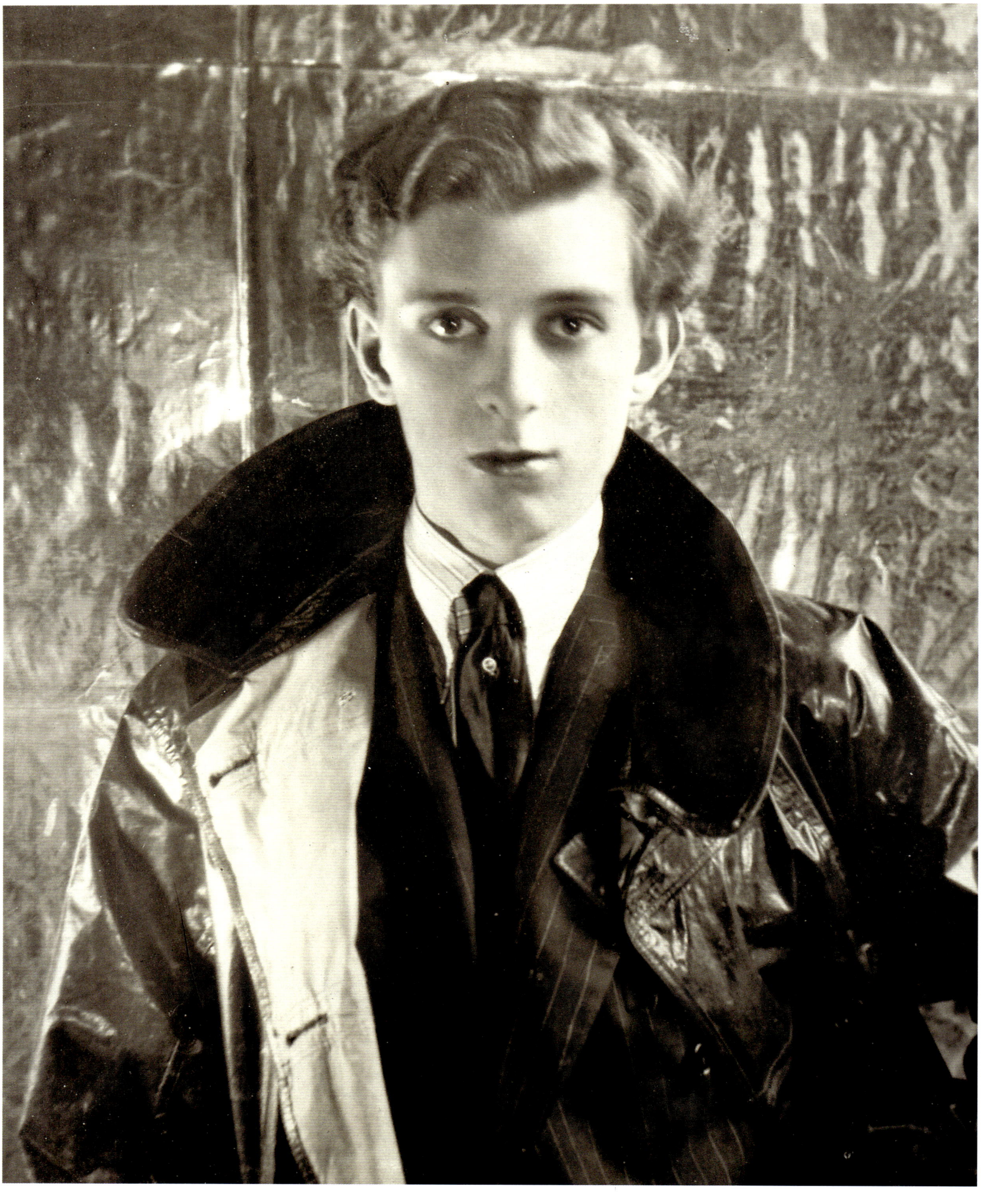

Cecil Beaton
Portrait of Stephen Tennant, 1927
Gelatin-silver print, 12 x 10 inches (30.5 x 25.4 cm)
Courtesy of Robert Miller Gallery, New York

Surrealist Diffusion: London (circa 1935)

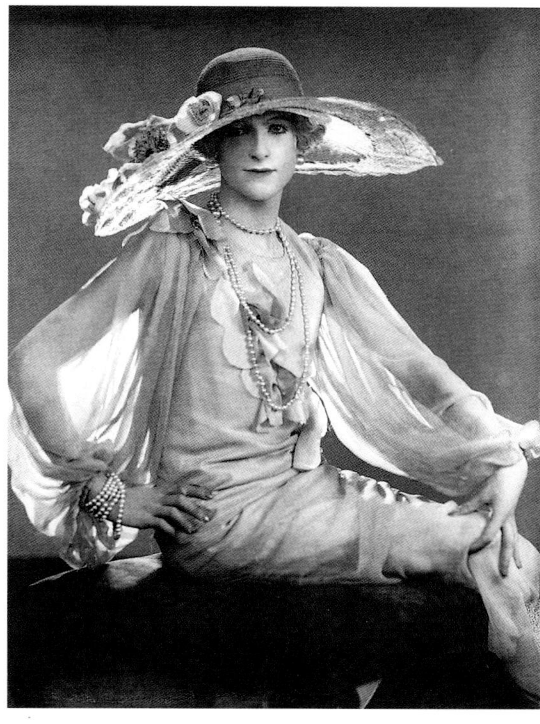

Dorothy Wilding
Cecil Beaton, 1925, in costume for *All the Vogue*, Cambridge Footlights revue
National Portrait Gallery, London

Gertrude Stein, the matriarch of expatriate Paris and modernist writing, pioneered a sensual literary style in which strangely juxtaposed words exude a variety of meanings, often deeply erotic. Like Cahun's, Stein's mature work celebrates sexual and gender ambiguity, and both women blossomed within the context of a lesbian relationship. In the mid-1930s, Cecil Beaton created a formal double portrait of Stein, in which her substantial presence is reiterated as if to suggest that the woman-behind-the-woman, her alter ego, is Stein herself. Beaton continues the game that Stein initiated when she published *The Autobiography of Alice B. Toklas* in 1933. Autobiography is a form in which the author's subject, the person whose character is developed, is the self. Toklas's "autobiography," which was written by Stein, subverts this relationship between author and subject, since the autobiographical writer and self are not contiguous, and because the book is Stein's memoir, told through Toklas's "voice." It is tempting to compare Beaton's double portrait with a decidedly more casual photograph, presumably taken at the same time, which reveals Toklas, slightly out-of-focus, in the proverbial wings. Here Alice takes the position of Gertrude's alter ego. Is Alice Gertrude or Gertrude Alice?

Beaton's double portrait of Stein recalls the frequent recourse, in his photographs, to mirror reflections, which made it possible to include himself in a portrait (hopefully, of someone grand).[32] This interest also seems to be linked to a delight in shimmering surfaces of all kinds—even glare—that emphasized the artifice of his images and promoted the status of his sitters as Olympian models divorced from pedestrian existence. As a society and fashion photographer, Beaton represented a particularly exaggerated femininity, the kind that frequently seems indistinguishable from drag. Certainly, he was conscious of the masquerade entailed; his own numerous cross-dressed self-portraits indicate a particular pleasure in constructing the self.[33] "I don't want people to know me as I am," he writes in a diary, "but only as I'm trying to be."[34] His professional endeavors were all in fields devoted to artifice—society portraiture; fashion photography; theater and film, for both of which he designed sets and costumes. To all of these he brought the rarefied sensibility of the dandy.[35]

Madame Yevonde, the professional name of Yevonde Cumbers Middleton, was a colleague in the field of portraiture. Her best work is a series of portraits of society women in the guise of Greek mythological goddesses.[36] Probably inspired by a costume ball, of which there were many in pre–World War II Paris and London, Yevonde did more than document fantastic outfits, such as that worn by Lady Dorothy Warrender, which was designed by Beaton's friend Oliver Messel. Yevonde combined her talent for the nascent Vivex color process with a Surrealistically inspired iconography that can, like Beaton's, become delightfully kitsch. Though part of a tradition in British portraiture dating back at least to Joshua Reynolds, in which aristocratic sitters are allegorically equated with mythological figures, the gusto with which Yevonde describes this project in her autobiography suggests a more personal investment.[37] An outspoken suffragist and supporter of women in the field of professional photography, she advocated color portraiture as the way of the future. Yevonde's *Goddesses* photographs heroize modern women, and may be linked to recurrent feminist attempts to identify historic role models—from Cahun's series on "Héroines" to Sackville-West's biographies of saints to Judy Chicago's compendium of foremothers featured in *The Dinner Party* (1979).[38]

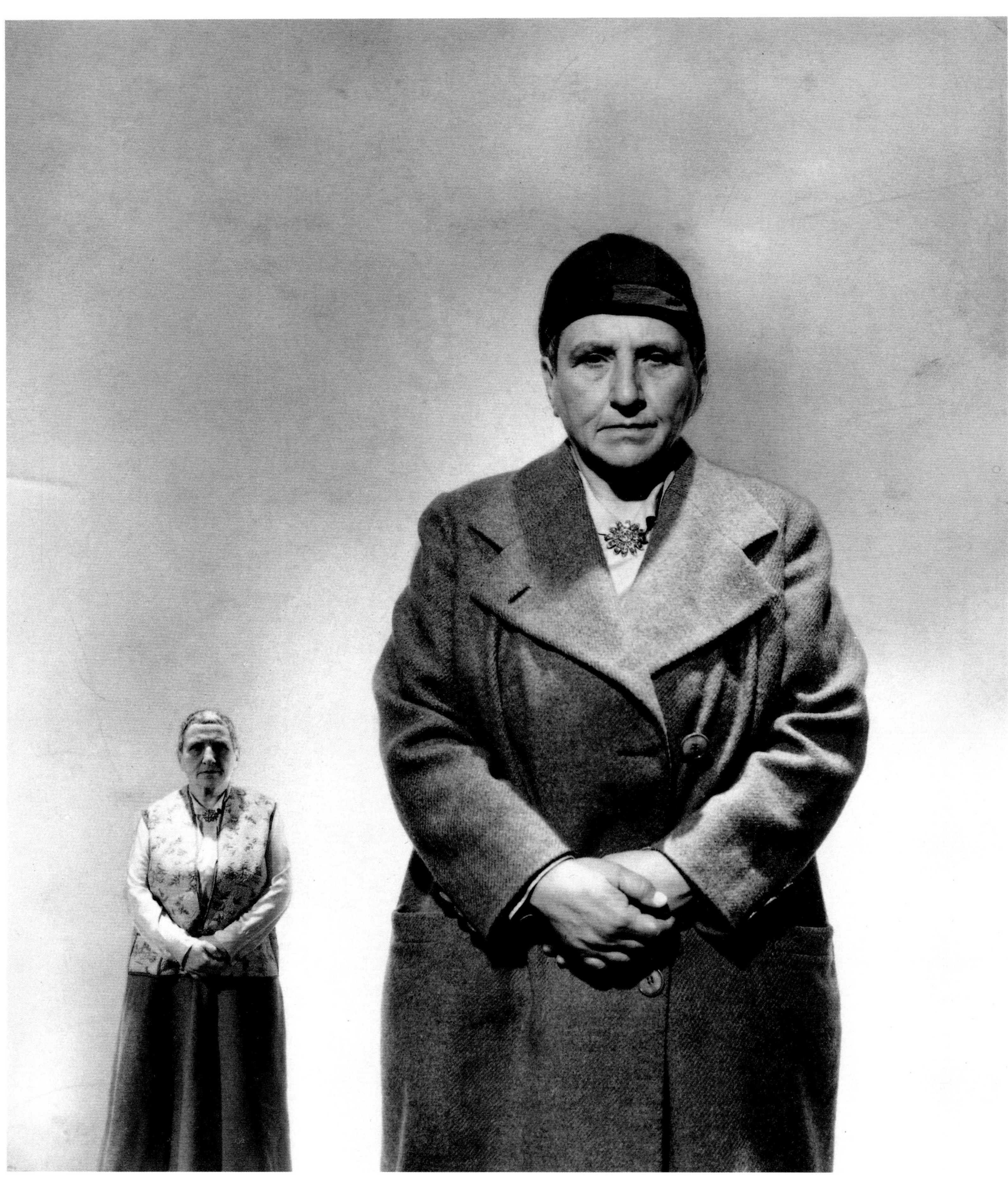

Cecil Beaton
Gertrude Stein, 1935
Airbrush on gelatin-silver print, 9 5/16 x 8 1/4 inches (23.6 x 21 cm)
Cecil Beaton Archive, Sotheby's London

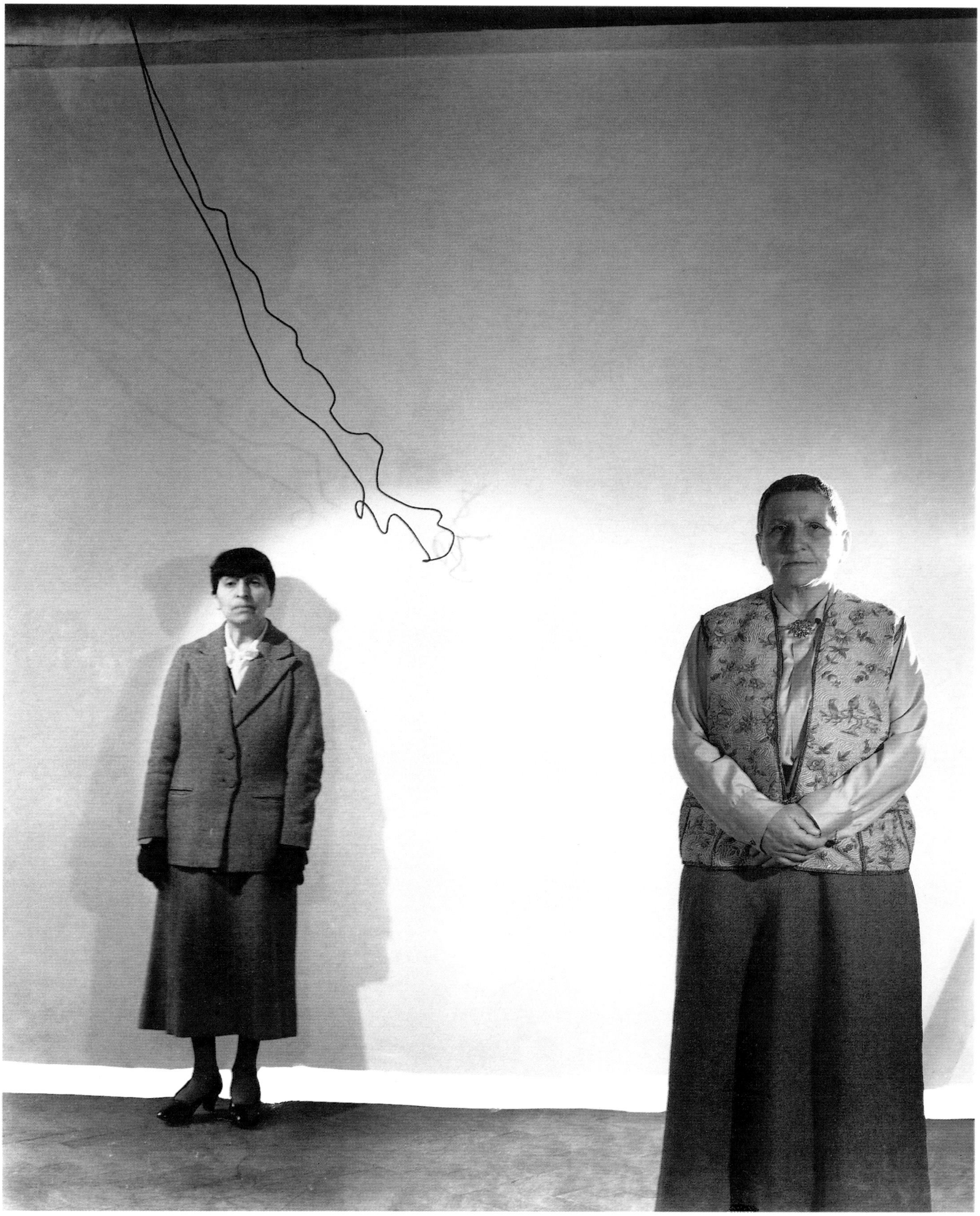

Cecil Beaton
Gertrude Stein and Alice B. Toklas, 1935
Gelatin-silver print, 8 11/16 x 7 1/4 inches (22 x 18.5 cm)
Cecil Beaton Archive, Sotheby's London

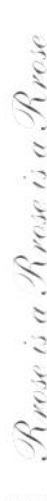

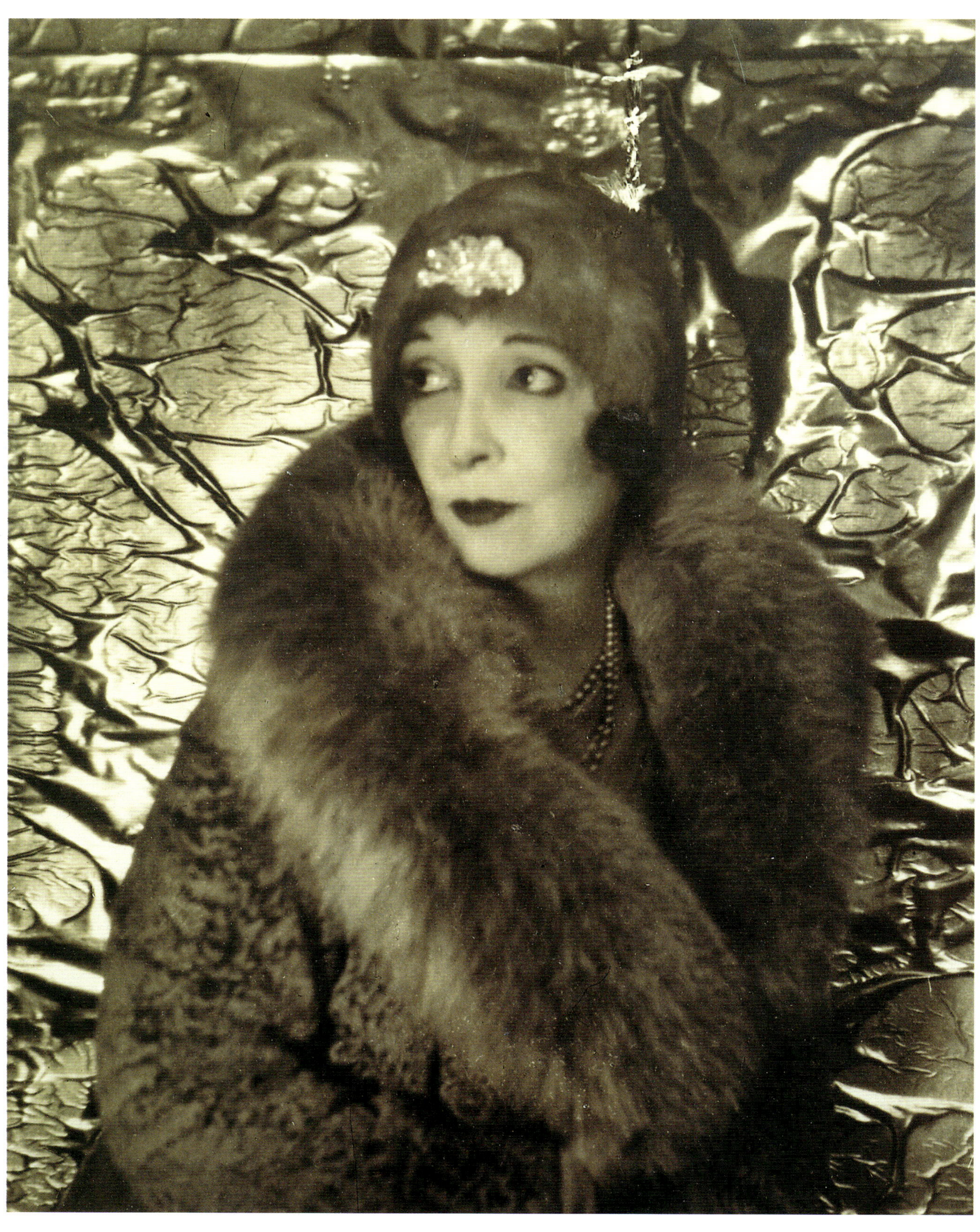

Cecil Beaton
Lady Lavery, ca. 1930
Gelatin-silver print, 13 3/16 x 11 1/4 inches (33.5 x 28.6 cm)
Courtesy of Robert Miller Gallery, New York

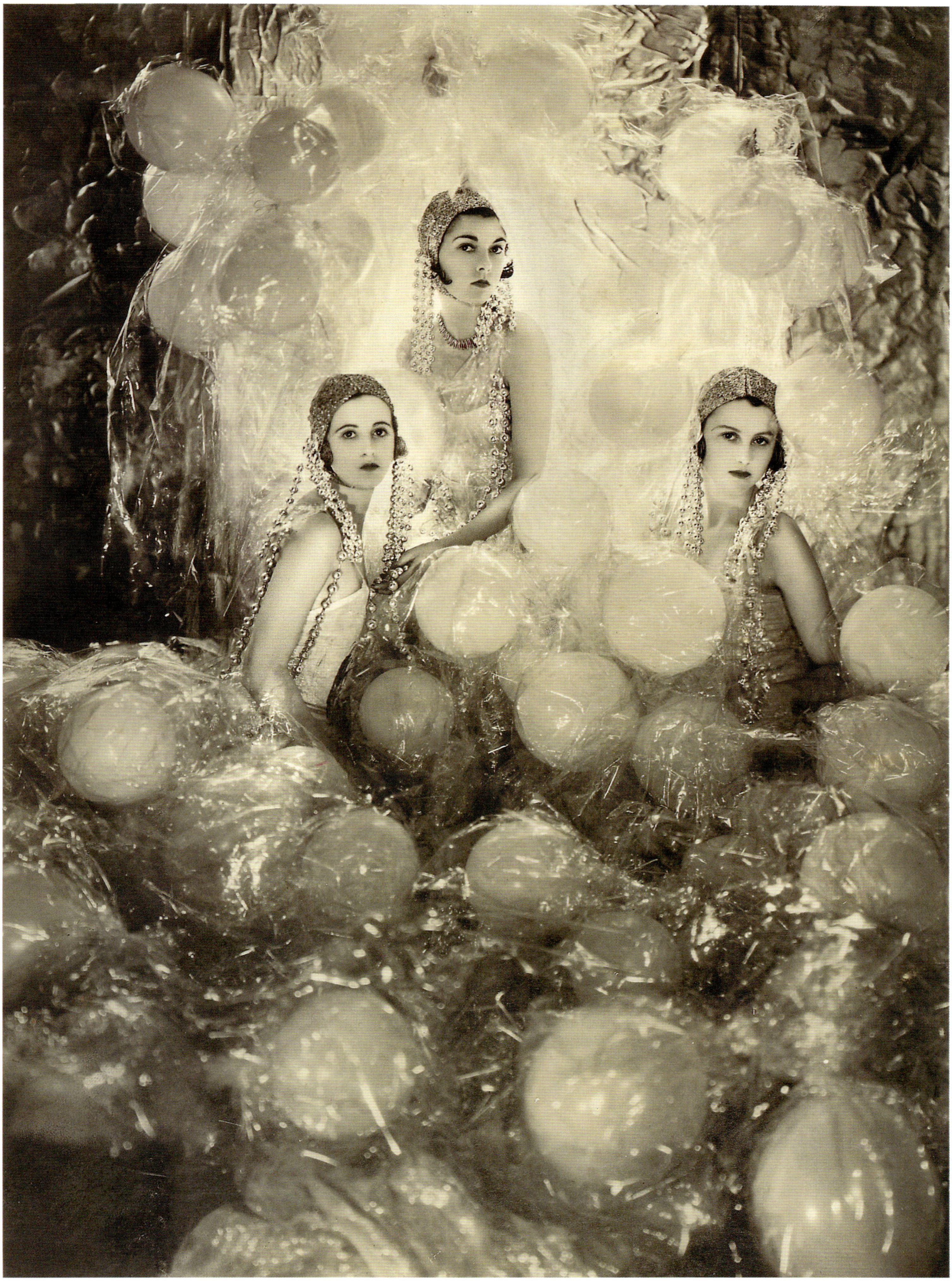

Cecil Beaton
Debutantes – Baba Beaton, Wanda Baillie-Hamilton and Lady Bridget Poulett, 1928
Gelatin-silver print, 19 13/16 x 13 13/16 inches (50.3 x 35.1 cm)
The J. Paul Getty Museum, Malibu

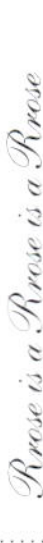

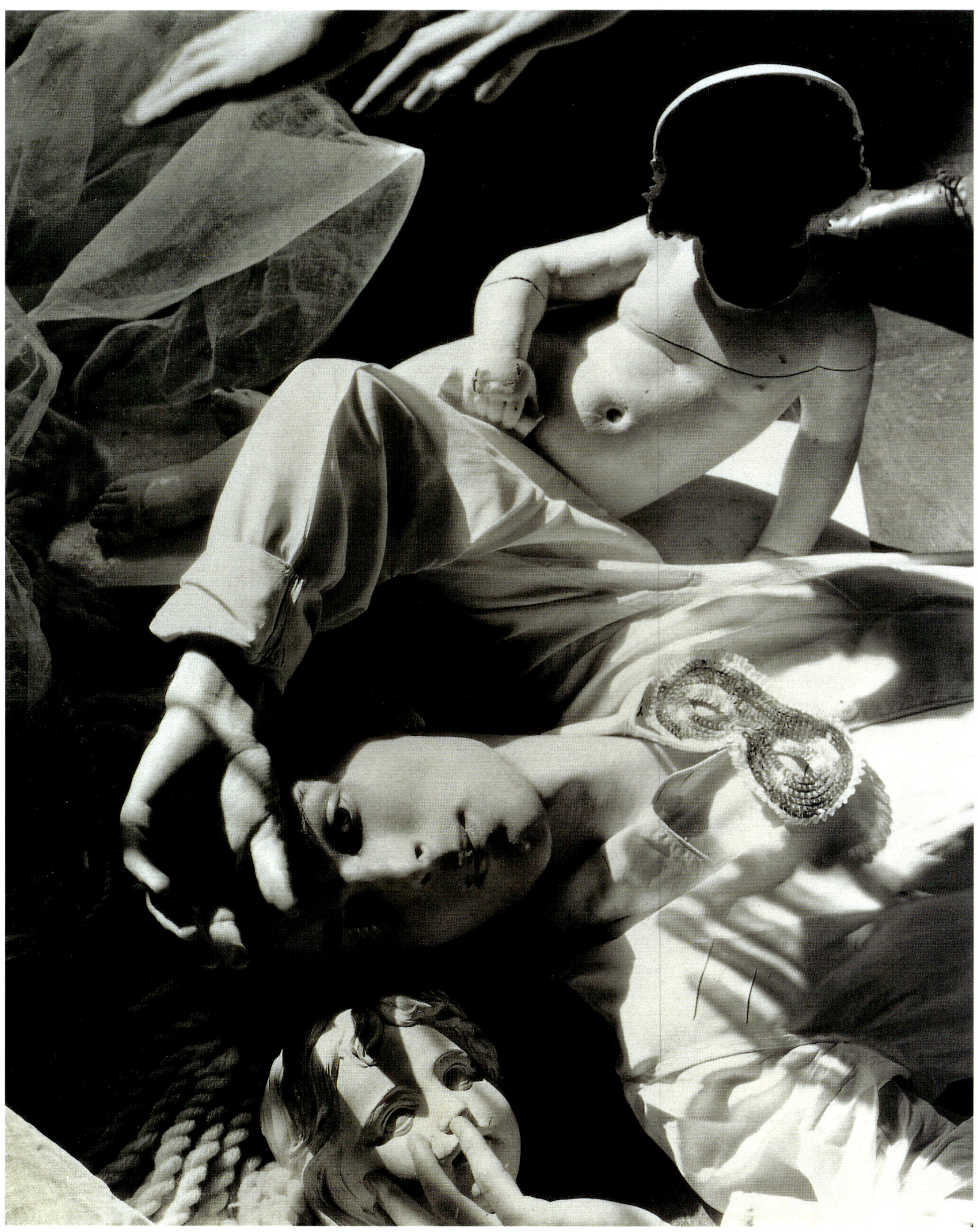

Cecil Beaton
Igor Markevitch, 1929
Gelatin-silver print, 9 ¾ x 7 ¹³⁄₁₆ inches (24.8 x 19.8 cm)
Cecil Beaton Archive, Sotheby's London

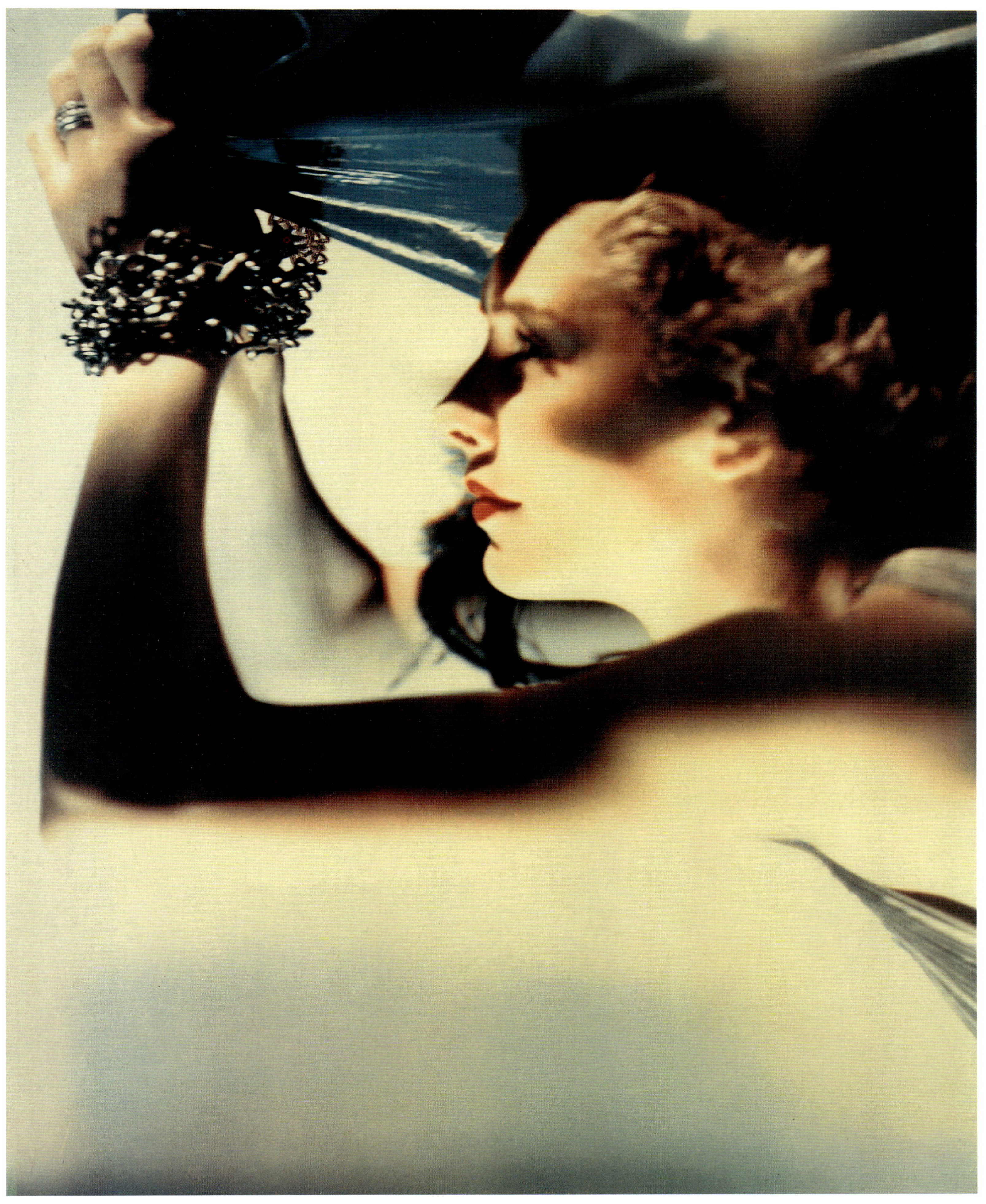

Madame Yevonde
Mrs. Richard Hart-Davis as "Ariel," from the *Goddesses* series, 1935
Vivex color print, 14 7/16 x 11 9/16 inches (36.6 x 29.3 cm)
National Portrait Gallery, London

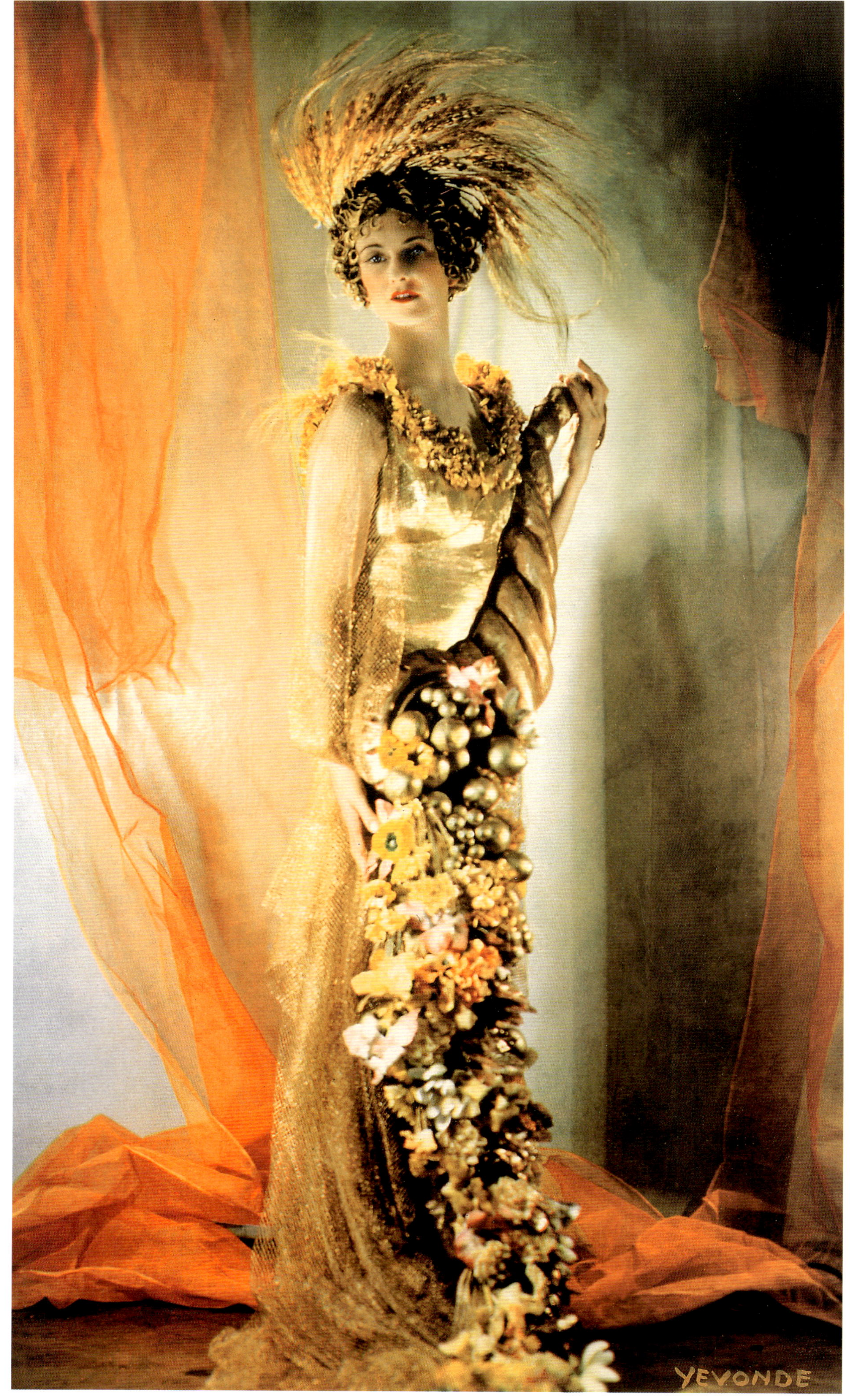

Madame Yevonde
Lady Dorothy Warrender as "Ceres," from the *Goddesses* series, 1935
Vivex color print, 14 13/16 x 8 11/16 inches (37.6 x 22.1 cm)
National Portrait Gallery, London

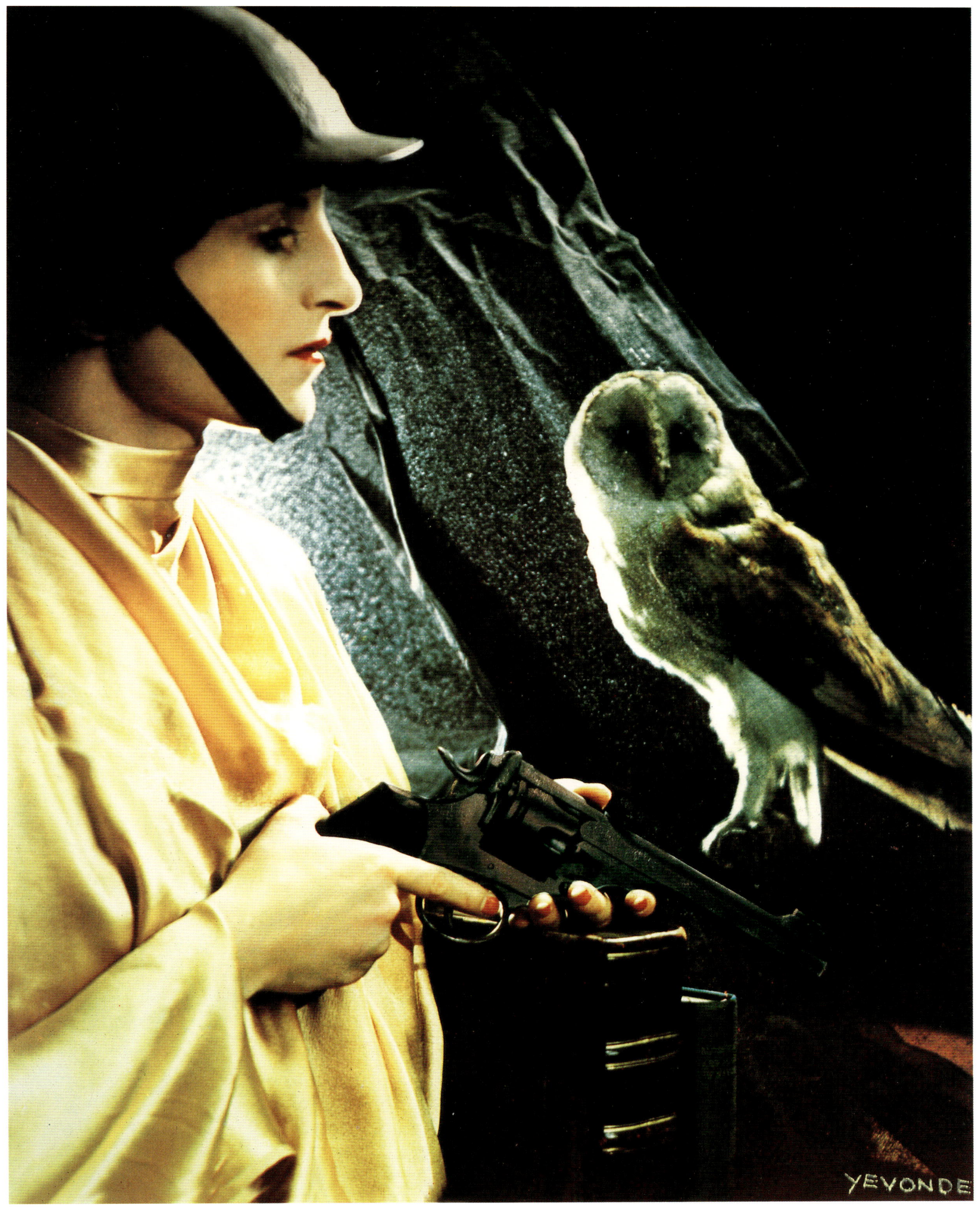

Madame Yevonde
Lady Michael Balcon as "Minerva," from the *Goddesses* series, 1935
Vivex color print, 13 ½ x 8 11/16 inches (34.2 x 22.1 cm)
National Portrait Gallery, London

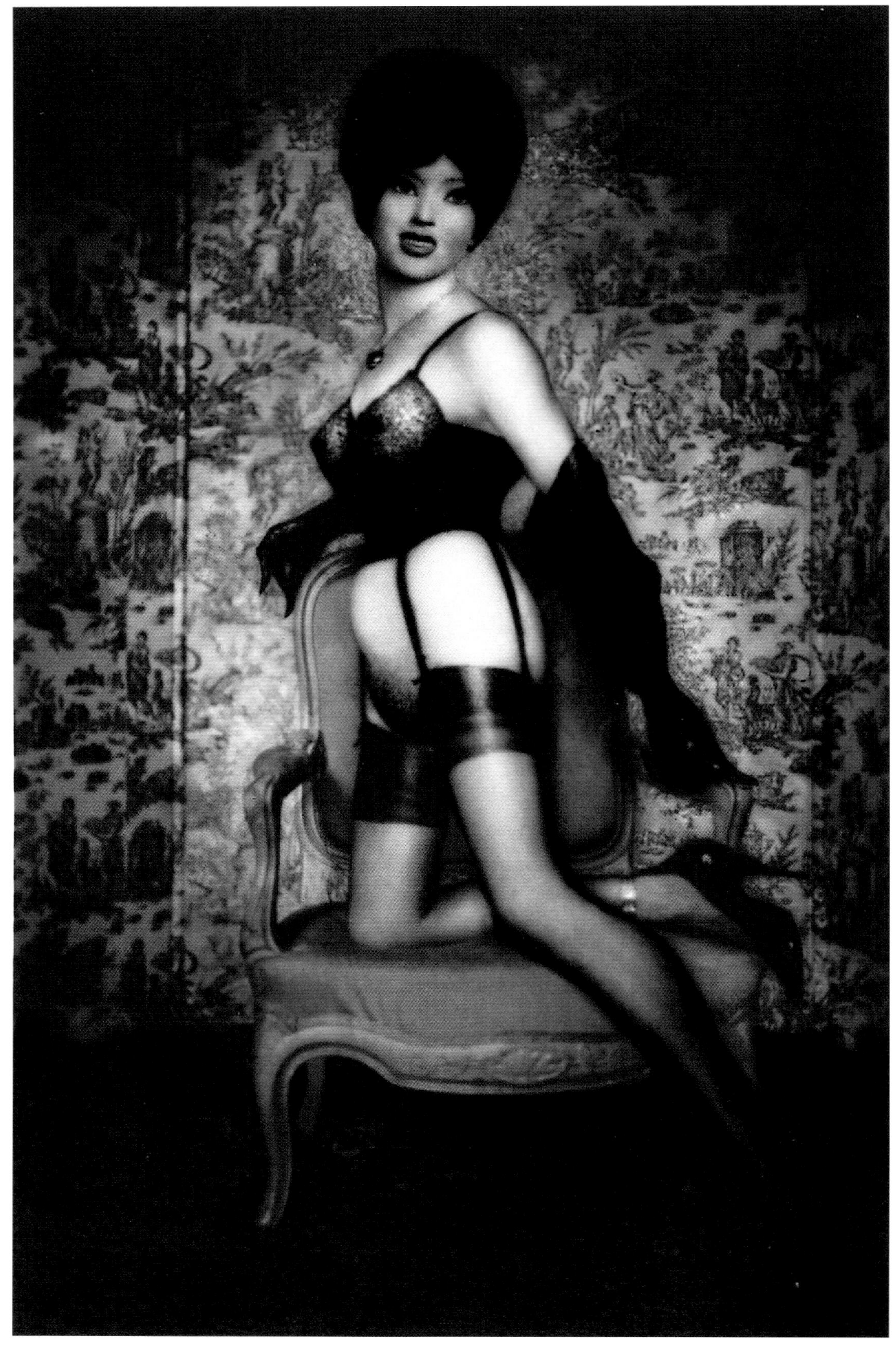

Pierre Molinier
Effigy (*Effigie*), 1970
Gelatin-silver print, 8 ⅞ x 5 ¹¹⁄₁₆ inches (22.5 x 14.5 cm), ed. 3/6
Musée National d'Art Moderne, Centre Georges Pompidou, Paris

2. An Interlude: Photographic Pleasure (The Work of Pierre Molinier as Fulcrum)

It is no doubt through the mediation of masks that the masculine and the feminine meet in the most acute, most intense way.
JACQUES LACAN, "What Is a Picture?" 1964[39]

The theoretical interest of perversion extends beyond the disruptive force it brings to bear upon gender. It strips sexuality of all functionality, whether biological or social . . . Perversion also subverts many of the binary oppositions upon which the social order rests.
KAJA SILVERMAN, "Masochism and Male Subjectivity," 1988[40]

The need of human beings to transcend "the personal" is no less profound than the need to be a person, an individual.
SUSAN SONTAG, "The Pornographic Imagination," 1967[41]

Speaking is always in some ways the speaking of a stranger through and as oneself.
JUDITH BUTLER, *Bodies that Matter*, 1993[42]

Non je suis lesbien.
PIERRE MOLINIER, when asked if he was homosexual, undated[43]

Shortly before his death, in 1855, Gérard de Nerval wrote "*Je suis l'autre*" (I am the other) under his engraved portrait.[44] By the end of the century, this sentiment, expressed by a poet who was frequently psychotically tormented, would become an emblem of the modern construction of identity. Photography fed this construction by providing multiple, frequent, and literal reminders of oneself as other, thus enforcing the notion of a kind of split personality: the one that sees itself looking at another one, which is itself.[45] An exceptional characteristic of the photograph is the power of direct address in portraiture, when the subject seems to be looking straight at you, the viewer. It is no accident that two of Roland Barthes's favorite photographs were intimate portraits of beloved women—one a childhood picture of his mother, the other Nadar's image of "his mother (or of his wife—no one knows for certain)."[46] Powerful emotions, eeriness and nostalgia, are aroused by the effigy of someone who is now dead. Yet we cling to the replica as a sort of talisman: this person, unseeing in the first place (become an image), whether dead, away, or grown older, is still before us, looking at us. Although, of course, paintings may conjure similar responses, the photograph's indexical relation to a being who was at one time before the camera seems to strengthen the intensity of the viewer's response.[47]

The pleasures of the photographic image are polymorphous, yet the various forms they take coalesce structurally around the dialectic of reality and fantasy—the index of the photograph versus the photograph as icon. The recognition of oneself in a photograph can serve to define oneself, to create an identifiable and distinct subject. This is the narcissistic pleasure of the mirror, in which we

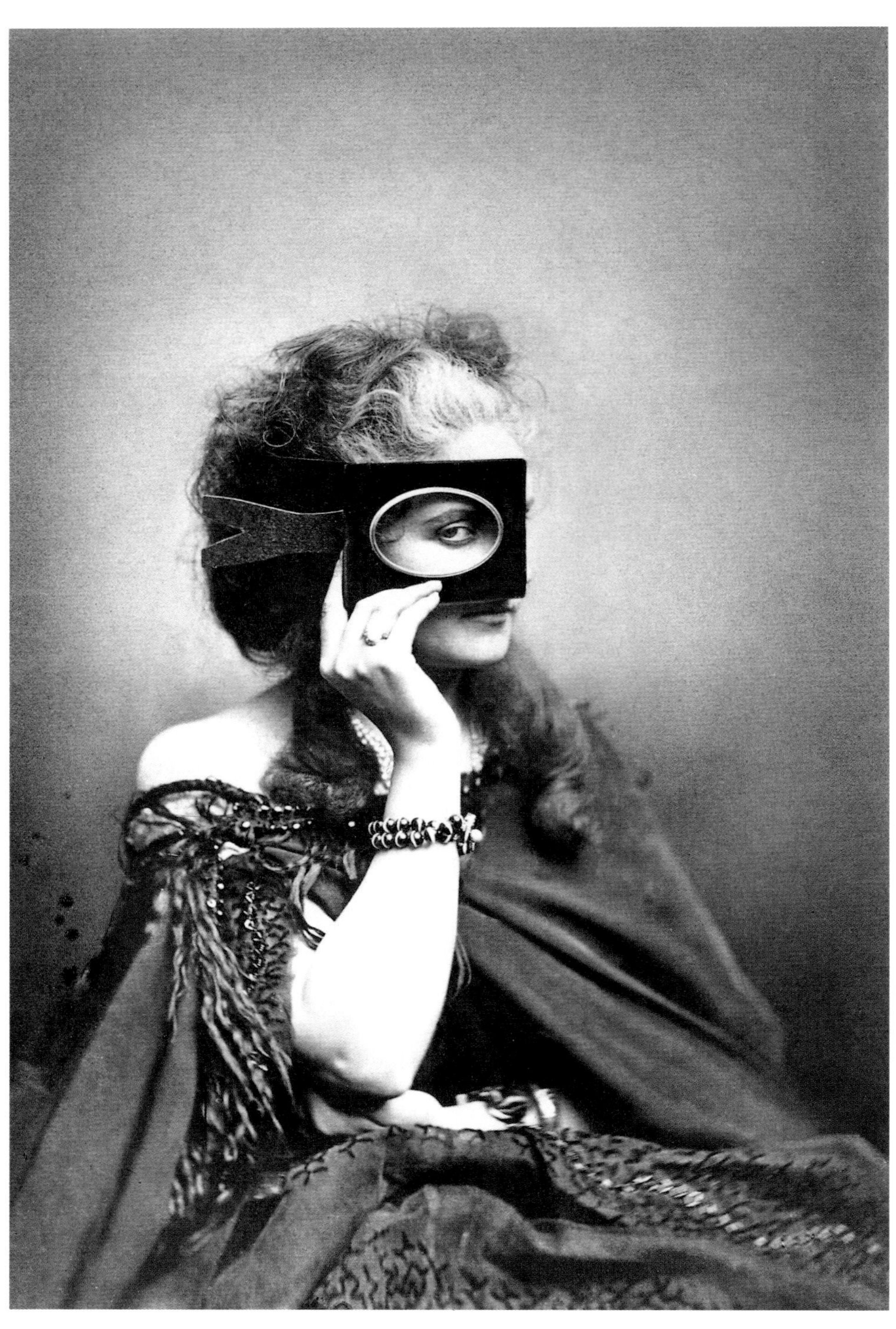

Pierre-Louis Pierson
Countess de Castiglione, ca. 1855 (printed 1940s)
Gelatin-silver print from glass negative, 7⅜ x 5 inches (18.7 x 12.7 cm)
The Metropolitan Museum of Art, New York, Gift of George Davis, 1948

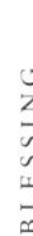

reassure ourselves of our existence. The mirror can also be a reminder of the pain of separation, of the loneliness that is individuality, of the loss of our first reflection in our mother's eyes. Photographic fantasy can assuage the ache of remembrance. It might show us a delirious image of disintegrated identity suggesting the blissful abandonment of subjectivity, its collapse into its (m)other. Or the photograph might present a perfect model self, our lost ego ideal. It can help us to enforce the psychic reconciliation of an untenable memory. Thus, the photograph becomes a fetish guarding against the reiteration of unacceptable perceptions.[48] The fact that the photograph is a trace or index of something that was once there gives it its reality effect—the sensation that it represents a truth. The fact that photographic means can be employed to create fictions, to promote surreal or fantastic illusions, to create fetishes that are fixed and transfix, is what makes the photograph an icon as well.

These aspects of photography may begin to suggest why it is compelling to look at, and, to a lesser extent, why it is a popular custom to create photographs. Regarding the latter, the dissemination of photographic equipment and technological improvements has allowed photography to be widely practiced and to have a particular private, personal usage as well as its public function. The line between the public and private status of photography is a fine one, somewhat comparable to the overlap between autobiography and fiction in Marcel Proust, for example. There is a trajectory in the history of photography that encompasses semi-intimate self-portraiture, which functions as a private pleasure, a personal tool of realizing the self, and yet frequently has an extra-personal, social, and artistic significance as well.[49] Contemporary appreciation of this type of photography is consistent with the modern esteem for the sketch and the journal, both of which were once considered modest private tools of the artist and writer, but which are now valued as independent works of art.

The photographic history of the pieces in this exhibition encompasses all manner of work in which a subject performs for the camera. Not surprisingly, this tradition, if it can be called that, is one characterized by compulsive repetition—there is never just one shot but rather always a seemingly endless parade of images. This is only partly due to the technical possibilities of the medium: the development of rolled film with its unfolding frames or the ability to repeatedly print an image. Instead, a more meaningful explanation for the sheer volume of images of this type, and the elaborately minute distinctions between each of them, is their compulsive motivation—the burning desire to achieve an unattainable goal. A momentary frisson is superceded by recurring desolation, and the circuit begins again.

From its inception, photography was perceived as an optimal means of obtaining portraits of public personages, the self, family, and friends. Its superb ability to accurately and quickly document the individual virtually replaced the portrait miniature in the mid-nineteenth century.[50] Before the Kodak era began in the 1890s, when photographic technology was sufficiently simplified to make it appealing to vast numbers of people, individuals who wished to document themselves without investing in the necessary photographic equipment might go to a studio or solicit an itinerant photographer to realize their portraits. For example, Hannah Cullwick in London and the Countess de Castiglione in Paris, though from very different social milieus, both quite actively directed the photographs they commissioned in the third quarter of the nineteenth century. These women's interest in their self-portraits was flavored by erotic tastes—in Cullwick's case, a desire for a masochistic image that would please her lover; for the countess, an apparently personal fetishistic delight in her own body.[51]

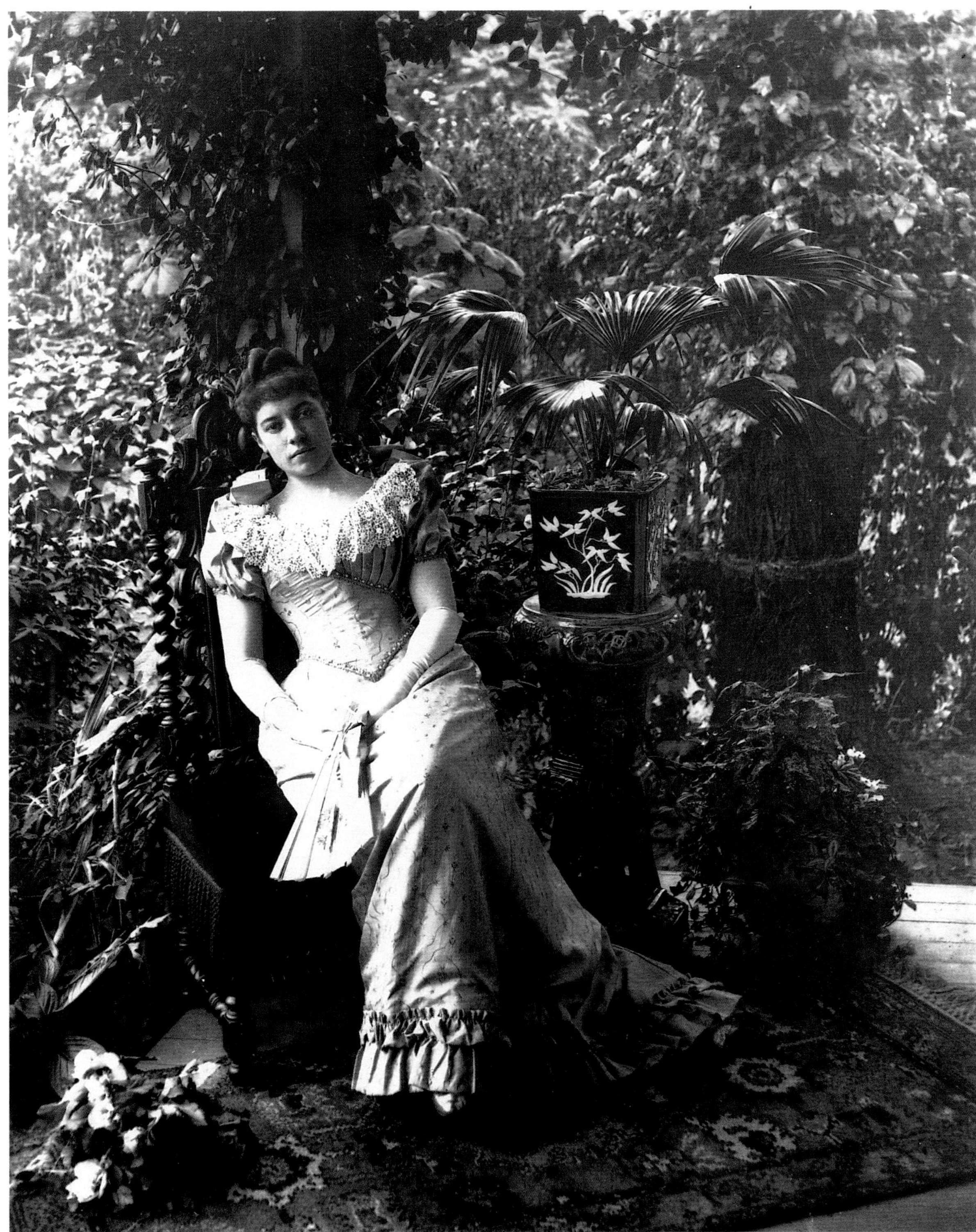

Alice Austen
Self-Portrait, Full Length with Fan, Monday, September 9th, 1892, 1892
Gelatin-silver print from glass negative,
8 $^{11}/_{16}$ x 6 $\frac{1}{2}$ inches (22 x 16.5 cm)
Courtesy of Staten Island Historical Society,
Alice Austen Collection

The relatively low cost of photographic, as opposed to painted, portraiture, permitted the development of the snapshot aesthetic, in which anyone could indulge their desire for self-images, not only for the formal portrait destined for posterity but also for more casual and playful representations. Experimentation and theatrical performance for the camera were fostered by the ease of photographic production. Thus Alice Austen might photograph herself on October 15, 1891 as a man and on September 9, 1892 as a woman.[52] Or the legacy of allegorical portraiture could be traced through the worker-genre 1920s self-portraits of the Morter Sisters, in which the women dressed as builder or housemaid, garnering prizes for their enigmatic depictions.[53] Then there are the countless private albums, many now dispersed or lost, in which anonymous photographers present themselves in their favored guises for personal delectation. The aesthetic pretensions organizing these images vary.

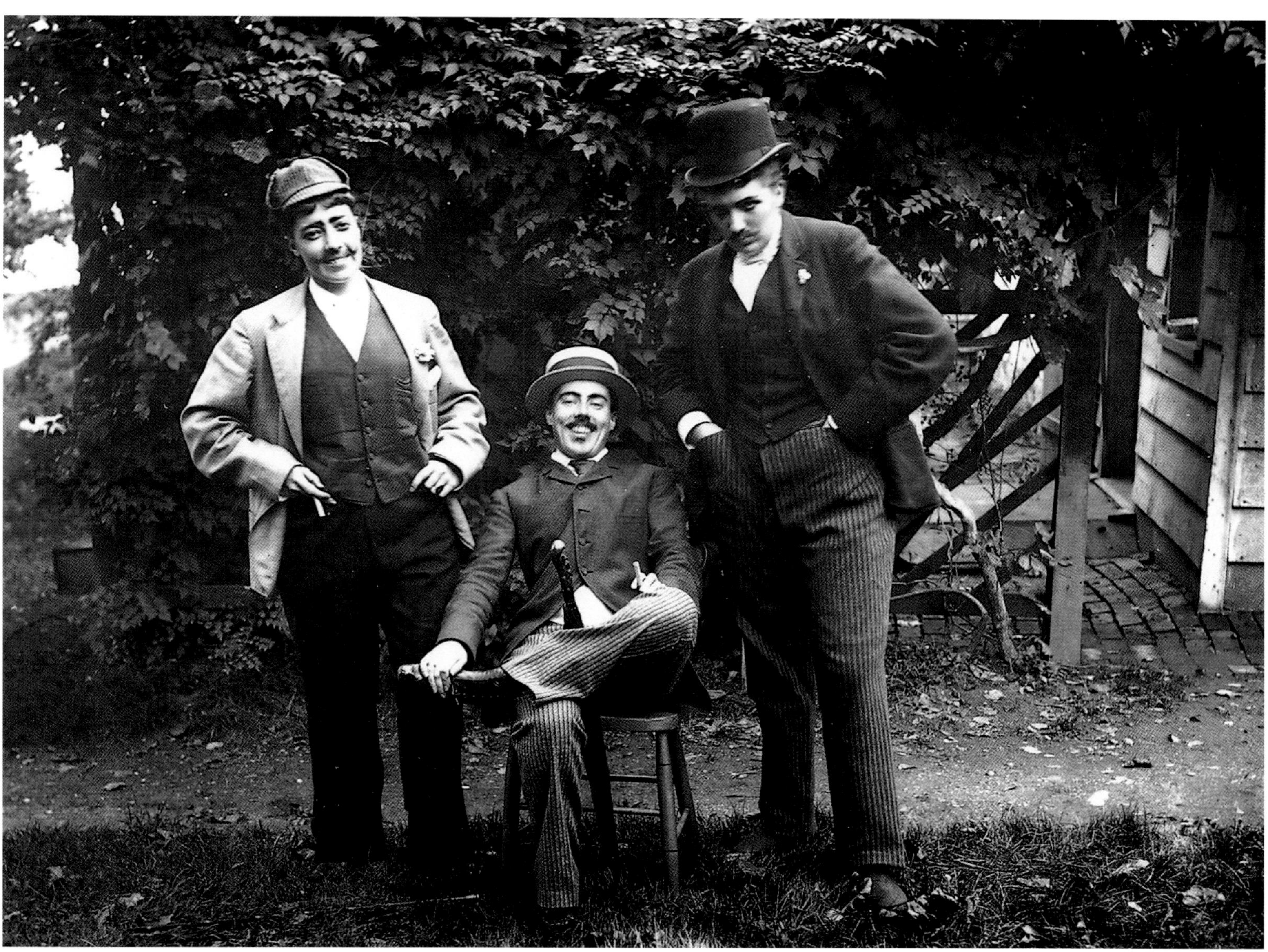

Alice Austen
Julia Martin, Julia Bredt and Self Dressed Up as Men, 4:40 pm, Thursday, October 15th, 1891, 1891
Gelatin-silver print from glass negative,
6½ x 8 9/16 inches (16.5 x 21.8 cm)
Courtesy of Staten Island Historical Society,
Alice Austin Collection

Nevertheless, the photographic work of Cahun or Pierre Molinier, an artist who created intricately manipulated self-portraits, should be situated in relation to this tradition of self-documentation. It is a tradition that would be invigorated by the Polaroid innovations of the 1960s, which provided instant gratification as well as the ability to shoot images without the need to have them developed at the neighborhood drugstore, and it would be transformed by the proliferation of the video camera, which maintains all the benefits of the Polaroid camera plus the incorporation of time and movement.

Memory is a creative process, which is now aided by photographs, such that it is difficult to discern which of your childhood recollections are "real" and which have been confused with photographs. Sensations generated by viewing a photograph might be entangled with memories sustained from later years. For example, you recall the clammy claustrophobia of that plastic Superman mask, which you are seen wearing in a photo taken at Halloween when you were four, conflating it no doubt with later Halloween memories. Or you "remember" insisting that your mother photograph you in your childish ideal of femininity, sporting curlers, lipstick, and high heels—however, perhaps what you remember is not asking to be photographed but your mother later telling you about it. Similarly, photographs that do not depict the past you wish to construct meet a violent end: you destroy the negatives of images that do not represent you as you want to be represented; you cut out the figure of a person you wish not to remember. Photography, as the record of a specific

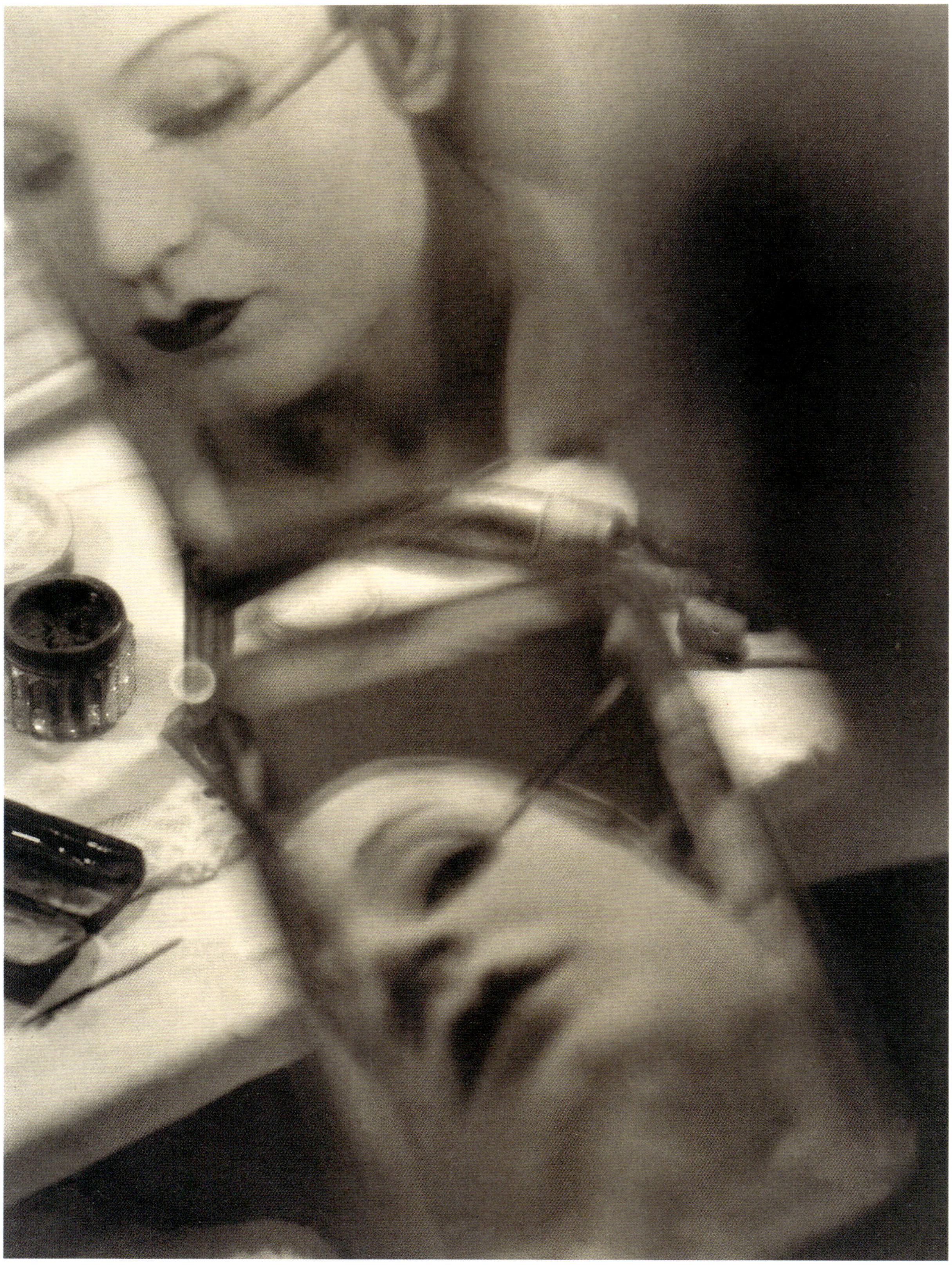

Man Ray

Barbette Making Up, 1928

Gelatin-silver print, 8 5/8 x 6 7/16 inches (21.9 x 16.4 cm)

The J. Paul Getty Museum, Malibu

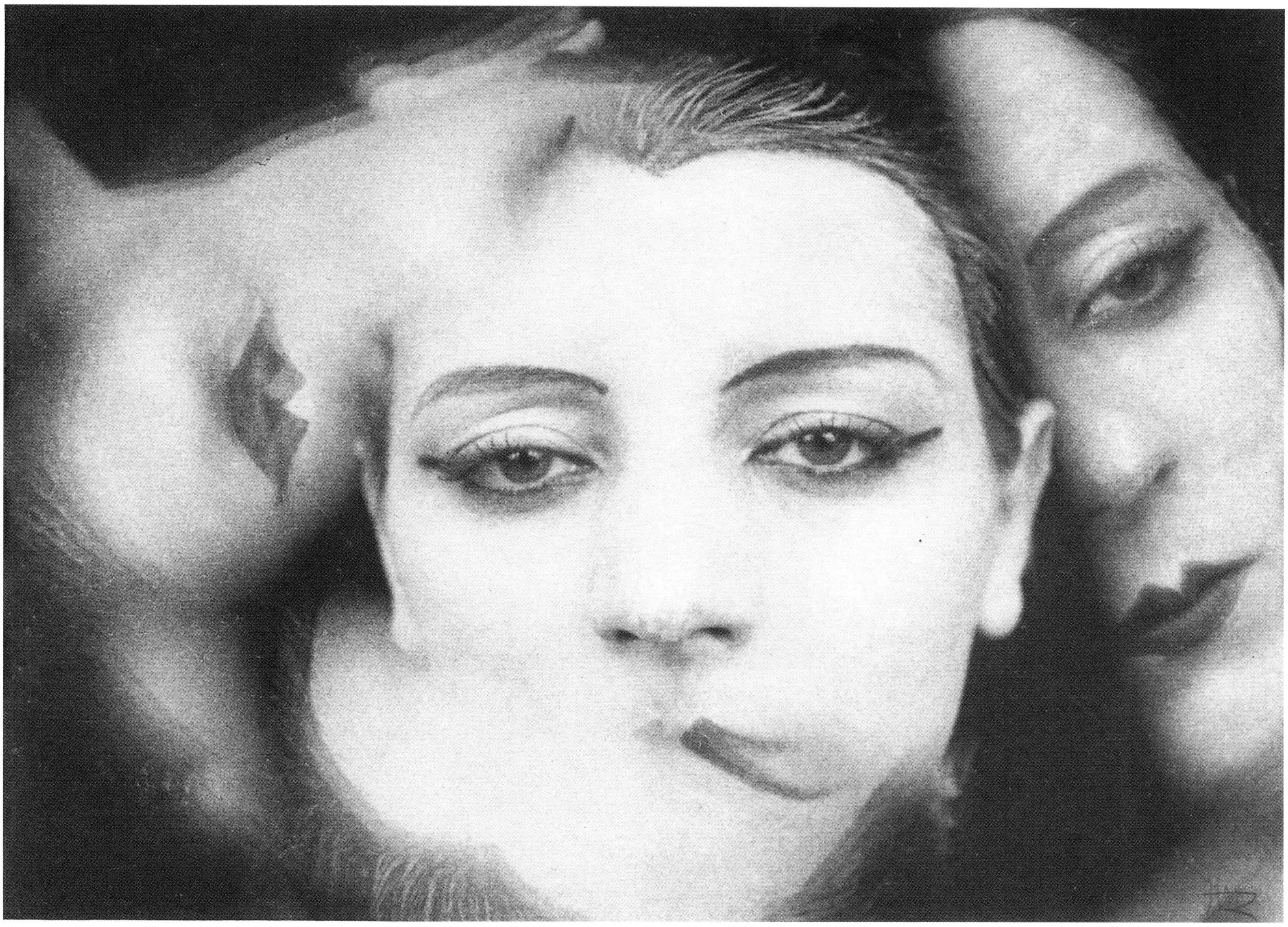

Man Ray
Kiki of Montparnasse, 1924
Gelatin-silver print, 8 3/4 x 11 13/16 inches (22.2 x 30 cm)
Musée National d'Art Moderne, Centre Georges Pompidou, Paris,
Gift of M. Lucien Treillard, 1981

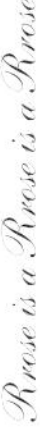

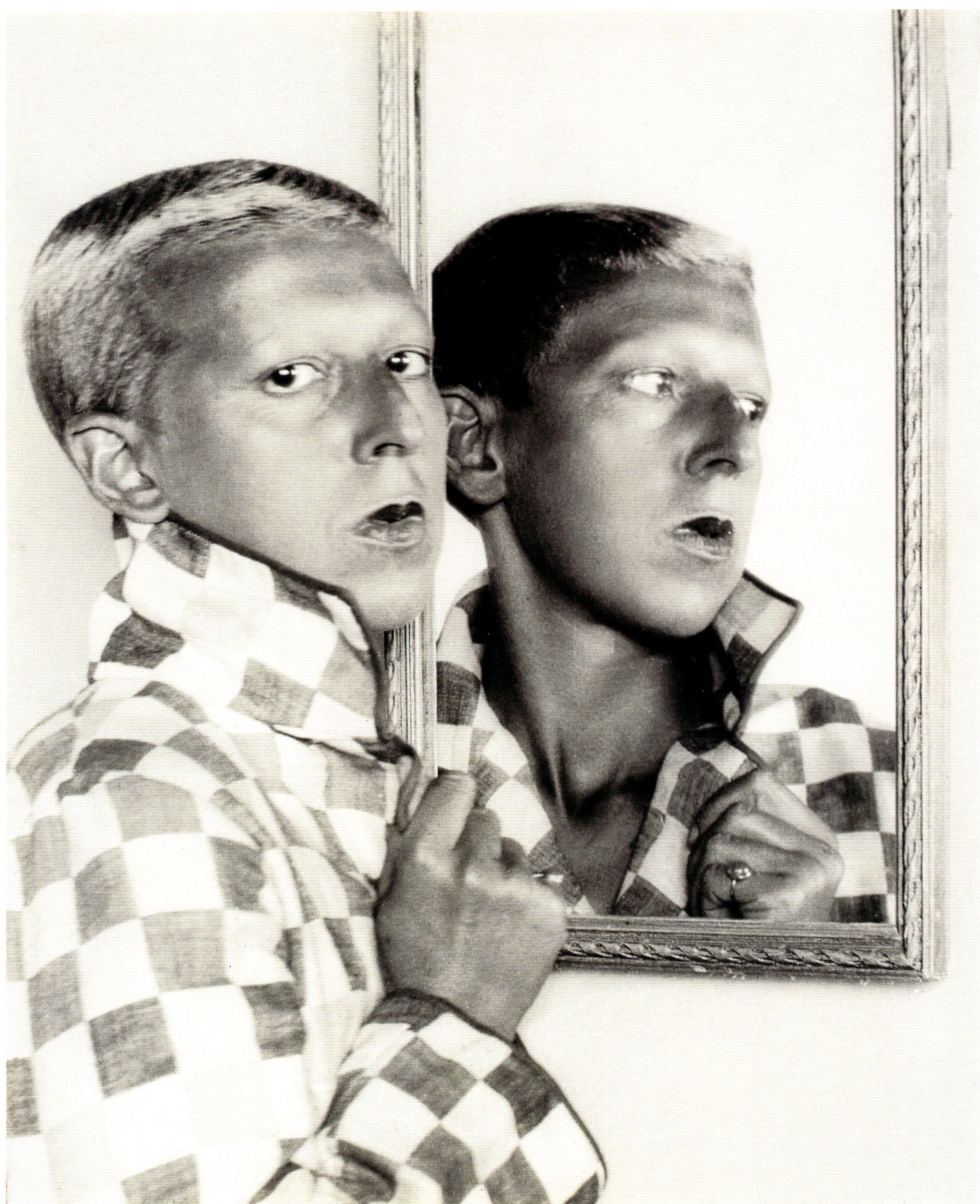

Claude Cahun
Self-Portrait, ca. 1928
Gelatin-silver print, 11 13/16 x 9 3/8 inches (30 x 23.8 cm)
Musée des Beaux-Arts de Nantes

moment that is by definition past, is structurally related to nostalgia and memory, which always seem uneasily headed for home.

It is from a lost moment of childhood that some photographs may derive their power: images that present a dispersed self, an amorphous and indistinct outline, recalling the euphoric experience of integration that a child feels with its mother.[54] This is a pleasure of bodilessness, of indistinguishable boundaries, that is echoed in a child's desire to spin out of control, out of itself, into delirium. This moment, however, is relatively short, for soon the child will see its reflection and begin to understand that it is a separate and distinct being, which is a cause for joy and also for mourning.[55]

Children must master this loss, must find a way to feel that they control their mother's separation and return, her distance and intimacy. Photographs seem to offer a means of organizing this original loss, which structures all losses including the ruin of one's youthful self, the painful passage of time, and ultimately death itself. Photographs thus become fetishes that deny the realities of existence. The prevalence of mirror images, doubled and multiple portraits, and pictures of otherworldly mannequins and dolls in photographic production can be explained, in part, as the natural union of subject and structure; fantastic fetish objects for a fetishistic medium, their uncanniness signals anxieties that the photograph attempts to contain.[56] These images embody the knowledge that the day will come when someone other than I will look at this picture of me; I will, thereby, have become the one who does not see.

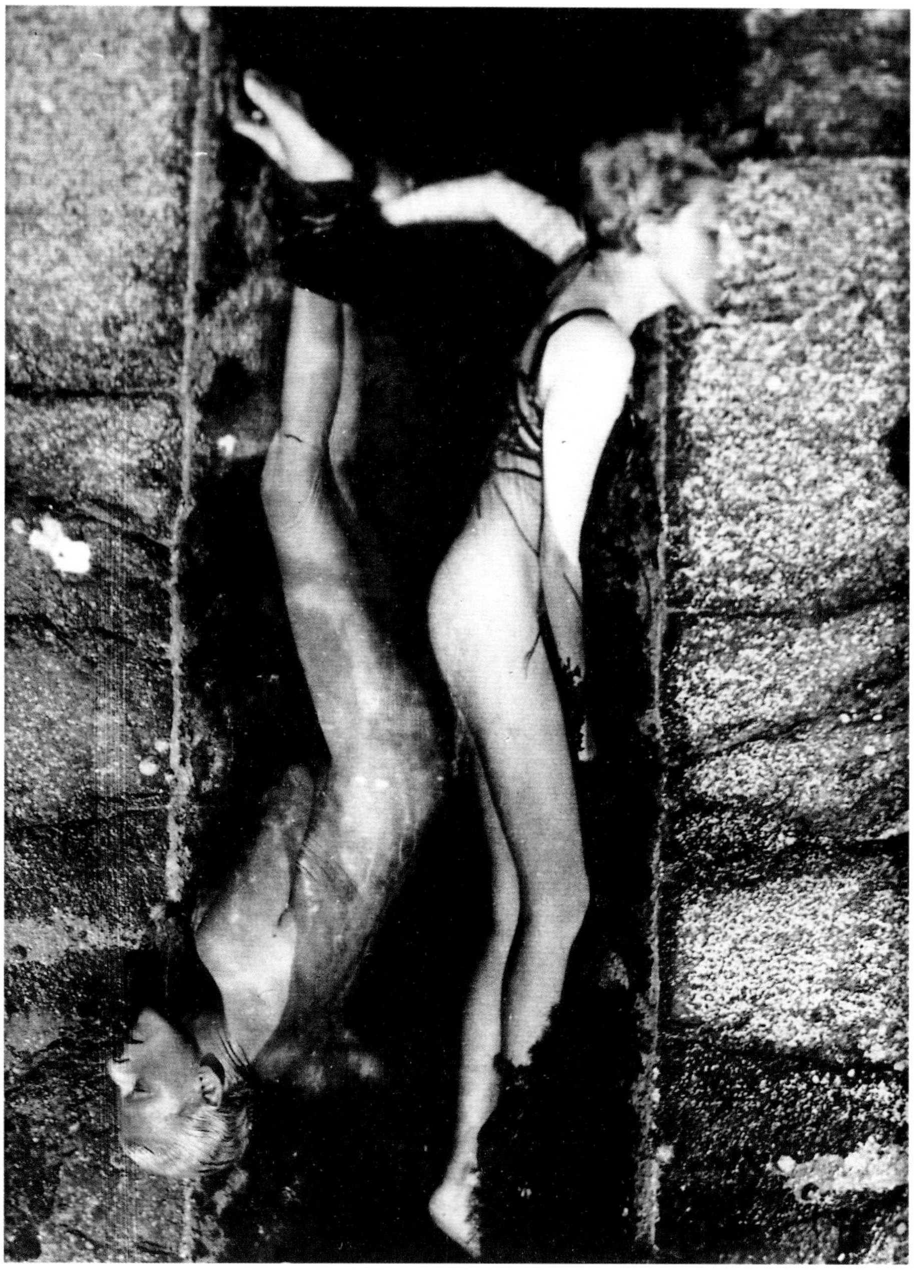

Claude Cahun
Untitled, 1928
Gelatin-silver print,
6 7/8 x 5 inches (17.5 x 12.8 cm)
Private collection, East Sussex, England

Freud conceived of fetishism as the process by which an adult manages his childhood fear that his mother was castrated—and that, therefore, he may be as well.[57] By denial, in other words, he insists that his mother, indeed, bears the phallus, and he develops various means through which he may continually reassure himself of this "fact." More broadly, the fetish is a sort of charm that wards off evil, that is enlisted to prevent feared outcomes. Sexually fetishistic practices for men encompass cross-dressing, in which the man "becomes" his mother and is, thereby, a woman with a penis; or obsessional attractions to specific articles of clothing or body parts that act as phallic substitutes. Certainly, there is erotic pleasure in these practices, though it is frequently laced with a shiver of anxiety.

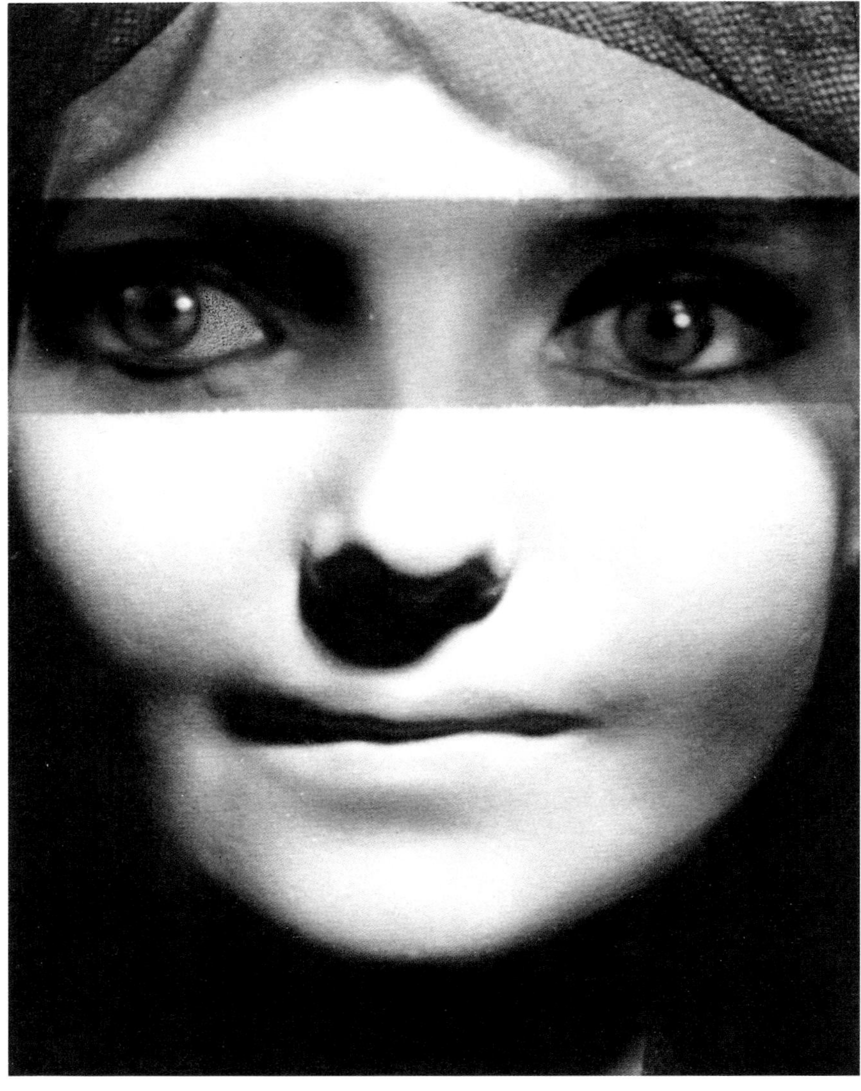

Man Ray
Aurélien, 1944
Gelatin-silver print, 5 11/16 x 4 7/16 inches (14.5 x 11.2 cm)
Musée National d'Art Moderne, Centre Georges Pompidou, Paris

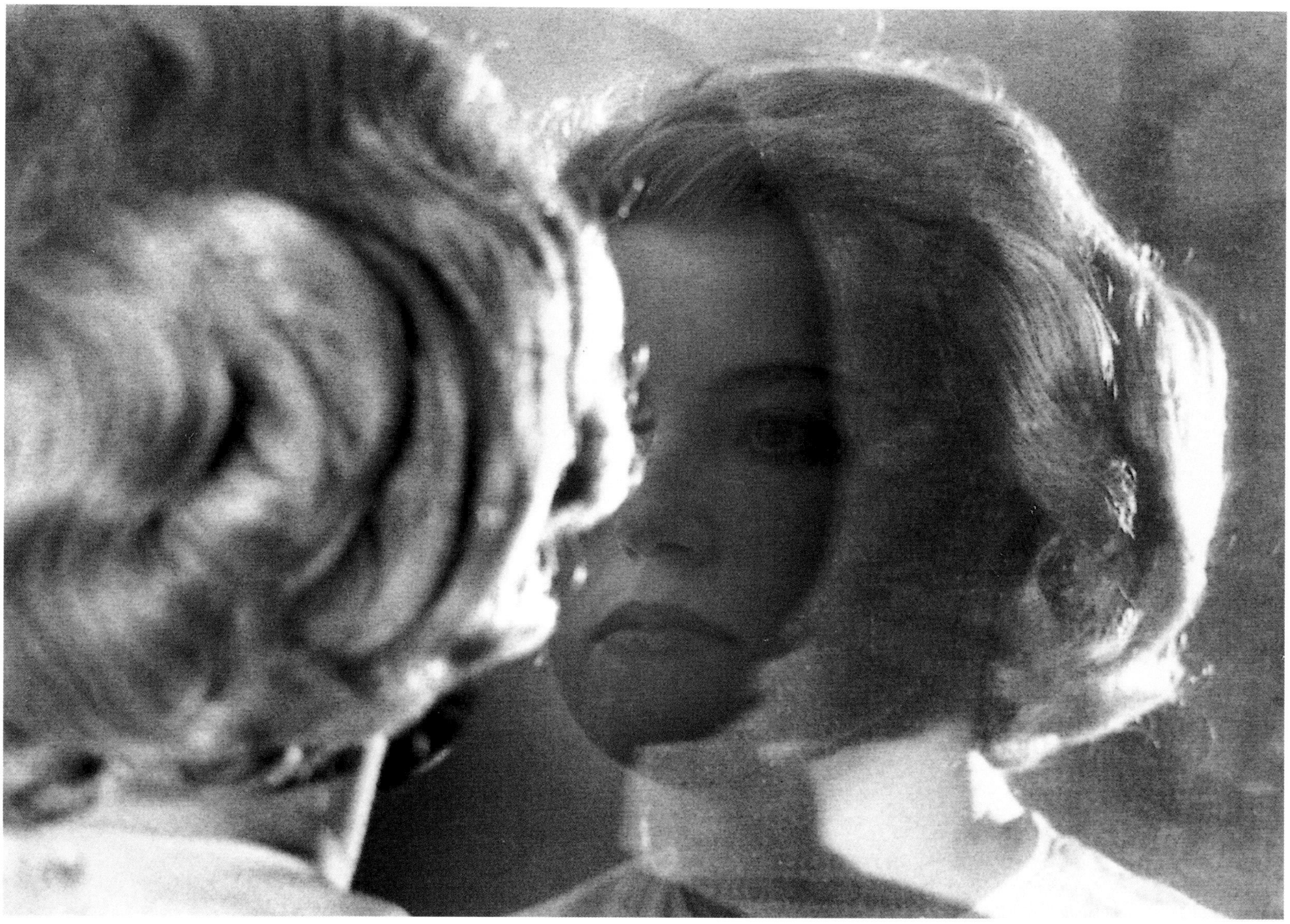

Cindy Sherman
Untitled Film Still, #56, 1980
Gelatin-silver print, 8 x 10 inches (20.3 x 25.4 cm), ed. 1/10
Collection of Jane B. Holzer

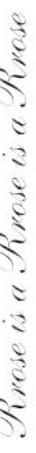

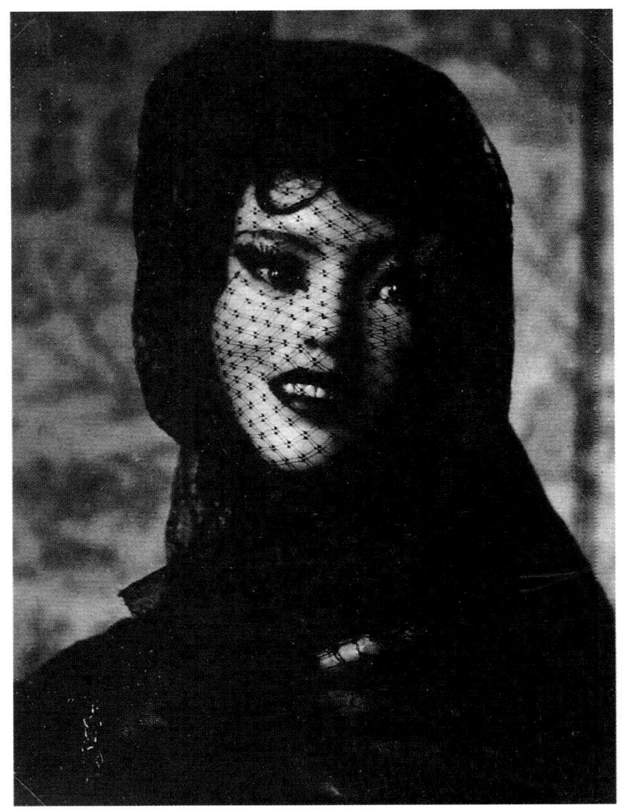

Pierre Molinier
The Doll (*La Poupée*), ca. 1970
Gelatin-silver print,
4¼ x 3⅛ inches (10.8 x 8 cm)
Musée National d'Art Moderne,
Centre Georges Pompidou, Paris

Born in 1900, Pierre Molinier trained as a painter whose taste ran to the sensual exoticism of Gustave Moreau.[58] In the mid-1960s, Molinier shifted his painterly concerns to photography, creating elaborate self-portraits constructed of animate and inanimate parts, a practice he continued until his death in 1976. His artistic process included taking photographs of himself, sometimes masked, dressed in corsets, stockings, and stiletto heels, as well as shots of friends. He then cut out the silhouettes of figures and body parts, which he recomposed and combined with photographs of mannequins to create fabricated portraits and fanciful collages. Through this process of cutting and recombination, which might require several intermediate generations, Molinier sought to achieve an ideal image of himself, as well as to realize his sexual fantasies. The erotic pleasure of his process is graphically indicated by maquettes he created in which the photographic paper literally penetrates another sheet, and by the lavish delicacy with which he embellished his prints. Through this marking and retouching, Molinier accentuated and improved upon desirable features, and eliminated the unwanted, in order to secure an impossible yet seemingly real persona who was "documented" in the final photograph.

Two key transformative procedures are reiterated in Molinier's self-portraits: one is his "becoming female" through the elimination of his penis, the addition of breasts, and his appearance in lingerie; the other is his ironization of masculinity through the proliferation of phallic objects, his fetishistic emphasis on legs, high-heeled shoes, and especially his prized invention—the shoe with dildo attachment. Through a symbolic castration that announces the feminine and the assertion of a

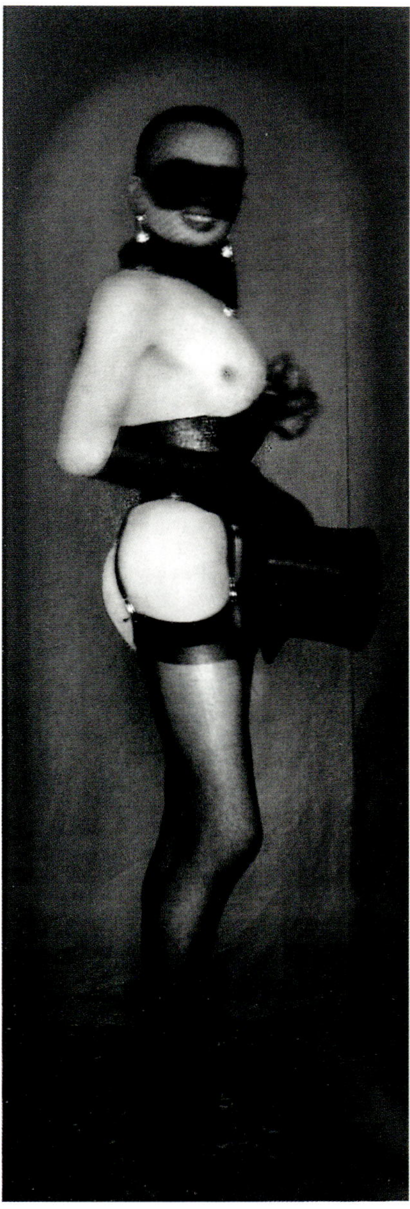

Pierre Molinier
Self-Portrait with Top Hat, late 1960s
Gelatin-silver print, 6¼ x 2⅛ inches
(15.9 x 5.4 cm)
Wooster Gardens, New York

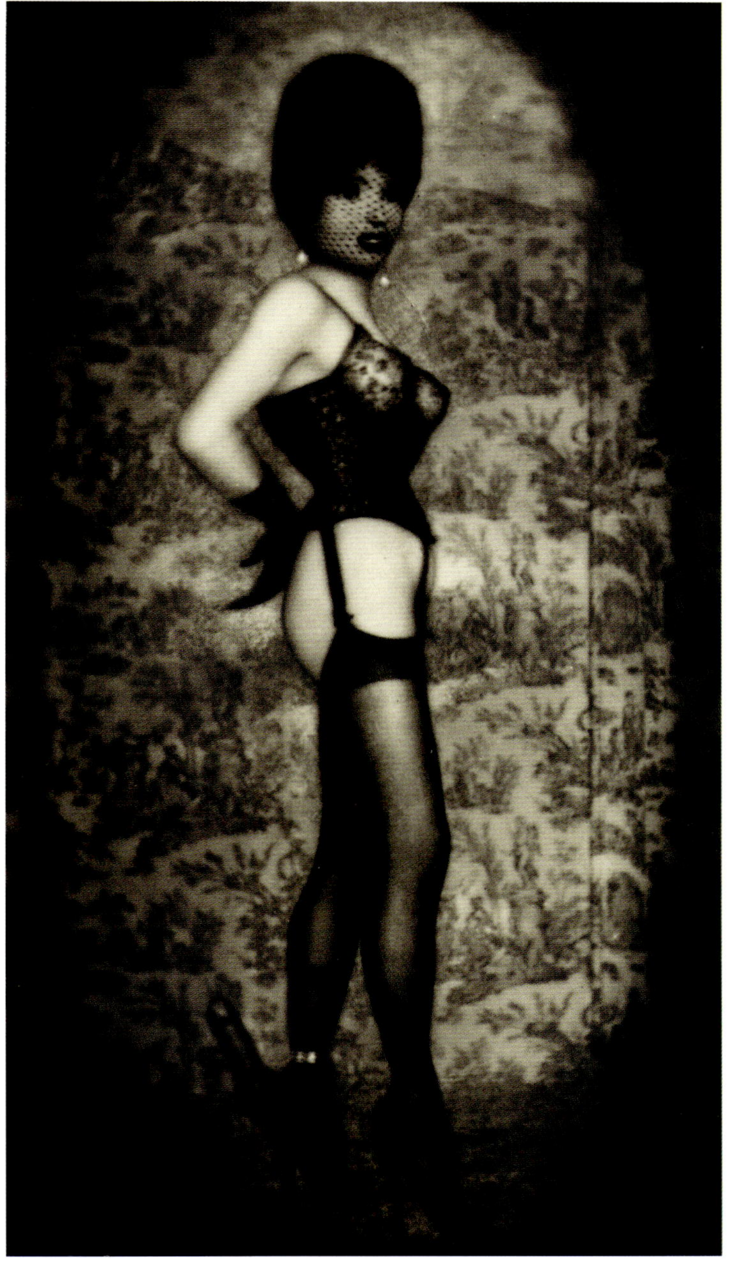

Pierre Molinier
The Spur of Love (*L'Eperon d'amour*), 1966–68
Gelatin–silver print, 6⅜ x 3¾ inches
(16.2 x 9.5 cm)
Courtesy of Ubu Gallery, New York

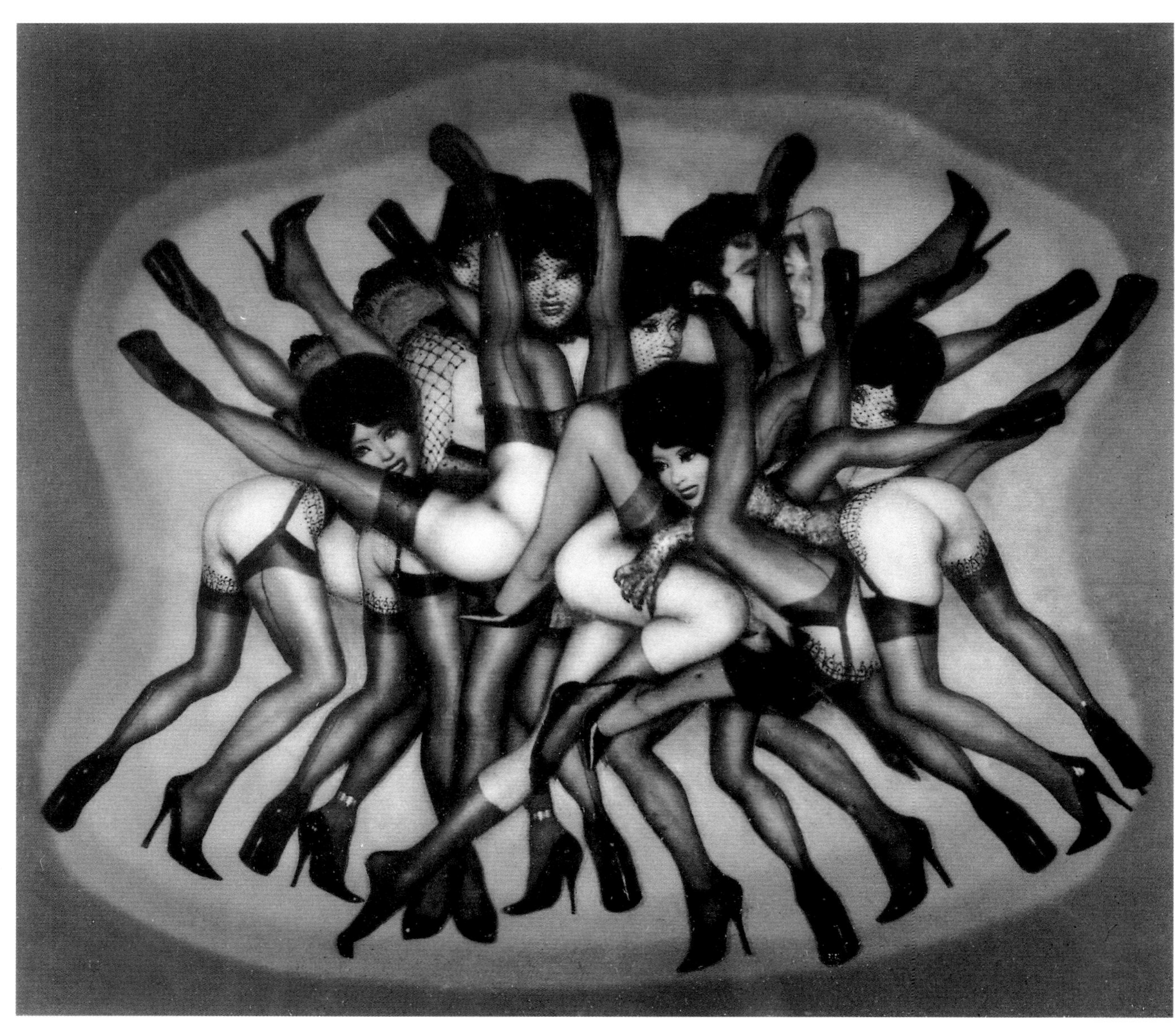

Pierre Molinier
Grand Melee (*Grande Mêlée*), late 1960s
Gelatin-silver print, 6 x 6⅞ inches (15.2 x 17.5 cm)
Wooster Gardens, New York

masculine presence through inorganic replicas, Molinier disrupts the codes of femininity and masculinity that would link bodily apparatus with gender definition. Peter Gorsen argues that "Molinier introduces himself in the pose of a shaman aesthetically amputating (retouching) his male genitals and replacing them with a godemiché [dildo], a prosthesis whose toy character and double nature ironize dominant male sexuality."[59] To understand why Molinier's images are so compelling, it is useful to recall Kaja Silverman's work on male masochism, in which she argues that the masochist wants to replace the authority of the father with the phallic mother, thereby denying the "law of the Father," which is imbricated with the "law of nature."[60] Since "nature" is the authority so frequently cited to lock individuals into socially predetermined roles, its subversion is greatly appealing to those stifled by its strictures. Visions of phallic mothers and castrated fathers, the proliferation of sexualities and genders, combat the repression of strict binary oppositions into male/female, masculine/feminine, father/mother. Such images graphically argue that no one actually has the phallus, that its power is a construction, and that you can make one for yourself.

Molinier's interactions with the last generation of Surrealists date from 1955, when he contacted André Breton and received an enthusiastic response. From its inception in the first manifesto of Surrealism, published by Breton in 1924, to its nominal end as an organized entity with Breton's death in 1966, Surrealism was profoundly engaged in investigating the body, sexuality, and the nature of desire.[61] Breton conducted inquiries into sexual practices and subjects, in various Surrealist journals, as early as 1928, when the first transcripts of "research" sessions were published in *La Révolution surréaliste*, to the late-1950s and mid-1960s investigations of striptease and the nature of eros.[62] Molinier participated in the later ventures, and his work was seen at that time as sympathetic with the concerns of Surrealism as articulated by Breton.[63] Unlike the legacy of twentieth-century abstraction, which privileged a search for transcendence through harmonious spiritual means, Surrealism sought transformation through disruption and was grounded in the material reality of the body. The name itself indicates a relationship to the real, and yet it is a realism made strange by its articulation of mental experience, this made manifest in visual and textual representation. Breton advocated a stream-of-conscious, unrepressed creative process that could be enhanced through the delirium induced by the folly of desire, among other things. He saw in Molinier's and other artists' work diverse attempts to transgress the confinement of bourgeois conformity and represent the pleasurable disorientation of passion. The scope of entries in the "Concise Lexicon of Erotism" that appeared in the catalogue for *L'Exposition InteRnatiOnale du Surréalisme*, a 1959 exhibition (directed by Breton and Duchamp) that included Molinier, demonstrates that all aspects of the erotic were within Surrealism's purview.[64]

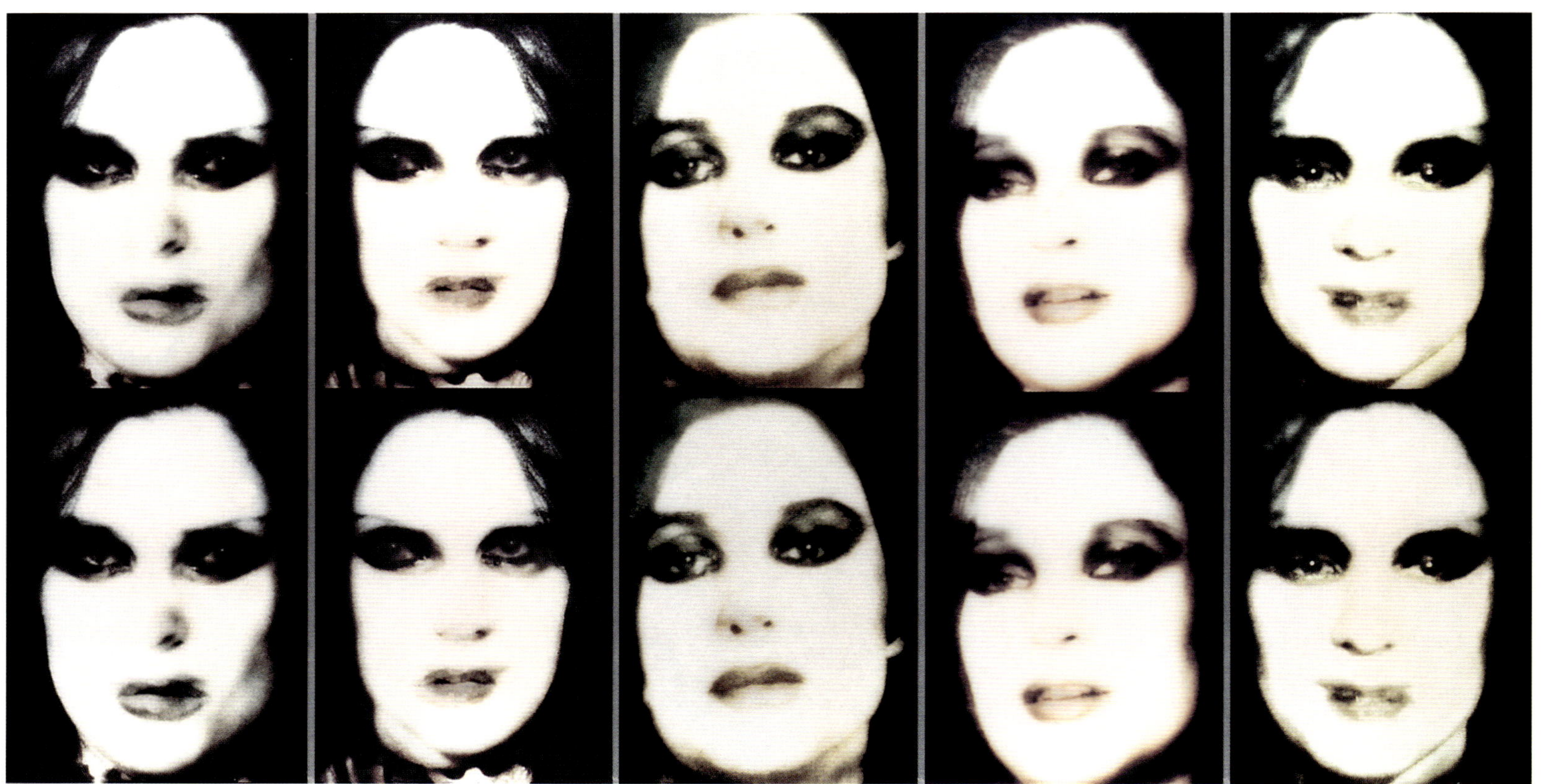

Katharina Sieverding
Transformer, 1973–74
Photographs, in five parts, each 59 7/16 x 24 inches (151 x 61 cm);
overall 59 7/16 x 120 1/16 inches (151 x 305 cm)
Deutsche Bank AG, Frankfurt

3. Some Photographic Work of the 1970s

It seems very evident that one person's narcissism has a great attraction for those others who have renounced part of their own narcissism and are seeking after object-love; the charm of a child lies to a great extent in his narcissism, his self-sufficiency and inaccessibility, just as does the charm of certain animals which seem not to concern themselves about us, such as cats and the large beasts of prey.

SIGMUND FREUD, "On Narcissism: An Introduction," 1914[65]

Are these photos for narcissistic or publicity purposes?

MICK JAGGER, as Turner in *Performance*, 1970[66]

I'm sure I'm going to look in the mirror and see nothing. People are always calling me a mirror and if a mirror looks into a mirror, what is there to see?

ANDY WARHOL, *The Philosophy of Andy Warhol: From A to B and Back Again*, 1975[67]

Yet it is not (it seems to me) by Painting that Photography touches Art, but by Theater.

ROLAND BARTHES, *Camera Lucida*, 1980[68]

Sexual Liberation and the Crisis of Masculinity

The "Great Masculine Renunciation" of sartorial finery that Flügel traced from the rise of the bourgeoisie during the French Revolution to 1930, when he published *The Psychology of Clothes*, seemed to be challenged in the 1960s. In a controversial 1965 article, "The New Mutants," critic Leslie Fiedler voiced a widespread alarm about the crisis in masculinity evidenced by the ambisexual clothing and long hair of rock stars and hippies.[69] The popular models of masculinity and femininity promoted by Hollywood in the 1950s—the sultry Ur-sensuality of Marilyn Monroe and other hypertrophied sex symbols, and the supermacho, predatory playboys in perfectly cut suits who chased them—gave way in the 1960s and 1970s to more androgynous ideals. The fashionable woman became a short-haired, boyish type like Twiggy or Edie Sedgwick, and men wore the long hair, caftans, and beads. Unisex clothing and hairstyles made distinguishing male from female a difficult prospect, which was a turn-on for some and a source of anxiety for others.

In 1974, the Swiss curator Jean-Christophe Ammann organized an exhibition, *"Transformer": Aspekte der Travestie*, that attempted to link manifestations of cross-dressing in popular music and contemporary art.[70] The exhibition was premised on a conception of travesty as a creative act, a means of expressing the self as multiple, and a critique of narrow bourgeois definitions of masculinity. In his catalogue essay, Patrick Eudeline traces the "outrage of traditional masculinity" in

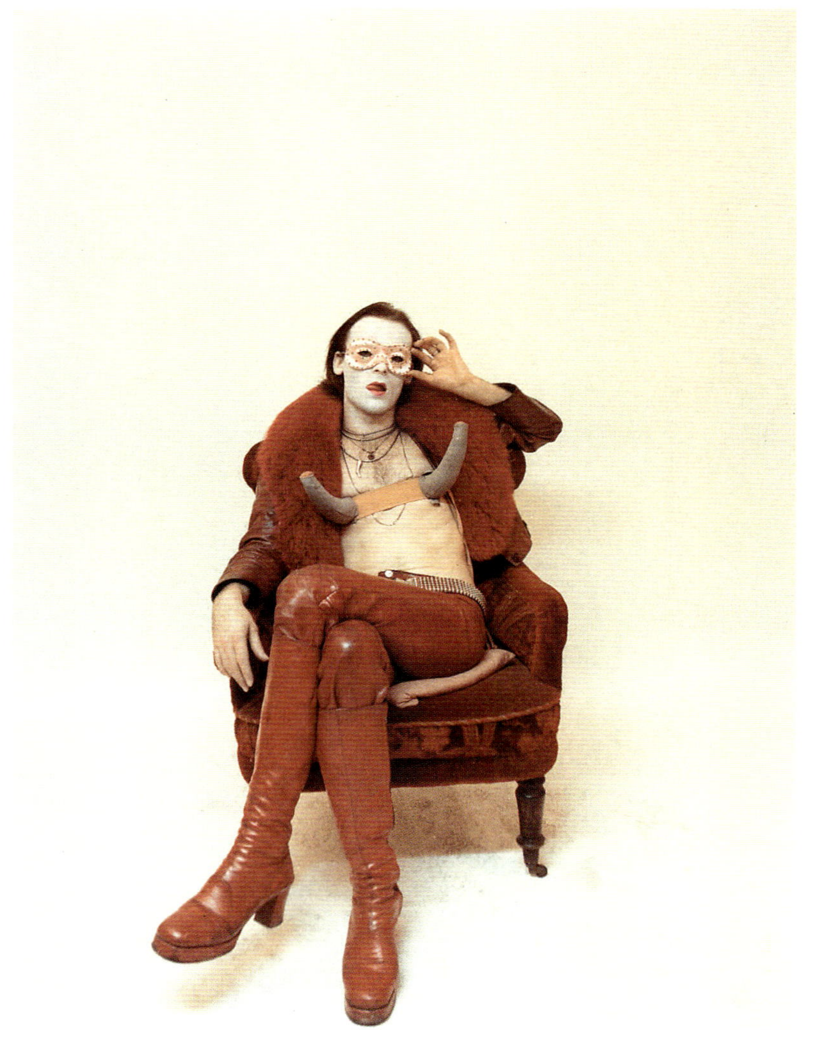

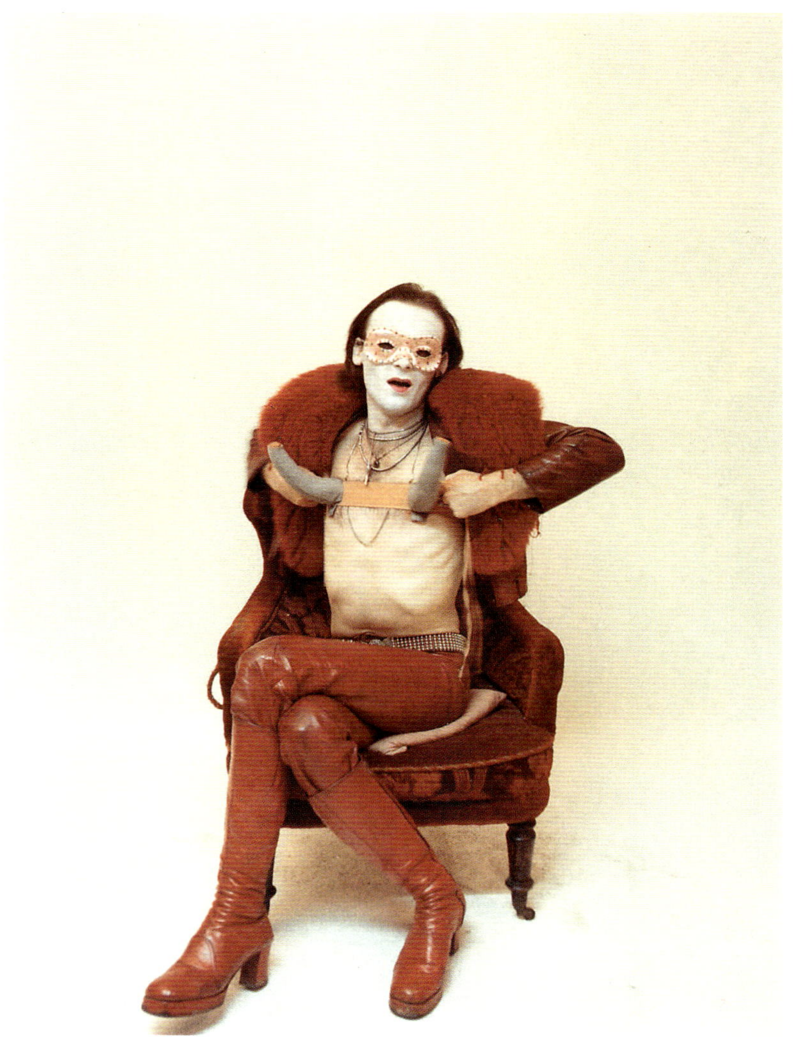

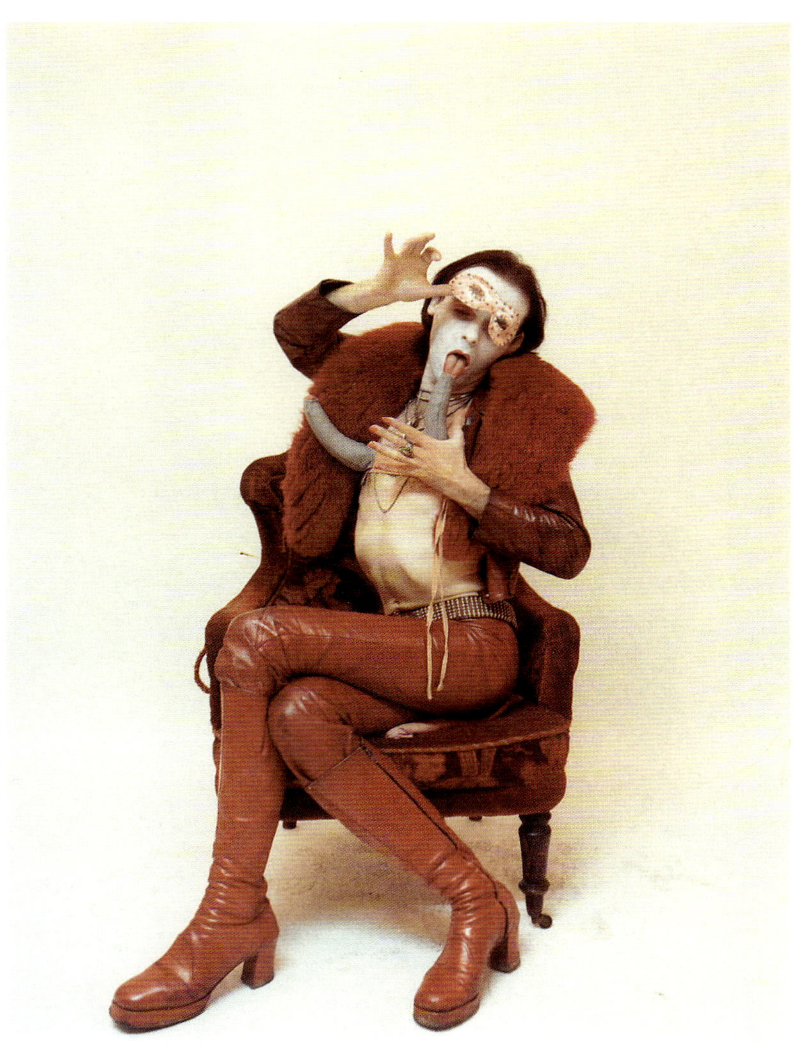

Jürgen Klauke
Transformer, 1973
Three color photographs, framed,
each 59 ⅞ x 53 ⅛ x 1 ⅛ inches (152 x 135 x 3 cm)
Courtesy of Galerie Bugdahn und Kaimer, Düsseldorf

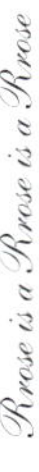

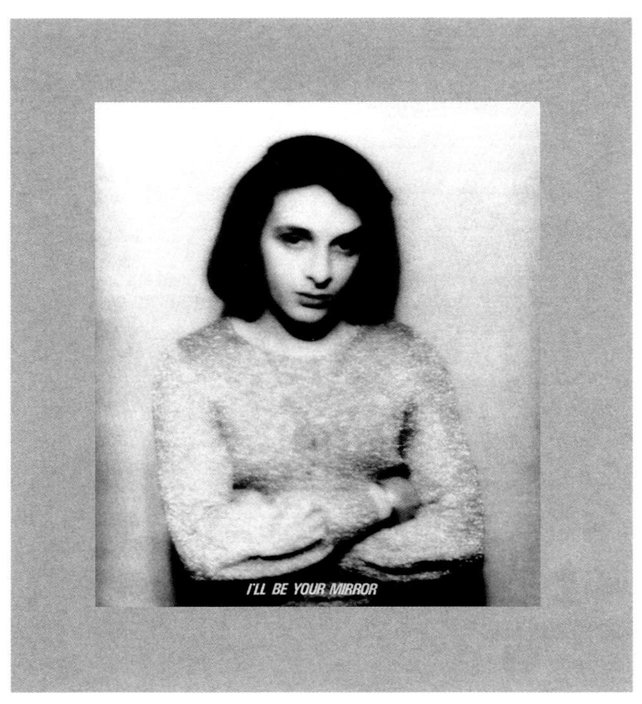

Urs Lüthi
I'll Be Your Mirror, 1972
Photograph on canvas,
39⅜ x 37⅜ inches (100 x 95 cm)
Private collection, Courtesy of
the artist

rock 'n' roll performance from its inception with Little Richard and Elvis Presley, to the second generation antics of the Rolling Stones and the Kinks, to the glitter rock of the early 1970s that included David Bowie and Lou Reed.[71] The exhibition borrowed its name from Reed's 1973 album *Transformer* (produced by Bowie), in which the singer chronicled urban life much as he had in the songs he wrote in the 1960s for the Velvet Underground. By referring to the title of Reed's album, Ammann was acknowledging Reed's reputation as the songwriter of drag queens—*Transformer* contained the hit drag anthem "Walk on the Wild Side." The catalogue opens with documentation of the performance-based photographic work of Continental European artists engaged with issues of transvestism, followed by sections on British and American rock performers and drag entertainers. In a brief mention in his preface, Ammann cites Man Ray's photograph of Duchamp as "Dame mit Hut" as a precursor.[72]

Reed's lyrics spoke for a generation fascinated by gender ambiguity, or confusion, and its pleasures. Artists included in "*Transformer*," such as Jürgen Klauke, Urs Lüthi, and Katharina Sieverding, voiced, in their work, a desire for a utopian conception of androgyny, in which they would embody a unified ambisexuality or realize a perfect union with their lover.[73] Lüthi and Sieverding produced photographic works in which they and their lovers appear almost identical. And Klauke created prostheses—phallic breasts and a strap-on vulva that he embellished with lipstick—that visualized a multiple sexual persona. Molinier's photographic montages, included with the work of these much younger artists, were characterized in the pages of the catalogue as representing their creator's attempt to achieve the state of perfection exemplified by the androgyne.[74]

The English word "transformer," Reed's motto, was imported by these young Swiss and German artists to describe the act of transcending binary gender definitions. Both Sieverding and Klauke used this word as the title of works initiated in 1973.[75] In 1972, Lüthi made a piece entitled *I'll Be Your Mirror*, which is also the name of a 1966 Velvet Underground song. It appears that, for these European artists, the new vision of gender transformation was emanating from America, communicated via a popular culture influenced by Andy Warhol and his involvement with drag queens.

Warhol's inspiration is registered in "*Transformer*" by the republication of a German article on the artist's 1972 film *Women in Revolt*, whose stars were the drag queens Jackie Curtis, Candy Darling, and Holly Woodlawn. However, it was only the most recent in a series of Warhol drag movies that included *The Chelsea Girls* (1966) and the Paul Morrissey–directed trilogy of *Flesh* (1968), *Trash* (1970), and *Heat* (1972). These films, along with Warhol's management of the Velvet Underground, the content of the band's songs, and its performances in the Exploding Plastic Inevitable shows, suggested Warhol's position at the forefront of "gender fuck dressing," in which identity, especially gender identity, was conceived as an impersonation, a role, a put-on.

Warhol's self-presentation, the antics depicted in his films, and, ultimately, the glitter rock he influenced are characterized by a delight in high camp. As Susan Sontag defined it in 1964, camp is "Being-as-Playing-a-Role. It is the farthest extension, in sensibility, of the metaphor of life as theater."[76] The camp aspect of glitter rock, its "*dandysme provocateur*," and the challenge it posed to

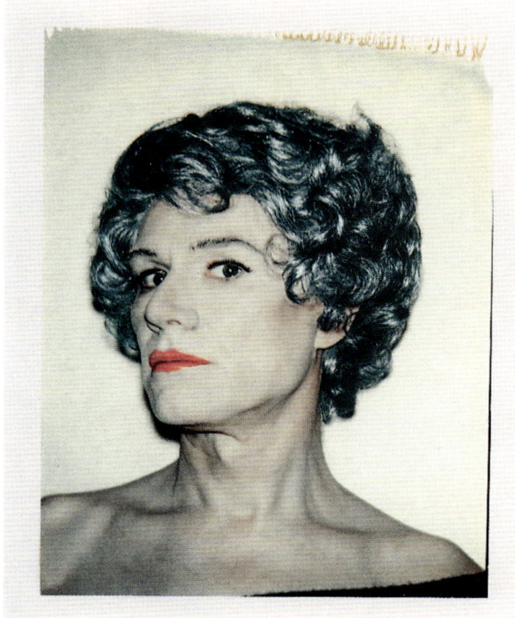
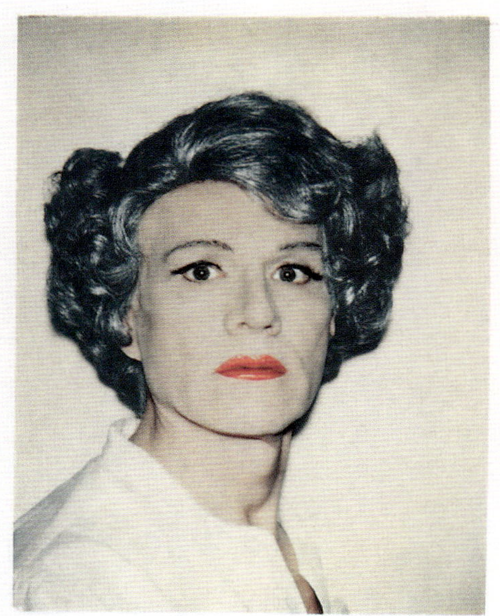
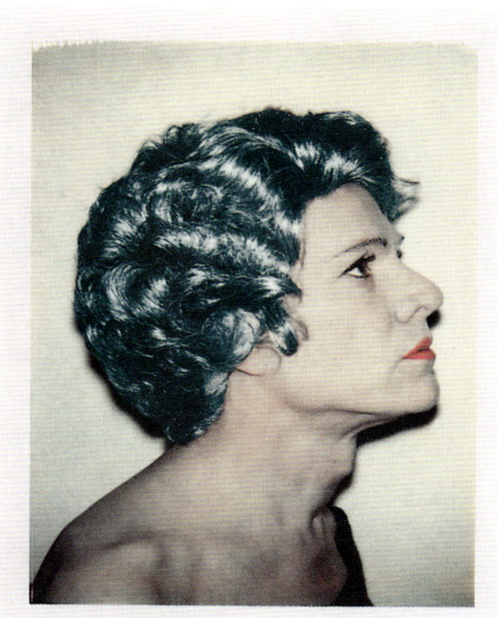

Andy Warhol
Self-Portraits in Drag, 1986
Polaroid photographs, each
3¾ x 2 ⁷⁄₁₆ inches (9.5 x 7.2 cm)
Musée National d'Art Moderne,
Centre Georges Pompidou, Paris

traditional masculinity through its derision of the sacrosanct masculine image was noted, in 1974, by Eudeline in his *"Transformer"* catalogue essay. Camp was a means through which rigidly defined patriarchal roles could be challenged through ridicule. This challenge was significantly informed by camp's relationship with flamboyant male homosexuality.

The entry of the camp sensibility into the mainstream, in the 1960s and 1970s, and its association with the artifice of female impersonators, must be seen in the context of the contemporaneous gay liberation movement.[77] Warhol's activities and glitter rock performance made visible, even marketed, the campy female impersonator as gay or bisexual idol. At a time when female impersonation was against the law in some American cities, presumably because it was perceived as the domain of homosexuals, and in light of the Stonewall Riots in 1969, gay-identified performance was not only a pleasurable but also a political act. Although critics, then and now, rightly point out that the campy self-presentation of pop stars was, for most, simply a marketing device, this does not totally negate the importance of the visibility of alternate gender presentations in mass culture.[78]

In an homage to Duchamp as Rrose Sélavy, Warhol appeared in drag in a 1981 photograph by Christopher Makos, *Altered Image*. Warhol subsequently incorporated a version of this photo into a centerfold project for *Artforum* magazine entitled *Forged Image*, in which he flanked the self-portrait in drag with a series of silk-screened dollar signs. Just as Rrose Sélavy's appearance on *Belle Haleine* suggests the deceitful replication of Helen of Troy (or the artifice of femininity itself), one reading of Warhol's *Forged Image* implies that the artist's identity is a forgery. But which part is duplicitous? Warhol's "altered image" is half-male and half-female: from the neck up he wears heavy "feminine" makeup and a blond wig, yet his attire is "masculine"; his pose is girlish, while his hands seem manly. It is not clear which elements are counterfeit (in fact, Andy in a wig is more normative than Andy in a tie), which supports the deduction that they all might be. In this way, his image suggests that gender identity is constructed and artificial. He also underscores the latent queer content in drag, a reading that is evacuated or oblique at best in Duchamp's gesture.[79]

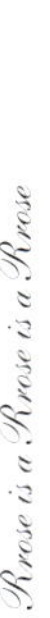

While the content of Warhol's films indicates that gender identity and sexuality are more complex than traditional Hollywood cinema has tended to represent, these movies, along with the artist's early 1960s silk-screen portraits, also suggest that all identity is a performance and that anyone can be a star. Warhol's portraits manifest a resolute disinterest in the notion that an introspective countenance represents the inner life of a sitter. Instead, the artist focuses on ready-made images that theatrically depict the self in its public guise, using found celebrity publicity pictures or photo-booth strips in which the not-yet-famous mug for the camera. His use of found images, and their repetition in the silk-screen process he employed to create his paintings, suggest the commodification of identity and reinforce its sense of artifice. By applying a grainy black-and-white image to variously colored grounds, Warhol emphasized the reproductive, photographic origins of the image. These were pictures of "real" people, the photo quality is an assurance of that, but their commodity status and artificiality are emphasized by the variety of color backgrounds. You could buy a Blue Marilyn, Gold Marilyn, or Green Marilyn—but they are all the same, the same "Marilyn," a construction of our expectations of celebrity.

Warhol also applied subsequent layers of color to highlight specific parts of the face. This application of veils of paint is a mode of covering, of obscuring and masking, which conforms with a conception of identity as masquerade. The frequent misalignment in the registration of the various silk-screened applications of paint notifies the viewer of a gap in the disguise, emphasizing a disjunction between mask and face. This slightly skewed registration, in conjunction with the garish coloring of lips and eyelids, often makes the portrait subject appear to be wearing makeup, to be in drag, whether it be Elvis, Mao, or Marilyn.

Warhol's 1963 silk-screen painting of multiple Mona Lisas is entitled *Thirty Are Better Than One*, and certainly from the point of view of the consumer, you can never have enough of anything. Desire is by definition unquenchable, but the more you have, the more you sustain the illusion that you are reaching satiation, even though you never do. Photography, with its potential for repetition, plays to this illusion, promoting the fantasy that, some day, perfection can be achieved. Gender identity is also conditioned by repetition, in that it entails the maintenance of a performance, one that must be reiterated in order to claim coherence. Sociologist Erving Goffman, who presented identity as a ritual of performance in his popular 1959 study *The Presentation of Self in Everyday Life*, later writes about the unfixity of gender:

> *What the human nature of males and females really consists of, then, is a capacity to learn to provide and to read depictions of masculinity and femininity and a willingness to adhere to a schedule for presenting these pictures, and this capacity they have by virtue of being persons, not females or males. One might just as well say there is no gender identity. There is only a schedule for the portrayal of gender.*[80]

Warhol's photo-based serial portraits share with portrait photography in general an attempt to fix the elusive, and frequently, especially in the 1970s, that slippery quality concerned identity itself. Perhaps it is to insure that the mirror will not be blank—a fear Warhol voiced—that the photographic self-portrait seems to take on the status of an obsession. The photo booth and the Polaroid camera allowed for the constant self-documentation of the "Me Generation," representing the farthest extension of the cult of individuality, when each person becomes his or her own god, a celebrity, a superstar. Much of the photographic work of the 1970s explores this aspect of contemporary society through the series and the grid format, which, through repetition, declare identity as manufactured.

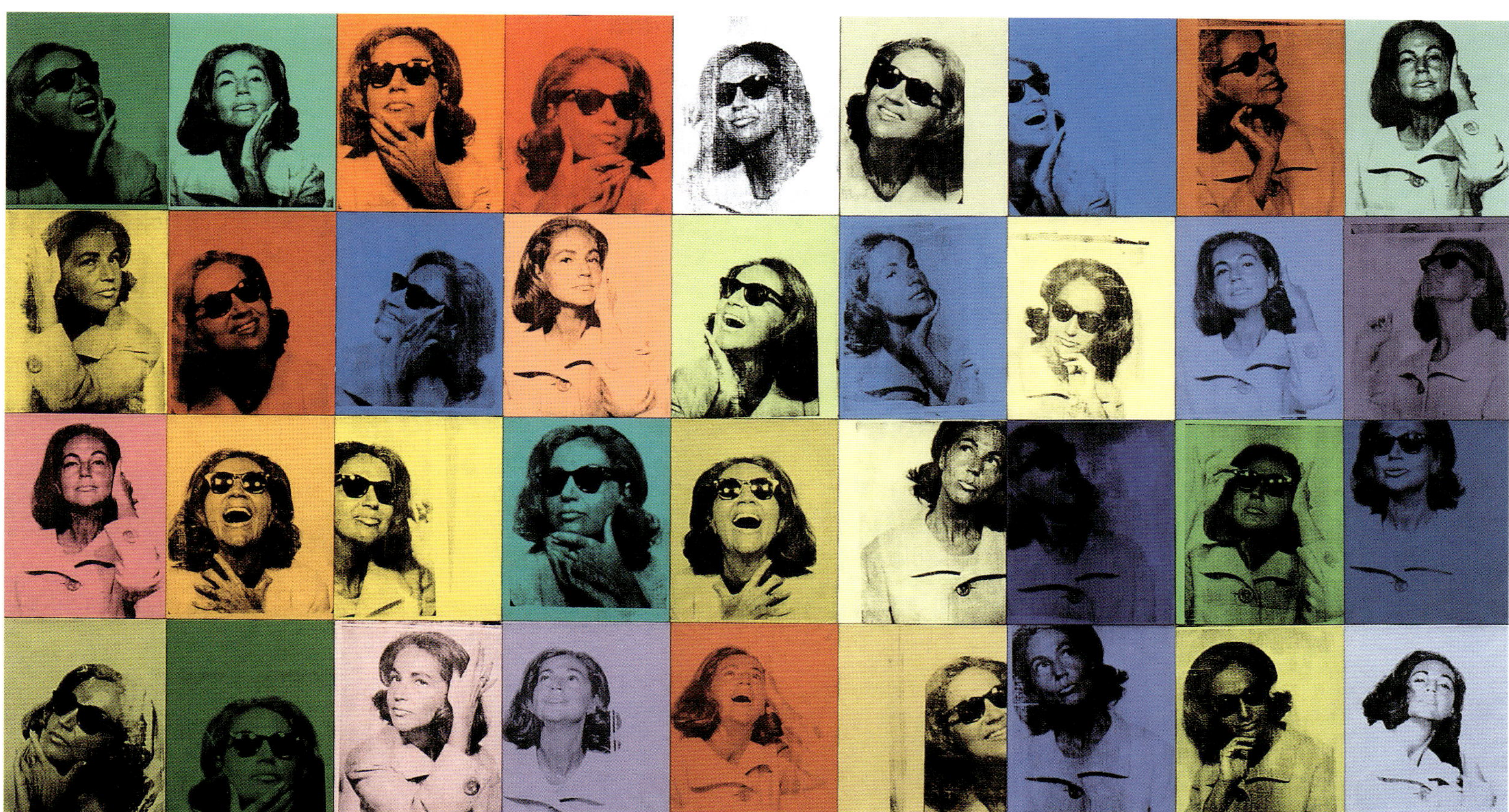

Andy Warhol
Ethel Scull 36 Times, 1963
Synthetic polymer paint silk-screened on canvas, 79 ¾ x 143 ¼ inches (202.6 x 363.9 cm)
Whitney Museum of American Art, New York, Gift of Ethel Redner Scull

The anxiety behind the play is captured in a scene in Wim Wenders's 1977 film *The American Friend*, when Dennis Hopper's troubled character, the eponymous protagonist of the film, shoots himself with a Polaroid over and over again, the exposed pictures fanning out around him on the pool table on which he lies.

Beginning in the late 1960s, Lucas Samaras created extensive series of Polaroid self-portraits and portraits. One of the earliest works, *Auto Polaroid* (1969–71), consists of eighteen prints arranged in a grid format.[81] In one image the artist appears in makeup and a long, blond wig; in another he is a tough guy dangling a cigarette from his mouth. Samaras is playing a grown-up game of dress-up, trying on various personae, all of them comically twisted. An artist deeply involved with the mechanics of fetishism—sexual, cultural, and religious—Samaras quite self-consciously explored the narcissism of the self, pursuing his investigations in a variety of media. The high theatricality of his photographic works acknowledges him as a student of the Happenings of the late 1950s and early 1960s. It also suggests the visceral power of photographic and reproductive media generally. In a 1969 film entitled *Self*, Samaras ate photographs of his father, mother, and sister.[82] Later, in his *Photo-Transformations* (1973–76), he manipulated the wet emulsion of the Polaroid, actually working on the photographic image, defacing and embellishing it, in the process embodying the urge to fix the image, to contravene the "real" and bend it into fantasy.

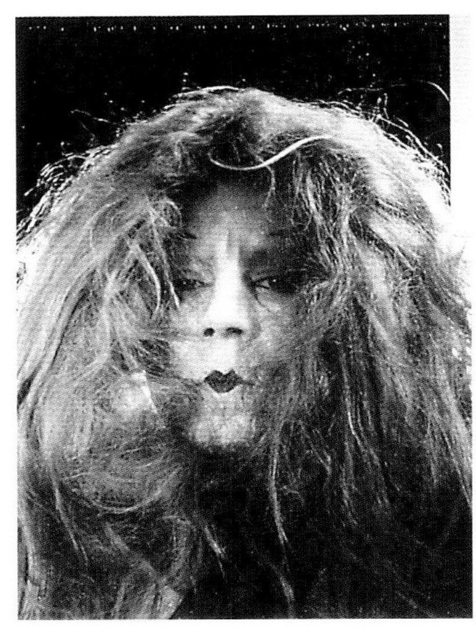
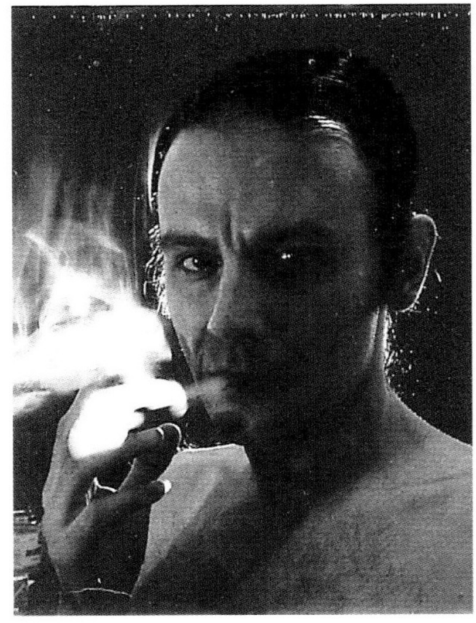
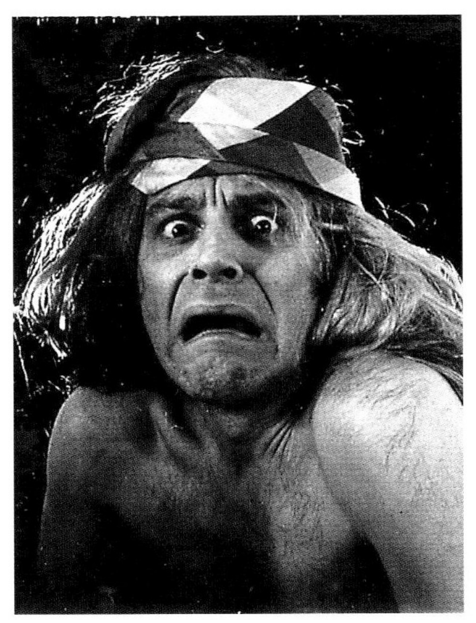
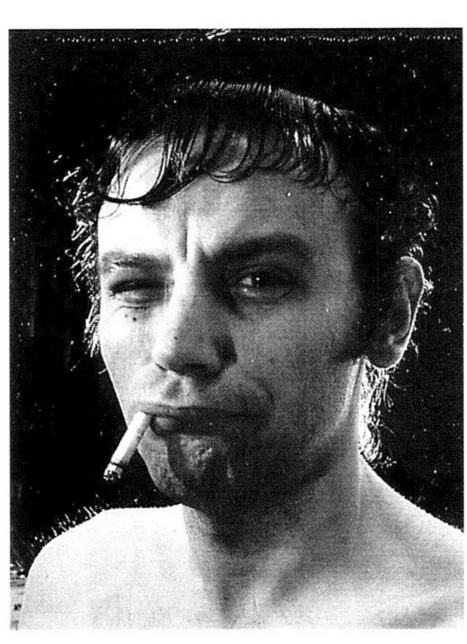
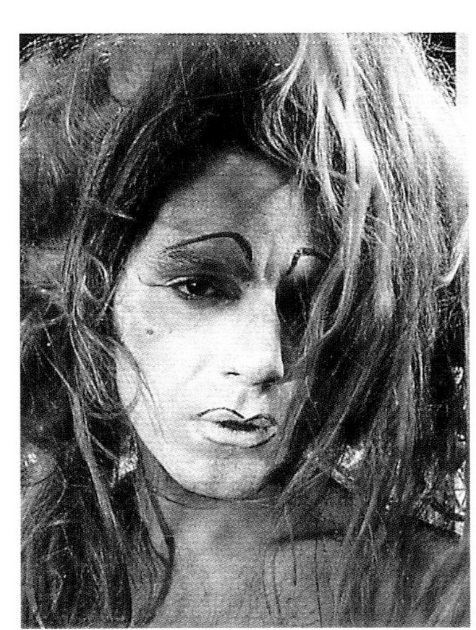
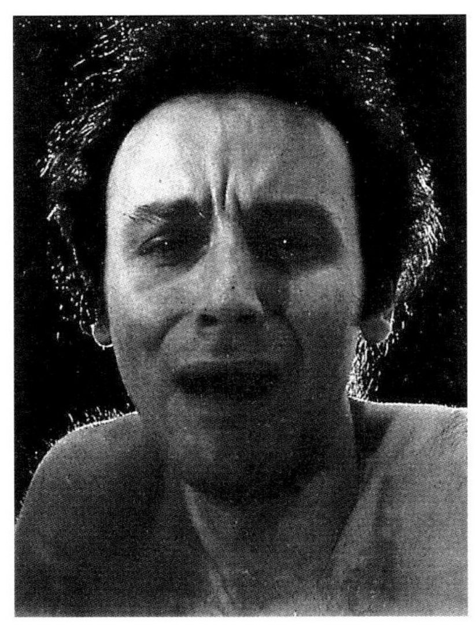
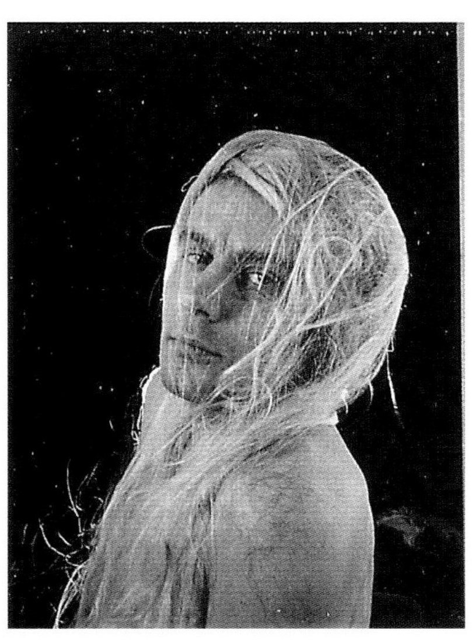
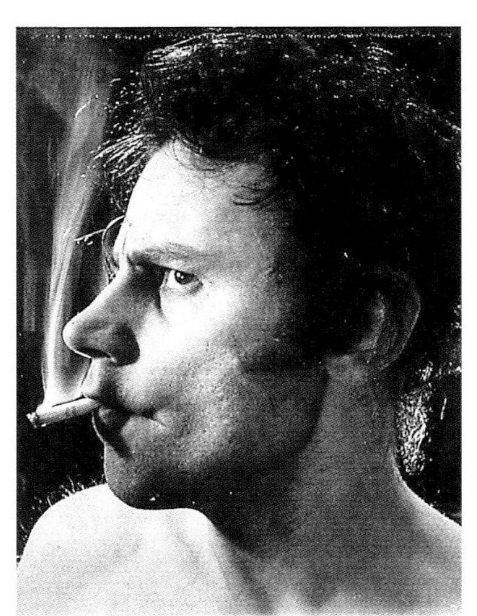
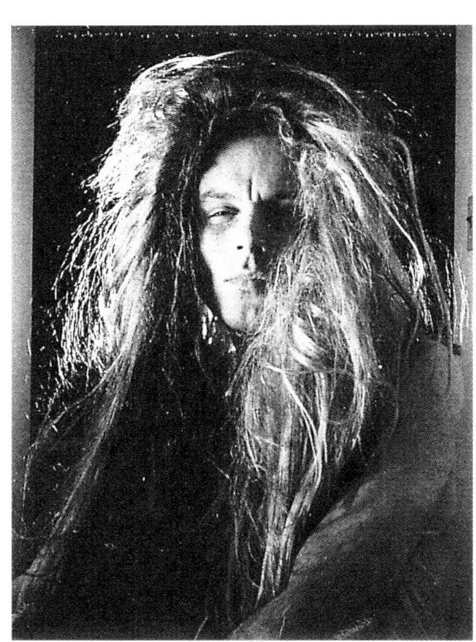

Lucas Samaras
Auto Polaroid, 1969–71
Eighteen black-and-white instant prints (Polapan), each 3¾ x 2 15/16 inches (9.5 x 7.4 cm); overall 14½ x 24¼ inches (36.8 x 61.6 cm)
The Museum of Modern Art, New York,
Gift of Robert and Gayle Greenhill

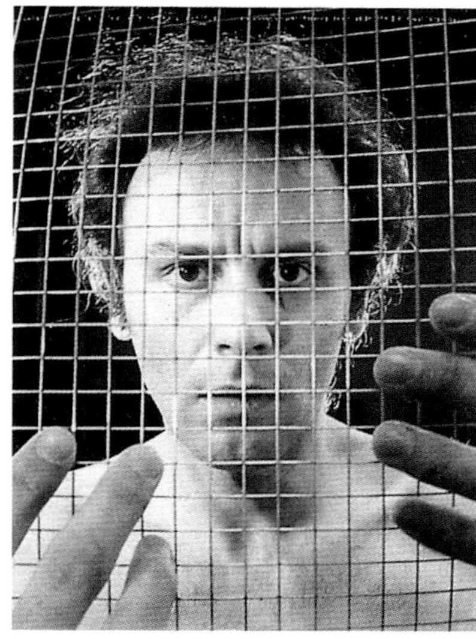

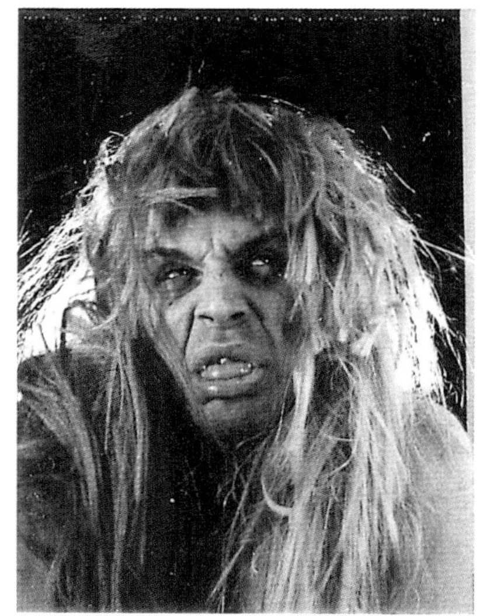

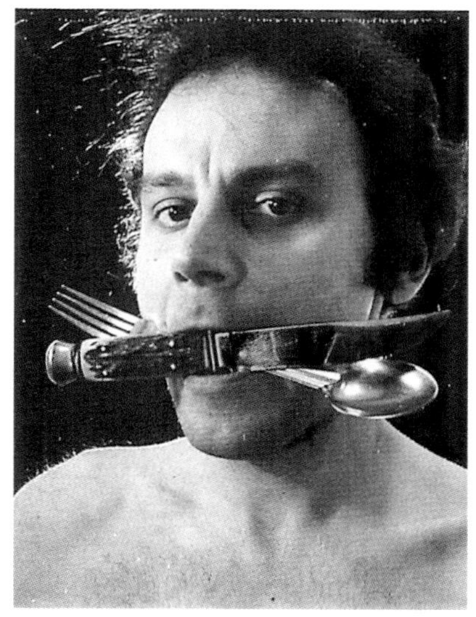

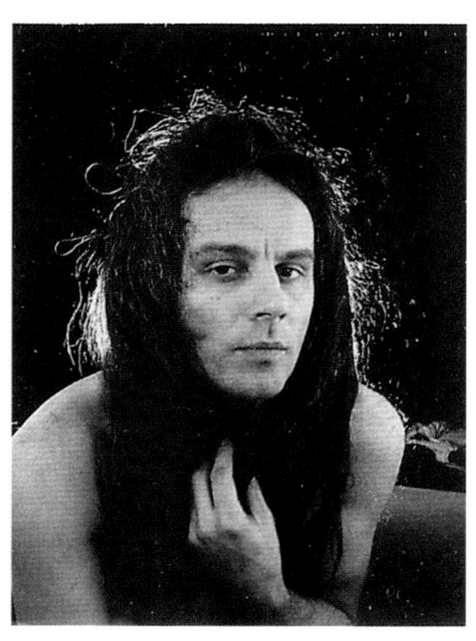

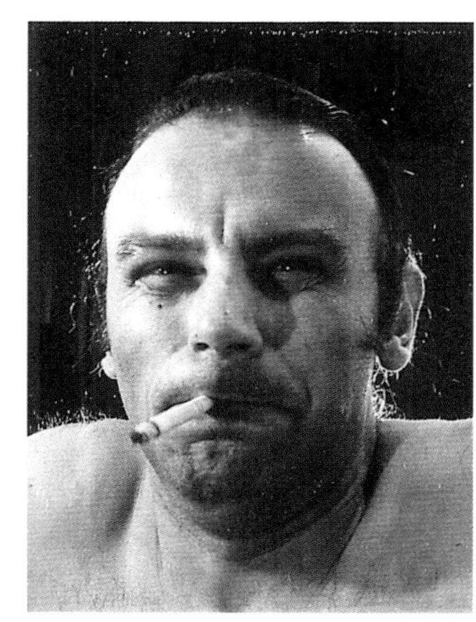

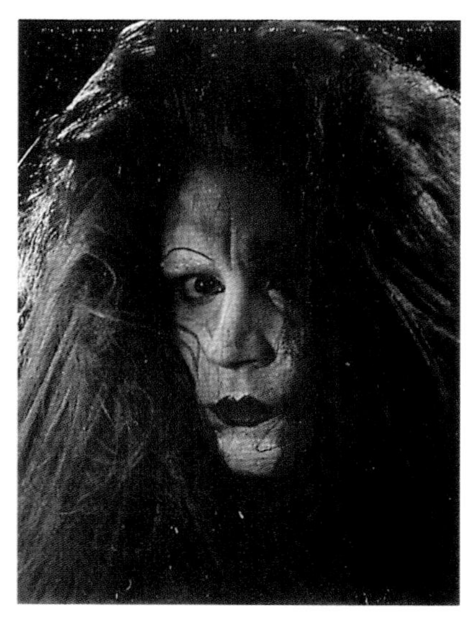

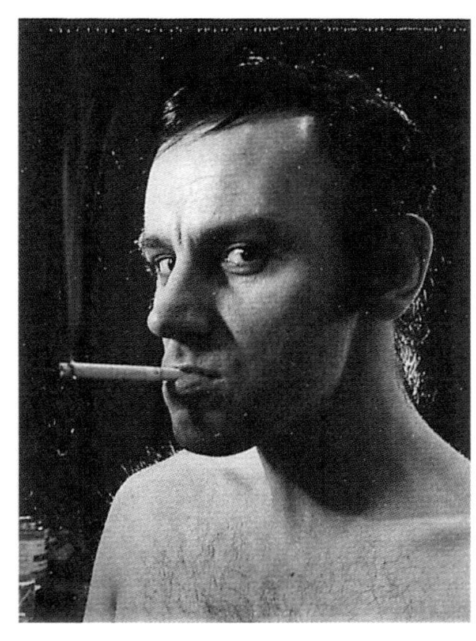

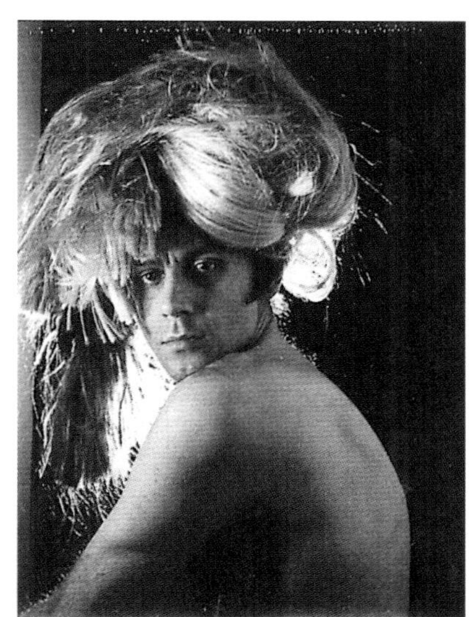

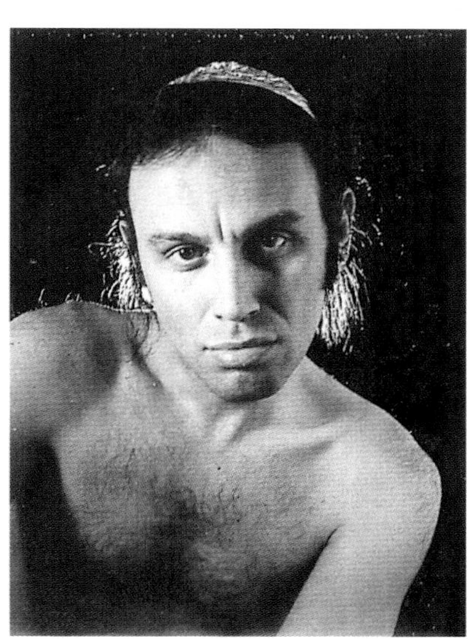

Feminism and the Masquerade of Femininity

Ammann's exhibition "*Transformer*" was exclusively concerned with male-to-female cross-dressing and conceived of the female impersonator as a model for artistic explorations of gender ambiguity, by, specifically, a male-born subject. It was premised on the notion of a revolt against traditional masculinity as represented by the uptight company man, who was probably the father of the artists and performers in the exhibition, and it championed the nascent gay liberation movement—again specifically that of men—in its implicit espousal of visibility as a means to assert identity.

Yet during the same period documented by "*Transformer*," a reemergent feminist movement was questioning the social construction of femininity. In 1975, Lucy Lippard published an article compiling numerous examples of Conceptual and performance-based artworks in which women examined the socially determined roles into which they were thrust as female subjects and experimented with alternate possibilities.[83] Performance artists such as Eleanor Antin created both male and female personae (Antin's repertory included The Ballerina, The King, The Black Movie Star, and The Nurse), who seem to literalize Goffman's notion of identity as performance. Many of these works demonstrate the elaborate artifice of femininity described and metaphorized in the ritual of makeup. The "construction chart" of Lynn Hershman's alter ego indicates the taxing social imposition that the masquerade of femininity entails, echoing Woolf's Orlando after her transformation from man to woman:

> *She remembered how, as a young man, she had insisted that women must be obedient, chaste, scented, and exquisitely apparelled. "Now I shall have to pay in my own person for those desires," she reflected; "for women are not (judging by my own short experience of the sex) obedient, chaste, scented, and exquisitely apparelled by nature. They can only attain these graces, without which they may enjoy none of the delights of life, by the most tedious discipline."*[84]

In her 1972 "album-collection" *The Voluntary Tortures* (*Les Tortures volontaires*), Annette Messager documents the myriad commercial methods available to women to make themselves more attractive to men. Messager, like Höch, appropriated the stereotypic representations of women in popular magazines and transformed them to her own ends. In another album-collection, *The Men-Women and the Women-Men* (*Les Hommes-Femmes et les Femmes-Hommes*, 1972), Messager playfully tampered with socially imposed gender definitions by inserting the images of male/female couples into other binary systems and subverting them. Positive reproductions are housed in the nominally private space of the album, while negative prints are exposed in the public domain of the wall, enframed. And, in each image, Messager has defiantly scribbled graffitilike defacements on the figures, drawing moustaches and beards on the women and accentuating the eyelashes and lips of the men, thereby making metaphorical husbands into wives and wives into husbands. This bifurcation of identity echoes Messager's self-defined personae, who include "Annette Messager Artiste" and "Annette Messager Collectionneuse," each the inhabitant of different areas of her house.[85] The album-collections are the product of the collector who rummages through the detritus of mass culture, incorporating it into her albums, thus compelling it to express what she wants it to, rather than simply allowing it to impose its homogenizing message on her.

There is a deadpan humor to Messager's work, which it shares with much of the post–Abstract Expressionist, Duchamp-inspired art that has flourished since the 1960s. Like the Dada and Surrealist laughter that it frequently resembles, however, it is not content simply to amuse but,

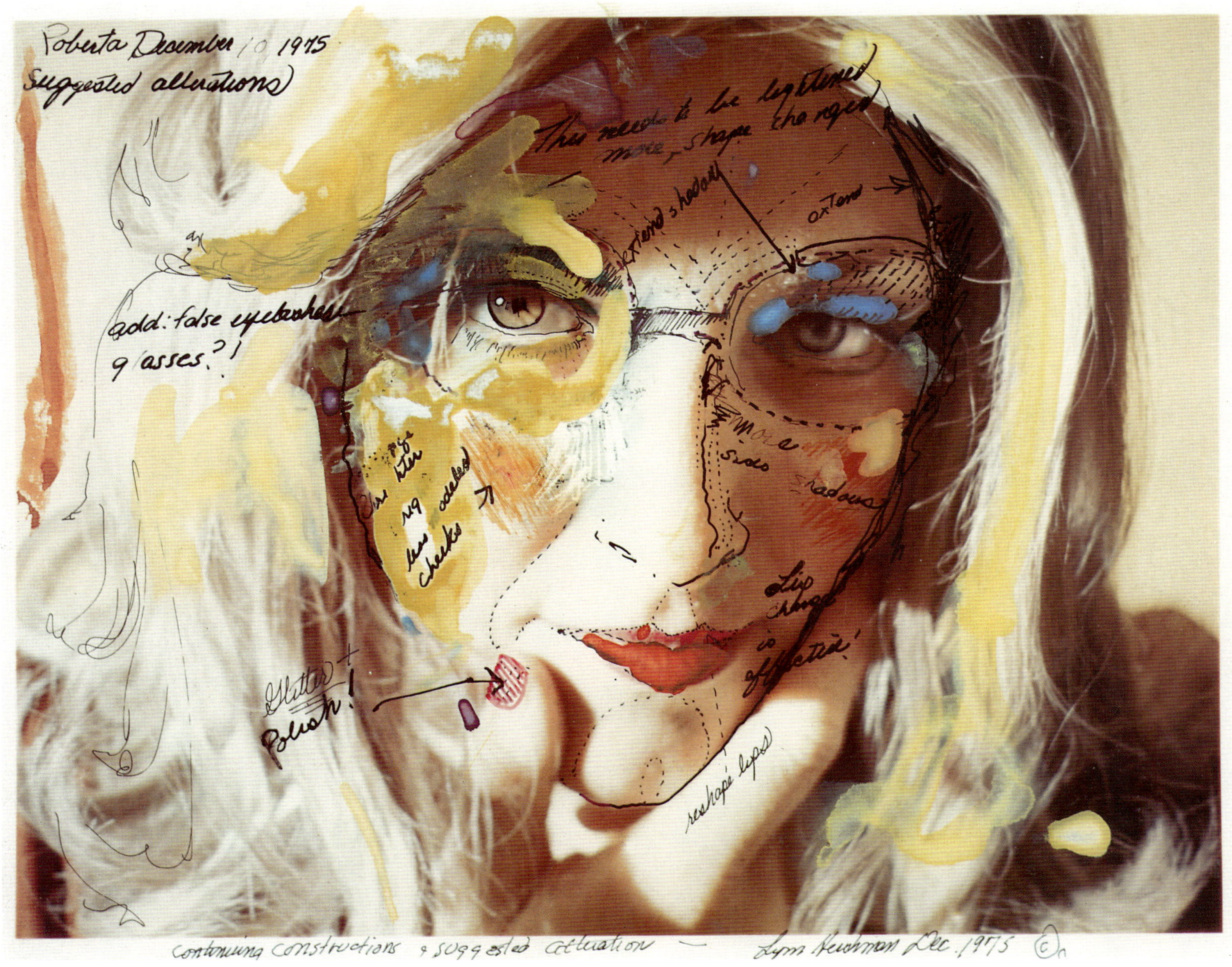

Lynn Hershman
Roberta's Construction Chart, 1975
C-print, 30 x 40 inches
(76.2 x 101.6 cm)
Courtesy of the artist

instead, has more or less clear critical implications. Laughter can be a disruptive act, expressing an in-your-face exuberance that only partially masks ridicule of its subject.[86] The works of the 1970s that play with and question gender identity often show—literally or metaphorically—their maker brimming with glee at the mockery she has made of traditional expectations. It is these artists' pleasure to refuse to conform, and to imagine another reality, one in which repressive conventions are overturned. It is here that the political implications of camp, as a rejection of a set of rules and its replacement with alternate conceptions, become clear. The critical potential of wit is often engaged in the work of artists who explore the definitions of femininity and masculinity in the 1970s.

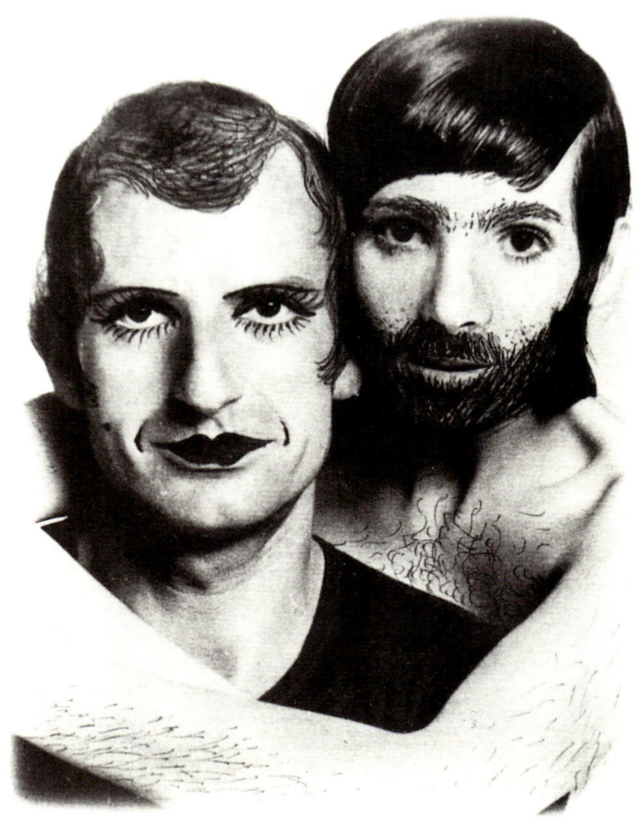

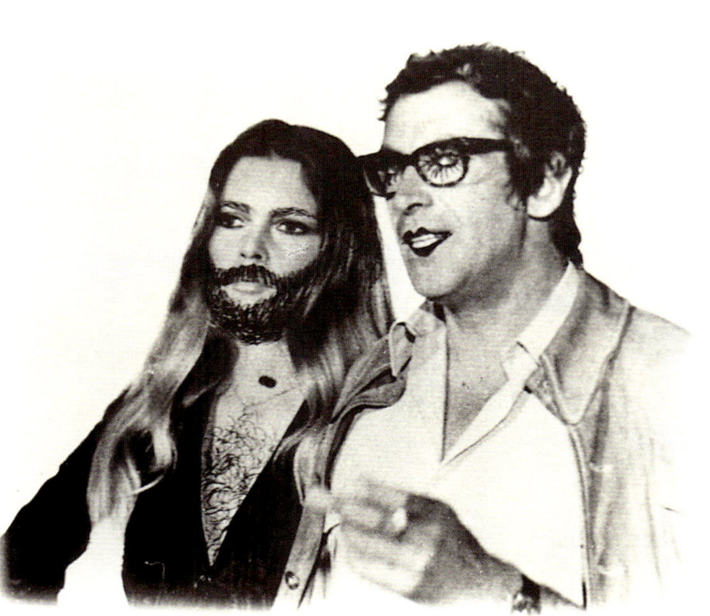

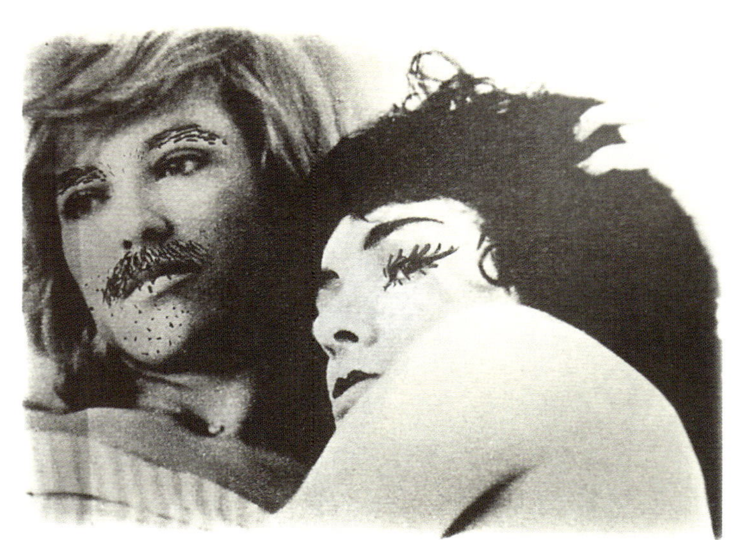

Annette Messager
The Men-Women and the Women-Men, Annette Messager Collector (Les Hommes-Femmes et les Femmes-Hommes, Annette Messager Collectionneuse), Album-collection No. 11 (details of album photographs), 1972
Nineteen photographs under glass and one album
Collection of the artist

facing page:
Annette Messager
The Men-Women and the Women-Men, Annette Messager Collector (Les Hommes-Femmes et les Femmes-Hommes, Annette Messager Collectionneuse), Album-collection No. 11 (installation detail), 1972
Nineteen photographs under glass, each maximum 7 1/16 x 5 7/8 inches (18 x 15 cm), and one album
Collection of the artist

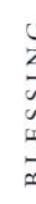

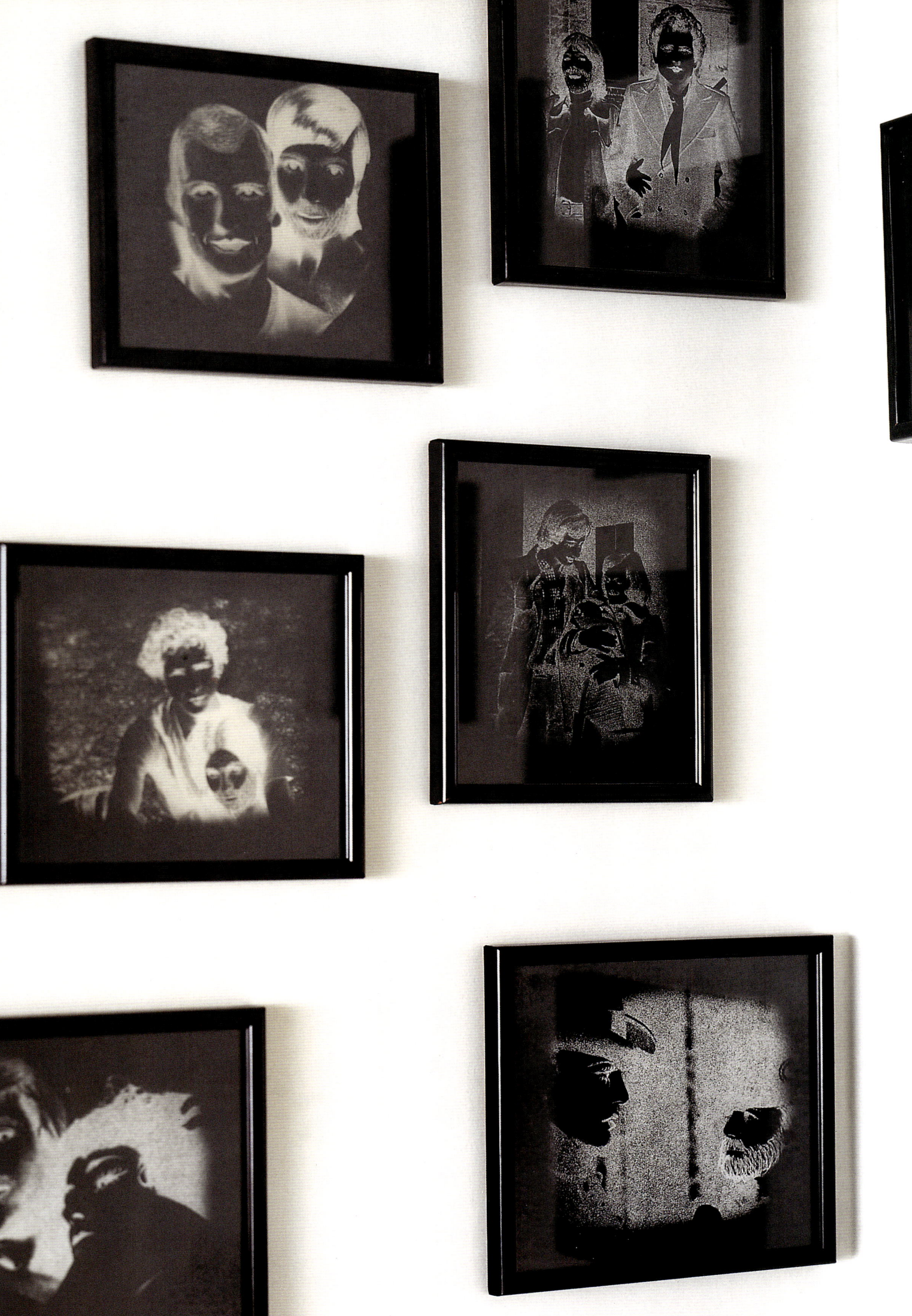

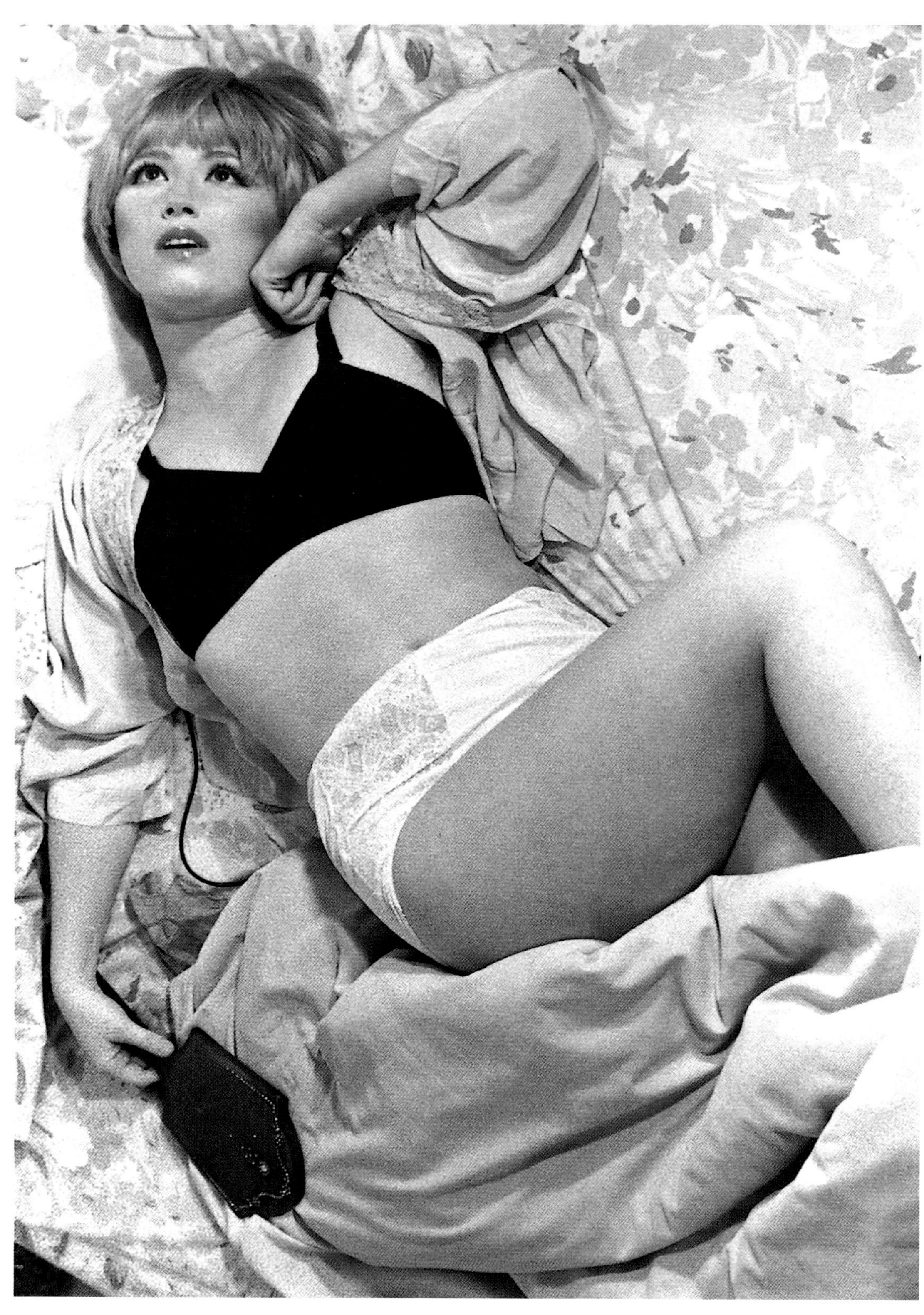

Cindy Sherman
Untitled Film Still, #6, 1977
Gelatin-silver print, 10 x 8 inches (25.4 x 20.3 cm), ed. 3/10
Collection of Samuel and Ronnie Heyman, New York

4. Some Contemporary Photographic Work

> **Not only are some people more masculine or more feminine than others, but some people are just plain more *gender-y* than others—whether the gender they manifest be masculine, feminine, both, or "and them some."**
>
> EVE KOSOFSKY SEDGWICK, "'Gosh, Boy George, You Must Be Awfully Secure in Your Masculinity!'" 1995[87]

> **There is a sense of freedom in having a desire that has never been labeled.**
>
> NAN GOLDIN, *The Other Side*, 1993[88]

Gender Fantasy

In her *Untitled Film Stills*, produced between 1977 and 1980, Cindy Sherman appropriated the format of black-and-white Hollywood publicity photographs. There is a deceptive nostalgic quality to the clothes and poses depicted in these images, and for a moment, we presume we are looking at some B-movie starlet whose films we cannot recall. However, the accumulated impact of the series, which includes sixty-nine pictures, forces the realization that this is a theater within a theater in which the performer is a *mannequin sans visage* whose representation is constructed through the artifice of wigs, makeup, costume, and distracted facial expressions. She is a familiar figure of spectacular femininity in melodrama, the damsel in distress who is perfectly cognizant she is being watched. She is that preposterous cinematic female victim-to-be who fixes her makeup and hair, presumably to prepare for her rescuer, instead of trying to escape the trauma that is about to befall her.

The conventions of the cinematic film still are brilliantly manipulated in Sherman's work, which is not to say they are transparent replicas that could ever be confused with the Hollywood version.[89] There is always something wrong, something off, about the picture, that highlights its artifice: a furnishing or accessory seems out of place, or is slightly too eccentric, enough to be distracting; a camera angle is too extreme. Or there are giveaways like a visible shutter-release cord or the reflection of a loft sprinkler system, which inform the viewer that this is an enactment. This is the work of a trickster; this is someone's fun and games.

There is also something troubling, something vaguely ominous, about the *Untitled Film Stills.* It is arguable that this is due to reading Sherman's later work back into these earlier photographs. Yet the "still" quality of the image suggests the quiet before the storm. Film stills can be shots from a movie or production pictures taken on the set. They tend to represent a fixed moment but may show some action. Sherman's pictures are frozen in the extreme, not so much in the way the action has been captured as that one has the sensation something is about to happen, or already has. The moment of pause, of anticipation, is fetishistically exaggerated, intensifying an anxiety fed by the slightly skewed quality, by those disjunctions unassimilable to our expectations. This photographic uncanniness is expressed in the frequent doubling, both within individual pictures, through the many mirror reflections and planted framed portraits, and the repetition of poses between various images.

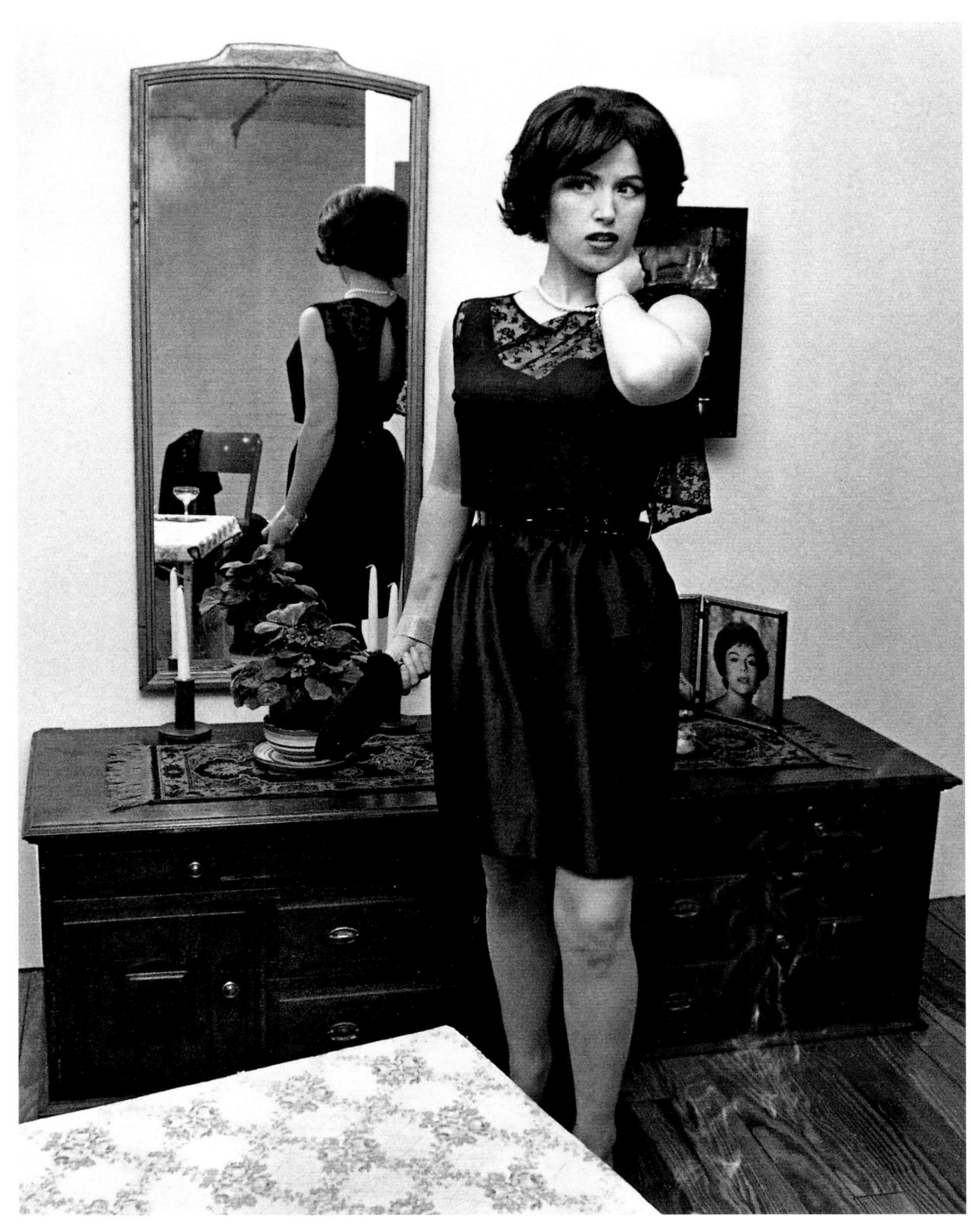

Cindy Sherman
Untitled Film Still, #14, 1978
Gelatin-silver print, 10 x 8 inches (25.4 x 20.3 cm), ed. 8/10
Collection of Carol and Paul Meringoff

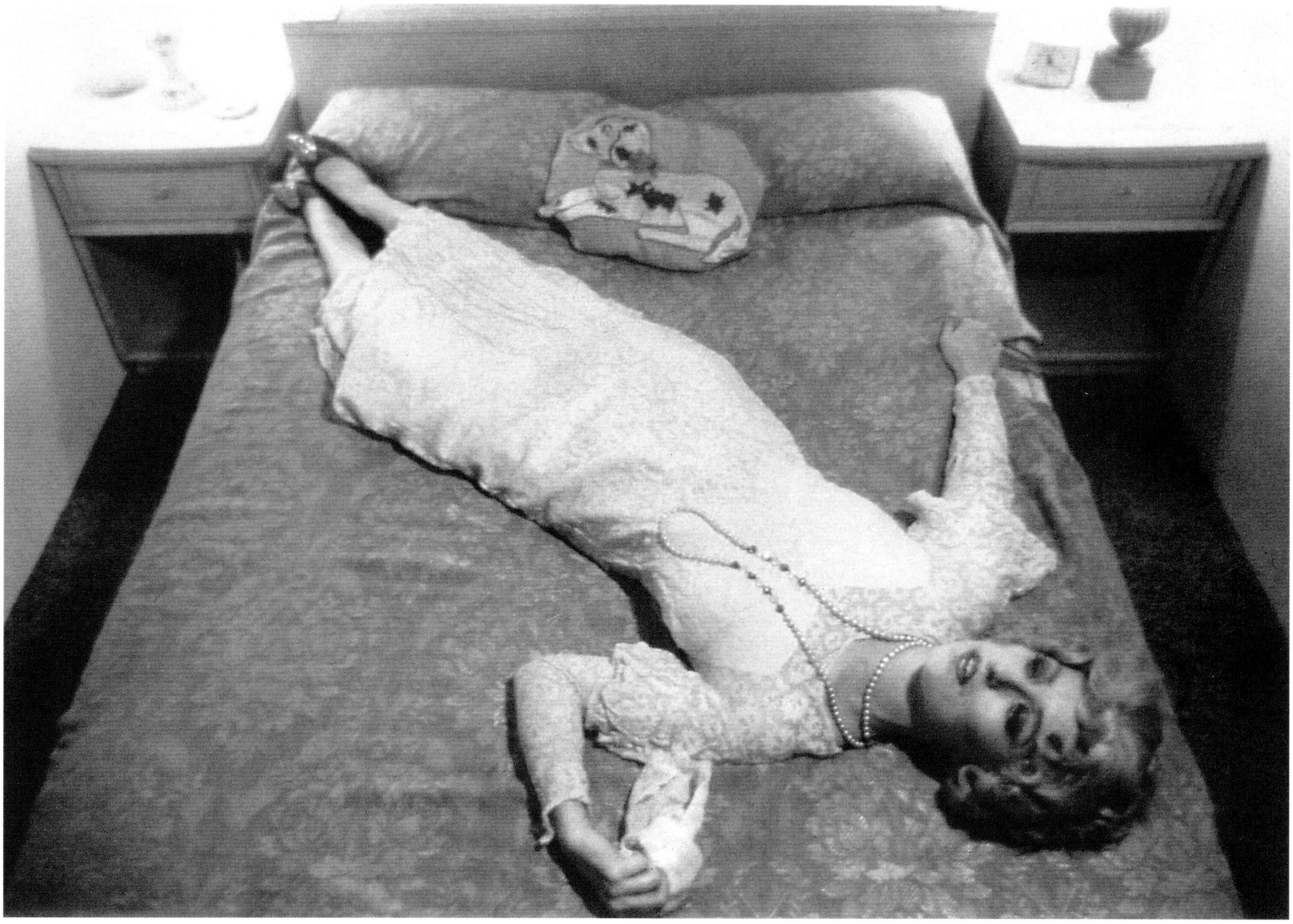

Cindy Sherman
Untitled Film Still, #11, 1978
Gelatin-silver print, 8 x 10 inches (20.3 x 25.4 cm), ed. 3/10
Collection of M. Anthony and Anne E. Fisher

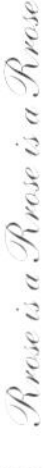

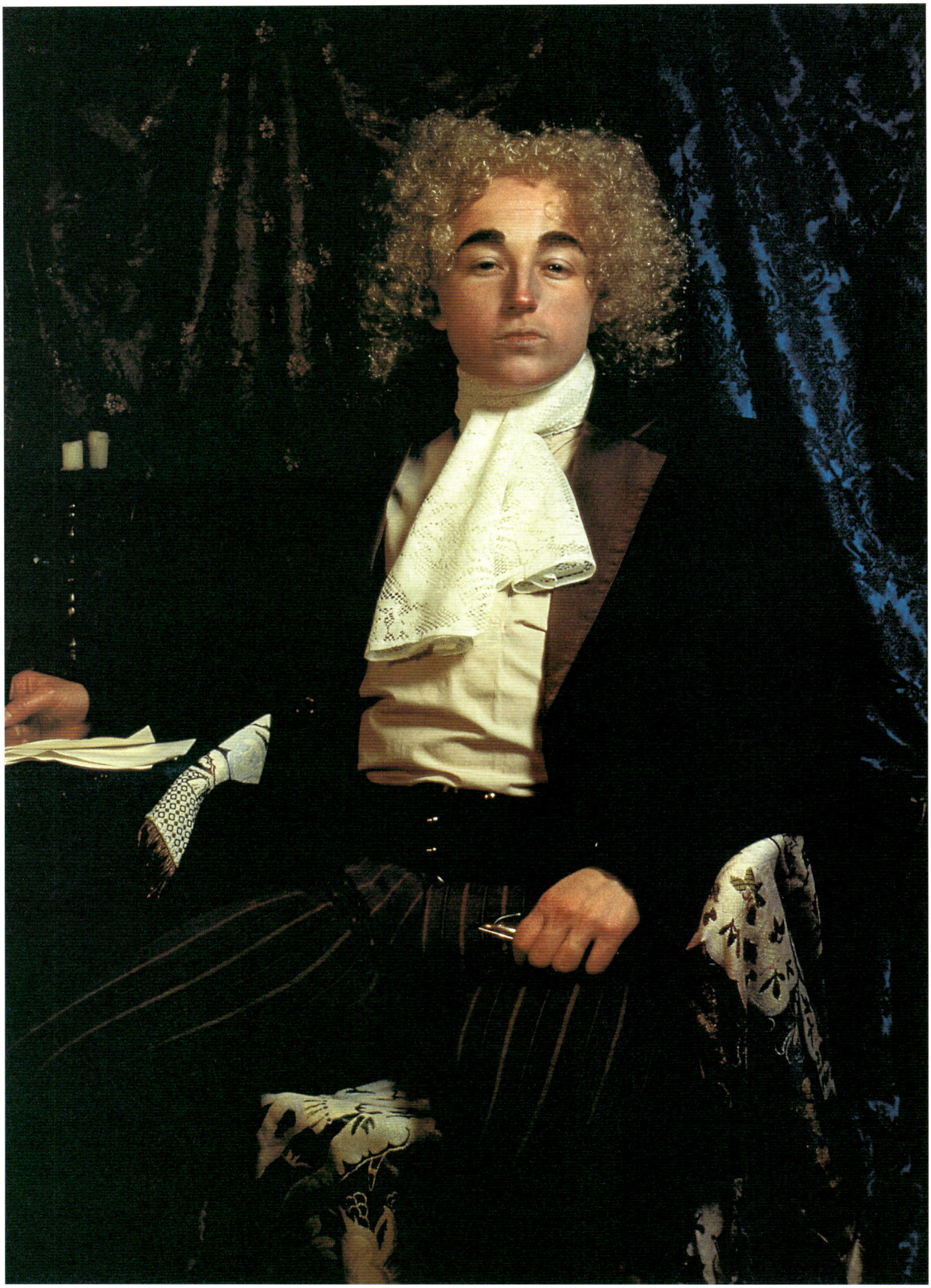

Cindy Sherman
Untitled, #201, 1989
Color photograph, 52 7/8 x 35 7/8 inches (134.3 x 91.1 cm), ed. 4/6
Collection of Beverly and Harris Schoenfeld

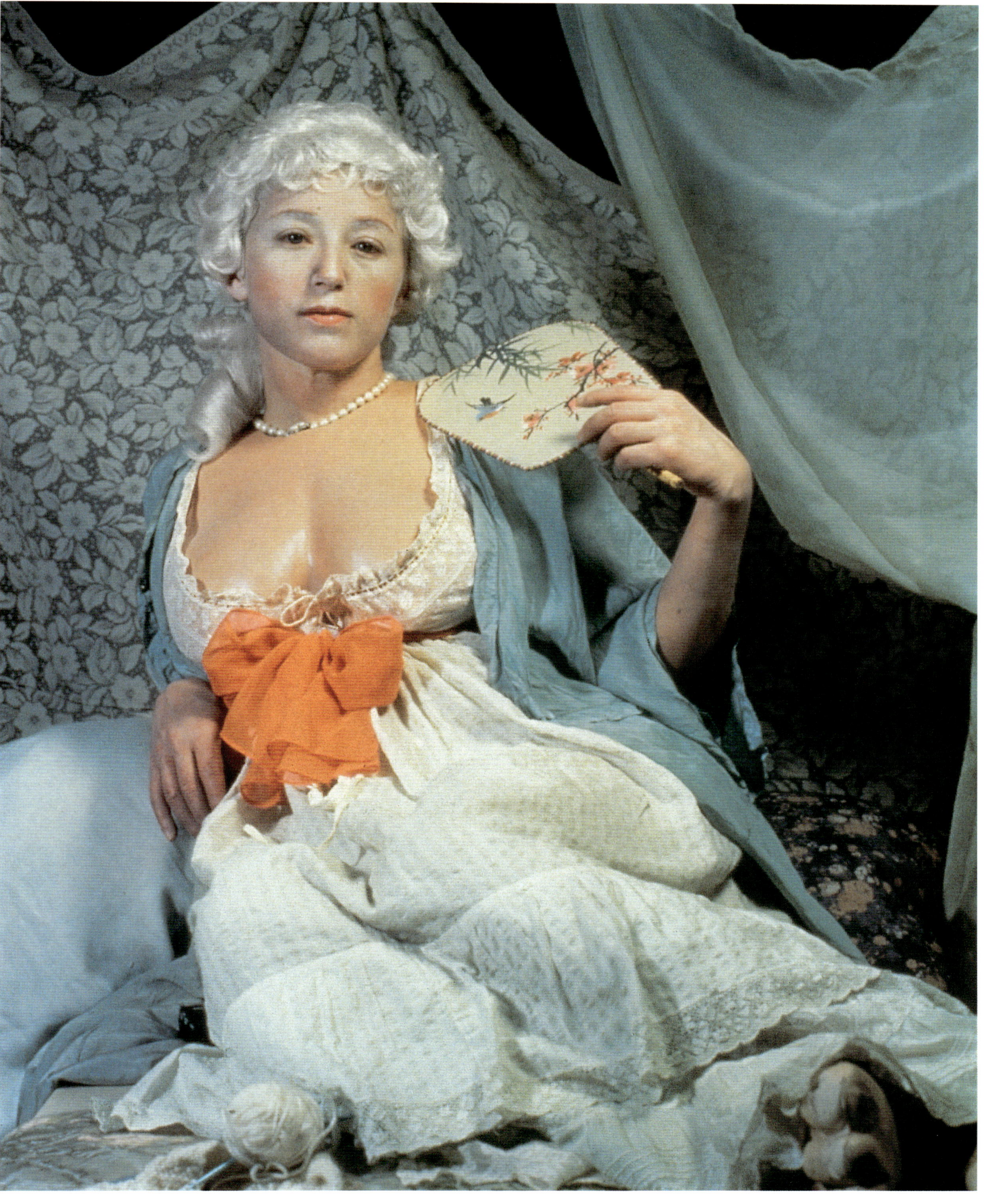

Cindy Sherman
Untitled, #193, 1989
Color photograph, 48 ⅞ x 41 15/16 inches (124.1 x 106.5 cm), ed. 5/6
Collection of William S. Ehrlich and Ruth Lloyds

In the *History Portraits* she began in 1988, Sherman created *tableau vivant* reenactments of masterpieces of art history, frequently drawing on the work of eighteenth-century painters of sensual leisure such as François Boucher.[90] In these images she plays with the artifice of period dress—the elaborate hairstyles of wigs and the powdery white makeup worn by both men and women—as well as the trappings of wealth that were an indicator of status, the fine tapestries and silks so prominently displayed in the period's portraits. The purposefully faked aspects of Sherman's pictures point to the artifice of painting itself, in which any liberty might be taken to flatter a sitter, but they also suggest a personal pleasure in the willfulness of their perverse disruption of the models from which they derive. The protagonists of the series are male and female, and most of the portraits include prosthetic body parts along with more conventional props, until, in Sherman's later work, the body is lost and the prostheses take over.

In mixed-media photographic tableaux dating from 1985, Yasumasa Morimura began to reenvision various masterpieces of Modernist art history, inserting himself in drag and disguise as all of the figures in paintings such as Edouard Manet's *Olympia* (1863). In 1988, Morimura recreated Rrose Sélavy in living color, in the process multiplying Duchamp's binary distinctions beyond the original male/female axis, to include ethnic and cultural dimensions and the manner in which these terms are sexualized. Morimura's insistent use of doubling (two hats, two sets of hands) summons the uncanny nature of fetishism, in which multiplication signals a preventative repetition to ward against castration and death, while it also magnifies the binary logic inherent to Duchamp's piece. Through the juxtaposition of hands and arms of different colors, and the obviousness of heavy white makeup (also exaggerated in Duchamp, mining the ancient historical convention equating whiteness with an ideal of femininity), Morimura signals the implication of sexuality in the constructs of race and ethnicity. The title of the piece, *Doublonnage (Marcel)*, suggests a variety of duplications, including Morimura's double of Duchamp, as well as a sense of the diffusion of Western culture and the way it is "dubbed" into other contexts. While writing himself into this exclusively Western Modernist history, Morimura also heightens the latent content in the original, the way in which race and ethnicity are subsumed or taken for granted in these works. Examining the marginalized often reveals the logic of dominant ideologies. Morimura forces the margins to the center, in the process compelling the viewer to acknowledge the ideological positions that inform the image that the artist reconstructs.

Matthew Barney, who integrates recorded performance and sculptural objects in his multimedia installations, also exhibits production photographs in "self-lubricating" plastic frames as independent artifacts from his videos. His enigmatic work presents various images of masculinity, particularly as represented in the arduous athleticism of professional sports, but including the realm of myth. Often he portrays an apparently male protagonist involved in a quest, whether rappelling along the walls of a gallery, enduring repeated punches, tap dancing into oblivion, or practicing blocking in drag.[91] The environments within which these events occur are frequently linked to ritualized contests of masculine endurance such as the race course and the football field.[92]

Barney has finished two videos of his projected five-part cycle, entitled *Cremaster*, after the muscle that retracts the testicles. The first movie produced, *Cremaster 4* (1994), involves an elaborate exploration of the binary logic of sexual differentiation, which is never finally resolved into complete difference or unity. It is as if Duchamp's *The Large Glass* metamorphosed into a fantastical Disneyesque walk-in storybook. In *Cremaster 4* and *Cremaster 1* (1995), the second film made in the series, Barney presents color-coded masculine and feminine symbols of bodily organs, as well as pro-

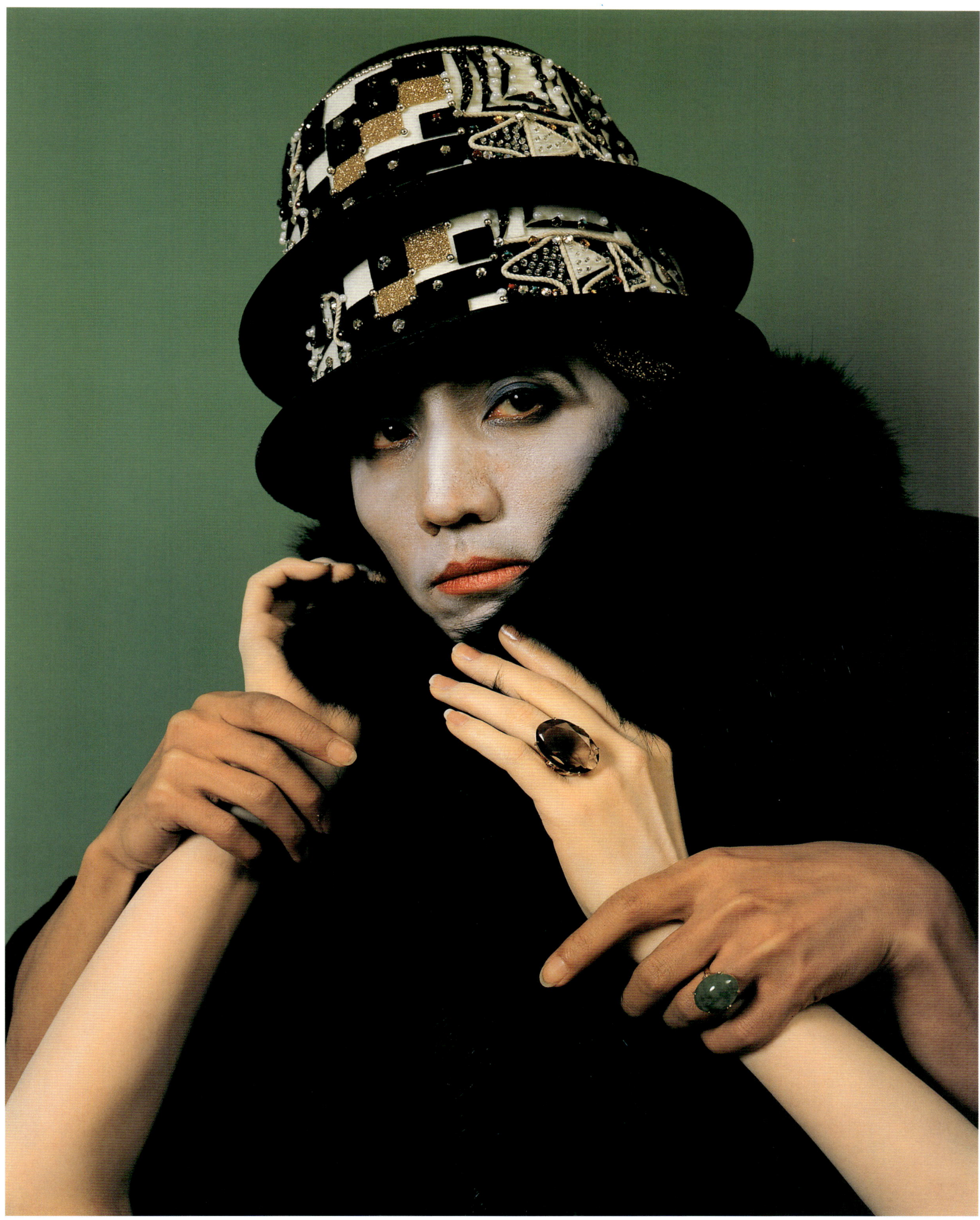

Yasumasa Morimura
Doublonnage (Marcel), 1988
Color photograph, 60 x 48 inches (152.4 x 121.9 cm)
Jedermann Collection, N.A.

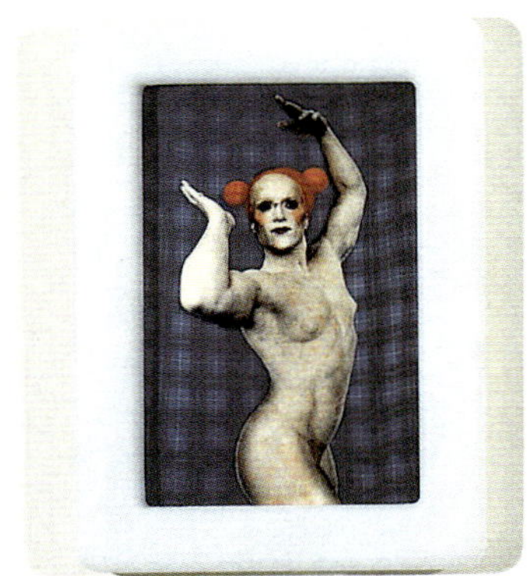
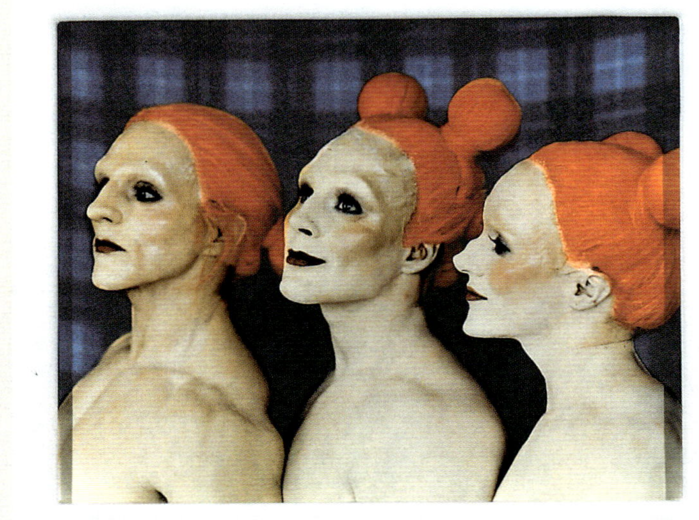
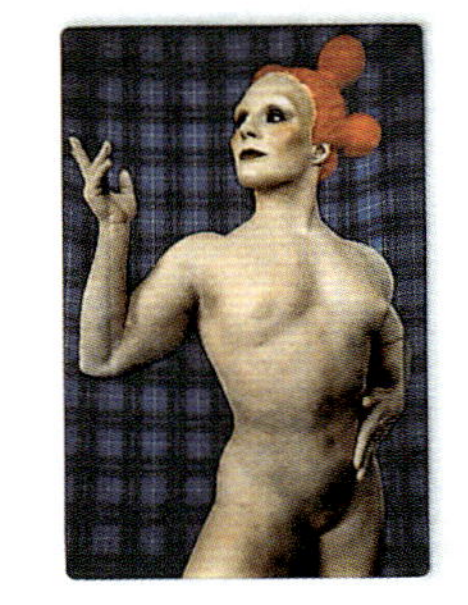
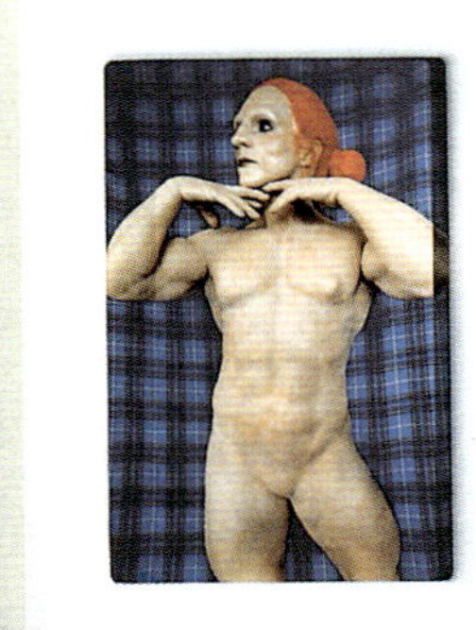

Matthew Barney
CR 4: Faerie Field, 1994
Four C-prints in self-lubricating plastic frames; three pieces,
each 17 ½ x 12 ¾ x 1½ inches (44.5 x 32.4 x 3.8 cm),
one piece 27 ½ x 33¼ x 1½ inches (70 x 84.5 x 3.8 cm), ed. AP 2/2
Courtesy of Michael James O'Brien

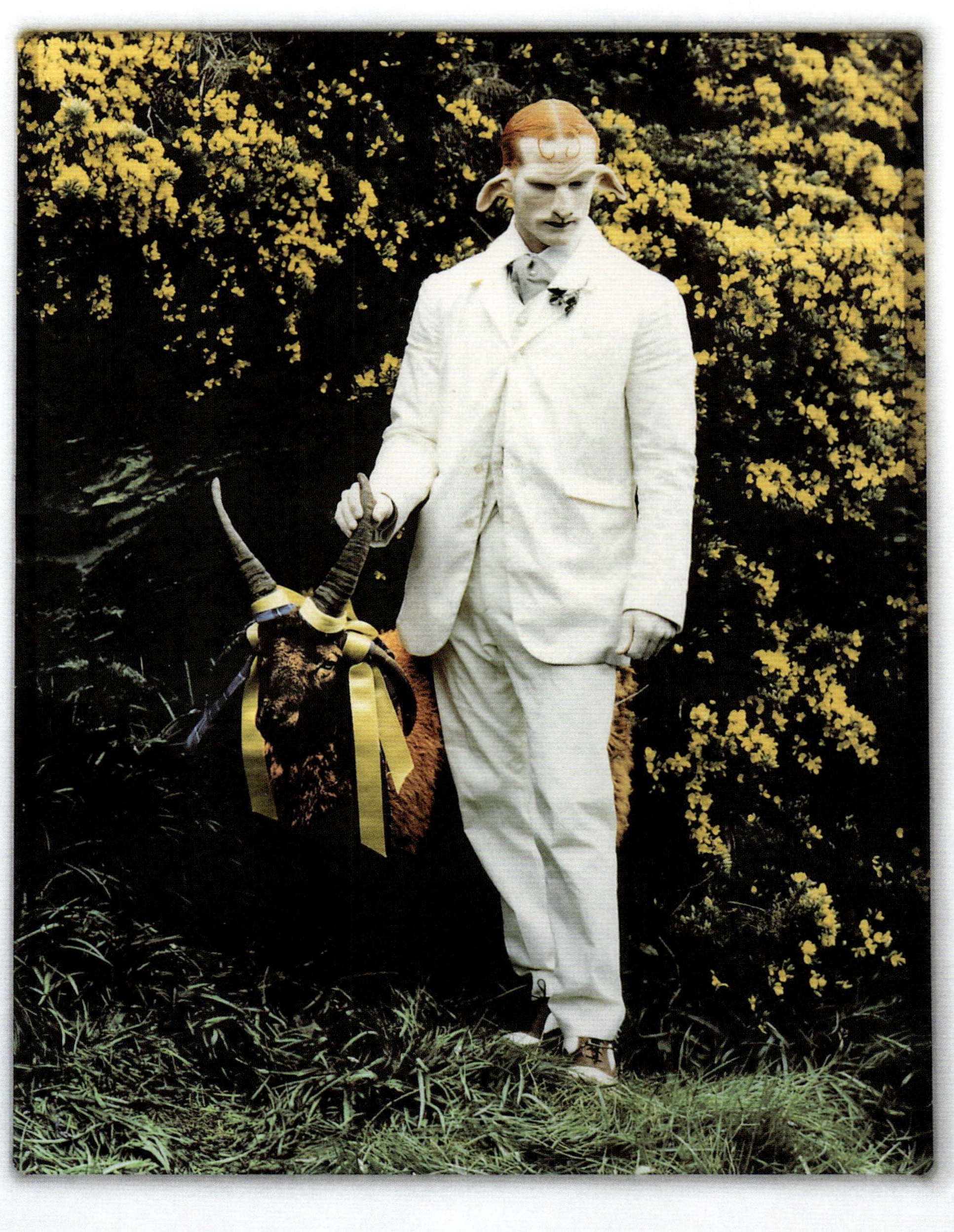

Matthew Barney
CR 4: Loughton Manual, 1994
C-print in self-lubricating plastic frame, 25 x 21 x 1½ inches
(63.5 x 53.3 x 3.8 cm), ed. 6/6
Private collection, New York

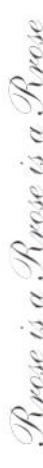

tagonists whose gender is not clearly defined. The settings and characters in these videos are surreally saturated with color and unusually costumed. Body makeup and prosthetics take the "Is she a he?" question to the *n*th-dimension—characters like the three faeries who accompany the Loughton Candidate in *Cremaster 4* and the satyrs in *Drawing Restraint 7* have a literal second skin. These beings are not male, not female; elements of dress or makeup may suggest masculinity or femininity, but, finally, these figures are so elaborately constructed that the most extreme indicators of "absolute" gender identification are nullified.

The legacy of body art, performance, and video of a generation earlier is apparent in works such as these by Sherman, Morimura, and Barney. But while their precursors were interested in real time, an integration of art with "real life," and an ethics of the ephemeral and the transitory, these artists' work is highly aestheticized, moving into another world, that of fantasy. The works of the late 1980s and 1990s often cite popular film and high-art sources, in the process purposefully subverting and happily perverting the traditional definition of gender while crossing the imaginary divide between high and low. All of these artists work in and against commercial fields concerned with theatrical artifice (as did Duchamp, Beaton, and Warhol, for example): they are each engaged with the fashion system; the Hollywood dream factory; and their integration and transmutation into art.[93]

Christian Marclay works with music and its visualization, in the process investigating media representations of music and its marketing by the music industry. For his *Body Mix* (1991–92) and *Masks* (1992) series, Marclay sewed found record album covers together, creating hybrid figures and visages out of multiple overlapping parts.[94] Viewing these series as a whole graphically underscores the modus operandi of advertising, summarized in the familiar adage "sex sells." Marclay's raw material, the album covers, characteristically fetishizes body parts, especially female. The same shots of headless torsos, long legs, and round buttocks are featured ad infinitum, an aspect highlighted by Marclay's strategy of conjoining the disparate parts. This technique also calls attention to the way the exotic other—represented by brown bodies and "ethnic" costumes—is called upon to feed the trope of music as sensual stimulation and particularly sensuality as the province of the ethnic and sexual other.

Marclay's engagement with montage, both in these works and his mixing of music in his performances, is rooted in Dada and Surrealist practice. His employment of the found object (album covers), and their juxtaposition to create new and surprising meanings, recall the photomontage of artists like Höch, as well as the Surrealist game of Exquisite Corpse, in which strange figures were forged through a process in which each participant added to a drawing without knowledge of what had come before.[95] Marclay's *Magnetic Fields*, a complex piece in the *Body Mix* series, gets its title from a text written by Breton and the poet Philippe Soupault, four years before the former published his first manifesto of Surrealism.[96] Soupault and Breton's text forecasts Surrealist practice, in the manner in which it juxtaposes prose fragments. Marclay's work mines this technique in numerous ways, combining seemingly disparate objects, images, and sounds, to expose tropes that are often taken for granted. The resulting disclosures may be compared to the insights we experience when learning another language or living in another culture; it is by comparing the difference in the way a thought is expressed or a social interaction is conducted that we become aware of what we never questioned, of what we took for granted. The tropes Marclay engages are the socially constructed distinctions between sound and sight; male and female; black and white; past and present.

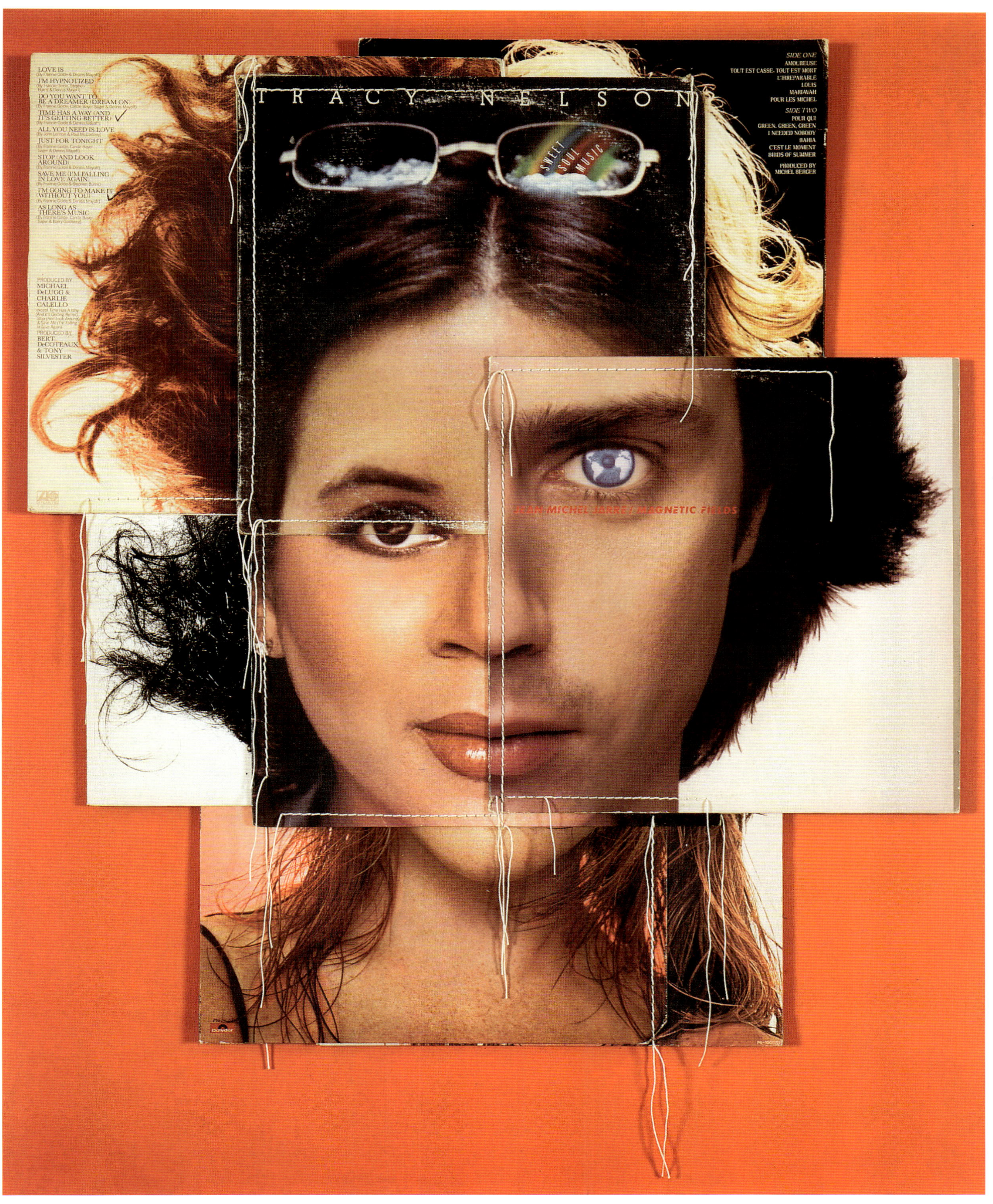

Christian Marclay
Magnetic Fields, from the *Body Mix* series, 1991
Record covers and cotton thread, 27¼ x 24½ inches (69.2 x 62.2 cm)
Collection of Joan and Gerald Kimmelman

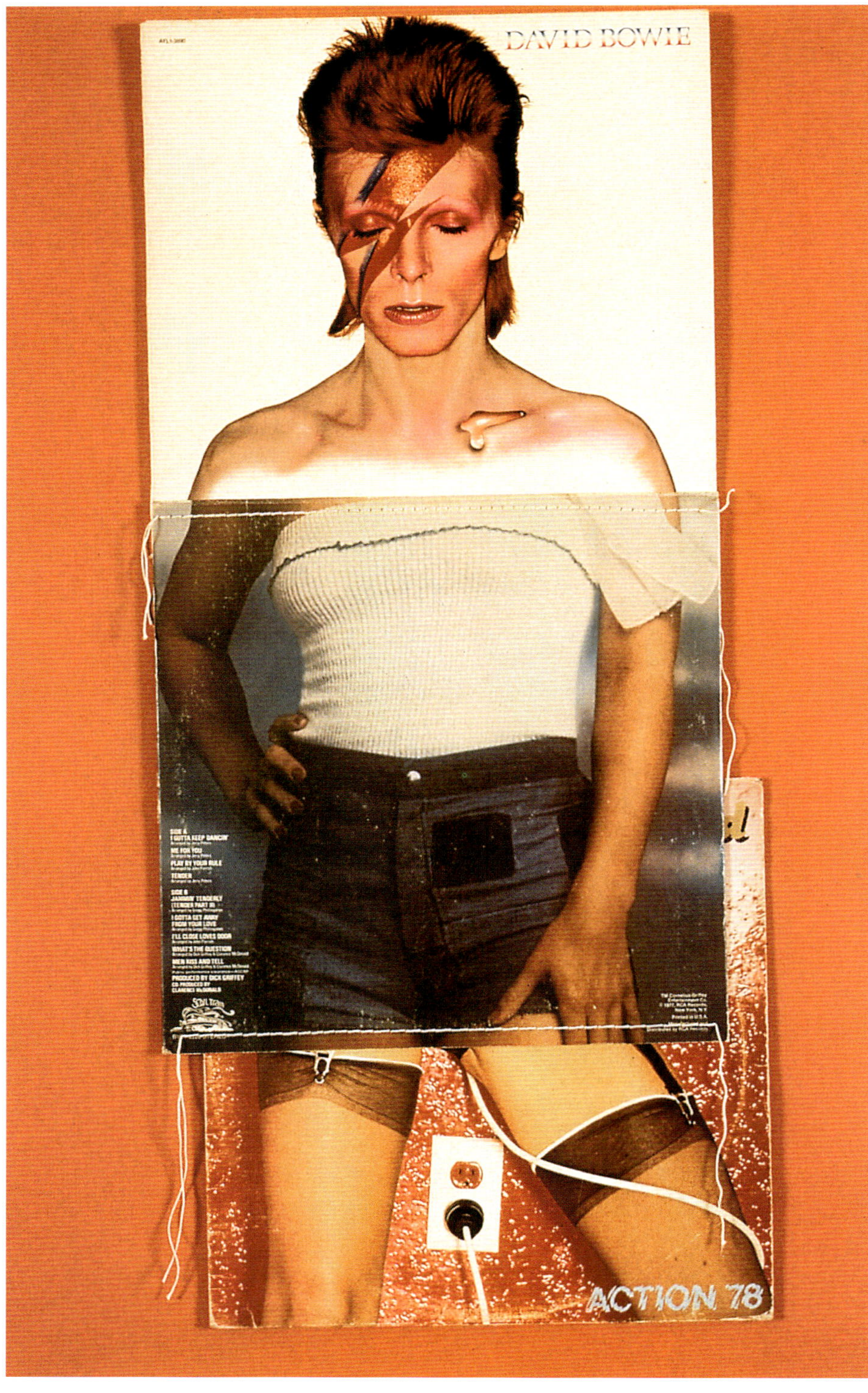

Christian Marclay
David Bowie, from the *Body Mix* series, 1991
Record covers and cotton thread, 29½ x 13¼ inches (74.9 x 33.7 cm)
Collection of the artist

The hybrid masculine and feminine creatures that Marclay fabricates in his *Body Mix* series recall the sexual and gender ambiguity often used to market pop music. *David Bowie* (1991) includes the singer's album cover depicting Aladdin Sane, one of Bowie's gender-bending personae of the early 1970s, whose name employs a Duchampian pun. Other works emphasize the conjunction of gender play and its appeal by incorporating album covers by stars who seem to shamanistically represent this realm of transformation to their fans, from Lou Reed, in his early 1970s packaging, to Michael Jackson, Prince, and Madonna.[97] The intriguing interplay of Marclay's combinations, while it creates impossible, humorous monsters, also demonstrates the meanings that already reside in the individual album covers. In other words, there can be no "normative" model without comparison to a socially constructed notion of an other, who is found wanting.

It is like that old *Twilight Zone* episode in which a post-operative woman, swathed in face bandages, expresses desperate hope that her plastic surgery has been successful. The bandages are removed, and as she and the doctor and nurses lament the horrible failure of the procedure, the audience sees, for the first time, that the "hideous" woman would be considered beautiful by contemporary human standards while the "normal" medical staff would be monstrous freaks. The moral of the story: the meaning of any characteristic is historically and socially contingent and not determined by some abstract law of "nature." Beauty does not reside in a feature, a nose, for example, but in constructed standards for noses.

The use of montage to create uncanny hybrids is facilitated by new technology in Inez van Lamsweerde's recent work. In various series produced since 1993, van Lamsweerde has elaborately posed models and recombined their parts, in the process creating photographically seamless images, perfectly real beings who are mysteriously and deceptively unreal. Van Lamsweerde plays with the codes of perfection manipulated by the fashion advertising industry, an industry that spurred the development of the paintbox computer technology she uses. Conventions of advertising that utilize bright shadowless lighting to suggest "realness" or the wholesome, and hence "truth," are employed by van Lamsweerde in the presentation of an alternate reality. The ecstatic reclining men in her four-piece series *The Forest* (1995) are puzzlingly strange. Upon close inspection it becomes apparent that some body parts are not scaled to the figure, and that a "male" subject wears nail polish and lip gloss. In fact, van Lamsweerde has mixed and matched female and male bodies. The artist, in collaboration with Vinoodh Matadin, also works in the fashion industry where she is known for editorial and advertising work that subverts expected codes. She presents men in the classically feminine pose of self-absorbed rapture—precursors range from Renaissance paintings of Danaë's Golden Shower to Hollywood publicity photographs of lounging starlets—as well as aggressively macho women whose gigantic stature dwarfs their surroundings.

Today, many artists engage the visual tropes of mass culture and the way in which gender is marketed. While their works "make strange" images whose very ubiquity enables them to be taken for granted, the artists show how peculiar (or arbitrary) the "original" images actually are. For example, watching Barney's *Cremaster 1*—which recalls a Busby Berkeley musical or the synchronized swimming in an Esther Williams movie—elicits the realization of how perverse those earlier films were and what that might suggest about the society from which they emerged. I do not, however, take perversion to be a pathology but rather a fascination with possibilities that lie outside social expectations of conformity, and a desire to disrupt rigidly defined roles for pleasurable ends. Contemporary "mainstream" interest in "gender trouble"—which is manifested in Hollywood movies, national magazines, and sitcoms to name just three popular arenas—overlaps with the widespread production of art that plays with gender.[98] This interest seems to be diversely motivated. There is a sense of curiosity, of fascination with gender as a site of potential and creativity. And then there is anxiety about the implications of the instability of sexual and gender assignments. This fear probably underlies the daily barrage of jokes ridiculing people who incorrectly read the gender and sexual identities of others,[99] accounting as well for the neat resolution of homosocial subtexts in big-budget movies into absolute heterosexual masculinity and femininity. And, finally, there is the assertion of visibility on the part of subjects who do not "fit" the socially acceptable categories delimited by dominant culture.

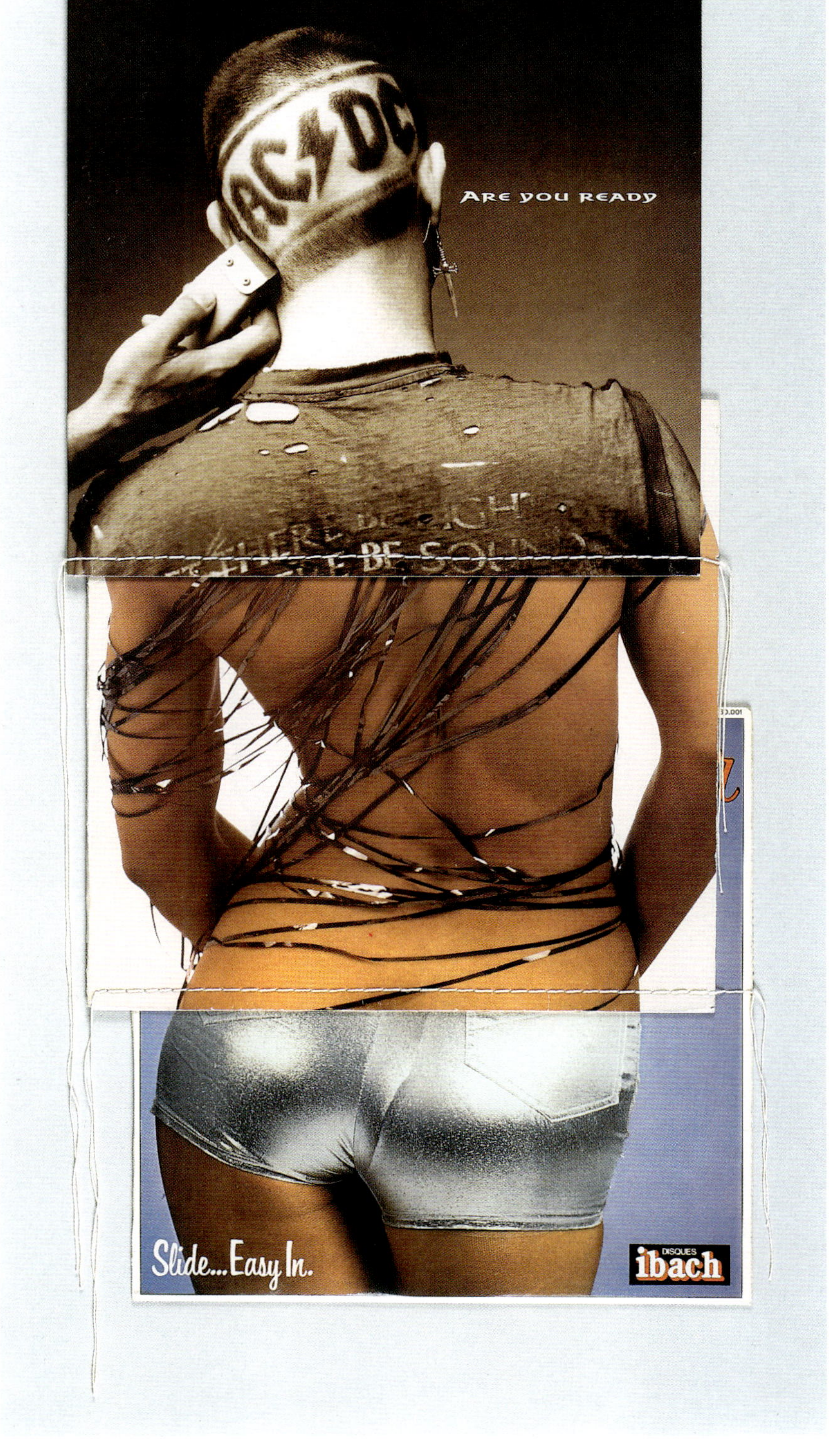

Christian Marclay
Slide Easy In, from the *Body Mix* series, 1992
Record covers and cotton thread, 27 x 13½ inches (68.6 x 34.3 cm)
Collection of the artist

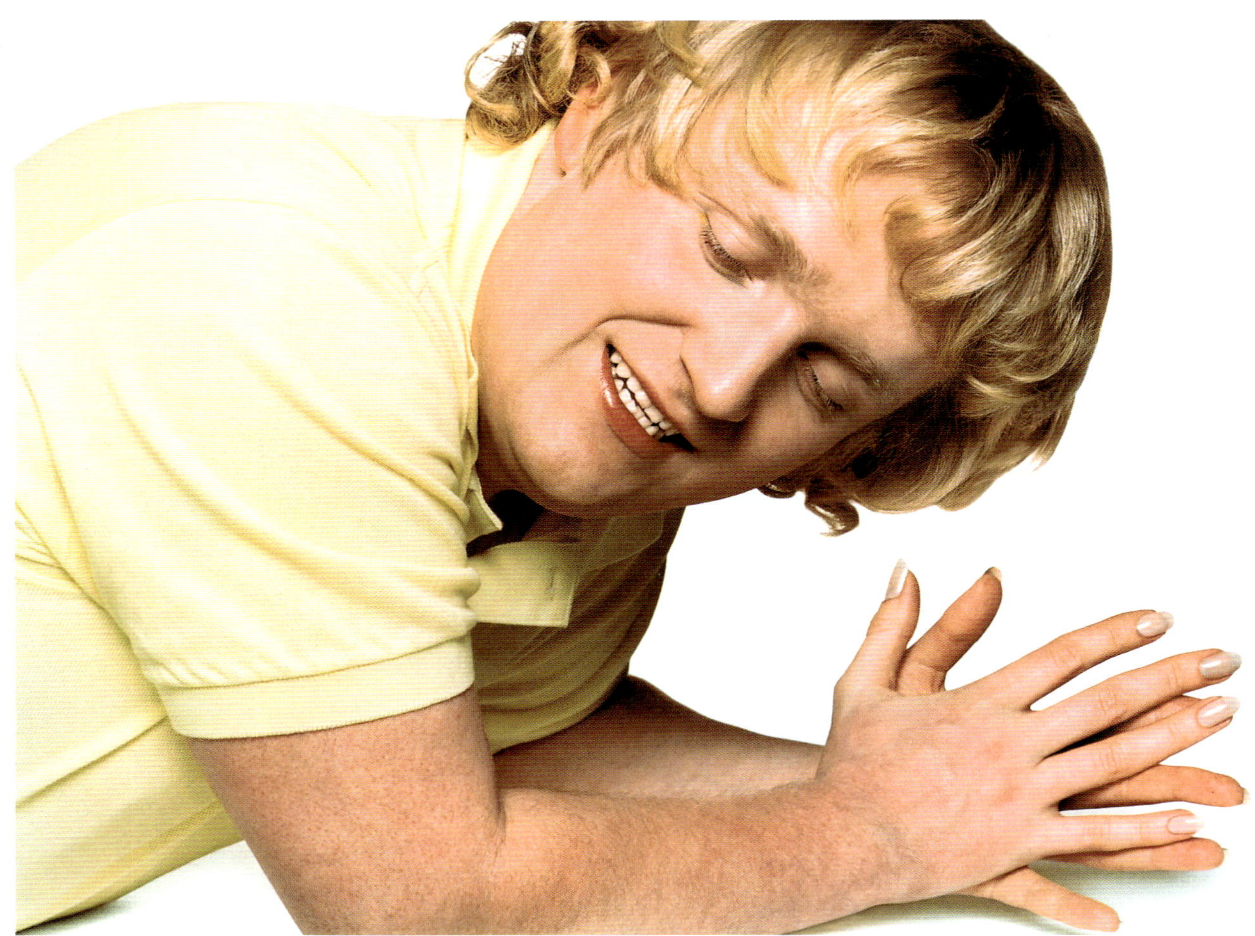

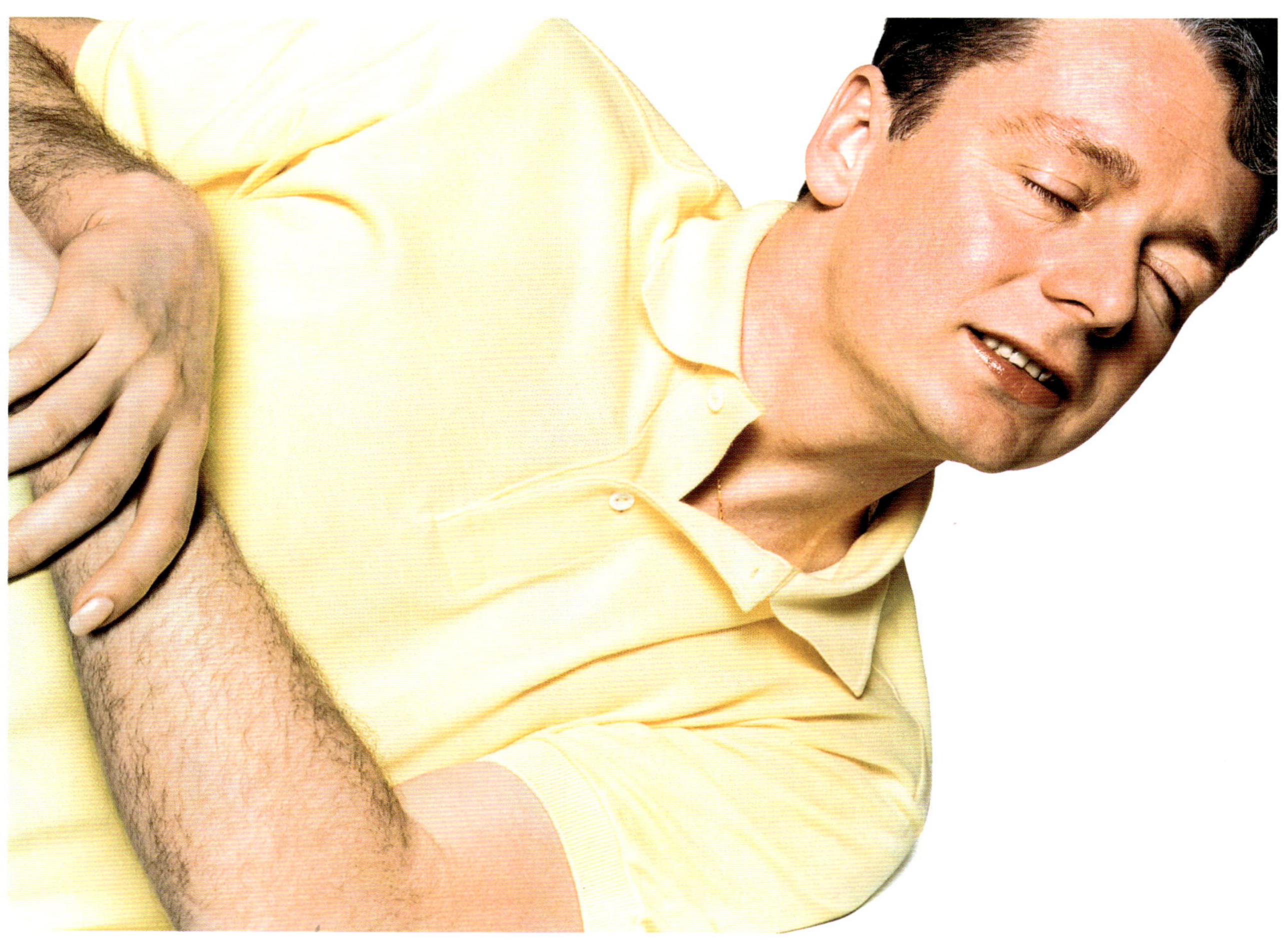

Inez van Lamsweerde
The Forest. Marcel, 1995
C-print in perspex, 53⅛ x 70⅞ inches (135 x 180 cm)
Courtesy of Matthew Marks Gallery, New York

Inez van Lamsweerde
The Forest. Rob, 1995
C-print in perspex, 53⅛ x 70⅞ inches (135 x 180 cm)
Courtesy of Matthew Marks Gallery, New York

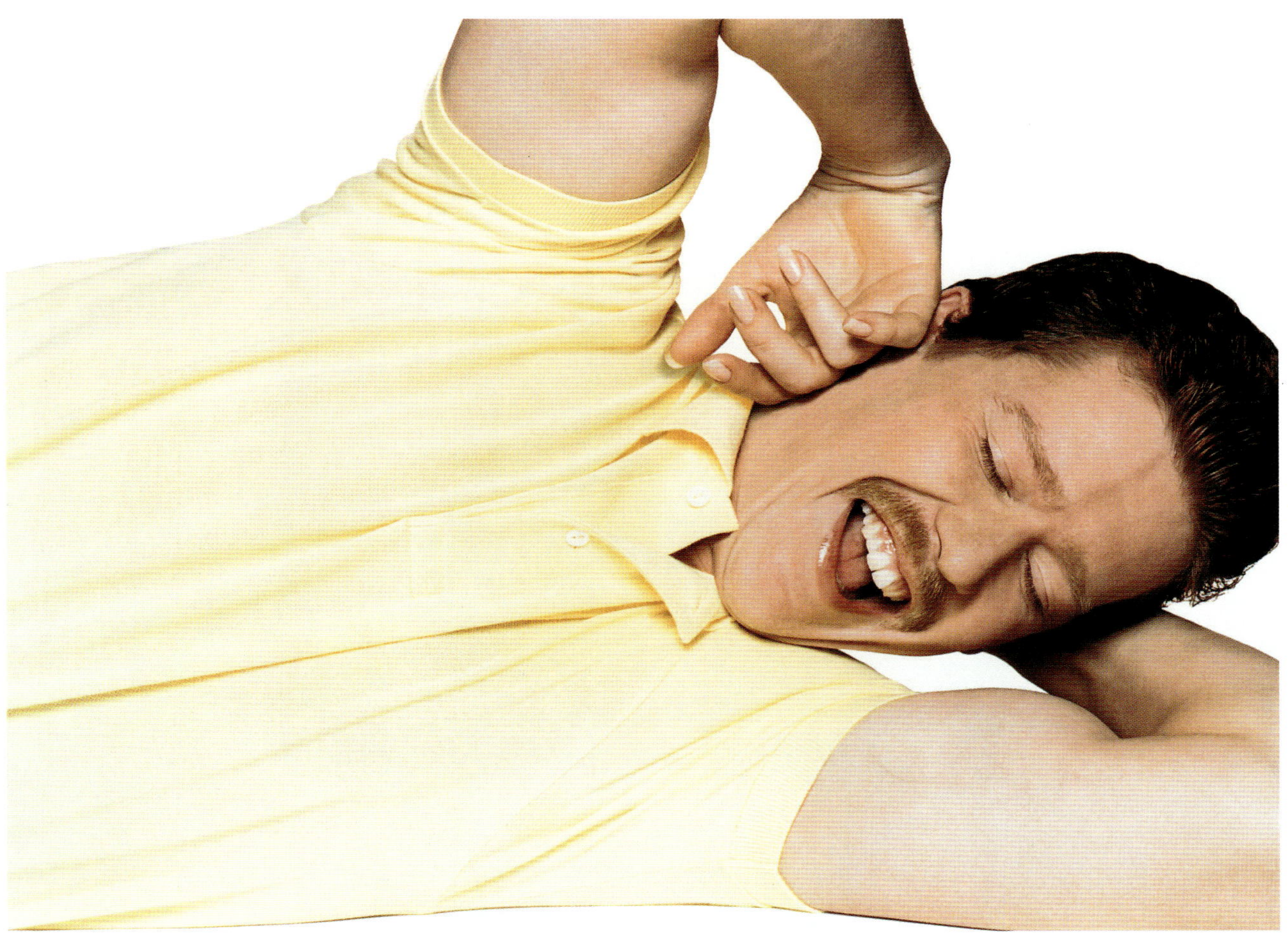

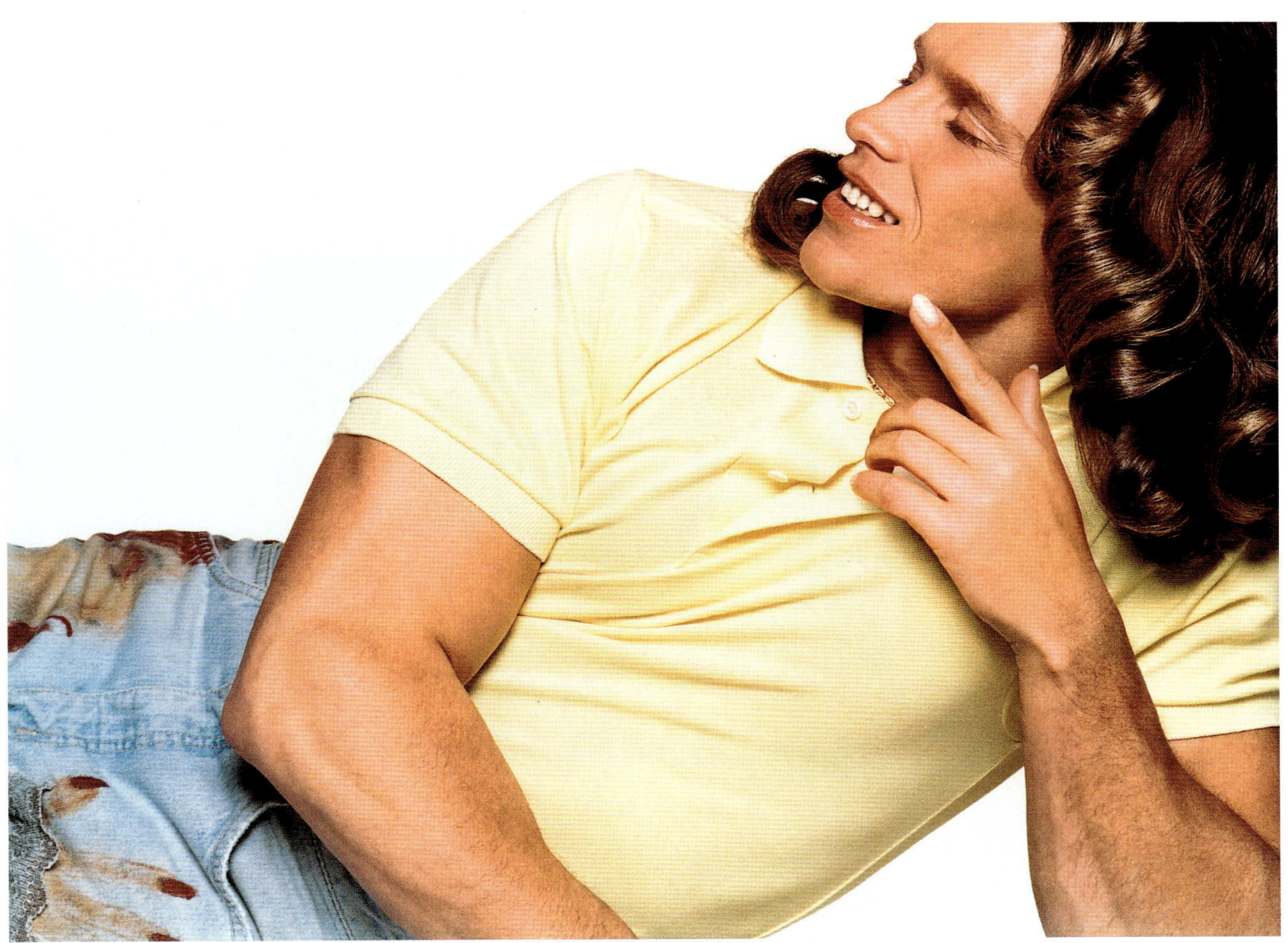

Inez van Lamsweerde
The Forest. Andy, 1995
C-print in perspex, 53 1/8 x 70 7/8 inches (135 x 180 cm)
Courtesy of Matthew Marks Gallery, New York

Inez van Lamsweerde
The Forest. Klaus, 1995
C-print in perspex, 53 1/8 x 70 7/8 inches (135 x 180 cm)
Courtesy of Matthew Marks Gallery, New York

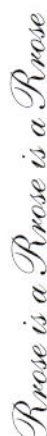

Queer Reality

In the early 1970s, Nan Goldin began taking photographs of drag queens and pre-op transsexuals who hung out at a Boston bar called The Other Side. Drag queens have been the subject of many twentieth-century photographers, including Brassaï, Lisette Model, Weegee, and Diane Arbus. Typically, this work is characterized by its voyeurism, in which the drag queen is presented as a debased theatrical personality alongside aging strippers and denizens of carnival sideshows. Pictures like these play into the realm of photography that delights in the documentation of the unusual, asserting the "realness" of the never-before-seen or the unimaginable, and allowing the viewer to stare, to ponder without shame, "Is it really a man? Does this person exist, or is it a trick?" These photographs feed the voyeur's yearning, which is not necessarily a predatory phenomenon, since the subjects in photographs like these are performers, or at least knew they were being photographed, and clearly many look quite pleased about it.[100]

Arguably some of these photographers, like painters before them, identified with the social alienation of their subjects. What distinguishes Goldin's photographs from the earlier images is her relationship with her subjects as well as their self-presentation. These are public pictures but also intimate ones, the result of time spent together. The legacy of Warhol's Factory lurks in the constant self-documentation, that repetition suggesting an attempt to fix identity, to hold up a mirror image of the self, to be who you want to be, to be "real," but, most of all, to be sure you exist. While the self-conscious ambition behind making the private public indicates the Warholian desire for celebrity, to be a star, hopefully for more than fifteen minutes, Goldin's pictures differ in the way they suggest a family album, a community, and a struggle with which the viewer is asked to empathize. This is a move away from the almost nihilistic insistence on surface, and nothing more, in Warhol's work. Goldin's documentation of her subjects' lives—including her own—is designed to humanize them, to refute the traditional view of their sexuality and gender presentation as pathological, in the spirit of the feminist adage, "The personal is the political." "Most people get scared when they can't categorize others—by race, by age, and, most of all, by gender," Goldin writes in her preface to *The Other Side*.[101] "The pictures in this book are not of people suffering gender dysphoria but rather expressing gender euphoria. This book is about new possibilities and transcendence."[102]

Goldin's photographs and those of other "Boston School" artists such as Philip-Lorca diCorcia and Shellburne Thurber are shot almost exclusively on-site, in the environments of the people documented.[103] They tend to indicate moments caught amid daily life and activities. Robert Mapplethorpe's pictures, on the other hand, while they similarly document his friends and lovers, are more frequently consciously contrived studio portraits. His images demonstrate the high value he placed on formal aesthetics. His portraits suggest the conventions of celebrity advertisements. Their flat backgrounds, tight cropping, iconic centrality, and minimal distracting detail focus all attention on the subject. Mapplethorpe's pictures announce a glistening perfection. Like Molinier's, his images of sex acts are gorgeously beautiful; they aesthetically exalt pleasure. Mapplethorpe's style of portraiture glorifies its subjects, in a way that is completely contrary to the moralizing implications of the "reality effect" that characterizes the gritty pictures of, for example, a photographer like Weegee.[104]

In 1991, Catherine Opie exhibited a series of portraits of friends in drag entitled *Being and Having*, a witty send-up of Lacan's theory of Symbolic sexual differentiation, in which the female is most commonly presumed to "be" the phallus, to represent the desire of the male, and men instead

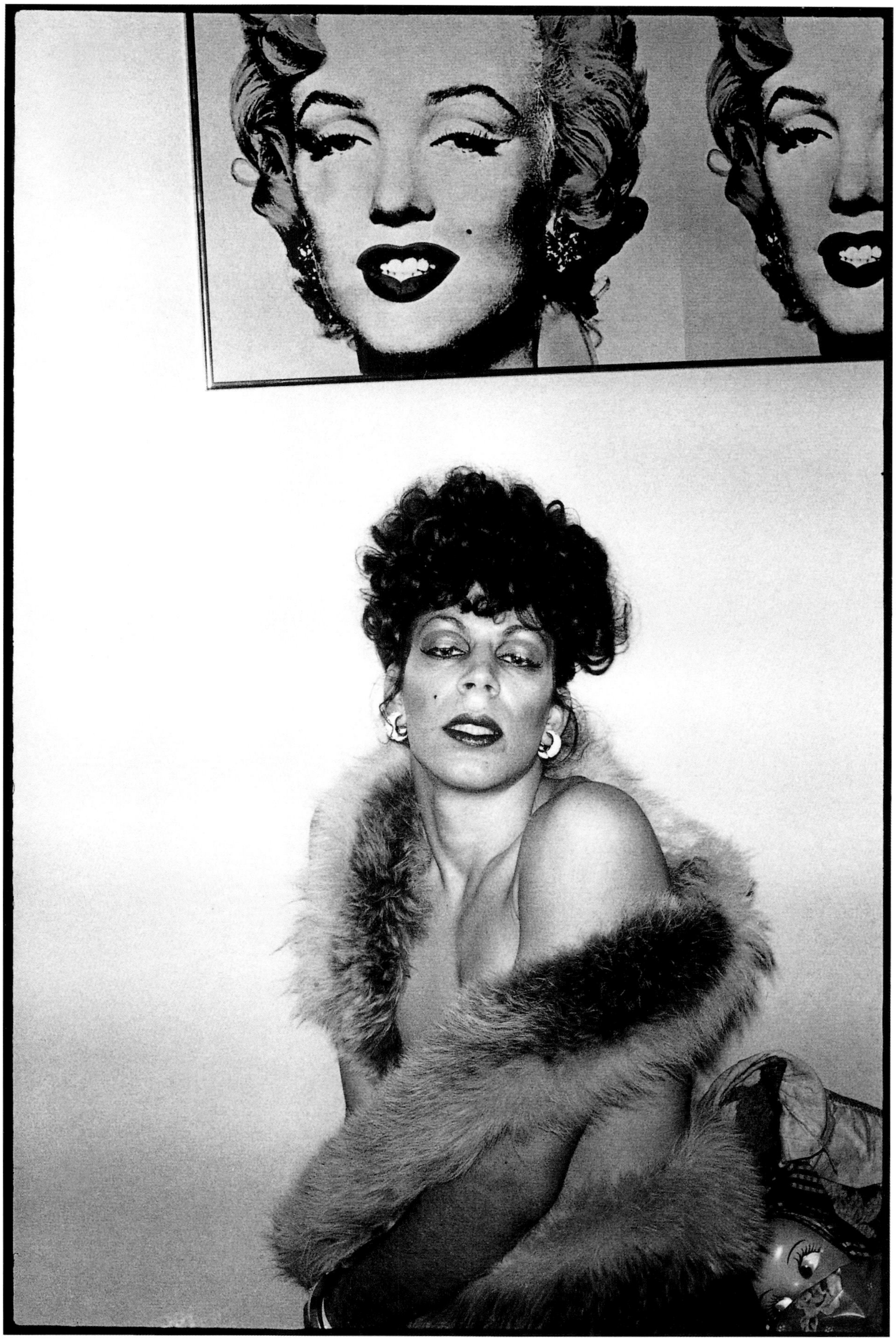

Nan Goldin
Ivy with Marilyn, Boston, 1973
Gelatin-silver print, 20 x 16 inches (50.8 x 40.6 cm)
Courtesy of the artist and Matthew Marks Gallery, New York

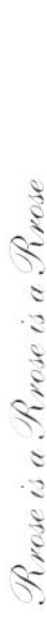

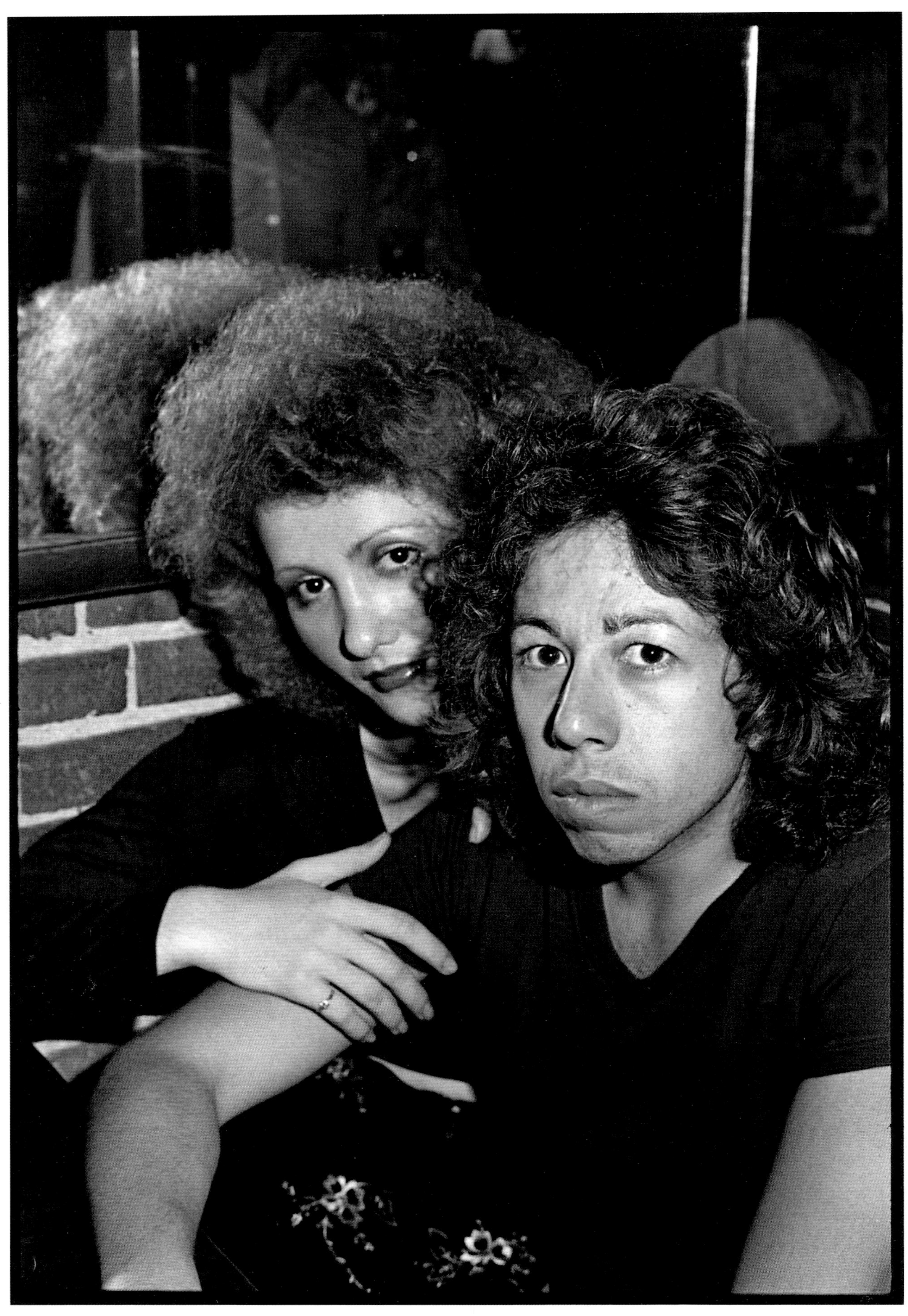

Nan Goldin
Pat and Denine in the Profile Room, Boston, 1973
Gelatin-silver print, 20 x 16 inches (50.8 x 40.6 cm)
Courtesy of the artist and Matthew Marks Gallery, New York

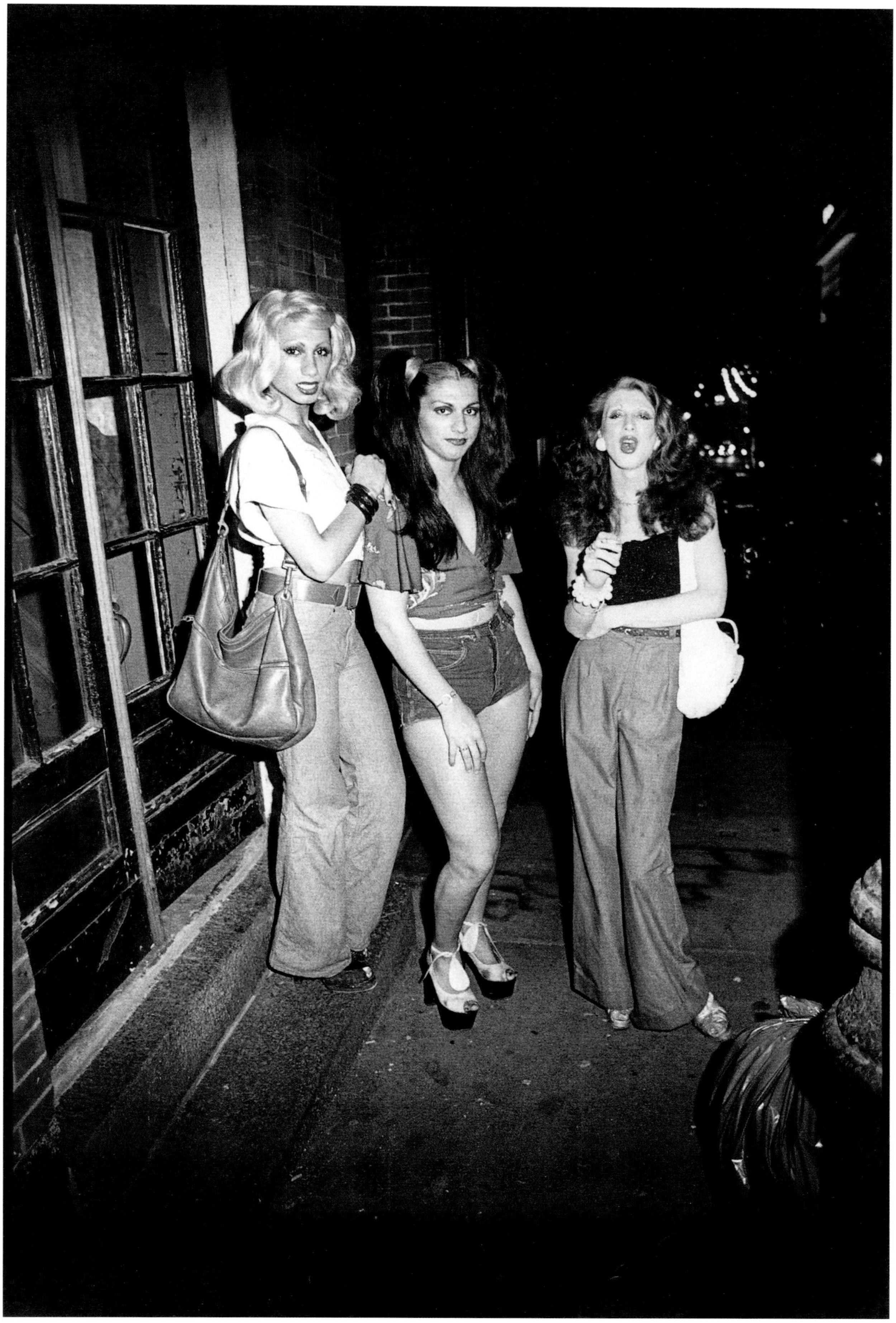

Nan Goldin
Marlene, Colette and Naomi on the street, Boston, 1973
Gelatin-silver print, 20 x 16 inches (50.8 x 40.6 cm)
Courtesy of the artist and Matthew Marks Gallery, New York

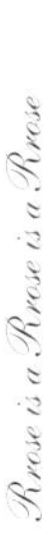

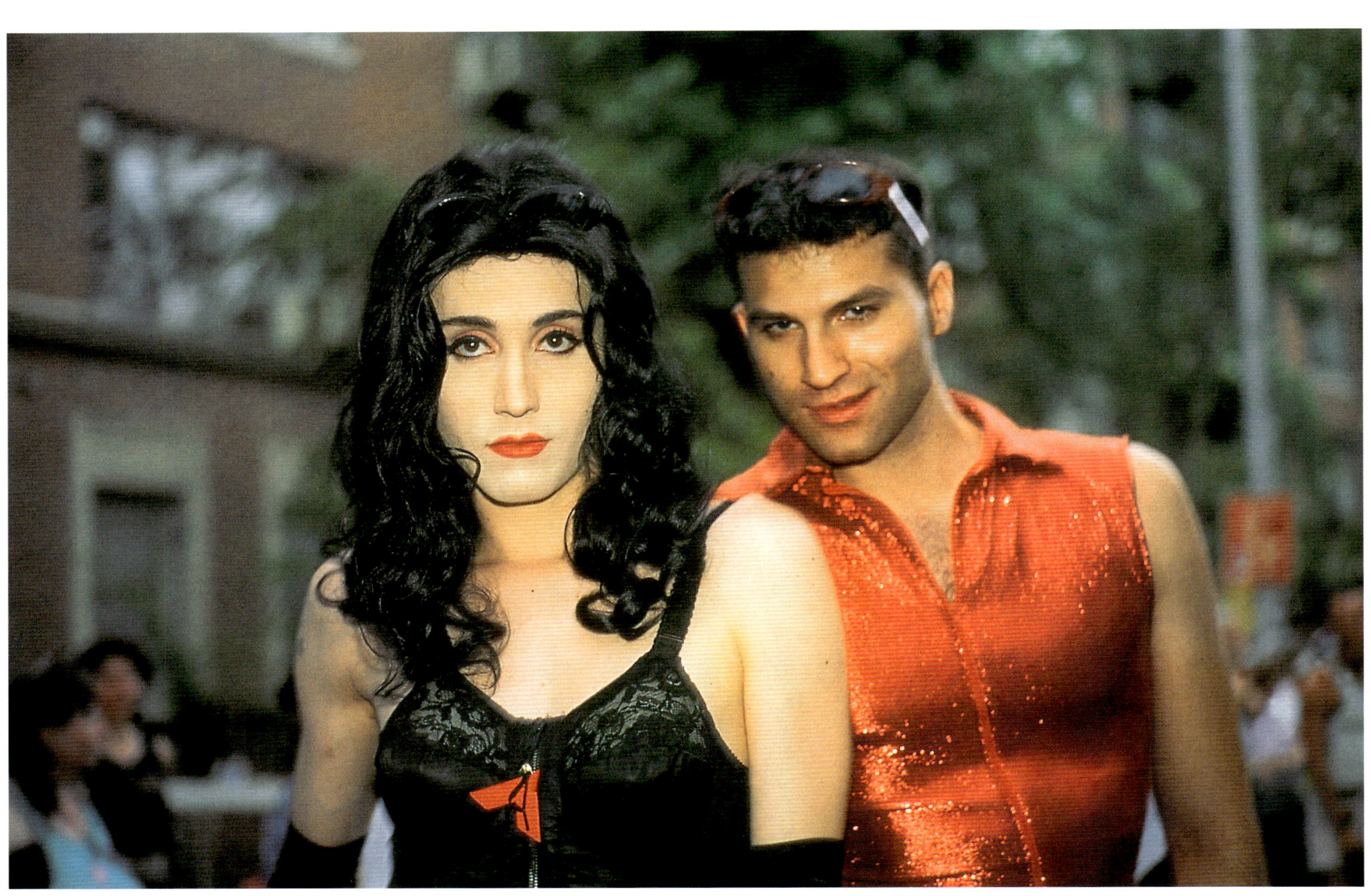

Nan Goldin
David and Mistress Formica at the Gay Pride Parade, NYC, 1991
Cibachrome print, 30 x 40 inches (76.2 x 101.6 cm)
Courtesy of the artist and Matthew Marks Gallery, New York

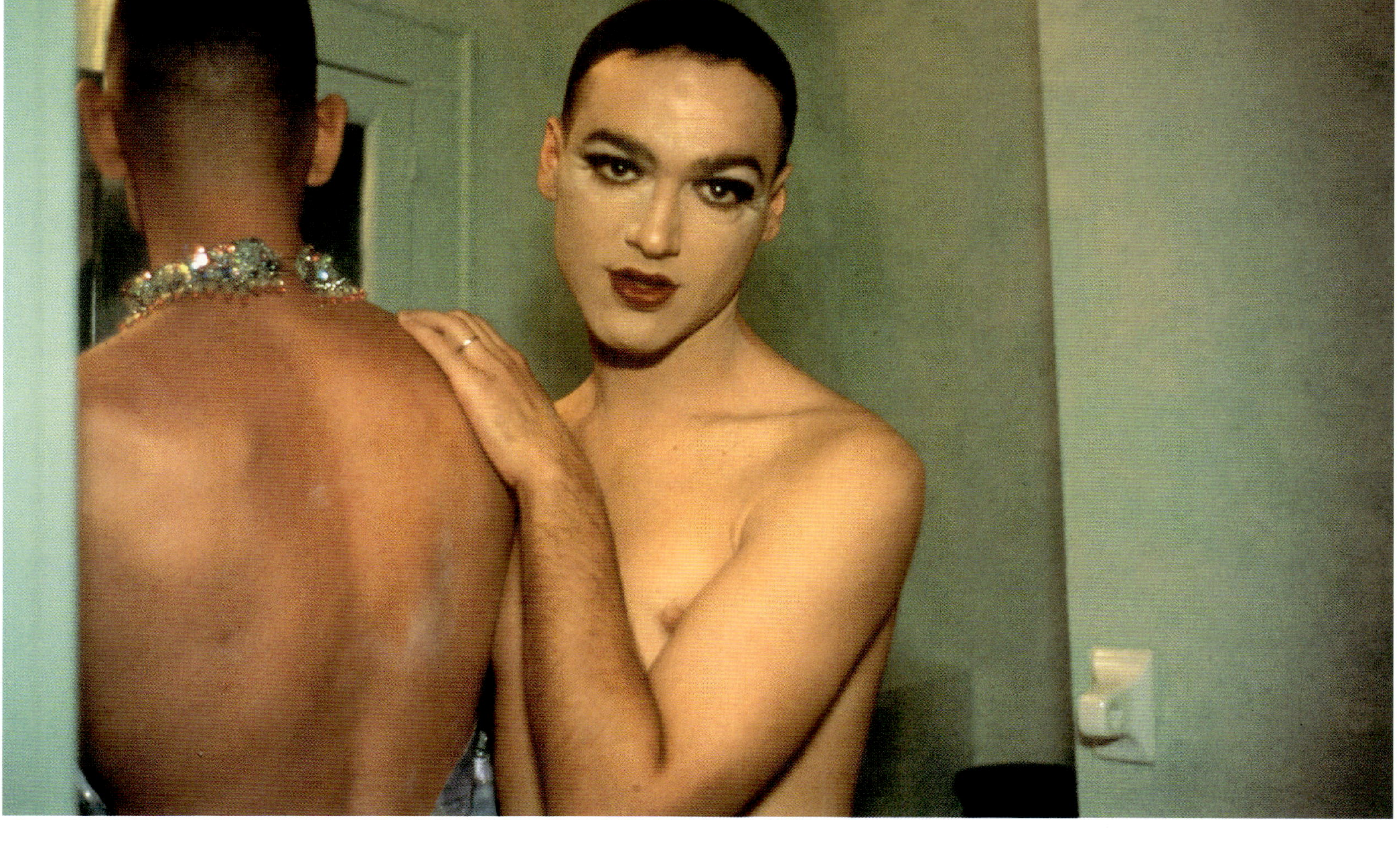

Nan Goldin
Jimmy Paulette and Tabboo! in the bathroom, NYC, 1991
Cibachrome print, 30 x 40 inches (76.2 x 101.6 cm)
Courtesy of the artist and Matthew Marks Gallery, New York

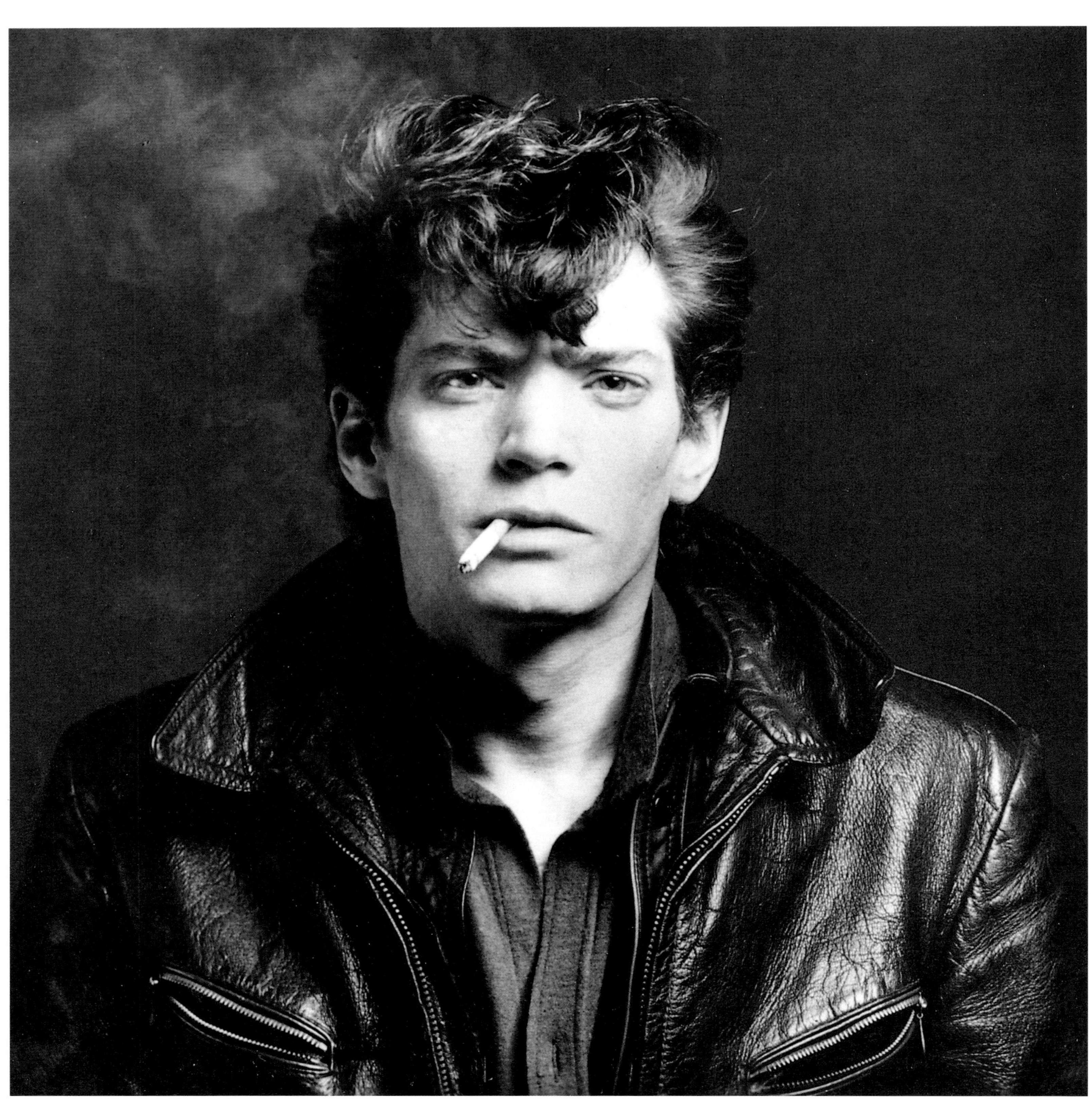

Robert Mapplethorpe
Self-Portrait, 1980
Gelatin-silver print, 20 x 16 inches (50.8 x 40.6 cm), ed. AP 3/3
Solomon R. Guggenheim Museum, New York,
Gift, The Robert Mapplethorpe Foundation

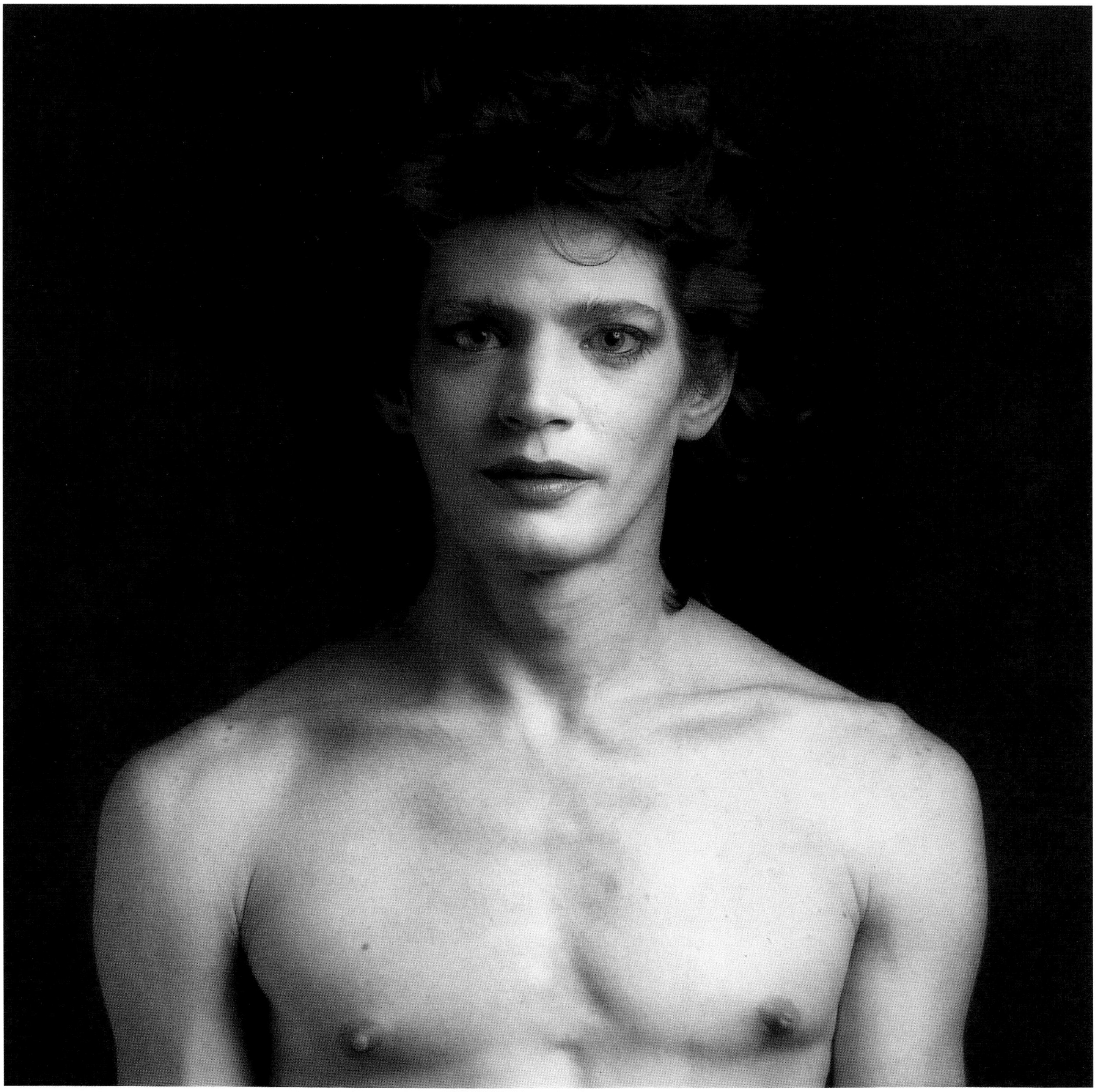

Robert Mapplethorpe
Self-Portrait, 1980
Gelatin-silver print, 20 x 16 inches (50.8 x 40.6 cm), ed. AP 2/3
Solomon R. Guggenheim Museum, New York,
Gift, The Robert Mapplethorpe Foundation

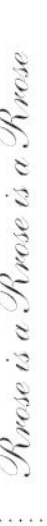

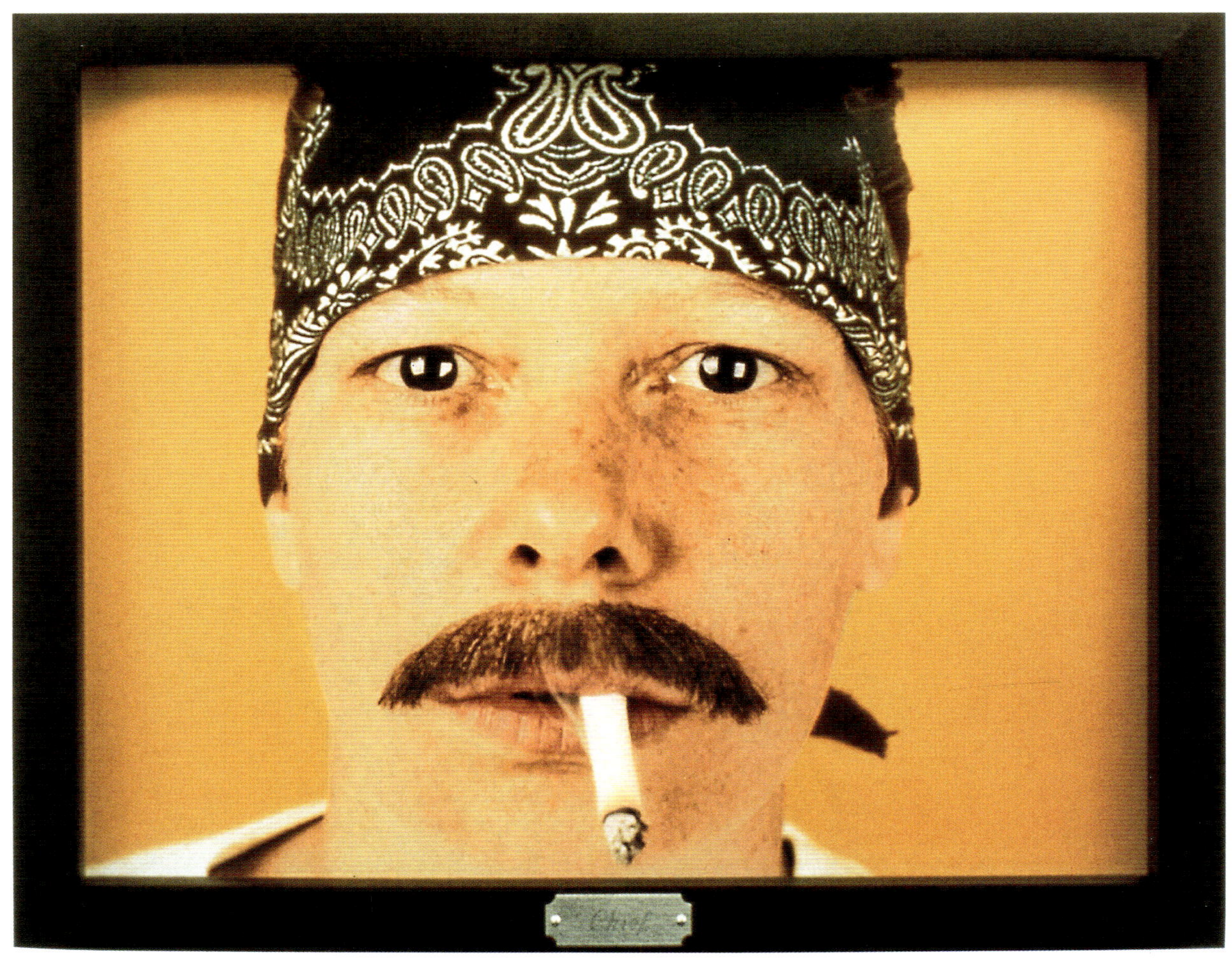

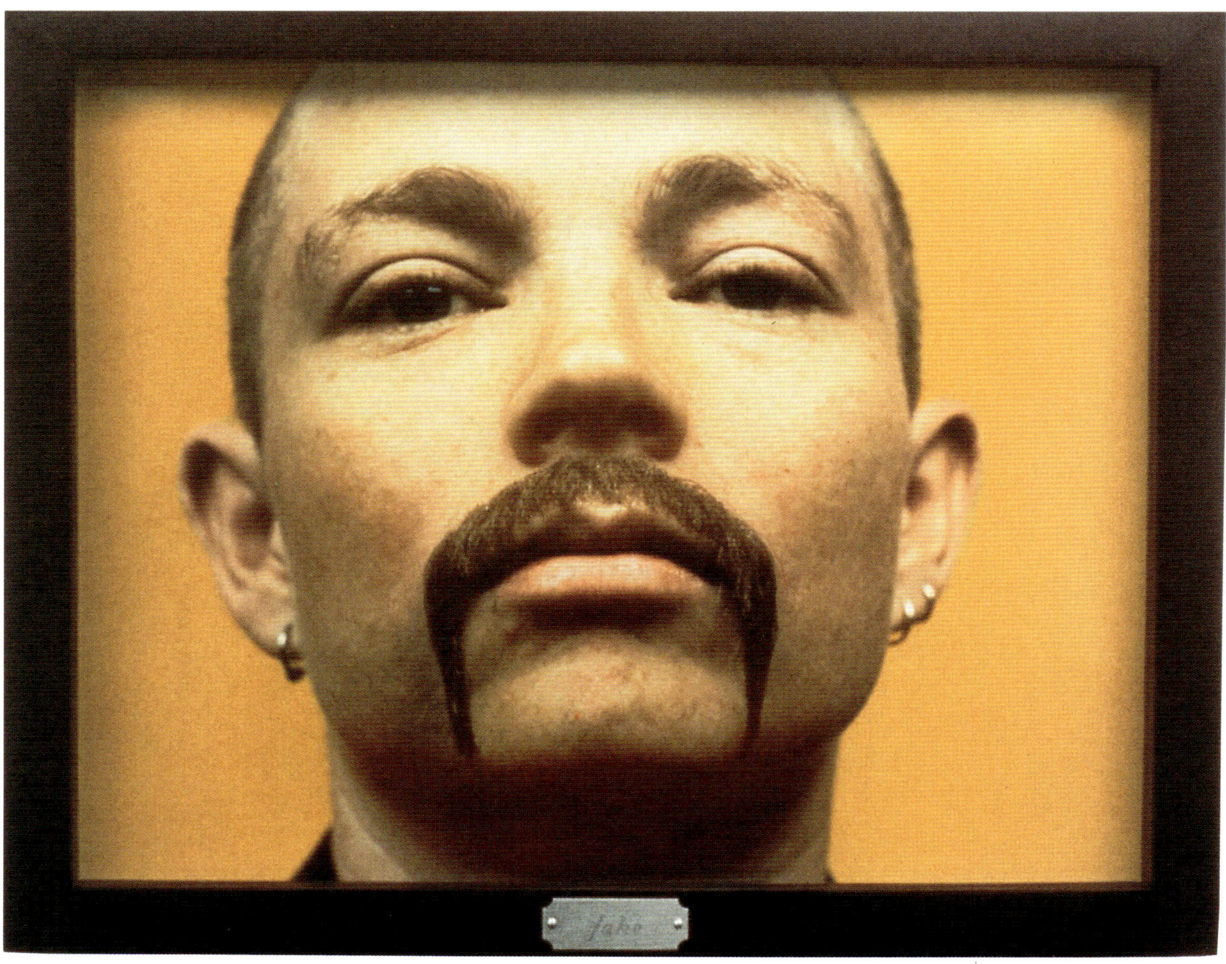

Catherine Opie
Chief, from the *Being and Having* series, 1991
Chromogenic print, framed, 17 x 22 inches (43.2 x 55.9 cm), ed. 3/8
Courtesy of Regen Projects, Los Angeles

Catherine Opie
Jake, from the *Being and Having* series, 1991
Chromogenic print, framed, 17 x 22 inches (43.2 x 55.9 cm), ed. 2/8
Collection of Fisher Stevens, Courtesy of Regen Projects, Los Angeles

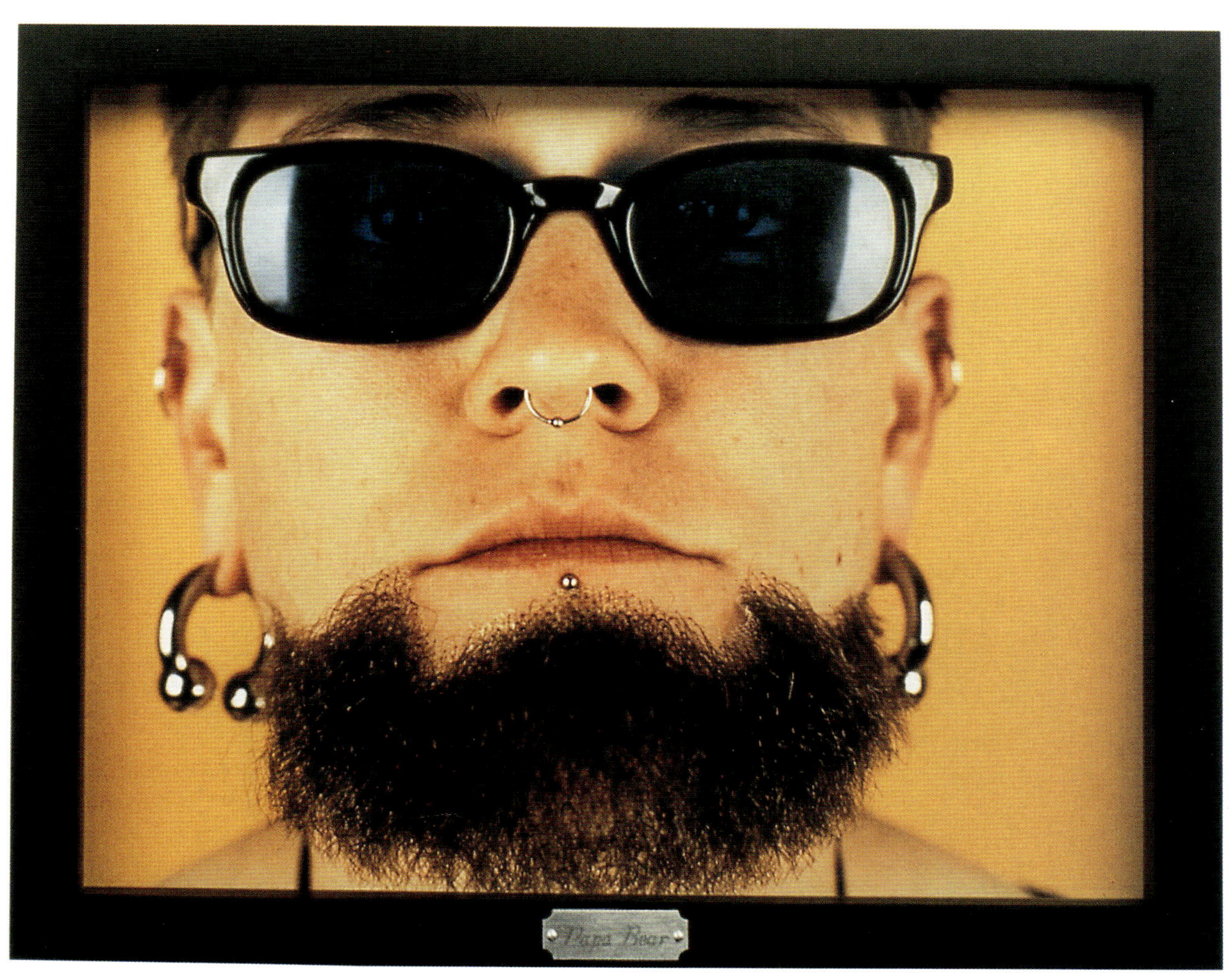

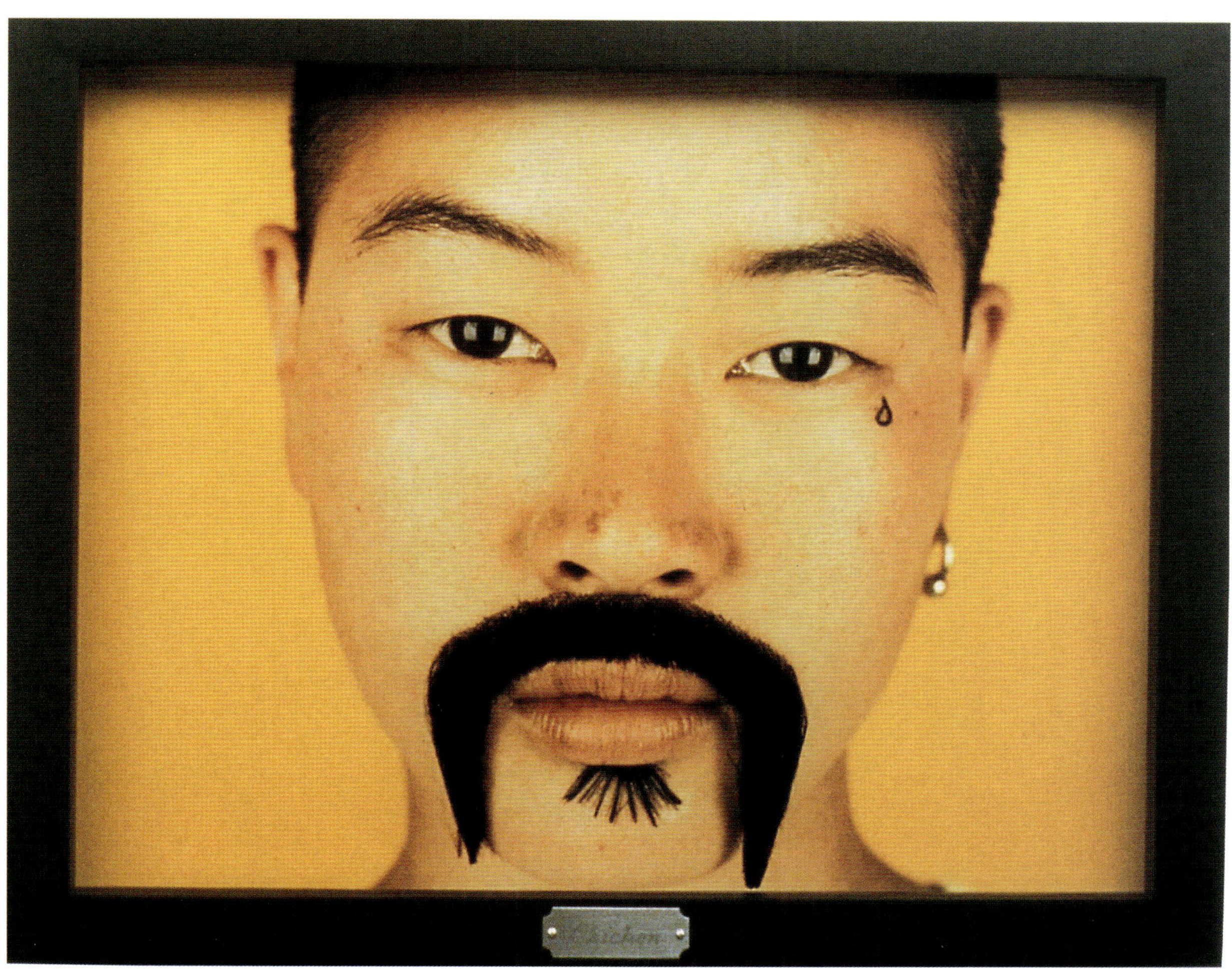

Catherine Opie
Papa Bear, from the *Being and Having* series, 1991
Chromogenic print, framed, 17 x 22 inches (43.2 x 55.9 cm), ed. 3/8
Courtesy of Regen Projects, Los Angeles

Catherine Opie
Chicken, from the *Being and Having* series, 1991
Chromogenic print, framed, 17 x 22 inches (43.2 x 55.9 cm), ed. 2/8
Collection of Patrick Breen, Courtesy of Regen Projects, Los Angeles

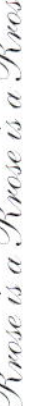

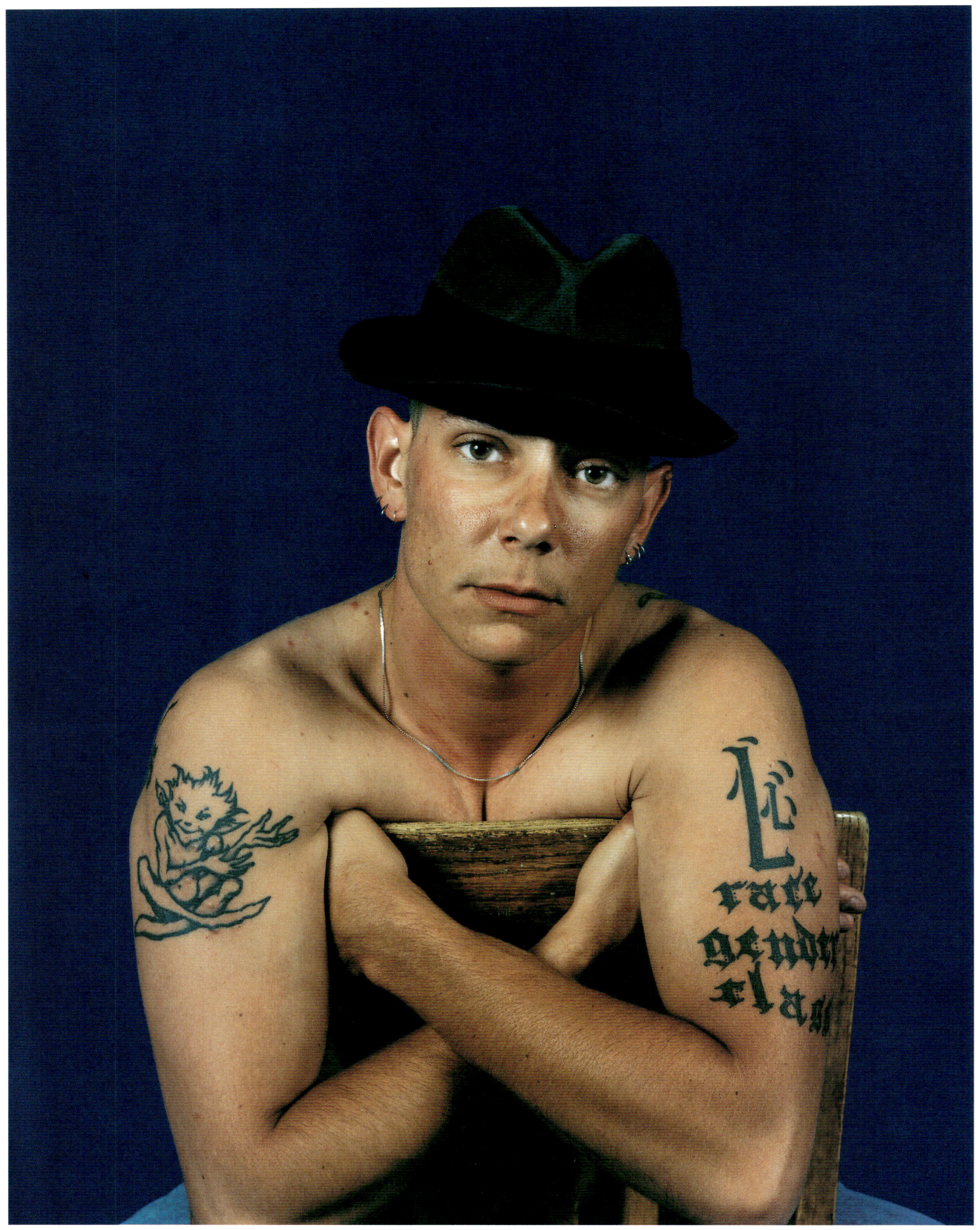

Catherine Opie
Mitch, 1994
Chromogenic print (Ektacolor), 18¼ x 14⅛ inches (46.4 x 35.9 cm)
Collection of Vivian Horan

to "have" the phallus. Sporting theatrical moustaches and goatees, the female-born subjects in these pictures pose as their masculine personae, which are named on metal plaques on the frames. In tight close-ups and glowing color, these are images of desirable subjects—but to whom? These women perform their "masculinity," they have the phallus, but they also represent the desire of an other—a female other—thus they are the phallus as well. Opie's series contests a logic that would see "being and having" as mutually exclusive, as neatly resolving into a female/male duality of heterosexual desire. Looking at the thirteen deadpan visages in this series also spurs the realization that male impersonation is a much rarer sight than the opposite. Drag queens have almost become cliché, and men cross-dressed as women commonly appear in films, television, and advertisements. Why is there such a dearth of popular images of female-to-male (FTM) gender-crossing? Is it somehow more problematic for a female-born subject to take on overt signs of masculinity than it is for a male-born subject to take on femininity? Could it be that femininity—the throwaway gender, that inscrutable extraneous otherness—is available for play, while masculinity, which symbolizes power, cannot be tampered with? In the 1970s, feminist artists investigated male impersonation as they questioned gender roles.[105] Opie's work of the 1990s examines gender in the context of sexuality and, specifically, lesbian desire. In her portraits of friends in the lesbian, transgender, and S/M communities, quietly dignified individuals pose in clear, warm light against simple, richly hued backdrops. Their pierced, tattooed, and shaved bodies announce their aesthetic and sexual pleasures, incidentally (perhaps) reinforcing a conception of the body as a site of personal intervention, where culture subsumes nature, biology is not destiny but, instead, a raw material with which we do what we will. Opie's carefully crafted images assert the viability of the subjects they represent, portraying individuals who have been all but invisible to "mainstream" society.

In 1987 and 1988, Lyle Ashton Harris created a series of self-portraits, entitled *The Americas*, in which he appears partially nude, wearing a blond wig, a boater hat, and white makeup. His whiteface persona inverts the blackface performance of minstrel shows, highlighting the way in which constructs of gender and sexuality are bound up with race. In nineteenth-century minstrelsy, white men caricatured African American subjects by wearing exaggerated black burnt-cork makeup.[106] They often also cross-dressed as women, thus impersonating both gender and race. Through these impersonations and the skits they performed, minstrel players frequently ridiculed both abolition and women's rights, suggesting the anxiety caused by the social dislocations of nineteenth-century American society. Thus, as cultural critic Kobena Mercer suggests, Harris's gender-bending whiteface persona "performs a version of black masculinity that signifies upon the grotesque pathos of the minstrel mask . . . and does so in such a way as to simultaneously evoke the masquerade of femininity as spectacle."[107] His white makeup is a mask, as are the mascara, lipstick, and blond wig he wears, and yet they are not. They signify identity and identification, which are variable and dependent upon who is looking and constructing a subject through that look.

In collaborative works dating from 1994, Harris reimagines a vision of community and nation that contests the mythology of the bourgeois nuclear family: European-descended, middle-class, with 2.4 children. Against a tricolor background that recalls the nationalist flag of Marcus Garvey's Universal Negro Improvement Association (UNIA), various couples iconically exemplify transformative visions of contemporary kinship. For example, in *Sisterhood*, Harris and Iké Udé present a dandy's archetype of feminine masculinity, appearing before a carved gilt throne fit for royalty. Taken together, these images disrupt traditional conceptions of race and gender, kinship and sexuality.

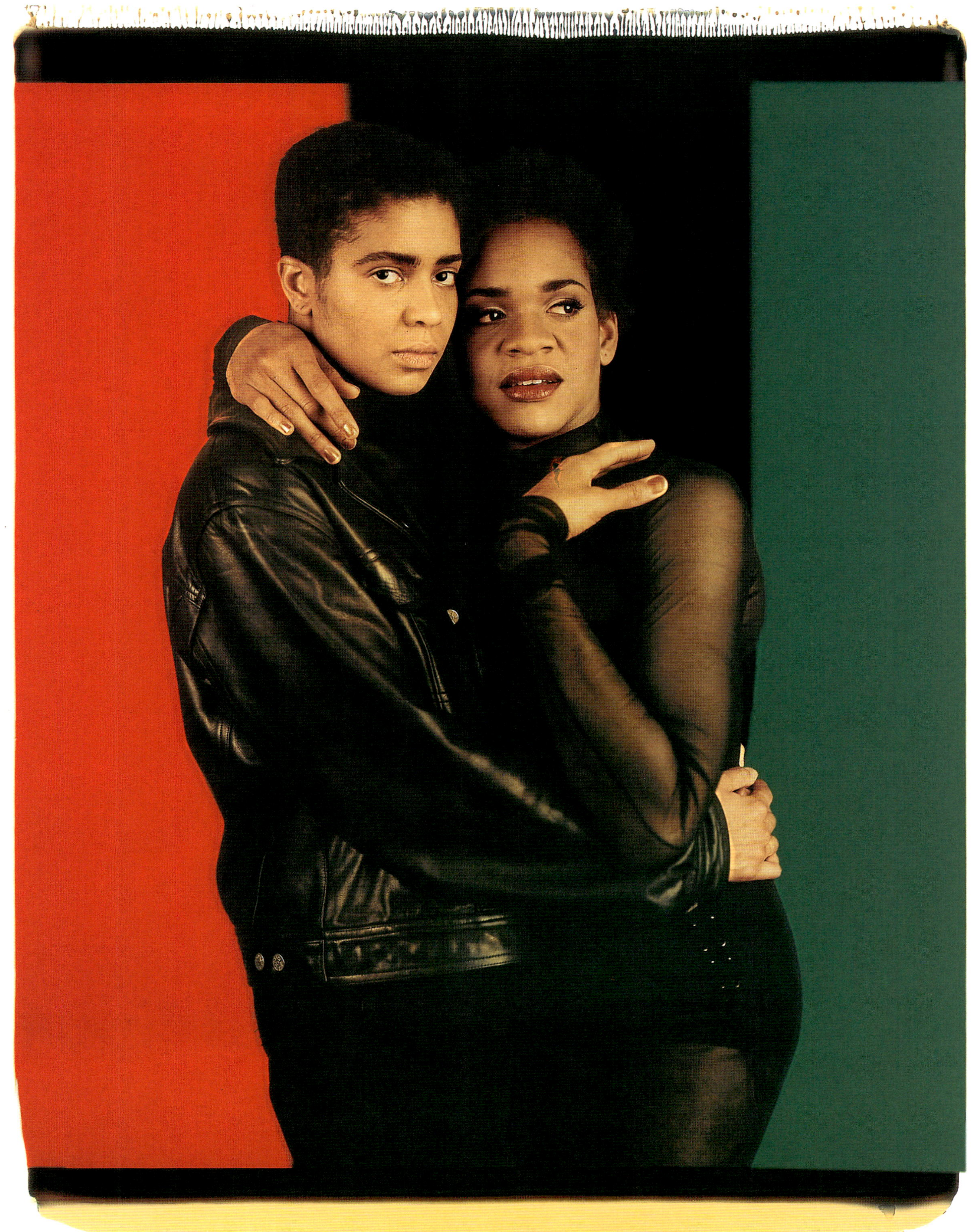

Lyle Ashton Harris and Alexandra Epps
Alex and Lyle, 1994
Polaroid photograph, 24 x 20 inches (61 x 50.8 cm)
Collection of Alexandra Epps, Courtesy of Jack Tilton Gallery, New York, and Margo Leavin Gallery, West Hollywood

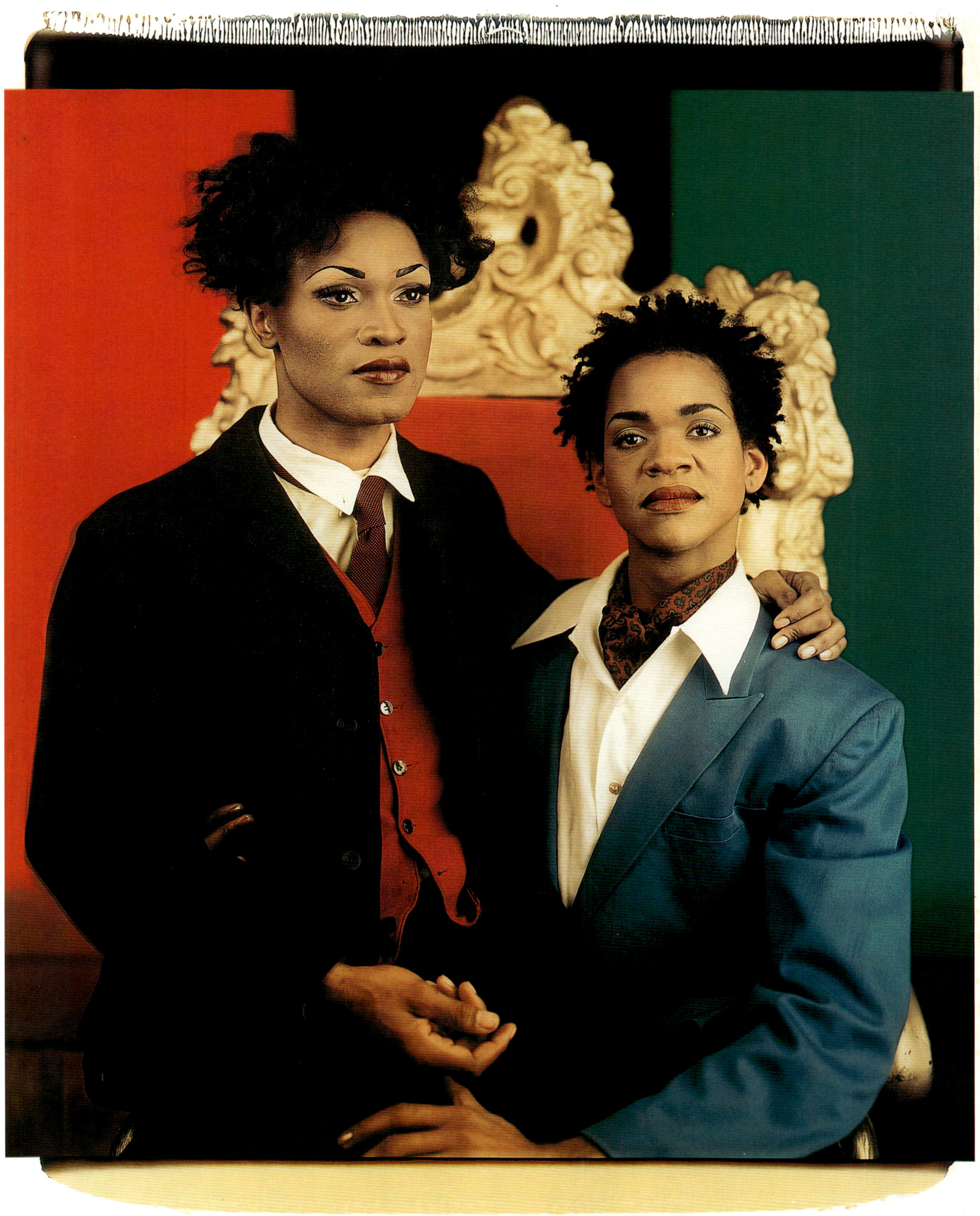

Lyle Ashton Harris and Iké Udé
Sisterhood, 1994
Polaroid photograph, 24 x 20 inches (61 x 50.8 cm)
Collection of Robert W. Conn, California

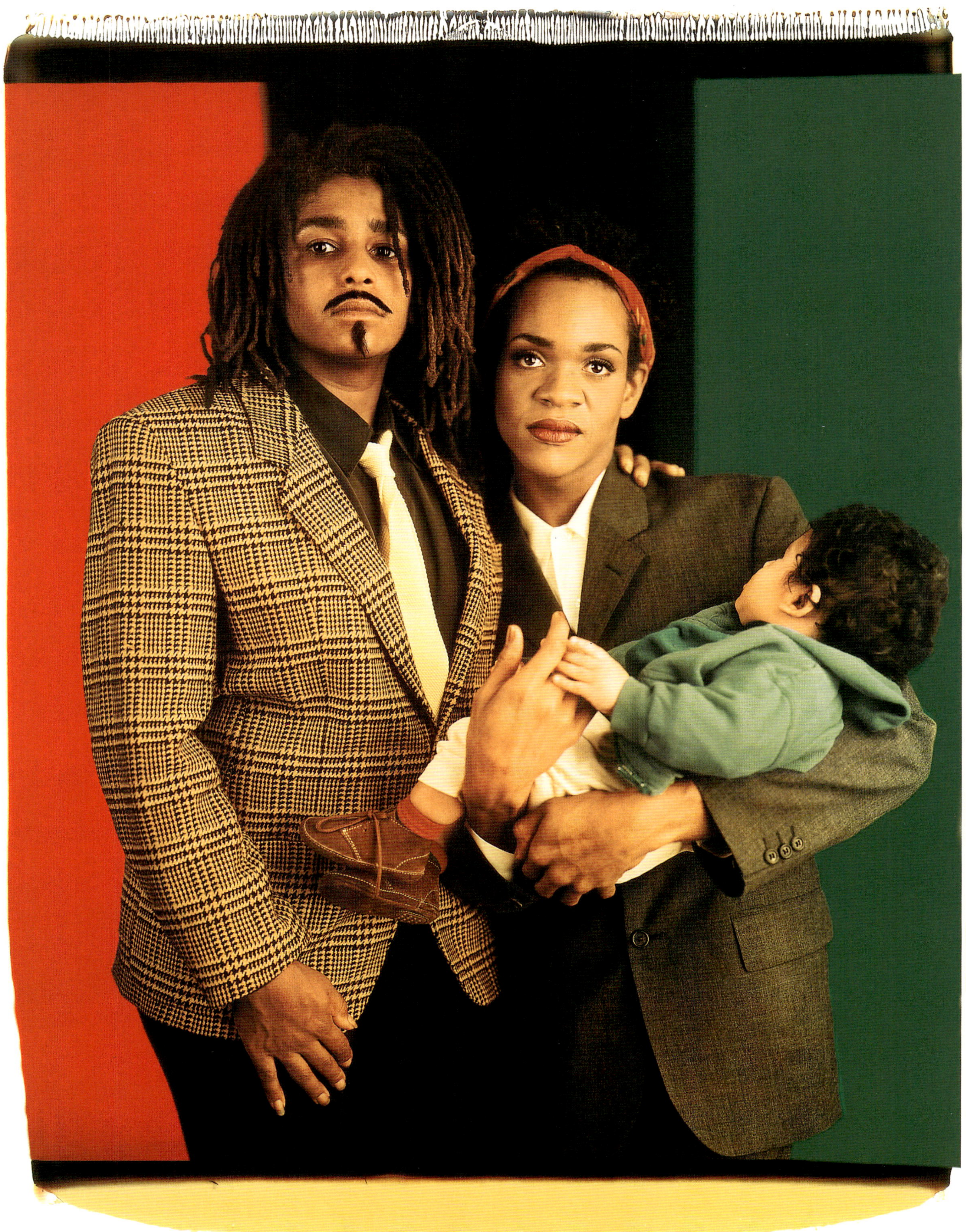

Lyle Ashton Harris and Renée Cox
The Child, 1994
Polaroid photograph, 24 x 20 inches (61 x 50.8 cm)
Courtesy of Jack Tilton Gallery, New York, and Margo Leavin Gallery, West Hollywood

Referring to a related collaboration with his brother, filmmaker Thomas Allen Harris, entitled *Brotherhood, Crossroads and Etcetera*, Harris states:

> *This collaboration with Thomas—using masquerade as our mode of transgression—is a way of expanding the notion of who can lay claim to the liberatory potential envisioned in the UNIA flag. We are challenging a construction of African nationalism that positions queers and feminists outside of the black family, the Million Man march and other black institutions.*[108]

Janine Antoni's 1993 triptych *Mom and Dad* is another type of family portrait. Three photographs document her parents, who appear both as themselves and made up as each other. Antoni, who applied the makeup, confounds the gender distinctions of her parents, taking on the question of gender roles at the site at which they are formed. It is with our parents that our first experiences of sexuality and gender are located. We see the reflection of ourselves through the eyes of our parents, and construct ourselves in and against those images. Antoni's piece indicates that these conceptions do not divide neatly into some "natural" dichotomy of paternal/maternal, male/female, masculine/feminine, or hetero/homo.

Whether in the mirror or in the image of the other, we each seek the reflection of our ideal self, the self we wish to be. In this way, we attempt to reinhabit the space in which we felt ourselves to "be," to "have," reflected in the gaze emanating from our parents' eyes. Ultimately, what we see in Antoni's triptych are the artist's parents, who, apparently, willingly sat for their daughter and who stare lovingly at her, at us.

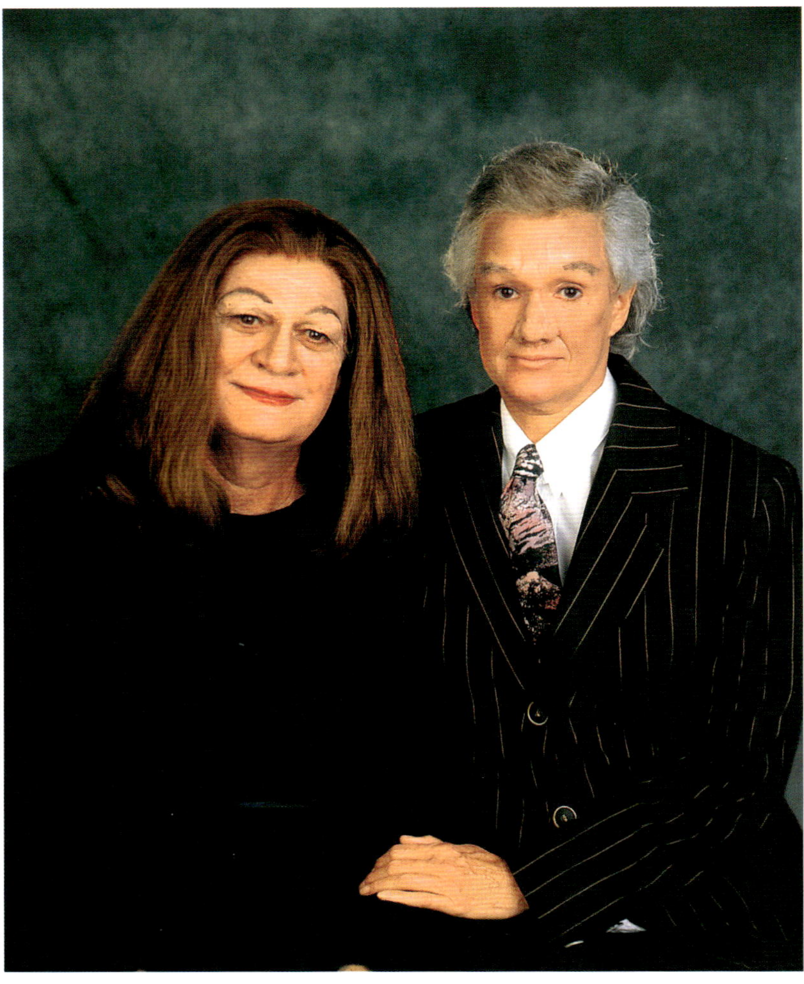

Conclusion

This exhibition and essay are informed by theories of gender and sexuality that, though developed throughout the course of the twentieth century, have been refined in the last decade or so. Our contemporary notions of gender and sexuality are, in fact, of quite recent origin: in some languages no distinction between the words presently exists, and the connotations of these and related terms are constantly shifting. So it is that the pretext of *Rrose is a Rrose is a Rrose*—"gender performance in photography"—is a contemporary lens through which the objects described herein have been viewed. As its author, I myself have engaged in my own utopian project of unification under the sign of difference.

Yet my position is not self-invented but, rather, reflects interests that are extensively represented in various media and venues. Why are these questions about identity so motivating now? We live in an age in which individual identity is widely conceived as an artificial performance, a conglomeration of signs through which we are (not necessarily willingly) fixed. Yet, at the same time, we claim these socially imposed identities in order to unite under a banner—the flag of "identity politics"—shared by others like us. We are caught in a new version of the old mind-body dilemma. We

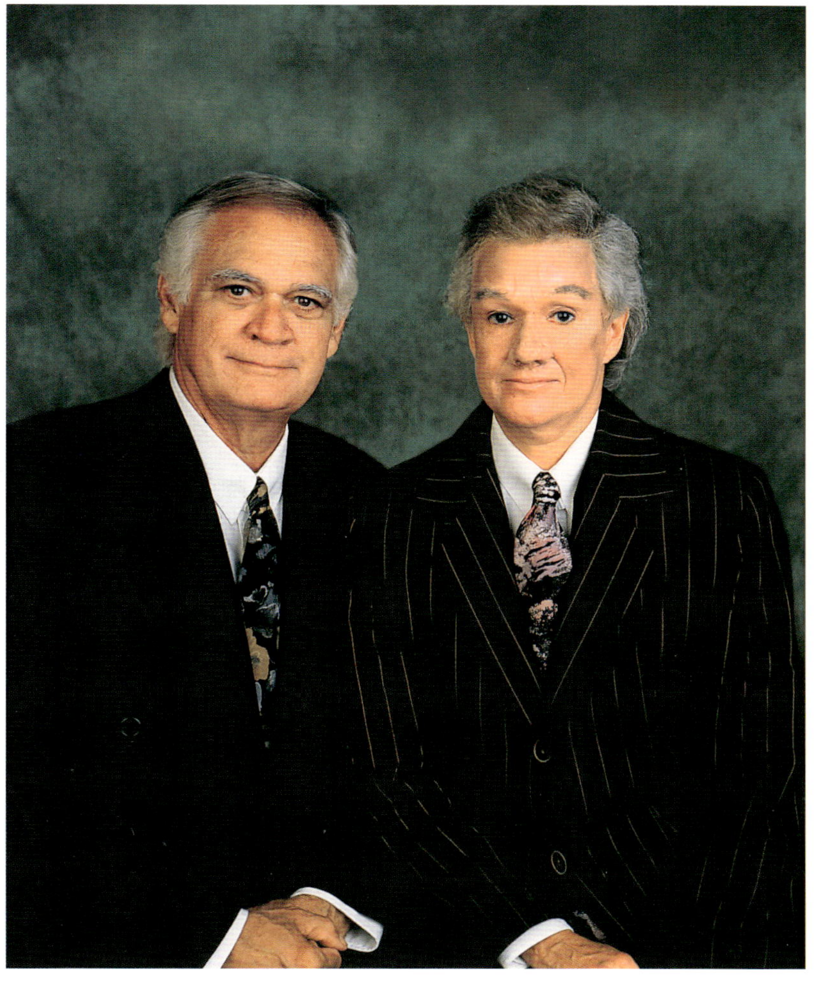

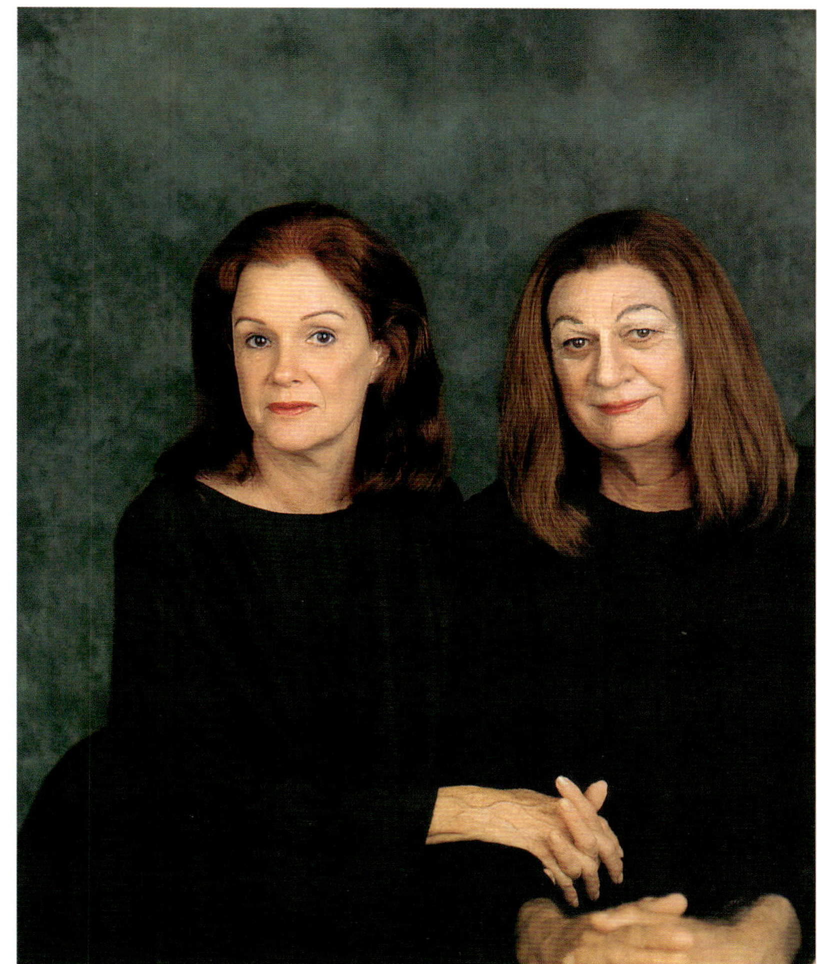

Janine Antoni
Mom and Dad, 1993
Mother, father, makeup;
each photograph 24 x 20 inches
(61 x 50.8 cm)
Solomon R. Guggenheim
Museum, New York, Gift,
International Director's Council

want our body to "be" and yet we assert the priority of the spirit (or language) over it; we are, and are not, our bodies.

The idea that we are fixed in language—that we perform according to the dictates of a system in which we are circumscribed—has a certain logical elegance, a compelling sense of "truth." However, there also lurks a secret dread of being caught like a fly in amber, without free will, without the ability to determine oneself. Perhaps it is to combat this dread that we insist on declaring ourselves, on underlining our subjectivity by defining our identity. In an era in which we have lost all belief in absolutes—in what is true, what is real, and the notion of objectivity itself—it is to the self that we turn to locate a corner of the universe that we can attempt to describe, not to determine it, not to extrapolate our experience to others, but simply to identify ourself as one individual and, thereby, insist upon its existence. Today, it seems that the shifting sand that is the self is the only thing we can be sure of.

The "author" has been resurrected after a much-touted death; however, this is an author without authority. In various fields of literary and visual production, authors look to themselves, voice themselves in the first person and represent their bodies, yet do not insist that these representations are necessarily identical to themselves. One is, and is not, one's self-presentation. The notion of authorial objectivity is not believed possible and is not a goal. Academic historians include first-person accounts in order to assert rather than obscure the motivation of their readings; documentary filmmakers show the trappings of the camera and the ways their presence changes the environment they record; and the line between fiction and memoir is willfully breached.[109] Critics charge the authors of these trends with "pathetic" narcissism, and yearn for a return to the godlike authority of the omniscient narrator and the "objective" reportorial voice, thereby wishing to ally the author's voice with the voice of the master. Instead, "narcissistic" authors, who use the first person and do not pretend to speak for everyone, to speak as if there is only one way to be, show, through their specific voices, that there should be no master.

Other critics (of the left rather than the right) argue that what is truly pathetic is holding to any notion of individuality and free will in the face of technological rationalization and the gigantic corporate entities, from governments to multinationals, that rule us. To focus on the body in this context is to indulge an escapist impulse—to create a mysterious and holy biological site—in a desperate attempt to counter the impersonality of modernity and the vision of self as an inconsequential cog in a great mechanical combine. In this critique, the presentation of an unusual, exotic, special, strange, or different self is perceived as misguided and as impossible a counter to capitalistic homogenization as the smashing of machines by the Luddites. There is something valid to this (cynical) reading. Certainly, the argument can be made that a love/hate relationship underlies the production of much art concerned with mass media and its mechanisms. The Dada-inspired works of artists such as Duchamp and Höch, as well as of Pop artists like Warhol, may, on some level, be understood as attempts to manage anxiety about the very mediums from which their imagery has been culled.[110]

However, underlying this critique is another master logic, which presumes that there is one correct form of critical discourse, and works that do not privilege it are retrograde. Henri Matisse aspired to create for the "businessman or writer" an art that would be "something like a good armchair in which to rest from physical fatigue."[111] This comment, which is cited with approval by some and censured by others, may be said to encapsulate the function of the art in this exhibition. Yet the crucial question is now not what does this art do, but who is it doing it for—who is in that armchair? Which brings us back full circle to Barthes's assertion of identity as taste, to the realization that "*my body is not the same as yours.*"[112] Nor is my pleasure.

Notes

1. Gertrude Stein, "Sacred Emily," in *Geography and Plays* (1922; New York: Something Else Press, 1968), p. 187.
2. Stein, "Next: Life and Letters of Marcel Duchamp," in ibid., pp. 405–06.
3. "Rrose Sélavy *née en 1920 à N.Y./nom juif? changement de/ sexe—Rose etant le nom le/ plus 'laid' pour mon gout personnel/et Sélavy le jeu de mots facile/C'est la vie —.*" Reproduced in Paul Matisse, ed., *Marcel Duchamp: Notes* (Boston: G. K. Hall, 1985), no. 286.
4. Marcel Duchamp, quoted in Katherine Kuh, "Marcel Duchamp" (interview), in *The Artist's Voice: Talks with Seventeen Artists* (New York: Harper & Row, 1962), p. 83; cited in Amelia Jones, *Postmodernism and the En-Gendering of Marcel Duchamp* (New York: Cambridge University Press, 1994), p. 154.
5. Hannah Höch created a photomontage entitled *Da Dandy* (1919).
6. Rose (with one "r") Sélavy first emerged as the copyright holder of *Fresh Widow* (1920), which Duchamp attributed to her. In 1921, the signature of Rrose Sélavy appeared on Francis Picabia's *L'Oeil Cacodylate* (1921). Parts of the present discussion, as well as small portions of sections 3 and 4 below, appear in modified form in Jennifer Blessing, "'Eros, c'est la vie': Fetishism as Cultural Discourse (Surrealism, Fashion, and Photography)," in *Art/Fashion*, exh. cat. (Milan: Skira, forthcoming 1997).
7. Rrose is also not Mary Garden, the opera singer who figured on the bottle's original label. See Nancy Ring, "New York Dada and the Crisis of Masculinity: Man Ray, Francis Picabia, and Marcel Duchamp in the United States, 1913–1921," Ph.D. diss., Northwestern University, Evanston, Ill., 1991, p. 239.
8. *New York Dada* (1921), quoted in Dawn Ades, "Duchamp's Masquerades," in Graham Clarke, ed., *The Portrait in Photography*, (London: Reaktion Books, 1992), p. 108.
9. In another context, Kenneth E. Silver notes that in *11 rue Larrey*, Duchamp illustrates that "'a door need not be either opened or closed.' It may be both." See Silver, "Modes of Disclosure: The Construction of Gay Identity and the Rise of Pop Art," in Donna De Salvo and Paul Schimmel, eds., *Hand-Painted Pop: American Art in Transition 1955–62*, exh. cat. (Los Angeles: Museum of Contemporary Art; and New York: Rizzoli, 1992), p. 183.
10. Note Duchamp's comments, quoted in Arturo Schwarz, *The Complete Works of Marcel Duchamp* (New York: Abrams, 1969), p. 477.
11. For a summary of causal explanations for the "Great Masculine Renunciation," including those of the writer who coined the phrase, J. C. Flügel, see Kaja Silverman, "Fragments of a Fashionable Discourse," in Tania Modleski, ed., *Studies in Entertainment* (Bloomington: Indiana University Press, 1986), pp. 138–52.
12. These circumstances included theatrical comedy and gay bars or clubs. An approximately contemporaneous anecdote drawn from a 1937 book demonstrates the strong disincentive for men to cross-dress:
An officer of the Federal Reserve Bank, asked what was adequate compensation for wearing his wife's hat to the office some morning, first answered, "Fifty thousand dollars." Then, after thinking it over for a moment, he said, "It would have to be as much as he could expect to earn the rest of his life, since afterward he could never expect to hold a position of financial responsibility again; and in the end he concluded that no price would be enough for the loss of prestige entailed." (Cited in Fred Davis, *Fashion, Culture, and Identity* [Chicago: University of Chicago Press, 1992], p. 41.)
13. I am indebted to Maud Lavin's ground-breaking study, *Cut with the Kitchen Knife: The Weimar Photomontages of Hannah Höch* (New Haven: Yale University Press, 1993); especially, see chapters 4 and 6.
14. For a germane analysis of Mikhail Bakhtin's arguments regarding the liberating space of the carnival, see Mary Russo, "Female Grotesques: Carnival and Theory," in Teresa de Lauretis, ed., *Feminist Studies/Critical Studies* (Bloomington: Indiana University Press, 1986), pp. 213–29.
15. Letter reproduced in Jones, *Postmodernism and the En-Gendering of Marcel Duchamp*, p. 121; discussed on p. 100.
16. For a useful review of Man Ray and Duchamp's collaborations, see *Conspiratorial Laughter/A Friendship: Man Ray and Duchamp*, exh. cat., with essay by Mason Klein (New York: Zabriskie Gallery, 1995).
17. See Cocteau's July 1926 *Nouvelle Revue française* article on Barbette, reprinted in *Le N[umér]o Barbette: Man Ray, photographies inédités; [texte par] Jean Cocteau; [avec un essai par] Francis Steegmuller* (Paris: Jacques Damase, 1980). Cocteau states that Man Ray made photos of Barbette's "metamorphosis" for him (pp. 9–10). This book also includes Francis Steegmuller's "A Visit to Barbette," previously published as appendix XIV in Steegmuller's *Cocteau: A Biography* (Boston: Little, Brown, 1970), pp. 523–29; this is a revised version of Steegmuller's article "Onward and Upward with the Arts: An Angel, A Flower, A Bird," *The New Yorker*, September 27, 1969, pp. 130–43.
18. *"Dans cette lumière magique du théâtre, dans cette boîte à malice où le vrai n'a plus cours, où le naturel n'a plus aucune valeur."* (*Le N[umér]o Barbette*, p. 23.)
19. Joan Riviere, "Womanliness as a Masquerade," *International Journal of Psychoanalysis* 10 (1929), pp. 303–13; reprinted in Victor Burgin, James Donald, and Cora Kaplan, eds., *Formations of Fantasy* (New York: Routledge, 1986), pp. 35–44.
20. See Jann Matlock, "Masquerading Women, Pathologized Men: Cross-Dressing, Fetishism, and the Theory of Perversion, 1882–1935," in Emily Apter and William Pietz, eds., *Fetishism as Cultural Discourse* (Ithaca: Cornell University Press, 1993), pp. 31–61.
21. See, for example, Michel Foucault, *The History of Sexuality*, vol. 1, trans. Robert Hurley (New York: Pantheon Books, 1978).
22. Brassaï, *Paris de nuit*, text by Paul Morand (Paris: Arts et Métiers, 1933); published in English as *Paris by Night*, trans. Gilbert Stuart (New York: Pantheon Books, 1987).
23. Brassaï, *The Secret Paris of the '30s*, trans. Richard Miller (New York: Random House/ Pantheon Books, 1976).
24. O. P. Gilbert, *Men in Women's Guise*, trans. Robert B. Douglas (London: Bodley Head, 1926); and Gilbert, *Women in Men's Guise*, trans. J. Lewis May (London: Bodley Head, 1932); cited in Jones, *Postmodernism and the En-Gendering of Marcel Duchamp*, p. 169. For an example of Gilbert's influence, see C. J. S. Thompson, *The Mysteries of Sex: Women Who Posed as Men and Men Who Impersonated Women* (1938; New York: Causeway Books, 1974); Thompson thanks Gilbert and M. M. Dowie in his preface.
25. Virginia Woolf, *Orlando: A Biography* (1928; New York: Harcourt Brace Jovanovich, 1956), p. 189.
26. J. C. Flügel, *The Psychology of Clothes* (1930; London: Hogarth Press and Institute of Psycho-Analysis, 1950).
27. Lavin, *Cut with the Kitchen Knife*, p. 128.
28. Claude Cahun's biographer François Leperlier notes Cahun's other pseudonyms such as Claude Courlis and Daniel Douglas. See Leperlier, "Claude Cahun," in *Mise en Scène: Claude Cahun, Tacita Dean, Virginia Nimarkoh*, exh. cat. (London: Institute of Contemporary Arts, 1994), p. 16.
29. Cahun, *Les Paris sont ouverts* (Paris: José Corti, 1934); Havelock Ellis, *L'Hygiène sociale*, vol. 1: *La Femme dans la société*, trans. Lucie [sic] Schwob (Paris: Mercure de France, 1929); and Cahun, *Aveux non avenus* (Paris: Editions du Carrefour, 1930). Marcel Schwob was a Symbolist critic and friend of Oscar Wilde. Sarah Bernhardt used Schwob's translation for her *Hamlet, en travesti*, which she performed in 1900.
30. Cahun also illustrated a nominal children's book with photographs of whimsical tableaux of objects: Lise Deharme, *Le Coeur de Pic* (Paris: José Corti, 1937).
31. *"Sous ce masque un autre masque. Je n'en finerai pas de soulever tous ces visages."*
32. For interesting insights on Cecil Beaton's use of mirrors and reflection, see David Alan

Mellor, "Beaton's Beauties," in Philippe Garner and Mellor, *Cecil Beaton: Photographs 1920–1970* (New York: Stewart, Tabori & Chang, 1995), pp. 8–58.

33. Though most often associated with theatrical roles, Beaton also preserved numerous cross-dressed self-portraits in his archives, which are now located at Sotheby's London.

34. Beaton, quoted in Terence Pepper, "Reviewing the Reviews of 'Cecil Beaton—The Authorised Biography' by Hugo Vickers," *Creative Camera* 252 (December 1985), pp. 11–12.

35. "Instead of the production of goods, Beaton, like Oscar Wilde and an earlier generation of dandies, put forward performance and the exhibition of the charismatic self." (Mellor, "Beaton's Beauties," p. 34.)

36. See Robin Gibson and Pam Roberts, *Madame Yevonde: Colour, Fantasy and Myth*, exh. cat. (London: National Portrait Gallery, 1990), especially Gibson's essay on the *Goddesses*, "Yevonde: Gradus and Parnassum," pp. 31–40.

37. [Madame] Yevonde, *In Camera* (London: Woman's Book Club, 1940), pp. 232 ff.

38. Cahun, "Héroïnes" [including Eve, Delilah, Judith of Holofernes, Helen of Troy, Sappho, Margaretha (Faust), Salomé], *Mercure de France*, no. 639 (February 1925); and "Héroïnes" [Sophie, Beauty], *Le Journal littéraire*, February 28, 1925; cited in *Claude Cahun Photographe*, exh. cat. (Paris: Musée d'Art Moderne, 1995), p. 165. For examples of Victoria [Vita] Sackville-West's biographies, see *Saint Joan of Arc* (Garden City, N.Y.: Doubleday, Doran, 1936); and *The Eagle and the Dove: A Study in Contrasts: St. Teresa of Avila, St. Therese of Lisieux* (Garden City, N.Y.: Doubleday, Doran, 1944). For Judy Chicago, see Amelia Jones, ed., *Sexual Politics: Judy Chicago's* Dinner Party *in Feminist Art History*, exh. cat. (Los Angeles: UCLA at the Armand Hammer Museum of Art and Cultural Center in association with University of California Press, 1996).

39. Jacques Lacan, "What Is a Picture?" in Lacan, *The Four Fundamental Concepts of Psycho-Analysis* (1973), ed. Jacques-Alain Miller, trans. Alan Sheridan (New York: W. W. Norton, 1981), p. 107.

40. Kaja Silverman, "Masochism and Male Subjectivity," *Camera Obscura* 17 (1988), p. 33; a "slightly different" version appears in *Male Subjectivity at the Margins* (New York: Routledge, 1992), pp. 185–213.

41. Susan Sontag, "The Pornographic Imagination," in Sontag, *Styles of Radical Will* (1969; New York: Doubleday, 1991), p. 70.

42. Judith Butler, *Bodies that Matter: On the Discursive Limits of "Sex"* (New York: Routledge, 1993), p. 242.

43. "No I am lesbian." Pierre Molinier, quoted in Jacques Donguy, "Molinier, homme et femme," *Canal* 32 (October 1979), p. 4; translated in *Pierre Molinier*, exh. cat. (London: Cabinet Gallery, 1993), p. 6. Note that Molinier has modified the French noun "*lesbienne*" to make it masculine.

44. Roger Cardinal, "Nadar and the Photographic Portrait in Nineteenth-Century France," in Clarke, ed., *The Portrait in Photography*, p. 207, note 13.

45. "Odd that no one has thought of the *disturbance* (to civilization) which this new action causes. I want a History of Looking. For the Photograph is the advent of myself as other: a cunning dissociation of consciousness from identity"; see Roland Barthes, *Camera Lucida: Reflections on Photography* (1980), trans. Richard Howard (New York: Hill and Wang, 1981), p. 12.

46. Ibid., p. 70; the caption on p. 68 reads, "Nadar: the artist's mother (or wife)." Nadar's photograph has traditionally been identified in this ambiguous way. Maria Morris Hambourg et al., *Nadar*, exh. cat. (New York: Metropolitan Museum of Art, 1995), pp. 53 and 73, assert that it represents the photographer's bedridden wife, Ernestine.

47. The terms "index" and "icon" describe types of signs in the semiotic system developed by C. S. Pierce; see Pierce, "Logic as Semiotic: The Theory of Signs," in *Philosophical Writings of Pierce*, selected and ed. with introduction by Justus Buchler (New York: Dover, 1955). Rosalind Krauss introduces Pierce's work in her essay on Brassaï's photographs; see Krauss, "Nightwalkers," *Art Journal* 41 (spring 1981), pp. 33–38. Krauss also discusses Surrealist photography with reference to Pierce in "Photography in the Service of Surrealism," in Krauss and Jane Livingston, *L'Amour fou: Photography and Surrealism*, exh. cat. (Washington, D.C.: Corcoran Gallery of Art; and New York: Abbeville Press, 1985), pp. 15–42.

48. Barthes, in *Camera Lucida*, is best at describing the fetishistic power of photographs, in terms that resonate with the memory of his mother. For a comparison of the fetishism of photography in relation to film, see Christian Metz, "Photography and Fetish," *October*, no. 34 (fall 1985), pp. 81–90; reprinted in Carol Squiers, ed., *The Critical Image* (Seattle: Bay Press, 1990), pp. 155–64.

49. The definition of private versus public photography is greatly complicated by rapidly changing historical conceptions of the status of the photographic medium. For instance, older examples of the kind of work presently under discussion were frequently mounted in albums for the enjoyment of the family and friends of the photographer. However, the number of people who viewed an album was often quite large, indicating that the photographs it held had a public status. Also, while the album was a format considered appropriate to photography, it did not preclude a reading of the photograph as a work of art (see, for example, the careers of the nineteenth-century photographers Julia Margaret Cameron and Lady Hawarden, whose prints were mounted in albums). Furthermore, it is only relatively recently that photographic prints have commanded the kind of prices that have led to the presentation of individual shots as "masterpieces," which encourages the disassembling of albums, much as medieval manuscripts were carved up in the past.

50. Here, I am including the daguerreotype in the rubric of photographic means of reproduction.

51. For Hannah Cullwick, see Heather Dawkins, "The Diaries and Photographs of Hannah Cullwick," *Art History* 10 (June 1987), pp. 154–87; for the Countess de Castiglione, see Abigail Solomon-Godeau, "The Legs of the Countess," *October*, no. 39 (winter 1986), pp. 65–108. Cullwick had herself photographed performing the most degrading household employments she could imagine (for example, scrubbing the exterior stairs to her house on her hands and knees). The erotics of class masquerade often inform photographic portraiture. This interesting subject, while related to the theme of this exhibition, is outside the scope of the present essay.

52. For Alice Austen, see Ann Novotny, *Alice's World: The Life and Photography of an American Original/Alice Austen, 1866–1952* (Old Greenwich, Conn.: Chatham Press, 1976). The photographs illustrated here are discussed in Susan Butler, "So How Do I Look? Women Before and Behind the Camera," in James Lingwood, ed., *Staging the Self: Self-Portrait Photography 1840s–1980s*, exh. cat. (London: National Portrait Gallery; and Plymouth, England: Plymouth Arts Centre, 1986), pp. 52–53.

53. Photographs by the Morter Sisters were exhibited in *Mesdames Morter: Striking Poses—Self-Portraits, 1918–1928*, at the Houk Friedman Gallery, New York (September 23–November 6, 1993).

54. I am referring here to a mother figure, not necessarily to a female subject.

55. This description of the child's development of identity is derived from Lacan. See Lacan, "The Mirror Stage as Formative of the Function of the I" (1949), in *Ecrits: A Selection*, trans. Alan Sheridan (New York: W. W. Norton, 1977), pp. 1–7. An earlier version of this paper appeared in *The International Journal of Psychoanalysis* 18

(January 1937) as "The Looking-Glass Phase." For a useful examination of Lacan's theory in relation to fashion photography, see Diana Fuss, "Fashion and the Homospectatorial Look," *Critical Inquiry* 18 (summer 1992), pp. 713–37.

56. For Freud's articulation of the significance of the uncanny, see Freud, "The 'Uncanny'" (1919), in *The Standard Edition of the Complete Psychological Works of Sigmund Freud*, ed. and trans. James Strachey (London: Hogarth Press, 1953–1974), vol. 17, pp. 219–52. For an examination of the uncanny dimension of Surrealist photography, see Krauss, "Corpus Delicti," in *L'Amour fou*, pp. 57–100. See also Hal Foster, *Compulsive Beauty* (Cambridge, Mass.: MIT Press, 1993).
57. Freud, "Fetishism" (1927), *Standard Edition*, vol. 21, pp. 152–57. Through this logic, women cannot be fetishists. In this regard, see Elizabeth Grosz, "Lesbian Fetishism?" in Apter and Pietz, eds., *Fetishism as Cultural Discourse*, pp. 101–15.
58. The best English-language reference on the artist is *Pierre Molinier*, exh. cat. (Winnipeg: Plug In Editions, 1993).
59. Peter Gorsen, "Hans Bellmer—Pierre Molinier: An Archaeology of Eroticism Against Technological Paranoia," trans. Michael Robinson, in Georg Schöllhammer and Christian Kravagna, eds., *Real Text* (Vienna: Ritter Klagenfurt, 1993), p. 256.
60. See, for example, Silverman's sympathetic discussion of Gilles Deleuze's conception of masochism, in her "Masochism and Male Subjectivity," pp. 56ff. For Deleuze's account, see Deleuze, *Masochism: An Interpretation of Coldness and Cruelty* (1967), trans. Jean McNeil (New York: George Braziller, 1971).
61. André Breton, "Manifesto of Surrealism" (1924), in *Manifestoes of Surrealism*, trans. Richard Seaver and Helen R. Lane (Ann Arbor: University of Michigan Press, 1969), pp. 1–47.
62. This research is collected and translated in José Pierre, ed., *Investigating Sex: Surrealist Research 1928–1932*, trans. Malcolm Imrie, with an afterword by Dawn Ades (New York: Verso, 1992).
63. "Une enquête sur le strip-tease," *Le Surréalisme, même* 4 (spring 1958), includes an illustration and a response by Molinier (pp. 58 and 62); another illustration appears in Gérard Legrand, "La Philosophie dans le saloon" (following "Le Striptease: Fin de l'enquête"), *Le Surréalisme, même* 5 (spring 1959), p. 61. Molinier's 1958 response is quoted in the "Strip-tease" entry in "Lexique succinct de l'érotisme," in *L'Exposition InteRnatiOnale du Surréalisme*, exh. cat. (Paris: Galerie Daniel Cordier, 1959), p. 140. Molinier also responded to "Une enquête sur la représentation érotique," *La brèche, action surréaliste*, no. 7 (December 1964), p. 94. His first Paris exhibition was at Breton's Galerie L'Etoile Scellée, in January 1956; the artist was then included in subsequent Surrealist exhibitions.
64. *L'Exposition InteRnatiOnale du Surréalisme*, pp. 121–42. Examples of entries in the "Lexique succinct de l'érotisme" range from "aphrodisiac" and "ardor," to "Gardner, Ava" and "Lee, Gypsy Rose," to "voluptuousness."
65. Freud, "On Narcissism: An Introduction" (1914), in *Standard Edition*, vol. 14, p. 89.
66. The quote is from the British film *Performance* (1970), directed by Donald Cammell and Nicholas Roeg, with James Fox as Chas, Mick Jagger as has-been rock star Turner, and Anita Pallenberg as his secretary/lover. Turner is responding to Chas's request to take Polaroid photos of him.
67. Andy Warhol, *The Philosophy of Andy Warhol: From A to B and Back Again* (New York: Harcourt Brace Jovanovich, 1975), p. 7; quoted in Cécile Whiting, "Andy Warhol, the Public Star and the Private Self," *Oxford Art Journal* 10, no. 2 (1987), p. 70.
68. Barthes, *Camera Lucida*, p. 31.
69. Leslie Fiedler, "The New Mutants," *Partisan Review* (fall 1965); reprinted in *Collected Essays of Leslie Fiedler*, vol. 2 (New York: Stein and Day, 1971), pp. 379–400. See also Susan Sontag's response in "What's Happening in America" (1966), reprinted in Sontag, *Styles of Radical Will*, pp. 193–204, especially pp. 199ff.

   The anxiety Fiedler expresses concerning the feminization of the contemporary male is complicated by his anxiety about the white male becoming Negro. The phenomenon of white rock 'n' roll bands emulating black performers is seen as a symptom, and a troubling one in the face of the civil rights movement:

   I am thinking of the effort of young men in England and the United States to assimilate into themselves (or even to assimilate themselves into) that otherness, that sum total of rejected psychic elements which the middle-class heirs of the Renaissance have identified with "woman." To become new men, these children of the future seem to feel, they must not only become more Black than White but more female than male. (p. 390)

   He goes on to discuss "the non-or anti-male," who is most likely "impotent or homosexual or both" (p. 391). His position's ambiguities are beyond the scope of this essay, but it is important to note the way in which race is gender-coded as masculine or feminine.
70. See *"Transformer": Aspekte der Travestie*, exh. cat. (Lucerne: Kunstmuseum, 1974).
71. Patrick Eudeline, "Le Phénomène du travesti dans la Rock Music," in *"Transformer,"* unpaginated.
72. Duchamp's work appears again in the *"Transformer"* catalogue, in the context of Katharina Sieverding's portfolio of photographic self-portraits, in which a detail of *Etant Donnés* is reproduced with the caption *"aux grandes étonnées/M. Duchamp."*
73. For a 1970s Jungian view of androgyny, see June Singer, *Androgyny: Toward a New Theory of Sexuality* (Garden City, N.Y.: Anchor Press/Doubleday, 1976).

   For contemporaneous investigations of androgyny in art, see, for example, Robert Knott, "The Myth of the Androgyne," *Artforum* 14 (November 1975), pp. 38–45 (also in this issue of *Artforum* are two other articles that deal with notions of androgyny, in Surrealism and contemporary art, respectively: Whitney Chadwick, "Eros or Thanatos—The Surrealist Cult of Love Reexamined," pp. 46–56; and Max Kozloff, "Pygmalion Reversed," pp. 30–37); and Elémire Zolla, *The Androgyne: Reconciliation of Male and Female* (New York: Crossroad/Thames and Hudson, 1981). See also *Androgyny in Art*, exh. cat. with text by Gail Gelburd (Hempstead, N.Y.: Emily Lowe Gallery, Hofstra University, 1982); and *Androgyn: Sehnsucht nacht Vollkommenheit*, exh. cat. (Berlin: Dietrich Reimer Verlag, 1986).

   For a critique of twentieth-century feminist engagements with the concept of androgyny, including 1970s positions, see Kari Weil, *Androgyny and the Denial of Difference* (Charlottesville: University Press of Virginia, 1992), pp. 144–69.
74. In the *"Transformer"* catalogue, the entry on Molinier relies substantially on Gorsen, *Pierre Molinier, lui-même: Essay über den surrealistischen Hermaphroditen* (Munich: Rogner & Bernhard, 1972).
75. Jürgen Klauke also titled a work *Ziggy Stardust* (1974).
76. Sontag, "Notes on 'Camp'" (1964), in Sontag, *Against Interpretation and Other Essays* (1966; New York: Farrar, Straus, Giroux, 1986), p. 280.
77. Popular interest in theatrical female impersonation in the early 1970s was manifested in a spate of publications that ran the gamut from superficial to scholarly. However, female impersonation continued to be denigrated as decadent or perverse when it was not performed by an ostensibly heterosexual subject. Contemporaneous publications on female impersonation include Gillo Dorfles et al., *Gli uni & gli altri: Travestiti e travestimenti nell'arte, nel teatro, nel cinema, nella musica, nel cabaret e nella vita quotidiana* (Rome: Arcana Editrice, 1976), which was also published in a French edition; picture books like Gilles Larrain, *Idols* (New York: Links, 1973); and the highly influential study by Esther

Newton, *Mother Camp: Female Impersonators in America* (Englewood Cliffs, N.J.: Prentice-Hall, 1972). Thompson's *The Mysteries of Sex*, the 1930s compendium of historical figures who cross-dressed cited in note 24 above was reprinted in 1974.

78. In his "*Transformer*" catalogue essay, "Die Geschlechterentspannung als Formprinzip und ästhetisches Verhalten," Gorsen criticizes the cooptation of intersexual subcultures (that of transvestites, gays, and transsexuals) by commercial interests, distinguishing pop culture's pseudo-transvestites from the "authentic" transvestite community, which was in the process of trying to identify itself in a positive rather than the traditionally negative way. For Gorsen, the pop transvestite manifestation is a fashion, while for the authentic transvestite cross-dressing represents a higher aspiration for a psychological ideal. See also Gorsen, "Intersexualismus und Subkultur," in Axel Matthes, ed., *Maskulin-Feminin* (Munich: Rogner & Bernhard, 1972; second rev. ed., 1975), pp. 93–137.
79. See also "For Rrose Sélavy and Belle Haleine—New York, 1973," in Anne d'Harnoncourt and Kynaston McShine, eds., *Marcel Duchamp*, exh. cat. (New York: Museum of Modern Art; and Philadelphia: Philadelphia Museum of Art, 1973), p. 227. Warhol's contribution to this catalogue consists of a photograph of the artist in a kind of barker's costume and black wig, inserted into what appears to be a group of drag queens.
80. Erving Goffman, *Gender Advertisements* (Cambridge, Mass.: Harvard University Press, 1979), p. 8 (in the chapter entitled "Gender Display"). See also Goffman, *The Presentation of Self in Everyday Life* (Garden City, N.Y.: Doubleday, 1959), p. 19 (in the chapter entitled "Performances"). Goffman's influence is cited by Kirk Varnedoe, "Introduction," in *Modern Portraits: The Self & Others*, exh. cat. (New York: Wildenstein, 1976), p. xxv, note 8.
81. The *Auto Polaroids* were first published in *Samaras Album*, exh. cat. (New York: Whitney Museum of American Art and Pace Editions, 1971).
82. This 22 ½-minute, 16-mm film was created with Kim Levin.
83. Lucy R. Lippard, "Transformation Art," *Ms.* 4 (October 1975), pp. 33–39; reprinted as "Making Up: Role-Playing and Transformation in Women's Art," in Lippard, *From the Center: Feminist Essays on Women's Art* (New York: E. P. Dutton, 1976), pp. 101–08.
84. Woolf, *Orlando*, pp. 156–57.
85. The album-collections were produced in her bedroom by "Annette Messager Collectionneuse."
86. In this regard, it is worthwhile to note Bakhtin's influential work on the carnivalesque in the work of François Rabelais: Bakhtin, *Rabelais and His World* (1965), trans. Hélène Iswolsky (Cambridge, Mass.: MIT Press, 1968). Russo summarizes the feminist reception of this work (as well as Riviere's on masquerade) in "Female Grotesques: Carnival and Theory," pp. 213–29. For an example of a polemical text of the 1970s that engages the feminist implications of laughter, see Hélène Cixous, "The Laugh of the Medusa," trans. Keith Cohen and Paula Cohen, *Signs* (summer 1976); reprinted in Elaine Marks and Isabelle de Courtivron, eds., *New French Feminisms: An Anthology* (New York: Schocken Books, 1981), pp. 245–64; this is a revised version of "Le Rire de la méduse," *L'Arc* (1975), pp. 39–54.
87. Eve Kosofsky Sedgwick, "'Gosh, Boy George, You Must Be Awfully Secure in Your Masculinity!'" in Maurice Berger, Brian Wallis, and Simon Watson, eds., *Constructing Masculinity*, with picture essay by Carrie Mae Weems (New York: Routledge, 1995), p. 16; this sentence begins, "One implication of work like Sandra Bem's is that . . ."
88. Nan Goldin, *The Other Side* (New York: Scalo Publishers, 1993), p. 7.
89. Nevertheless, at least one art critic made this mistake, as Krauss notes in her book *Cindy Sherman* (New York: Rizzoli, 1993), p. 17.
90. For example, Cindy Sherman's *Untitled, #193* is compared to Boucher's *Madame Boucher on a Chaise Longue* (1743) in Christa Schneider, *Cindy Sherman: History Portraits* (Munich: Schirmer/Mosel, 1995), p. 18. Schneider deals exclusively with the *History Portraits* that depict female subjects.
91. The works referred to are, respectively, Matthew Barney's *Blind Perineum* (1991), *The Jim Otto Suite* (1990), *Cremaster 4* (1994), and *Radial Drill* (1991).
92. The works referred to are, respectively, Barney's *Cremaster 4* (1994) and *Cremaster 1* (1995).
93. For examples of each artist's engagement with fashion, see Sherman's *Fashion* series (1983–84, and ongoing); Yasumasa Morimura's *Sister* photos (1991); and Barney's use of designer clothes in his videos (an interesting precursor is Jean Cocteau's film *The Blood of a Poet* [*Le Sang d'un poète*, 1930], in which Barbette wears Chanel.) For more or less obvious references to Hollywood, see, for example, Sherman's *Untitled Film Stills*; Morimura's *Actress* photographs (1996), in which he emulates movie goddesses from Marilyn Monroe to Joan Crawford; and Barney's Busby Berkeley references in *Cremaster 1*, as well as his exhibitions of production photographs from the video.
94. See Wayne Koestenbaum's interesting essay on this work, "Corpse on a Pink Record Cover Dancing Upside Down," in *Masks*, exh. cat. (Rome: Valentina Moncada, 1992), unpaginated.
95. For contemporary examples of the Exquisite Corpse game, see *The Return of the Cadavre Exquis*, exh. cat., with texts by Ingrid Schaffner, Charles Simic, and Mary Ann Caws (New York: Drawing Center, 1993).
96. André Breton and Philippe Soupault, *Les Champs magnétique* (Paris: Au Sans Pareil, 1920).
97. Compare this with Morimura's 1994 *Psychoborg* series on Madonna and Michael Jackson. Christian Marclay ironizes the notion of rock star as shaman or godlike figure in his iconically columnar and cruciform *Body Mix* pieces and related sculptural constructions such as *Skin Mix I* (1990).
98. Note, in this regard, the recent explosion of books about drag: for example, F. Michael Moore, *Drag! Male and Female Impersonators on Stage, Screen and Television: An Illustrated World History* (Jefferson, N.C.: McFarland, 1994); Roger Baker, *Drag: A History of Female Impersonation in the Performing Arts* (London: Cassell, 1994); and Catherine Chermayeff, Jonathan David, and Nan Richardson, *Drag Diaries* (San Francisco: Chronicle Books, 1995). See also the more scholarly contributions on cross-dressing such as Julia Epstein and Kristina Straub, eds., *Body Guards: The Cultural Politics of Gender Ambiguity*, (New York: Routledge, 1991); Lesley Ferris, ed., *Crossing the Stage: Controversies on Cross-Dressing*, (New York: Routledge, 1993); Marjorie Garber, *Vested Interests: Cross-Dressing & Cultural Anxiety* (New York: Routledge, 1992); and Vern L. Bullough and Bonnie B. Bullough, *Cross Dressing, Sex, and Gender* (Philadelphia: University of Pennsylvania Press, 1993).

Today, books and articles with the word "gender" in their titles seem innumerable; see, for example, Richard Ekins and David King, eds., *Blending Genders: Social Aspects of Cross-Dressing and Sex-Changing* (New York: Routledge, 1996); and Holly Devor, *Gender Blending: Confronting the Limits of Duality* (Bloomington: Indiana University Press, 1989).
99. In a random sample during a single night of watching national television, I counted at least one joke per show, ranging from a man trying to convince his son to trade in his Barbie for a GI Joe, with the final revelation that the man had dressed up as a girl when he was a child; and a woman who tries to seduce a middle-aged bureaucrat until he refers to his "husband of many years," which elicits the audience's laughter (October 9, 1996, NBC).
100. It is interesting to note, in this regard, Sedgwick's provocative discussion of the genesis of shame and its relationship to perfor-

mance, in her essay "Queer Performativity: Henry James's *The Art of the Novel*," *GLQ: A Journal of Lesbian and Gay Studies* 1, no. 1 (1993), pp. 1–16.

101. Goldin, *The Other Side*, p. 6.
102. Ibid., p. 8.
103. See Lia Gangitano, ed., *Boston School*, exh. cat. (Boston: Institute of Contemporary Art, 1995).
104. I refer loosely here to Barthes's articulation of the reality effect in literature. See his essay "The Reality Effect" (1968), in Barthes, *The Rustle of Language*, trans. Richard Howard (New York: Hill and Wang, 1986), pp. 141–48.
105. Note Nayland Blake's distinctions between the use of drag in the 1970s and the present in "Curating in a Different Light," in Nayland Blake, Lawrence Rinder, and Amy Scholder, eds., *In a Different Light: Visual Culture, Sexual Identity, Queer Practice*, exh. cat. (San Francisco: City Lights Books; and Berkeley: University Art Museum and Pacific Film Archive, University of California at Berkeley, 1995), pp. 31–33.
106. For information on the minstrel shows, see Robert C. Toll, *Blacking Up: The Minstrel Show in Nineteenth-Century America* (New York: Oxford University Press, 1974); and Robert C. Allen, *Horrible Prettiness: Burlesque and American Culture* (Chapel Hill: University of North Carolina Press, 1991), pp. 163–78. See also Garber, "Black and White TV: Cross-Dressing the Color Line," in *Vested Interests*, pp. 267–303.

    When African American performers began to form minstrel companies in the late 1860s, they also wore blackface. A complicated circuit, which started with whites constructing black characters by shoehorning elements of black American slave culture into European minority stereotypes, came to be reclaimed by blacks who redeployed the minstrel conventions, eventually for black audiences.
107. Kobena Mercer, "Busy in the Ruins of Wretched Phantasia," in *Mirage: Enigmas of Race, Difference and Desire*, exh. cat. (London: Institute of Contemporary Arts, 1995), p. 32. I thank Lyle Ashton Harris for bringing this essay to my attention.
108. Harris, quoted in Michael Cohen, "Lyle Ashton Harris," *Flash Art* 29 (May–June 1996), p. 107.
109. For a journalistic account of the autobiographical aspects of current academic writing in the field of literary criticism, see, for example, Adam Begley, "The I's Have It," *Linguafranca* 4 (March–April 1994), pp. 54–59. On the contemporary breakdown of the distinction between fiction and memoir, see, for example, James Atlas, "The Age of the Literary Memoir Is Now: Confessing for Voyeurs," *The New York Times Magazine* (special issue, "True Confessions: The Age of the Literary Memoir," with portraits by Goldin, Harris, and Catherine Opie, among others, interspersed with family snapshots), May 12, 1996, pp. 25–27; and Bill Buford, "The Seductions of Storytelling: Why is Narrative Suddenly So Popular?" *The New Yorker*, June 24 and July 1, 1996, pp. 11–12.
110. In this light, Warhol's professed desire to be a machine could be equated with the defense mechanism of identifying with the enemy. The rise of performance and body art, with its emphasis on real time and the artist's corporeal presence, might be viewed as a reaction to anxiety about advances in computer technology and space exploration, as evidenced in contemporaneous films such as *2001: A Space Odyssey* (Stanley Kubrick, 1968), and the profound fear manifested in many of David Bowie's lyrics, such as *Major Tom*.
111. Henri Matisse, "Notes of a Painter" (1908), in Herschel B. Chipp, *Theories of Modern Art: A Source Book by Artists and Critics* (Berkeley: University of California Press, 1968), p. 135: *What I dream of is an art of balance, of purity and serenity devoid of troubling or depressing subject matter, an art which might be for every mental worker, be he businessman or writer, like an appeasing influence, like a mental soother, something like a good armchair in which to rest from physical fatigue.*
112. See the epigraph at the start of this book, from *Roland Barthes by Roland Barthes* (1975), trans. Richard Howard (Berkeley: University of California Press, 1994), pp. 116–17.

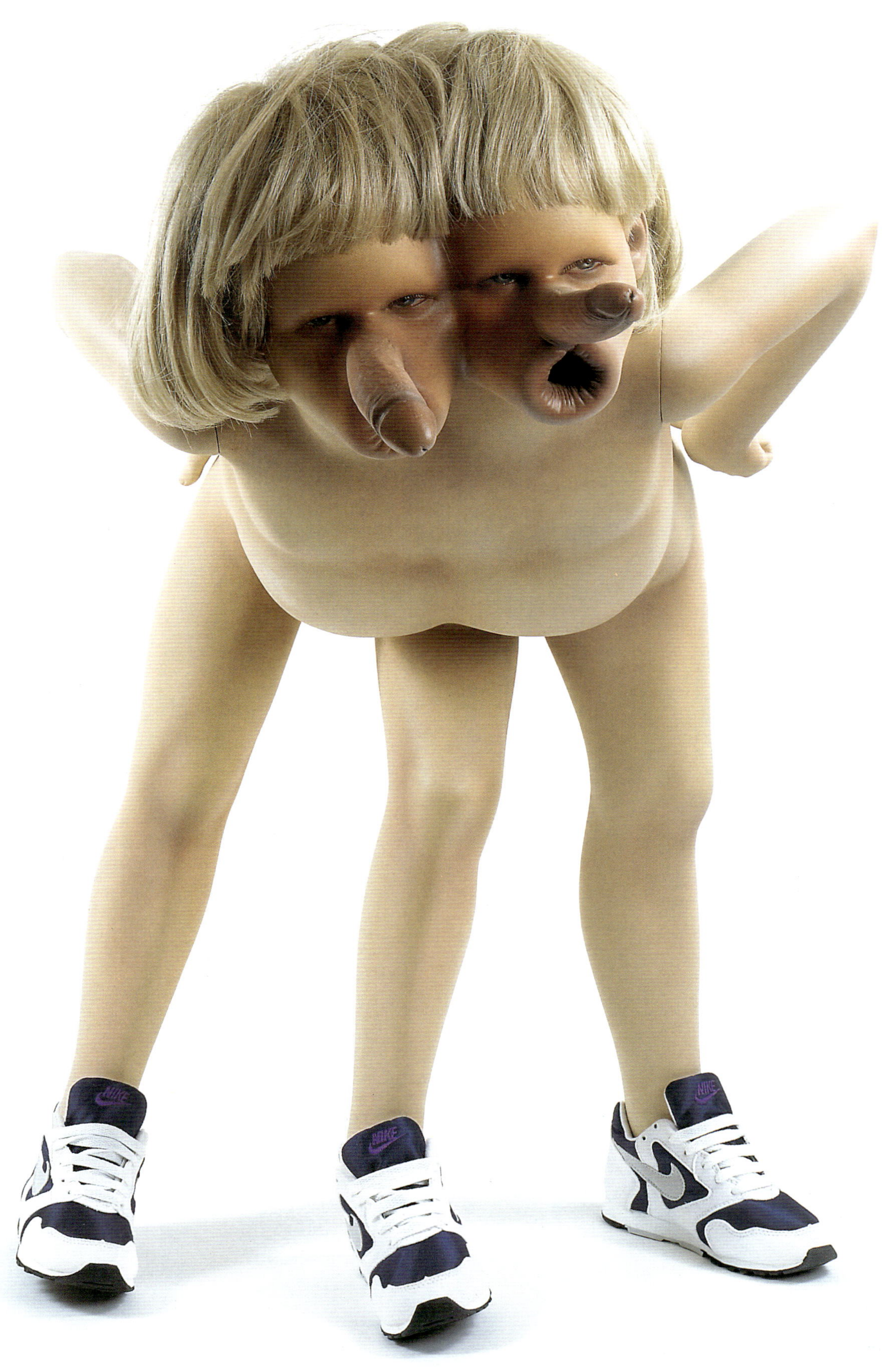

Dinos and Jake Chapman
Fuckface Twin, 1995
Fiberglass, resin, and paint, 33 7/16 x 21 1/4 x 26 3/8 inches (85 x 54 x 67 cm)
Deste Foundation, Athens, Courtesy of Victoria Miro Gallery, London

Death Masks

CAROLE-ANNE TYLER

Queer photography, indeed, these pictures of an underworld or another world, an alternative past or future where identities as we know them have been burlesqued, cut up, and collaged anew in unusual, sometimes grotesque and frightening, sometimes beautiful combinations. *I'll Be Your Mirror* (1972), Urs Lüthi's cross-dressed self-portrait promises us, offering an image of ourselves we would not recognize, a double we would deny, like Nan Goldin's drag queens, Hannah Höch's man-woman *Tamer*, or the masquerading self-portraits of Claude Cahun, Robert Mapplethorpe, and Cindy Sherman. Perhaps more disturbing still are Jürgen Klauke's cyborg bodies with penis nipples, or Dinos and Jake Chapman's "Siamese Twat . . . Fuckface Twin / Two-faced Cunt / Cunt-chops . . . zygotic acceleration, biogenetic de-sublimated libidinal model,"[1] child mannequin sculptures sprouting adult penises, anuses, and vaginas in surprising places, numbers, and combinations, along with extra heads, torsos, arms, and legs. Are these the faces of desires from which our own (and perhaps their other) faces shield us, desires incompatible with gender—or race or class—as custom fixes them? What do we make of these queer beings—and what does that make of us? Where might desire take us, theirs (as we imagine it) and ours? We gaze at these pictures as into a developing tray, wondering what identities might take shape when the chemistry of desire is so complex. Can we ever secure a comfortable identity, get "back to the future" as if we knew it, as Marty McFly—the hero played by Michael J. Fox in Robert Zemeckis's series of films about the oedipal adventures of masculinity—strives to do? Like him, we must all cross the tenses and tensions of identity in those paradoxes of time travel that make up life itself, aporias more insoluble than the film suggests.

The circle McFly moves in might seem very far indeed from that of Gertrude Stein's famous line, "Rose is a rose is a rose is a rose,"[2] or from Marcel Duchamp's feminine alter ego, Rrose Sélavy, the muse for this exhibition together with Stein's rose. Yet all three, like the exhibition itself, point to the necessity and impossibility of fixing identity through representation, however often we repeat it. We figure ourselves out of our figures of ourselves because identity is always under (re)construction; no name can do us justice when it has forgotten our future—and, unlike McFly, it never can remember it. As biographers and autobiographers know, every identity is retroactive. Identity comes to us from the future, rather than the past, and is *what will have been*, a defensive editing of the past (even the past of the body in transsexual and cosmetic surgeries) to make it all come out right, with the proper ending—for that moment. "I" will be another all too soon, as performance artist Orlan demonstrates in the surgical reconstructions of herself she stages in operating rooms (fittingly termed "theatres" in British usage, which seems to acknowledge the common presence of observers at medical spectacles).

Only the end of life itself provides closure for this process. As literary critic Frank Kermode reminds us in a book on time and narrative, death is what gives us the sense of an ending:

Gertrude Stein's letterhead (detail), n.d.
Beinecke Rare Book and Manuscript Collection, Yale University, New Haven, Yale Collection of American Literature

Men, like poets, rush "into the middest," in medias res, *when they are born; they also die* in mediis rebus, *and to make sense of their span they need fictive concords with origins and ends, such as give meaning to lives and to poems. The End they imagine will reflect their irreducibly intermediary preoccupations. They fear it, and as far we can see have always done so; the End is a figure for their own deaths.*[3]

Stein once made a similar observation. "In writing a story one had to be remembering," she writes, "but . . . realizing the existence of living beings actually existing did not have in it any element of remembering so the time of existing was not the same as in the novels."[4] Identity is finalized when we are past revising it and have become our obituary, the story of our life, which is actually written and revised by others in a process that can end only with the death of history.

Walter Benjamin claims that all storytelling is such an obituary. "The nature of the character in a novel cannot be presented any better than is done in this statement, which says that the 'meaning' of his life is revealed only in his death," he writes.

But the reader of a novel actually does look for human beings from whom he derives the "meaning of life." Therefore he must, no matter what, know in advance that he will share their experience of death: if need be their figurative death—the end of the novel—but preferably their actual one.[5]

The stream of life and the language that would represent it is punctuated by some other, who places the final period that makes of each a "period," something with a definite shape, a beginning, middle, and end from which identity emerges as the significance of it all. Death is the point of view of the meaning of life, to which life looks ahead. We are subjected to it; it makes us human subjects, as Sigmund Freud emphasizes in his theory of a death drive, which he articulates to account for the aggression that exceeds the pleasure and reality principles and is fundamentally masochistic. Who or what have we been for that other who sees us from beyond our grave, who makes our death mask, who must finish us off to represent us in that murderous still-life of "identity"? The gaze of the other kills and embalms us, as does the photographer, according to Roland Barthes, and yet we sit still for it; we even collaborate with it: "The photograph represents the very subtle moment when, to tell the truth, I am neither subject nor object but a subject who feels he is becoming an object: I then experience a micro-version of death (of parenthesis): I am truly becoming a specter."[6] Film theorist Christian Metz also affirms a connection between death and photography, asserting that "the snapshot, like death, is an instantaneous abduction of the object out of the world into another world, into another kind of time—unlike cinema, which replaces the object, after the act of appropriation, in an unfolding time similar to that of life."[7]

Each shot makes us into a hunter's trophy or a taxidermist's triumph, catching us in a "natural pose" as what we are "supposed" to be. Yet we believe portraits show us as we really are: "Leibovitz was able to find the essence of these athletes," a *Time* magazine editor asserts of Annie Leibovitz's photos of 1996 Olympians.[8] Her gaze fixes them in heroic impostures, as they "strike a pose," to echo Madonna's phrase in "Vogue," projecting themselves into images of an ideal. Barthes draws our attention to this mimicry through which we express ourselves for others:

In front of the lens, I am at the same time: the one I think I am, the one I want others to think I am, the one the photographer thinks I am, and the one he makes use of to exhibit his art. In other words a strange action: I do not stop imitating myself.[9]

Richard Avedon remarks on this facet of portraiture when he argues that "Rembrandt must have been acting when he made his own self-portraits. . . . Not just making faces, but always, throughout his life, working in the full tradition of performance."[10] Rembrandt displays not the essence but the appearance, the death masks that disguise the desires of the living being, impostures we scrutinize for clues about the man, duped by their "lifelike" qualities. Robert Mapplethorpe's self-portraits solicit a similar scrutiny, as he masquerades in turn as a female impersonator in 1980, a terrorist with a machine gun in 1983, and finally death itself in a 1988 photo that invites a comparison between his face and the skull crowning the walking stick he grips. Only the small skull and fist in the photo's foreground are in sharp focus; while his disembodied face in the middle ground is luminous in the otherwise velvety blackness of the image, the soft focus suggests he is already fading, disappearing. Is this death within his grasp what Mapplethorpe really is? It is literally his support and more "lifelike" (solid-seeming, tangible, and "realistic") than the face dissolving into darkness.

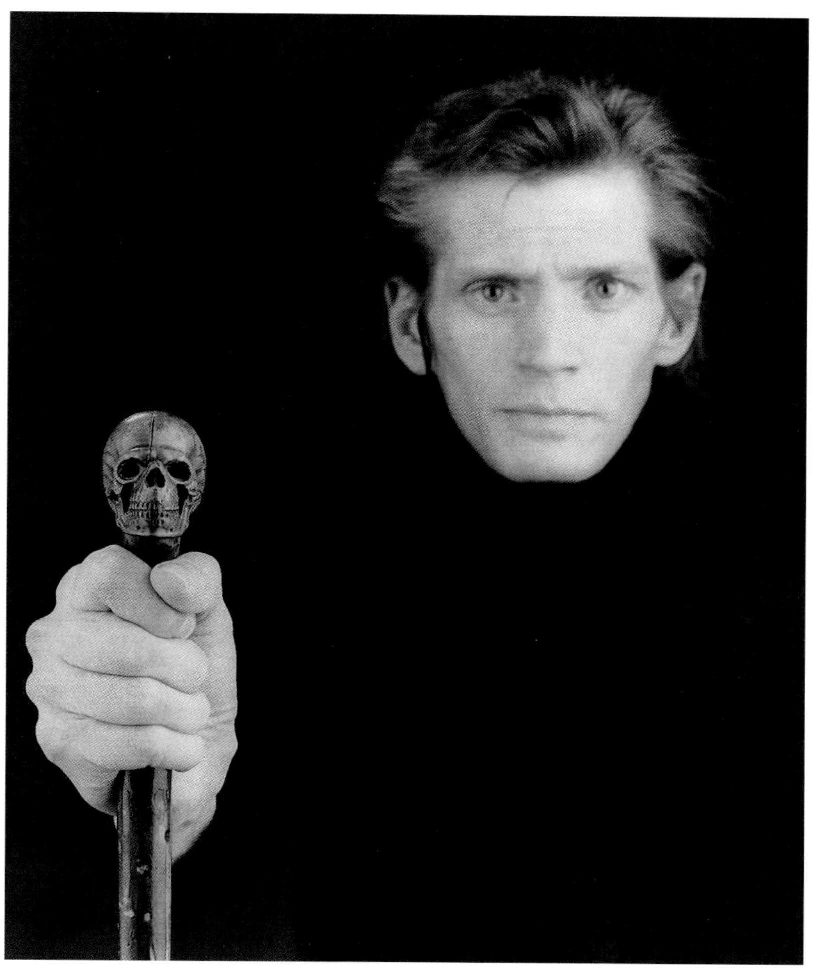

Robert Mapplethorpe
Self-Portrait, 1988
Gelatin-silver print,
24 x 20 inches (61 x 50.8 cm)
Courtesy of The Robert Mapplethorpe Foundation, New York

The portrait artist in any medium is condemned to the cliché of the "lifelike" as a kind of talisman or fetish with prophylactic powers against the threat of death, as Barthes notes of the photographer, who, he writes, must resort to "contortions to produce effects that are 'lifelike' . . . to keep the Photograph from becoming Death."[11] They are gestures drawn from a museum of gestures, preserved in art—the aesthetic as stereotype, as art critic Rosalind Krauss says[12]—but also in the theater of everyday life, as is suggested by Barthes's use of quotation marks to signal the artifice of the "lifelike" as a time-worn pose. Furthermore, the contortions Barthes describes are not those of the photographer but of the model who responds to the demands of the photographer, who can stand in for all the others for whom Barthes and the rest of us posture. They make something—perhaps something different—of the poses we hope to impose on them. "[T]hey make me," Barthes reiterates,[13] as he describes his performances for the eyes of the other, and indeed, they quite literally make him, for there is no identity without that mortifying gaze "through which . . . I am *photographed*," according to Jacques Lacan.[14] We are all exhibitionists, soliciting the other's gaze as confirmation of our existence; as the title of Sandra Bernhard's 1990 film of cross-race and cross-gender performances declares, *Without You I'm Nothing.* We desire the other's desire; with his or her gaze framing and caressing us, our contours are consolidated, we *are.* This is the generative dimension of photography: it performs (into being) what it seems to reflect. Art historian John Tagg notes that it was through the taking of a photograph that the making of a bourgeois subject occurred. Photography represented and reproduced the status of those with the status to be photographed: they could afford to pay for the privilege, unlike the lower orders, even if they could not sit for a portrait in oils, as aristocrats did.[15] Like Tagg, sociologist Pierre Bourdieu draws attention to photography's performativity. He argues that it creates the family unity it depicts, gathering the group together to be preserved forever in the family snapshot, whatever the rifts that precede and succeed it. "Photography itself," he asserts, "is most frequently nothing but the reproduction of the image that a group produces of its own integration."[16]

What else is the "being" of the Diane Arbus photo *A naked man being a woman, New York City* (1968) if not a performance for a gaze that fixes an imposture? Caught in the act that transforms "him" to "her," with nothing to hide (since nudity is the very figure of self-revelation), the subject passes for what the other helps to make of him. The shutter and the frame slice like knives; he is castrated, stripped of the organ that signifies his pretense, whose trace is the title's own insistence on his doubleness. As a "naked man being a woman" he is actually *being* a naked man being a woman for that gaze that sees what is not even there in the picture except as a suspicious rereading of its signs. This is a second castration, one that deprives the would-be deceiver of the power of masquerade itself. "She's a He," proclaims a recent ad for Sauza "Commemorativo" tequila, performing the same double gesture of un/veiling the female impersonator. The other cuts me down to size, fits me to a pattern, stitches me to "me," an image that does not quite fit, like the emperor's new clothes. Mastery is the tailor's, as Buffalo Bill, one of the killers in *The Silence of the Lambs* (Jonathan Demme, 1991), knows, which is why he tries to seize it for himself. A would-be self-made woman, he repeatedly steals the skins of "real girls" ("r.g.'s" in transsexual slang) in which to dress himself. Psychoanalyst Eugénie Lemoine-Luccioni points out that kleptomania frequently has been described as the "feminine form" of fetishism, in which the woman takes things to make up for what she "lacks,"[17] experiencing an orgasmic pleasure in the theft. Like every fetishist, Buffalo Bill believes that with the right outfit, anything is possible. For him, a woman's skin is the finest fabric, and there is the added pleasure of the cut. If his mad basement burlesque involves cutting up the woman to mock her as well as mimic her, it is because fetishism is characterized by a double attitude. As Freud explains, the fetishist both worships and castrates his fetish object, knows and ignores the fact that its magic properties are in his eyes only.[18] Buffalo Bill can never be the master tailor, the one who fixes these properties so all may witness them; even a night-blinded female detective can see to that, sewing up the case with a shot that makes him the picture of the pervert as sociopathic criminal.

The law is the master who coauthors me by authorizing "me," providing me with a name and an image of myself with which I am urged to identify from the first moment I am held up in front of the mirror and told to see the pretty baby, the one who is not quite "me" but who nonetheless represents me. Mastery is that of the other who subjects me, alienates me, and constitutes me. It belongs to the one whose wish that we imitate a particular object we take as the law of our own desire, which literally subjects us, but it also belongs to that object we mimic, whose mastery alienates us from the master's desire, having captivated it. If we could imitate this alter ego well enough, we might become it, overcoming our difference from it, if only for those we can dupe, to whom we have implicitly assigned the power to judge.

That is the tragicomic message of *Paris Is Burning* (Jennie Livingston, 1991), a documentary about African American and Latino voguers who impersonate the primarily white and feminine ideals touted by our media culture and judge each other's "realness" with respect to those ideals. But they also judge the realness of the real women they teach to emulate them: Willie Ninja, one of the "mothers" or heads of a house of voguers, runs a modeling school for the very women after—and before—whom he models himself. "I'm trying to bring their femininity back and bring some grace and poise. You know, whether they become models or not, it's nice to know because it's more attractive to men," he explains. This statement might be taken as evidence for the assertion of performance-studies scholar Peggy Phelan that if these gay men valorize femininity, "the architecture of that femininity . . . is thoroughly masculine,"[19] operating in the service of patriarchy and capitalism (the women are commodities, deeply identified with the clothing and other accoutrements of a pleasing style that they consume for the men who will "consume" them). A recent television commercial for a California clothing-store chain offers women viewers a transvestite role model with whom they can compete through commodity consumption. Proclaiming "If Clothestime can make Mark look this good, imagine what we can do for you," the commercial implicitly levels the field by making everyone a gender "player," rather than the real thing, soliciting a serious investment in the commodity as fetish and prosthesis.

American-literature historian Eric Lott outlines the double of such scenarios in his book on blackface minstrelsy. "I take as normative a long, conflicted history of racial exchange that significantly 'blackened' American culture as it creolized African cultural imports, a history that in one sense makes it difficult to talk about expropriation at all," he writes.

> *Black performance . . . was precisely "performative," a cultural invention, not some precious essence installed in black bodies, and for better or worse it was often a product of self-commodification . . . sometimes developed . . . in tandem with white spectators.*[20]

The result was "racially mixed forms that both did and did not read as 'black.'"[21] As Lott explains, one black Shakespearean, Ira Aldridge, incorporated into his act an imitation of a white minstrel's imitation of him because it sold well,[22] while the dances of the black blackface minstrel Juba included imitations not only of other minstrels' dances but even of his own famous dance, according to Susan Willis.[23] In a similar gesture during the first broadcast of her short-lived weekly TV variety show in 1987, Dolly Parton announced that if she had been born a man, she would be a female impersonator. Which is the master or original and which the copy in these möbius movements of simulation, in which race and gender are joint productions, imitations of others' imitations of oneself, veering in the direction of self-parody? *Paris Is Burning* invites just such reflection by cross-cutting between scenes of "real people" and their impersonators until we are no longer certain which is which. The Cheryl Lynn song to which the soundtrack compulsively returns, "Got to Be Real," becomes an ironic commentary on an impossible demand.

Yet it is one with which every American is taxed, as political scientist Michael Rogin sees it. The European immigrant to America is transformed into a white American through imposture, as were the Irish immigrants who constituted a large percentage of the original blackface minstrels in the nineteenth century. Blackface is "synecdochal for Hollywood," Rogin argues; it "gives America its meaning—self-making through role-playing—in *Holiday Inn*, *Swanee River*, and *Dixie*"[24] and a host of other films. Through blackface the immigrant and minstrel is reborn into that mythic moment of imaginary harmony before the Civil War when racial difference split America into quarrelsome factions. Like the phoenix—or Cinderella—the immigrant rises from the ashes, leaving behind the burnt cork of blackface, and is assimilated into an implicitly white American culture of upward mobility by changing one mask for another. If Americans are self-made, it is when they play a role scripted by others—a role that frees them from an earlier ("un-American") image in whose grip they were caught. We are all condemned to such mimicry, according to psychoanalysis and other theories of identity that construe it as a performative social construction rather than an expression of a pregiven or essential self. "Performatives are forms of authoritative speech: most performatives . . . are statements that, in the uttering, also perform a certain action and exercise a binding power," Judith Butler explains, giving as an example of this "the promise," whose words change the relationship and identities of both the speaker and auditor.[25] All discourses are finally performative like promises;

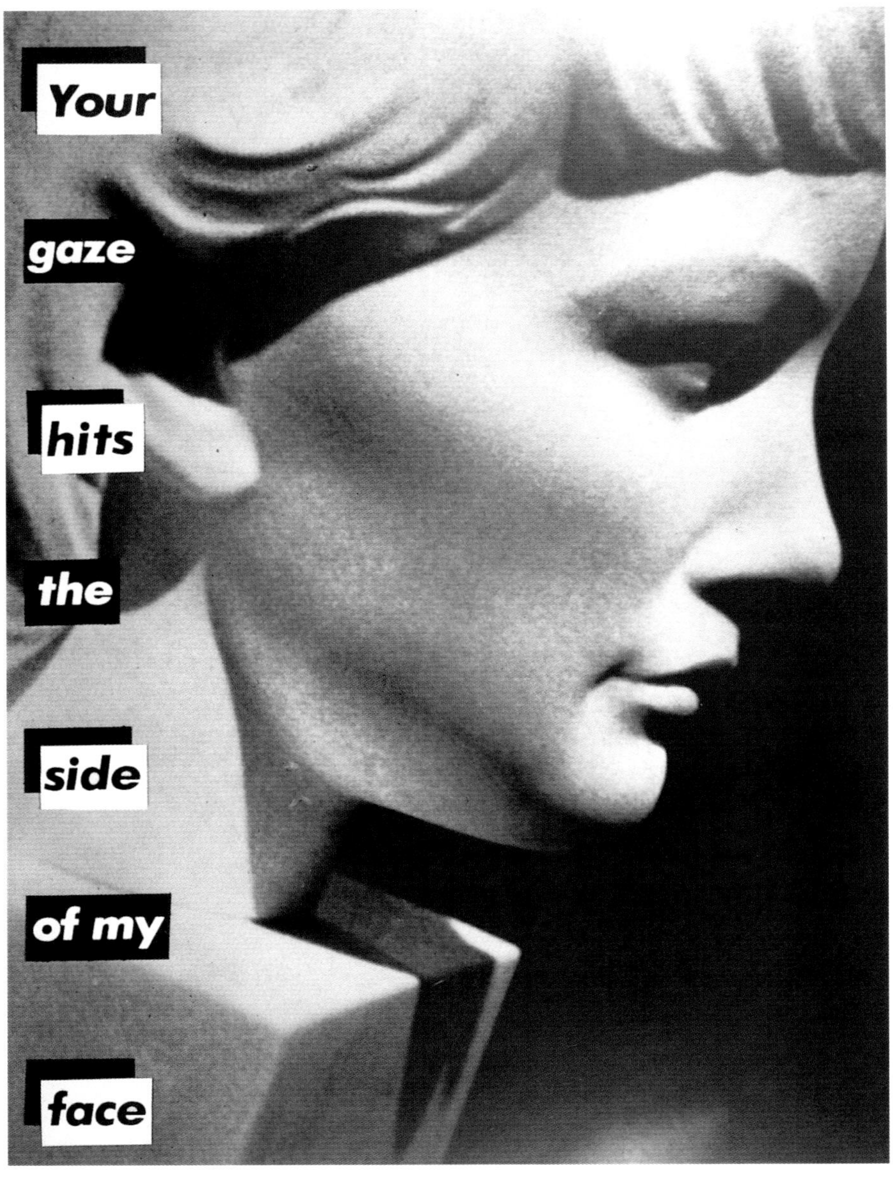

Barbara Kruger
Untitled (Your gaze hits the side of my face), 1981
Photograph, 55 x 41 inches
(139.7 x 104.1 cm)
Courtesy of Mary Boone Gallery, New York

they produce what they name, including the subject who is named "I" in the statements that he or she utters. Paradoxically, Butler writes, "the discursive condition of social recognition *precedes and conditions* the formation of the subject: recognition is not conferred on a subject, but forms that subject."[26] A person is the impersonation an other recognizes as the self; there is nothing more genuine behind that mask, as there is in the sociological theory of role-playing developed by Talcott Parsons, in which the subject is assumed to exist before and beyond the role.[27]

That the self actually is a mask is implicit in the Freudian notion of the ego as a projection of the surface of the body the subject recognizes in the mirror or in others with whom he or she is encouraged to imagine a resemblance (such as those of the "same" class, race, or gender). I imitate such projections as my self and thereby shape my self. I am an imprint of my mirror image, a copy without an original, like a photograph. There is no ego before such mimicry, no original given to "self-expression," like the hunchback inside Benjamin's chess-playing machine in the first of the "Theses on the Philosophy of History,"[28] or the artist whose genius breathes life and "soul" into the formulae of a genre painting. The violence of the gaze that pins me to the captivating image I appropriate as it expropriates me (or, rather, whatever there was before the picture that represents "me") is caught by Barbara Kruger in *Untitled* (*Your gaze hits the side of my face*) (1981), a photomontage of a stone bust of a woman upon which Kruger has collaged the words "Your gaze hits the side of my face." The woman has been petrified by the other she would please (and in a patriarchal society that takes heterosexuality for granted, we read this addressee as a male spectator), turned into the statue in which her self is projected for some Pygmalion. She literally "makes up" her face, a mask of cosmetics and expressions she dons as a lure and a shield in the "feminine masquerade" psychoanalysts such as Joan Riviere and Lacan[29] have discussed and that many feminists have linked to an alienating sexual and commodity fetishism assigned to women. The woman disappears into the props and prostheses through which she exhibits herself as the "good object." They are an integral part of the orthopedic armature that is the substance of her (and any other) ego, for they have entered into her dreams and fantasies, a process therapists also encourage in young amputees; as Elaine Scarry explains, the amputees are advised to sleep with their artificial limbs.[30]

Yet the failure of such prophylactics is always imminent, as they (and the woman they help make visible) become the stuff of nightmares. Cindy Sherman explores the reversion of the fetish to the phobic object in her recent work with the detritus of femininity (dropped compacts, half-eaten candy, oozing makeup), monstrous hybrid figures with snouts and other grotesqueries, and feminine

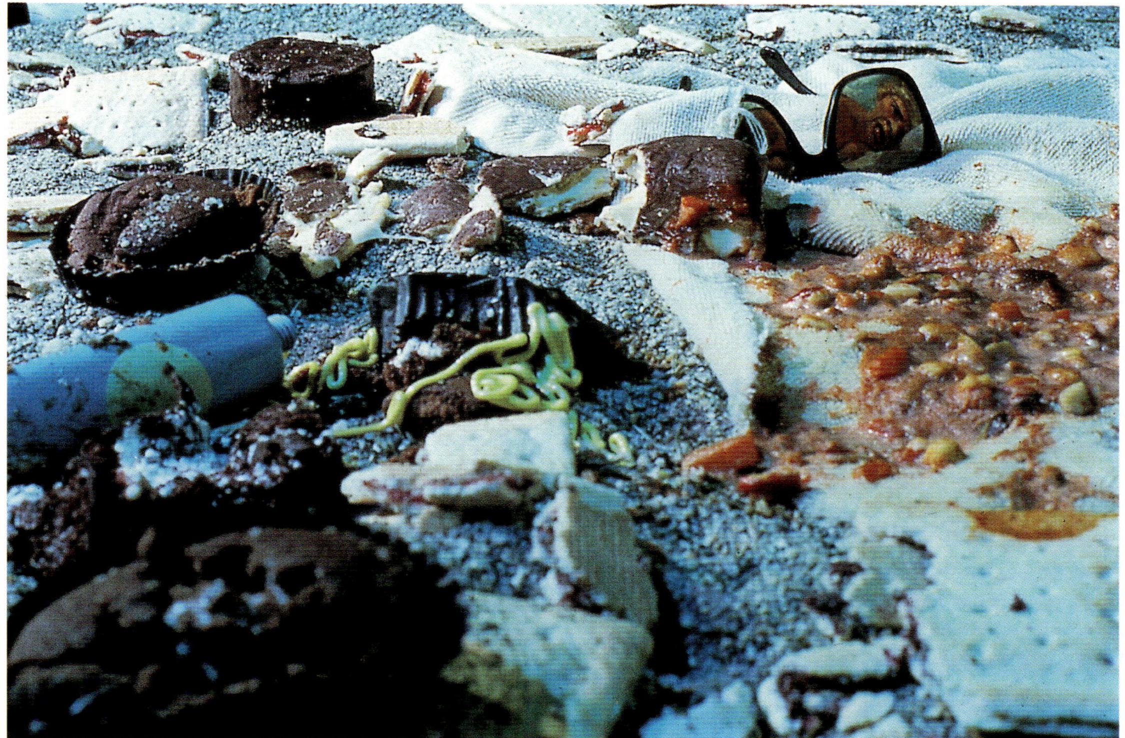

Cindy Sherman
Untitled, #175, 1987
Color photograph,
47½ x 71½ inches (120.7 x 181.6 cm)
Courtesy of the artist and
Metro Pictures, New York

puppets and rubber body parts, all of which substitute for the woman to whom they allude, who is otherwise absent. The feminine roles or poses Sherman performs in her earlier *Untitled Film Stills* (1977–80) function similarly. There is something uncanny about them, not despite but because of their familiarity. The woman is her own double and ours, at once a lifeless automaton compelled to mechanically repeat a feminine gesture or stereotype and a living being who represents "all our suppressed acts of volition which nourish in us the illusion of Free Will," as Freud says of the doppelgänger.[31] What desires do her clichés conceal or, more terrible still, express? These masquerades evoke all the ambivalence a fetish does because they function as such, especially in the stolen moment of a photograph. As Metz explains, photography is predisposed to function fetishistically because of its theft of life itself from its movement in and of time, which is suggested by the photo's two key features, "smallness [of temporal size], possibility of a lingering look."[32] Photographs frame and immobilize something we want to see that blocks out something we are afraid to see, something any movement, as the mark of time and life, might reveal. We keep the photographic image in our hearts and wallets to screen us from what we fear: the death and destruction toward which we are headed and for which, in fact, we also wish, the loss of the whole and wholly lovable self that woman's feminine difference all too often signifies in a sexist culture.

Racial difference, too, signifies ambiguously, even in the minstrel performance whose caricatures are intended to annul the threat an oppressed group might represent. According to Rogin, in minstrelsy, "Black mimicry, black performance, the black mask, the technique by which the subjugated group kept its distance and mocked its oppressor, was itself expropriated and made into a blackface performance for whites."[33] Yet minstrelsy, like assimilation, could never finally secure white mastery because in both the identity of the performer and the spectator remains in question. In the phrase of postcolonial-studies scholar Homi Bhabha, they are "not quite/not white,"[34] like the subjects of colonial mimicry. In such mimicry there is at once a resemblance and a difference, each of which menaces the colonizer's identity. How secure is "whiteness" if others can perform it well—and what are they playing at when they fail to do so? Conversely, if minstrels can pass for what they are not, if they are "passed" by those who are fooled by their performances, are they really what they think they are? In *My Geisha* (Jack Cardiff, 1962), Shirley MacLaine becomes what she believes she is only pretending to be, a submissive woman who puts men first, through her performance of a stereotype of

Japanese feminine passivity, which she initially imitated to confirm her superiority over both her male dupes and the "real" geishas. Who is fooling whom, who is assimilating whom, in these masquerades prompted by cross-cultural exchanges? At once parody and imitation they threaten the racial difference they constitute. Blackface is not only racist caricature but hip-hop identification, the "wigger" the white parents of TV talk shows fear their teenager is becoming, whose style is as much a rebuke to adult values as was that of the hipster (Norman Mailer's "white negro") of an earlier generation. Whiteface is both the passing of the tragic mulatta and mulatto (their lives and deaths chronicled by William Faulkner, Fannie Hurst, and Nella Larsen, among others), and the parodies of Whoopi Goldberg, Eddie Murphy, and some of the voguers of *Paris Is Burning*, who like most female impersonators poke fun at what they love (camp is the in/sincerest form of flattery). I can never be certain of the meaning of the mimicry of the other who is not quite not me because contrary to the Platonic dictum, appearances are not sufficiently deceiving. We are not taken in by them; if the other puts on a good show, we suspect he or she is up to something offstage. Freud illustrates this paradox with the joke about the man who wonders why his friend has told him he is going to Cracow so he will think the destination is Lemberg when it really is Cracow.[35]

Because identities are performative social constructions, they cannot be safeguarded. The signifiers of race or gender can be stolen, counterfeited, or serve as another currency altogether, as historian Barbara Fields reveals in a probably apocryphal but nevertheless telling story about an American journalist's interview with the late Papa Doc Duvalier of Haiti. Inquiring what proportion of the Haitian population was white, the journalist was very surprised to learn it was as high as ninety-eight percent and repeated the question to be certain Duvalier had heard it correctly. "Struggling to make sense of this incredible piece of information," Fields writes,

> *the American finally asked Duvalier: "How do you define white?" Duvalier answered the question with a question: "How do you define black in your country?" Receiving the explanation that in the United States anyone with any black blood was considered black, Duvalier nodded and said, "Well, that's the way we define white in my country."*[36]

Just as it is possible to be black in one country and white in another, one can also change sex by crossing a border, as did transsexual Renée Richards. She was able to compete as a woman in European tennis tournaments during the same period she was defined as a man by the U.S. Tennis Association and the Women's Tennis Association and so denied permission to play in the women's U.S. Open.

Border crossings skew identity and the laws that would determine them. We serve different masters in different times and places, which makes tricksters of us all as our identities are revised and we die again into a new picture, another obituary, in which we are seen in a different light. Yet where is our agency in this? It seems we cannot resist being shot and framed for something—or someone—we did not "do." We are abducted and alienated from ourselves by the other's mastery, to which the death drive submits us, silenced by the obituary in which the other's redemption, rather than our own, is at stake as our life is chronicled. "For every image of the past that is not recognized by the present as one of its own concerns threatens to disappear irretrievably," Benjamin writes in the fifth of the "Theses on the Philosophy of History."[37] We all make ourselves through what we make of others as they make something of us in a relationship that is bilateral but not reciprocal, since the partners are neither complements nor equivalents. The violence of these appropriations, however mutual, is necessarily felt as such. The gaze of the other appears to rob us of our self-image; it steals the very soul we discover only in its reflection. Perhaps there is no better contemporary example of this than the star and his or her fans, whose worship is the source of the star's brilliance. Paradoxically, their love deprives the star of the "aura" it creates, that "unique phenomenon of a distance" things once had before they were subject to mechanical reproduction, according to Benjamin,[38] as are stars and other mass-produced commodities. The star is always dying into the lifeless trademark fans both demand and reject; the star must be continually reinvented as "new and improved" in order to rekindle the flames of devotion that are the star's life itself burning out.

Stars and their fans are alter egos, binary companions exerting a deadly attraction on one another, as Michael Jackson's music video *Speed Demon* (1989) reveals. In it, Jackson declares war on the commodified self that belongs to his fans, who would trap him in his trademark "image." He disguises himself in a rabbit outfit to escape his admirers, who aggressively stalk him wherever he goes, then morphs into several other figures (something Jackson has done in "real life" through his multiple surgeries) before finally having a showdown with himself in a dueling dance of Jackson representations: the trademark Jackson "look" and the disguise that according to Willis is actually Brer Rabbit, a trickster figure of black folk culture. As Willis and many other cultural theorists see it, the commodity fetish, like the sexual fetish, screens us from difference, both the other's and our own, which our double or alter ego represents, because "all moments and modes are merely incorporated into its infinite seriality."[39] Willis argues that in *Speed Demon* we do not get another mechanical reproduction of a slightly "new and improved" Jackson minstrel figure who sells us a "difference" that is really the same, negating the explosive potential inherent in transformation."[40] Instead, for her, Brer Rabbit figures the resistance to the black commodification that began with slavery and included minstrelsy.

However, Jackson's trickster is actually another trademark, for he is also Bugs Bunny and the Brer Rabbit of the Uncle Remus tales, like minstrelsy commodifications of black culture for white audiences. The rabbit is no more authentically black than the Jackson image is; both are cultural masks, and even the gesture of defiance is the spectacle staged for a price: the "moonwalk" dance as a modern update of the minstrel's (as Juba's was an imitation of white imitations of his). Willis herself later says the rabbit is Jackson's "exaggerated, folksy, blackface alter ego,"[41] undermining the authenticity she has assigned it. In *Speed Demon*, the minstrel merely moves from mask to mask, immobilized in none of them. The commodity fetish splits into the black vernacular and mass-mediated forms—but which is which if none are finally authentic? Having begun with the assumption that "Michael Jackson" is a trademark in which a black man is alienated, Willis closes by refiguring that image as his "self" and transferring alienation to the trickster mask he dons to escape it, a reversal symptomatic of her desire for an authentic self, one existing before or beyond the commodity and the gaze of the paying spectator.

Willis's gesture denies the ambiguity of the Jackson video, of Jackson himself, and of all commodity fetishes—including "art"—which are sites of struggle over meaning, identity, and desire. As Lacan explains, "The human subject, the subject of the desire that is the essence of man . . . knows how to play with the mask as that beyond which there is the gaze"[42] as a cause of desire, which is that portion of the death drive unsatisfied by whatever it is we see in or show to the other. It makes for a relationship in which something is always lacking, as the other finds us "wanting" (in both senses of the word). Identities are limited, while the drive is boundless; it would tear off all the masks and resolve the differences between self and other by escaping identity and representation altogether. Willis argues that it is just such a desire that motivates Jackson's surgical reconstructions. He is morphing into something amorphous, something whose androgynous and "beige" qualities homogenize the gender and racial differences that are a source of social tension in the United States today. As Willis explains, Jackson resolves these conflicts through the "magical erasure"[43] of difference itself. In effect, he performs a quasi-Hegelian synthesis that seems like a "queer" update of the "melting pot" metaphor for America.

It is just this amorphous quality of the "queer" to which many feminist, lesbian, and gay scholars object. They are critical of a subject like Buffalo Bill, who, in Hannibal Lecter's view, would posit a self beyond the boundaries and border crossings we associate with identities and their transgression. Buffalo Bill is neither homosexual nor transsexual but instead desires to escape gender altogether, to be "*horsexe*" (outside sex), "*toujours ailleurs*" (always somewhere else), as psychoanalyst Catherine Millot claims all transsexuals do, given the fantasies she finds they share of being secret agents in the camp of the other, perpetually in disguise, at once both sexes and neither.[44] We see a similar wish to escape the limitations of having an identity in Marjorie Garber's assertion that the transvestite is a third term beyond sexual difference as a binary construct,[45] and in African Americanist scholar Michael Awkward's praise of Michael Jackson for the androgynous beige morphing that troubles Willis. According to Awkward, Jackson is both a "transracial" hybrid[46] and a transvestite who resists being reduced to a "single color" or sex.[47] Jacques Derrida and Michel Foucault also share this desire for a reification and personification of what Garber has termed "category crisis"[48] and offer the hermaphrodite as their counterpart to the transvestite and transracial hybrid. In Herculine Barbin, the nineteenth-century French medical curiosity whose case he published, Foucault discovers and celebrates "the happy limbo of a non-identity,"[49] which for Barbin proved unlivable (s/he eventually committed suicide). In *Spurs: Nietzsche's Style*, Derrida dreams of "the hermaphroditic spur (*éperon*) of a phallus"[50] that would "invaginate" itself for the Neitzschean man "becoming woman," who plays with Truth, including the truth of gender, as a fetish like a woman's veil, beneath which there is proof neither of castration, nor anticastration. Truth is instead in style itself, which hides nothing.

Critics of queer theory and identity resist these utopian impulses to "fix" a self-difference that undoes identity. They have decried in particular a queer theory that posits gender as stable and unified, while it celebrates sexuality as queer, ambiguous, and changing. When queer theory and queer subjects represent themselves in terms of a liberating transcendence of confinement and the completion of more limited critical identities and projects (such as feminism), they replicate the masculinism and sexism they would supercede. Feminist theorist Biddy Martin expresses her concern about such queer vanguardism:

> *I am worried about the occasions when antifoundationalist celebrations of queerness rely on their own projections of fixity, constraint, or subjection onto a fixed ground, often onto feminism or the female body, in relation to which queer sexualities become figural, performative, playful and fun. In the process, the female body appears to become its own trap, and the operations of misogyny disappear from view.*[51]

Martin emphasizes that unmasking gender performativity does not do away with it; a queer theory in which sexuality displaces gender cannot account for the enduring power of gender.[52] Articulating a similar complaint about the "queer," feminist philosopher Elizabeth Grosz and literary theorist Leo Bersani note that unless they work with a concept of sexual difference, queers cannot do justice to homosexual specificity, which Grosz and Bersani define as same-sex object choice.[53] Butler shares these reservations, reminding us that a theory of sexuality without gender cannot account for the practices of some of the sexual minorities queer studies would wish to address, including sex workers and transsexuals.[54]

"Implicit in these constructions of queerness, I fear, is the lure of an existence without limit, without bodies or psyches,"[55] Martin writes. Like the vampire, the queer who has transcended identity has no reflection, no alter ego as a love object mirroring a lovable self. Such a queer is Hegel's "Absolute Spirit" of desire, having purged it of any imaginary demands for love. Beyond love and self-love, sublimating the dross of particular objects whose fascinations impede the death drive's self-realization, including the ego as a projection of the body, queer desire becomes pure Thanatos, an energy liberated from the erotic ties that bind, which it aggressively dissolves. When the death drive is realized, the libidinal energy captivated by the image we love as ourselves is released into entropic decay and the inhuman chemistry that ultimately drives desire.

"Do I have to give up me to be loved by you?" asks Kruger's photomontage *Heart (Do I have to give up me to be loved by you?)* (1988). The question appears over an extreme close-up of myocardial tissue, which might signify either the less than human meat to which the "I" has been reduced by the other, the "you." However, it might also signify the living essence of the self that is behind all the masks the "I" assumes, beyond the narcissism in desire that has attached us to the human form we receive from the other, that lovable self in which our love alienates us. For, as feminist film scholar Kaja Silverman observes, "Although at the deepest recesses of its psyche the subject has neither identity nor nameable desire, the fantasmatic and the *moi* [the ego] together work to articulate a mythic but determining vision of each."[56] Thanatos is always fused with Eros, according to Freud: "It escapes detection unless its presence is betrayed by its being alloyed with eros."[57] The death drive is the aggressive impulse in any desire. It is directed against those we love, not just those we hate, destroying and renewing all relationships and identities (we make ourselves over both when we are in love and when we are over it, done with trying to be what the other wanted).

Paradoxically, however, the death drive's negativity also queers its own identity. In saying "no" even to its no, Thanatos affirms something it preserves for a future negation, which at once masks and expresses it: life itself. The death drive has no authentic face. It is the rending and rendering of the face of desire that Eros assumes, a death mask. Death must appear through a living desire, which we only know through what signifies it: a pressure or tension in an erotogenic zone, an aim or action to relieve it, and an object choice that facilitates that aim, all of which figure in fantasy as the figure or representation of desire. "*Desire itself is a defence against desire*," Slavoj Zizek explains; "the desire structured through fantasy is a defence against . . . this 'pure', trans-phantasmatic

Barbara Kruger
Heart (Do I have to give up me to be loved by you?), 1988
Photographic silkscreen on vinyl, 111½ x 111½ inches (283.2 x 283.2 cm)
Collection of Emily Fisher Landau, Courtesy of Mary Boone Gallery, New York

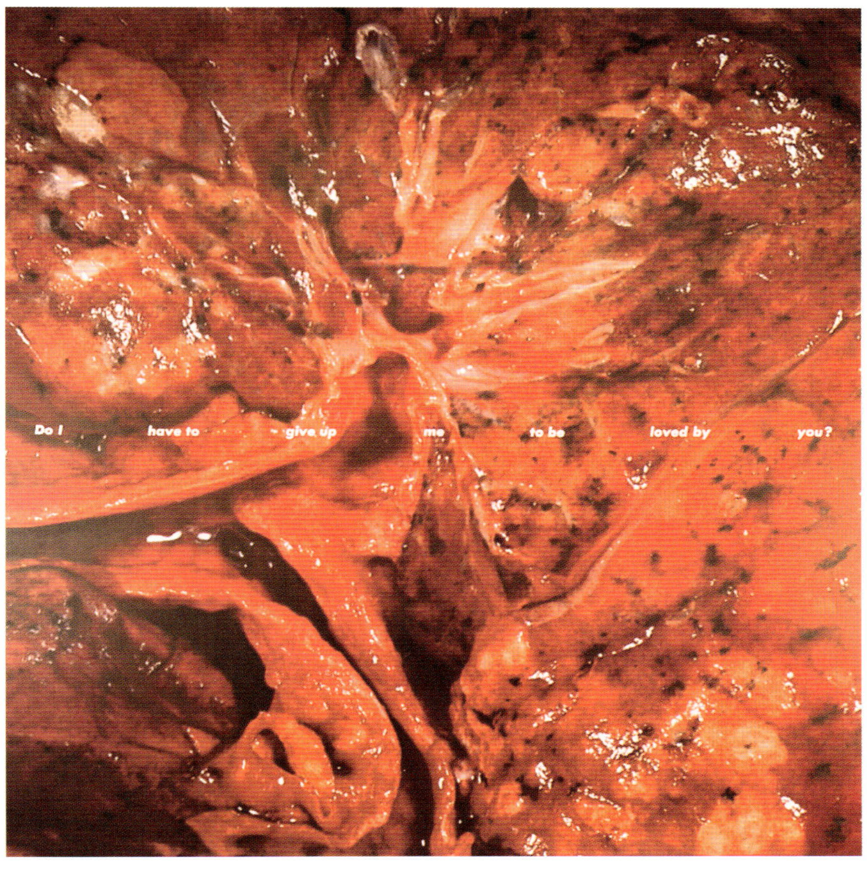

desire (i.e. the 'death drive' in its pure form)."[58] Desire is alienated in life and representation, yet only exists through them as their disruption, something Marcel Duchamp conveys when he renames himself Rrose Sélavy, or "*éros c'est la vie*" (eros that is life). The desire that is not quite visible in him as Marcel Duchamp or even in his transvestic feminine alter ego, the other figure or face he assumes, expresses itself as the extra "r" that transforms Rose into "eros" (pronounced "R-rose" in French), the repeated *R* of Stein's repeated roses in her circular rose poem. The sound of this *R* breaks through "the mortiferous layer of the pose,"[59] as Barthes explains of the noise of the camera.

For Stein, too, the noise of the apparatus of representation resurrects the thing entombed in the dead sign, cracking its fetishistic carapace. "Rose is a rose is a rose is a rose," Stein writes, framing a hole with the edges of the letters whose repetitions, like an incantation, would charm the thing out of the nothing they shape. That zero renews the mystery of being: "I think that in that line the rose is red for the first time in English poetry for a hundred years,"[60] she asserts. Seeking a language of verbs without the nouns that stifle the being of things, a "continuous present" that would be the language of pure being rather than the lifeless posturing of signs, Stein would refuse the simulations and sarcophagi in which the performative becomes a pale reflection of its own doing, a citation or representation of what it promises to create. Painters and sculptors too have dreamed of an art of gestures purged of representation, striving for a godlike originality in which the artist creatively transcends the codes of the medium in an act of authentic self-expression. The latex and foam "pours" of Lynda Benglis in the late 1960s and early 1970s constitute one such effort of pure performativity.

But there is no pure performative that is not always already a citation, as Derrida argues in his critique of J. L. Austin's speech act theory:

> *For, finally, is not what Austin excludes as anomalous, exceptional, "non-serious," that is* citation *(on the stage, in a poem, or in a soliloquy), the determined modification of a general citationality—or rather, a general iterability—without which there would not even be a "successful" performative? Such that—a paradoxical, but inevitable consequence—a successful performative is necessarily an "impure" performative, to use the word that Austin will employ later on when he recognizes that there is no "pure" performative.*[61]

We are all minstrels. There is at once self-expression and self-alienation in our self-images and the love objects that help define them. The voices of the dead speak through us. We are condemned to use their words to represent the desire that we are, which is figured as the sense of something behind our masks, or the difference between them, the death we mask with life and its roles and fetishes.

Notes

1. Dinos and Jake Chapman, *Chapmanworld* (London: Institute of Contemporary Arts, 1996), p 7.
2. Gertrude Stein, "Sacred Emily" (1913), in *Geography and Plays* (1922; New York: Something Else Press, 1968), p. 187.
3. Frank Kermode, *The Sense of an Ending: Studies in the Theory of Fiction* (1967; Oxford: Oxford University Press, 1981), p. 7.
4. Stein, "Portraits and Repetition," in Stein, *Lectures in America* (New York: Random House, 1935), p. 181.
5. Walter Benjamin, "The Storyteller: Reflections on the Works of Nikolai Leskov" (1936), in Benjamin, *Illuminations*, ed. Hannah Arendt, trans. Harry Zohn (New York: Schocken Books, 1969), pp. 100–01.
6. Roland Barthes, *Camera Lucida: Reflections on Photography* (1980), trans. Richard Howard (New York: Hill and Wang, 1981), p. 14.
7. Christian Metz, "Photography and Fetish," in Carol Squiers, ed., *The Critical Image: Essays on Contemporary Photography* (Seattle: Bay Press, 1990), p. 158.
8. "Gallery of Glory: A Portfolio by Annie Leibovitz," *Time*, July 22, 1996, p. 79.
9. Barthes, *Camera Lucida*, p. 13.
10. Richard Avedon, "Borrowed Dogs," in Ben Sonnenberg, ed., *Performance and Reality: Essays from Grand Street* (New Brunswick, N.J.: Rutgers University Press, 1989), p. 16.
11. Barthes, *Camera Lucida*, p. 14.
12. Rosalind Krauss, "A Note on Photography and the Simulacral," in Squiers, ed., *The Critical Image*, p. 22.
13. Barthes, *Camera Lucida*, p. 14.
14. Jacques Lacan, *The Four Fundamental Concepts of Psycho-Analysis* (1973), trans. Alan Sheridan (New York: W. W. Norton, 1978), p. 104.
15. John Tagg, *The Burden of Representation: Essays on Photographies and Histories* (Amherst: University of Massachusetts Press, 1988), pp. 34–59.
16. Pierre Bourdieu, *Un Art moyen: Essai sur les usages sociaux de la photographie* (Paris: Editions de Minuit, 1965), p. 48.
17. Eugénie Lemoine-Luccioni, *La Robe: Essai psychanalytique sur le vêtement* (Paris: Editions du Seuil, 1983), p. 117.
18. Sigmund Freud, "Fetishism" (1927), in Freud, *Sexuality and the Psychology of Love*, ed. Philip Rieff, trans. Joan Riviere (New York: Collier Books, 1963), p. 219.
19. Peggy Phelan, *Unmarked: The Politics of Performance* (New York: Routledge, 1993), p. 95.
20. Eric Lott, *Love and Theft: Blackface Minstrelsy and the American Working Class* (Oxford: Oxford University Press, 1993), p. 39.
21. Ibid., p. 48.
22. Ibid., p. 46.
23. Susan Willis, "I Want the Black One: Is There a Place for Afro-American Culture in Commodity Culture?" in Willis, *A Primer for Daily Life* (London: Routledge, 1991), p. 126.
24. Michael Rogin, "'Democracy and Burnt Cork': The End of Blackface, the Beginning of Civil Rights," *Representations* 46 (spring 1994), p. 8.
25. Judith Butler, *Bodies that Matter: On the Discursive Limits of Sex* (New York: Routledge, 1993), p. 225.
26. Ibid., pp. 225–26.
27. Talcott Parsons, *The Social System* (Glencoe, Ill.: Free Press, 1951).
28. Benjamin, "Theses on the Philosophy of History" (1940, published 1950), in Benjamin, *Illuminations*, p. 253.
29. Lacan, "The Meaning of the Phallus" (1966), in Juliet Mitchell and Jacqueline Rose, eds., *Feminine Sexuality: Jacques Lacan and the école freudienne*, trans. Jacqueline Rose (New York: W. W. Norton, 1982), pp. 225–46.
30. Elaine Scarry, "The Merging of Bodies and Artifacts in the Social Contract," in Gretchen Bender and Timothy Druckrey, eds., *Culture on the Brink: Ideologies of Technology* (Seattle: Bay Press, 1994), p. 95.
31. Freud, "The 'Uncanny'" (1919), in Freud, *On Creativity and the Unconscious: Papers on the Psychology of Art, Literature, Love, Religion*, ed. Benjamin Nelson, trans. Alix Strachey (New York: Harper Torchbooks, 1958), p. 142.
32. Metz, "Photography and Fetish," p. 155.
33. Rogin, "'Democracy and Burnt Cork'," p. 8.
34. Homi Bhabha, "Of Mimicry and Man: The Ambivalence of Colonial Discourse," *October*, no. 28 (spring 1984), p. 132.
35. Freud, *Jokes and Their Relation to the Unconscious* (1905), ed. and trans. James Strachey (New York: W. W. Norton, 1963), p. 115.
36. Barbara Fields, "Ideology and Race in American History," in J. Morgan Kousser and James McPherson, eds., *Region, Race, and Reconstruction: Essays in Honor of C. Vann Woodward* (Oxford: Oxford University Press, 1982), p. 146.
37. Benjamin, "Theses on the Philosophy of History," p. 255.
38. Benjamin, "The Work of Art in the Age of Mechanical Reproduction" (1936), in Benjamin, *Illuminations*, p. 222.
39. Willis, "I Want the Black One," p. 123.
40. Ibid.
41. Ibid.
42. Lacan, *The Four Fundamental Concepts of Psycho-Analysis*, p. 107.
43. Willis, "I Want the Black One," p. 120.
44. Catherine Millot, *Horsexe: Essai sur le transsexualisme* (Paris: Point Hors Ligne, 1983), p. 61.
45. Marjorie Garber, *Vested Interests: Cross-Dressing & Cultural Anxiety* (New York: Routledge, 1992), p. 16.
46. Michael Awkward, *Negotiating Difference: Race, Gender, and the Politics of Positionality* (Chicago: University of Chicago Press, 1995), p. 186.
47. Ibid., p. 190.
48. Garber, *Vested Interests*, pp. 16–17.
49. Michel Foucault, "Introduction," in Herculine Barbin, *Herculine Barbin: Being the Recently Discovered Memoirs of a Nineteenth-Century French Hermaphrodite* (1978), trans. Richard McDougall (New York: Pantheon Books, 1980), p. xiii.
50. Jacques Derrida, *Spurs: Nietzsche's Style* (1978), trans. Barbara Harlow (Chicago: University of Chicago Press, 1979), p. 129.
51. Biddy Martin, "Sexualities without Genders and Other Queer Utopias," *diacritics* 24, nos. 2–3 (summer–fall 1994), p. 104.
52. Martin, "Extraordinary Homosexuals," *More Gender Trouble: Feminism Meets Queer Theory*, special issue of *differences* 6, nos. 2–3 (summer–fall 1994), pp. 101–02.
53. Elizabeth Grosz, "Experimental Desire: Rethinking Queer Subjectivity," in Joan Copjec, ed., *Supposing the Subject* (London: Verso, 1994), p. 14; and Leo Bersani, *Homos* (Cambridge, Mass.: Harvard University Press, 1985), p. 58.
54. Butler, "Against Proper Objects," *More Gender Trouble*, p. 11.
55. Martin, "Extraordinary Homosexuals," p. 123.
56. Kaja Silverman, *Male Subjectivity at the Margins* (New York: Routledge, 1992), pp. 5–6.
57. Freud, *Civilization and Its Discontents* (1930), ed. and trans. James Strachey (New York: W. W. Norton, 1961), p. 81.
58. Slavoj Zizek, *The Sublime Object of Ideology* (London: Verso, 1989), p. 118.
59. Barthes, *Camera Lucida*, p. 15.
60. Stein, *Writings and Lectures* 1911–1945, ed. Patricia Meyrowitz (London: Owen, 1967), p. 7.
61. Derrida, "Signature Event Context," in Derrida, *Margins of Philosophy* (1972), trans. Alan Bass (Chicago: University of Chicago Press, 1982), p. 325.

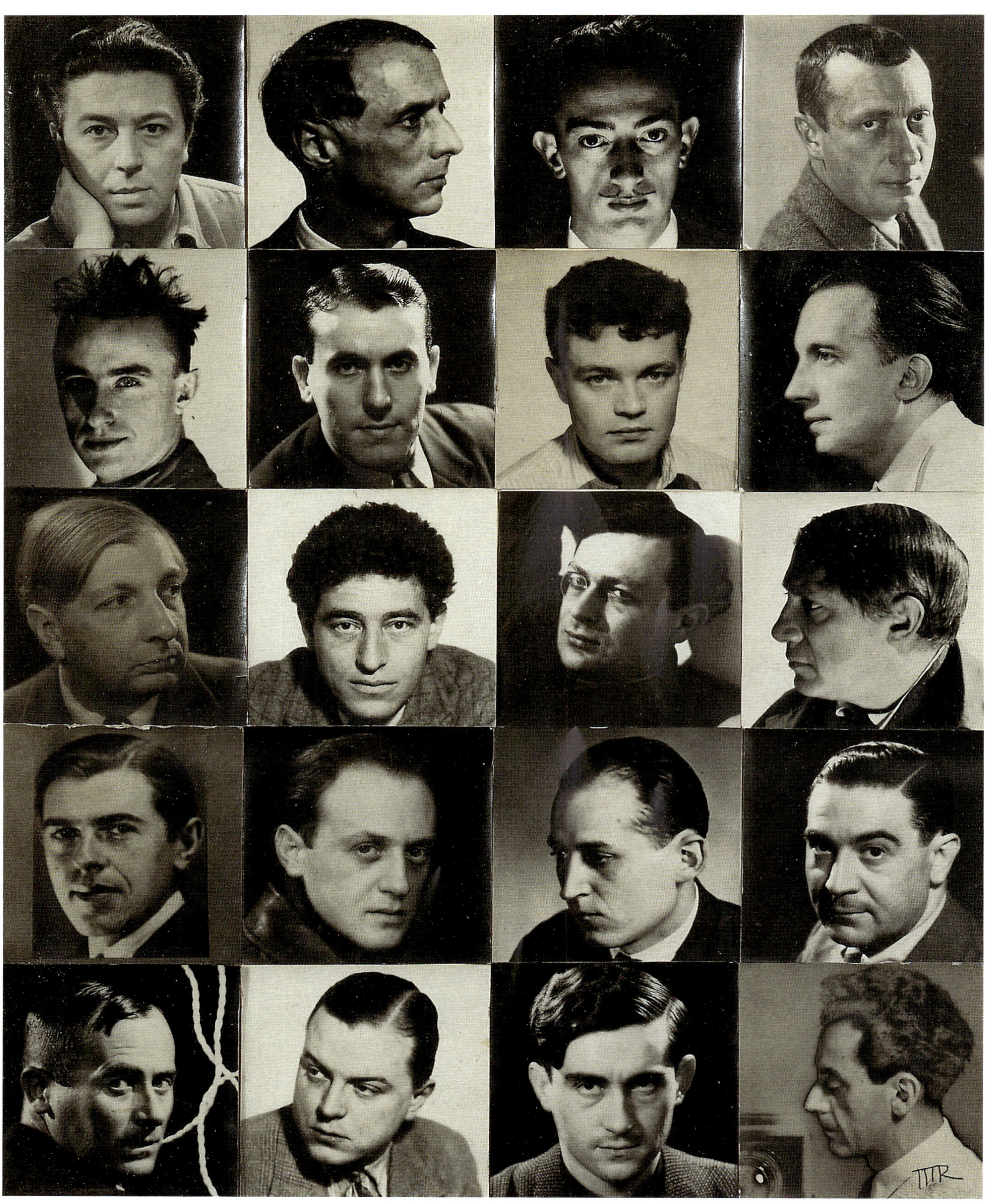

Man Ray
Surrealist Chessboard (*L'Echiquier surréaliste*), 1928
Photomontage of twenty vintage photographs, 18 ⅛ x 11 ⅞ inches (46 x 30.2 cm)
Arturo Schwarz Collection, Milan

Femininities-Masquerades

SARAH WILSON

The time may have come to valorize women's ideas at the expense of men's, whose bankruptcy has achieved a tumultuous climax today.
ANDRÉ BRETON, *Arcane 17* (Quebec), 1944

To those of you who are women this will not apply—you are yourselves the problem.
SIGMUND FREUD, "Femininity," 1933

Our Fin-de-Siècle

Orlando, Virginia Woolf's transsexual heroine, stands at a temporal and cultural crossroads—she looks back in her various guises to the past; she anticipates our future.[1] In France, too, transsexual stories go back to Joan of Arc, man-maid of Orleans, and are reincarnated in the present in the performance artist Orlan. Two terrains whose paths cross: sexual difference, cultural difference. All have their being under the aegis of patriarchy and the conflict of essence versus existence, "nature or nurture." "One is not born but rather becomes, a woman," as Simone de Beauvoir wrote.[2] This is a history whose origins begin neither in our century nor in the age of chivalry but in fantasy as the aftermath of the revolution against a legendary matriarchy. There, at least, a vision of a female Golden Age existed.[3] The eternal sex war represented in art and literature is a less glorious tale.[4]

In etymology, even before mythology, woman has been placed on the side of evil: on the garter of Niki de Saint-Phalle's *Hon/Elle* (*Hon/She*, 1966) is written "*Honi soi qui mal y pense*" (Evil to him who evil thinks), the motto of the Order of the Garter. The catalogue for the London exhibition *Bad Girls* tells us that the Middle English word "baeddel" means "*homo utriusque, hermaphrodita*" and that its derivative "baedling" may be defined as "effeminate fellow, womanish man."[5] Likewise, *féminisme*, which entered the French language in 1837, had a disturbing twin meaning: on the one hand, it indicated the political movement to acquire rights for women, including enfranchisement, but, alternatively, it defined "the aspect of a male individual who presents certain female secondary sexual characteristics," a state thought to be especially dangerous for the male intellectual or artist. (So Charles Baudelaire's *Les Fleurs du mal* becomes *Les Fleurs du mâle*.[6]) It was not until the late nineteenth century that the French word *artiste* acquired a possible resonance for either sex.

The primordial subject of the male artist has been the female nude, a tradition ratified by the institutions of academy and salon as well as the "professions" of model and prostitute (Edouard Manet's Olympia, Emile Zola's Nana, Honoré de Balzac's Belle Noiseuse). Yet implicit in his own professionalism is the artist's capacity for *Bovaryisme* (Gustave Flaubert's "*Madame Bovary, c'est moi*"), for an identification with that flesh, a penetrating of that female anatomy, in order to understand

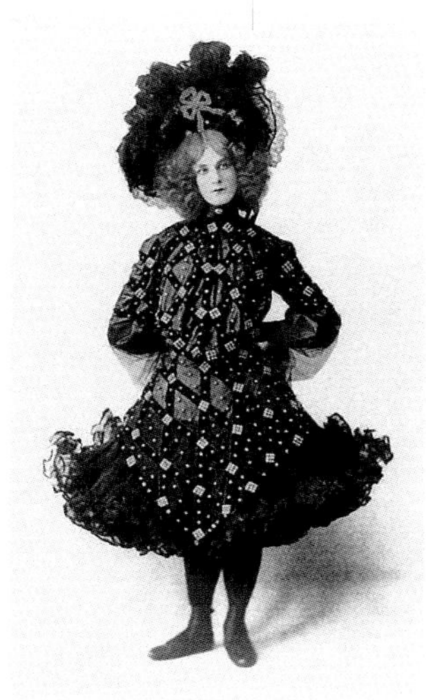

Anonymous
The Man with the Diamond Dress, 1920
Gelatin-silver print
Courtesy of the Library of Congress, Washington, D.C.

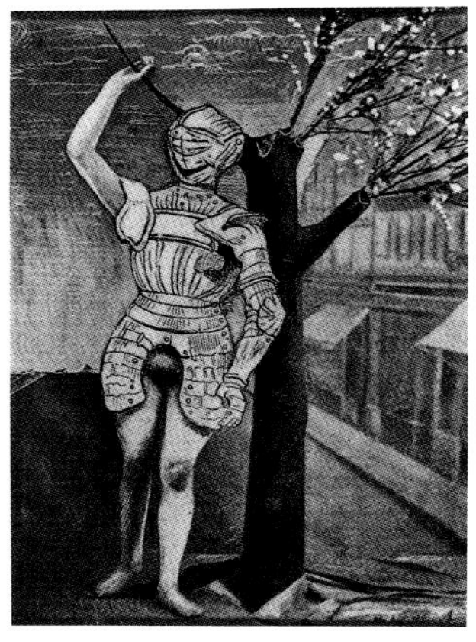

Max Ernst
Vanity Fair, 1920
Collage with photograph, gouache, and india ink, 5 15/16 x 4 1/8 inches (15 x 10.5 cm)
Collection of Morris Philipson, New York

from within its contours, softness, thoughts. His love of and desire for this female created object is none other than a sign, an extension of himself and his prowess. Next to *Bovaryisme* stands the myth of Pygmalion: the artist's kiss of life symbolizing his hermaphroditic self-sufficiency. Constantin Brancusi's phallic, polished *Princesse X* (1916) is the perfect exemplar. Sexual cross-identification is a complex affair, wherein gender itself may be defined as a melancholic structure. The body and the visage of woman is created by the male artist as a mask; a mask that Judith Butler, rephrasing Lacan, describes, in *Gender Trouble,* as "part of the incorporative strategy of melancholy, the taking on of attributes of the object/Other that is lost, where loss is a consequence of a refusal of love."[7]

The constructs and masks of masculinity, explored through the expanding field of gender studies, now qualify all constructions of patriarchy, both political and intellectual. Yet our fin-de-siècle mirrors its precursor: on the threshold of a new century our gaze is transfixed, Janus-like, on the past as well as the future. The proliferation of publications in this field today finds both its origins and its reflection in the explosion of nineteenth-century sexology and its impact on contemporaneous criminal, medical, nascent psychoanalytic, literary, and pornographic discourses—the very matrices of the birth of modernism.

Such texts as Balzac's *Sarrazine* (1830), Théophile Gautier's *Mademoiselle de Maupin* (1835), Arthur Schopenhauer's *Uber die Weiber* (Of woman, 1851), and Jules Michelet's *La Femme* (1859), to Rachilde's *Monsieur Venus* and Joris-Karl Huysmans's *A Rebours* (both 1884), Oscar Wilde's *The Picture of Dorian Gray,* and Joséphin Peladin's *Le Gynandre* (both 1891), found their reflections in Symbolist and decadent painting and sculpture and, later, in the new realms of photography and cinema. These texts posit a world of gender indeterminacy that has found its response not only in the work of Marcel Duchamp or Woolf, in Roland Barthes's *S/Z* (1970) or Michel Foucault's study of Herculine Barbin (1978), but also in the popular culture of today, including such films as *Tootsie* (Sydney Pollack, 1982), *Victor/Victoria* (Blake Edwards, 1982), and *Yentl* (Barbra Streisand, 1983).[8]

Beyond or beneath the erotic or the pornographic, it is the problem of differentiation, of gender indeterminacy and its many masks, that lies at the core of this exhibition. For both sexes within patriarchy, the feminine becomes prioritized as the site of masquerade. And beyond personal guises and disguises, one is dealing with serious issues—love, hate, and death. Looking back again to the gestation of the modern (in the womb of Olympe de Gouges, perhaps, guillotined for promoting the rights of woman?[9]), what has been called "gender trouble" started to perturb the linearity of first Cartesian, then Darwinian thought, of Schopenhauerian pessimism and its aftermath. Friedrich Nietzsche's profound misogyny was reflected in the writings of Otto Weiniger and the succession of earnest sexologists and degeneracy theorists who came after him; their researches were, subsequently, subsumed in both the grand Freudian narrative of this century and, alas, the racial theories of fascism.[10] The "psychological 'gynecide' advocated by the turn of the century male intellectual avant-garde" came first.[11] But if literal gynecide was unthinkable, it only took a few decades for genocide to be industrialized; the individual and mass psychotic structures that facilitated this event irrevocably qualify Sigmund Freud's oedipal paradigms and his "norms."[12]

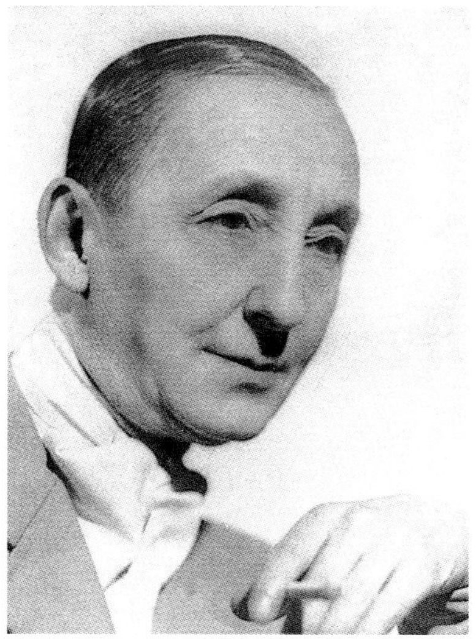

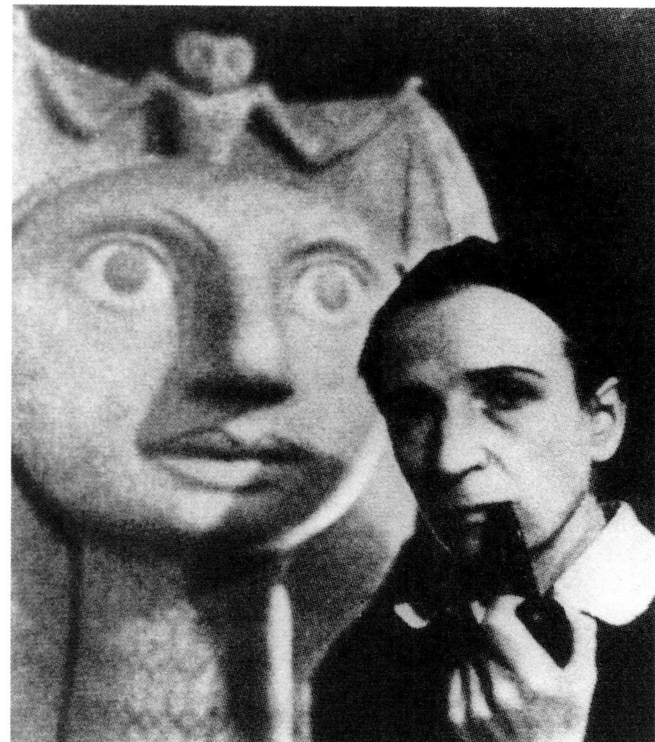

Marlow Moss
Courtesy of Courtauld Institute of Art Witt Library, London

Hans Anton Prinner
Reproduced in *View* 6, no. 1 (February 1946), p. 27

Amazons/Américaines

Cubism only tentatively restored the empiricism of the grid, quavering under the sexually inscrutable gaze of Pablo Picasso's Michaelangelesque *demoiselles d'Avignon*, at a time when Parisian analyses of woman, conflating the "scientific" with the frankly pornographic, demonstrated a profound malaise.[13] Such was Dr. Caufeynon's *Histoire de la femme, son corps, ses organes, son développement au physique et au moral, ses séductions, ses attraits, ses aptitudes à l'amour, ses vices, ses aberrations sexuelles, saphisme, nymphomanie, clitorisme, les déséquilibres de l'amour, inversion sexuelle, etc., etc.* (History of woman, her body, her organs, her physical and moral development, her seductive features, her attractions, her propensities for love, her vices, her sexual aberrations, sapphism, nymphomania, clitorism, perturbations in love, sexual inversion, etc., etc., 1904).[14] His publication anticipated the translations in France, in 1909, of Havelock Ellis's *Sexual Inversion* (1909) and, in 1910, of Magnus Hirschfeld's *Die Transvestiten* (1910). Hirschfeld's *Sexualpathologie* (1917–20), translated in 1918, contained additional transsexual/transvestite case histories. The androgyne entered Cubism with Marc Chagall and metamorphosed as the double figure of Terence/Thérèse, a character in Guillaume Apollinaire's music-hall farce *Les Mamelles de Tiresias* (The breasts of Tiresias, 1917), elevating the genre to the avant-garde with a piquant, pronatalist topicality.

World War I—whose mechanization of battle brought shell shock and mass death for men—created a polarization of sexual roles in Europe. Yet this polarization only ratified fearful nineteenth-century stereotypes, carrying them more powerfully into the twentieth century, as the "the girls who stayed at home" were neglected for more fantasmatic images of the great (patriotic) mother.[15] France, in 1918, did not yet know the "new woman"; with New York Dada, the problem of the crossing of sexual difference with cultural difference registered at the very outset. "The 'Nude descending a Stairway' is not a woman. Neither is it a man,"[16] declared Duchamp. In New York, woman in the studio did not follow the mistress/prostitute/model paradigm. It was American Woman, powerful, glamorous, enfranchised, "her husband in the role of slave-banker,"[17] who drove Duchamp and Francis Picabia into the melancholic trope of the "*machine célibataire*" (bachelor machine). The insatiate *vaginae dentatae* of Picabia's protestant "Young American Girls" were depicted via imagery of their cars; Duchamp and Picabia encountered not only young girls but also powerful widows, extravagant eccentrics such as the Baronesss Elsa von Freytag-Loringhoven, with her "artistic" clothes, black lipstick, wooden birdcage round her neck (with live canary), and French *poilu* (soldier's helmet).[18]

Duchamp's retreat from painting and his philosophy of "delay" was not only antiretinal and onanistic but also photographic, cinematic, translinguistic, and, of course, transsexual. Far from being an exception, Rrose Sélavy was representative of a new metropolitan subjectivity. Back in France, Victor Margueritte's *La Garçonne* (1922), a moralizing tale of France's new boyish woman, sold 20,000 copies in its first four days and was read by twelve to twenty-five percent of the adult French population. A decade is spanned between *La Garçonne* and Colette's *Ces Plaisirs* (1932): "Eleanor Butler would curse as she jacked up the car and would have her breasts amputated."[19] Overt bisexuality or homosexuality was now chic; masked balls were a form of superior conspicuous consumption. "Women have looked the same for two years. By day they look like boys and by night they look like female impersonators,"[20] Janet Flanner wrote from Paris for *The New Yorker*, in 1926. Even Marxists took note: in "Notes sur la morale sexuelle en France," published in 1925, Jean Montrevel analyzed "Christianity, monarchy, chivalry, syphilis, court life, and, in the last instance, capitalism" with an exemplary class-consciousness—until his envoi: "A word on feminism: this doctrine is the predilection of lazy women with intellectual pretensions. . . . The amazon will always be an exception and physiology will always impose its laws. Everything within the normal constitution of woman gravitates around one central function: the reproduction of the species."[21]

Individual tragedy lay, of course, behind the story of each war widow, broken engagement, the thousands of spinsters created as a result of the male casualties of World War I. Resulting changes in employment patterns found their echo in the moves toward emancipation voiced by the still-disfranchised women of France. The jazz-society stereotypes and music-hall caricatures of the *garçonne* turned dour as the decade progressed. And with the low franc came the so-called *Américaines*: Djuna Barnes, Jane Heap, Lee Miller, Gertrude Stein, and their English sisters, Eileen Agar, Nancy Cunard, Marlow Moss, Paule Vézelay. Lesbians, aviators, writers, painters, photographers. "Amazons" or "*Américaines*"—the terms were almost identical.

Womanliness as a Masquerade

Both literary and artistic London and the British Psychoanalytic Society were dependent on strong, intellectual women. In 1929, the year of the second Surrealist manifesto, one year after Woolf's *Orlando: A Biography*, the elegant Joan Riviere, Woolf's Bloomsbury contemporary, the translator into English of Freud and Melanie Klein, published the now celebrated text "Womanliness as a Masquerade." Referring at first to Ernest Jones's article "The Early Development of Female Sexuality" (1927), which claimed an inherent bisexuality in each person and heterosexual and homosexual types of female development, and to Leo Ferenczi's theories of compensatory behavior (homosexual men exaggerating their heterosexuality), Riviere progressed to the notion of "womanliness" itself as a masquerade adopted "to avert anxiety and the feared retribution from men," discussing the cases of "an American woman engaged in a work of a propagandist nature, which consisted principally in speaking and writing" and a "wife and mother, a university lecturer in an abstruse subject," who would address her male colleagues in particularly feminine clothes.[22] In each case, the conclusion is that the woman who wishes to possess the father's penis is "seized by horrible dread" and, fearing retribution, offers herself sexually as propitiation.[23] Riviere's embrace of the strictures of her discipline and its great fathers accounts for her evident neglect of both the necessary social negotiations of these emancipated, achieving women and the irony of her text's autobiographical dimensions.

Adopting the scrupulously "scientific" tone of her male counterparts, Riviere used psychoanalysis as a masquerade to hide any possible feelings of identification with her subjects. Her conclusions, nonetheless, were devastating: "Womanliness could therefore be assumed and worn as a mask, both to hide the possession of masculinity and to avert the reprisals expected if she was found to possess it."[24] Furthermore, should one ask where to draw the line between "genuine womanliness" and the "masquerade," she replied, "My suggestion is not, however, that there is any such difference; whether radical or superficial, they are the same thing."[25]

This 1929 text, which has been so crucial for developing theories of sexuality, desire, spectatorship, and gender games in the United States and Great Britain since the 1970s, now generating work on "the masculine masquerade,"[26] is apparently little-known in France. Was this a case of ignorance, protectionism, or merely redundancy in the light of contemporaneous Surrealist explorations? Riviere's equivalent in France, Freud's protector and translator, Marie Bonaparte shared Riviere's personal problems of self-definition within the context of strict Freudian orthodoxy. Freud himself called Bonaparte "quite outstanding, a more than just half masculine female" (her obsession with operations on her clitoris is notorious). Did Bonaparte choose to ignore Riviere's revolutionary definition of female masquerade because it upset Freud's very basic categorizations? Freud's *On Female Sexuality* (1931) used terms subsequently reformulated by Bonaparte as "true women," "women who accept" ("*acceptatrices*," children replace penis envy), "women who deny" ("*renonciatrices*," mere spinsters) and "women who take their revenge" ("*revendicatrices*").[27]

Bonaparte's translations of Freud circulated widely in interwar Paris, compounding the climate of "delirium" in Surrealist circles and beyond.[28] Another woman, however, must be rescued from history: Agnès Masson. While a faithful disciple of Havelock Ellis, Masson had the intelligence in her writing to see beyond the merely pathological, devoting the first chapter of her book on transvestism, *Le Travestissement: Essai de psychopathologie sexuelle* (1935), to the age-old *cultural* origins of this behavior: "in history, literature, ethnography."[29] She moved impressively through the list of those who immortalized transvestism by description or in practice: Plato, Xenophon, Lucien, Theocritus, Virgil, Horace, Catullus, Juvenal, Tiresias, Achilles, the Amazons, the Scythians, the Cynedes, Caligula, Nero, Heliogabalus . . . arriving finally in *la douce France*, land of the fictitious Pope Joan and a bevy of colorful transvestites: the Abbé de Choisy, Gautier's Mademoiselle de Maupin, King Henri II, and the Chevalier d'Eon (secret agent of Louis XV in the English and Russian courts), not forgetting George Sand or Sarah Bernhardt. Anticipating Foucault, Masson discussed the cultural nature of sexuality: homosexuality in Ancient Greece, the trope of cross-dressing and disguise central to Renaissance literature (William Shakespeare), moving from François Rabelais's boy "page-girls" to the works of Balzac and Rachilde. Yet the contemporary situation, characterized by an "epidemic" of transvestite novels, she dated to the aftermath of World War I, the emergence of so-called "virile women" (*femmes-viriles*), and the current popularization of sex and psychoanalysis. Of Masson's subsequent case histories, sixty-two out of sixty-seven were translations from other sources, for example, "Observation 26 (Hirschfeld)": "Artist. Aged 40; quite feminine. Succubus [sits on top]

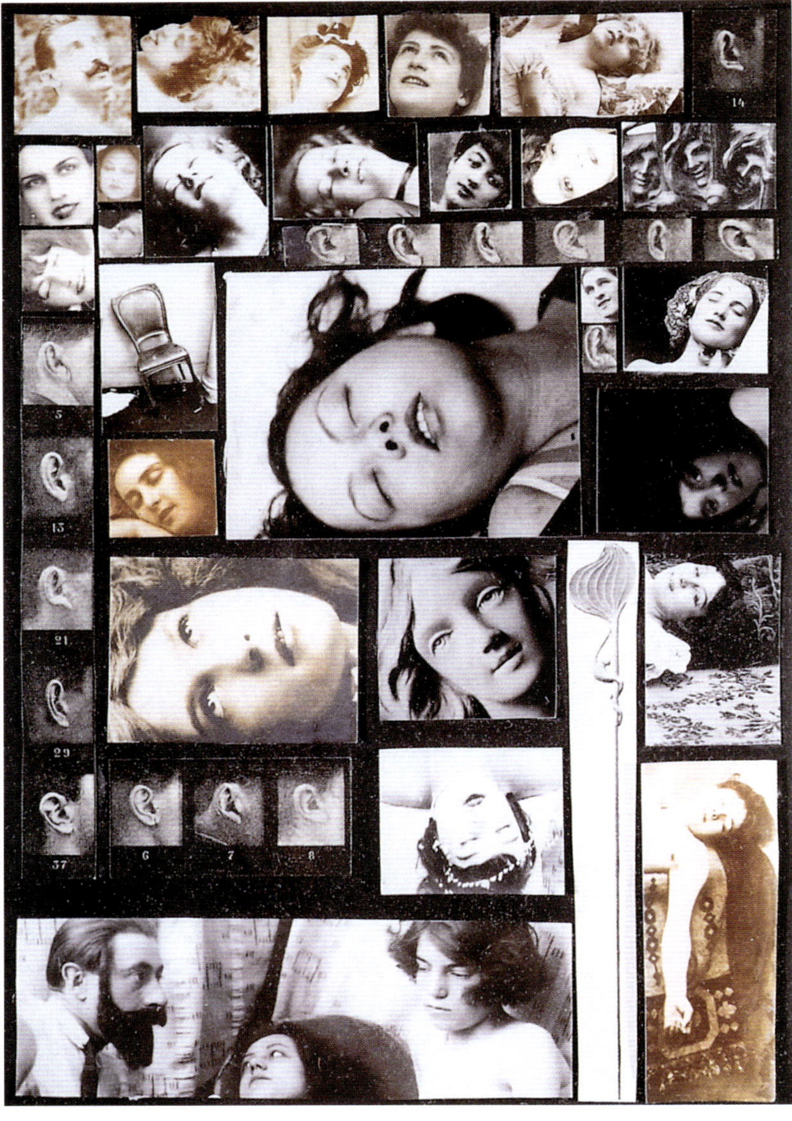

Salvador Dalí
The Phenomenon of Ecstasy
(Le Phénomène de l'extase), 1933
Photomontage,
10 ⁹⁄₁₆ x 7 ⁵⁄₁₆ inches (27 x 18.5 cm)
Isidore Ducasse Fine Arts

during coitus."[30] Ludicrous as this may sound to late twentieth-century sensibilities, Masson's work participated in the interwar discourse on transsexuality and masquerade within which the Surrealist movement must be resituated.

Surrealist Masquerades: Open Eyes/Downcast Eyes

The Surrealist movement, with its cult of woman, *l'amour fou* (mad love), exhibitionism, fetishism, sadomasochism—but, above all, no homosexuality—was thus formed in a lesbian and transvestite Paris itself constituted through war loss and an immense melancholy. It may be conceptualized as a series of masks and gazes, its literary nature constantly in competition with the "phallogocularcentric."[31] Despite the Surrealists' proclaimed desire for revolution, emancipation, free love, they resoundingly rejected the threatening New Woman of Paris, the *Amazone* or the *garçonne*, preferring their muses, from Kiki de Montparnasse to Gala, and only the most compliant *Américaines* (Lee Miller), whose modest, downcast eyes prelude the sexually ecstatic. Indeed, Salvador Dalí's *The Phenomenon of Ecstasy* (*Le Phénomène de l'extase*, 1933) must be read as a return, via female masquerade, of the repressed. The ecstatic female women constitute a mask of displacement, concealing the hysterical man (note the frantic, stabbing pattern of repetition in the collage). Compare the twenty-eight Surrealist men who surround the portrait of the assassin Germaine Berton (a photomontage of 1924), or the twenty illuminated and penetrating glances of the men in Man Ray's *Surrealist Chessboard* (*L'Echiquier surréaliste*, 1928). Sixteen pairs of male eyes are closed (in intellectual withdrawal or masturbatory fantasy?) in René Magritte's painting *I Do Not See the [Woman] Hidden in the Forest* (*Je ne vois pas la [femme] cachée dans la forêt*), which may be read in conjunction with the famous Surrealist survey "Recherches sur la sexualité" (1928).[32] This frank investigation, published in the journal *La Révolution surréaliste*, was in itself a stunning instance of purported textual "openness" actually revealing closure: the Stalinist model of the cell, self-criticism, exclusion extending to the refusal of all "abnormalities." Moreover, it is a classic case of the link between what is fashionably called "homosociality" (boy talk) and "homosexual panic"—the potential fear that suppressed homoerotic/homosexual relations will become explicit.[33] Think of Dalí and Federicó García Lorca, the Max Ernst/Paul Eluard relationship, the suicide of the homosexual René Crevel, who detailed his love of "nocturnal boys" in *Moi et mon corps* (1925), and, above all, André Breton's generally "seductive" behavior toward men despite his virulent homophobia.

Surrealism equals pederasty; this equation was made by writers Paul Claudel, Ilya Ehrenburg, and Jean-Paul Sartre, with his parody of Breton as the homosexual "leader" Achille Berton (Breton's Achilles heel?). Homosexual panic was frantically near the surface. Man Ray was the most brilliant and knowing male exegete of Surrealist doublespeak. He illustrated Breton's concept of *explosante-*

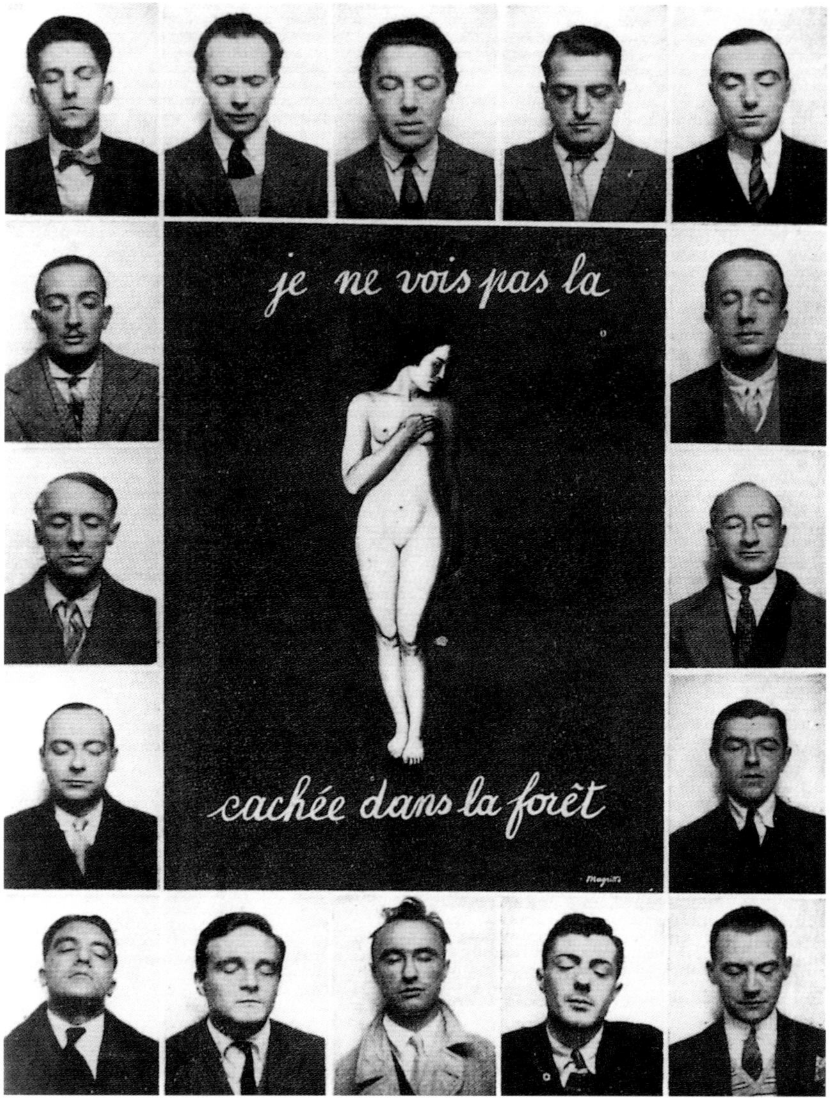

fixe as a flurry of Loïe Fuller–like veils—but he knew how woman's phallicism would symbolically reassert itself. So, for example, Tristan Tzara's text "D'un certain automatisme du goût" (On a certain automatism of taste, 1933) was illustrated by Man Ray's portraits of metonymically vaginal/phallic hats on invisible women: "It's the hat that makes the man," a case in which "the masking of femininity slips irresistibly into the conditions of male spectatorship."[34] The indeterminate boundaries between art and fashion in Surrealism, its penetration of the worlds of Elsa Schiaparelli and *Vogue* and *Harper's Bazaar* is precisely because of the role played by dress and disguise in Surrealist masquerade.[35] The Surrealist mannequins exhibited at the Galerie des Beaux-Arts in 1938 were inspired by Robert Couturier's disturbing, draped precursors in the Pavillon de l'Elégance at the Paris World Fair of 1937, operating through reversal and perversion rather than complicity with fashion magazine notions of beauty. Duchamp's severe "virilized mannequin" in tailored jacket is a case in point.

René Magritte
I Do Not See the [Woman] Hidden in the Forest (*Je ne vois pas la [femme] cachée dans la forêt*), from *La Révolution surréaliste*, no. 12 (1929)

In her nudity, too, Surrealist woman participated in a game of truth. The idealized woman might be displayed with open eyes as a solarized nude for *Harper's Bazaar* or with the downcast eyes of modesty, as in the well-known Man Ray photograph of the naked Meret Oppenheim *Veiled Erotic* (*Erotique voilée*, 1933), hiding behind the wheel of the printing press as it symbolically besmirches her. Woman as an allegory of truth is played off against "woman" as an allegory of "deception" (hence truth equals deception: the abolition of philosophy itself). Together with the sociological evidence of the sex war of the 1920s and 1930s and the idealizing structures of the Surrealists' residual Catholicism, the Nietzschean input as regards the Surrealist intellectuals Georges Bataille, Duchamp, and Picabia is indisputable. Behind the extravagance of Nietzsche's misogynistic statements, Jacques Derrida has analyzed an appalling triple bind, inherited by the Surrealists, that far surpasses Riviere's analysis in its sophistry:

> *1. The woman, taken as a figure or potentate of falsehood, finds herself censured, debased and despised. In the name of truth and metaphysics she is accused here by the credulous man who, in support of his testimony, offers truth and his phallus as his own proper credentials. . . .*
>
> *2. The woman is censured, debased and despised, only in this case it is as the figure or potentate of truth. In the guise of the Christian, philosophical being she either identifies with the truth, or else she continues to play with it at a distance, as if it were a fetish, manipulating it, even as she refuses to believe in it, to her own advantage. Whichever, woman, through her guile and naivety (and her guile is always contaminated by naivety), remains nonetheless within the economy of truth's system, in the phallogocentric space. . . . The woman, up to this point then, is twice castration: once as truth and once as nontruth.*

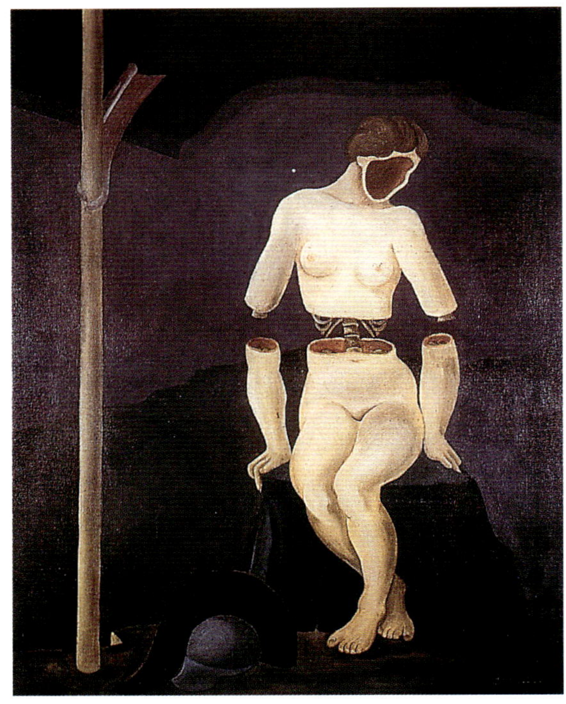

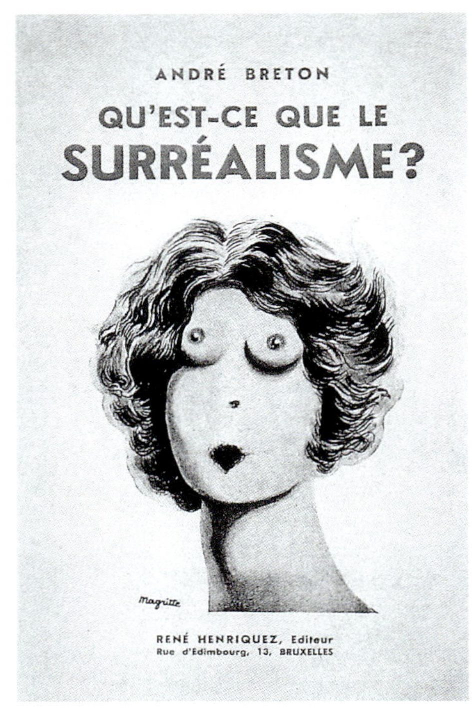

Marc Eemans
The Sawed-up Woman
(*La Femme sciée*), n.d.
Oil on canvas, 36¼ x 28¾ inches
(92 x 73 cm)
Collection of Carl Laszlo, Basel

René Magritte
The Rape (*Le Viol*), cover of
André Breton's *Qu'est-ce-que*
le surréalisme? (Brussels: René
Henriquez, 1934)

> *3. . . . Beyond the double negation of the first two, woman is recognized and affirmed as an affirmative power, a dissimulatress, an artist, a dionysiac. And no longer is it man who affirms her. She affirms herself, in and of herself, [and] in man. Castration, here again, does not take place. And anti-feminism, which condemned woman only so long as she was, so long as she answered to man from the two reactive positions, is in its turn overthrown.*[36]

Derrida posits the problem of theorizing itself around the "heterogeneity of style . . . if these three types of statement are to form an exhaustive code."[37] I would argue that the proliferation of female representations and styles in Surrealism, and its theories from *l'amour fou* to the female revolution posited by André Breton in *Arcane 17*, are attempting to do just this.[38]

The solution? Gynecide—the metaphoric chopping up of images of woman. *"Femme sans teste tout en est bon"* (A headless women is all to the good)[39] runs the French proverb that Max Ernst surely knew: "An effective Muse is a Muse that is killed, not once, but over and over again, her power is to be both powerful and dead, present and absent, a severed and yet unsevered head."[40] Surrealism is organized around endless decapitations, the fetishization of female body parts—above all, no face, no eyes, no look—from Ernst's pioneering hacked-up or blinded nudes in *L'Eléphant Celebes* (1921), *The Wavering Woman* (*La Femme chancelante*, 1923), and the collage-novel *La Femme 100 têtes* (The hundred-headless woman, 1929), to the obscene *The Sawed-up Woman* (*La Femme sciée*, n.d.) by the second-rate Marc Eemans, which was celebrated in the highly unanalytic exhibition catalogue *La Femme et le surréalisme*.[41] The most blatant replacement of downcast eyes by body parts is in Magritte's *The Rape* (Le Viol) of 1934, which Breton employed metonymically to define Surrealism itself in reproducing it on the cover of *Qu'est-ce que le surréalisme?* (What is Surrealism?) in 1934. Again, one confronts a double bind: the invitation to rape turns into the phallic woman, her look reinstated. Magritte's apotropaic desire for self-protection paradoxically creates Surrealism's most powerful image of the Medusa or Gorgonic gaze.[42] With Bataille's metamorphic *Histoire de l'oeil* (Story of the eye, 1928), Hans Bellmer's dismembered dolls, even Duchamp's *Etant Donnés* (1946–66), the gaze masquerading as vagina, supplicant and sugar pink or displaced and sealed, still terrifyingly reasserts itself.

Agar, Miller, Oppenheim, Valentine Penrose, these creative women (Nietzsche's third category; Riviere's category of masqueraders) caused problems for the Surrealists. The muses—so often complicit in their aspiration for the role of fetish[43]—were, nonetheless, on the attack. While Agar's *Angel*

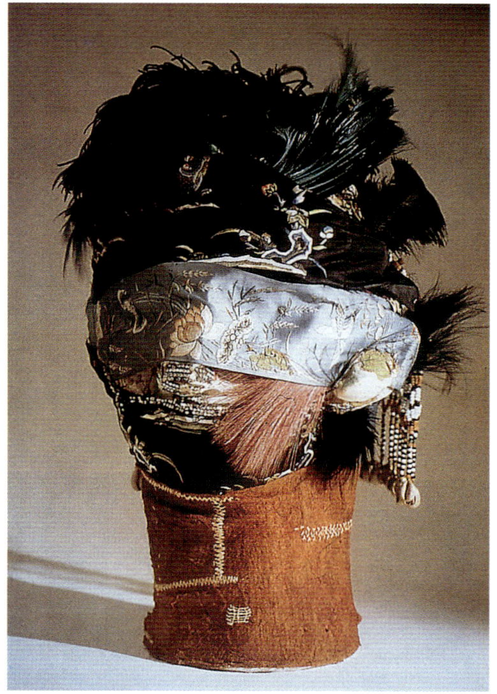

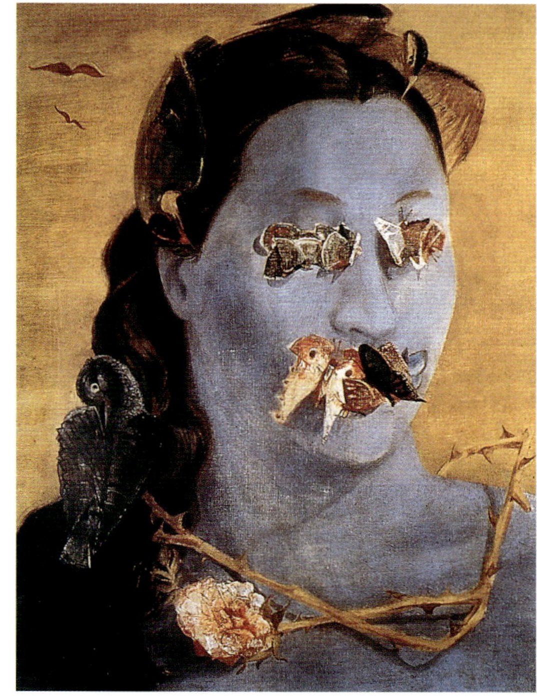

Eileen Agar
Angel of Anarchy (second version), 1940
Plaster cast covered with mixed media, 27 ⁹⁄₁₆ x 12 x 12 inches (70 x 30.5 x 30.5 cm)
Tate Gallery, London

Roland Penrose
Winged Domino (Portrait of Valentine), 1937
Oil on canvas, 23 7⁄16 x 17 ¹¹⁄₁₆ inches (59.5 x 45 cm)
Private collection, England

of Anarchy (1940) feminized and masked her husband's bust in furs, feathers, silks, and diamanté, Roland Penrose's *Winged Domino (Portrait of Valentine)* (1937) shows the theatrical, carnival-grotesque aspects of "femininity as masquerade." This act of seduction or compensation was not, however, Valentine's idea; on the contrary, the masking gesture, the blue, dead skin, the butterfly-shaded eyes have been imposed by her husband. She reads as fetishized object. Yet if we identify with Valentine as subject, her downcast eyes invite us to contemplate the mystery of her unshared subjectivity as a creative woman poet, something that Penrose found to be a stumbling block. The "exhaustive codes" are more complex than Riviere imagined.

Claude Cahun was a pioneering code-scrambler, a Surrealist woman who was never a muse. With perverse delight, she played with a range of masks in her self-reflexive photographs: the poet (her profile portrait so close to that of her uncle, the critic Marcel Schwob), the narcissist, the lesbian, the aviator (parodying Breton), the sportswoman with her slogan, "Don't kiss me, I'm in training," the blond, Aryan maiden, the pseudo-infant, identifying with Lise Deharme's son, Pic, in her photographs for Deharme's children's book *Le Coeur de Pic* (Pic's heart, 1937). While Man Ray retained the traditional artist/model paradigm, photography itself, technically the medium of black/white inversion, becomes for Cahun the medium that records the "exhaustive code"—and its reversability. Cahun's intervention in the Breton/Aragon political debate on Communism, her tract on the role of poetry, *Les Paris sont ouverts* (Place your bets, 1934), is remarkable, both for its intellectual incisiveness and its surtitles at the heads of pages, which are evidently self-referential: "POETRYREVEALSHERSECRETKEEPSHERSECRET . . . SHEREVEALSIT? . . . SHEKEEPSIT? . . . SHHHE."[44] Two structuring grand narratives, Freudianism and Marxism, the dream versus political revolution, were at stake. Cahun perceived the dilemma with clarity and an ironic wealth of reference, parodying the seriousness of an essentially competitive male squabble. Breton's brief acknowledgment of her writing is especially double-edged when one considers that the intellectuality of *Les Paris sont ouverts*—Cahun's means of attracting not just his attention but his mind and his pen—was part of the doomed strategy of her unrequited love. Breton preferred "objective chance," madness, and domination in his sexual choices (Nadja, Jacqueline Lambda), masquerading, of course, as monogamous, romantic love. Cahun retreated to Jersey, in the Channel Islands, with her friend Suzanne Malherbe, in 1937, finding creative peace—until war, the Nazis, brutality, and terror devastated her life.[45]

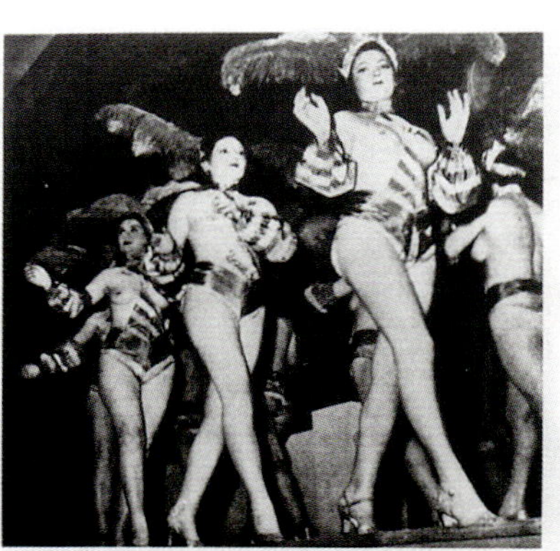

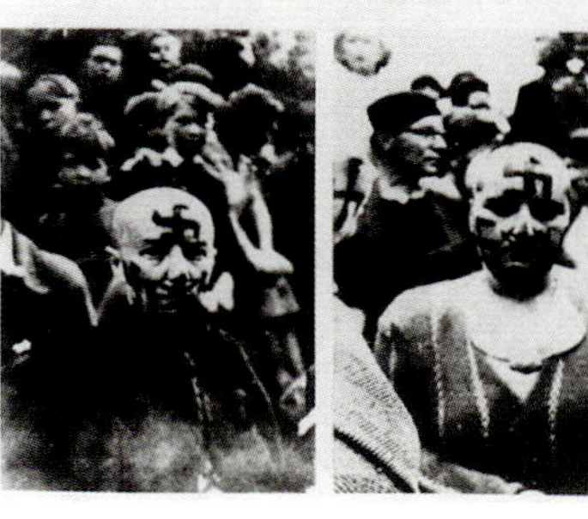

Images from Jean Eparvier, *A Paris sous la botte des nazis* (Paris: Editions Raymond Schall, 1946), reproduced in *View* 6, no. 1 (February 1946), p. 9

One Becomes a Woman? De Beauvoir or Genet?

Enfranchised at last, French womanhood went to the polls in 1945, in a period when the "Rights of Man" contrasted strikingly with the savage treatment of female "collaborators," who had their heads shaved and were tarred and paraded publicly during the post-Occupation purge. It was another fetishized, this time forced, masquerade, "a carnival of uglies," an expression of the humiliation of the French male during the War. The Surrealists saw the appalling photographs as fair game for a 1946 issue of the journal *View*, which was published by Charles Henri Ford in New York. "The Shaved Woman," a poem written by the female transsexual sculptor Hans Anton Prinner in February 1945, echoed the litany of insults: "—Slut!—Whore!—Carcass!—Dungheap!—Disgusting!—Pile of shit!—Look at her!"[46] The poem's form, a tribunal recalling the trial of Joan of Arc, expresses a sado-masochistic rage echoed in the artist's stylized engravings.

Despite state closure of the brothels in 1946, French society still functioned on a sexual economy of bourgeois marriage versus the "seduction" of mistresses and prostitutes. The froufrou of Christian Dior's New Look, the "Miss Tabou" beauty contests in Saint-Germain-des Prés, the historical costume dramas in the theaters and the cinema, the taste for a "Fantastic 40s," all played their role in characterizing the reborn Frenchwoman. The excess of femininity in these masquerades contrasted acutely with the new cult of ugliness in art: the awkward, scratched surfaces of Germaine Richier's bronzes, Jean Fautrier's scarred and iridescent *Hostages* (*Otages*), followed by his *Nudes* (*Nus*) in 1955, and Jean Dubuffet's hideous *Olympia* of the *Ladies' Bodies* (*Corps des dames*) series. (In 1948, 600,000 "ladies" were working in Paris, two years after the official closure of the brothels.[47]) These are violent and misogynistic works, despite their mock insouciance. They correspond in their interiority and dissolution not only to Maurice Merleau-Ponty's embodied "cogito" but also to an archetypal enunciation, made by Jean-Paul Sartre, in 1940, in a chapter in *L'Imaginaire* on the work of art: "The real is never beautiful." To desire a woman, "We must forget that she is beautiful, because desire is a plunge into the heart of existence, into what is contingent and most absurd."[48] Desire—or an infantile, aggressive rage—spreads out contiguously with painterly matter in the *Ladies' Bodies*, attempting to obliterate the subject-ground relationship by engulfing it. Dubuffet invokes with both humor and terror the devouring mother: his "dames" are the mothers of Niki de Saint-Phalle's *Nanas* of the 1960s.

Niki de Saint-Phalle
The Death of the Patriarch
(*La Mort du patriarche*), 1962/72
Paint and mixed media,
90 ⁹⁄₁₆ x 43 ⁵⁄₁₆ (230 x 110 cm)
Courtesy of the artist

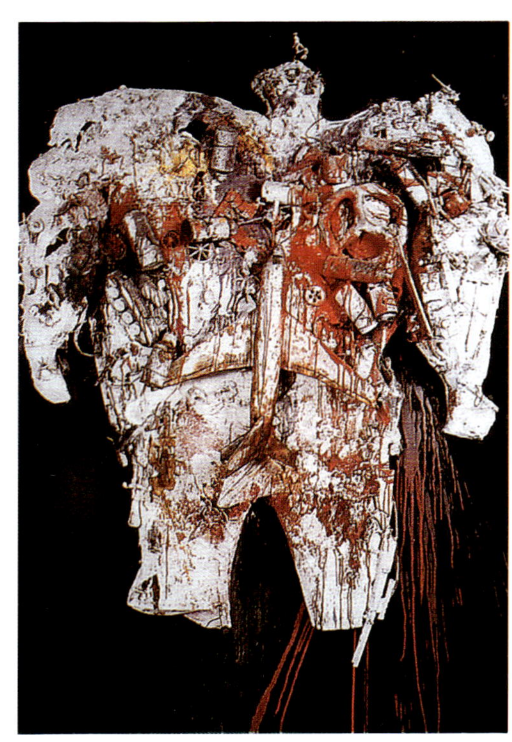

Manet's *Olympia*—the "female gorilla" as she was called in 1865—now irradiated the Jeu de Paume museum with her erotic beauty. The impact of ugliness in the new art displaced the cult of female beauty, marking the inscription of the terrible caesura of World War II—massacre overwhelming masquerade: "Ugliness, as an inscription of time in the heart of a picture, asserts itself doubtlessly as a 'surface,' eroded, withered, worn, not to say flayed."[49] We are reminded that *laedere*, one possible root for the French *laid* (ugly) means "to wound."[50] De Beauvoir's *Le Deuxième Sexe* (The second sex), serialized in *Les Temps modernes* from May 1948 and published in 1949, was a sociological and scholarly tour-de-force: 22,000 copies were sold in its first week of publication. Here, de Beauvoir redefined Sartre's fluctuatingly sexed "Other": "He is the Subject, he is the Absolute—she is the Other."[51] Ironically, she appropriates Sartre's own vocabulary to challenge the pseudo-objectivity of the male philosophical voice. The impact of *Le Deuxième Sexe* coincided, in France, with that of the Kinsey reports on male and female sexuality[52] and the new expressions of the feminine embodied in the gaminelike singer-actress Juliette Greco, the child-woman Brigitte Bardot, and novels such as Françoise Sagan's *Bonjour Tristesse* (1955). It has been argued, however, that Sartre's own horror of the "viscous" nature of the biological female[53] penetrated the writings of de Beauvoir, whose position was shown to falter with her half-hearted critique of the Marquis de Sade (a hero for Bataille, Pierre Klossowski, Jean Paulhan, and the Surrealists). Her book *Brigitte Bardot ou le syndrome de Lolita* (published in English as *Brigitte Bardot and the Lolita Syndrome*, 1960) could do nothing to stop the rise of the new child-woman—a welcome distraction from colonial war in Algeria.[54] Man Ray, in an exasperated exposé, published in 1958, contrasted the dark existentialist waif (Greco) with the blond Marilyn Monroe, quoting Dior's lipstick ads and Paulhan's preface to Pauline Réage's *Histoire d'O* (1954): "All is sex in them [women] even the spirit. They must be continually fed, washed, painted with makeup and beaten."[55] The next *Exposition InteRnatiOnale du Surréalisme*, in 1959, which was devoted to Eros, signaled the continuing fascination with woman as fetish.[56] Oppenheim's transformation of her own food-bedecked body into a cannibalistic feast at the opening was the embodiment of Eros as woman to be devoured. In contrast, de Saint-Phalle's androgynous sculpture *The Death of the Patriarch* (*La Mort du patriarche*, 1962/72), an equally Arcimboldesque landscape of planes, missiles, and dismembered dolls, demonstrated, at last, a creative intelligence who could take and transform the masquerade of female decoration as consumption into a terrifying metaphor for the war-scarred and hideous body of France, making explicit the links between women, toys, rape, colonialism, and cannon fodder. For France, she went far beyond Betty Friedan's analyses in *The Feminine Mystique* (1963), with its description of "the Happy Housewife Syndrome,"[57] which had supplanted de Beauvoir's *Le Deuxième Sexe*.

De Beauvoir, whose femininity was governed by intellectual competitiveness, "existential" interiority, and a climate of postwar austerity, had little sympathy with mascara, let alone the deep structures of feminine masquerade. Jean Genet, however, embraced with dazzling extravagance the world of flowers, of silks, of sensuality, the camp of female movie stars and transvestites. His melancholy anticipates our own; it is the transgressive sexuality of Genet and of Antonin Artaud that generated the deconstructive vision of gender today. Genet's "Fragments," of 1954, a suicidal, Mallarméan prose poem, is surely the most moving testimony to human sexuality produced in mid-century. It is a passionate exegesis of homosexuality in riposte to Sartre's preposterous vision of "pederasty" as self-willed. Genet insists that he experiences his state as "a theme of guilt" and that "inversion is lived in a solitary state." "The homosexual" he writes, "rejects woman, who, ironically, wreaks her vengeance by reappearing inside him, putting him into a dangerous fix. They call us effeminate. Banished, sequestered, hoaxed, Woman, through our gestures and intonations, seeks and finds the day: our body, suddenly riddled, becomes unreal."[58]

The 1960s and After

The following year, in 1955, Pierre Molinier's meeting with Breton heralded, strangely, a volte-face in the Surrealist's previously hostile stance toward transsexuality and sexual deviance.[59] In a reversal of the Pygmalion myth, the female figures in Molinier's Surrealist paintings became transformed into his own transvestite image: photographs of the 1960s and 1970s, taken with an automatic timer, display Molinier as both dominatrix and succuba. These photos may be compared, in both terms of the

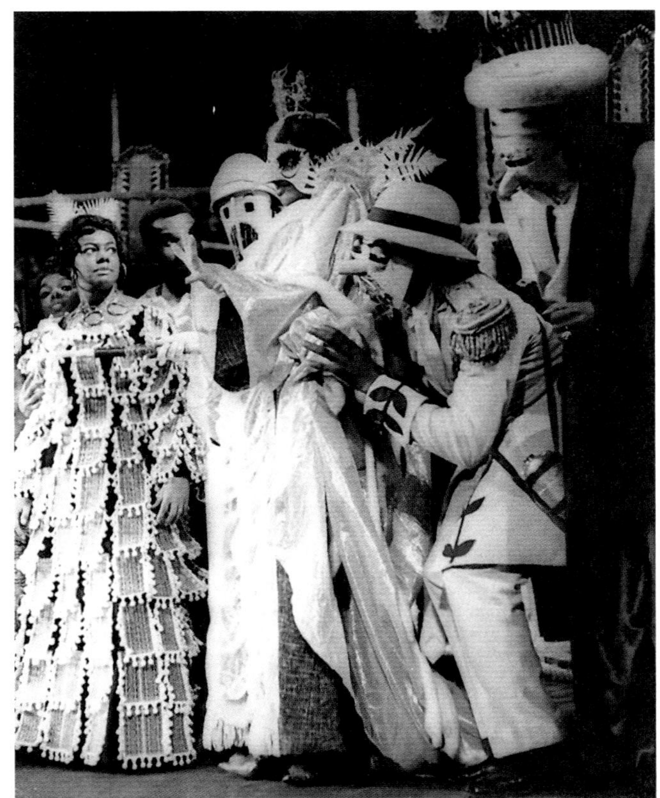

Performance of Jean Genet's *The Blacks* (*Les Nègres*), Royal Court Theatre, London, May 30, 1961
Roger Blin Archives

"anagrammatic" principle of their poses and gender confusion (Molinier used female masks and, eventually, female models), to the later work of Bellmer, such as *Girl-Phallus* (*Fille-Phallus*, 1968), although Molinier's concern with pornographic realism was more of its time than Bellmer's waspish gentlemen's erotica. In his tableaux, Molinier accentuated his handmade accessories, his autosodomizing dildo fetishes, his female rubber masks, photographing himself against the patterned eighteenth-century *toile de Jouy* wallpaper of his studio-boudoir, which evoked the ambience of a cheap hotel. Revealing its intimacies, this world became a bridge to a new generation fascinated, as one critic wrote, with "the desire to be doubled, androgyne, bisexual, that we may experience the sexual ecstasies of the other."[60] Besides the Surrealists, well-known transvestites, homosexuals, and transsexuals who were part of the Paris revue scene flocked to see him. In 1964, Hanel Koeck and Maryat (Emmanuelle Arsan, author of *Emmanuelle*, 1970) arrived and posed, intertwined as lesbian muses, for Molinier's photograph *Communion of Love* (*Communion d'amour*, 1968). And, in 1974, the future painter Luciano Castelli collaborated with Molinier on a photo series.[61] During the 1970s, a period in the art world marked by an explosion of confessional self-representations, a transvestite undercurrent was growing—Michel Journiac's two 1972 series *Trap for a Transvestite* (*Piège pour un travesti*) and *Homage to Freud* (*Hommage à Freud*), in France, and Urs Lüthi's "he" and "she" personae, in Germany—parallel to the concerns of Andy Warhol and his fellow artists in the United States.[62]

Genet's role as precursor in the articulation of 1960s homosexual concerns should not be underestimated. That his work had a direct influence on the Americans, such as filmmaker Kenneth Anger, who lived in Paris during the 1950s, is not in doubt. But the climate of camp and growing sexual explicitness in the United States at the time of Genet's "arrival" is significant. The year 1954 saw the American publication of Genet's *The Maids* and *Deathwatch*, with a preface by Sartre:

> *By virtue of being false, the woman acquires a poetic density. Shorn of its texture and purified, femininity becomes a heraldic sign, a cipher. As long as it was natural, the feminine blazon remained embedded in woman. Spiritualized, it becomes a category of the imagination. Anything can be a woman: a flower, an animal, an inkwell. . . . Such is the initial direction of his derealization: a falsification of femininity. . . . These fake women who are fake men, these*

women-men who are men-women, this perpetual challenging of masculinity by a symbolic femininity and of the latter by the secret femininity which is the truth of all masculinity, are only the faked groundwork.[63]

In the New York art world, the heroic period of Abstract Expressionism was drawing to a close. Only recently has the rise of Pop art been seen not merely as a figurative and popular celebration of consumer opulence, but as "closely allied with burgeoning gay identity in the art worlds of New York and London."[64] Kenneth E. Silver has compared "the master equation of Abstract Expressionism"—"tough, non-literary serious art" made by "rough hewn, spontaneous, male artists"[65] with the transitional work of Jasper Johns and the high camp of Warhol: "painting with balls" versus Johns's *Painting with Two Balls* (1960). He analyzed this painting's gesturalism mummified in encaustic as a "counter-castration" and described Johns's tributes to the homosexual poets and painters Hart Crane, Charles Demuth, Marsden Hartley, Frank O'Hara, and Walt Whitman. He compared Johns's masquerade of masculinity, the bronze-painted Ballantine Ale cans of 1960, with Warhol's "outrageously female" Campbell's Soup cans: "In a Duchampian transference, women *and* men who never did their own shopping or cleaning were sent to the Stable Gallery and Leo Castelli's to buy Campbell's and Brillo, just like Mrs. Warhola and the vast majority of American women."[66] In the time between Clement Greenberg's notorious "Avant-garde and Kitsch," of 1939, and Susan Sontag's "Notes on 'Camp,'" of 1964 ("Dandyism in the age of mass culture"[67]), high Modernism had been short-circuited. In fact, the tongue-in-cheek, "camp" attitude of Roy Lichtenstein's comic-strip females may be read as the precursor, "close in spirit (and possibly intention), to Cindy Sherman's *Untitled Film Stills* from the late 1970s and early 1980s."[68] These photographic masquerades are, of course, contemporary with Diane Arbus's hermaphrodites and with Warhol's photographic self-portraits in drag.

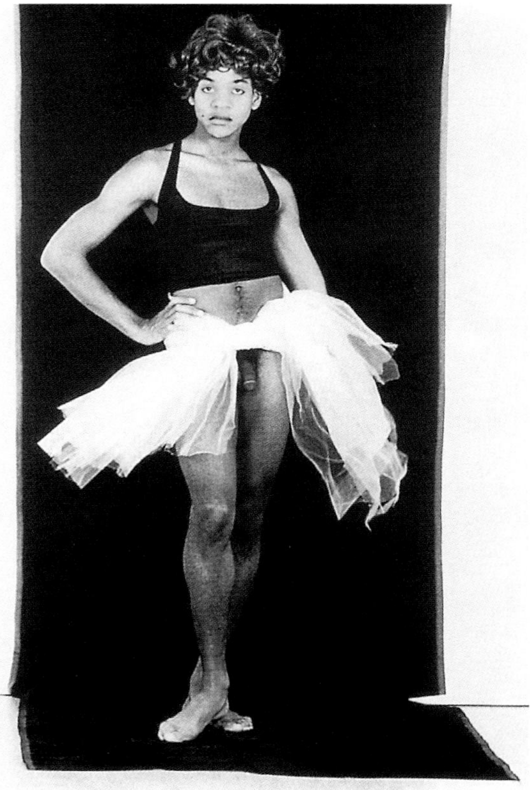

Lyle Ashton Harris
Construct #10, 1989
Black-and-white silver mural print, 72 x 36 inches (182.9 x 91.4 cm)
Courtesy of Jack Tilton Gallery, New York

Back in Europe, de Saint-Phalle's 1966 show, *Hon*, at the Moderna Museet, in Stockholm, invited the public joyously and transgressively to explore the body of a giant Nana via a vagina and enter into a huge womb of delights. It anticipated a cultural climate that allowed the *First International Exhibition of Erotic Art*, in Sweden in 1968, and the *Second International Exhibition of Erotic Art*, in Denmark in 1969, to be held in public, tax-supported museums, which were visited by over 250,000 people. These celebratory shows were naive if optimistic in their conception; female viewers were invited to be voyeurs at a spectacle designed to appeal "not only to the gonads but to the mind." They were also more explicit than any previous or subsequent museum show, containing such works as Tom Wesselmann's *Bedroom Painting No. 20* (1969), which is dominated by an enormous dark brown phallus.[69] The sense of urgency conveyed by these shows may be compared to that revealed in much American writing on feminist art in the 1970s. Yet, who now remembers the 1972 *Festival of Women in the Arts* at Cornell University, in Ithaca, New York, or the Erotic Art Gallery, in New York.? Discussions shifted from overtly "feminist" creations—the sexualized flowers of Georgia O'Keeffe, or Judy Chicago's classic *Dinner Party* (1979)—to works that were both more violent and more gender-sophisticated. De Saint-Phalle's film *Daddy* (1972), with its incest theme and scenes of women masturbating or being masturbated, was shown in New York in the early 1970s.[70] Louise Bourgeois's semi-abstract *Trani Episode* (1971–72) was exhibited

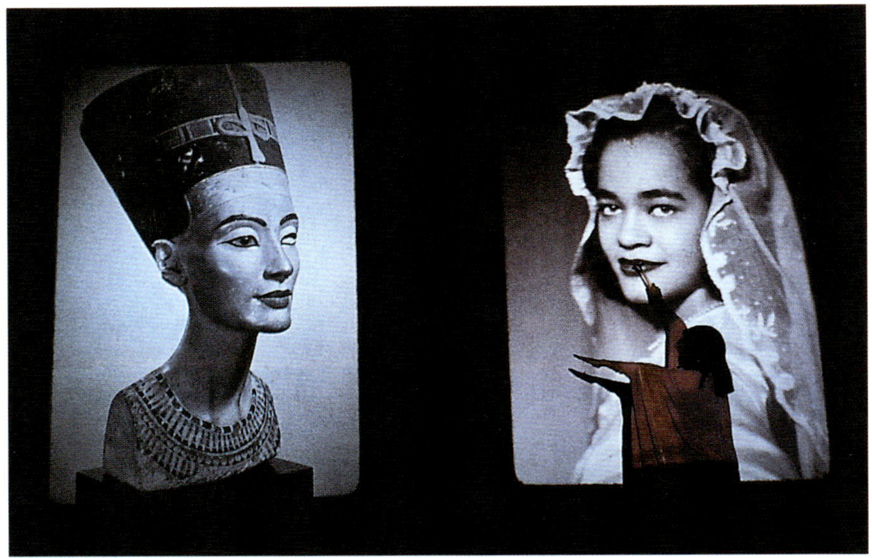

Lorraine O'Grady
Nefertiti/Devonia Evangeline, 1981
(first performed October 1980)
Courtesy of the artist

with Marge Helenchild's *Vulva Hammock* and Shelly Lowell's *Slice of Life*, an Oldenburgian pie with meringue-peak nipples. Bourgeois's phallic white marble *Cumulus No. 1* (1962), now in Paris, must be reimagined in its 1973 New York context of *Metaphorical Cunts and Measured Cocks.*[71]

Black Male

Frantz Fanon's virulent *Peau noir, masques blancs* (Black skin, white masks) was published in Paris in 1952.[72] Henceforth, color and colonialism became issues inextricably linked with sex and power. Two years later, Jean Rouche's film *Les Maîtres fous* (The mad masters) profoundly shocked a select Parisian audience with its reportage of a black African ritual and transsexual parody of colonialist rule in the Gold Coast, climaxing in frenzied scenes of possession, spittle, and blood.[73] The film was a direct inspiration for Genet's play *Les Nègres* (*The Blacks*), which was performed in Paris and London in 1959, and subsequently in New York, where more than 1,400 performances between 1961 and 1964 set an off-Broadway record, stunning and delighting a largely black audience: "White Genet imagines black actors imagining caricature Whites who imagine stereotype Niggers."[74] At the height of his involvement with Angela Davis and the Black Panthers (recalled in his posthumous work, *Un Captif amoureux* [Prisoner of love, 1986][75]), Genet refused categorically to speak about his theater work. Once again, however, he seems a precursor.

The macho dimension of the civil rights and black power movements clashed with the rise of feminism in the 1970s. Nevertheless, despite "the overwhelmingly male focus of black American art,"[76] by the mid-1970s, the woman artist Adrian Piper was doing performances on the streets of New York. In the 1975 *Mythic Being* series, the masquerade was drag: an Afro wig, bell bottoms, dark sunglasses. Piper recorded the "animosity, fear and indifference she experienced as a radicalized male subject."[77] Her photo-offset posters declared: "I embody everything you most hate and fear." As Genet would say (inversely): "Changing sex doesn't consist merely in subjecting one's body to a few surgical adjustments: it means teaching the whole world, forcing upon it, a change of syntax."[78] Lorraine O'Grady's contacts with Piper and Surrealism engendered her 1980 performances as "Mlle. Bourgeoise Noire"—a perfect response, after a twenty-year gap, to Genet's *The Blacks.* O'Grady paraded in a tiara and ball gown, holding a cat-o'-nine-tails in her begloved hands, with which she whipped herself as she declaimed a liberation manifesto for black artists. With her performance *Nefertiti/Devonia Evangeline* (1980), she continued the extension of work on femininity and the masquerade beyond gender to issues of race and history; at the same time, the personal resonance of allusions to the tragic death of her sister preserved the performance from the banalization of much of the "post-postmodern."[79]

Yet Genet's notion of a change, a fundamental "*détournement*" of syntax, implies an underlying signification beyond transsexualism: with the reversibility of display, the possible abolition of the "reality" of sex altogether. What Genet experienced as personal tragedy was leavened, in New York, by the ironic transposition of cultural and sexual codes, and has been transformed, in today's era of constant sexual exposure and pseudo-celebration, into a universe of simulation. The substitution of "porn for sex and sex for porn" implies the breakdown of the polarity of active/passive "and with it the hetero-homo distinction since there is no longer any reality of 'sex' itself to be compared with."[80] In the chapter "A World of Penises" in his recent book *Male Impersonators*, Mark Simpson cites Jean Baudrillard: "Where the distinction between poles can no longer be maintained, one enters into simulation, and hence into absolute manipulation."[81] This tendency to abolish polarities, to conflate boundaries, to "live the simulation," impinges directly on the art world, whose very raison d'être is to provide fantasy representations, alternative "realities," networks, encounters. The sexual tantalizations of reversability as an ethos have supplanted a pornography of arousal based on a promise of "real" sex: Robert Mapplethorpe's (decapitated) *Man in a Polyester Suit* (1980) is displaced, almost a decade later, by Lyle Ashton Harris's black male as ballerina in gauze tutu and curly blond wig. The equation of the black male with the feminine (made as early as 1860 by Theodore Tildon[82]) is evidently the corollary to the hypermasculinization of black culture in rap, sports, and cinema.[83] The 1994 exhibition *Black Male*, at the Whitney Museum of American Art, New York, demonstrated both this shift toward reversibility with Harris's generation, and a corresponding move toward reality as "simulation." The boundaries between the museum, popular culture, the documentary, and the star system became blurred, with the incorporation within the show of videos of the beating of Rodney King, of O. J. Simpson, and of the Senate testimony of Anita Hill and Clarence Thomas. Hence, the impossibility of defining a territory for "the culture of the museum," in what has been categorized by Arthur and Marilouise Kroker as a "panic exhibition" within the "fuzzy set" of the simulacra of American culture.[84] In this context, how possible are calls for a new authenticity?[85]

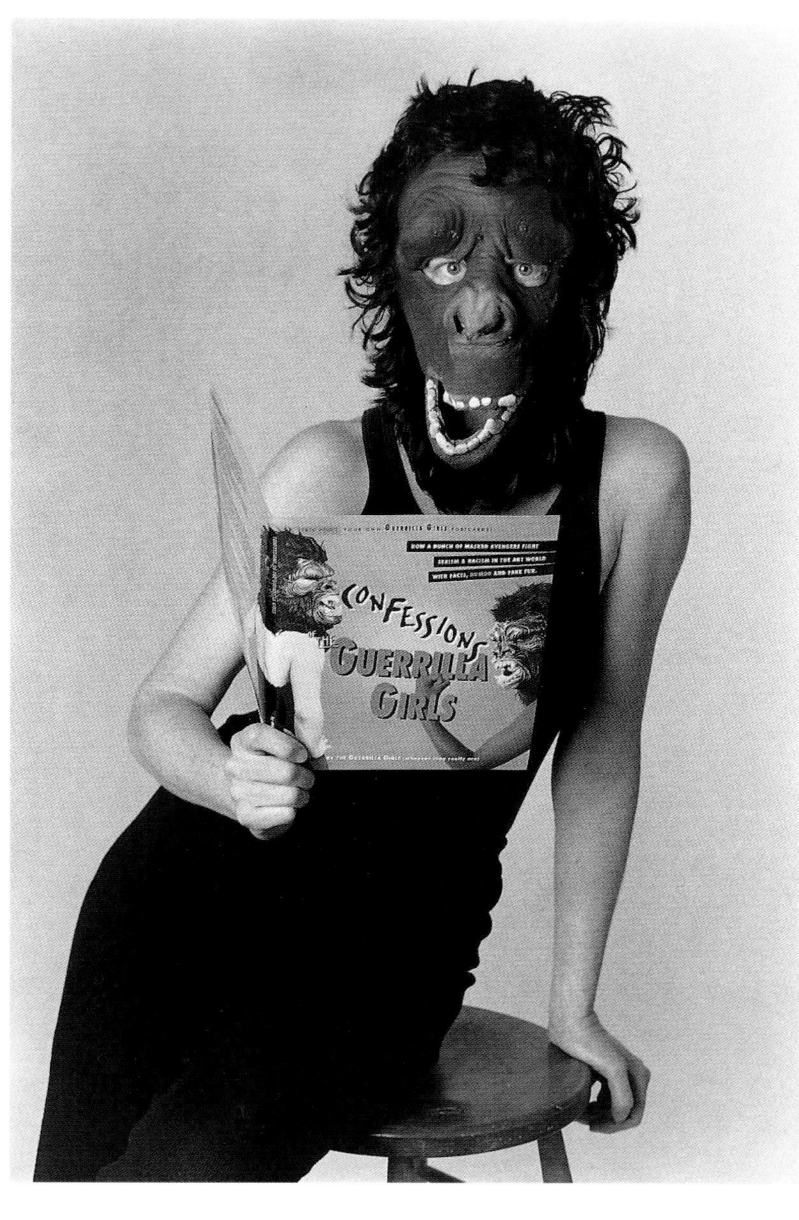

Guerrilla Girls
Confessions of the Guerrilla Girls, 1995
Courtesy of the Guerrilla Girls

Guerrilla Girls?

"A World of Penises" foresting the jungles of both art and popular culture is predicated, alas, upon exclusivity. The masculine masquerade, as Genet so well understood, seeks ultimately to engulf and ceaselessly to obliterate the always-recurring feminine.[86] Guerrilla action was called for as long ago as 1969 by Monique Wittig, in her novel *Les Guérillières*,[87] a pioneering and poetic sapphic text, too reminiscent, perhaps, of Pierre Louÿs's exoticism and ultimately unconvincing in its moments of erotic frenzy. The American Guerrilla Girls, masked and metropolitan, know that politics and statistics are the real game: "Facts, humor and fake fur." They materialized "mysteriously in the dark of night of 1988," in outraged response to *An International Survey of Painting and Sculpture*, an exhibition at the Museum of Modern Art, New York, in which, of 169 artists, a mere thirteen were women.[88] None has ever revealed the identity behind the mask of her assumed persona: Romaine Brooks, Frida Kahlo, Tina Modotti, Gertrude Stein. As Lee Krasner declared: "We secretly suspect that all women are born Guerrilla Girls. It's just a question of helping them discover it."[89] The Guerrilla Girls have traveled to Barcelona, Basel, Berlin, Dublin, Graz, Helsinki, Oslo, Ulm, and Vienna. They have yet to visit Paris.

The philosopher Yves Michaud recently outlined the cultural and political shifts that have broken the eternal London-Paris-New York love triangle. He described the French version of feminism as a battle lost: the "impression of déjà-vu," something that has had its moment, which is now in the past.[90] This is certainly not true of Orlan's current reputation in the United States, but in continental Europe, a patriarchal, canonic vision dominates. Thus the 1993 catalogue for de Saint-Phalle's retrospective in Bonn could, with impunity, declare: "Through a knowledge that is of a rather intuitive kind, she looks at what the great artists of modern art preceding her have produced. With innocence, like a blithe spirit, she borrows from them, as if she were picking flowers in a beautiful garden."[91] Where were the Guerrilla Girls when they were most needed?

Orlan
Orlan Before Saint-Orlan
(Orlan avant Sainte-Orlan), 1988
Acrylic on canvas,
executed by Publidécor,
photograph by Joël Nicolas
118 ⅛ x 78 ¾ inches (300 x 200 cm)
Courtesy of the artist

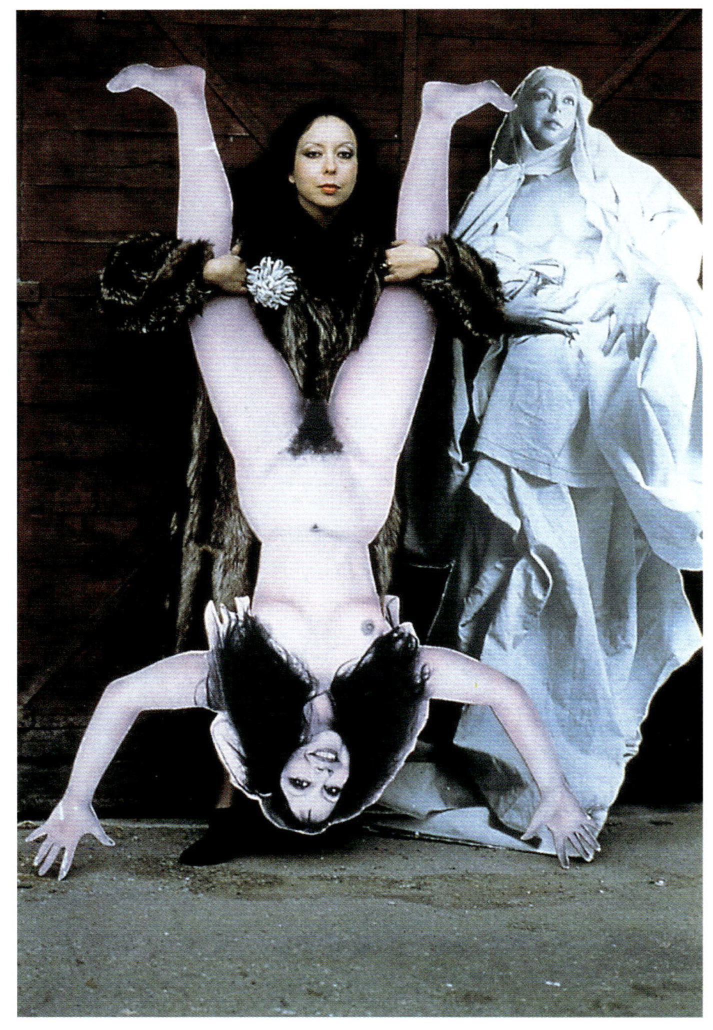

Despite the definitive survey exhibition *fémininmasculin*, which appeared at the Centre Georges Pompidou in 1995, the antifeminist position of the 1970s generation persists in France. The very words "feminism" or "feminist" are experienced as a form of bad taste, particularly with regard to the marginalized "spectacle" of charismatic women writing—Hélène Cixous, Luce Irigaray, Julia Kristeva[92]—who are far from idolized in Paris. Derision is the mask of insularity.

From Orlan to the Millennium

In the ancient and Catholic country of France, Orlan blasphemously manages her own metamorphosis, her own refiguration, her own woman-to-woman transsexualism: "This woman tells us that the Madonna is a transvestite."[93] Beneath baroque draperies, the artist/madonna reveals a breast; the breast of the whore becomes the

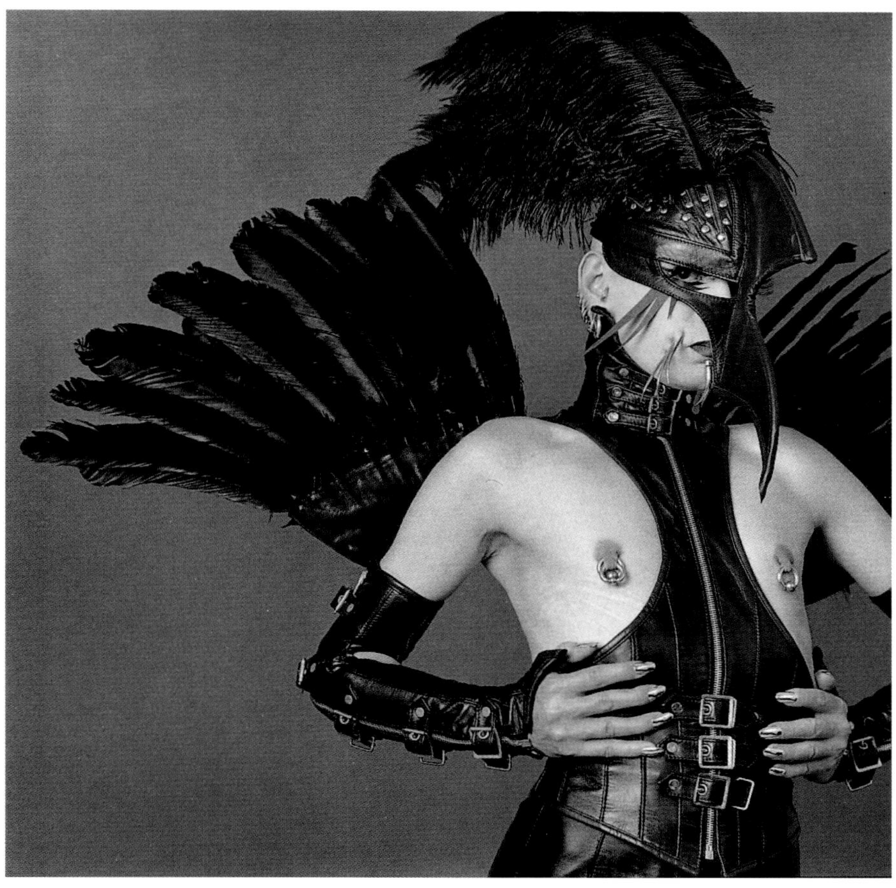

Nicholas Sinclair
Fabian, 1995
Gelatin-silver print,
14 x 14 inches (35.6 x 35.6 cm)
Courtesy of the artist

single breast of the Amazon. Orlan strips finally to the nude to "give back to the nude the sexual charge it has lost."[94] (Her version of the Pygmalion myth can dispense entirely with the redundant male artist.) Orlan's canvas is synonymous with the soiled sheets of her repudiated trousseau. She works with canonic texts—Freud's Medusa, with Eugénie Lemoine-Luccioni, who has pointed out the transsexuality of saints and thus the sacred as well as the profane aspects of transsexuality: "I have an angel's skin but I am a jackal; . . . a crocodile's skin but I am a puppy, a black skin but I am white; a woman's skin but I am a man; I never have the skin of what I am. There is no exception to the rule because I am never what I have."[95] For Orlan, desire now reaches beyond skin-deep masquerade, beyond the mythical feminine stereotypes of Europa, Psyche, Venus, Mona Lisa, beyond even the series *The Re-incarnation of Saint-Orlan* (*La Ré-incarnation de Sainte-Orlan,* 1993)—to the transgressive, anamorphic sacrifices of serial plastic surgery. This aesthetic vision of opening wounds, broadcast worldwide via satellite TV,[96] shows how "the universe penetrates us through the rents in our body,"[97] as the mystic Simone Weil wrote. Orlan's work develops beyond gender questions related to the knife, into realms of genetic manipulation, computer montage, and virtual reality.[98]

And, meanwhile, nostalgically, from Matthew Barney in evening dress (*Radial Drill*, 1991), to Robert Gober's *Wedding Gown* (1989) or bisexual torso-vest (*Untitled*, 1990), and Jana Sterback in her male *Hairshirt* (1993), art "clothes" are extending beyond the masculine or the feminine masquerade to become transsexual prosthetics. Reciprocally, the worldwide community of transvestites and transsexuals photographed by Nan Goldin—the extended "family" of her book *The Other Side* (1993)—are differentiated from their soft-porn fellows only by the artist's eye.[99] Does Goldin's *Kim in Rhinestones, Paris* (1991) belong to the annual Parisian Salon of Eroticism or to the art museum? And what of Nicholas Sinclair's extravagant fauna, who came in the flesh with leather, rings, and glitter to animate the opening, in Brighton, of the exhibition *Fetishism*?[100] As the boundaries of the museum collapse, gender is transgressed: each Amazon, each man in a diamond dress, celebrates a passing beauty as well as the masquerade itself, and, in an age of HIV/AIDS, the transience of a sadder bohemia, in which the virtuality of the image is the only immortality. On the threshold of the year 2000, *The Other Side* summons the beyond; and the polyvalence of masquerade fuses with the pathos of endless quotation: "Exhibitionism? Narcissism? Sport? Theater? Deviation? Inversion? Infantilism? Competitiveness? Pride? Sincerity? Imposture? Doubtless, it's Love."[101]

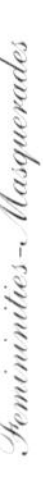

Notes

A substantially different version of this essay was published as "Féminités-Mascarades," trans. Charles Penwarden and Marie-Noëlle Ryan, in *fémininmasculin*, exh. cat. (Paris: Centre Georges Pompidou and Gallimard/Electa, 1995), pp. 291–311. Unless otherwise noted, all translations from the French are by the author.

1. Virginia Woolf, *Orlando: A Biography* (1928; New York: Harcourt Brace Jovanovich, 1956).
2. Simone de Beauvoir, *The Second Sex* (1948), trans. and ed. H. M. Parshley (New York: Alfred A. Knopf, 1993), p. 281: "It is civilization as a whole that produces this creature, intermediate between male and eunuch, which is described as feminine."
3. See Johann Joachim Bachofen, *Das Mutterrecht* (Stuttgart: Krais & Hoffmann, 1851).
4. Heinrich Cornelius Agrippa's *Sur la supériorité des femmes* (written 1509, published 1529), ed. B. Dubourg (Paris: Denvy Livres, 1986), was violently attacked by François Rabelais in his *Le Tiers-livre* (1546), called, at the time, "the antifeminist manifesto of the century." For subsequent iconography, see Laure Beaumont-Maillet, ed., *La Guerre des sexes* (Paris: A. Michel, 1984); and *Der Kampf der Geschlechter: Der neue Mythos in der Kunst, 1850–1930*, exh. cat. (Cologne: DuMont, 1995).
5. Laura Cottingham, "What's So Bad About Em?" in *Bad Girls*, exh. cat. (London: Institute of Contemporary Arts, 1993), p. 59, note 2. Cottingham's uses "bad" to mean positive, Dionysiac, anticonservative, ironic, humorous, and so on.
6. Definition quoted in Naomi Schor, "Feminism and George Sand: Lettres à Marcie," in Judith Butler and Joan W. Scott, eds., *Feminists Theorize the Political* (London: Routledge, 1992), p. 41.
7. Butler, *Gender Trouble: Feminism and the Subversion of Identity* (New York: Routledge, 1990), p. 48.
8. See Marjorie Garber, *Vested Interests: Cross-Dressing & Cultural Anxiety* (New York: Routledge, 1992), pp. 4–9, 77–84.
9. See Olympe de Gouges's tragically unrealized "Déclaration des droits de la femme et la citoyenne," in Avril de Sainte-Croix, *Le Féminisme* (Paris: V. Giard et E. Brière, 1907), pp. 24–25.
10. In this essay, I concentrate artistically on France, Great Britain, and the United States. While the psychoanalytic story is a tale of Vienna, Paris, and New York, the "German story" is central to the sexological aspects of my thesis. See Gert Hekma, "'A Female Soul in a Male Body': Sexual Inversion as Gender Inversion in Nineteenth-Century Sexology," in Gilbert Herdt, ed., *Third Sex, Third Gender: Beyond Sexual Dimorphism in Culture and History* (New York: Zone Books, 1994), pp. 213–39; and the surprisingly German emphasis of Guy Hocquenghem's *Race d'Ep! Un siècle d'images de l'homosexualité* (Paris: Hallier, 1979).
11. For the gynecide-to-genocide progression, see Bram Dijkstra, *Idols of Perversity: Fantasies of Feminine Evil in Fin-de-Siècle Culture* (New York: Oxford University Press, 1985), especially the conclusion, pp. 400–01. Let us remember, emblematically, Berty Albrecht, who published in the journal *Le Problème sexuel* in 1934, and whose mutilated body was found in the garden of the Fresnes prison in 1946, a victim of Nazi genocide.
12. For the twentieth-century proto-Nazi German context, see Klaus Theweleit, *Male Fantasies*, vol. 1: *Women, Floods, Bodies, History* (1977), trans. Stephen Conway, in collaboration with Erica Carter and Chris Turner (Minneapolis: University of Minnesota Press; and Oxford: Basil Blackwell, 1987). See vol. 2: *Male Bodies: Psychoanalyzing the White Terror* (1978), trans. Erica Carter and Chris Turner, in collaboration with Stephen Conway (Minneapolis: University of Minnesota Press; and Oxford: Polity Press, 1989), for Theweleit's critique of Freud's normative paradigms (p. 213), and for the Freudian taboo on involving the patient's body in treatment (p. 261).
13. For a discussion of the androgyny of the *demoiselles*, see David Lomas, "A Canon of Deformity: *Les Demoiselles d'Avignon* and Physical Anthropology," *Art History* 16, no. 3 (September 1993), pp. 424–46.
14. *Histoire de la femme . . .* (1904; Paris: Côté Femmes Editions, 1989). Dr. Caufeynon [Jean Fauconney] wrote over 100 works from 1901 to 1950, including *Histoire de l'homme* (1903).
15. See Theweleit, *Women, Floods, Bodies, History*, for the complex repertoire of idealized and denigrated images relating war and women; and Anna Bailey, "A Time of Transition: Female Representation in France, 1914–24" (M.A. thesis, Courtauld Institute of Art, London, 1991).
16. Marcel Duchamp, in an interview with Nixola Greeley-Smith, *The Evening World*, April 4, 1916; quoted in Francis M. Naumann, *New York Dada: 1915–1923* (New York: Harry N. Abrams, 1994), p. 102.
17. Duchamp, in an interview in the *New York Tribune*, September 12, 1915; quoted in Amelia Jones, *Postmodernism and the En-Gendering of Marcel Duchamp* (New York: Cambridge University Press, 1994), p. 284.
18. Naumann, *New York Dada*, pp. 168ff.
19. In speaking of Eleanor Butler, Colette suggests a Parisian reincarnation of the famous nineteenth-century Welsh lesbian couple, Butler and Sarah Ponsonby, the so-called Ladies of Llangollen. *Ces Plaisirs* was republished in 1941 as *Le Pur et l'impur*. See Colette, *The Pure and the Impure* (1941), trans. Herma Briffault (New York: Farrar, Straus and Giroux, 1975), pp. 114–29.
20. Janet Flanner, quoted in Anna Chave, *Constantin Brancusi: Shifting the Bases of Art* (New Haven: Yale University Press, 1993), p. 106. Chave also cites Natalie Barney's Sapphic festivals in the "Temple d'Amitié" and Jane Heap in male drag at a party in Brancusi's studio.
21. Jean Montrevel, "Notes sur la morale sexuelle en France," *Clarté*, no. 73 (1925), p. 15.
22. Joan Riviere, "Womanliness as a Masquerade," *The International Journal of Psychoanalysis* 10 (1929), pp. 303–13; reprinted in Victor Burgin, James Donald, and Cora Kaplan, eds. *Formations of Fantasy* (New York: Routledge, 1986), pp. 35–44.
23. Ibid., Riviere, p. 37.
24. Ibid., p. 38.
25. Ibid.
26. Much work was done following the reappearance of Riviere's article in Hendrik M. Ruitenbeek, ed., *Psychoanalysis and Female Sexuality* (New Haven: College and University Press, 1966). See, for example, Laura Mulvey, "Visual Pleasure and Narrative Cinema," *Screen* 16, no. 3 (1975), pp. 6–18; and Mary Ann Doane, "Film and the Masquerade: Theorising the Female Spectator," *Screen* 23, nos. 3–4 (1982), pp. 74–84. See also, Butler, "Lacan, Riviere, and the Strategies of Masquerade," in Butler, *Gender Trouble*, pp. 43–57; and Butler's extended bibliography, p. 159, note 18.
27. For Riviere and Marie Bonaparte, see Lisa Appignanesi and John Forrester, *Freud's Women* (London: Weidenfeld and Nicholson, 1992), pp. 329–48, 353–65. Marie Bonaparte's *La Sexualité de la femme*, which leans heavily on a 1920s and 1930s bibliography, did not appear until 1951 (Amer. ed., *Female Sexuality*, trans. John Redker [New York: International Universities Press, 1953]). Bonaparte would have been familiar with Richard Goldschmidt's December 1931 lectures at the Faculté des Sciences, "Le Déterminisme du sexe et l'intersexualité." In 1932, Freud's discourse on "Féminité" appeared and was included in *Nouvelles Conférences sur la psychanalyse* (1932), translated by Anne Berman, in 1936.

28. See Elisabeth Roudinesco, "Traductions des oeuvres de Freud en langue française entre 1920 et 1940," in *La Bataille de cent ans: Histoire de la psychanalyse en France*, vol. 1 (Paris: Editions de Seuil, 1982), pp. 481–83.
29. See Agnès Masson, *Le Travestissement: Essai de psychopathologie sexuelle* (Paris: Hippocrate, 1935). The preface was written by René Laignel-Lavaltine, Masson's professor, who published on the femininity of the Abbé de Choisy in the journal *Paris-Medical* in 1919, subsequently devoting himself, at the Sainte-Anne hospital, to the study of the "more or less developed lack of polarization" among the patients—that is, the abundance of bearded women, symptoms of virilism, endocrine malfunctions, etc.
30. Ibid., p. 65. France's ethnographic craze had its reflection in Masson's account of the ritual character of castration, homosexual, and other practices by Native Americans, Eskimos, and Tahitians. See also Roland d'Eck, *De la pluralité sexuelle* (Paris, 1931); and Gregorio Maranon, *Evolution de la sexualité et des états intersexuels* (Paris, 1931); cited in René Colla, *Le Travestissement habituel* (Paris: Edition de la faculté de médicine de Paris, 1956).
31. For a discussion of the notion of "phallogocularcentrism," see Martin Jay, *Downcast Eyes: The Denigration of Vision in Twentieth-Century French Thought* (Berkeley: University of California Press, 1993). Surrealist art refutes his thesis.
32. The "Recherches sur la sexualité" were originally published in *La Révolution surréaliste*, nos. 10–11 (1928). They are collected and reprinted in José Pierre, ed., *Investigating Sex: Surrealist Research 1928–1932*, trans. Malcolm Imrie (New York: Verso, 1992).
33. For "homosexual panic," see Garber, *Vested Interests*, p. 137, discussing Edward J. Kempf's coinage of the term in 1920 and its currency today, thanks to the writing of Eve Kosofsky Sedgwick.
34. See Tristan Tzara, "D'un certain automatisme du goût," *Minotaure* 3–4 (1933); and also, the analysis by Briony Fer, "The Hat, the Hoax, the Body," in Kathleen Adler and Marcia Pointon, eds., *The Body Imaged* (New York: Cambridge University Press, 1993), pp. 161–73.
35. J. C. Flügel's article "Clothes Symbolism and Clothes Ambivalence" (discussing polyphallic symbolism and female exhibitionism, etc.) precedes Riviere's 1929 article in *The International Journal of Psychoanalysis* 10 (1929), pp. 205–17. Roland Barthes's essay "Masculin-Féminin-Neutre," an early version of *S/Z*, was the prelude to his *Système de la mode*, written from 1957 to 1963 and published in 1967; see Barthes, *The Fashion System*, trans. Matthew Ward and Richard Howard (New York: Farrar, Straus and Giroux, 1983). See also Eugénie Lemoine-Luccioni, *La Robe: Essai psychanalytique sur le vêtement* (Paris: Editions du Seuil, 1983); and Richard Martin, *Fashion and Surrealism*, exh. cat. (New York: Fashion Institute of Technology and Rizzoli, 1987).
36. Jacques Derrida, *Spurs: Nietzsche's Styles* (1978), intro. Stefano Agosti, trans. Barbara Harlow (Chicago: University of Chicago Press, 1979), p. 97.
37. Ibid., p. 99.
38. André Breton, *Arcane 17* (1944).
39. The proverb is represented as a decapitation in an anonymous copper engraving, circa 1660, reprinted in Beaumont-Maillet, ed., *La Guerre des sexes*, p. 8. This must have been the generic source for Max Ernst's *La Femme 100 têtes*.
40. Barbara Johnson, *A World of Difference: Disfiguring Poetic Language* (Baltimore: Johns Hopkins University Press, 1983), p. 114; quoted in Chave, *Constantin Brancusi*, p. 291.
41. *La Femme et le surréalisme*, exh. cat. (Lausanne: Musée cantonal des Beaux-Arts Lausanne, 1987).
42. To decapitate is to castrate, according to Freud. From the woman's point of view, "The tusked Gorgon is *the eye which eats*." See Camille Paglia, *Sexual Personae* (New Haven: Yale University Press, 1990), p. 50.
43. See Jacqueline Rose, *Sexuality in the Field of Vision* (London: Verso, 1986): "Woman is taken to desire herself but only through the term which precludes her" (p. 212); and Garber, *Vested Interests*, on female fetishism and fetish envy, pp. 126–27.
44. Claude Cahun, *Les Paris sont ouverts* (Paris: José Corti, 1934).
45. See François Leperlier, *Claude Cahun* (Paris: Jean-Michel Place, 1992).
46. Hans Anton Prinner was a female transvestite sculptor, whose true sexual identity was unknown to many in the art world. See Hans Anton Prinner, *La Femme tondue*, illustrated with eight engravings (Paris: APR, 1946); and Alain Brossat, *Les Tondues: Un carnaval moche* (Paris: Editions Manya, 1993).
47. The 600,000 prostitutes indicated an increase of 200,000 since the War (figures quoted in *Combat*, September 12, 1947).
48. Jean-Paul Sartre, *L'Imaginaire* (Paris: Gallimard, 1940), pp. 372–73.
49. Murielle Gagnebin, *Fascination de la laideur: L'en deça psychanaltytique du laid* (1978; Paris: Editions Champ Vallon, 1994), p. 259.
50. Ibid.
51. De Beauvoir, *The Second Sex*, p. xvi, challenging Emmanuel Levinas in *Le Temps et l'autre*: "Otherness reaches its full flowering in the feminine."
52. Kinsey's report on male sexuality was published in France in 1948; the report on female sexuality (1953) came out in French in October 1954. Bonaparte's *La Sexualité de la femme* appeared in 1951. See Isabelle Moreau, *Mon comportement sexuel: Une française répond au questionnaire Kinsey* (Paris: Editions Jean Froissart, 1953). The impact of film is another dimension; see, for example, Gina Lombroso, *L'Ame de la femme* (Paris: Payot, 1947); or Lombroso, "De la vamp à la femme," special number of *L'Ecran* (February–March 1958).
53. Sartre's characterization of the viscous and feminine "revenge of the *en-soi*," expressed in *Etre et le néant* (1943) was challenged by Suzanne Lilar, in *A propos de Sartre et l'amour* (Paris: Grasset, 1967), p. 77; see also Dorothy MacCall, "Existentialisme ou féminisme?" *Sartre*, special issue of *Obliques* (1979), pp. 311–20.
54. De Beauvoir, *Brigitte Bardot and the Lolita Syndrome*, trans. Bernard Frechtman (New York: Reynal & Company, 1960).
55. Man Ray, "Des chats et des magnolias," *Le Surréalisme, même*, no. 1 (1958), p. 7.
56. See *Exposition InteRnatiOnale du Surréalisme (EROS)*, exh. cat. (Paris: Galerie Daniel Cordier, 1959).
57. Betty Friedan, *The Feminine Mystique* (1963; New York: W. W. Norton, 1983).
58. Jean Genet, "Fragments," *Les Temps modernes* (August 1954), pp. 200, 203.
59. Pierre Molinier's solo show at the Galerie de l'Etoile Scellée, in 1956, was arranged by Breton, who wrote the preface to the catalogue; Molinier subsequently contributed to *Le Surréalisme, même* and exhibited at the international exhibitions of Surrealism in 1959 and 1965.
60. Gérard Durozoi, "Molinier, entre l'amour et la mort," *Canal* 32, no. 4 (October 1979), a response to Molinier's retrospective at the Centre Georges Pompidou, Paris.
61. See Jean-Louis Poitevin, "Pierre Molinier: De la photographie comme extase," *Clichés*, no. 59 (1989), pp. 54–59; and Peter Gorsen, "The Artist's Desiring Gaze on Objects of Fetishism," in *Pierre Molinier: Comme je voudrais être*, exh. cat. (London: Cabinet Gallery, 1993), p. 37. Gorsen points to the important show *"Transformer": Aspekte der Travestie*, which was at the Kunstmuseum in Lucerne, Switzerland, in 1974, and traveled to Graz, Austria, and Bochum, West Germany, in

1974–75. See also Pierre Petit, *Molinier: Une vie d'enfer* (Paris: Editions Ramsay/Jean Jacques Pauvert, 1992).

62. See, for example, Severo Sarduy, "Les Travestis: Kallima sur un corps: Toile, idole," *Art Press*, no. 20 (September–October 1975), pp. 12–13. In 1971, Guy Hocquenghem founded the Front Homosexuel d'Action Révolutionnaire. Subsequently, he published *Le Désir homosexuel* (Paris: Editions Universitaires, 1972); and *Race d'Ep!*

63. Sartre, preface to Genet, *The Maids and Deathwatch: Two Plays*, trans. Bernard Frechtman (New York: Grove Weidenfeld, 1983), pp. 10-15.

64. Kenneth E. Silver, "Modes of Disclosure: The Construction of Gay Identity and the Rise of Pop Art," in *Hand-Painted Pop: American Art in Transition, 1955–1962*, exh. cat. (Los Angeles: Museum of Contemporary Art; and New York: Rizzoli, 1993), pp. 178–203.

65. Ibid., p. 181.

66. Ibid., p. 197.

67. Susan Sontag, "Notes on 'Camp'" (1964); reprinted in Sontag, *Against Interpretation and Other Essays* (New York: Farrar, Straus and Giroux, 1986), p. 116.

68. Dick Hebidge, "Fabulous Confusion: Pop before Pop?" in *Hand-Painted Pop*, p. 234; see also Laura Mulvey, "A Phantasmagoria of the Female Body: The Work of Cindy Sherman," *New Left Review*, no. 188 (July–August 1991), pp. 136–51.

69. See the reprint of the catalogues to both exhibitions, *The Complete Book of Erotic Art*, compiled by Phyllis and Eberhard Kronhausen (New York: Bell Publishing, 1987).

70. *Daddy* was shown in London at the Hammer Cinema in November 1972; the revised version was shown, in April 1973, at the eleventh New York Film Festival.

71. Maryse Holder, "Another Cuntree: At Last, a Mainstream Female Art Movement," *off our backs* (September 1973); reprinted in Arlene Raven, Cassandra Langer, and Joanna Frueh, eds., *Feminist Art Criticism: An Anthology* (New York: G. K. Hall, 1993), pp. 1–20.

72. Frantz Fanon, *Peau noir, masques blancs* (Paris: Editions du Seuil, 1952); *Black Skin, White Masks*, trans. Charles Lam Markmann (New York: Grove Press, 1967). Compare Norman Mailer's very disturbing polemic *The White Negro* (1957; San Francisco: City Lights Books, 1959).

73. *Les Maîtres fous*, a film astonishing in its implications, is contextualized by Paul Stoller, René Prédal, and Ingrid Eisen, in C. W. Thompson, ed., *L'Autre et le sacré: Surréalisme, cinéma, ethnologie* (Paris: Editions Harmattan, 1995).

74. Jean Decock, "Les Nègres aux U.S.A.," in *Genet*, special issue of *Obliques* (1989), p. 48; for Decock's entire article, see pp. 48–50. For French reception of Genet's play, see Maurice Lecuyer, "*Les Nègres* et au-delà," in ibid., pp. 44–47. See also Edmund White, *Jean Genet* (New York: Alfred A. Knopf, 1993), pp. 490–508.

75. Genet, *Prisoner of Love* (1986), trans. Barbara Bray (Hanover, N.H.: University Press of New England; and Middletown, Conn.: Wesleyan University Press, 1989).

76. See *Black Male: Representations of Masculinity in Contemporary Art*, brochure and exh. cat. (New York: Whitney Museum of American Art, 1994).

77. Lowery Stokes Sims, "Aspects of Performance by Black American Women Artists," in Raven, Langer, and Frueh, eds., *Feminist Art Criticism*, p. 209.

78. Genet, *Prisoner of Love*, p. 150. The translator, Barbara Bray, does not translate "afin qu'il vous désign" (so the world can classify you), and Genet's "obligatoire détournement syntaxique" is more complex (perverse) than "change of syntax."

79. Sims, *Aspects of Performance*, p. 215.

80. Mark Simpson, *Male Impersonators: Men Performing Masculinity* (London: Cassell, 1994), p. 142.

81. Jean Baudrillard, *Simulations*, trans. Paul Foss, Paul Patton, and Philip Beitchman (New York: Semiotext(e), 1983), p. 57; quoted in ibid.

82. See Elisabeth Lebovici, "A quel débat 'Black Male' s'expose-t-il à New York?" *Libération*, December 10–11, 1994, p. 32.

83. Simpson's devastating analysis of football (*Male Impersonators*, pp. 69–93), with its revelation of the hidden feminine, could fruitfully be extended into the arena of the "black male."

84. For the concept of "panic" and its links with a culture of "simulacra," see Arthur and Marilouise Kroker, "Panic Sex in America," and "Theses on the Disappearing Body in the Hyper-Modern Condition," in Arthur and Marilouise Kroker, eds., *Body Invaders: Panic Sex in America* (New York: St. Martin's Press, 1987), pp. 10–19, 20–34.

85. I see bell hook's 1992 essay "Reconstructing Black Masculinity," in Andrew Perchuck and Helaine Posner, eds., *The Masculine Masquerade: Masculinity and Representation*, exh. cat. (Cambridge, Mass.: MIT Press, 1995), pp. 67–88, as a key example of this "framing" problem.

86. While *The Masculine Masquerade* (ibid.) is an exemplary exploration of new literature and imagery, male masquerade surely dates back to display in the "men's hut" and the very origins of andocracy.

87. Monique Wittig, *Les Guérillières* (1969), trans. David Le Vay (New York: Viking, 1971).

88. The situation has not been any better in Europe. For example, the exhibition *Douze ans d'art contemporain en France*, at the Grand Palais, Paris, from May to September 1972, included two female artists and seventy men.

89. See the Guerrilla Girls, *Confessions of the Guerrilla Girls*, with an essay by Whitney Chadwick (New York: HarperCollins, 1995), p. 21.

90. See texts by Marcia Tucker on the United States; Lisa Tickner and Griselda Pollock (the pioneer of British feminist art history), on Great Britain; Rosie Huhn, on France; and Nicole Dubreuil-Blondin, on Canada, in Yves Michaud, ed., *Féminisme, art et histoire de l'art* (Paris: Ecole nationale supérieure des Beaux Arts, 1994).

91. Pontus Hulten, "Working with Fury and with Pleasure," in *Niki de Saint-Phalle*, exh. cat. (Stuttgart: Hatje, 1992), p. 13. De Saint-Phalle's show was installed above Hulten's quasi-millennial survey of twentieth-century art, *Territorium Artis*, which opened at the Kunst- und Ausstellungshalle der Bundesrepublik Deutschland Bonn, in 1992, and included four women and 106 men.

92. For a discussion of this marginalization, see Stephen Frosh, *Masculinity and Psychoanalysis* (New York: Routledge, 1994), pp. 28ff; for a now dated example, take Derrida's self-contradictory assertion: "Deconstruction is certainly not feminist," in *Critical Exchange*, no. 17 (winter 1985), p. 30.

93. See Dominique Gilbert Laporte, "A une amazone . . . ," in *Lea Lublin/Orlan: Histoires saintes de l'art* (Cergy: Lacertidé, 1985), unpaginated.

94. See Orlan's "Citations-situation," in collaboration with Hubert Besacier, for the symposium "Mesonges" (1979).

95. Lemoine-Luccioni, *La Robe*, p. 95; see also ibid., pp. 122–23. For the transsexuality of saints, see ibid., Chapter XI, "Orlan," pp. 133–45, where her source is Louis Réau, *Iconographie de l'art Chrétien* (Paris: Presse Université de France, 1959). Of course, the mythicizing of gender differentiation is at the root of the Old Testament Genesis and, subsequently, of the Cabala.

96. Orlan's seventh operation, *Omniprésence*, part of the *Re-incarnation de Sainte-Orlan* series (1993), was performed on July 11, 1993. The next operation will be done in Japan. See Sarah Wilson, "L'Histoire d'O: Sacred and

Profane," in Sarah Wilson et al., *Orlan* (London: Black Dog Publishing, 1996), pp. 7–17.

97. Simone Weil, quoted by Marisa Vescovo, in *Gina Pane*, exh. cat. (Pays de la Loire: F.R.A.C., 1991), p. 38.

98. See *Les Vingt Ans de pub et de ciné de Sainte-Orlan*, exh. cat. (Basse-Normandie: Centre d'Art Contemporain, 1990); Barbara Rose, "Is It Art? Orlan and the Transgressive Act," *Art in America* 81, no. 2 (February 1993), pp. 82–87; and, for a psychoanalytic interpretation, Parveen Adams, "This Is My Body," in *Suture—Phantasmen der Vollkommenheit*, exh. cat. (Salzburg: Salzburger Kunstverein, 1994), pp. 48–56.

99. On Nan Goldin, see Michael Bracewell, "Making Up Is Hard to Do," *Frieze*, no. 12 (1993), pp. 32–37.

100. Anthony Sheldon, ed., *Fetishism: Visualising Power and Desire*, exh. cat. (Brighton: Brighton Museum and Art Gallery, 1995). The exhibition, which ran from April to July 1995, included a foyer show of Nicholas Sinclair's photographs. See also Nicholas Sinclair, *The Chameleon Body: Photographs of Contemporary Fetishism*, with texts by David Alan Mellor and Anthony Sheldon (London: Lund Humphries, 1996).

101. Walerian Borowczyk, preface to André Berg's book of soft-porn transvestite photographs, *Créatures* (Nyons: Le Club du Livre Secret; and Paris: Pink Star, 1982).

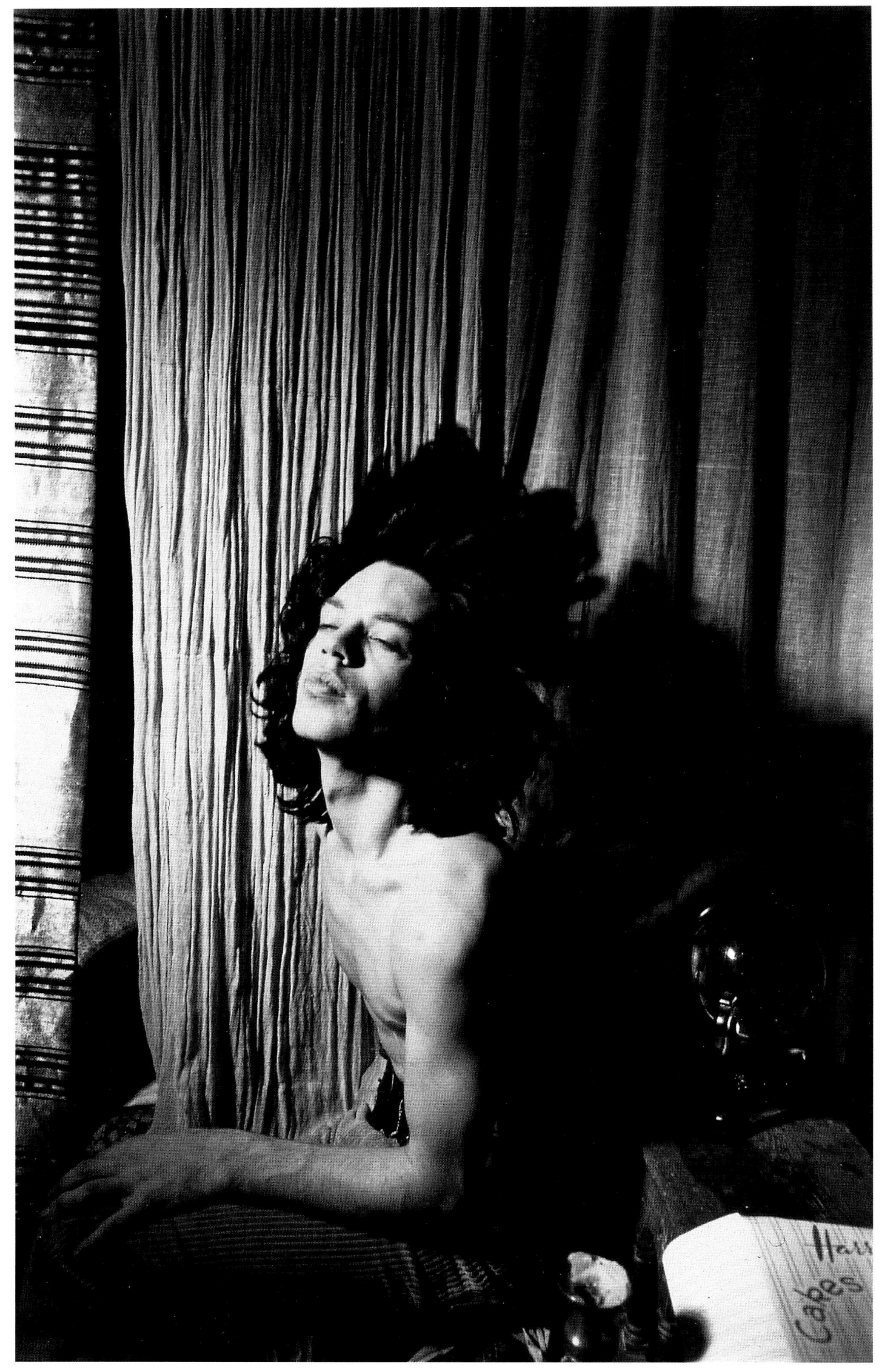

Cecil Beaton
Mick Jagger on the set of *Performance*, 1968
Courtesy of Cecil Beaton Archive, Sotheby's London

Performing the Body in the 1970s

NANCY SPECTOR

Rebel, you've torn your dress
Rebel, your face is a mess
Rebel, how could they know?
Hot tramp, I love you so!

You've got your mother in a whirl, 'cause she's
Not sure if you're a boy or a girl
Hey babe, your hair's alright
Hey babe, let's stay out tonight
DAVID BOWIE, "Rebel, Rebel," 1974

Nothing is real, everything is permitted.
MICK JAGGER as Turner in *Performance*, 1970

Prologue: The Legacy of Duchamp

In 1967, Michael Fried published his now famous essay "Art and Objecthood," in which he dismissed Minimalist sculpture as overtly *theatrical* because, in order for it to exist as an artwork, the physical presence of a viewer over a period of time was required.[1] The corporeal implications of work by Carl Andre, Donald Judd, and Robert Morris, among others of that generation, disrupted what Fried, an acolyte of Greenbergian Modernism, valued—the absolute "presentness" of an art form that adheres to the specificities of its own medium.

Inadvertently, Fried's critique of theater as that which "lies between the arts" presaged the emergence of radically new forms during the 1970s that emphatically defied categorization by medium and dramatically engaged the temporal process.[2] The decade witnessed the emergence of artistic models that were recognized for their preoccupation with time, transformation, and the body. For instance, in 1970, Dennis Oppenheim slept on Jones Beach for five hours to induce a second-degree burn;[3] in 1971, Chris Burden invited a colleague to shoot him in the arm with a .22-caliber rifle;[4] in 1973, Gina Pane slashed her forearm with a razor blade, forcing thorns from cut roses into each wound;[5] and, in 1974, Marina Abramović ingested medications for acute catatonia and schizophrenia as part of a seven-hour performance.[6]

Fried's prophetic, albeit negative, understanding of the phenomenological nature of Minimalism was overlooked during the 1970s by critics eager to link the new body-related art to pres-

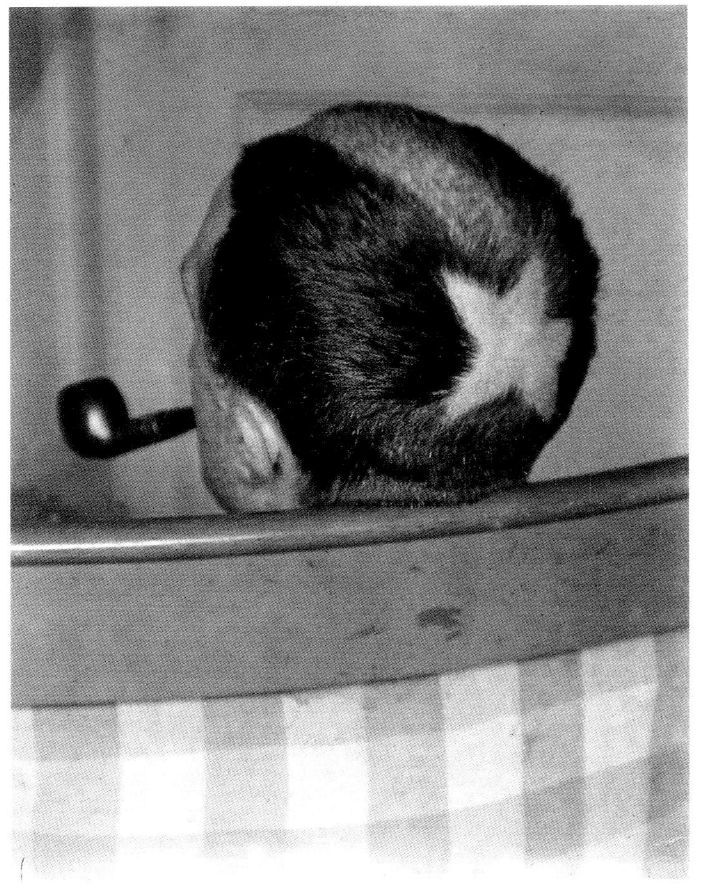

Man Ray
Duchamp Tonsured (by Georges de Zayas), 1921
Gelatin-silver print,
4¾ x 3‰ inches (12.1 x 9 cm)
Private collection, Courtesy of Howard Greenberg Gallery, New York

tigious historical sources. Thus, early artistic prototypes such as Futurist theater and Dada soirees were cited, and analogies were continually drawn between the new work and that of Marcel Duchamp. In particular, references were made to *Tonsure* (1919/21), the piece in which Duchamp shaved the hair on the back of his head into a star shape.[7] (*Tonsure* refers, in both French and English, to the ritualistic practice of shaving the heads of those entering ecclesiastical orders or religious cults.) This precocious parody of the art world's then only marginally burgeoning "star system" was considered a paradigm for the conflation of self and object intrinsic to the new body art.[8] Because, in *Tonsure*, Duchamp had constructed an image with and on his own person, the work was espoused as a key predecessor to contemporary work involving performances conducted in private or for the public, acts of self-mutilation, and/or acts of self-transformation.

However, two critical aspects of the piece relevant to 1970s body art were not discussed in this context. First, Duchamp had devised the emblematic alteration to his coiffure strictly for the camera. And second, two different photographs of his star-shaped bald spot[9]—dated 1919 and 1921—document the artist's self-conscious metamorphosis into "cult" object:[10] the dual versions of the image sequentially and conceptually bracket Duchamp's unveiling, in 1920, of his feminine alter ego, Rrose Sélavy. At the time Duchamp conceived this particular presentation of self—as an inductee into an unspecified sect, whether religious or secular—he was ruminating about a complete change in identity. Thinking back on the period, he said that he had considered switching his religious affiliation from Christian to Jewish but had not found any enticing Jewish names to adopt. Instead, he opted to swap genders: "Why not change sex? It was much simpler," he mused.[11] And thus was born his female other, the fashionable flapper Rrose Sélavy. In light of these recollections, one might wonder which cult Duchamp was preparing himself for with his star-shaped tonsure. Could it have been that age-old and not so secret cult of transvestism, with its tantalizing elision of binary thought?[12]

These interpretive details—the performative, the photographic, and the inversion of gender roles—intersect in and around *Tonsure* and its retroactive relationship with art of the 1970s. Together, the three motifs compose a provocative theoretical constellation through which to contemplate the body art of this period and its surviving documentation. This conceptual matrix does not encompass all forms of body-related art, however, but rather that performed expressly to be documented—whether by photographic, video, or cinematic means—and that which entailed some form of transvestism—either female to male, male to female, or somewhere in between. Beyond identifying art-historical instances of this convergence between embodied art and gender representation—which is not particularly difficult, given the plethora of such work in the 1970s—the real challenge lies in determining what these examples might reveal about subjectivity, sexual difference, gender division, desire, and visual pleasure—both then and now.

A Note on Photography: Documentation as Art Form in the 1970s

In the wake of Pop and Minimalism—genres that each contained the seeds of institutional critique—many contemporaneous artists felt compelled to discover new ways to supplant the autonomous art object and its commodification by the museum and gallery system. The strategies of "dematerialization" and dispersal that emerged by the end of the 1960s in response to this challenge were numerous and disparate. Variations on Earth art, Process art, body art, Postminimalism, Conceptualism, and Arte Povera evolved in both the United States and Europe, introducing to the vocabulary of visual art processes of distribution; elements of time and corporeality; linguistic analysis; and a mythology of materials. What linked these dissimilar and seemingly incongruous practices was photography, a medium that served to chronicle and display this otherwise ephemeral work.

As a medium long marginalized within the art-historical hierarchy, photography was embraced during the 1970s as the transgressive medium par excellence.[13] Its mechanical reproducibility, its low cultural status, and its mimetic capabilities offered artists a more or less debased vehicle through which to transmit ideas without necessarily creating aestheticized objects.[14] Because fine-art photography had joined the cultural canon of Modernism by the 1920s and was thus enshrined in the collections of such venerable institutions as New York's Museum of Modern Art,[15] artists of the 1970s were more inclined to expropriate the style of photojournalism as a model for their analytic endeavors (even though, by the 1960s, photojournalism was itself considered art photography).[16]

The documentary photograph was adapted not only by artists wishing to bypass conventionally aestheticized mimetic systems, but also by those who co-opted its representational codes of "vérité" and instantaneousness to record events enacted primarily for the camera, particularly those executed as preconceived episodes or as performances in the privacy of the studio.[17] Formulated through what A. D. Coleman has called the "directorial mode," the artfully constructed mise-en-scène of much conceptually oriented photographic work of the 1970s parodies photography's romance with reportage and reportage's claims to truth.[18] Many of the artists who employed this "directorial" strategy—Vito Acconci, Eleanor Antin, Jürgen Klauke, Bruce Nauman, Oppenheim, Adrian Piper, and Lucas Samaras, among them—structured their work around the presentation of self in photographic terms, either physically altering their bodies, performing some predetermined task, or acting the part of a fictional character. In order to convey and preserve the notion of time in such work, which was rendered static by the photographic freeze-frame, multiple images and descriptive texts were often used. In a number of cases, as in work by Acconci, Antin, Dan Graham, Rebecca Horn, Nauman, and William Wegman, private performances were recorded on videotape or Super-8 film, which, though structurally different from photography, shares its mimetic faculties and was thus well suited for the "(photo)documentation" of performative exercises.[19] In reassessing photo-based body art of the 1970s, it is essential to differentiate between the photographic documentation of theatrical events staged publicly for an audience—examples include work by Abramović and Ulay, Burden, Joan Jonas, Paul McCarthy, Pane, Rachel Rosenthal, and Carolee Schneemann—and the purposely choreographed construction of self (or selves) for the camera alone, with the photograph itself constituting the core of the artwork. This distinction is being emphasized here in order to foreground the particular historical matrix in question: the collusion among body art, photography, and gender performance during the 1970s.[20]

Historical and Cultural Contexts: Acting Out in the 1970s

It is not by coincidence that the concept of self—as something to construct, reconstruct, and deconstruct—came under such scrutiny during the 1970s. It was a time when the borders between self and other were under interrogation from within—the women's liberation movement, the civil rights movement, and the gay and lesbian rights movement were in various stages of formation, and all introduced burning questions about social, racial, and sexual identity. Furthermore, the United States' controversial involvement in the Vietnam War forced the issue of self and other into a politicized arena in which oppositions were premised on perceived ideological and nationalistic differences. And, finally, the 1960s counterculture had passionately embraced the concept of personal transformation, even transcendence, through mind-expanding drugs, rock 'n' roll, and free sex. Its utopian ideals—from communal living to ecological awareness and military passivism—advocated, at least on the surface, union between self and other, unless that other was considered to be part of the "establishment."

Despite the acute social and political upheavals of 1960s America—namely, the escalation of the Vietnam War, the battle for civil rights, and the assassinations of President Kennedy, Robert F. Kennedy, Martin Luther King, Jr., and Malcolm X—the decade ended on a relatively optimistic note. In 1969, American astronauts Neil Armstrong and Buzz Aldrin made their historic walk on the moon; the "Stonewall" rebellion in New York's Greenwich Village initiated the modern-day gay and lesbian rights movement; the Woodstock Music Festival triumphed as three days of peace and harmony; and the women's liberation movement was solidified across the country through "consciousness raising" groups, community-based education, and grass-roots politics. The United States Food and Drug Administration's approval of the birth control pill in 1960 granted women unprecedented control over their own bodies and helped to usher in a new age of sexual freedom. During the ensuing decade, a politics of pleasure emerged that endorsed sexual indulgence as a force to counter dominant modes of oppression. Articulated by the social theoretician Herbert Marcuse as early as 1955, this libidinal economy argued for a desublimation of instinctive energies as an antidote to social ills.[21] The "anything goes" sensibility of the 1960s, however naive it may seem in retrospect, was rooted in a profound desire for social change, one that upheld racial and/or sexual equality as criteria for cultural renewal. This belief was even reflected in fashion with the emergence of "unisex" dressing, that paean to androgyny as a utopian state of bisexed being.

The dawn of the 1970s was anything but auspicious, however. When the United States invaded Cambodia during the first year of the decade, it became apparent that the Vietnam War was far from over. Previously peaceful demonstrations against U.S. military intervention in Southeast Asia turned bloody when the National Guard opened fire on students protesting at Kent State University in 1970. Youth culture, with its faith in the liberatory excesses of drugs and rock music, encountered a harsh reality check the same year when two of its cultural icons—Jimi Hendrix and Janis Joplin—died from drug overdoses. These episodes were not exactly sobering; the emancipatory inclinations that defined and eventually dated the 1960s continued throughout the 1970s, albeit with a slightly ironic edge. The sexual subculture of the preceding decade, replete with drag queens, butch dykes, and transsexuals, crept into the popular imagination through mainstream films and rock music. What was essentially outlawed in 1960s cinematic representation—take, for example the censorship of independent filmmaker Jack Smith's *Flaming Creatures* (1962)—was embraced during the 1970s in such movies as Michael Sarne's *Myra Breckinridge* (1970), Nicholas Roeg and Donald Cammell's *Performance* (1970), Sidney Lumet's *Dog Day Afternoon* (1975), and Jim Sharman's *Rocky Horror Picture Show* (1975). Granted, Smith's unabashed celebration of transvestism and polymorphous sexuality was erotically explicit, but the film's confiscation by the police had more to do with the instability of gender roles it portrayed than with any frontal nudity.[22] By the time Tim Curry appeared as the mad scientist sporting a red corset and fishnet stockings in *Rocky Horror* and Chris Sarandon wore a white gown and veil as a "bride" in *Dog Day Afternoon*, audiences had grown more accustomed to on-screen references to homosexuality, gender mutability, and cross-dressing.

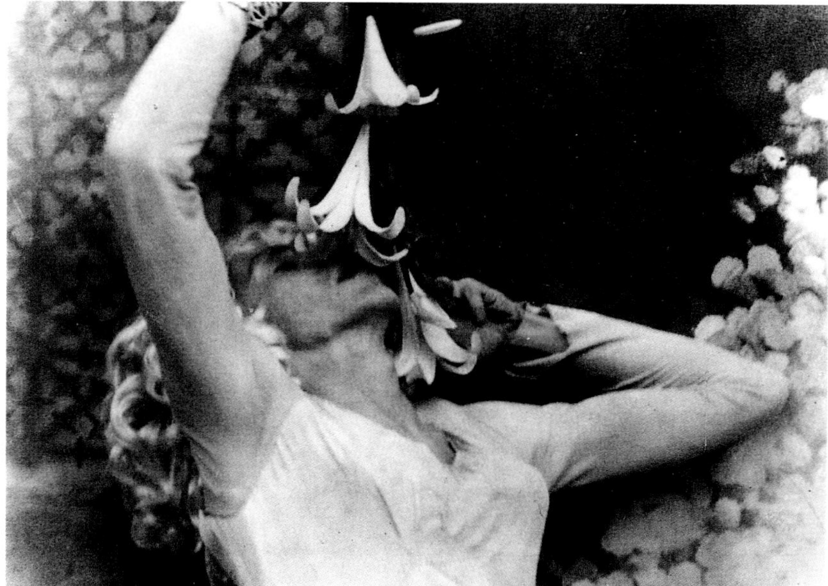

Jack Smith
Film still from *Flaming Creatures*, 1962
Courtesy of Anthology Film Archives, New York

Rock musicians had long embraced travesty as a mode of performance, but more as a means to signify (and package) social transgression than to express the radical implications of true sexual and gender ambiguity. The 1970s witnessed the rise of such enigmatic pop stars as David Bowie, Brian Eno, Mick Jagger, the New York Dolls, and Iggy Pop, whose theatrical personae embodied gender indeterminacy.[23] Their performances as feminized males, complete with eye makeup, lipstick, platform heels, and fetishistic costumes, did not alienate their presumably largely heterosexual audiences. On the contrary, their male-to-female travesty was relatively unthreatening, if not entirely seductive, given their commercial success, and it proved that the Marcusean principle of sexual desublimation was a highly marketable strategy. Despite the popularity of androgynous rock 'n' roll, however, it was rare to encounter the female-to-male version in mainstream contemporary music. The only example that comes to mind is Patti Smith, who was photographed in drag by Robert Mapplethorpe for the cover of her *Horses* album in 1975. Too feminine in appearance to "pass" as a man, Smith played the part of the androgyne with perfect punk coolness; her wrinkled white shirt, open black tie, disheveled hair, and pale complexion made a statement against the marketing of female rock stars as sex symbols.

While the feminized male was easily accepted as a pop star,[24] the masculine or "phallic" female did not (and still does not) fit comfortably within the social codes that determine cultural visibility. The same double standard held true for visual artists working with the body during the 1970s; while the men were free to possess their own self-representations, altering appearances at will and playing with gender roles, women who experimented with similar strategies were more often criticized, if not dismissed, for self-indulgent or narcissistic behavior. In fact, the contradictory critical responses to work by male and female artists who dealt with photographic representations of gender and its inherent mutability are quite telling in their division along gender lines and the suppositions they reveal about "artistic" uses of the body.

Body Art and "Gender Trouble"

The concept of "body art" was first articulated (as "body work") by artist/critic Willoughby Sharp in the premiere issue of *Avalanche*, the magazine he founded with Liza Beár in 1970 to cover recent developments in contemporary culture. In his analysis of the topic, Sharp attempts to delineate the parameters of this aesthetic practice, which he defines simply as the "use of the artist's own body as sculptural material."[25] Identifying four subcategories of the genre—"body as tool," "body as place," "body as backdrop," and "body as prop"—Sharp insists that the physicality of the work far outweighed any expressive or autobiographical content it might have. He considered the artist's body as nothing more than a vehicle to perform the action of intransitive verbs: to cut, to skip, to gag, to run, to walk, to jump, and so on.[26] With this explanation, Sharp effectively dismisses the possibility of artistic subjectivity or the presence of psychological content in the work. Furthermore, all of the artists he discusses—including Acconci, Terry Fox, Barry Le Va, Richard Long, Nauman, and Oppenheim—are male, though he certainly feels no need to explain this segregation by gender. The maleness of the artist has always been presupposed, unless stated otherwise. Nevertheless, many women artists were also using their bodies in their art at this time, if not before. Jonas, Yayoi Kasuma, and Schneemann, for instance, had been producing body-based performance work since the mid-1960s.[27] And by the beginning of the 1970s, a culture of feminist performance art emerged in Southern California with the establishment, by Judy Chicago, of the Feminist Art Program at Fresno State College, where artists such as Suzanne Lacy and Faith Wilding created their first performance pieces.[28]

It can be said, without overgeneralizing, that a "universalizing" single-sex discourse around body art prevailed through much of the decade. In 1974, feminist critic Lucy Lippard devoted an article in *Art in America* to an overview of performance work by women, in which she discusses the impossibility of female artists using their own bodies without also using their *selves*, and that these selves were impossible to divorce from gender identification. Lippard also notes that women artists in Europe (such as Abramović, Horn, and Pane) were encouraged early on to utilize their physical beings in ephemeral, performance work by the "male establishment," who wished to avoid competition in the more profitable areas of painting and sculpture.[29] Four years later, British art historian and feminist Lisa Tickner wrote another essay dealing exclusively with women's body art and its sexual politics, in which she, like Sharp before her, divides body-related work into separate categories in order to encompass the range of conceptual strategies in practice during the decade. In contrast to Sharp's pragmatic and formalist groupings, however, these classifications—"Vaginal Iconography," including work by Chicago, Betty Dodson, and Miriam Schapiro; "Transformations and Processes," including work by Antin, Pane, and Piper; and "Parody: Self as Object," including work by Lynda Benglis, Schneemann, and Hannah Wilke—explicitly recognize the subjective, psychological, and critical facets of body-related art by women, not to mention its anatomical aspects.[30]

Sharp's exclusion of women from his roster of avant-garde "body" artists mining new aesthetic territory may have been motivated by a desire to colonize an already occupied realm of artistic practice. But it may also have been a function of a subconscious attempt to neutralize an art form that, by its very nature, is inextricably linked to issues of the human body and its representation—namely, eroticism and sexual identity. Sharp's emphasis on formal concerns—"In body works the body per se is not as important as what is done with the body"[31]—would have been more difficult to convey if he had included contemporaneous women's body art in his discussion. Throughout the history of Western art, the female body has been rendered as *the* object of desire, a site for scopophilic identification. The very gesture of painting or sculpting has been considered, in itself, a libidinous act, for it makes manifest—through the brush stroke or chisel mark—the desiring (traditionally, male) gaze.[32] Due to cultural assumptions of male-gendered spectatorship, any representation of the female form was (and still is) connotatively loaded. In contrast, representations of the male body seem, like language itself, universalizing and ideologically transparent.[33]

Acconci's early comments about his experiments with body-related work advanced the kind of depersonalized rhetoric expounded by Sharp. In a 1972 interview in *Avalanche*, he says that when he began making art, "the initial attempts were very much oriented to defining my body in a space, finding a ground for myself, an alternate ground to the page ground I had as a poet."[34] And he points out that the body he displayed in works such as *Following Piece* (1969) had a very "neutralized presence."[35] In retrospect, Acconci questioned this approach to the presentation of self and his avoidance at the time of any references to individual subjectivity. In an interview in 1977, he admits:

> *I always wonder about my use of self in earlier pieces. It's always seemed like a very generalized self. Very recently when I see a lot of work by women dealing with self, it seems a really specific self. Compare it to some of my stuff and it seems like, my god, as if mine is a general, abstract kind of male abstracting notion. A generalized almost grandiose self.*[36]

Formalizing discourse aside, there are elements in Acconci's performative work from the early 1970s that actually problematize the presentation of the masculine subject as an ontologically coherent being. When observed from the theoretical vantage point of today—informed by poststructuralist and feminist concepts of subjectivity as provisional, sexually ambivalent, and estranged—Acconci's practice may be regarded as a highly critical, deconstructive venture. The embodied pieces in which he *performed* his own masculinity—either by overemphasizing it or casting it into doubt, even casting it away—introduced the possibility that gendered identity might be contingent, a "theatrical" construction sustained by repetitive demonstration.[37] And it is this component of Acconci's praxis that may be considered in tandem with coterminous projects by feminist body artists, who were similarly performing their own sexual identity to question its socially prescribed, purportedly "biological," origins. By acting out sexual difference in self-consciously performative situations, both male and female artists put in motion potentially disruptive play, while underscoring the oppressive reality of always already existing gender roles.

In thinking together the long-segregated modes of male and female body art in the 1970s—body art that involved sexual travesty and its representations—it is possible to detect a subtle breakdown of the binary model of gender, with its coercive codes of behavior, visual appearance, and sexual orientation. It did not occur to any of the American critics who were analyzing and/or attacking embodied art at the time to read male and female practices simultaneously as being complementary and provocative in their fusion. However, in one invective against body art, critic Max Kozloff does go halfway, asserting that "in that art area where sexual and political neuroses masquerade, the most revealing images or presences are of males transposing themselves into females."[38] What he fails to mention is the other side of the coin: the number of equally important women artists evocatively transposing themselves by imitating the male gender.

The piece that best demonstrates the interrogation of gender binarism in Acconci's oeuvre is *Conversions (Parts I–III)* (summer 1971), private performances recorded on Super-8 film and in pho-

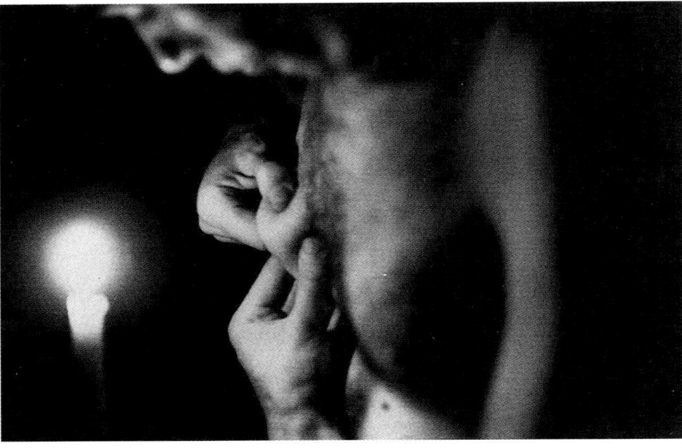

Vito Acconci
Conversions (Part I: Light, Reflection, Self-control), summer 1971
Black-and-white print from Super-8 film
Courtesy of Barbara Gladstone Gallery, New York

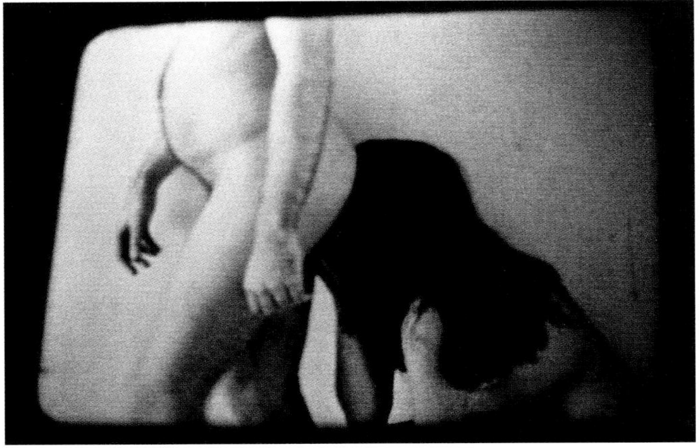

Vito Acconci
Conversions (Part III: Association, Assistance, Dependence), summer 1971
Black-and-white print from Super-8 film
Courtesy of Barbara Gladstone Gallery, New York

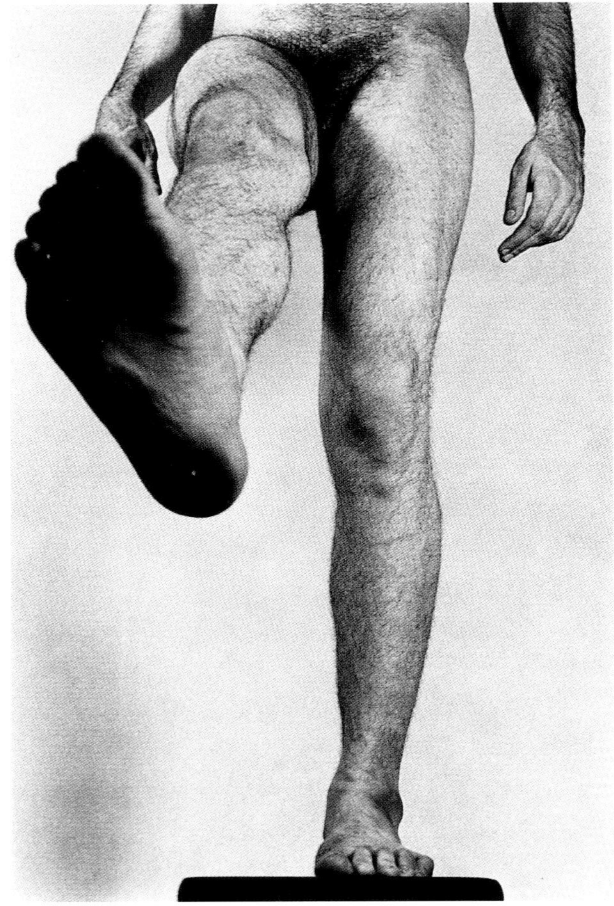

Vito Acconci
Conversions (Part II: Insistence, Adaptation, Groundwork, Display), summer 1971
Black-and-white print from Super-8 film
Courtesy of Barbara Gladstone Gallery, New York

tographic/text panels, in which the artist attempted to feminize his unquestionably male body. In the first sequence of the film, Acconci spends forty-eight grueling minutes burning off the hair around each of his nipples, which he then pulls and massages in a futile effort to create female breasts.[39] The next section shows the artist performing simple calisthenic exercises—walking, running in place, bending, squatting, etc.—with his penis tucked between his legs, hidden from sight, metaphorically castrated.[40] But the charade of transsexuality is always apparent. The visible triangle of pubic hair on Acconci's purposefully handicapped body only approximates a woman's; unable to accomplish all his tasks perfectly, Acconci ends up revealing his penis as much as concealing it. In the third and final section of *Conversions*, Acconci tries to hide his penis once again, but this time in the mouth of the woman (his girlfriend Kathy Dillon) kneeling behind him. "When I'm seen from the front," he explains, "the woman disappears behind me and I have no penis, I become the woman I've canceled out."[41] While Acconci's alleged negation of his female partner, who he claimed to have become, has been interpreted as a classic illustration of the Lacanian phallus inscribing itself over the effaced (and lacking) woman, other readings are viable.[42] As Amelia Jones points out in her significant study of male embodied art from the 1970s, Acconci's willingness to efface his own masculinity, while simulta-

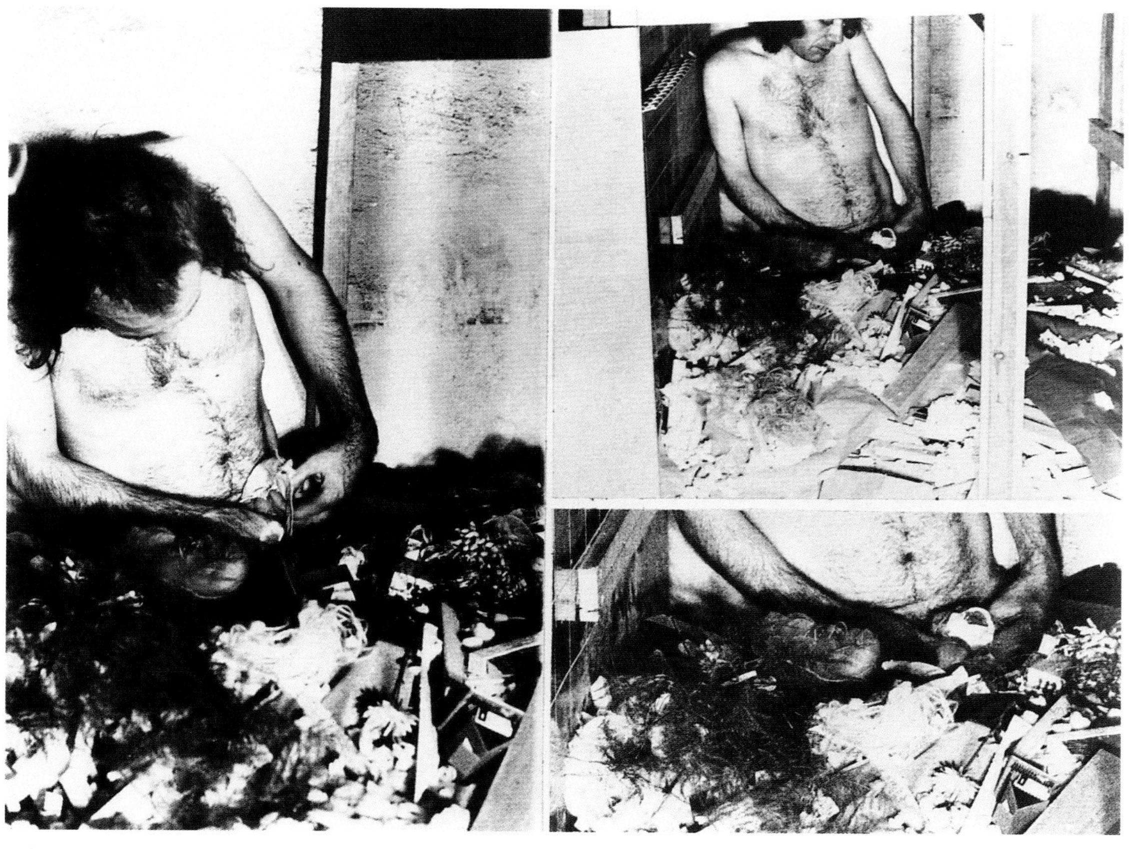

Vito Acconci
Trappings, October 14, 1971
Performance/installation photograph
Courtesy of Barbara Gladstone Gallery, New York

neously enacting the cancellation of his partner's femininity, foregrounds our understanding of the ontological instability of all sexual identities.[43]

In another body work dating from 1971 entitled *Trappings* (which is recorded in photographs), Acconci played out and parodied, in an emphatically self-deprecating manner, the sacrosanct and overdetermined connection between masculinity, the penis, and the phallus. Sitting naked in a closet filled with items associated with femininity and childhood—a "location for regressive activity"—the artist dressed up his penis in doll's clothes and talked to it as if it were a playmate. The calculated absurdity of the situation allowed Acconci to disrupt the seamless integration of masculinity and phallic privilege. No longer veiled, the penis/phallus was shown, in masquerade, as the psychosocial construct it is.[44]

While it was not yet theorized during the early 1970s, the notion that subjectivity and sexual identity may be performative rather than substantive found expression in Acconci's work, even if only intuitively. In 1971, the year he completed his work on *Conversions* and *Trappings*, Acconci claimed:

> *I'm using art as a means of changing myself, as a means of breaking out of a category. I am categorized as male. Now I'm trying to change that category, [to] open up the possibility of being female. There are structures that limit things. An art work might be a means to see and examine possibilities that these structures have eliminated. So I use art as an instrument to break through these structures. That's why I'm always stressing the idea of an art work as a means to improve, to correct, to open myself up, to make myself vulnerable. . . . The goal is to break out of spiritual and social confines as well. . . . I want to build up an idea of life—the idea that people can change from one role to another. People don't have to be limited by roles, they don't have to be rigidly enclosed in categories.*[45]

Acconci's flagrant libidinalization of performative work brought to the fore art criticism's misgivings about visual pleasure, qualms that were expressed far more aggressively in contemporaneous critiques of embodied work by women artists.[46] Condemned by both Modernism's disdain for corporeal identification and feminism's suspicions of the desiring male gaze, art that alluded to the pleasures of the flesh was often marginalized, and then overlooked, in ensuing histories of postwar art.[47] Because visual pleasure has been such a taboo subject, specific aspects of Acconci's work—which is being considered here as a case study—are simply not discussed in the critical literature. For instance, the scheme he devised in *Conversions* to hide his penis in the mouth of a female accomplice cannot really be thought separately from the heterosexual eroticism it suggests. Also, the kind of self-effacement he enacts cannot be theorized without considering the masochistic side of eroticism it invokes. The question can thus be posed: why should investigations of sexual identity, played out across the physical body as a site of shifting, performative personae, not be libidinal in orientation? And, furthermore, why should the gesture of demystifying supposedly fixed, ontological constructs of gender not be pleasurable for artist and viewer alike?

Other examples of embodied work by male artists who flaunted gender indeterminacy elicit such queries about visual pleasure, the artist's complicity in its production, and the audience's receptivity to it. The early photographic self-constructions of the German artist Jürgen Klauke and the Swiss artist Urs Lüthi reveal both men independently exploring polymorphous sexual identities for their cameras. Klauke's photographic series *Physiognomies* (*Physiognomien*, 1972–73) shows the artist posing in various theatrical guises, which range from intensely female to questionably male, in an effort to dislodge accepted ideas of normative gendered behavior. "The never-ending search for my/our identity is an underlying theme here," he explains in a recent interview.[48] According to Klauke, his goal at the time was "to lustfully claim female identity or any form of 'otherness,' and therefore question 'eternal masculinity' and 'eternal femininity'; i.e. to break through conventional, limited views of how things should be."[49] Similarly, Lüthi deployed travesty in his performative photographs as a strategy to symbolize the transgressive potential of self-transformation. In a "self-portrait" as a woman (or highly feminized male), entitled *I'll Be Your Mirror* (1972), the artist directly implicates the viewer in his transposition of genders, suggesting that the fluid state depicted may reflect the ambivalence at the core of all subjectivities. While not as aggressive or farcical as Acconci's play with masculinity, Klauke's and Lüthi's works problematize gender binarism with equal passion. The fetishistic elements employed in the photographs—from veils and flowers to makeup—are seductive tools used to lure the viewer into identification with (or desire for) the figures portrayed. The visual pleasure offered is located in the dizzying gaps between what is represented, what is seen, and what is known.

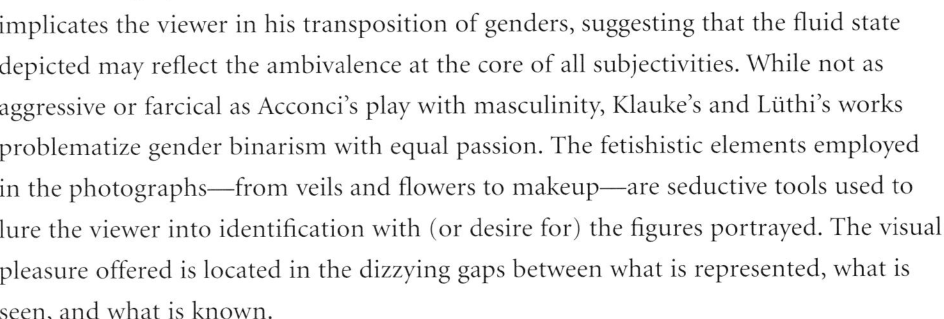

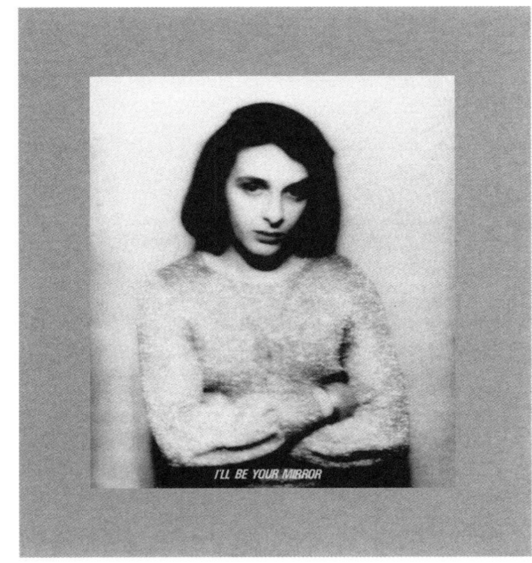

Urs Lüthi
I'll Be Your Mirror, 1972
Photograph on canvas,
39 ⅜ x 37 ⅜ inches (100 x 95 cm)
Private collection, Courtesy of the artist

Both Klauke's and Lüthi's early efforts to emulate the feminine other in order to create a truly liberatory art reflect theories of transvestism advanced by author Marjorie Garber in her 1992 book, *Vested Interests: Cross Dressing & Cultural Anxiety*, in which she states, rather idealistically, that cross-dressing can actually abolish the binarism behind cultural representation by causing a "category crisis" through its disruption of established gender boundaries. Transvestism, in Garber's view, introduces into the system the prospect of a "third term," which, as a "mode of articulation," creates a new "space of possibility."[50] Accordingly, the cross-dressed body refuses to conform to the social dictate of either/or, man or woman, and thus acts as a site of social resistance through the confusion it causes. In Garber's view, the visual codes of gender difference are thereby obscured and frustrated. However, there is a fine line between subversion and reinvestment. Transvestism—lately appropriated by the fashion industry as a titillating, yet marginal,

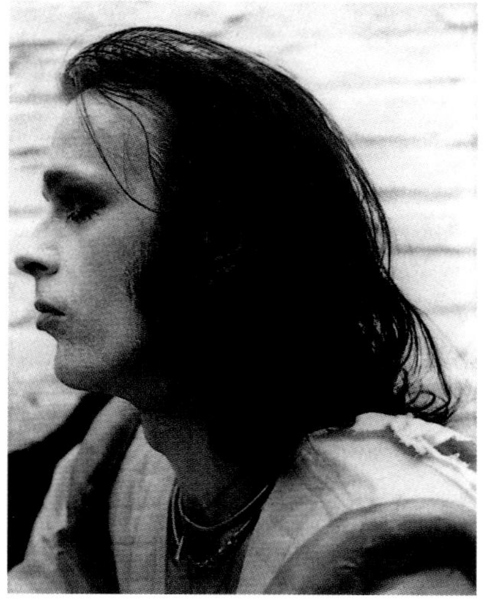

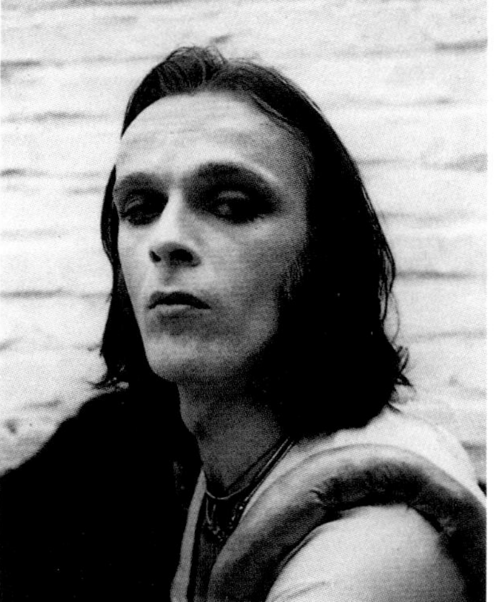

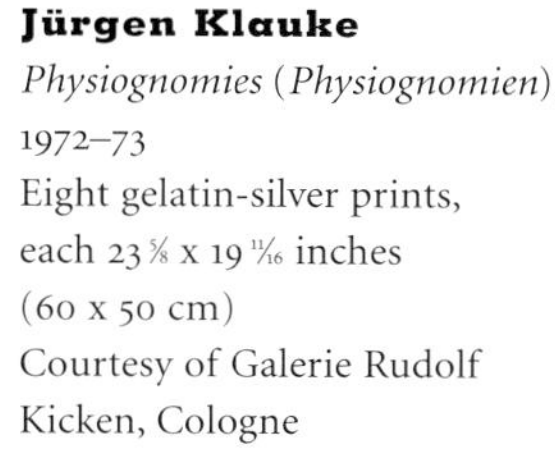

Jürgen Klauke
Physiognomies (*Physiognomien*),
1972–73
Eight gelatin-silver prints,
each 23 5/8 x 19 11/16 inches
(60 x 50 cm)
Courtesy of Galerie Rudolf
Kicken, Cologne

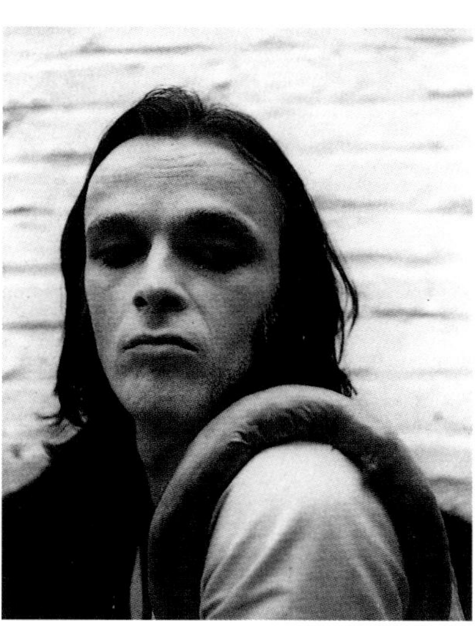

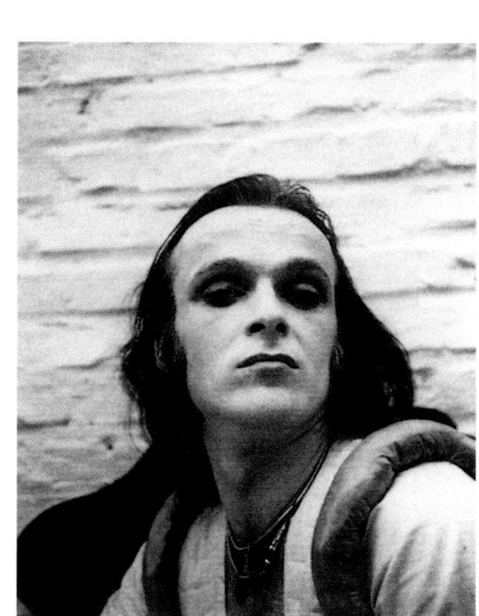

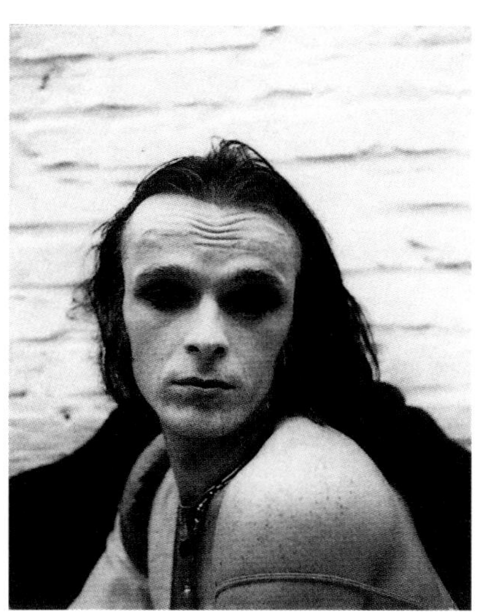

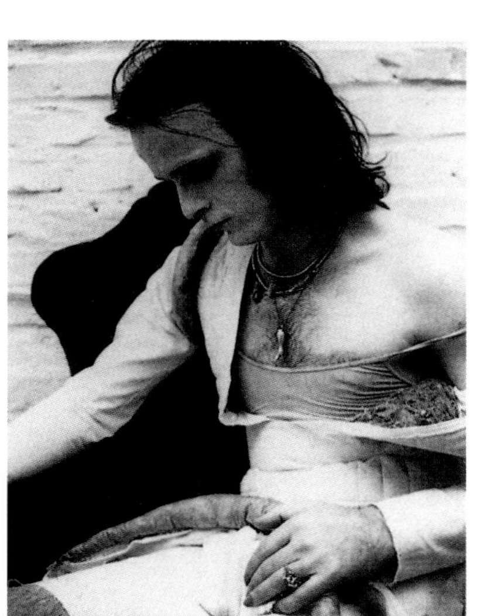

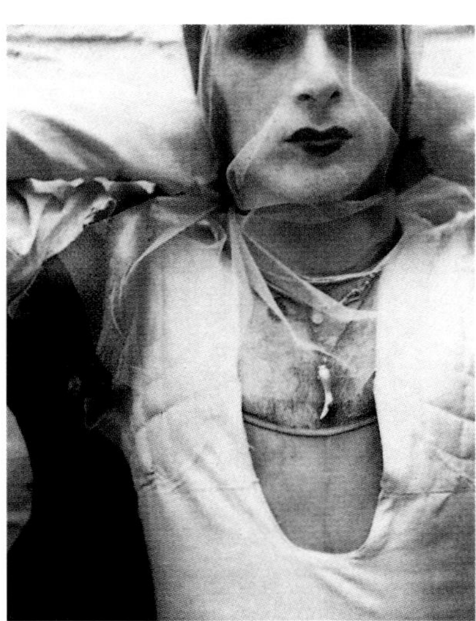

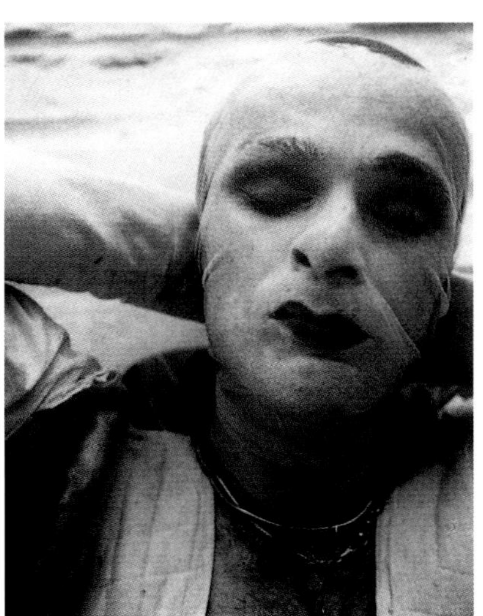

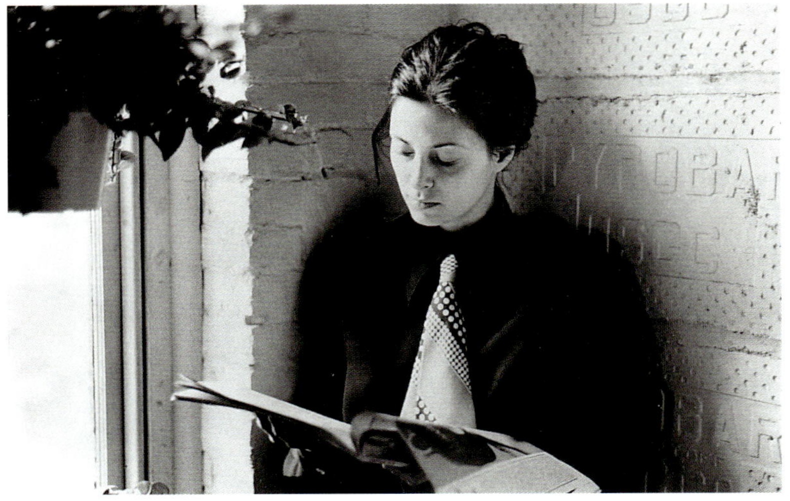

Hannah Wilke
Portrait of the Artist in His Studio, 1971
Performalist self-portrait with Claes Oldenburg
Courtesy of Ronald Feldman Fine Arts, New York

mode of countercultural defiance—simply recirculates and reinstates pregiven signs.

The polemics of pleasure, desire, and libidinal identification in art intensified during the 1970s when the work in question was made by a woman, particularly if she exploited her own body in the process. Because women have been traditionally inscribed as objects-to-be-seen, "unrepresentable except as representation,"[51] female-authored displays of the feminine body—even in cases when the presentation is transgendered—were particularly threatening to the (male) art establishment. Even some feminist critics found that supporting women's embodied art was difficult when the work equivocated between being a parodic critique of sexual objectification and an "essentialist" celebration of female sexuality.[52] The conundrum they encountered was whether it was conceivable to disengage the actual, physical body of a woman from the patriarchal construct of woman-as-representation.[53] For instance, Wilke, an artist who performed her own femininity to the point of caricature, also utilized the codes of drag to further comment on the power structure inherent in gender difference. One of her initial "performalist self-portraits," which displays a self composed for the camera, shows Wilke dressed as a man in black shirt and patterned tie—her long, wavy hair (an attribute she often flaunted in her "feminine" guise) clipped back, out of sight.[54] In place of her distinctively seductive gaze at the camera-cum-viewer—which she repeatedly exploited to obscure the difference between complicity and parody—her attention is fixed on the art journal she holds in her hands. The title of the photograph, *Portrait of the Artist in His Studio* (1971), indicates that Wilke, at this formative stage in her career, fully intended to claim for herself the artistic authority so indelibly linked to masculine privilege. In 1976, Wilke crossed genders again to tackle what Jones called "the construction of a highly invested 'father' figure of postmodern practice"—Marcel Duchamp—in a performance and subsequent film entitled *Through the Large Glass.*[55] Presented at the Philadelphia Museum of Art, where Duchamp's *The Bride Stripped Bare by Her Bachelors, Even (The Large Glass)* (1915–23) is housed, Wilke staged a measured and deliberately slow striptease behind the glass "painting." Wearing the signature attire of a gentleman dandy—white suit with vest, white fedora, and white silk scarf—the artist visually identified herself with both the onanistic, self-contained, and infinitely productive "bachelor machine" in the lower realm of *The Large Glass* and the ever-virginal bride in the upper. Filmed directly through the glass panes of the

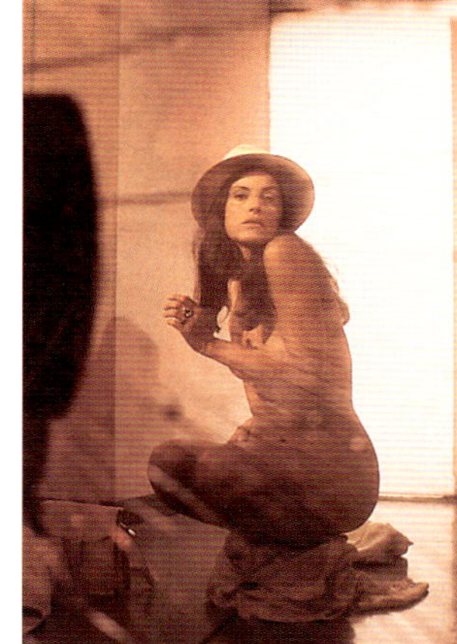

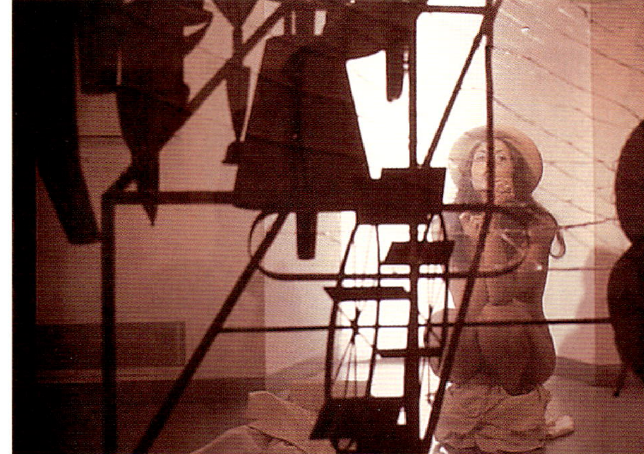

Hannah Wilke
Through the Large Glass, 1976
Film stills from a performance at Philadelphia Museum of Art
Courtesy of Ronald Feldman Fine Arts, New York

work, Wilke's striptease—from dapper man to alluring woman—can be read as a metaphoric and eroticized joining of the forever separated domains of bachelor and bride. Her striptease-as-marriage ceremony symbolically reclaimed for women the rite of (pro)creativity long appropriated by male artists.[56]

Sculptor and video artist Lynda Benglis also employed transgender codes to challenge the equation between masculinist authority and creative agency. In *Document*, a video from 1972, Benglis draws a moustache on a photograph of her face that is taped to a blank video monitor and writes copyright notices, which she then traces and retraces, across the bottom of the monitor's screen. Raising issues of originality and artistic entitlement here, she was only warming up for a gesture that would rock the art world. In 1974, Benglis placed a series of self-produced advertisements for one-person gallery exhibitions, each of which featured her own constructed photographic self-portrait. These ads followed in a tradition of mostly male artists posing for their exhibition announcements, often in overtly macho scenarios, which she first parodied in 1973 in her own invitations to three one-person shows at the Portland Center for the Visual Arts, in Oregon; the Jack Glenn Gallery in Corona Del Mar, California; and The Clocktower, in New York. On each invitation she reproduced a childhood snapshot of herself wearing a traditional Greek evzone outfit, complete with white leggings and skirt. Benglis's recuperation of this photo, in which she posed in male military attire that today appears quite feminine, reveals an interest in gender masquerade. Her ensuing advertisement for an exhibition at the Paula Cooper Gallery, in New York, inaugurated the series labeled "sexual mockeries," which were intended to investigate gender ambiguity and sexual role playing, while lampooning the art-world star system.[57] Posed in quintessentially butch attire—jeans, man's shirt, black jacket, and aviator sunglasses—Benglis is shown leaning against an old Porsche with close-cropped hair and a smirk. For the invitation to this show, Benglis commissioned Annie Leibovitz to photograph her in a classic, Betty Grable cheesecake pose—with her nude back to the viewer, arms folded behind her head, and jeans down around her high-heeled ankles. The culmination of the "sexual mockeries" was an advertisement run in the November 1974 *Artforum*, which showed Benglis entirely oiled up and naked, save for a pair of glamour-girl sunglasses and a gigantic, plastic dildo held at genital level.[58] Her brazen expropriation of the penis, albeit an exceptionally fake one, served to ironically deflate the organ's alleged alignment with the "phallus"[59] and to grant her access to masculinist authority and the artistic agency associated with it. Hermaphrodite par excellence, Benglis appears in this photograph as a metaphoric fusion of the Duchampian bride and bachelor, claiming for herself the authorial rights enacted by the self-enclosed, self-satisfying bachelor machine.[60]

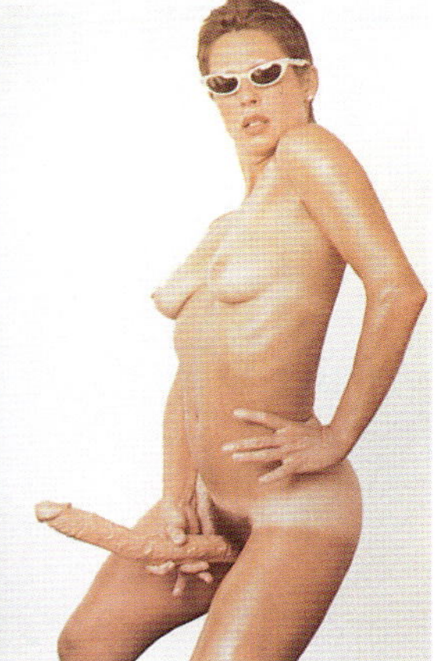

Lynda Benglis
Advertisement in *Artforum* 13 (November 1974)

The media outrage generated by Benglis's advertisement is indicative of how profoundly defensive the critical community—including both mainstream and feminist writers—was about attacks on its authority. A group of *Artforum* editors thought it necessary to publish a letter expressing their chagrin over Benglis's gesture, stating that the ad was an "object of extreme vulgarity" and a

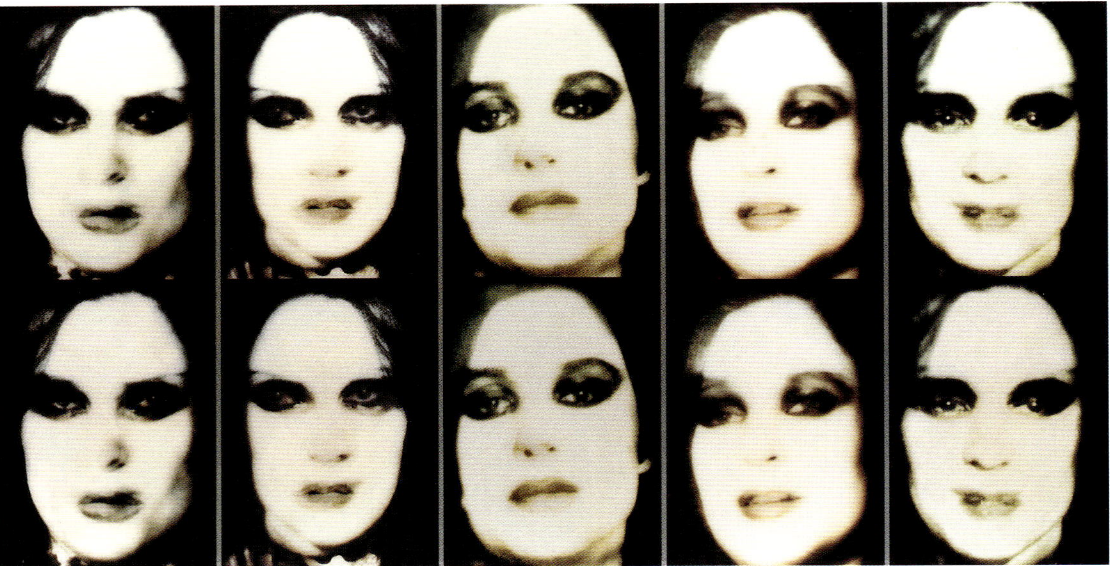

Katharina Sieverding
Transformer, 1973–74
Photographs, in five parts,
each 59 7/16 x 24 inches
(151 x 61 cm); 59 7/16 x 120 1/16 inches
(151 x 305 cm) overall
Deutsche Bank AG, Frankfurt

"shabby mockery of the aims" of the women's liberation movement.[61] And Cindy Nemser attacked Benglis in an issue of *The Feminist Art Journal*, declaring that her gesture was anything but liberatory:

> *True her organ may be the most majestic in size but it is still only plastic. Her image may be tough and forbidding but look where she places it—smack on the first page (and at her own cost) of the most establishment of art magazines thus making a frantic bid for male attention. . . . She may convince herself and other naives that she is saying "Fuck you" to the men but she is still only using her lovely woman's body to say "Fuck me," and thereby making herself doubly tantalizing to those who like their sex served up with S&M overtones.*[62]

The numerous other responses—both derogatory and supportive—proved just how dangerous was the territory that Benglis defiantly explored in this series of self-portraits. As Jones comments, Benglis constructed herself as "an active female subject in wild abandon" who became "that which *should not be seen*: woman as desirable body, woman with penis, woman with phallus, woman as self-producer, woman in control of the critical gaze."[63]

In addition to Wilke and Benglis, in the 1970s, many other women artists explored transgender themes in their performative work as a strategy to symbolically invert sexual binarism and to expose the masquerade at the heart of gendered identity. The German artist Katharina Sieverding, for instance, used her own photographic self-portrait to create series upon series of large-scale, masklike, solarized images. In *Transformer* (1973–74), gender boundaries were completely blurred by the artist, who manipulated photographs of herself and her partner so that one cannot be distinguished from the other; the female image intimates the male, and the male the female. The resulting "portraits" convey the arbitrary division between self and other, suggesting that both genders may be present in any individual.[64] Sieverding approached transvestism as a means of "communication" that could expose "roles, repressions . . . and self-extension." "The conquest of another gender," she explains, "takes place in oneself."[65] Beginning in 1973, the Conceptual artist Eleanor Antin created a number of dramatis personae—including a black ballerina formerly with Sergey Diaghilev's Ballet Russe, a heroic nurse from the Crimean War, and a seventeenth-century bearded king—whose obsessional autobiographies she performed live, as well as in a series of videos and antique-seeming photo albums. Approaching both the objectivity of history and the infallibility of identity as myths to debunk, Antin used her fictional characters to comment on the provisional (and gendered) nature of "reality." Conceptual artist Adrian Piper also created transgendered performative personae, which she deployed during the early 1970s to disrupt cultural stereotypes of both sexual and racial difference. In 1970, she executed a series of performance works, entitled *Catalysis*; dramatically altering her person by wearing stench-ridden clothes and assuming other codes for the economically downtrodden, she inserted herself into the social environment to confront the disenfranchisement of those perceived as other. Then, five years later, Piper posed, complete with Afro and moustache, as a streetwise black male known as the *Mythic Being* in order to enter the community and experience life as an African American man—experiencing both the liberation she felt in the empowered male role and the racist fears her presence provoked in the whites around her. Documented in a series of photographic and painted posters, some of which utilize comic-strip "bubble" thoughts, one portrait of the *Mythic Being* is accompanied by the phrase: "I embody everything you most hate and fear." Another photograph bears the floating thought, "I hate you for doing this to me, and myself for allowing it to happen."[66] In this work, Piper ripped open the gender dichotomy that preoccupied feminist representation in the 1970s, interjecting the problem of racial difference into an already inflammatory mix of divergent ideologies, sexualities, and class-based issues that has plagued the modern-day women's movement from its inception.

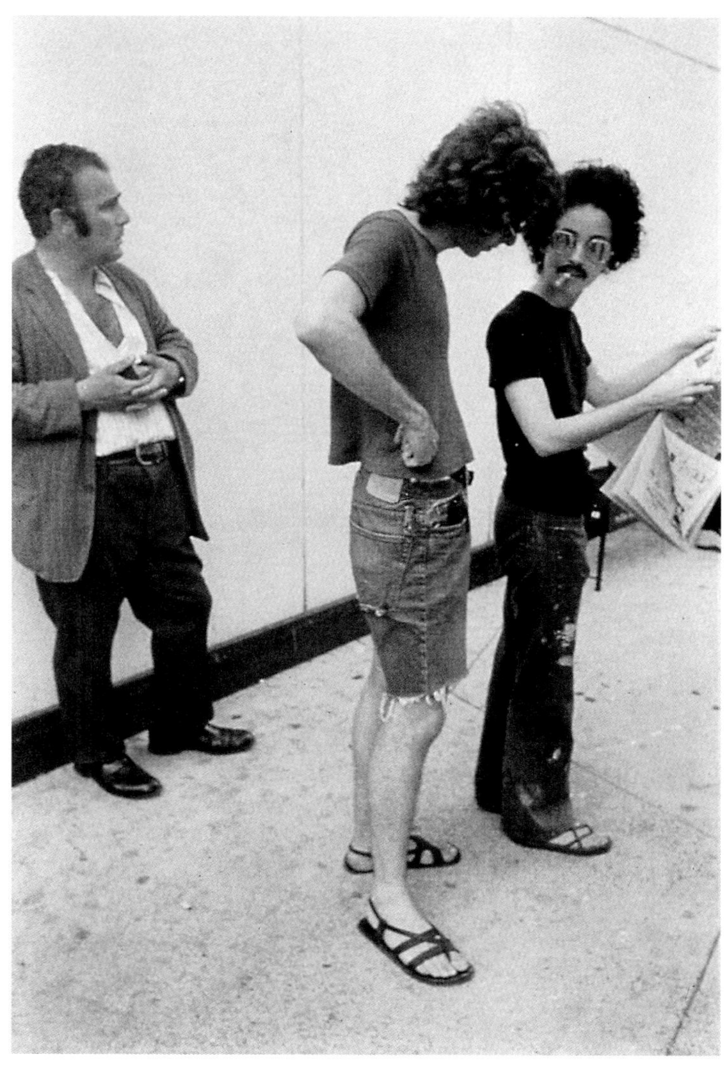

Adrian Piper
Mythic Being: Getting Back #1, 1975
Courtesy of John Weber Gallery, New York

The advent of performance-based "self-portraiture" in the 1970s anticipated the critical impulse, so popular in the 1990s, to proclaim all identity as performative rather than natural, stable, or ontologically determined. Fueled by poststructuralism's concept of the decentered subject, postmodernism's distrust of master narratives, and feminism's skepticism about essentialist ideologies, performativity has evolved as a significant critical tool today.[67] Philosopher and gender theorist Judith Butler's pivotal work in the field has fostered an understanding that gender "is in no way a stable identity or locus of agency from which various acts proceed."[68] Rather, as she explains, "it is an identity tenuously constituted in time—an identity instituted through a *stylized repetition of acts*."[69] These "acts" are bodily functions, gestures, and movements that generate the image of an immutable gendered subjectivity, which adheres to socially and politically determined codes of behavior. This illusionary gendered self is, according to Butler, just a "constructed identity, a performative accomplishment which the mundane social audience, including the actors themselves, come to believe."[70] Gender is not, however, just a theatrical convention to be acted out at will; rather, it is *performative*, which means, in Butler's words, that gender identity is "real only to the extent that it is performed."[71] The potential for disruption in this delusional system relies on the self-conscious and subversive repetition of already repetitious acts—the use of mimicry, parody, and the like.

In thinking through the issues of 1970s body art, in which both male and female artists emphatically performed their own genders as well as that of the other, one is struck by the precociousness of the entire enterprise. It is clear that artists such as Acconci, Benglis, and Wilke could not have predicted the contemporary theorizations of performance that are informing so much recent feminist and queer thinking and, in turn, their impact on art criticism. However, one *can* infer from the artists' carefully crafted photographic documents that the mimetic "performativity" of gender *was* rehearsed, if not foregrounded, in the body art of the 1970s. Perhaps this is why the art and culture of that decade—with its emphasis on time, liminality, shifting identities, and sexuality—has become so trenchant again in the 1990s.

Notes

1. Michael Fried, "Art and Objecthood," *Artforum* 5, no. 10 (June 1967), pp. 12–23.
2. Art critic and theorist Douglas Crimp points out, in his pivotal essay "Pictures," that the most radical art produced throughout the decade following Fried's "Art and Objecthood" was precisely that which invoked the theatrical in its involvement with time and bodily tendencies. Such artistic strategies of the 1970s included, but were by no means limited to: the real-time systems of Hans Haacke; the task-based activities of Abramović and Ulay, Vito Acconci, Chris Burden, and Bruce Nauman; the excavations in nature of Walter De Maria, Nancy Holt, Dennis Oppenheim, and Robert Smithson; the orgiastic theater of Günter Brus, Hermann Nitsch, and Rudolf Schwarzkogler; and the staged social confrontations of Adrian Piper and Martha Rosler. See Crimp, "Pictures," *October*, no. 8 (spring 1979), pp. 75–88.
3. *Reading Position for a Second Degree Burn* is illustrated in Ann Goldstein and Anne Rorimer, *Reconsidering the Object of Art: 1965–1975*, exh. cat. (Los Angeles: Museum of Contemporary Art; and Cambridge, Mass.: MIT Press, 1995), p. 189. Oppenheim reclined on the sand with a large, hardcover book open across his chest, the five-hour exposure to the summer sun leaving him sunburned save for the expanse of skin covered by the book. Oppenheim likened allowing his skin to change pigment to the process of being painted.
4. Burden's *Shoot* was staged in the F Space Gallery in Santa Ana, California. Documentation of this work can be found in *Chris Burden: A Twenty-Year Survey*, exh. cat. (Newport Harbor, Calif.: Newport Harbor Museum of Art, 1988). Because of its sensational character, *Shoot* was perhaps the most infamous performance work of the 1970s. Although Burden had apparently requested that the marksman merely graze his arm with the bullet, in actuality he suffered a deep wound. For many, the violence inherent in this piece came to exemplify performance art in general, which tended to be associated with brutality, self-mutilation, and intemperance.

   For an examination of performance art, thought through the psychoanalytic model of masochism, see Kathy O'Dell, *Toward a Theory of Performance Art: An Investigation of Its Sites* (Ph.D. diss., City University of New York, 1992; and Ann Arbor, Mich: UMI Research Press, 1996).
5. This action was part of Gina Pane's performance *Azione sentimentale*, which was staged at the Galleria Diagramma, in Milan. A photograph from the performance is reproduced in Catherine Millet, "L'Espace du corps," in *L'Art au corps: Le corps exposé de Man Ray à nos jours*, exh. cat. (Mac: Galeries contemporaines des Musées de Marseille, 1996), p. 179.
6. Abramović's performance, entitled *Rhythm 2*, was staged in the Gallery of Contemporary Art in Zagreb, Yugoslavia, in 1974. It is documented in Friedrich Meschede, ed., *Abramović* (Stuttgart: Edition Cantz, 1993), pp. 56–63.
7. Marcel Duchamp's *Tonsure* is discussed in at least four of the major texts dealing with the emergence of body art during the 1970s: Cindy Nemser, "Subject-Object Body Art," *Arts Magazine* 46 (September–October 1971), p. 39; Lea Vergine, *Il corpo come linguaggio (La "Body-art" e storie simili)*, trans. Henry Martin (Milan: Giampaolo Prearo Editore, 1974); Ira Licht, *Bodyworks*, exh. cat. (Chicago: Museum of Contemporary Art, 1975), unpaginated; and François Pluchart, *L'Art corporeal*, exh. cat. (Paris: Editions Rodolphe Stadler, 1975), unpaginated.
8. A note on terminology: I refer to the corporeal artwork discussed in this text as "body art," "performative art," and "embodied art," but these terms are by no means codified. Time-based art from the 1970s that involves the body as subject, object, and sculptural medium has been categorized in a number of ways: "bodyworks," "performance art," "body art," and "embodied art," for instance. My choice of the word "performative" over the more commonly used "performance" differentiates ephemeral, durational work created specifically for the camera from that presented to a live audience.
9. The 1919 photo was attributed to a photographer named Bacci (in Pluchart, *L'Art corporeal*, unpaginated); the photo dated 1921 was taken by Man Ray.
10. See O'Dell, *Toward a Theory of Performance Art*, pp. 374–75, for a brief discussion of the ideology of the star system considered in conjunction with Duchamp's *Tonsure*. She also points out that it was during the 1970s that Duchamp was officially ordained into the cult of the artist with his first major retrospective in the United States at the Museum of Modern Art, New York, in 1973, and the Philadelphia Museum of Art, in 1973–74 (p. 415, note 15).
11. See Pierre Cabanne, *Dialogues with Marcel Duchamp*, trans. Ron Padgett (New York: Viking Press, 1971), p. 64.
12. Marjorie Garber has investigated the historical and literary correlations between the Judeo-Christian tradition and transvestism, from liturgical vestments and cross-dressed saints to Gothic novels such as Matthew Lewis's *The Monk* (1796). Her discussion about the historical feminization of the Jewish male is particularly provocative in light of Duchamp's remarks regarding religious conversion and gender identification. See the section "Jew, Woman, Homosexual," in the chapter "Religious Habits," in Garber, *Vested Interests: Cross-Dressing & Cultural Anxiety* (New York: Routledge, 1992), pp. 224–33.
13. For a detailed examination of photography's relationship to Conceptual art during the 1970s, see Jeff Wall, "'Marks of Indifference': Aspects of Photography in, or as, Conceptual Art," in Goldstein and Rorimer, *Reconsidering the Object of Art*, pp. 247–67.
14. While that may have been the case during the early 1970s, a market for "conceptual photography" has emerged during the past few years that has proven quite challenging to dealers and curators alike. Photographs by artists such as Acconci and Oppenheim were not necessarily issued in editions, nor were they conceived as "original" objects. Rather, prints were made on demand for exhibitions, publications, and the rare sale, and were usually dated to the time of inception. As Wall succinctly explains:

    Paradoxically . . . photography could emerge socially as art only at the moment when its aesthetic presuppositions seemed to be undergoing a withering radical critique apparently aimed at foreclosing any further aestheticization or "artification" of the medium. Photoconceptualism led the way toward a complete acceptance of photography as art—autonomous, bourgeois, collectible art—by virtue of insisting that this medium might be privileged to the negation of that whole idea. (Ibid., p. 252.)
15. See Christopher Phillips, "The Judgement Seat of Photography," in Joan Copjec, Douglas Crimp, Rosalind Krauss, and Annette Michelson, eds., *October: The First Decade, 1976–1986* (Cambridge, Mass.: MIT Press, 1987), pp. 257–93; originally published in *October*, no. 22 (fall 1983), pp. 27–63.
16. Wall, "'Marks of Indifference'," pp. 248–58. My argument here about Conceptual photography's critical relationship to reportage is indebted to Wall's pivotal essay on the subject.
17. Artists active during the 1970s such as Jan Dibbets, Dan Graham, Douglas Huebler, Gordon Matta-Clark, Ed Ruscha, and Smithson also utilized the pictorial codes of photojournalism to parody and thus distance their work from its claims to mimetic truth and aesthetic value. They did not, however, turn routinely to performance as a strategy for constructing their photographic imagery. The staged or "theatrical" photograph is one subgenre of Conceptual photography.
18. A. D. Coleman, "The Directorial Mode: Notes Toward a Definition," *Artforum* 15, no. 1 (September 1976), pp. 55–61. Wall cites Bruce Nauman's photographs, such as *Failing to Levitate in the Studio* (1966), as an example of Conceptual photodocumentation:

    The photographer's studio, and the generic complex of "studio photography," was the antithesis against which the aesthetics of reportage were elaborated. Nauman changes the terms. Working within the experimental framework of what was beginning at the time to be called "performance art," he carries out photographic acts of reportage whose subject matter is the self-conscious, self-centered "play" taking place in the studios of artists who have moved "beyond" the modern fine arts into the new hybridities. (Wall, "'Marks of Indifference'," p. 254.)

19. After the portable videotape recorder was introduced in the United States in 1965, video became a "new perceptual instrument" and one of the leading mediums for artists involved with body art and its documentation.

    For a discussion of video's role in American art of the late 1960s and early 1970s, see John G. Hanhardt, "Beyond Illusion: American Film and Video Art, 1965–75," in *The New Sculpture: 1965–75*, exh. cat. (New York: Whitney Museum of American Art, 1990), pp. 29–39. Hanhardt claims that artists such as Acconci, Lynda Benglis, Joan Jonas, and Nauman all articulated the body in their artworks within a space conceived specifically for the video camera.

    For a theoretical analysis of video as a "psychological" mode of reproduction, see Rosalind Krauss, "Video: The Aesthetics of Narcissism," *October*, no. 1 (spring 1976), pp. 50–64. Written in the relatively early years of video's use by artists, Krauss's text reads the medium through a psychoanalytic model and posits the body (ego) as the critical third term between camera and monitor.

20. It is important to note, however, that many of the artists discussed in this essay worked (and still work) in both publicly staged "performance art" and performative self-representation for the camera.

21. For an analysis of how Herbert Marcuse's writings on liberation and desublimation (in particular, his *Eros and Civilization*, 1955) influenced art of the 1960s and its association with the counterculture, see Maurice Berger, *Labyrinths: Robert Morris, Minimalism, and the 1960s* (New York: Harper & Row, 1989), pp. 12–13, 61–62.

22. See Juan A. Suárez's discussion of Jack Smith's *Flaming Creatures* in the chapter "Drag, Rubble, and 'Secret Flix': Jack Smith's Avant-Garde against the Lucky Landlord Empire," in Suárez, *Bike Boys, Drag Queens, Superstars: Avant-Garde, Mass Culture and Gay Identities in the 1960s Underground Cinema* (Bloomington: Indiana University Press, 1996), pp. 181–213. Suárez points out that other films of the time, such as Kenneth Anger's *Scorpio Rising* (1964), Barbara Rubin's *Christmas on Earth* (1963), and Carolee Schneemann's *Fuses* (1967), were censored for sexual explicitness, but none received the official condemnation by a congressional hearing conferred upon *Flaming Creatures.*

23. The analogy between transvestite rock and gender performance in the visual arts during the 1970s was not lost on curator Jean-Christophe Ammann, who organized the exhibition *"Transformer": Aspekte der Travestie*, in 1974, for the Kunstmuseum Luzern, in Switzerland. Participants in the exhibition included artists as well as musicians: David Bowie, Luciano Castelli, The Cockettes, Brian Eno, Mick Jagger, Urs Lüthi, Marco, Werner Alex Meyer, Pierre Molinier, the New York Dolls, Luigi Ontani, Walter Pfeiffer, Andrew Sherwood, Katharina Sieverding, and Andy Warhol.

24. The same holds true for the 1980s and 1990s, during which performers such as Boy George, Michael Jackson, and George Michael, have been embraced by the music industry. Even "heavy metal" bands, which caricature tropes of masculinity, construct their stage personae with layers of heavy makeup, teased hair, skintight clothing, and platform heels. This is pointed out by Andrew Ross in "Uses of Camp," in Ross, *No Respect: Intellectuals and Popular Culture* (New York: Routledge, 1989), p. 164.

25. See Willoughby Sharp, "Body Works," *Avalanche* 1 (fall 1970), pp. 14–17. Describing what he christened "body work," Sharp writes: *Variously called actions, events, performances, pieces, things, the works present physical activities, ordinary bodily functions and other usual and unusual manifestations of physicality. The artist's body becomes both the subject and object of the work. The artist is the subject and object of the action. Generally the performance is executed in the privacy of the studio. Individual works are mostly communicated to the public through the strong visual language of photographs, films, videotapes and other media, all with strong immediacy of impact.* (p. 14)

    The category "body art" first appeared in the *Art Index* in 1971.

26. In his analysis of body art, Sharp employs a vocabulary that was more or less common parlance in art-critical circles of the 1970s, particularly in discussions of Process and Earth art. In a subsequent article on body art, Nemser follows Sharp's formal approach, dividing the work into two categories: the investigation of the body as a closed system to effect physical or psychological change, or the investigation of the body as it interacts with various aspects of the empirical world as sculptural material or tool; see Nemser, "Subject-Object Body Art," pp. 38–42.

27. There were also a number of European male artists working with the body during the 1960s who were not mentioned in Sharp's article, such as the Viennese Aktion artists. While his text is oriented specifically to work by American artists, Sharp does refer to Joseph Beuys and Yves Klein as sources for the more recent body work in America.

28. For an overview and detailed chronology of women's performance work, see Moira Roth, ed., *The Amazing Decade: Women and Performance Art in America 1970–1980* (Los Angeles: Astro Artz, 1983). Also, for a long-awaited examination of Schneemann's career, see the recently published *Carolee Schneemann: Up to and Including Her Limits*, exh. cat. (New York: New Museum of Contemporary Art, 1996), with essays by Dan Cameron, David Levi Strauss, and Kristine Stiles.

29. See Lucy Lippard, "The Pains and Pleasures of Rebirth: European and American Women's Body Art," in Lippard, *From the Center: Feminist Essays on Women's Art* (New York: E. P. Dutton, 1976), pp. 121–38; originally published in *Art in America* 64, no. 3 (May–June), pp. 73–81. Lippard points out: *"Neutral" art made by women still has little chance of making it into the market mainstream, while the male establishment, unsympathetic to women's participation in the art world as equal competitors, has approved (if rather patronizingly and perhaps lasciviously) of women working with their own, preferably attractive, bodies and faces.* (p. 123)

30. Lisa Tickner, "The Body Politic: Female Sexuality and Women Artists Since 1970," *Art History* 1 (June 1978), pp. 236–47.

31. Sharp, "Body Works," p. 17.

32. For an analysis of the paint brush as phallus, see Carol Duncan, "The Aesthetics of Power in Modern Erotic Art," in Arlene Raven, Cassandra Langer, et al., eds., *Feminist Art Criticism* (Ann Arbor, Mich.: UMI Research Press, 1988), p. 62.

33. Mira Schor discusses this representational phenomenon as revolving around the Lacanian distinction between the phallus and the penis and the fact that the "the phallus can only play its role as veiled." Historical representations of the male nude were conceptualized or idealized through geometric canons of proportion: "Man is the measure of all things." But the visibility of the penis was rarely privileged. Rather, its "lack" was rendered in image after image of nude women—as goddesses, nymphs, or prostitutes. And if woman's "lack" (of the penis/phallus) is foregrounded, then man's is hidden, even forgotten. Thus, the phallus, as power, language, and law, is his to claim. See Schor, "Representations of the Penis," *M/E/A/N/I/N/G*, no. 4 (November 1988), pp. 3–5. Jacques Lacan's quote is from "The Meaning of the Phallus" (1958), cited in Juliet Mitchell and Jacqueline Rose, eds., *Feminine Sexuality: Jacques Lacan and the école freudienne*, trans. Jacqueline Rose (New York: W. W. Norton, 1982), p. 82.

34. Acconci, quoted in "Excerpts from Tapes with Liza Beár" (interview), *Avalanche* 6 (fall 1972), p. 71. This special issue of *Avalanche* is entirely devoted to Acconci's work.
35. Ibid., p. 72.
36. Interview with Bruce Barber, dated January 7, 1977, unpublished manuscript, unpaginated. I would like to thank Bruce Barber for sharing this material with me.
37. Early on, Acconci acknowledged the theatrical character of his work, indicating an interest in the writings of Erving Goffman, who proposed that all social interaction was premised on the paradigm of performance, with protagonists and antagonists each adopting the appropriate dramatic role. In 1972, Acconci stated:
It's recently occurred to me that a lot of my stuff could be related to actor's rehearsal techniques. And it's obvious why. But the sources I draw from, at least for notes on pieces, range from concrete methodology to general systems people, sociologists: Erving Goffman's work on interaction, for example, which is all done in a kind of theatrical metaphor—he talks about people setting up "performance areas" when they meet. ("Tapes with Liza Beár," p. 71.)
Acconci is referring to Goffman's influential book *The Presentation of Self in Everyday Life* (New York: Doubleday, 1959).
38. Max Kozloff, "Pygmalion Reversed," *Artforum* 14, no. 3 (November 1975), p. 37.
39. In a text published with photographs of the action, Acconci describes his efforts:
I'm stopping the candle at my breast, burning the hairs. . . . The breast is hairless: I am pulling at it, making it supple, flexible—an attempt to develop a female breast. (*Avalanche* 6 [fall 1972], p. 26.)
40. About this section, Acconci writes:
Extending the sex change: exercising my new body, adapting myself to my new conditions . . . I need time to persist in my appearance, to develop ease in that appearance (static camera—I'm in one position in front of it—or I'm walking to it away from it—I'm forced to play up to the camera—my performance depends on an attempt to handle, control, personal information. (Ibid., p. 28.)
41. Quoted in Judith Russi Kirchner, *Vito Acconci: A Retrospective: 1969–1980*, exh. cat. (Chicago: Museum of Contemporary Art, 1980), p. 15.
42. Schor completely dismisses Acconci's *Conversions* as a display of narcissistic male empowerment:
He seeks to strip away all signs of maleness: first the hairs off his breasts, then the penis from his body. But he has a penis and must put it someplace—in a disappeared woman. So the phallus reinscribes itself over the erased/lacking woman, even as the penis is hidden, as usual. (Schor, "Representations of the Penis," p. 8.)
In an unpublished M.A. thesis, Laura A. Brunsman argues for a Lacanian reading of all of Acconci's early performance work. She reads *Conversions (Parts I–III)* through the model of the "mirror–stage," suggesting that Acconci was enacting the "metaphorical castration . . . that leads toward increasing interaction with an Other and ultimately to the development of gender identity." See Brunsman, *A Critical Study of Vito Acconci and the Psychology of Narcissism in his Body and Performance Works: 1969–1975* (M.A. thesis, University of Washington, 1990), pp. 104–05.
43. Amelia Jones, "Dis/playing the Phallus: Male Artists Perform Their Masculinities," *Art History* 17, no. 4 (December 1994), p. 566. My ideas about performative art by male artists in the 1970s are indebted to Jones's groundbreaking work, which is cited throughout the remainder of this essay.
44. Writing about this piece, Acconci states:
I have only myself to work with—turn in on myself—I'm dividing myself in two—turn my penis into another person. I can dress my penis here—the space is scaled to it: toy houses, toy animals—it functions side by side with them—I can throw myself into its world: my body's draped with color, smoothness. I'm talking to it—my words are addressed to me . . . my words are addressed to the penis (it has a life of its own, it's far enough away from me to talk to it). For the entirety of this text, see *Avalanche* 6 (fall 1972), p. 57.
45. Cindy Nemser, "An Interview with Vito Acconci," *Arts Magazine* 45, no. 5 (March 1971), pp. 21–23.
46. In particular, Acconci's infamous performance/installation *Seedbed* (1972) at the Sonnabend Gallery, in New York, caused great critical controversy. Although beyond the scope of this essay, for it did not involve any gender transference, the piece entailed the artist's daily activity for the duration of the show: hidden under a false floor, Acconci masturbated while fantasizing about the visitors walking above him.
47. Jones examines the issue of visual pleasure in her study of women's performance art from the 1960s and 1970s. She argues that feminism's refusal to perpetuate the codes associated with male visual pleasure effectively dismissed the significance of women's art that involved the performance of the body. She situates feminism's militant call to disown representations of bodily desire in Laura Mulvey's highly influential article from 1975, "Visual Pleasure and Narrative Cinema." See Jones, "Postfeminism, Feminist Pleasures, and Embodied Theories of Art," in Joanna Frueh, Cassandra L. Langer, and Arlene Raven, eds., *New Feminist Criticism, Art, Identity, Action* (New York: HarperCollins: 1994), pp. 16–41 (hereafter referred to as "Postfeminism").
48. Quoted from an interview with Jürgen Klauke by Peter Weibel, "Self-Identity and Otherness," trans. Baker and Harrison, in *Jürgen Klauke/Cindy Sherman*, exh. cat. (Munich: Sammlung Goetz; and Stuttgart: Cantz Verlag 1994), p. 35.
49. Ibid.
50. Garber, *Vested Interests*, p. 11.
51. The phrase is Theresa de Lauretis's, quoted in Rebecca Schneider, "After Us the Savage Goddesses: Feminist Performance Art of the Explicit Body Staged, Uneasily, Across Modernist Dreamscapes," in Elin Diamond, ed., *Performance and Cultural Politics* (New York: Routledge, 1996), p. 157.
52. Lippard expressed her concern with this dilemma in 1974:
There are ways and ways of using one's own body, and women have not always avoided self-exploitation. A woman artist's approach to herself is necessarily complicated by social stereotypes. I must admit to a personal lack of sympathy with women who have themselves photographed in black stockings, garter belts, boots, with bare breasts, bananas, and coy come-hither glances. Parody it may be . . . but the artist rarely seems to get the last laugh. A woman using her own face and body has a right to do what she will with them, but it is a subtle abyss that separates men's use of women for sexual titillation from women's use of women to expose that insult. (Lippard, "Pains and Pleasures of Rebirth," pp. 124–25.)
53. Schneider, "After Us the Savage Goddesses," p. 159.
54. The term "performalist self-portrait" is Wilke's and was the title originally given to her photographs shown at the Washington Project for the Arts in 1979. She continued to use the term to "credit the many people who assisted her in her self-portraits, her performances, and other conceptual works in which she posed and directed herself." Quoted from Thomas H. Kochheiser, ed., *Hannah Wilke: A Retrospective*, exh. cat. (Columbia: University of Missouri Press, 1989), p. 167.
55. Jones, "Postfeminism," p. 32. The performance was held on June 15, 1976. The film in which it was included was part of a larger film project on Duchamp titled *C'est la Vie Rrose*, directed for German television by Hans-Christof Stenzel.
56. Lippard expresses her concern over the criticism wielded against Wilke, while also managing to criticize the artist as well:
I must say that I admire the courage of women with less than beautiful bodies who defy convention and become particularly vulnerable to cruel criticism, although those women who do happen to be physically well-endowed probably come in

for more punishment in the long run. . . . Hannah Wilke, a glamor [sic] girl in her own right who sees her art as "seduction," is considered a little too good to be true when she flaunts her body in parody of the role she actually plays in real life. . . . Since the women's movement, [she] has begun to do performances in conjunction with her sculpture, but her own confusion of her roles as beautiful woman and artist, as flirt and feminist, has resulted at times in politically ambiguous manifestations that exposed her to criticism on a personal as well as on an artistic level. (Lippard, "Pains and Pleasures of Rebirth," pp. 125–26.)

This kind of critical writing is a good example of feminism's discomfort with embodied art. Granted, Lippard (p. 125) does point out the double standard—that Acconci's self-indulgent antics are considered art while those by an attractive woman artist are considered acts of narcissism, but she was selective in what she would approve.

57. Details and reproductions of Lynda Benglis's series of advertisements can be found in Susan Krane, *Lynda Benglis: Dual Natures*, exh. cat. (Atlanta: High Museum of Art, 1991), pp. 39–46.
58. Benglis produced this image in dialogue with Robert Morris, who was her lover at the time. It should, therefore, be read in concert with his self-portrait poster made on the occasion of a one-person exhibition, in 1974, at the Castelli-Sonnabend Gallery, in New York. Clad in the vestments associated with S/M sexuality—spiked dog collar, heavy chains, and military helmet—Morris's greased and muscular torso appears as a surrogate for the penis itself. Ever present and always veiled, the phallus asserts itself here within acceptable visual codes, for it is the man who invokes it. For further details of the Morris-Benglis collaboration, see ibid., p. 42. Morris's poster is reproduced on p. 40. For a discussion of this image and its relation to the veiled phallus, see Schor, "Representations of the Penis," p. 9; and Jones, "Postfeminism," p. 34.
59. Jones, "Postfeminism," p. 33.
60. Benglis comments on the "hermaphroditic" character of the image:

    I was alluding to something: mocking art and the sexual "hype" advertising. My intention was to mock the idea of having to take sides—to be either a male artist or a female. . . . I was involved with how I could mock both sexes. The idea of the hermaphrodite is ideal because then you employ and embody without contradicting. The condition is a contradiction in itself. You embody the perfect condition in a neither/nor state. I had to take a mocking stance with the glasses because to me it's an impersonal state—not to reveal anything. (Quoted in Krane, *Lynda Benglis*, p. 42.)
61. The *Artforum* editors were Lawrence Alloway, Max Kozloff, Rosalind Krauss, Joseph Masheck, and Annette Michelson. For the text of the letter and commentary about it, see ibid., pp. 59–60, note 95.
62. Nemser, "Lynda Benglis—A Case of Sexual Nostalgia," *The Feminist Art Journal* 3, no. 4 (winter 1974–75), p. 7.
63. Jones, "Postfeminism," p. 34.
64. This explanation was provided by the artist in a conversation with the author on November 2, 1996.
65. Katharina Sieverding, quoted in Lippard, "Pains and Pleasures of Rebirth," p. 128.
66. For a description of the ten-part series *The Mythic Being I/You (Her)* (1974–75), see Jane Farver and Lowery S. Sims, *Adrian Piper: Reflections 1967–1987*, exh. cat. (New York: Alternative Museum, 1987).
67. See Elin Diamond's "Introduction," in Diamond, *Performance and Critical Theory*, pp. 4–5, for a discussion of performativity as a "crucial critical trope" of the 1990s.
68. Judith Butler, "Performative Acts and Gender Constitution: An Essay in Phenomenology and Feminist Theory," in Sue-Ellen Case, ed., *Performing Feminisms: Feminist Critical Theory and Theatre* (Baltimore: Johns Hopkins University Press, 1990), p. 270. See also Butler, *Gender Trouble: Feminism and the Subversion of Identity* (New York: Routledge, 1990).
69. Butler, "Performative Acts and Gender Constitution," p. 270.
70. Ibid., p. 271.
71. Ibid., p. 278.

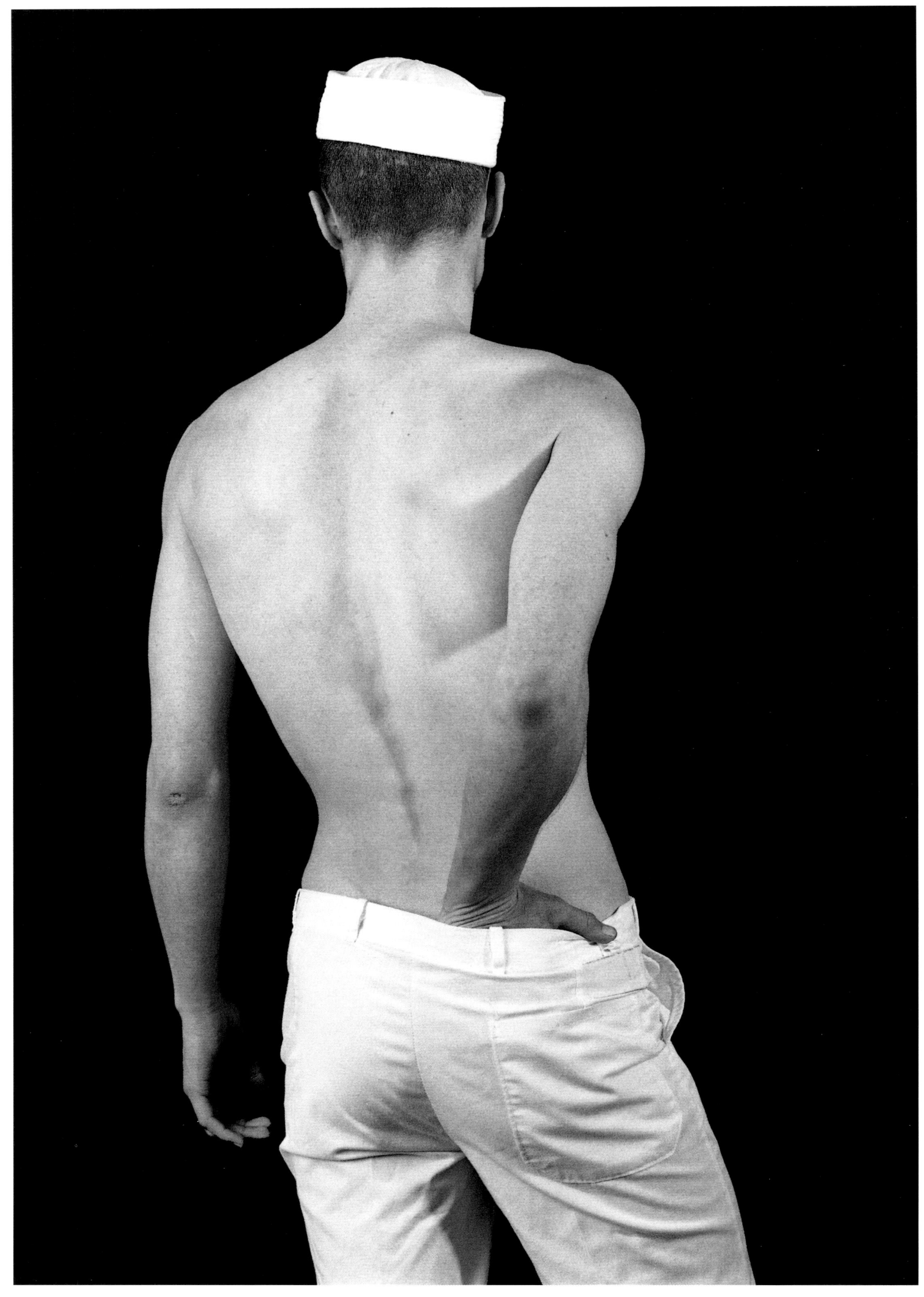

Della Grace
Jack's Back, 1994
Gelatin-silver print, 24 x 20 inches (61 x 50.8 cm)
Courtesy of the artist

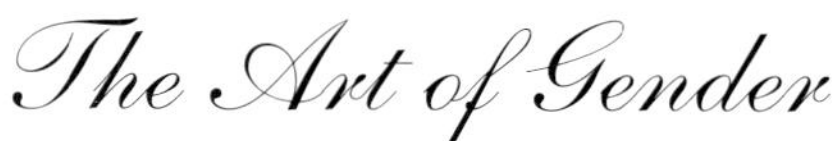

The Art of Gender

JUDITH HALBERSTAM

Bathrooms, Butches, and the Aesthetics of Female Masculinity

Bathrooms

Recently, on my way to give a talk in Minneapolis, I had to make a connection at Chicago's O'Hare airport. Feeling the need to use the facilities, to freshen up, to relieve myself, and other euphemisms, I strode purposefully into the women's bathroom. No sooner had I entered the stall than someone was knocking on the door: "Open up, security here!" As soon as I spoke, the two guards realized their error, mumbled apologies, and took off. I understood immediately what had happened. Once again, I had been mistaken for a man or a boy, and some woman (fearing what exactly?) had called security. On that same trip, in Denver's new airport, the same sequence of events was repeated.

Needless to say, the policing of gender within bathrooms is intensified in the realm of the airport, where people are literally moving through space and time in ways that cause them to want to stabilize some boundaries (gender) even as they traverse others (state). However, having one's gender challenged in the women's rest room is a frequent occurrence in the lives of many androgynous or masculine women. Indeed, it is so frequent that one wonders whether the category "woman" when used to designate public functions is completely outmoded.[1]

It is no accident that travel hubs become zones of intense scrutiny and observation. But gender policing within airport bathrooms is merely an intensified version of a larger "bathroom problem." The bathroom problem makes all its participants aware of otherwise invisible gender standards and their violation and brings us all up against the laws that bind women to femininity. The accusation, "You're in the wrong bathroom," really says two different things. First, it announces that your gender seems at odds with your sex (your apparent masculinity or androgyny is at odds with your supposed femaleness); second, it suggests that single-gender bathrooms are only for those who fit clearly into one category (male) or the other (female).

The frequency with which I and others I know are mistaken for men in public bathrooms suggests that a large number of feminine women spend a large amount of time and energy policing masculine women. Something very different happens, of course, in the men's public toilet, where the space is more likely to become a sexual cruising zone than a site for gender repression. Lee Edelman, in an essay about the interpenetration of nationalism and sexuality, argues that "the institutional men's room constitutes a site at which the zones of public and private cross with a distinctive psychic charge."[2] Noting the significance of the juxtaposition of public urinals with private stalls, Edelman comments: "Indeed, the effort to provide a space of privacy interior to the men's room itself, a space that would still be subject to some degree of public regulation and control, had encouraged by 1964 the increasing popularity of the coin-operated toilet stall within the public washroom."[3] The men's room, in other words, constitutes both an architecture of surveillance and an incitement to desire, a space of potential homosocial interaction and homoerotic interaction.

Sex-segregated bathrooms may be necessary to protect women from male predations, but they also produce and extend a rather outdated notion of a public/private split between male and female society.[4] The bathroom is a domestic space beyond the home that comes to represent domestic order, or a parody of it, out in the world. The women's bathroom accordingly becomes a sanctuary of enhanced femininity, a "little-girl's room" to which one retreats to powder one's nose or fix one's hair. The men's bathroom signifies as the extension of the public nature of masculinity—it is precisely *not* domestic even though the names given to the sexual space of the bathroom—such as "cottage" or "tearoom"—suggest it is a parody of the domestic. The codes that dominate within the women's bathroom are primarily gender codes; in the men's room they are sexual codes. Private gender versus public sex, discretely repressive versus openly sexual, bathrooms beyond the home take on the proportions of a gender factory. Marjorie Garber comments upon the liminality of the bathroom in *Vested Interests: Cross-Dressing & Cultural Anxiety* in a chapter on the perils and privileges of cross-dressing. Here, Garber discusses the very different modes of passing and cross-dressing for cross-identified genetic males and females,[5] and she observes that the rest room is a "potential waterloo" for both female-to-male (FTM) and male-to-female (MTF) cross-dressers and transsexuals.[6] For the FTM, the men's room represents the most severe test of his ability to pass, and advice frequently circulates within FTM communities about how to go unnoticed in male-only spaces. Garber notes: "The cultural paranoia of being caught in the ultimately wrong place, which may be inseparable from the pleasure of 'passing' in that same place, depends in part on the same cultural binarism, the idea that gender categories are sufficiently uncomplicated to permit self-assortment into one of the two 'rooms' without deconstructive reading."[7] It is worth pointing out here (if only because Garber does not) that the perils for passing FTMs in the men's room are very different from the perils of passing MTFs in the women's room. On the one hand, the FTM in the men's room is likely to be less scrutinized because men are not quite as vigilant about intruders as women, for obvious reasons. On the other hand, if caught, the FTM may face some version of gender panic from the man who discovers him, and it is quite reasonable to expect and fear violence in the wake of such a discovery. The MTF, by comparison, will be more scrutinized in the women's room but possibly less open to punishment if caught. Because the FTM ventures into male territory with the potential threat of violence hanging over his head, it is crucial to recognize that the bathroom problem is much more than a glitch in the machinery of gender segregation and is better described in terms of the violent enforcement of our current gender system.

Garber's reading of the perilous risks of using rest rooms for both FTMs and MTFs develops out of her introductory discussion of what Jacques Lacan calls "urinary segregation."[8] Lacan, we may recall, uses the term to describe the relations between identities and signifiers, choosing the simple diagram of the rest-room signs "Ladies" and "Gentlemen" to show that, within the production of sexual difference, primacy is granted to the signifier over that which it signifies; in more simple terms, naming confers rather than reflects meaning. In the same way, the system of urinary segregation creates the very functionality of the categories "men" and "women." While rest-room signs seem to serve and ratify distinctions that already exist, in actual fact these markers produce identifications within these constructed categories. Garber latches onto the notion of urinary segregation because it helps her to describe the processes of cultural binarism within the production of gender; for Garber, transvestites and transsexuals challenge this system by resisting the literal translation of the signs "Ladies" and "Gentlemen." Garber uses the figures of the transvestite and the transsexual to show the obvious flaws and gaps in a binary gender system; the transvestite as interloper creates, for Garber, a "third space of possibility" within which all binaries become unstable.[9] Unfortunately, as in all attempts to break a binary by producing a third term, Garber's third space tends to stabilize the other two. Edelman also turns to Lacan's term "urinary segregation" in his discussion of the "tearoom," but he uses Lacan's diagram to mark heterosexual anxiety "about the potential inscriptions of homosexual desire and about the possibility of knowing or recognizing whatever might constitute 'homosexual difference.'"[10] While for Garber, it is the transvestite who marks the instability of the markers "Ladies" and "Gentlemen," for Edelman, it is the passing homosexual who does so.

Both Garber and Edelman, interestingly enough, seem to fix upon the men's room as the site of these various destabilizing performances. As I am arguing here, however, focusing exclusively on the drama of the men's room avoids the much more complicated theater of the women's room. Garber writes of urinary segregation: "For transvestites and transsexuals, the 'men's room' problem is really a challenge to the way in which such cultural binarism is read."[11] She goes on to list some cinematic examples of the perils of urinary segregation, discussing scenes from *Tootsie* (Sydney Pollack, 1982), *Cabaret* (Bob Fosse, 1972), and *Female Impersonator Pageant* (1975). Garber's examples are odd illustrations of "the men's-room problem" if only because at least one of her examples, *Tootsie,* demonstrates gender policing in the women's room. Also, Garber makes it sound as if vigorous gender policing happens in the men's room while the women's room is a more benign zone. She notes, "In fact, the urinal has appeared in a number of fairly recent films as a marker of the ultimate 'difference'—or studied indifference."[12] Obviously, Garber is drawing a parallel here between the conventions of gender attribution within which the penis marks the "ultimate difference"; however, by not moving beyond this remarkably predictable description of gender differentiation, she overlooks the main distinction between gender policing in the men's room and in the women's room. Namely, in the women's room, not only the MTF but *all* gender-ambiguous females are scrutinized, while in the men's room, biological men are rarely deemed out of place. Garber's insistence that there is a third space of possibility occupied by the transvestite closes down the possibility that there may be a fourth, fifth, sixth, or one-hundredth space beyond the binary. In fact, the "women's-room problem" (as opposed to the "men's-room problem") indicates a multiplicity of gender displays even within the supposedly stable category of "woman."

What gender, then, are the hundreds of people born female who are consistently not read as female in the women's room? And since so many women clearly fail the women's-room test, why have we not begun to count and name the genders that are clearly emerging at this time? One could answer this question in two ways: On the one hand, we do not name and notice new genders because as a society we are committed to maintaining a binary gender system. On the other hand, we could also say that the failure of "male" and "female" to exhaust the field of gender variation actually ensures the continued dominance of these terms. Precisely because virtually nobody fits the definitions of male and female, the categories gain power and currency. Finally, as I suggested in relation to Garber's arguments about transvestism, "thirdness" merely balances the binary system and, furthermore, tends to homogenize many different gender variations under the banner of "other."

It is remarkably easy in this society to not look like a woman; it is relatively difficult, by comparison, to not look like a man. So another question posed by the bathroom problem might be, what makes femininity so approximate and masculinity so precise? Or to pose the question with a different spin, why is femininity easily impersonated or performed while masculinity seems resistant to imitation? Of course, this formulation does not easily hold and, indeed, quickly collapses into the exact opposite: Why is it, in the case of the masculine woman in the bathroom, that one finds the limits of femininity so quickly while the limits of masculinity in the men's room seem fairly expansive?

We might tackle these questions by thinking about the effects, social and cultural, of reversing gender typing. In other words, what are the implications of male femininity and female masculinity? In "Reading the Male Body," Susan Bordo laments that "when masculinity gets symbolically 'undone' in this culture, the deconstruction nearly always lands us in the territory of the degraded, while when femininity gets symbolically undone, the result is an immense elevation in status."[13] This changes the terms of gender irreversibility slightly; here Bordo seems to suggest that even a hint of the feminine sullies male masculinity while all masculinizations of femaleness are elevating. (I think my bathroom example proves that this is not so.) Her examples of elevated masculine females include the heroines of *Thelma and Louise* (Ridley Scott, 1991), Linda Hamilton in *The Terminator* (James Cameron, 1984), and Sigourney Weaver in *Aliens* (Ridley Scott, 1986). It is not difficult to see that what renders these performances of female masculinity quite tame is their resolute heterosexuality. When and where female masculinity conjoins with possibly queer identities, it is far less likely to meet with approval. It is important when thinking about gender variations like male femininity and female masculinity not simply to create another binary. In Bordo's reading, masculinity everywhere and always signifies power; in alternative models of gender variation, female masculinity is not simply the opposite of female femininity nor is it a female version of male masculinity. Rather, as we shall see in some of the artwork and gender performances discussed below, very often the unholy union of femaleness and masculinity produces wildly unpredictable results.

Butches

Many theorists have observed that gender is a technology, one that works to obscure the mechanisms by which gender is rendered natural. In other words, the apparent "givenness" of gender is its technology, and while femininity often manifests as technical effect or simply as artificial, masculinity draws its power from its seeming stability and organic qualities. Judith Butler, for example, following Monique Wittig, writes in *Gender Trouble: Feminism and the Subversion of Identity*: "To be male is not to be 'sexed'; to be 'sexed' is always a way of becoming particular and relative, and males within this system participate in the form of the universal person."[14] The systems that sustain the conflation of maleness and universality are various, of course, but can generally be described as compulsory heterosexuality within capitalism. While Garber, as we saw, feels that the only way out of the cultural binarism of gender is to valorize a disruptive third term, Wittig believes that the very categories "man" and "woman" must be refused and resisted. Butler, on the other hand, refuses to invest in either thirdness or the utopian ungendered space, arguing for the proliferation of gender performances within parodic repetition. In a project on alternative masculinities, such as mine, it does not make sense to go with Wittig's call for the abolition of gender or with Garber's "third space of possibility"; and yet, while the notion of parodic performance as theorized in *Gender Trouble* may be the obvious starting point for all attempts to cast masculinities without men, we need a more descriptive account than Butler's of the places within representation where corporeality and performance conspire to produce masculinity with a difference.

One might begin by pointing out that it is relatively simple to expose the mechanisms of even dominant male masculinity; indeed, the most masculinist of film genres, the action-adventure film, does so all the time. For example, we could look to the most recent James Bond film, *Goldeneye* (Martin Campbell, 1995), for a representation of the technology of masculinity. In *Goldeneye*, Bond battles the usual array of bad guys: Commies, Nazis, mercenaries, and a superaggressive, violent femme type. He puts on his usual performance of debonair action-adventure hero and has his usual supply of gadgetry to aid him—a retractable belt, a bomb disguised as a pen, a laser-weapon watch, and so on. But there is something curiously lacking in this latest Bond flick, namely, credible masculine power. Bond's boss, M, is a noticeably butch older woman who calls Bond a dinosaur and chastises him for being a misogynist and a sexist. His secretary, Miss Moneypenny, accuses him of sexual harassment, his male buddy betrays him and calls him a dupe, and, ultimately, women seem not to go for his charms—bad suits and lots of sexual innuendo—which seem as old and as ineffective as his gadgets. Masculinity, in this rather actionless film, is primarily prosthetic and, in it and countless other action films, has little if anything to do with biological maleness. It signifies more often as a technical special effect. In *Goldeneye*, it is M who most convincingly performs masculinity, and she does so partly by exposing the sham of Bond's own performance. It is M who convinces us that sexism and misogyny are not necessarily part and parcel of masculinity even though historically it has become difficult, if not impossible, to separate masculinity from the oppression of women. The action-adventure hero should embody an extreme version of normative masculinity, but, instead, we find that excessive masculinity turns into a parody or exposure of the norm. Since masculinity tends to manifest as natural gender itself, the action flick, with its emphasis on prosthetic extension, actually undermines the heterosexuality of the hero even as it extends his masculinity. So, in *Goldeneye*, Bond's masculinity is linked not only to a profoundly unnatural form of masculine embodiment but also to gay masculinities. In the scene in which Bond goes to pick up his newest set of gadgets, a campy and almost queeny science nerd gives Bond his brand-new accessories and demonstrates each one with great enthusiasm. It is no accident that the science nerd is called Agent Q. We might read Agent Q as a perfect model of the interpenetration of queer and dominant regimes. Q is indeed an agent—a queer subject who exposes the workings of dominant heterosexual masculinity. The gay masculinity of Agent Q and the female masculinity of M provide a remarkable representation of the absolute dependence of dominant masculinities upon minority masculinities.

Minority masculinities and femininities destabilize binary gender systems in many different locations. As many feminist and antiracist critics have commented, femininity and masculinity signify as normative within and through white, middle-class, heterosexual bodies. Richard Fung, for example, writing about gay male porn, suggests that pornographic narrative structures assume a white male viewer who embodies a normative standard of male beauty and male desirability. Within this scopic field, porn characterizes black men as excessively sexual and wholly phallic and Asian men as passive and asexual.[15] Films by artists of color that disrupt this representational code—*Looking for Langston* (Isaac Julien, 1988) and *Tongues Untied* (Marlon Riggs, 1989), for example—can undo the hierarchic relations between dominant and minority sexualities. They also have the power to reorganize masculinity itself.

Other assaults upon dominant gender regimes come from queer butch art and performance, which might include drag king shows, butch theatrical roles, or art featuring gender-variant subjects. In terms of drag king performances, stars like Elvis Herselvis or Tony Las Vegas (performed by Julie

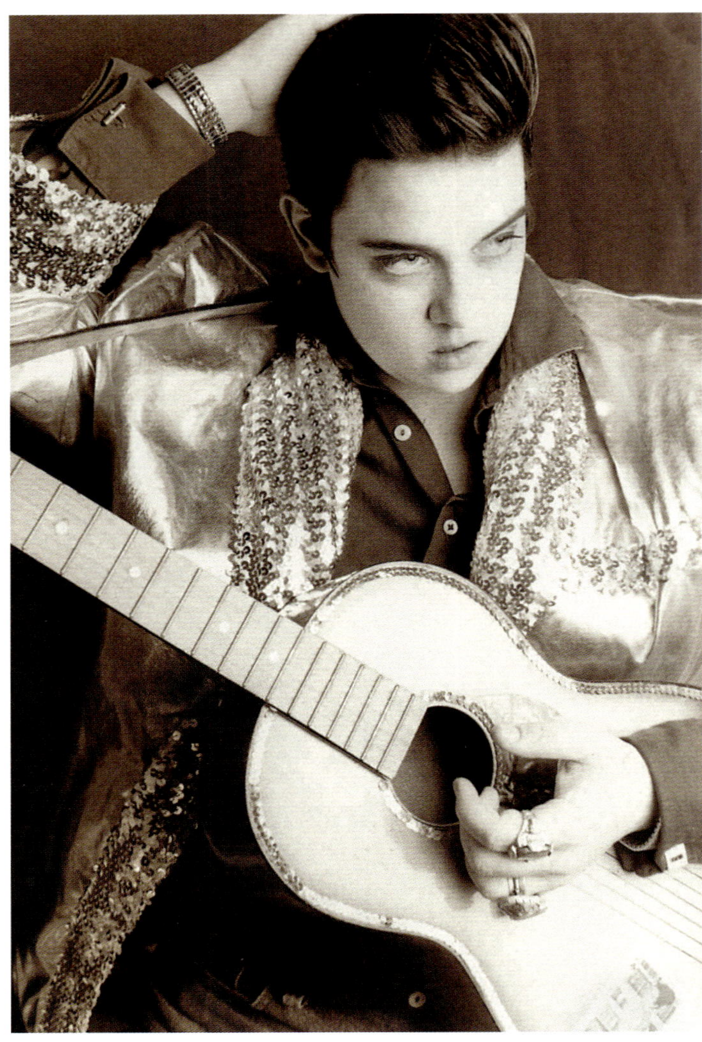

Elvis Herselvis
1990
Photographed by Phyllis Christopher

Wheeler) turn dominant masculinity around by parodying male superstardom and working conventional modes of performed sexism and misogyny into successful comedy routines. As Tony Las Vegas, for example, Wheeler manages to parody masculinity by performing its most unnatural and obviously staged aspect: sexism. Exhorting the audiences in dyke clubs to "show us yer tits" and standing far too close to other women onstage with him, Tony reeks of the tricks of misogyny. Tony's manipulations of a stagy and theatrical masculinity draw attention not simply to the performative aspect of masculinity but also to the places where nonperformativity has ideological implications. In other words, by exposing smarmy male attentions to females as staged, the drag king refuses any construction of misogyny as the natural order of things.

In one of the very few articles in print on the topic of drag kings, Sarah Murray asks provocatively: "Why hasn't drag developed into a distinct theatrical genre among lesbians in the United States?"[16] She answers her own question by drawing upon conventional notions of lesbian invisibility and by remarking on the "naturalization of the masculine." She states correctly, "A woman has less to grab on to when doing individual drag."[17]

Obviously, my argument about the apparent stability of male masculinity concurs with Murray's analysis. I also agree with her that the forms of masculinity available for parody tend to be either working-class masculinities (the construction worker, for example) or explicitly performative middle-class masculinities like the lounge lizard. Furthermore, the masculinities that offer up subversions of recognizably dominant male masculinity tend to be nonwhite. Where we diverge, however, is on the topic of lesbian masculinities themselves. Murray finds butch iconicity to be less about redefining masculinity and more about appropriating male power. She reduces butchness to an historical marker of lesbian visibility that belongs to 1950s lesbian communities but not to contemporary queer dyke culture, and she suggests that lesbians, ultimately, "don't feel free to play with the masculine the way gay men play with the feminine."[18]

I would respond to these arguments by saying, first, that it is crucial to recognize that masculinity does not belong to men, has not only been produced by men, and does not properly express patriarchy. A popular misunderstanding of lesbian butchness depicts it as either an appropriation of dominant male masculinity or an instance of false consciousness in which the butch simply lacks strong models of lesbian identity. What I am trying to show in this essay (and what is demonstrated in the longer project of which it is a part) is that what we call "masculinity" has also been produced by women, by specifically masculine women, who are gender deviants and often lesbians. For this reason, it is inaccurate and indeed regressive to make masculinity into a general term for "behavior associated with males." To argue then, as Murray does, that women do not feel free to play with masculinity is to position masculinity as something separate from all lesbian women, as something they may play with but not a quality they may express or embody. Second, in relation to Murray, butch identity has a complicated relation to notions of lesbian community and lesbian visibility and, partic-

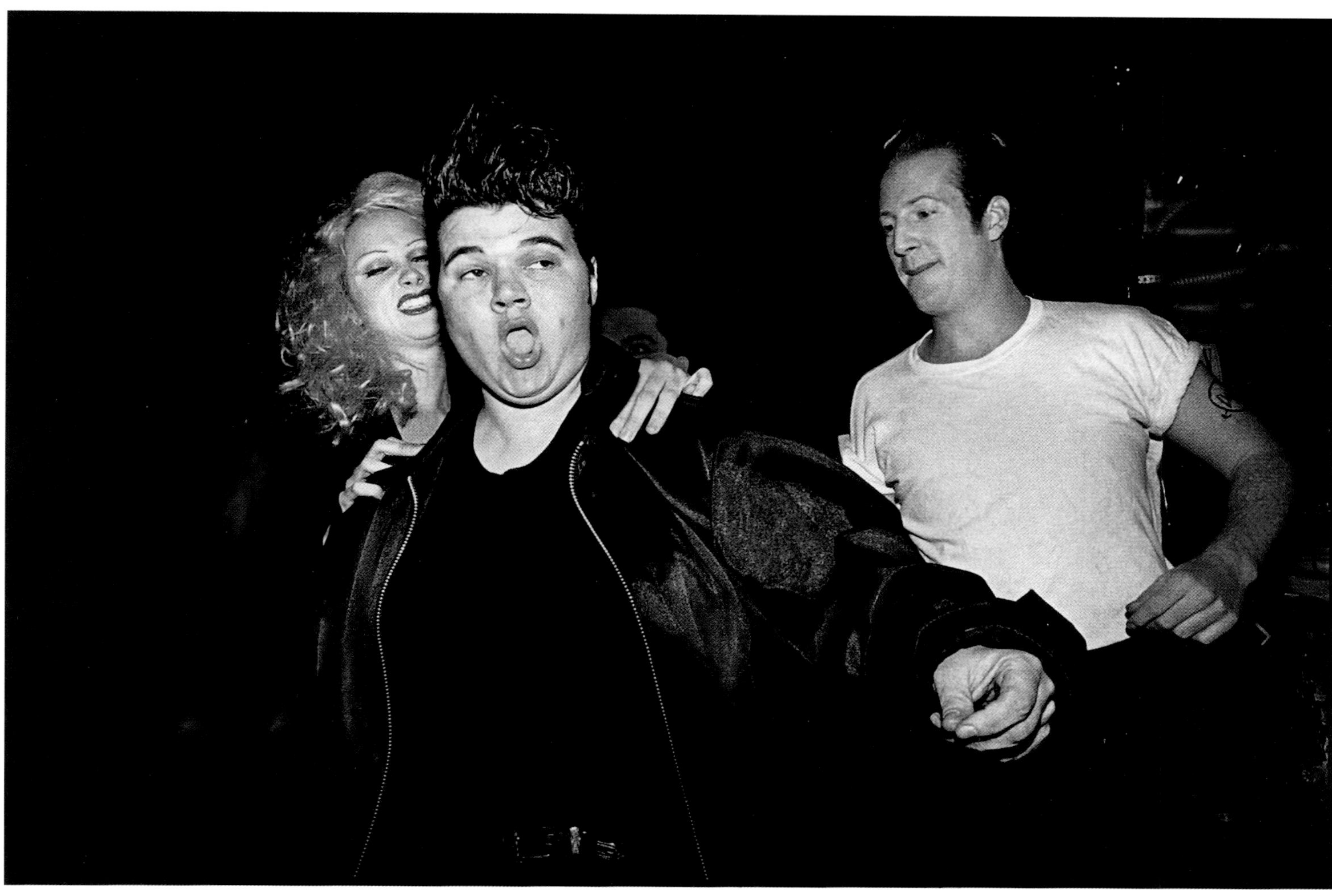

Betsey L. A. Gallagher
Murray Hill and Penelope Tuesdae as John Travolta and Olivia Newton-John, 1996
Gelatin-silver print,
16 x 20 inches (40.6 x 50.8 cm)
Photographed by Tanya Braganti

ularly, to lesbian drag. Since so little has been written on lesbian masculinity that does not reduce it to a stereotype of the lesbian or a pathetic parody of maleness, we have yet to determine what its relations might be to either lesbian or transgender definition. Furthermore, butches may not be the most appropriate women to do male drag. Murray avoids any substantive discussion of transgenderism in her article because she cannot account for what happens when drag is not a costume but represents part of an identity effect. When she does mention transgender figures like Billy Tipton, she incorrectly and imprecisely characterizes them as "female" and uses feminine pronouns to talk about their performed identities. To be perfectly clear, butches, and transgender butches in particular, do not wear male clothing as drag—they embody masculinity. For this reason, some of the best drag king performances may actually come from femme drag kings like Shelley Mars, performers who maintain a disjuncture between gender and performed gender.

In a slightly different kind of butch theater, a queer performance-art piece called *You're Just Like My Father* (1995), Peggy Shaw represents female masculinity as a pugnacious and gritty staging—that is, restaging—of family dynamics via the butch daughter. There is no question here that Shaw's masculinity is part and parcel of her lesbianism rather than a drag identity. Shaw becomes her mother's substitute husband and her lovers' substitute fathers and brothers and constructs her own masculinity by reworking and improving the masculinities she observes around her. She moves easily back and forth between various personae: she is the fighter, the crooner, the soldier, the breadwinner, the romeo, the patriarch. In each of these roles, Shaw makes it clear that she is a female-bodied person inhabiting each role and that each role is part of her gender identity. In order to play among a variety of masculine identifications, Shaw, furthermore, is not forced to become her father or to appropriate his maleness; she is already "just like" her father and their masculinities exist on parallel planes.

The Art of Gender

The fleshing out of female masculinities has not been limited to theatrical arenas. In the photographic work of artists like Catherine Opie and Della Grace, we can watch the female body becoming masculine in stunning and powerful ways. Opie's lush photographic portraits of members of dyke, transgender, and S/M communities put a particular version of female masculinity on display. In one of her early projects, entitled *Being and Having*, Opie created a series of framed portraits of mustachioed or bearded faces set against startling yellow backdrops. In each shot, the camera zooms in on the model's face (often even cropping the top of the head), bringing the spectator right up against a face that, despite its proximity, remains gender ambiguous. The close-up articulates what feels like an intimacy between model and artist, an intimacy, moreover, that is not readily available to the viewer.

In many of the portraits, the camera comes close enough to the model's face to reveal the artificiality of the facial hair; in others, the facial hair appears to be real, setting up a visual trap: we may pause to wonder whether we are looking at a male or a female face. In many of the commentaries on Opie's work, in fact, critics insist that its complexity relies upon the "operations that almost unconsciously take place when we determine whether we are looking at a man or a woman."[19] But, if we look at her photographs within a larger context of productions of female masculinity, the ambiguity, or binarism, of gender seems spectacularly irrelevant. Indeed, in this context, these portraits are not simply ambiguous—they are resolute images of female masculinity, in which, as Opie puts it, her cross-dressing models take their performances "both into the bedroom and out to public spaces. They are, I suppose, exhibitionists, and their scene has become a public spectator sport."[20]

Opie's images of bearded, pierced, and tattooed dykes and transgender men create a powerful visual aesthetic of alternative masculinities. While Opie's work is often compared to Diane Arbus's because both take as subject so-called misfits and freaks, she vigorously denies such a comparison:

> *I try to present people with an extreme amount of dignity. I mean, they're always going to be stared at, but I try to make the portraits stare back. That's what the relationship is all about. I mean, it's not like Diane Arbus or anything like that. Some of the portraits look very sad, I think they have this distant gaze but they are never pathetic.*[21]

Opie's insistence that her portraits "stare back" creates an interesting power dynamic not only between photographer and model but also between image and spectator. The power of the gaze in an Opie portrait always, and literally, rests with the image: the perpetual stare challenges the spectator's own sense of gender congruity, even of self. Indeed, this gaze replicates the hostile stares that the model probably faces every day in the street. One reviewer of Opie's 1994 show, *Portraits*, commented that the isolation of each subject within the stylized frame of the photograph, with its brilliant color backdrop, transforms them into "abstract signs" and leaves the spectator free to be a voyeur.[22] But such an assessment ignores the disorienting effect of these pictures—the subjects are positively regal in their opulent settings, and their colorful displays of tattoos and body markings single them out for photographic glory. The stare of the spectator is forced to be admiring and appreciative rather than simply objectifying and voyeuristic. The tattoos, piercings, and body modifications that mark the Opie model become in her portraits far more than the signifiers of outlaw status. Whether we are confronted with the hormonally and surgically altered bodies of transgender men or the tattooed and pierced and scarred skin of the butch dyke, we look at bodies that display layered and multiple identifications, adding a gender dimension unassimilable within the boundaries of "man" or "woman."

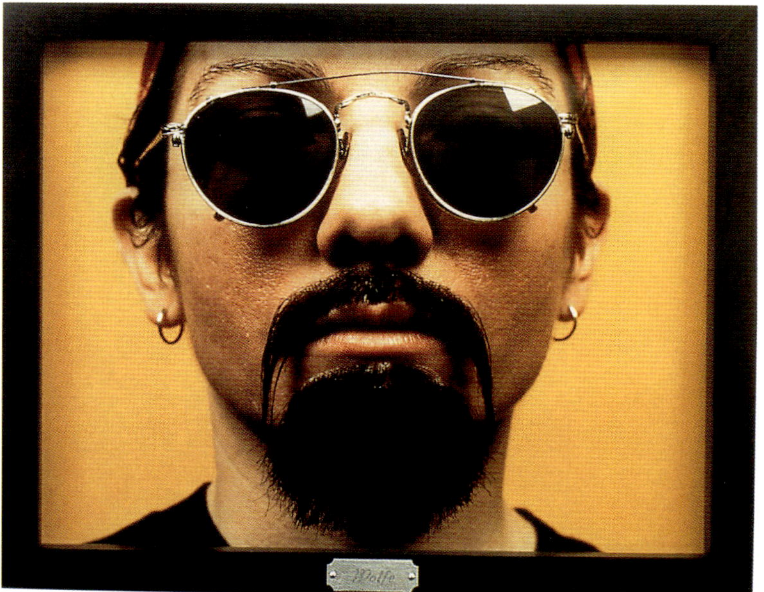

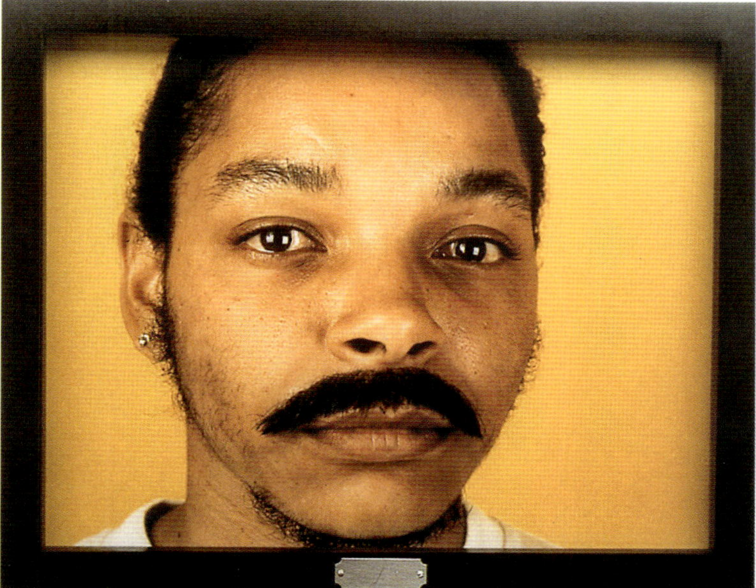

Catherine Opie
Wolfe, from the *Being and Having* series, 1991
Chromogenic print, framed, 17 x 22 inches (43.2 x 55.9 cm)
Courtesy of Regen Projects, Los Angeles

Catherine Opie
J., from the *Being and Having* series, 1991
Chromogenic print, framed, 17 x 22 inches (43.2 x 55.9 cm)
Courtesy of Regen Projects, Los Angeles

Grace's images of gender-ambiguous bodies are, like Opie's, stylized portraits in the Mapplethorpe tradition. However, in many of Grace's photographs an action defines gender ambiguity in relation to a set of sexual practices. Her photos often feature two or more bodies in play, and we thus see gender as a complex set of negotiations between bodies, identities, and desire. In *Triad* (1992), for example, three shaven and bald female bodies are intertwined in a three-way embrace. The pallor of the bodies and the smoothness of the shaven skin turn skin to marble, refusing the traditional softness of femininity. Grace frequently affords her subjects an almost mythical treatment, photographing them in classical costume or titling the photographs after mythological subjects, and, as does Opie, she always grants her models dignity, power, and beauty even as she exposes them to the gaze.

In her photographs of butch bodies, Grace borrows from gay male erotic imagery to construct a context for an unself-conscious female masculinity. In *Jack's Back* (1994), we see a sailor with his back toward us. He wears white Navy-issue pants and a white cap and has a hand tucked into his waistband. The back of the head is closely shaven, the shoulders are broad and manly. This image could have been plucked from Paul Cadmus or Rainer Werner Fassbinder's *Querelle* (1982) or the image bank of gay erotica. However, the back belongs to Jackie, a beautifully built and tightly muscled butch whom Grace has photographed repeatedly. In *Jack Unveiled* (1994), we now see Jackie head on, wearing khaki pants and pulling an army T-shirt over her head. While the model's face is still partially obscured, her torso (Jack's front) is exposed. The breasts are just pronounced enough to mark Jackie as a "woman," but they are small enough and the torso is muscular enough to keep the ambiguity intact.

Opie also uses back shots to make gender unreadable. In *Dyke* (1994), we see a torso set against an elaborate backdrop. The word "DYKE" is tattooed in Gothic script just below the neckline of a head of very short hair. On the one hand, the inscription dispels gender ambiguity by declaring the body lesbian, but on the other hand, given the many multigendered images of dykes that Opie has produced, the word "DYKE" gives very few clues as to what the front of this body might look like.

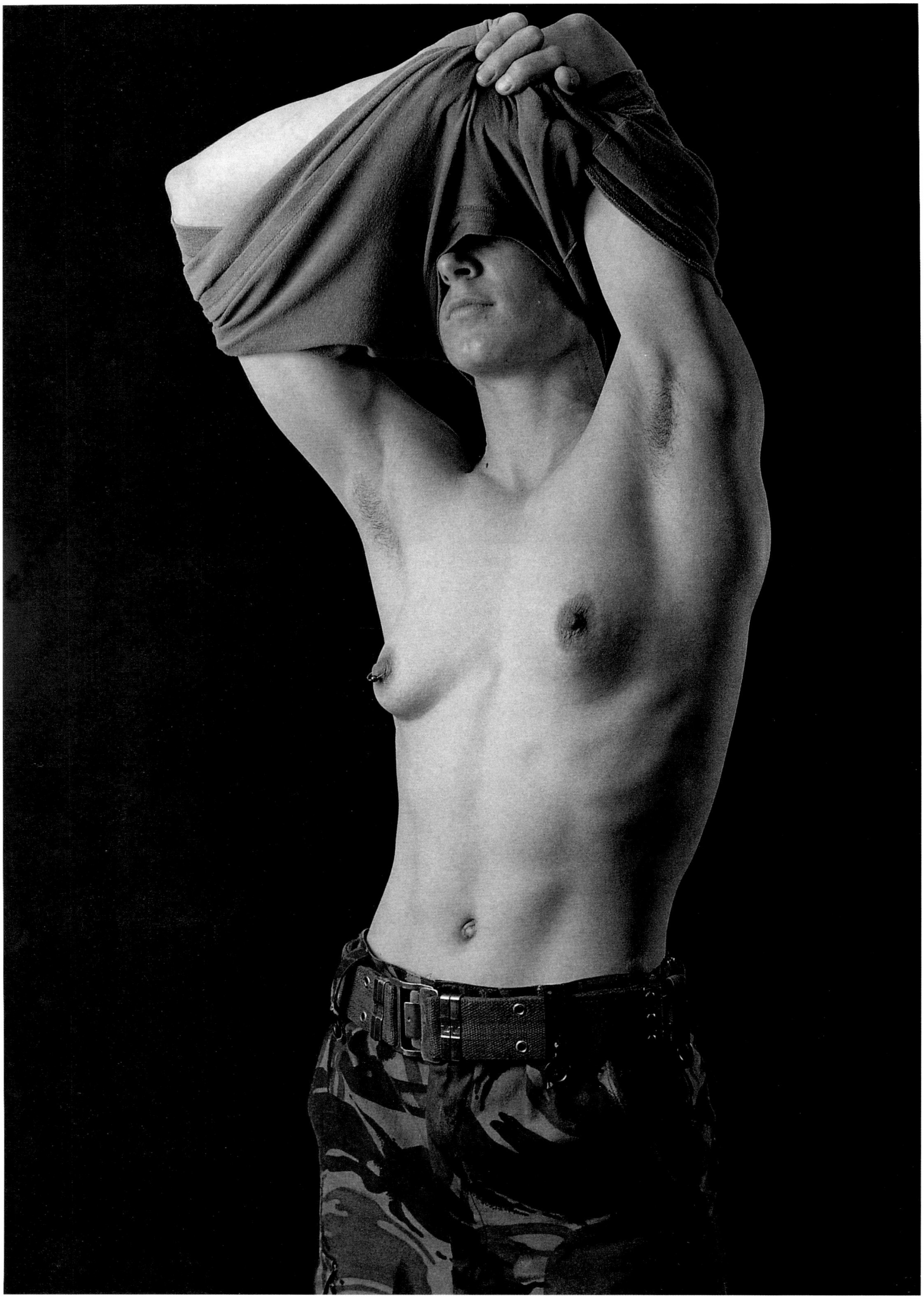

Della Grace
Jack Unveiled, 1994
Gelatin-silver print, 24 x 20 inches (61 x 50.8 cm)
Courtesy of the artist

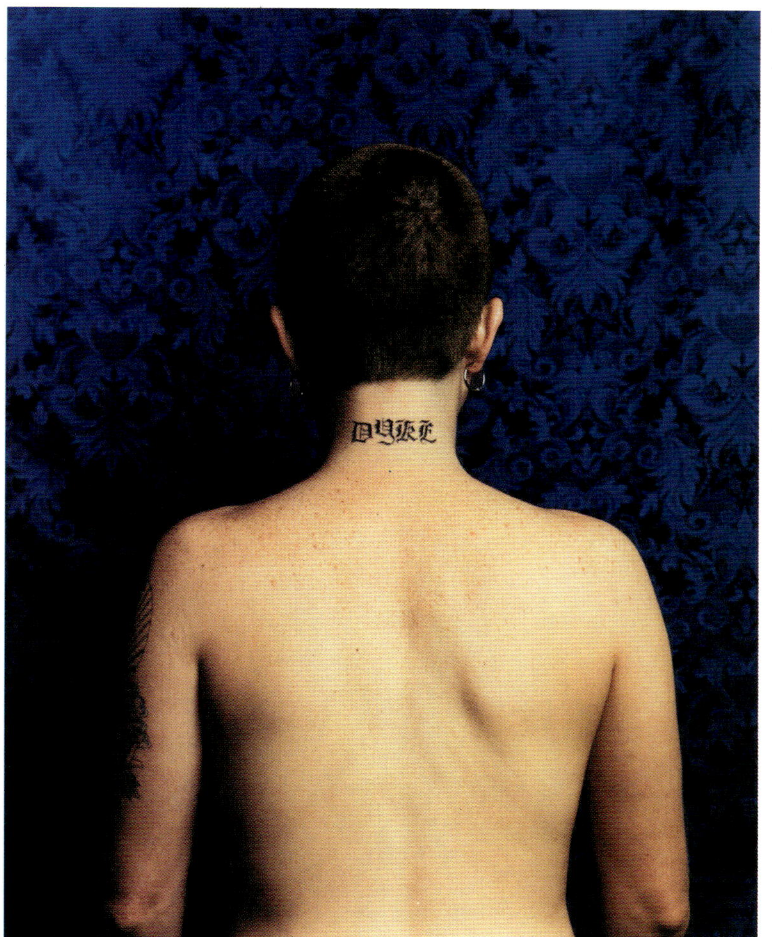

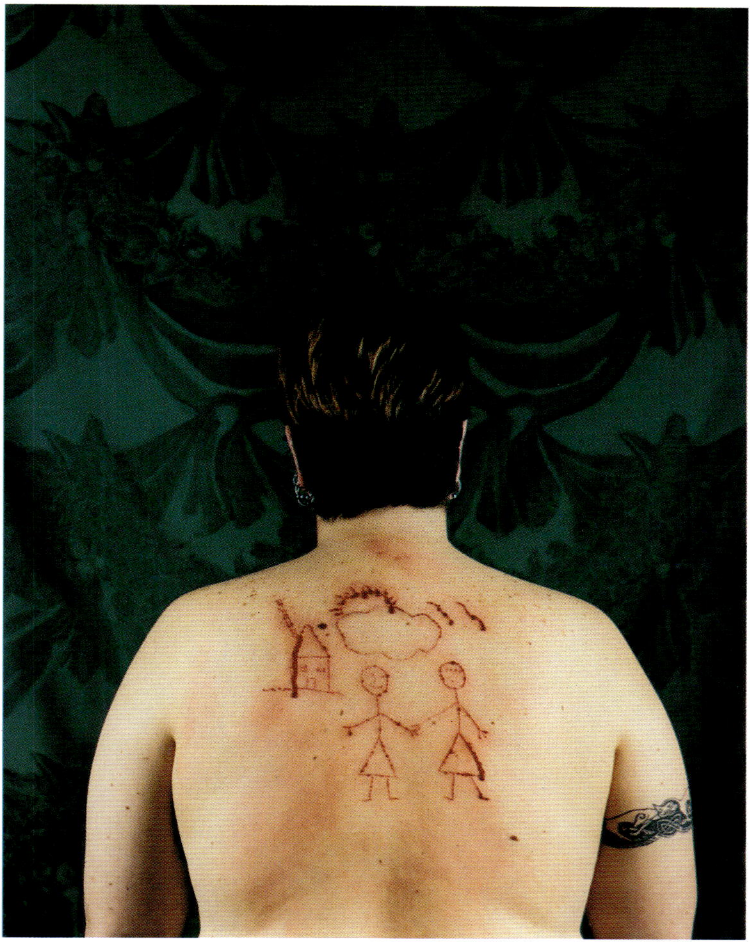

Catherine Opie
Dyke, 1992
Chromogenic print,
40 x 30 inches (101.6 x 76.2 cm)
Courtesy of Regen Projects,
Los Angeles

Catherine Opie
Self-Portrait, 1993
Chromogenic print,
40 x 30 inches (101.6 x 76.2 cm)
Courtesy of Regen Projects,
Los Angeles

Opie's and Grace's "back art" is a refusal to engage with the all-too-easy game of gender ambiguity. They want gender literally to be a surface for inscriptions, words and drawings, art and desire. In another back shot, *Self-Portrait* (1993), Opie exposes her own back to view. Cut into the skin is a childlike image of two stick figures in skirts holding hands, standing in front of a stick house, below a bubble cloud. The picture, seemingly etched in blood, sits uncomfortably close to one of Opie's arm tattoos. Turning the back into a canvas, Opie dispels curiosity about what the front of the body might reveal. As the artist notes about this self-portrait: "It says a lot of different things. One of them is that I have my back to you."[23] While so many of Opie's photographs literally return the gaze with piercing stares, the back shots circumvent the question of the gaze, allowing a space to open up for both gender variation and different inscriptions of the sexed body.

Opie's cuttings and the tattoos and scars on the bodies of both Opie's and Grace's models stand in direct opposition to another recent and popular image of gender bending created by the photographer Annie Leibovitz. Demi Moore appeared on the cover of the August 1992 *Vanity Fair*, naked but for a painted man's suit. Inside the magazine were further pictures of Moore, still wearing the painted suit and leaning over the body of a sleeping man, her husband, Bruce Willis. These photographs were considered innovative and challenging when they were first published, but if we juxtapose Leibovitz's images of Moore's painted body with the gender art of Opie and Grace, we will be reminded of how fiercely heterosexual and gender invariant popular culture tends to be. Moore's body suit precisely fails to suggest even a mild representation of female masculinity precisely because it so anxiously emphasizes the femaleness of her body. While Opie's and Grace's portraits often make no effort to make femaleness visible, the Moore images represent femaleness as that which confers femininity upon even the most conventional of masculine facades (the suit). By contrast, the female masculinity in the work of Opie and Grace offers a glimpse into worlds where alternative masculinities make an art of gender.

Queer Futures

In this essay, I have tried to chart the implications of gender policing and gender performances within public spaces and to map them onto a utopian vision of radically different bodies and sexualities. By making such a move, I do not wish to suggest that we can magically wish into being a new set of properly descriptive genders that would put pressure on the outmoded categories of male and female. Nor do I mean to suggest that by simply desegregating public toilets we will change the function of dominant genders within heteropatriarchal cultures. However, it seems to me that there are some very obvious spaces in which gender difference, as conventionally described, simply does not work and that the breakdown of gender as a signifying system in these arenas can be exploited to hasten the proliferation of alternate gender regimes in other locations. From drag kings to spies with gadgets, from butch bodies to FTM bodies, gender and sexuality and their technologies are already excessively strange. It is simply a matter of keeping them that way.

Notes

An earlier, and substantially different, version of this essay, entitled "Techno-Homo: Bathrooms, Butches, and Sex with Furniture," was published in Melody Calvert and Jennifer Terry, eds., *Processed Lives* (New York: Routledge, 1997).

1. The continued viability of the category "woman" has already been challenged in a variety of academic locations: Monique Wittig, most notably, argued that "lesbians are not women" in her essay "The Straight Mind," in Wittig, *The Straight Mind and Other Essays* (Boston: Beacon Press, 1992), p. 121. Wittig claims that since lesbians are refusing primary relations to men, they cannot occupy the position "woman." In another philosophical challenge to the category "woman," transgender philosopher Jacob Hale uses Wittig's radical claim to theorize the possibility of gendered embodiments that exceed male and female; see Hale, "Are Lesbians Women?" *Hypatia* 11, no. 2 (spring 1996), pp. 94–121. Elsewhere, Cheshire Calhoun suggests that the category "woman" may actually "operate as a lesbian closet"; see Calhoun, "The Gender Closet: Lesbian Disappearance under the Sign 'Woman,'" *Feminist Studies* 21, no. 1 (spring 1995), pp. 7–34.
2. Lee Edelman, "Tearooms and Sympathy or, The Epistemology of the Water Closet," in *Homographesis: Essays in Gay Literary and Cultural Theory* (New York: Routledge, 1994), p. 158.
3. Ibid., p. 159.
4. Some people are currently writing about the social construction of gender within the operation of sex-segregated bathrooms. Barbara Cruikshank, for example, is presently working on a project, called "Flushing Gender: Public Toilets and Public Life," that tries to expand upon gender-based exclusion in public toilets to think about other exclusionary public space.
5. For an examination of differing notions of genetic and biological gender, see, for example, Anne Fausto-Sterling, "The Five Sexes: Why Male and Female Are Not Enough," *The Sciences* 33 (March–April 1993), pp. 20–24.
6. Marjorie Garber, *Vested Interests: Cross-Dressing & Cultural Anxiety* (New York: Routledge, 1992), p. 47. Obviously, Garber's use of the term "waterloo" makes a pun out of the drama of bathroom surveillance. While the pun is clever and even amusing, it is also troubling. The constant use of puns throughout the book has the overall effect of making gender crossing sound like a game or at least trivializes the often life-or-death processes involved in cross-identification. This is not to say that gender can never be a "laughing matter" and must always be treated seriously but only to question the use of the pun as a theoretical method.
7. Ibid.
8. Ibid. pp. 13–16.
9. Although Garber never uses this precise term in her text, it does appear in the index (ibid., p. 441). For a discussion of the "third" in more general terms, see ibid., pp. 9–13.
10. Edelman, "Tearooms and Sympathy," p. 160.
11. Garber, *Vested Interests*, p. 14.
12. Ibid.
13. Susan Bordo, "Reading the Male Body," *Michigan Quarterly Review* 32, no. 4 (fall 1993), p. 721.
14. Judith Butler, *Gender Trouble: Feminism and the Subversion of Identity* (New York: Routledge, 1990), p. 113.
15. Richard Fung, "Looking for My Penis: The Eroticized Asian in Gay Video Porn," in Bad Object Choices, ed., *How Do I Look? Queer Video and Film* (Seattle: Bay Press, 1991), pp. 145–68.
16. Sarah Murray, "Dragon Ladies, Draggin' Men: Some Reflections on Gender, Drag and Homosexual Communities," *Public Culture* 6, no. 2 (winter 1994), p. 344.
17. Ibid., p. 356.
18. Ibid., p. 360.
19. David Pagel, "Catherine Opie," *Art Issues* (September–October 1994), p. 45.
20. Anna Maria Smith, "The Feminine Gaze: Photographer Catherine Opie Documents Lesbian Daddy/Boy Subculture," *The Advocate*, November 19, 1991, p. 83. This is a great early review of Opie's work, although the title "The Feminine Gaze" seems to insist on the femininity of all things produced by women. Let's face it, there is nothing feminine about this work.
21. Russell Ferguson, "Catherine Opie with Russell Ferguson" (interview), *Index* 1, no. 2 (April 1996), p. 29.
22. Michael Cohen, "Catherine Opie—Regen Projects," *Flash Art* 27, no. 179 (December 1994), p. 98.
23. Ferguson, "Catherine Opie," p. 30.

drag racing

I have to take you elsewhere, with an image of me, age seven, sitting on the back porch of our brownstone in the Bronx, waiting for a father who would never arrive. It's vague now; but I remember that mother is silent, reading, staring with a resolute familiarity through her glasses at another book, as if she had been here before and was seeking refuge there, again. I think my brother was reading too, or maybe we were both running around playing. And if I wasn't playing, I was hiding in my room where I spent an increasing amount of time. We were getting ready to go to the park, or down south to Charleston, somewhere, and our bags were packed, sitting by the door, ready since eight a.m. It was now two. He never came, and in a terrible sense I am still waiting for him, maybe we each are, busying ourselves with exteriors, trying to figure out how to manage absence. Now I understand that not only were we waiting for father, we were resisting the idea of him.

What I have come to realize is that, not only does this image offer up notions of sentimentality and longing, but it also suggests a stirring of resistance. The resistance in that room was different from the longing. Beneath the serene veneer was an insurgent tension—a series of subtle, rebel acts were in process (reading, running around, hiding), which set up a mechanism through which we could each cope with the idea that father would not come, and that our waiting was in vain. At age seven I was consciously creating a mechanism, a strategy for how to deal with the very real presence of my body and the absence of another's.

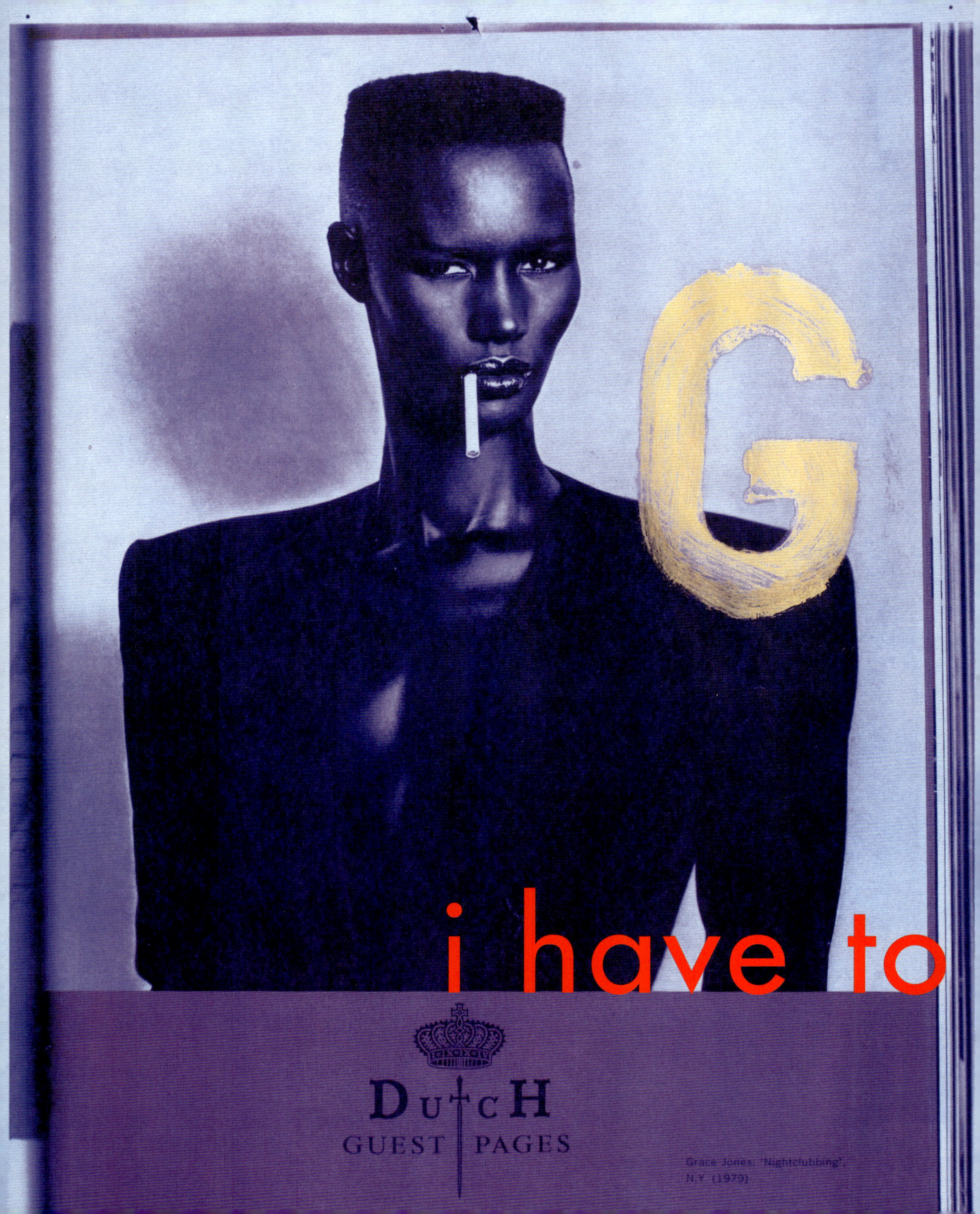

G

i have to

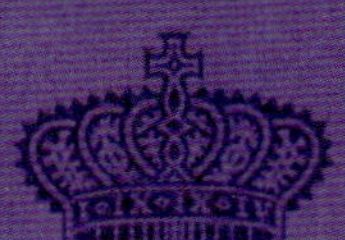

DUTCH
GUEST PAGES

Grace Jones: 'Nightclubbing',
N.Y (1979)

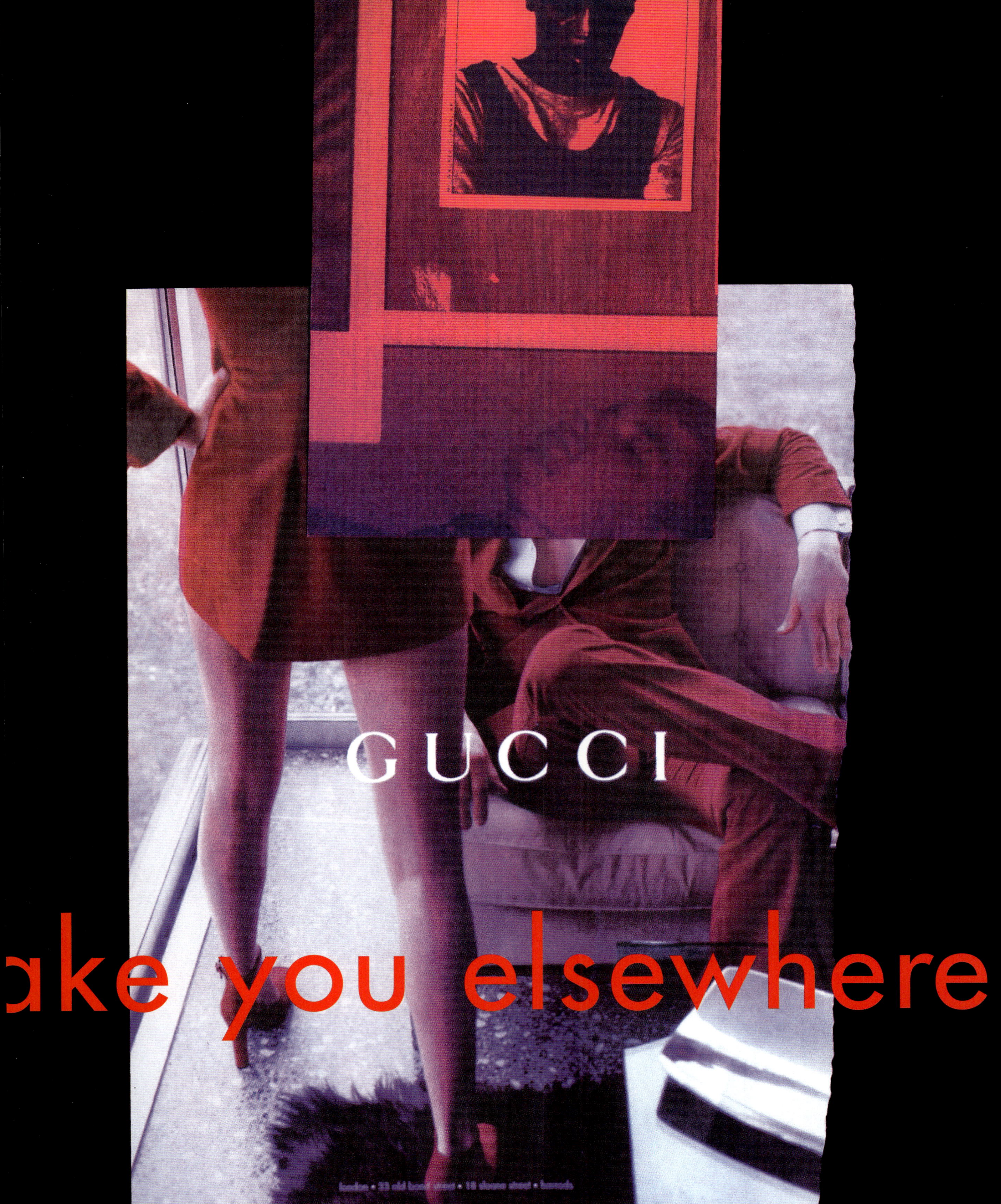
GUCCI
ake you elsewhere

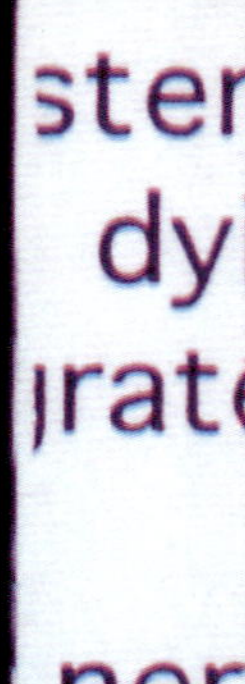

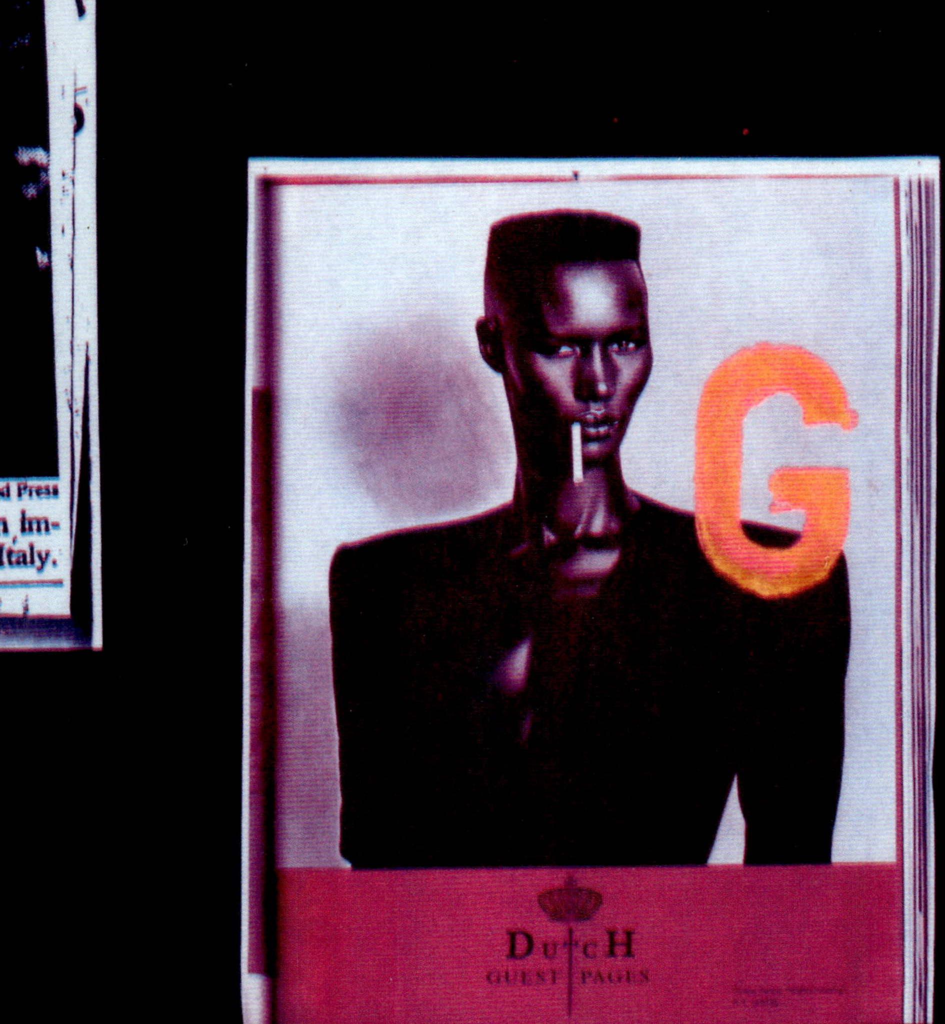

what

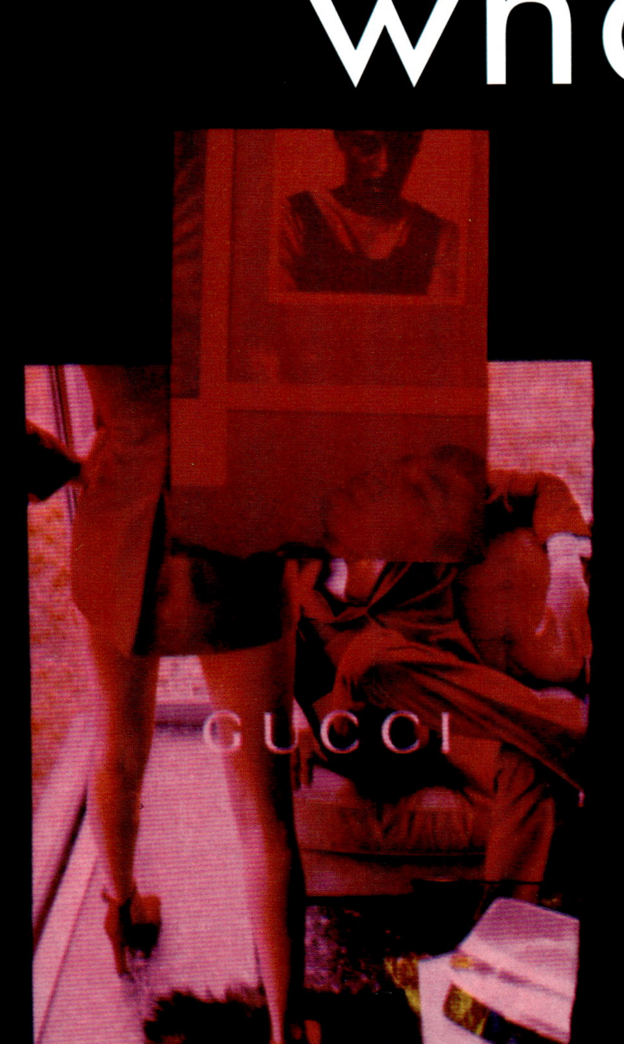

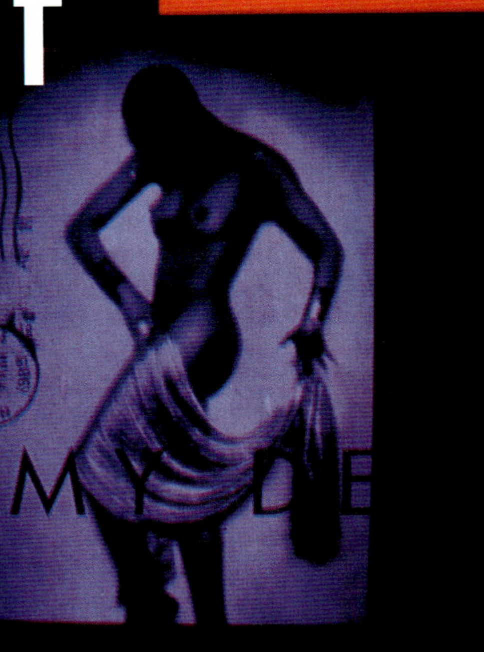

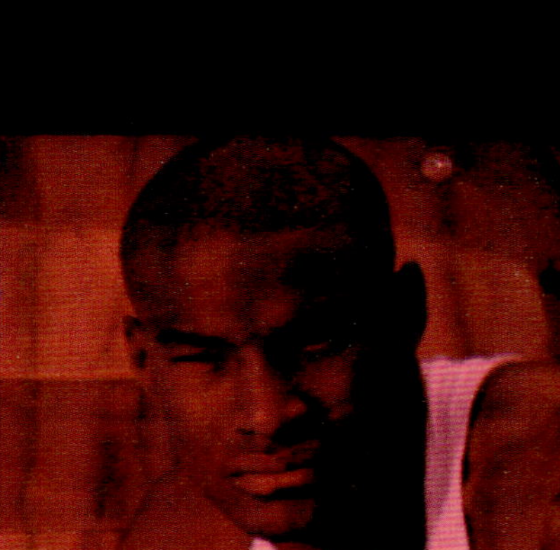

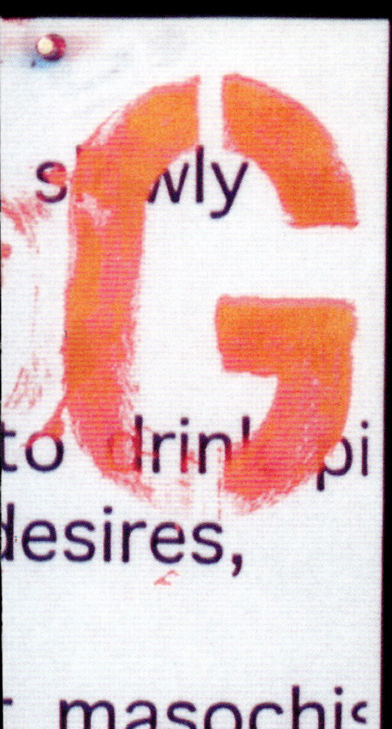

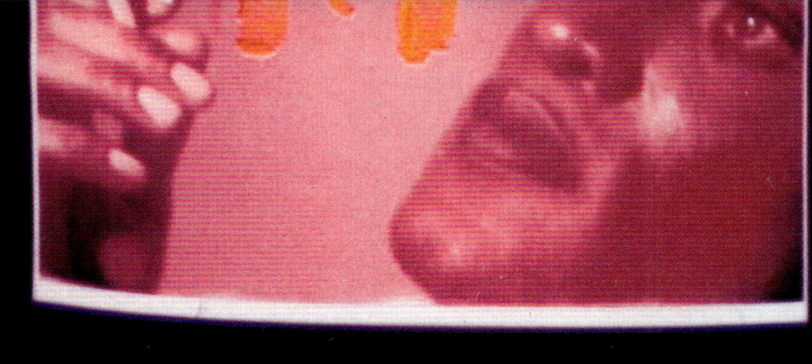

THE BONDS OF LOVE

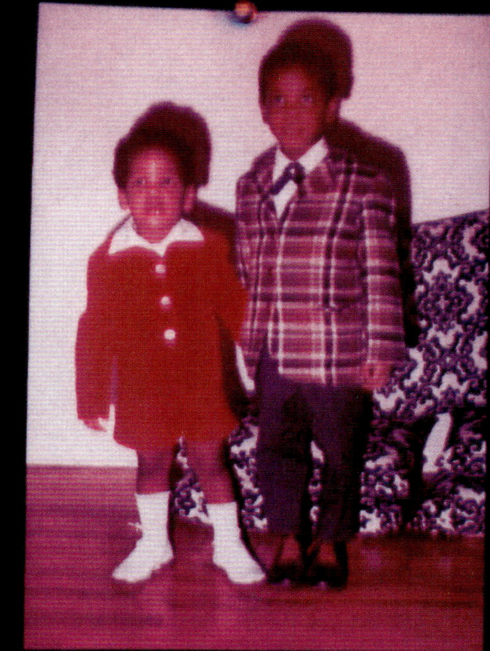

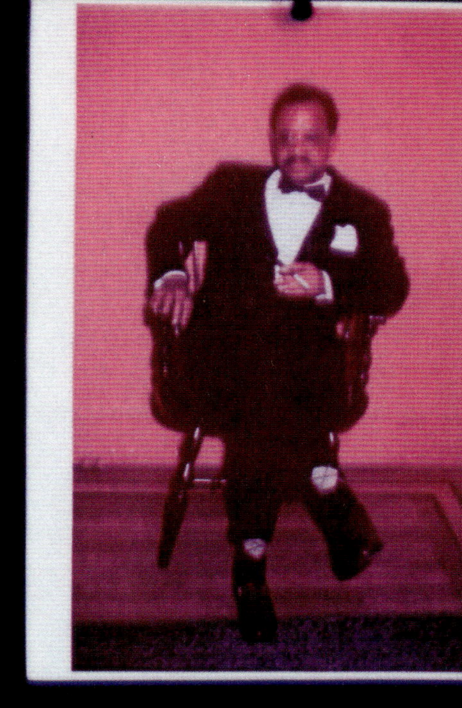

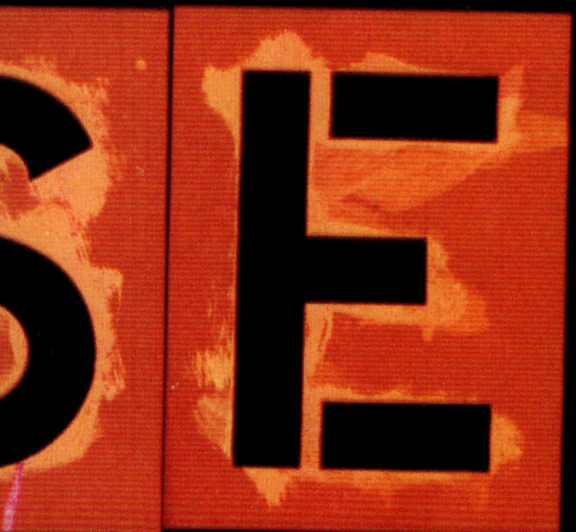

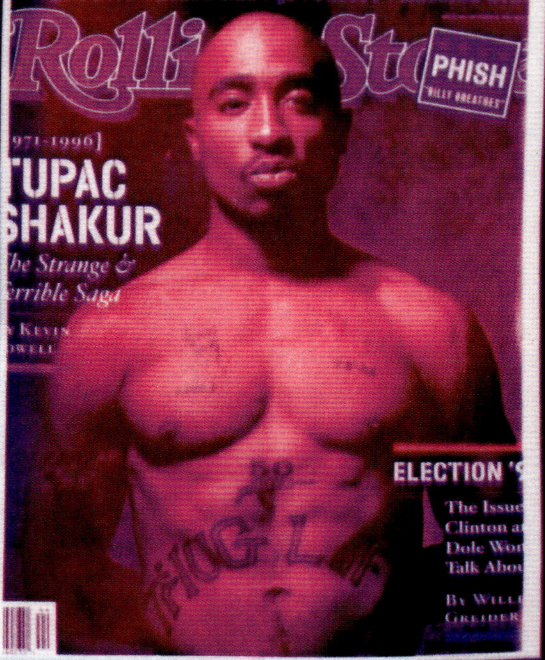

ud in the mid-
uggles in New
Baltimore. W
gs of her wherea
d died of a crac
hat fucked me
uldn't even cry, man. I felt I needed
ddy to show me the ropes, and I did
ve one."

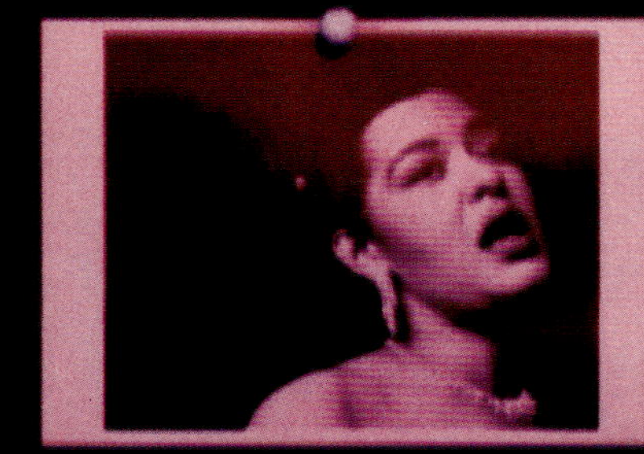

Boygina, bo
Booty, boog
Cupcakes, C

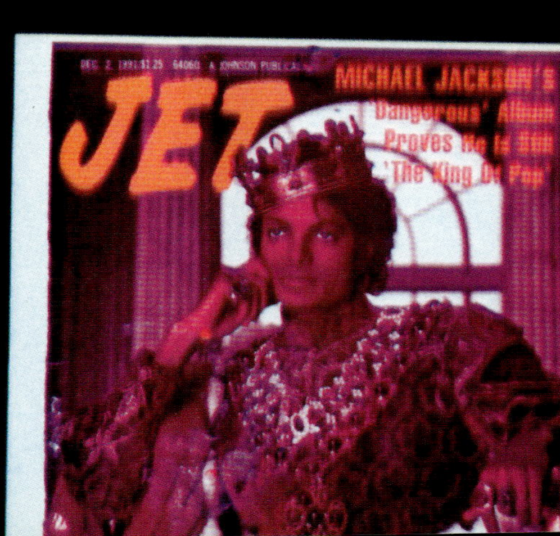

Boygi

Booty

Cupca

russy
na, bo
boog
es. C

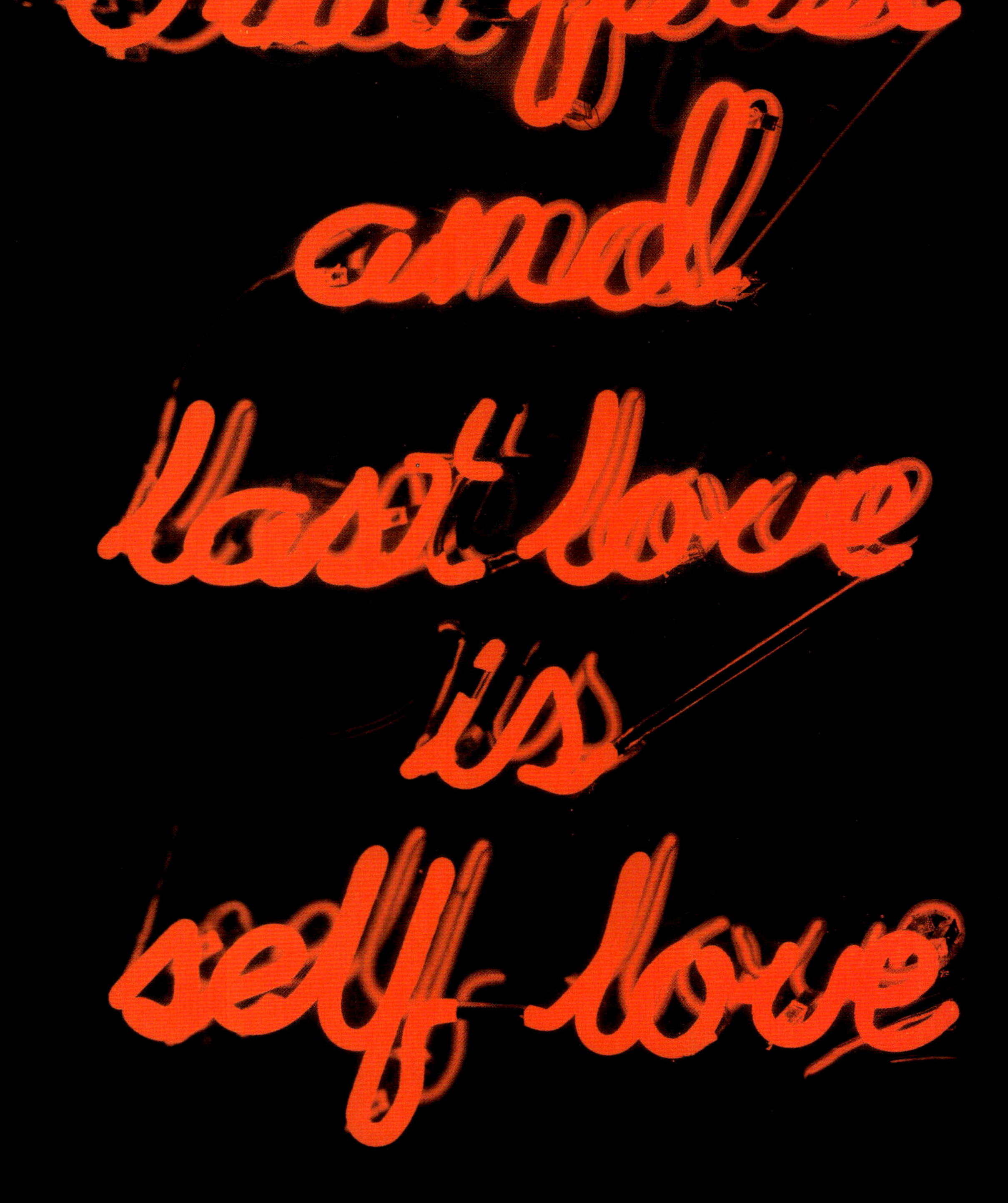

Our first
and
last love
is
self love

was resisting

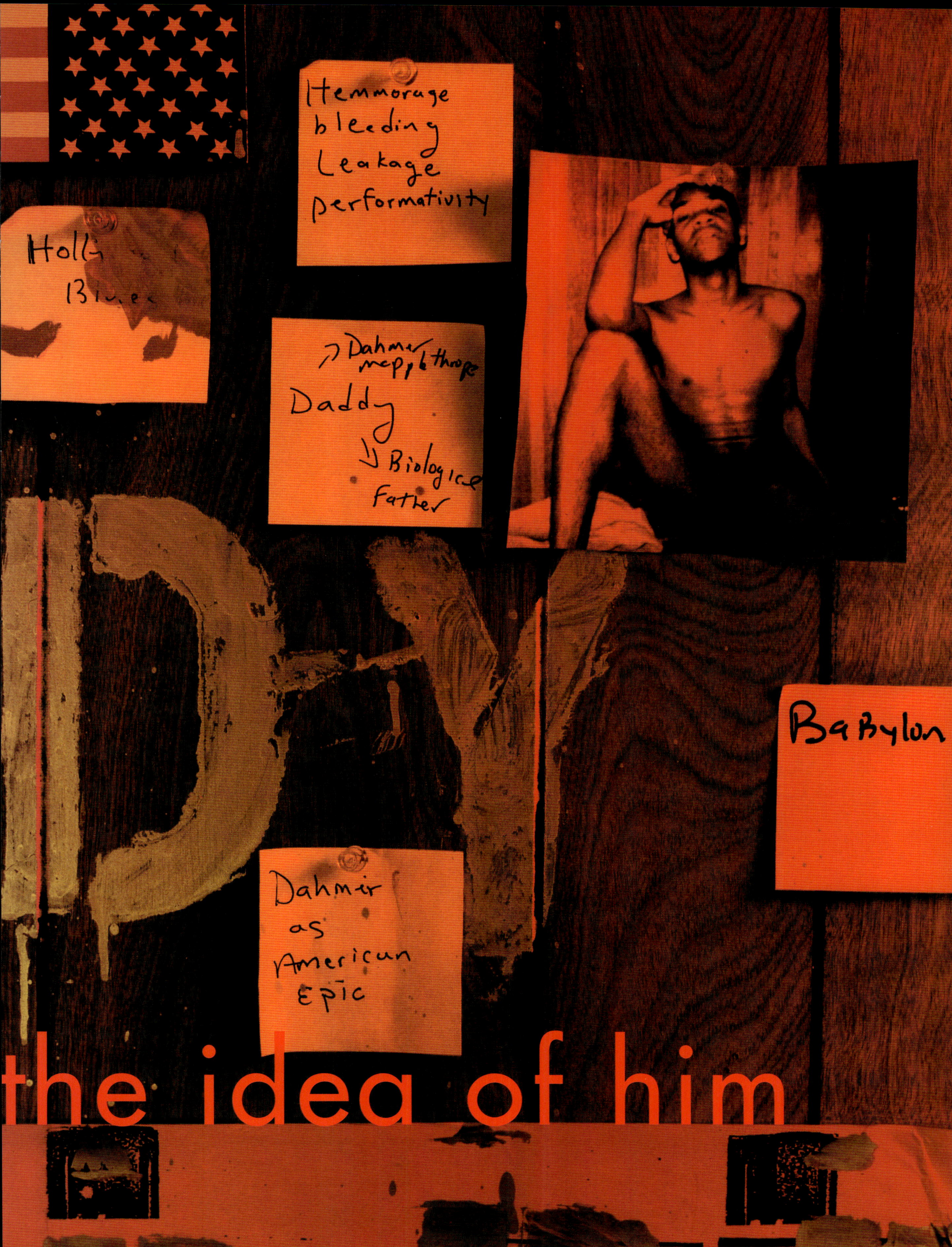
Hemmorage
bleeding
Leakage
performativity
Dahmer
Daddy
Biological
Father
Babylon
Dahmer
as
American
Epic
the idea of him

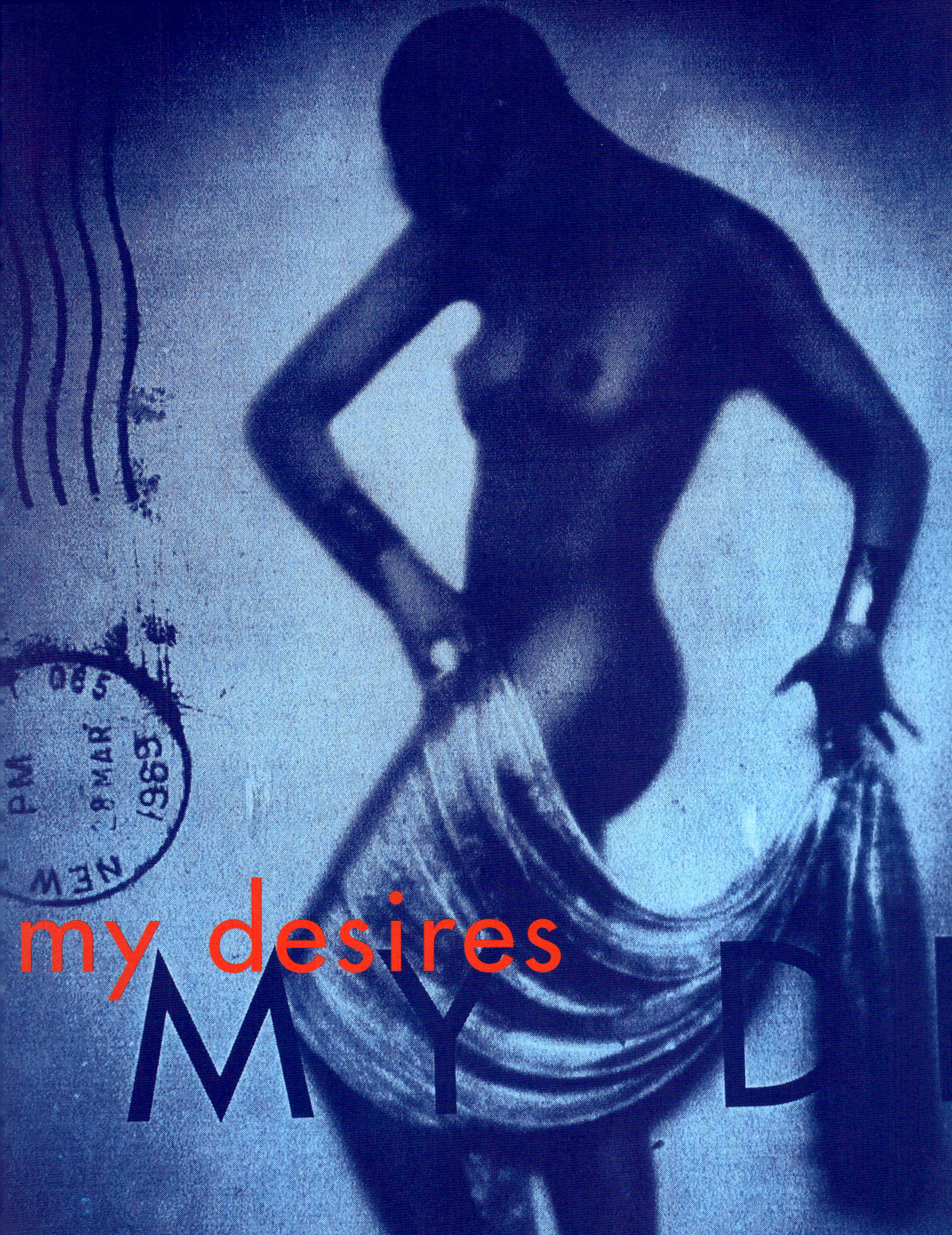

085
PM
8 MAR
1969
NEW
my desires
MY D

tence

dying, s wly

rate.

dying

nerve to drin p

e my desires,

closet masoch

Each man sees
but can not
so they kill

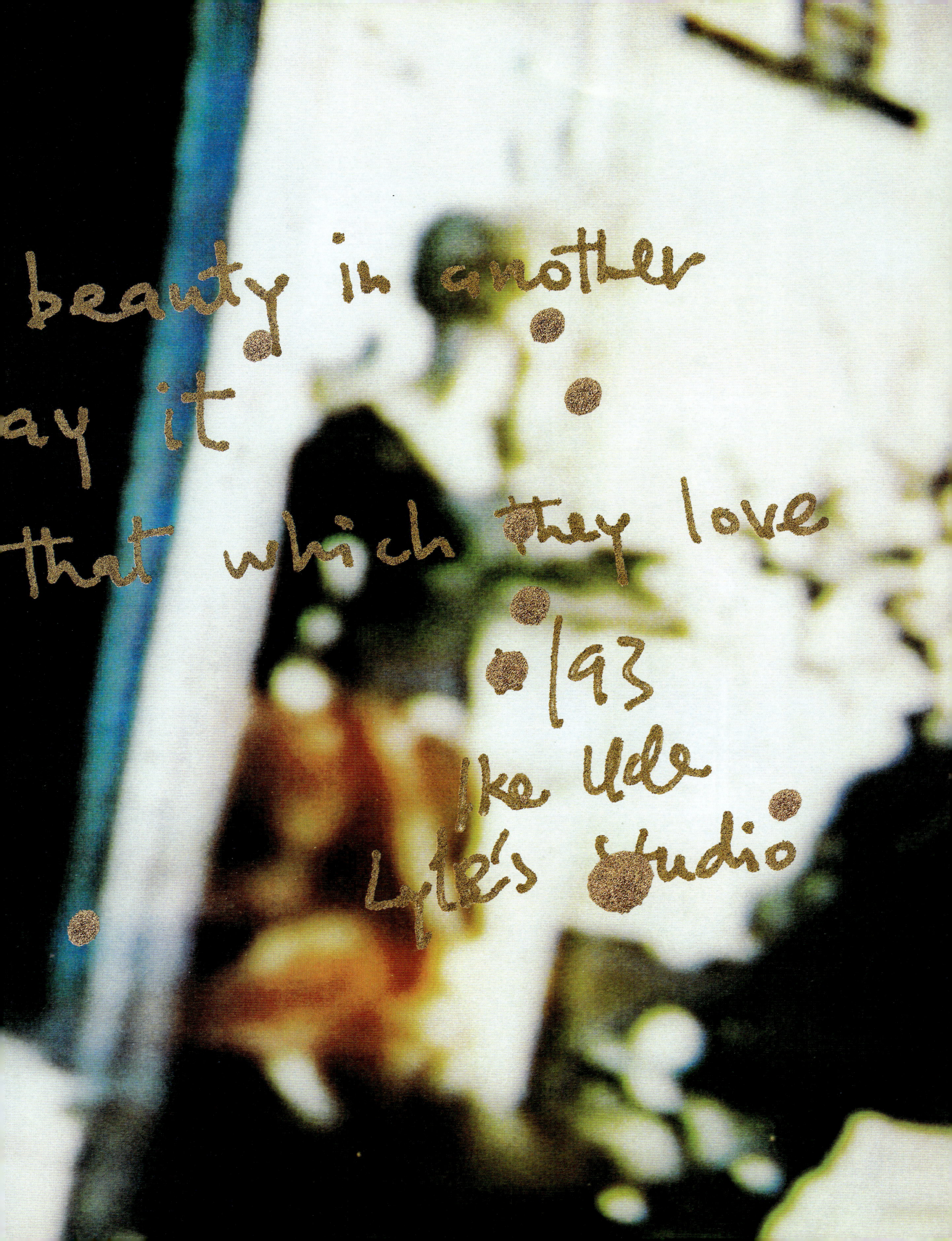

beauty in another

ay it

that which they love

/93

Ike Ude

Lyle's studio

Artists' Biographies

TRACEY BASHKOFF,
SUSAN CROSS,
VIVIEN GREENE,
AND J. FIONA RAGHEB

The biographies that follow are for the artists featured in the exhibition. For more information about them as well as other artists discussed and illustrated in this book, see sources listed in the notes accompanying each essay.

Janine Antoni

(b. January 19, 1964, Freeport, Bahamas)

Janine Antoni began working on process-oriented pieces that take physical activities as their point of departure while a graduate student at the Rhode Island School of Design, Providence. Since receiving an M.F.A. with honors in sculpture in 1989, she has continued to invest her projects with both a temporal and corporeal element, creating work that makes manifest otherwise ephemeral processes and reveals the ways in which our experiences of the body have been socially and culturally conditioned. In drawing upon intimate rituals—such as eating, bathing, sleeping, and washing—whose meanings are constituted in the communal sphere, she positions her work on the border between private and public realms.

Gnaw, Antoni's first solo exhibition, in 1992, is emblematic of the artist's efforts to engage her art with the experiential realm of the body. While the 600-pound cubes of lard and chocolate that partially comprised the installation evoke ready associations with the industrially fabricated forms of their Minimalist forebears, their geometric lines bear the disfiguring marks of Antoni's teeth, the traces of an act both critical and humorous. Yet the artist's choice of materials distances these cubes from their Modernist lineage while linking them to the highly gendered spaces of the physical world. This association was reinforced by a display housing the masticated remains of lard and chocolate, which had been transformed, respectively, into lipsticks and the heart-shaped vacuum packaging in which chocolates are frequently sold—objects of consumer desire that also mediate one's relationship to the body.

A rich tissue of art-historical precedents is woven through Antoni's work, reflecting her acute awareness of history and its patriarchal constitution. In its reinterpretation of artistic techniques through the body, *Gnaw* recalls Eleanor Antin's *Carving: A Traditional Sculpture* (1972), in which the artist "sculpted" her figure by means of a rigorous diet regimen. Indeed, in the use of her own body as a source of art making and the private experience on which she draws, Antoni is most indebted to feminist art of the 1970s. This lineage is clearly evoked in *Loving Care*, first presented in 1992, in which Antoni "mops" or "paints" the floor with her dye-soaked hair, recalling Mierle Laderman Ukeles's *Maintenance Art* series from the mid-1970s. Like this earlier series, Antoni's performance confuses the distinctions between art and work. By also interjecting notions of feminine beauty, Antoni is able to interrupt conventional equations concerning the female body and to reveal how the experience of that body is overdetermined by a host of societal forces.

Whether sculpted with her teeth, modeled with her tongue, or painted with her hair, Antoni's art operates in the space between object and performance, where the body is the site of contested meanings. Her work has been the subject of solo exhibitions in 1995 at the Centre for Contemporary Arts, Glasgow, and the Irish Museum of Modern Art, Dublin, and has been presented in numerous group exhibitions throughout the United States and Europe, including *Aperto '93* of the Venice *Biennale*; the 1993 Whitney *Biennial*; *Cocido y Crudo* at the Museo Nacional Centro de Arte Reina Sofía, Madrid, in 1994; and *PerForms: Charles Ray, Jana Sterbak, Janine Antoni* at the Institute of Contemporary Art, Philadelphia, in 1995. In 1996, her achievements were recognized with The IMMA/Glen Dimplex Artists Award, administered by the Irish Museum of Modern Art, as well as with her nomination for The Hugo Boss Prize, administered by the Guggenheim Museum. Antoni lives in New York. – J. F. R.

Suggested Readings

Cottingham, Laura. "Janine Antoni: Biting Sums Up My Relationship to Art History." Interview with Janine Antoni. *Flash Art* 26, no. 171 (summer 1993), pp. 104–05.

Janine Antoni/Matrix 129. Exh. brochure. Hartford, Conn.: Wadsworth Atheneum, 1996.

Slip of the Tongue. Exh. cat. Glasgow: Centre for Contemporary Arts; and Dublin: Irish Museum of Modern Art, 1995.

Matthew Barney

(b. March 25, 1967, San Francisco)

Matthew Barney graduated in 1989 from Yale University, New Haven. Since then, he has created work that fuses sculptural installations with performance and video. His singular vision foregrounds the physical rigors of sport and its erotic undercurrents to explore the limits of the body and sexuality. In this, the artist's work reflects his own past as an athlete, while also being attuned to a new politics of the body evident in the work of many contemporary artists. Barney's ritualistic actions unfold in hybrid spaces that evoke at once a training camp and medical research laboratory, equipped as they are with wrestling mats and blocking sleds, sternal retractors and speculums, and a range of props often cast in, or coated with, viscous substances such as wax, tapioca, and petroleum jelly. Indeed, his earliest works, created at Yale, were staged at the university's athletic complex. Within this alternative universe, Barney's protagonists—including an actor dressed as Oakland Raider Jim Otto, and the artist himself naked or cross-dressed—engage in a metaphoric dance of sexual differentiation.

Barney's exploration of the body draws upon an athletic model of development, in which growth occurs only through restraint: the muscle encounters resistance, becomes engorged and is broken down, and in healing becomes stronger. This triangulated relationship between desire, discipline, and productivity provides the basis for Barney's meditation on sexual difference. These athletic and sexual references converge in Otto's jersey number "00," which becomes a leitmotif for the artist's ongoing exploration of a polymorphous sexuality. Woven cipherlike throughout Barney's work, this motif variously appears as if marking elapsed time in his videos, and in altered form as a single oblong, resembling a football field. For the artist, however, the oblong represents "the orifice and its closure—or the body and its self-imposed restraint." Homonymic with the word "auto," Otto also suggests autoeroticism, or a closed, self-sufficient system.

Barney's *Cremaster* project—named for a testicular muscle—transports these concerns to an Arcadian realm populated by faeries, satyrs, and chorus girls. Broadcast on Dutch television and screened at several film festivals, *Cremaster 4* (1994) and *Cremaster 1* (1995) are the first two videos produced in a projected series of five that allegorize the stages in the sexual differentiation of an embryo. Blending athleticism and choreography with an ineffable symbology of sexuality, these elaborately styled videos create an alternative cosmology of sexual differentiation that presents "a million different zones of sexual articulation."

In 1991, at the age of twenty-four, Barney was honored with a solo exhibition at the San Francisco Museum of Modern Art. The Museum Boymans-van Beuningen, Rotterdam, organized a solo exhibition of his work that toured Europe throughout 1995 and 1996. In addition to *Documenta IX* and numerous other group exhibitions, Barney has been included in many international exhibitions, such as the 1993 and 1995 *Biennial* exhibitions at the Whitney Museum of American Art, New York, and *Aperto '93*, for which he was awarded the Europa 2000 Prize. Barney lives in New York and is currently at work on *Cremaster 5*, the third installment of his video cycle to be produced. – J. F. R.

Suggested Readings

Goodeve, Thyrza Nichols. "Travels in Hypertrophia." Interview with Matthew Barney. *Artforum* 33, no. 9 (May 1995), pp. 66–71, 112, 117.

Parkett 45 (1995). Issue devoted to Matthew Barney, Sarah Lucas, and Roman Signer.

Saltz, Jerry. "The Next Sex." *Art in America* 84, no. 10 (October 1996), pp. 82–91.

Wakefield, Neville. "Matthew Barney's Fornication with the Fabric of Space." *Parkett* 39 (1994), pp. 118–24.

Cecil Beaton

(b. January 14, 1904, London; d. January 22, 1980, Broadchalke, England)

Cecil Beaton attended private schools before enrolling at Cambridge University in 1922. There he concentrated on photography and theatrical endeavors, activities he would pursue energetically throughout his life. In 1925, Beaton moved to London and began to execute photographic portraits of that city's high society. Beaton's theatrical inclinations led him to orchestrate luxuriant portraits that fuse reflective surfaces and rococo costuming, his posed sitters sometimes emerging as sexually ambiguous figures. Appropriating conventions from Victorian and Edwardian photography—which he collected from childhood—as well as Modernist photographic trends, he devised a signature style that was simultaneously romantic and innovative.

Beaton's success in creating glamorous images ushered him into the worlds of film and fashion; by 1928, both British and American *Vogue* were among his clients. Not only well-received in the commercial realm, Beaton was the sole British photographer to be shown in the 1929 avant-garde *Film und Foto* exhibition, organized by the Deutsches Werkbund in Stuttgart. He also achieved recognition for a number of photographic publications, beginning in 1930 with a collection of portraits of the social and entertainment elite, *The Book of Beauty*. In 1937, he photographed the Duke and Duchess of Windsor's wedding portraits as well as royalty and the aristocracy for the coronation of George VI. Beaton continued to portray the British royal family over the next four decades. During World War II, the Ministry of Information engaged Beaton to photograph the war both in Britain and abroad. The resulting images were in a more documentary style.

Notwithstanding his diverse photographic undertakings, Beaton's interest and professional involvement in theater did not wane, and he extended his talents beyond the stage to include designing costumes and scenery for films. The result of Beaton's one foray as a playwright, *The Gainsborough Girls*, opened in 1951 in Brighton, but received little acclaim. In 1956, the photographer embarked upon a series depicting cinema icons such as Marilyn Monroe and Grace Kelly. Beaton maintained ties with Hollywood, and his designs for the costumes in the film *Gigi* (Vincente Minnelli, 1958) won him an Academy Award. He also designed the costumes and sets for George Cukor's 1964 film version of *My Fair Lady* (as he did for the original 1956 stage production), this time attaining two Academy Awards. A renowned dandy himself, Beaton was esteemed by the extravagantly styled generation of the 1960s, and photographed many of its celebrities, including rock idol Mick Jagger and Pop artist Andy Warhol.

In 1968, Beaton curated his own retrospective at London's National Portrait Gallery and in 1972 was knighted by Queen Elizabeth II. Despite a stroke in 1974, he recovered and persevered with his art until his death in 1980. Most recently, in 1986 London's Barbican Centre organized a retrospective of Beaton's oeuvre. – V. G.

Suggested Readings

Cecil Beaton: A Retrospective. Edited by David Mellor. Exh. cat. New York: Little Brown, 1986.

Garner, Philippe, and David Mellor. *Cecil Beaton: Photographs 1920–1970.* New York: Stewart, Tabori and Chang, 1995.

Brassaï [Gyula Halász]
(b. September 9, 1899, Brassó, Hungary [now Brasov, Romania]; d. July 8, 1984, Nice)

Born Gyula Halász and later deriving his pseudonym from the name of his native town, Brassaï was the son of a university professor of French literature. He forged an early connection with Paris when his family moved there in 1903 for his father's year-long sabbatical. He studied art at the Képomuvészeti Foiskola in Budapest (1918–19) and the Akademische Hochschule, Berlin-Charlottenburg (1921–22), where he received his degree and met Vasily Kandinsky, Oskar Kokoschka, and László Moholy-Nagy.

Brassaï moved to Paris in 1924 and worked intermittently as a correspondent for German and Hungarian newspapers. By 1930, he had started photographing Paris by night, recording solitary views of abandoned streets as well as the bohemian life of the city's cafés and dance halls and its demimonde of criminals, homosexuals, transvestites, and prostitutes. Though Brassaï's photographs appear to be completely candid, his subjects were generally aware of his presence and frequently posed, to some degree, for these portrayals. In 1933, Brassaï's pictures of Paris were published as *Paris de Nuit* (Paris by night), a book subsequently distributed worldwide in numerous languages.

Brassaï was a free-lance photographer for a wide variety of publications, from the Surrealist journal *Minotaure* to the fashion magazine *Harper's Bazaar*. Beginning in the 1930s, he portrayed such twentieth-century cultural icons as Salvador Dalí, Henri Matisse, Henry Miller, and Pablo Picasso. His contact with these literary and artistic figures later led him to publish books such as *Conversations avec Picasso* (Conversations with Picasso, 1964). Brassaï's other significant photographic projects include a series on Parisian graffiti and documentary images taken during his travels to foreign countries.

Brassaï was also a sculptor, draughtsman, set designer, writer, and filmmaker. His 1956 film *Tant qu'il y aura des bêtes* (So long as there are animals; released in English as *Lovers and Clowns*) earned a prize at the Cannes Film Festival. Brassaï has been honored by several major exhibitions; among the most important of those held during his lifetime was a retrospective at the Museum of Modern Art, New York, in 1968, which traveled to Australia, New Zealand, and South America. – V. G.

Suggested Readings

Brassaï. Exh. cat. New York: Museum of Modern Art, 1968.

Brassaï: Vom Surrealismus zum Informel. Exh. cat. Barcelona: Fundació Antoni Tàpies, 1994.

Krauss, Rosalind. "Nightwalkers." *Art Journal* 4, no. 1 (spring 1981), pp. 33–38.

Claude Cahun [Lucy Renée Mathilde Schwob]
(b. October 25, 1894, Nantes; d. December 8, 1954, Saint-Hélier, Jersey, English Channel Islands)

Lucy Renée Mathilde Schwob was born into an intellectual family. She studied at Oxford (1907–08) and the Sorbonne (around 1914), majoring in literature and philosophy, although she never graduated. A photographer and a writer, she began to create photographic self-portraits around 1912 and published her first article in the *Mercure de France* at the age of twenty. In approximately 1917, she adopted the pseudonym Claude Cahun, the last name taken from her maternal grandmother. She visited Paris frequently, finally moving there in 1922 with her stepsister, lifelong partner, and sometime-collaborator Suzanne Malherbe (who signed herself Marcel Moore).

In Paris, Cahun briefly engaged in theatrical pursuits, while continuing to contribute to literary journals. In 1930, she produced *Aveux non avenus* (Avowals not admitted), a book of prose poetry and photomontages made in collaboration with Malherbe. Cahun espoused leftist politics and played a role in the Surrealist movement, probably joining the Association des Ecrivains et Artistes Révolutionnaires by the end of 1932. Her pamphlet on the possibility of revolutionary poetry, *Les Paris sont ouverts* (Place your bets), appeared in 1934. Along with André Breton and Georges Bataille, she was a founding member of Contre-Attaque, a group established in 1935 in response to the threat of Fascism.

In her self-portraits, Cahun frequently presented herself costumed, made up, or masked as various personae, including a life-size "doll" and a Turandot-like figure. There is no evidence that she ever exhibited any of these photographs, so it is likely that they were made chiefly for her own personal use. She is known to have exhibited her assemblages of objects in the 1936 *Exposition surréaliste d'objets* at Charles Ratton, a gallery in Paris. In conjunction with this exhibition, *Cahiers d'art* published her article regarding the premise of the show, "Prenez garde aux objets domestiques" (Beware of household objects). Cahun's photographs of still-life tableaux served as illustrations for a 1937 children's poetry book by Lise Deharme, *Le Coeur de Pic* (Pic's heart).

In 1937, Cahun and Malherbe moved to the Isle of Jersey, where both had summered as children, and mounted their own propaganda campaign against the Nazis, anonymously dispersing written messages throughout the island. They were eventually captured and condemned to death in 1944 by the Gestapo, but the war ended before they could be executed. Cahun remained on Jersey until her death in 1954. It is only recently, through such publications as Edouard Jaguer's 1982 *Les Mystères de la chambre noire: Le Surréalisme et la photographie* and the 1985 exhibition *L'Amour Fou: Photography and Surrealism* at the Corcoran Gallery of Art, Washington, D.C., that Cahun's virtually unknown photographs were rediscovered. – V. G.

Suggested Readings

Claude Cahun: Photographe. Exh. cat. Paris: Musée d'Art Moderne de la Ville de Paris and Jean-Michel Place, 1995.

Leperlier, François. *Claude Cahun: L'Écart et la métamorphose.* Paris: Jean-Michel Place, 1992.

Lichtenstein, Therese. "A Movable Mirror: Claude Cahun." *Artforum* 30, no. 8 (April 1992), pp. 64–67.

Marcel Duchamp

(b. July 28, 1887, Blainville-Crevon, France; d. October 2, 1968, Neuilly, France)

Along with his siblings Jacques Villon, Raymond Duchamp-Villon, and Suzanne Duchamp, Marcel (Henri-Robert-Marcel) Duchamp embraced an artistic career, going in 1904 to study for a year at the Académie Julian in Paris. In 1912, he painted his seminal Cubist work, *Nude Descending a Staircase, No. 2* (*Nu descendent un escalier, n° 2*), which caused an uproar when exhibited the next year at New York's Armory Show.

Though initially a painter, Duchamp soon became interested in working in three dimensions. Selecting the most banal objects he could find and recontextualizing them, Duchamp gave ordinary props of modern life a new and often incongruous significance—experiments that led to the creation of his renowned "readymades." In 1913, Duchamp began work on one of his most significant pieces, *The Bride Stripped Bare by Her Bachelors, Even* (*The Large Glass*), which he intermittently worked on until 1923, deliberately leaving it incomplete.

Duchamp's intense interest in, and aptitude for, mathematics and scientific studies led him to experiment with the construction of a multiplicity of three-dimensional, sometimes mechanical, creations during the course of his career. Because he considered the conceptual aspect of his work at least as significant as its tangible embodiment, Duchamp dedicated intensive thought to and made copious notes, drawings, and plans for his pieces. His love for complex logic is also evidenced by his other lifelong enterprise, the game of chess, which he sometimes played to the exclusion of art.

Following the outbreak of World War I, Duchamp made the first of many extended trips to New York, where he developed steadfast friendships with artist Man Ray, with whom he would later collaborate, and collectors Katherine Dreier and Walter and Louise Arensberg, who became lifelong patrons. Back in Paris in 1918, Duchamp joined the Dada group. In 1920, he returned to the United States and engaged in constructing visual and written puns. One consequence of this practice was the fashioning of his female alter ego, Rrose Sélavy. This alternate identity was photographed by Man Ray, appeared in some of Duchamp's own work, and was the pseudonym by which he signed a number of pieces. In 1921, together with Man Ray, he produced the only issue of *New York Dada*, which also contained an article by Tristan Tzara.

In the 1930s, Duchamp became involved with the Surrealists in Paris. Among other endeavors, he designed publications for works by fellow artists and writers. In 1936, he was included in the *Fantastic Art, Dada, Surrealism* exhibition at the Museum of Modern Art, New York. The following year, he had his first solo show, at the Arts Club of Chicago. Duchamp also assisted landmark collectors such as Peggy Guggenheim in the organization of exhibitions. In 1942, he made New York his permanent home, and from 1946 to 1966, at a time when it was believed that he had given up art making for chess, he secretly worked on his last large-scale work, known as *Etant Donnés*.

As an artist, writer, and cultural arbiter, Duchamp played a pivotal role in the shaping of twentieth-century culture. With the 1959 English translation of Robert Lebel's monograph *Marcel Duchamp*, a generation of emerging artists became acquainted with Duchamp's oeuvre and was significantly influenced by it. The first major retrospective devoted to the artist, which he was alive to witness, was the 1963 *Marcel Duchamp: A Retrospective Exhibition*, organized by Walter Hopps at the Pasadena Art Museum. – V. G.

Suggested Readings

Marcel Duchamp. Edited by Anne d'Harnoncourt and Kynaston McShine. Exh. cat. Philadelphia: Philadelphia Museum of Art; and New York: Museum of Modern Art, 1973.

Marcel Duchamp. Exh. cat. Milan: Palazzo Grassi and Bompiani, 1993. English edition.

Schwartz, Arturo. *The Complete Marcel Duchamp*. London: Thames and Hudson; and New York: Abrams, 1969.

Nan Goldin

(b. September 12, 1953, Washington, D.C.)

Nan Goldin's interest in photography began as a means of remembering the details of her daily existence. She left her home in her teenage years to escape the lingering effects of her older sister's suicide, moving in with foster families and attending an alternative school outside Boston. There, Goldin was given a Polaroid camera and began photographing friends and acquaintances in an effort to secure memories of them, much as she struggled to preserve recollections of her dead sister. Goldin's engagement with photography persisted, and in 1977, she earned a B.F.A. and Fifth-Year Master's Certificate from the School of the Museum of Fine Arts in Boston.

Goldin began exhibiting her photographs at the age of nineteen. The slide presentations for which she would later become known began of necessity during her art-school years, when the lack of a darkroom forced her to turn to slides. These shows were presented in various environments—from the bars where she worked in Provincetown to the Mudd Club and other underground venues in New York, where she relocated in the late 1970s. *The Ballad of Sexual Dependency*, the work for which she is perhaps best known, began as, and remains, a constantly evolving slide show of several hundred images accompanied by a music track. Chronicling the gritty lives and relationships of her "re-created family," the work provides an intimate glimpse of disaffected men and women sleeping, having sex, lounging around, and otherwise living their lives—suggesting volatile narratives of desire and frustration, played out most frequently in bed. For Goldin, the juxtaposition of slides with a soundtrack that has included such songs as "My World Is Empty Without You" and "You Don't Own Me" serves to clarify her interest in the sexual dynamics of relationships. The slide show has also been presented in videotape format and was published in book form in 1986.

Whether exhibited as prints or slide shows, Goldin's photographs reveal her milieu with a directness and immediacy in keeping with her personal relationships with her subjects. They spring directly from her life and her obsessive need to record it, constituting a self-described "diary" rather than a programmatic study. *The Other Side: 1972–92*, a body of work published in 1993, evolved from photographs she began taking in the early 1970s while living with drag queens in Boston and frequenting the Other Side, a drag bar. Capturing the unconventional relationships of drag queens and transsexuals, these unstudied, brightly hued photographs share the same concerns that inform *The Ballad of Sexual Dependency*. If, as Goldin maintains, relationships are predicated on a universal struggle between autonomy and dependency—a struggle that is complicated by the construction of gender roles—then the ultimate autonomy comes from redefining such distinctions. As evidenced in these candid photographs of the "third sex," gender is a malleable construct that can be enlisted to alter the dynamics that characterize conventional and unconventional relationships alike.

Goldin's work has been included in numerous exhibitions both in the United States and abroad, including *Pleasures and Terrors of Domestic Comfort* at the Museum of Modern Art, New York, in 1991, and the Whitney *Biennial* in 1993 and 1995. She has been the recipient of the Camera Austria Prize for Contemporary Photography in 1989, the Brandeis Award in Photography in 1994, and numerous other awards. In 1996, her work was the subject of a solo exhibition at the Whitney Museum of American Art, New York, which included *All By Myself*, a slide show that takes the artist herself as its sole subject. Goldin lives in New York. – J. F. R.

Suggested Readings

Goldin, Nan. *The Ballad of Sexual Dependency*. Edited by Nan Goldin, Marvin Heiferman, Mark Holborn, and Suzanne Fletcher. New York: Aperture, 1986.

———. *The Other Side: 1972–1992*. Edited by David Armstrong, Nan Goldin, and Walter Keller. Zurich: Scalo, 1993. In English.

Kozloff, Max. "The Family of Nan." *Art in America* 75, no. 11 (November 1987), pp. 39–43.

Nan Goldin: I'll Be Your Mirror. Edited by Nan Goldin, David Armstrong, and Hans Werner Holzwarth. Exh. cat. New York: Whitney Museum of American Art; and Zurich: Scalo, 1996.

Lyle Ashton Harris
(b. February 6, 1965, New York)

Lyle Ashton Harris grew up in the Bronx, but as a teenager briefly moved to Dar es Salaam, Tanzania, with his mother and older brother, filmmaker Thomas Allen Harris. Influenced by a family of what he has called "fanatically devoted" amateur photographers, Harris also experimented with the camera, but it was not until his undergraduate years at Wesleyan University in Middletown, Connecticut, after a liberating visit to his brother Thomas in Amsterdam, that Harris switched his major from economics to art. During that time, the artist created his first body of photographs, *The Americas* (1987). Harris received an M.F.A. from the California Institute of Arts in Valencia in 1990. In New York, he completed the National Graduate Photography Seminar at the Tisch School of the Arts of New York University in 1991 and the Whitney Independent Study Program in 1992.

In 1989, Harris completed a series of gelatin-silver prints entitled *Constructs,* which portray the artist in a sequence of poses that challenge the tenuous distinctions between genders. This series was presented at the Whitney Museum of American Art, New York, in the exhibition *Black Male: Representations of Masculinity in Contemporary Art,* in 1994; and the UCLA at Armand Hammer Museum of Art and Cultural Center, Los Angeles, in 1995. In 1994, the artist was given his first New York solo exhibition, *The Good Life,* at Jack Tilton Gallery. This installation integrated enlarged family photographs in vintage ektachrome by Albert Sydney Johnson, Jr., Harris's grandfather, with oversized color Polaroid portraits created by Harris in collaboration with friends and family. Using as subjects Renée Cox (with whom he shared a studio), his brother Thomas, Margaret Nelson, George Rush, Dread Scott, Iké Udé, and himself, Harris created portraits of real and imagined figures of American and African-diasporic culture. Throughout his work, Harris questions fictions of race, sexuality, and gender as well as of family and cultural history. In 1995, a comprehensive selection of Harris's photographs was exhibited in *Masculine Masquerade* at the MIT List Visual Arts Center, Cambridge, Massachusetts. The selection included works from Harris's 1994 collaboration with his brother Thomas, *Brotherhood, Crossroads, and Etcetera,* which depicts mirrorlike images of the artists embracing, nude and in full makeup with guns. A reflection on a well-known photograph of Black Power icon Huey Newton, this series, Harris states, engages "the ambivalence around desire, envy, compassion and death that we are dealing with as two brothers who love each other critically."

Harris's most recent work, an installation called *The Watering Hole* (1996), explores interracial desire and consumption in American culture by focusing on serial killer Jeffrey Dahmer and his victims. Harris presents elegiac photographic images of "bulletin-board" collages that consist of cutouts of sports, entertainment, and fashion advertisements, news clippings, vintage pornography, self-portraits, and handwritten notes alluding to exploitation and self-destruction, racism and redemption, violence and pleasure. In addition, Harris and collaborator Tommy Gear created kaleidoscopically repeating images of "Narcissus" at the watering hole, giving the object of desire his own subjectivity.

The artist has been awarded numerous grants and fellowships, including a WESTAF/NEA Fellowship in 1991, and has exhibited internationally. Recent group exhibitions of note include *Face Value: American Portraits,* a traveling show organized by the Parrish Art Museum, Southampton, New York, in 1995; *Mirage: Enigmas of Race, Difference, and Desire,* a traveling exhibition that premiered at the Institute of Contemporary Arts in London in 1995; and *Persona,* presented at the Renaissance Society at the University of Chicago, and the Kunsthalle Basel in 1996. Harris lives in Los Angeles. He has been a member of the faculty of the Otis College of Art and Design, Los Angeles, since 1994. – S. C.

Suggested Readings

Cohen, Michael. "Lyle Ashton Harris." *Flash Art* 29, no. 188 (May–June 1996), p. 107.

Cotter, Holland. "Art after Stonewall: Twelve Artists Interviewed," *Art in America* 82, no. 6 (June 1994), pp. 63–64.

Face Value: American Portraits. Exh. cat. Southampton, N.Y.: Parrish Art Museum; and New York: Flammarion, 1995, p. 31.

Lyle Ashton Harris. Exh. cat. Caracas: Centro de Arte Euroamericano; and Coral Gables, Fla.: Ambrosino Gallery, 1996. In English and Spanish.

Mercer, Kobena. "Dark and Lovely: Black Gay Image Making." In Kobena Mercer, *Welcome to the Jungle: New Positions in Black Cultural Studies.* New York: Routledge, 1994, pp. 221–32.

Hannah Höch
(b. November 1, 1889, Gotha, Germany; d. May 31, 1978, Berlin-Heiligensee)

Hannah (Johanne) Höch left Gotha in 1912 to study applied arts at the Kunstgewerbeschule, Berlin-Charlottenburg, for two years. Her education was interrupted by World War I, but she resumed her studies in 1915 at Berlin's Staatlichen Lehranstalt des Kunstgewerbemuseums, where she met Raoul Hausmann, who became her artistic collaborator and companion until 1922.

To support herself in Berlin, Höch began working part time in 1916 for the publishing company Ullstein Verlag, where she remained for ten years making handicraft patterns, lettering, and illustrations for brochures and magazines. Höch produced her first collage in 1916, and two years later started fashioning photomontages that utilize clippings taken from the type of illustrated women's magazines published by Ullstein. Rather than depicting the "New Woman," Höch constructed images that confronted the ambiguities inherent in that notion of the modern woman propagated by Weimar society.

Through her association with Hausmann, Höch became a peripheral member of the Berlin Dada group, participating in performances it staged and contributing works to its first exhibition, held at the Graphischen Kabinett of I. B. Neumann in 1919. She then showed photomontages, sculptures, and a poster in the *Erste Internationale Dada-Messe* exhibition in Berlin in 1920. Many of her works, along with the majority of those exhibited, satirized the Weimar Republic. Höch persisted in this vein of social and political commentary and, from 1923 to at least 1934, made photomontages that address themes of "otherness," notably those of female identity, androgyny, and ethnography.

After the dissolution of the Berlin Dada group, Höch became affiliated with International Constructivism and befriended Kurt Schwitters. From 1920 until 1931, Höch contributed paintings to various annual Berlin exhibitions, such as that held by the Novembergruppe. From 1926 to 1929, the artist lived in The Hague, The Netherlands, where, in 1929, she had her first solo show before returning to Berlin. That same year, Höch was included in the international photography exhibition *Film und Foto*, organized by the Deutsches Werkbund in Stuttgart. A significant exhibition of her photomontages was held in Brno, Czechoslovakia, in 1934, but at this point her artistic career was brought to a halt by a thyroid illness. Höch did not exhibit again until 1945. Two years before her death, in 1976, a retrospective was held at the Musée d'Art Moderne de la Ville de Paris and the Nationalgalerie, Berlin. Most recently, in 1996, the Walker Art Center, Minneapolis, mounted a major Höch exhibition, which traveled to the Museum of Modern Art, New York, in 1997. –V. G.

Suggested Readings

Hannah Höch 1889–1978: Ihr Werk, ihr Leben, ihre Freunde. Exh. cat. Berlin: Berlinische Galerie and Argon, 1989.

Lavin, Maud. *Cut with the Kitchen Knife: The Weimar Photomontages of Hannah Höch.* New Haven: Yale University Press, 1993.

The Photomontages of Hannah Höch. Exh. cat. Minneapolis: Walker Art Center, 1996.

Jürgen Klauke

(b. September 6, 1943, Kliding, near Cochem an der Mosel, Germany)

Trained as a graphic artist at the Fachhochschule für Design und Kunst in Cologne, Jürgen Klauke graduated in 1970, during a period of cultural upheaval that had reached its apogee in the student demonstrations of 1968. Seeking a new identity apart from bourgeois conventions, many artists—rejecting the academic tradition that painting had come to represent—favored a practice that engaged real life more directly. For Klauke, photography provided a means to negotiate this new territory.

Since the early 1970s, Klauke has been engaged in a continuous exploration of identity outside the conventional accounts of sexuality. While his early publication *I & I (Daily Sketches and Photo Sequences)* (*Ich & Ich [Tageszeichnungen und Fotosequenzen]*, 1972) combined erotic drawings and diaristic commentary with photographs, photography soon became Klauke's main means of giving objective form to his subjective impulses and erotic obsessions.

The titles of Klauke's early photographic series—such as *Self-Performance* (1972–73), *Transformer* (1973), and *Masculin/Feminin* (1974)—all convey a sense of negotiation and symbiosis of the self. *Self-Performance*, a twelve-part work, shows Klauke undergoing a transformation of sexual identities, appearing at times virginal and at others debauched. Accessorized with the trappings of S/M rituals and appendages that mimic both male and female genitalia, these sexually transgressive poses—photographed in a coolly straightforward manner—suggest a fluid and multidimensional sexuality. Klauke's use of the sequence further underscores the performative aspect of the work. In 1975, the artist presented the first of several related performances, which were a logical outgrowth of the photographs.

In probing the mutable nature of identity, Klauke's work refutes facile notions concerning photography's ability to capture both the "truth" and a fixed identity—beliefs that were promulgated, in part, through German photographer August Sander's early twentieth-century series of representative types based on social backgrounds and occupations. In contrast, Klauke's oeuvre suggests a tacit endorsement of more contemporary theorizations that gender is not an innate biological trait but instead a fictional construction that is "performed" and may be modified at will. His more recent work reveals a shift toward an exploration of identity within a broader social context, abandoning a highly individual eroticism in favor of an almost depersonalized assessment of the subject in society.

Klauke's work has been the subject of solo exhibitions at the Museum Boymans-van Beuningen, Rotterdam, in 1987; the Museum Ludwig, Cologne, in 1987; the Staatliche Kunsthalle, Baden-Baden, in 1992; and the Kunstmuseum Düsseldorf in 1992. Klauke lives in Cologne, where he teaches at the Kunsthochschule für Medien. – J. F. R.

Suggested Readings

Jürgen Klauke/Cindy Sherman. Exh. cat. Munich: Sammlung Goetz; and Ostfildern: Cantz, 1994. In English and German.

Jürgen Klauke, Eine Ewigkeit ein Lächeln: Zeichnungen, Fotoarbeiten, Performances 1970/86 (Jürgen Klauke, An Eternal Smile: Drawings, Photographical Works, Performances 1970/86). Edited by Andreas Vowinckel and Evelyn Weiss. Exh. cat. Cologne: DuMont Buchverlag, 1986. In English and German.

Jürgen Klauke, Fotosequenzen 1972–1980: Die Schwarz-Weiss Sequenzen. Frankfurt: Betzel-Verlag, 1982. In English and German.

Jürgen Klauke: Sonntagsneurosen. Edited by Jochen Poetter. Exh. cat. Ostfildern: Cantz; and Baden-Baden: Staatliche Kunsthalle, 1992. In English and German.

George Platt Lynes
(b. April 15, 1907, East Orange, New Jersey; d. December 6, 1955, New York)

George Platt Lynes benefited from a private education and attended Yale University, New Haven, for a single semester in 1926. His earliest ambition was to be a literary publisher and, during his first trip to France, in 1925, he developed a friendship with writer and arts patron Gertrude Stein. She supported his aspirations and provided him with an entrée into the sphere of the intellectual avant-garde. Lynes originally took up photography in 1927 as a secondary activity, but it soon became his principal occupation. On a subsequent visit to France, in 1928, he photographed eminent cultural figures, among them Jean Cocteau, and saw the work of Surrealist photographers such as Man Ray.

In New York, Lynes was initially identified with the Surrealist movement, particularly since he received the endorsement of the prominent gallery owner Julien Levy, who represented several established Surrealist photographers. Through Levy, Lynes gained significant exposure, which allowed him to open a professional studio by 1932. His reputation burgeoned and by 1934 he was executing portrait and fashion commissions, the latter often informed by Surrealist principles. In these compositions, Lynes made use of backdrops, props, and poses to suggest a dreamlike world, blurring the boundaries between commercial and fine-art photography. Lynes also photographed ballet dancers and, in 1935, was hired to make promotional images for George Balanchine's American Ballet Theatre in New York. In many of his fine-art images, Lynes explored homoerotic themes by focusing on male nudes, sensual images that are occasionally explicit in their depiction of gay sexuality.

Lynes's popularity reached its apex in 1941 with a retrospective held at the Pierre Matisse Gallery, New York, which featured more than two hundred portraits. At that time, he became more involved in pursuing his personal photographic projects and grew increasingly dissatisfied with commercial work. The erotic male nudes Lynes continued to create in private constitute a body of work that is unique—especially given the photographer's professional stature—because of its positive portrayals of homosexuals and in its adherence to male nudity as subject matter. Lynes's work would become a role model for later photographers such as Robert Mapplethorpe.

In an effort to revitalize his career, Lynes moved to Los Angeles in 1946 to assume the position of Chief Photographer for *Vogue* magazine's studio in Hollywood. However, financial difficulties obligated him to return to New York in 1948. Although Lynes was unsuccessful in resuming his former career due to changing tastes in photography, his work was of great interest to Dr. Alfred C. Kinsey, who began collecting it around 1950 in conjunction with his research on gay-male sexuality. After his death in 1955, Lynes's photographs were largely forgotten except for the 1960 portrait exhibition *George Platt Lynes, Portraits 1931–1952* at the Art Institute of Chicago. In fact, it was not until the early 1980s that his oeuvre began to receive critical attention, with an exhibition at Boston's Institute of Contemporary Art, *George Platt Lynes: Photographic Visions*, and the publication of *George Platt Lynes: Photographs 1931–1955*. – V. G.

Suggested Readings

Crump, James. *George Platt Lynes.* Boston: Little Brown, 1993.

Prokopoff, Stephen. *George Platt Lynes: Photographic Visions.* Exh. cat. Boston: Institute of Contemporary Art, 1980.

Woody, Jack. *George Platt Lynes: Photographs 1931–1955.* Pasadena, Calif.: Twelvetrees, 1981.

Man Ray [Emmanuel Radnitsky]
(b. August 27, 1890, Philadelphia; d. November 18, 1976, Paris)

Emmanuel Radnitsky grew up in Brooklyn. In New York, he studied art at the National Academy of Design, the Art Student's League, and the nontraditional Ferrer Center, where George Bellows and Robert Henri taught. In 1914, by which time he had abbreviated his full name to Man Ray, he married the Belgian writer Adon Lacroix; the union lasted four years, during which time Lacroix influenced his intellectual development. In 1915, Man Ray was introduced to Marcel Duchamp, newly arrived from Paris, who became a lifelong friend and collaborator. That same year, he had his first solo show, at the Daniel Gallery, New York, and first used photography to document the works exhibited there. Man Ray subsequently mastered the medium as an art form and, in 1917, created his first *cliché-verre*, a photographic image derived from drawing on a glass negative.

In the winter of 1920, Man Ray executed the first of several artful photographs of Duchamp posing as his feminine alter ego, Rrose Sélavy. In the summer of 1921, Man Ray moved to Paris and met the members of the proto-Surrealist circle at the Café Certà. In his first Parisian solo exhibition, in 1921 at the Dada bookstore and gallery Librairie Six, he presented work in several mediums: paintings, "aerographs," collages, and objects. During the 1920s, Man Ray photographed the denizens of Montparnasse, the thriving artistic quarter of Paris in which he lived. Among his subjects were the notorious artists' model Kiki (Alice Prin)—who became his lover—and the transvestite trapeze performer Barbette. To earn his livelihood in Paris, Man Ray turned to commercial photography, accepting commissions from fashion magazines and portraying the cultural and aristocratic circles he had begun to frequent. He concurrently produced photographs in a more strictly artistic vein and contributed images to Surrealist journals.

Man Ray's innovative approach to photography, combined with a fortuitous darkroom accident, led to his discovery of the photogram (a photograph produced by placing objects on light-sensitive paper) sometime in the winter of 1921–22. He experimented extensively with this particular technique, which he called "rayography." Man Ray continued to work in multiple genres, adding film to his repertoire in 1923 with *Retour à la raison* (Return to reason), realized for his friend Dadaist poet Tristan Tzara. In 1929, Man Ray entered into a collaborative relationship with the photographer Lee Miller, who was his assistant, model, student, and lover until 1932. It was with Miller that Man Ray devised the process of solarization (tone reversal in the photographic print). In 1934, his now-celebrated book *Photographs by Man Ray 1920 Paris 1934* was published in Paris.

Garnering further international recognition, in 1936 the expatriate artist was included in both the landmark *International Surrealist Exhibition* at the Burlington Galleries, London, and *Fantastic Art, Dada, Surrealism* at the Museum of Modern Art, New York. Wartime exigencies forced Man Ray to repatriate in 1940, but rather than remain in New York, he moved to Los Angeles, where his work was well received. Man Ray returned permanently to Paris in 1951. He received the gold medal in recognition of achievement in photography at the 1961 Venice *Biennale*, and in 1976 was awarded the Order of Artistic Merit by the French government. – V. G.

Suggested Readings

Foresta, Merry, et al. *Perpetual Motif: The Art of Man Ray*. Exh. cat. Washington, D.C.: National Museum of American Art, Smithsonian Institution; and New York: Abbeville Press, 1988.

Livingston, Jane. "Man Ray and Surrealist Photography." In Rosalind Krauss and Jane Livingston, *L'Amour fou: Photography and Surrealism*. New York: Abbeville, 1985, pp. 115–47.

Man Ray. *Self Portrait*. Boston: Little Brown, 1963.

Robert Mapplethorpe

(b. November 4, 1946, Floral Park, New York; d. March 9, 1989, Boston)

Robert Mapplethorpe left home in 1962 and enrolled at the Pratt Institute, Brooklyn, in 1963, where he studied painting and sculpture and received his B.F.A. in 1970. During this time, he met artist, poet, and musician Patti Smith. She encouraged his work and posed for numerous portraits when they lived together in Brooklyn and in the Chelsea Hotel in Manhattan, a gathering place for artists, writers, and musicians in the early 1970s.

It was not Mapplethorpe's original intention to be a photographer, and from 1970 to 1974, he mainly made assemblage constructions that incorporate images of men from pornographic magazines with found objects and painting. In order to create his own images for these collages, Mapplethorpe turned to photography, initially using a Polaroid SX-70 camera. Interested in portraiture, Mapplethorpe worked as a staff photographer for Andy Warhol's *Interview* magazine. He also produced album covers for Smith and the group Television, and at the same time photographed socialites and celebrities such as John Paul Getty III and Carolina Herrera.

Two of Mapplethorpe's friends were influential in his continuing exploration of photography as a means of art making. He met John McKendry, Curator of Prints and Photography at the Metropolitan Museum of Art, New York, in 1971. The curator bought Mapplethorpe his first camera and persuaded him to take up photography full time. Mapplethorpe traveled to Europe for the first time with McKendry, where he was introduced to many of the collectors who later became sitters for portraits. Curator and photography collector Sam Wagstaff, who he met in 1972, became Mapplethorpe's friend and eventual lover, encouraging the photographer's development, gallery associations, and career course. They remained close until Wagstaff's death in 1986.

Mapplethorpe had his first substantial shows in 1977, both in New York: an exhibition of photographs of flowers at the Holly Solomon Gallery and one of male nudes and sadomasochistic imagery at the Kitchen. Mapplethorpe's diverse work—homoerotic images, floral still lifes, pictures of children, commissioned portraits, mixed-media sculpture—is united by the constancy of his approach and technique. The surfaces of his prints offer a seemingly endless gradation of blacks and whites, shadow and light, and regardless of subject, his images are both elegant and provocative. In the mid-to-late 1980s, returning to the sculptural use of photography seen in his early assemblages, Mapplethorpe created sensual diptychs and triptychs of photographs printed on fabric and luxurious cloth panels. In 1988, four major exhibitions of his work were organized: by the Stedelijk Museum, Amsterdam; the Whitney Museum of American Art, New York; the Institute of Contemporary Art, University of Pennsylvania,

Philadelphia; and the National Portrait Gallery, London. Mapplethorpe died due to complications from AIDS in 1989.

The Institute of Contemporary Art's retrospective continued to travel after Mapplethorpe's death. Although the exhibition had sparked no controversy at its first two venues, the threat of right-wing objections to the photographs of S/M and homoerotic acts prompted officials at the Corcoran Gallery of Art in Washington, D.C., to cancel the show two weeks before its scheduled opening. The exhibition instead traveled to the Washington Project for the Arts (W.P.A.), Washington, D.C., where it received record attendance. – T. B.

Suggested Readings

Barrie, Dennis. "The Scene of the Crime." *Art Journal* 50, no. 3 (fall 1991), pp. 29–32.

Celant, Germano. *Mapplethorpe*. Exh. cat. Milan: Electa, 1992. In English.

Kardon, Janet. *Robert Mapplethorpe: The Perfect Moment*. Exh. cat. Philadelphia: Institute of Contemporary Art, University of Pennsylvania, 1988.

Marshall, Richard. *Robert Mapplethorpe*. Exh. cat. New York: Whitney Museum of American Art in association with New York Graphic Society Books, 1988.

Christian Marclay

(b. January 11, 1955, San Rafael, California)

Though born in the United States, Christian Marclay was raised in Geneva, Switzerland, where he studied at the Ecole Supérieure d'Art Visuel. Returning to the States in 1977, Marclay attended the Massachusetts College of Art in Boston, where he earned a B.F.A. in 1980. While in school, Marclay became interested in performance art as well as music, and was particularly inspired by the liberating punk-rock scene.

The marriage of art and music has been the defining characteristic of Marclay's career ever since. Like his objects and site-specific installations, which often combine and juxtapose disparate elements of art and musical culture, Marclay's DJ performance pieces at such venues as the Kitchen and La Mama in New York and cultural institutions throughout Europe use "mixing" techniques to create unusual fusions of music. Similar to the found objects he orchestrates in his visual art, Marclay reuses existing recordings as well as everyday sounds to produce new music.

Shuttling between these different arenas, Marclay maintains a fresh perspective in both his music and visual art. In his sculpture, Marclay recontextualizes the paraphernalia of musical culture such as speakers, audiotape, and instruments, often transforming familiar objects into unexpected, Duchampian assemblages. His first works done in the early 1980s were made of recycled records manipulated into visually stimulating and often humorous sculptures. Marclay's later *Body Mix* (1991–92) series, featuring collaged album jackets, questions the fixed nature of identity as well as the object. With their exquisite-corpse-like combinations of male and female body parts, his overlapping, sewn-together album covers refashion stereotyped images of race and gender into strange, erotic hybrids. Marclay had previously mounted groupings of covers on boxy, wooden skeletons. *Skin Mix I* and *II* (both 1990) are styled into totemlike sculptures, highlighting the hollow and artificial aspects of these commercial objects.

Like these theatrical unions, the artist has at times "fashioned" himself into a chameleon—a compilation of consumers' disparate desires. In 1994, Marclay depicted himself in a series of five concert announcements installed in the streets of Geneva. In each poster, the artist is dressed in the stereotypical garb of a certain type of musician (jazz, classical, rock). The series, called *False Advertising*, attracted a diverse group of individuals, each of whom was surprised to discover not the particular concert he or she had expected but an exhibition of the posters. The group was compelled to confront its preconceptions and to rethink the standard visual clues that had manipulated them.

Marclay's work has been exhibited nationally and internationally since 1983. Examples of his sculpture were included in the Whitney *Biennial* in 1991, and in 1995 the artist represented Switzerland at the Venice *Biennale*. Marclay has had notable solo exhibitions at the Hirshhorn Museum and Sculpture Garden, Smithsonian Institution, Washington, D.C., in 1990; the Fri-Art Centre d'Art Contemporain Kunsthalle, Fribourg, Switzerland, in 1994; the Cleveland Center for the Arts in 1995; and the Musée d'Art et d'Histoire, Geneva, in 1996. The artist will be given a solo exhibition at the Kunsthaus Zürich in fall 1997 in conjunction with the Preis für Junge Schweizer Kunstgesellschaft. Marclay lives in New York. – S. C.

Suggested Readings

Christian Marclay: Amplification. Exh. cat. Bern: Office Fédéral de la Culture, 1995. In English, French, German, and Italian.

Christian Marclay. Exh. cat. Berlin: Daadgalerie; and Fribourg: Fri-Art Centre d'Art Contemporain Kunsthalle, 1994. In English, French, and German.

Cruz, Amada. "Directions: Christian Marclay." Exh. brochure. Washington, D.C.: Hirshhorn Museum and Sculpture Garden, Smithsonian Institution, 1990.

Seliger, Jonathan. "Christian Marclay." *Journal of Contemporary Art* 5, no. 1 (spring 1992), pp. 64–76.

Vogel, Sabine. "In Record Time." *Artforum* 29, no. 9 (May 1991), pp. 103–07.

Annette Messager

(b. November 30, 1943, Berck, France)

Annette Messager's early artistic interests were encouraged by a father she has described as a Sunday painter and collector. Influenced by the many trips to churches and museums she made throughout Europe as a child, Messager moved to Paris in the early 1960s to attend the Ecole des Arts Décoratifs, where she was greatly influenced by the radical intellectual atmosphere of the May 1968 rebellion.

Inspired in equal turns by the subversive qualities of Surrealism and an early attraction to Catholicism, Messager began to create reliquarylike objects in art school. In keeping with her interest in "secret objects," she began making eclectic personal diaries in the early 1970s that include collections of her own signature, needlework, expense records, as well as photographs satirizing women's tortuous beauty rituals and other social conventions. Deriding the separation of art and life, Messager signed these works, made in her bedroom, "Annette Messager Collectionneuse" to differentiate them from the works made in her studio, which she signed "Annette Messager Artiste." Over the years, Messager has assumed several titles, including "Practical Woman," "Trickster," and "Peddler."

Throughout her prolific and diverse career, Messager has maintained an interest in the dual nature of things. Her use of taxidermy and photography—mediums that suspend objects between life and death—can be seen as a metaphor for the gaps the artist tries to close between other accepted dichotomies. In referencing the human form, for example, Messager uses ambiguity to free gendered bodies from fixed meaning, allowing them to speak for themselves.

In many series made during the 1980s, Messager manipulated photographs of isolated body parts, enlarging, fragmenting, painting, and drawing over them to form strange monsters, imaginary landscapes, and fantastic identities. Messager also began adding text to her works, writing repetitive mantras down the wall in colored pencil, or weaving threads of words in weblike arrangements. Memory and menace coexist in Messager's dualistic universe. *The Pikes* (*Les Piques*, 1991–93), a garden of spikes and impaled dolls, is at once ominous and carnivalesque, while *Penetration* (*Pénétration*, 1993–94), a forest of brightly colored internal organs made of stitched and stuffed cloth, mediates between funhouse and slaughterhouse, impishly perverting the viewer's notions of the hideous and the divine.

In 1989, Messager had her first touring retrospective, which originated at the Musée de Grenoble. Most recently, in 1995, the Los Angeles County Museum of Art and the Museum of Modern Art, New York, organized a major retrospective of the artist's work, which also traveled to the Art Institute of Chicago in 1996. Messager lives in Malakoff, France. – S. C.

Suggested Readings

Annette Messager: Comédie tragédie, 1971–1989. Exh. cat. Grenoble: Musée de Grenoble, 1989. In French and German.

Annette Messager: Faire des histoires/Making Up Stories. Exh. cat. Toronto: Mercer Union and Cold City Gallery, 1991. In English and French.

Conkleton, Sheryl, and Carol S. Eliel. *Annette Messager.* Exh. cat. Los Angeles: Los Angeles County Museum of Art; and New York: Museum of Modern Art, 1995.

Gourmelon, Mo. "Arbitrated Dissections: The Art of Annette Messager." *Arts Magazine* 65, no. 3 (November 1990), pp. 66–71.

Rowlands, Penelope. "Art that Annoys." *Artnews* 94, no. 8 (October 1995), pp. 132–35.

Pierre Molinier

(b. April 13, 1900, Agen, France; d. March 3, 1976, Bordeaux)

Pierre Molinier grew up in the small town of Agen, where he went to the local art school and took evening courses at the Ecole des Beaux-Arts. To augment the limited artistic training available to him, he apprenticed with his father, a painter, and with a sculptor named Pierre Augustin de Fumadelles. After a brief interlude in Paris, Molinier moved to Bordeaux in 1923 and established his permanent residence there. Molinier was a painter for most of his career, first creating landscapes in a Post-Impressionist style, then delving into abstraction, and, in 1936, adopting a more Surrealistic idiom. Photography was merely a means for him to document his work until about 1950, when he began to execute self-portraits.

In 1955, Molinier approached Surrealist leader André Breton, who consequently gave him a solo exhibition at his new Parisian gallery, l'Etoile Scellée, in January 1956. Following this, the artist contributed to Breton's periodical, *Le Surréalisme, même*, and showed his paintings in several Surrealist exhibitions. Molinier's encounter with Surrealism proved to be a creative catalyst for the artist, who dedicated himself in 1964 almost exclusively to photography and to photomontages that concentrated on sexually transgressive themes.

Primarily for his own pleasure, Molinier crafted photographic scenarios that depict himself and other models wearing copious makeup or female masks and costumed in leather corsets, stockings, and stiletto heels while employing props such as mannequins or handmade dildos. When constructing his virtually seamless photomontages, Molinier obfuscated the gender and identity of the figures through repeated technical manipulations.

In 1967, Molinier met and collaborated with Hanel Koeck, who was affiliated with the Vienna Actionists, and his little-known photography soon become popular with European artists of the early 1970s. As a consequence, he was included in the Kunstmuseum Luzern's exhibition *"Transformer": Aspekte der Travestie* in 1974–75. Molinier remained active as a photographer until his death by suicide in 1976. In 1979, the Musée National d'Art Moderne, Centre Georges Pompidou, Paris, held a retrospective of his work. – V. G.

Suggested Readings

Durant, Mark Alice. "Lost (and Found) in a Masquerade: The Photographs of Pierre Molinier." *Exposure* 29, nos. 2–3 (1994), pp. 27–35.

Molinier: Peinture, photos et photomontages. Exh. cat. Paris: Fondation Aquitaine and Musée National d'Art Moderne, 1979.

Molinier, Pierre. *Pierre Molinier.* Exh. cat. Winnipeg, Canada: Plug in Editions, 1993. In English and French.

Petit, Pierre. *Molinier: Une Vie d'enfer.* Paris: Ramsay/Jean-Jacques Pauvert, 1992.

Yasumasa Morimura

(b. June 11, 1951, Osaka)

Yasumasa Morimura received a B.A. from Kyoto City University of Art in 1975 and studied visual design there in 1978. Since 1985, he has been using photography to investigate the complex cultural and economic exchanges between East and West that have influenced contemporary Japanese identity. Reacting to the profusion of Western images in Japan's visual vocabulary, Morimura re-creates, as both homage and critique, the masterpieces he knew—through reproductions—as a youth. Using methods that include photography, over-painting, and computer imaging, Morimura transports himself into the center of such iconic works as Edouard Manet's *Olympia* (1863), Rembrandt's *The Anatomy Lesson of Professor Nicolaes Tulp* (1632), and Goya's *The Third of May, 1808* (1814), inserting an Asian subjectivity into a European narrative.

As early as 1986, Morimura, a consummate drag artist, began drawing parallels between fictions of race and gender. In works such as *Doublonnage (Marcel)*, his 1988 interpretation of Man Ray's portrait of Marcel Duchamp's female alter ego, Rrose Sélavy, in which gender is indicated by costume and jewelry and race invoked through makeup, Morimura denies these categories as natural or predetermined. As the artist's work has become even more concerned with identity as performance, his impersonations and props have become more extravagant, rivaling in still photography the most elaborate theatrical and cinematic productions. (His brightly colored tableaux can measure up to eight by eleven feet.)

In 1991, Morimura also addressed the economic factors shaping Japanese identity, satirizing upper-class Japanese women obsessed with Western status symbols in the photographs of himself, costumed in Chanel and Louis Vuitton, from the *Sister* series. The artist also began reworking documentary photography at this time, and again expanded his use of pop-culture imagery in 1994 with his *Psychoborgs*, various incarnations of Michael Jackson and Madonna. Morimura elaborated on the theme of the entertainer with his *Actress* series of 1996, in which he faithfully restaged stills from various American, European, and Japanese film classics. Whether he is playing Marilyn Monroe in *The Seven Year Itch* (Billy Wilder, 1955) or the Infanta Margarita in Velázquez's *Las Meninas* (1656), Morimura undermines the colonizing gaze of the historical Western, white male subject by corrupting accepted "truths" of gender, race, beauty, culture, and the self with his impeccable illusions.

Morimura had his first solo show at a museum in 1992 at the Museum of Contemporary Art, Chicago, which subsequently traveled to the Carnegie Museum of Art, Pittsburgh. Other significant solo exhibitions have been organized by the Fondation Cartier pour l'Art Contemporain, Paris, in 1993; the Hara Museum, Hara, and the Ginza Art Space, Tokyo, in 1994; and the Yokohama Museum of Art in 1996. Morimura lives in Osaka. – S. C.

Suggested Readings

Bonami, Francesco. "Yasumasa Morimura: Double Exposure." *Flash Art* 25, no. 163 (March–April 1992), pp. 82–83.

Gumpert, Lynn. "Glamour Girls." *Art in America* 84, no. 7 (July 1996), pp. 62–65.

Morimura Yasumasa: The Sickness unto Beauty—Self-Portrait as Actress. Exh. cat. Yokohama: Yokohama Museum of Art, 1996. In English and Japanese.

Wright, Beryl J. *Options 44: Yasumasa Morimura.* Exh. brochure. Chicago: Museum of Contemporary Art, 1992.

Catherine Opie

(b. April 14, 1961, Sandusky, Ohio)

Moving from Ohio at the age of thirteen, Catherine Opie spent her teenage years in Rancho Bernardo, California, a neighborhood on the outskirts of San Diego. Following high school, she moved to San Francisco and began to explore her childhood interest in photography. Enrolling at the San Francisco Art Institute, Opie focused on documentary photography, a preference influenced early on by the work of Lewis Hine and later by the work of artists such as Bernd and Hilla Becher, Walker Evans, and Dorothea Lange. After receiving her B.F.A. in 1985, Opie returned to Southern California, earning an M.F.A. from the

California Institute of Arts in Valencia in 1988. Though her master's degree show and other early work were documentary projects on planned communities, Opie had already begun taking—though not exhibiting—photographs of her friends and other members of the leather and fetish community.

Being and Having, Opie's earliest series of intimate portraits intended for a public audience, were included in her first solo exhibition in New York, in 1991. These head shots depicting women with mustaches and beards were intended as performative pieces that at times allow the viewer to see the artifice behind the masculine masquerade. Opie's more colorful *Portraits* of 1994, however, are straightforward homages to individuals and couples in the little-represented lesbian S/M community. These formal and dignified bust- and full-length portraits gained Opie considerable attention at the 1995 Whitney *Biennial*.

Expanding her investigation of community, Opie began a series of photographs of the Los Angeles freeways in 1994. Like her portraits, which focus a fresh lens on the queer community and standard definitions of gender, the artist's vision of these thoroughfares challenges expected notions of landscape and beauty and again brings into view what is often excluded. In her panoramic black-and-white platinum prints, Opie imbues these monuments of industrialization with a surprising romanticism.

In 1995, Opie began a series devoted to Hollywood Hills house facades. The photographs capture a variety of homes, which are often seen up close and cropped, a formal approach similar to that of her earliest portraits. In this series, however, Opie inverts her previous critiques of perception and hints at the perversion of the seemingly ordinary. Opie's images reassess attitudes toward and representation of various "fringe" and familiar communities.

The artist's work has recently been represented in numerous group exhibitions, including, in 1994, *Persona Cognita*, at the Museum of Modern Art at Heide, Australia, and *Oh Boy, It's a Girl*, at the Kunstverein München, Munich, and the Kunstraum, Vienna; *fémininmasculin: Le Sexe de l'art*, at the Centre Georges Pompidou, Paris, in 1995; and *Persona* at the Renaissance Society at the University of Chicago, and the Kunsthalle Basel in 1996. Opie lives in Los Angeles. – S. C.

Suggested Readings

Fullerton, Kim, and Sky Gilbert. *Fabrications*. Exh. cat. Toronto: Toronto Photographers Workshop, 1996.

Persona Cognita. Exh. cat. Heide, Australia: Museum of Modern Art at Heide, 1994, pp. 18–19, 41–43.

Rugoff, Ralph. *Transformers*. Exh. cat. New York: Independent Curators Incorporated, 1994, pp. 22–24.

Smith, Anna Marie. "The Feminine Gaze: Photographer Catherine Opie Documents a Lesbian Daddy/Boy Subculture." *The Advocate*, November 19, 1991, pp. 82–83.

Lucas Samaras

(b. September 14, 1936, Kastoria, Macedonia, Greece)

In 1948, Lucas Samaras and his mother moved from Greece to West New York, New Jersey, where they joined his father, who had emigrated to the United States in 1939. Samaras became an American citizen in 1955 and in the same year was admitted to Rutgers University in New Brunswick, New Jersey. Studying with Allan Kaprow and George Segal until 1959, Samaras experienced the development of Kaprow's junk-filled environments and multimedia performance events, which came to be known as Happenings. In 1959, he entered Columbia University, New York, and studied art history under Meyer Shapiro.

Samaras participated in a number of Happenings at New York's Reuben Gallery, where he met Jim Dine, Red Grooms, and Claes Oldenburg, and proceeded to show with other pioneer Pop artists in the second *New Forms* exhibition at New York's Martha Jackson Gallery in 1960. The autobiographical content of his work differentiated Samaras from the Pop artists. He expanded his interest in the performative aspects of contemporary art by attending the Stella Adler Conservatory of Acting and continued producing work that embraced diverse mediums such as painting, sculpture, assemblage, and film. In 1969, he gave an advanced sculpture seminar at Yale University and completed a short film, *Self*, with Kim Levin. He taught in the art department of Brooklyn College from 1971 to 1972.

Samaras's first explorations into photography, in 1969, were his *AutoPolaroids*, black-and-white Polaroid self-portraits that depict him performing for the camera nude or costumed, vamping and mugging. In 1973, he discovered that the image could be altered and distorted by manipulating the emulsion of the unique photograph immediately after it emerged from the camera. These pioneering *Photo-Transformations* opened up new possibilities for Samaras, who used the swirling, rippling, scratched, and patterned surfaces to give psychological dimension to his work. In the mid-1980s, Samaras further pushed the boundaries of photography by incorporating double exposures into his oeuvre. He continues to experiment with new technology and formats in instant photography to rework questions about the nature of identity and portraiture.

In 1983, a retrospective of Samaras's photographs was presented at the Centre Georges Pompidou, Paris; the Frankfurter Kunstverein; the International Center of Photography, New York; and the Serpentine Gallery, London. In 1992, the Museum of Modern Art, New York, showed an extensive collection of the artist's photographs. Samaras lives in New York. – T. B.

Suggested Readings

Lifson, Ben. *Samaras: Photographs, 1969–1986.* New York: Aperture, 1988.

Lucas Samaras: Objects and Subjects, 1969–1986. Exh. cat. New York: Abbeville Press, 1988.

Lucas Samaras: Photos Polaroid Photographs 1969–1983. Exh. cat. Paris: Musée National d'Art Moderne, Centre Georges Pompidou, 1983. In English, French, and German.

Cindy Sherman

(b. January 19, 1954, Glen Ridge, New Jersey)

Cindy Sherman emerged onto the New York art scene in the early 1980s as part of a new generation of artists concerned with the codes of representation in a media-saturated era. Having graduated from State University College, Buffalo, in 1976, she moved to New York the following year, at a time when the authority of the Modernist paradigm was coming under increasing scrutiny. Amid debates surrounding authorship and the role of originality, the condition of the photographic image, and the increasing commodification of art, Sherman's work was quickly embraced in the early 1980s and framed within the contemporary feminist critique of patriarchy.

Sherman's reputation was established on the basis of her *Untitled Film Stills*, a series of black-and-white photographs from the late 1970s in which the artist depicted herself dressed in the guises of clichéd B-movie heroines. In photograph after photograph, Sherman was ever present, and yet never really there—her ready adaptation of a range of personae highlighting the masquerade of identity. Her appropriation of the space on both sides of the lens destabilized the traditionally gendered opposition between artist and model, object and subject—one that had been theorized by film critics in terms of spectatorship and its gendered codes of looking.

If the *Untitled Film Stills* elicited debate concerning the construction of woman-as-image, the photographs Sherman made throughout the mid-1980s served to perpetuate this discourse. Her *Centerfolds* (1981) and *Fashion* (1983–84) series elaborated the codes of what film theorist Laura Mulvey termed the "to-be-looked-at-ness" of female representation. Emulating the signifiers of the centerfold, the closely cropped photographs reveal a body that is available to the camera and bathed in a vivid light. Sherman's choice of gendered genres compounds the voyeuristic impression established in the works.

Feeling pigeonholed by the feminist discourse that surrounded her work, Sherman gradually dispensed with representations of the female, often removing herself from the picture and moving toward more fantastic and lurid imagery, as in her *Fairy Tales* and *Disasters* series from the mid-to-late 1980s. The ever-increasing market for her photographs also prompted this turn, challenging her to attempt to create work that was "unsaleable" due to its visceral depictions of vomit, body parts, and grotesque fairy tales. Simultaneously, she instilled the works with a heightened sense of artifice created by garish colors and gaps that reveal the fiction behind the illusion.

Throughout her career, Sherman has appropriated numerous visual genres—including the film still, centerfold, fashion photograph, historical portrait, and soft-core sex image—while disrupting the operations that work to define and maintain their respective codes of representation. In addition to numerous group exhibitions, her work was the subject of solo exhibitions at the Stedelijk Museum, Amsterdam, in 1982; and the Whitney Museum of American Art, New York, in 1987. Most recently, a retrospective organized by the Museum Boymans-van Beuningen, Rotterdam, traveled throughout Europe in 1996 and 1997. Sherman lives in New York and is at work on a feature-length horror film. – J. F. R.

Suggested Readings

Cindy Sherman. Exh. cat. New York: Whitney Museum of American Art, 1987.

Cindy Sherman. Exh. cat. Rotterdam: Museum Boymans-van Beuningen, 1996. In English and Dutch.

Cindy Sherman: Photographic Work 1975–1995. Edited by Zdenek Felix and Martin Schwander. Exh. cat. Munich: Schirmer Art Books, 1995. In English.

Krauss, Rosalind. *Cindy Sherman: 1975–1993.* New York: Rizzoli, 1993.

Katharina Sieverding

(b. November 16, 1944, Prague)

After spending one year (1963–64) at the Hochschule für Bildende Künste, Hamburg, Katharina Sieverding enrolled at the Staatliche Kunstakademie, Düsseldorf, where she studied until 1967 with Teo Otto. While at school, Sieverding also worked on set designs and construction for theatrical performances at venues such as the Burgtheater, Vienna, the Schauspielhaus, Düsseldorf, and the Deutsche Oper, Berlin. She continued her studies at the Kunstakademie through 1972 under the direct tutelage of Joseph Beuys. Beuys's emphasis on the creation of the artist's persona is evident in Sieverding's early photographic work, which features large-scale, close-up self-portraits that vary endlessly as she changes makeup, lighting, and focus.

In the mid-1970s, Sieverding began making monumental photographic tableaux that combine images and text. She came to New York in 1976 to participate in the Whitney Museum of

American Art's Independent Study Program and remained in Manhattan to become a member of the Graduate Faculty of Political and Social Science of the New School for Social Research in 1977. She traveled throughout the United States and Canada in 1977, lecturing, performing, and creating installations at institutions such as the Minneapolis College of Art and Design, the Los Angeles Institute for Contemporary Art, and Concordia University, Montreal.

Sieverding returned to self-portraiture in the early 1980s, creating close-cropped and abstracted works that are connected to the masklike images she produced in the 1960s and early 1970s. From 1990 to 1992, Sieverding was visiting professor at the Hochschule für Bildende Künste in Hamburg, where she created a work that was chosen by the jury organized to fill the renovated Reichstag in Berlin. *Memorial* (*Mahnmal*, 1990), a monumental photograph of a solar eruption—Sieverding's proposed memorial to the persecution in 1933 of non-Nazi members of the German parliament—provocatively explores the country's political past and present.

In 1992, Sieverding moved to Berlin to teach at the Hochschule der Künste and a year later executed a controversial billboard project for Kunstwerke, a Berlin arts complex that houses exhibition and studio space. Installed in 500 locations around Berlin, the billboard depicted a black-and-white image of a woman's face surrounded by knives, arranged as if thrown by a circus performer. In large text superimposed on the image was a headline taken from a German newspaper: "Deutschland wird deutscher" (Germany is becoming more German). Many billboards were defaced or removed.

Sieverding's work was shown in *Documenta 5*, Kassel, in 1972. She has had solo exhibitions at the Stedelijk Van Abbe Museum, Eindhoven, The Netherlands, in 1979; the Städtische Kunsthalle Düsseldorf in 1980; the Kasseler Kunstverein, Kassel, in 1987; Artspace, San Francisco, in 1988; and the Nationalgalerie, Berlin, in 1992. Sieverding has been chosen to represent Germany at the 1997 Venice *Biennale*. She lives in Düsseldorf. –T. B.

Suggested Readings

Garrels, Gary. *Photography in Contemporary German Art: 1960 to the Present*. Exh. cat. Minneapolis: Walker Art Center, 1992.

Sieverding. Exh. cat. Ostfildern: Cantz, 1992. In English and German.

Solomon-Godeau, Abigail. "The Face of Difference." In *Katharina Sieverding: Eine Installation*. Exh. cat. Regensburg: Museum Ostdeutsche Galerie, 1993, pp. 11–24. In English and German.

Inez van Lamsweerde

(b. September 25, 1963, Amsterdam)

Inez van Lamsweerde studied fashion at the Mode Akademie Vogue (1983–85) and photography at the Gerrit Rietveld Akademie (1985–90), both in Amsterdam, and in 1992 moved to New York for a one-year residency at P.S. 1, the Institute of Contemporary Art. Since her first series in 1991, which depicted women dressed as if posing for pin-ups in unremarkable urban sites scattered throughout the northern Dutch city of Groningen, van Lamsweerde has mimicked the glossiness of fashion magazines and retail catalogues in order to target myths of beauty and eroticism and to question assumptions about gender roles.

Van Lamsweerde has received public commissions and support for projects since 1992, when she produced a controversial city-funded billboard for a drawbridge in Amsterdam. The photograph of a sensuously posed woman confronted motorists when the bridge was raised, leading it to be defaced with graffiti accusing the artist of sexism—a critique that fell somewhat flat since it has always been van Lamsweerde's tactic to subvert the vocabulary of commercial photography for her own critical purposes.

Van Lamsweerde often employs high-tech working methods to seamlessly alter her models' body parts. In the four works that comprise her 1993 series *Thank You Thighmaster*, she has removed body hair, genitals, and nipples from the images of nude female models by using a Quantel paintbox computer program. The disquieting plasticized figures that are the result of these complex alterations suggest a loss of individuality and eroticism. Van Lamsweerde's 1995 series *The Forest* subtly examines gender identity. In these works, parts of the bodies of the men portrayed have been replaced with those of women—a subtle blurring of masculine and feminine that is emphasized by the models' carefully styled hair and faces.

Van Lamsweerde works concurrently as a successful commercial fashion photographer and has shot, in collaboration with Vinoodh Matadin, the collections of John Galliano, Helmut Lang, Hervé Leger, Véronique Leroy, and Vivienne Westwood. Here, too, she alters the appearance of her models—elongating body parts, eliminating blemishes, or duplicating figures. She has been showing and publishing her work in Amsterdam since 1990, and in 1992 was awarded the Photography Award of the Netherlands (PANL) and the European Kodak Awards for the categories of Fashion and People/Portraits. Her work has been seen in exhibitions at the Centraal Museum, Utrecht, in 1993; the Stedelijk Museum Bureau, Amsterdam, in 1993; the Kunstverein Salzburg, in 1994; and the Musée d'Art Moderne de la Ville de Paris in 1994. Van Lamsweerde lives in Amsterdam and New York. – T. B.

Suggested Readings

Inez van Lamsweerde. Exh. cat. Zurich: Kunsthaus Zürich, 1996. In English and German.

Schorr, Collier. "Openings: Inez van Lamsweerde." *Artforum* 33, no. 2 (October 1994), pp. 96–97.

Turner, Jonathan. "Inez van Lamsweerde: Vanity Fear." *Artnews* 93, no. 9 (November 1994), p. 75.

Andy Warhol [Andrew Warhola]
(b. August 6, 1928, Pittsburgh; d. February 22, 1987, New York)

Andy Warhol attended Pittsburgh's Carnegie Institute of Technology (now Carnegie Mellon University), enrolling in the Department of Painting and Sculpture. Upon graduating in 1949, Warhol moved to New York, where he embarked upon a successful and lucrative career as a commercial artist, executing advertisements and illustrations throughout the 1950s. During this period, he shortened his name.

Warhol first gained critical attention as a fine artist in the early 1960s with paintings and sculptures that feature iconic representations of the mundane products purchased by the American consumer, as well as images of idolized celebrities such as Marilyn Monroe. These works, like the majority of Warhol's oeuvre, were done in multiple versions that not only exemplify the artist's interest in seriality, but also his enthrallment with popular culture, stardom, and mass production. In keeping with the latter, Warhol frequently utilized mechanical means, like the photographic silk-screen process, to create his art.

Warhol's studio, appropriately dubbed "The Factory," was the locus of convergence for notorious characters belonging to the counterculture of the 1960s and early 1970s. Warhol proclaimed the more glamorous and outrageous of these individuals "Superstars." Ranging from socialite Edie Sedgwick to transvestite Candy Darling (James Slattery), they appear in Warhol's films and photographs from this period. Warhol's first true foray into photography occurred in 1964 with the *Photobooth* pictures. For these, he simply prompted subjects to pose in a photo booth, where their photographs were automatically taken. Sometimes Warhol would employ the film camera as one would a regular camera, producing film portraits, called *Screen Tests*, in which a person would be asked to sit motionless for the three-minute duration of a reel of film. The *Screen Tests* were sometimes intended to reveal whether the subject had the potential to be the next Superstar in a Warhol movie. In 1968, Warhol was shot and almost killed by a woman who had appeared in one of his films.

Warhol was obsessed with recording everything around him, finding the most banal actions mesmerizing. He carried a camera and tape recorder with him constantly, and eventually kept a detailed diary, which he dictated over the phone to an assistant. He usually had a stationary camera (first film and then video) set up in his studio to capture staff and visitors performing daily activities. Around 1970, the Polaroid Big Shot became Warhol's primary camera, and with it he took a gargantuan number of Polaroids that encompass nudes, self-portraits, and portraits. The portrait Polaroids were often the source for the commissioned silk-screened works of famous personalities and wealthy society figures that Warhol created until his death. From 1976 to 1986, he also produced stitched photographs, which consist of multiple identical pictures sewn together to create a single image.

A prolific artist, Warhol experimented successfully with myriad methods of reproduction during his lifetime, also generating books, apparel, *Interview* magazine, and cable-television shows. He died prematurely in 1987, following gallbladder surgery. Warhol's legacy has been recognized in many exhibitions worldwide. In 1989, *Andy Warhol: A Retrospective* was held at the Museum of Modern Art, New York, and in 1994 an institution dedicated to the artist, The Andy Warhol Museum, opened in Pittsburgh. A large-scale interdisciplinary exhibition, *Andy Warhol: A Factory*, is planned for spring 1998 at the Guggenheim Museum SoHo. – V. G.

Suggested Readings

Andy Warhol: A Retrospective. Edited by Kynaston McShine. Exh. cat. New York: Museum of Modern Art, 1989.

Andy Warhol Photobooth Pictures. Exh. cat. New York: Robert Miller Gallery, 1989.

Andy Warhol Polaroids 1971–1986. Exh. cat. New York: Pace/MacGill Gallery and The Andy Warhol Foundation for the Visual Arts, 1992.

Koch, Stephen. *Andy Warhol Photographs.* Exh. cat. New York: Robert Miller Gallery, 1986.

Madame Yevonde [Yevonde Cumbers Middleton]
(b. January 5, 1893, London; d. December 22, 1975, London)

Yevonde Cumbers attended boarding schools in England and Belgium, completing her education at the Sorbonne in Paris. At seventeen, she joined the suffragette movement, marking the beginning of her commitment to women's causes. On an impulse, she decided to study photography and apprenticed with the portrait photographer Lallie Charles from 1911 to 1914.

Cumbers established a studio of her own in London in 1914 and, taking the professional name of Madame Yevonde, proceeded to earn a living as a portrait photographer, contributing to society magazines such as *The Sketch* and *The Tatler*. In 1920, she married playwright Edgar Middleton. Madame Yevonde periodically lectured on photography and, in 1921, was the first woman to address the Congress of the Professional Photographers Association, London, with her lecture "Photographic Portraiture from the Women's Point of View." Around 1925, she extended her commercial endeavors to include advertising.

Tiring of black-and-white photography, Madame Yevonde began experimenting with the Vivex color process in the early 1930s, ingeniously placing colored cellophane and filters over the camera lens and modulating the lighting to obtain specific tones and vibrant hues. She exhibited her celebrated *Goddesses* series in her studio in July 1935. The "goddesses" were society women costumed as Greek and Roman deities and posed against backdrops of imaginative props in fantastical and artful compositions. Influenced by the Surrealists and especially Man Ray, whose work became known in Britain in the mid-1930s, Madame Yevonde also began creating still lifes in 1936 that depict unusual juxtapositions of objects.

Though grief stricken by her husband's death in 1939, Madame Yevonde did not curtail her artistic activities. Her autobiography, *In Camera*, was published in 1940. In the same year, the Royal Photographic Society (of which she had been a member since 1921) named her a Fellow for her work in color photography. Madame Yevonde continued to explore diverse photographic techniques throughout her life, producing solarized photographs in the late 1950s and early 1960s. In 1973, as a tribute for her eightieth birthday, a major retrospective in London, *Sixty Years a Portrait Photographer*, was organized by the Royal Photographic Society.—V. G.

Suggested Readings

Gibson, Robin, and Pam Roberts. *Madame Yevonde: Colour, Fantasy, and Myth*. Exh. cat. London: National Portrait Gallery, 1990.

Salway, Kate. *Goddesses and Others: Yevonde, A Portrait*. London: Balcony Books, 1990.

[Madame] Yevonde. *In Camera*. London: Women's Book Club, 1958.

Index of Reproductions

Reproductions are listed by page number.

Contributors

JENNIFER BLESSING is Assistant Curator at the Solomon R. Guggenheim Museum, where she specializes in Surrealism and postwar European art. Her publications include essays on Claude Cahun, Marc Chagall, Peggy Guggenheim's collection, paparazzi photographs, Gypsy Rose Lee, and most recently, "'Eros, c'est la vie': Fetishism as Cultural Discourse (Surrealism, Fashion, and Photography)," in *Art/Fashion*, exh. cat. (Skira, 1997). She is currently writing an essay on Gina Pane.

JUDITH HALBERSTAM is Associate Professor of Literature at the University of California, San Diego, where she teaches nineteenth-century fiction, queer theory, and cultural studies. She is the author of *Skin Show: Gothic Horror and the Technology of Monsters* (Duke University Press, 1995) and is currently finishing a book on "female masculinity." She writes film reviews for *Girlfriends Magazine.*

LYLE ASHTON HARRIS is a lecturer on Autobiography and Visual Culture at Otis College of Art and Design, Los Angeles, and Art Center College of Design, Pasadena. His writings and interviews have appeared in international journals, including *Flash Art*, *Art in America*, *aRude*, and *Afterimage*, and will be published in *The Passionate Camera: Photography and the Bodies of Desire*, ed. Deborah Bright (Routledge, forthcoming). Harris is represented by Jack Tilton Gallery, New York, and Margo Leavin Gallery, Los Angeles, and has completed several editorial photography projects for *The New York Times Magazine.*

NANCY SPECTOR is Associate Curator at the Solomon R. Guggenheim Museum, where she specializes in contemporary art. Exhibitions she has curated at the museum include retrospectives of Felix Gonzalez-Torres and Rebecca Horn. She is currently co-curating the first Berlin *Biennial*, which is scheduled for summer 1998. She writes frequently on issues in contemporary visual culture for the museum and international art publications.

CAROLE-ANNE TYLER is Associate Professor of English at the University of California, Riverside, where she teaches courses in film and visual culture, gender and sexuality, literary theory, and modern literature. She is the author of *Female Impersonation* (Routledge, forthcoming); portions of which appeared in *differences: a journal of feminist cultural studies*; *Inside/Out: Lesbian Theories, Gay Theories*, ed. Diana Fuss (Routledge, 1991); and *Theory between the Disciplines: Authority, Vision, Politics*, ed. Martin Kreiswirth and Mark A. Cheetham (University of Michigan Press, 1990).

SARAH WILSON is a lecturer in twentieth-century art history at the Courtauld Institute of Art, University of London, where she specializes in postwar European art. Since 1981 she has collaborated on major exhibitions with the Centre Georges Pompidou in Paris, contributing texts on postwar French art, Max Ernst, Kurt Schwitters, art and sexuality, and art and politics, while also publishing extensively in Britain and abroad. She is the author of *When Modernism Failed: Art and the Politics of the Left in France, 1930–1956* (Yale University Press, forthcoming).

Photo credits

Photo credits are listed by page number.
viii, courtesy of the artist and Metro Pictures; *6*, courtesy of Sotheby's London; *7*, © 1996 The Detroit Institute of Arts; *8*, courtesy of Sotheby's London; *9*, © Nan Goldin, courtesy Matthew Marks Gallery, New York; *10*, © Museum Boymans-van Beuningen; *11*, © Yevonde Portrait Archive, England; *12*, © 1997 Artists Rights Society (ARS), New York / ADAGP / Man Ray Trust, Paris; *13*, © 1996 The Museum of Modern Art, New York. © Gilberte Brassaï; *14*, © George P. Lynes II; *15*, photo by Ilona Ripke. © 1997 Artists Rights Society (ARS), New York / VG Bild-Kunst, Bonn; *18*, *20*, © Philadelphia Museum of Art. © 1997 Artists Rights Society (ARS), New York / ADAGP / Man Ray Trust, Paris; *21*, © 1997 Artists Rights Society (ARS), New York / ADAGP, Paris / Estate of Marcel Duchamp; *22*, photo by Photothèque des Musées de la Ville de Paris. © 1997 Artists Rights Society (ARS), New York / ADAGP, Paris; *24*, *25*, top, *25*, bottom, © 1997 Artists Rights Society (ARS), New York / VG Bild-Kunst, Bonn; *26*, © 1996 Kunsthaus Zürich. All rights reserved. © 1997 Artists Rights Society (ARS), New York / VG Bild-Kunst, Bonn; *27*, © 1997 Artists Rights Society (ARS), New York / VG Bild-Kunst, Bonn; *28*, © 1922 The Metropolitan Museum of Art. © 1997 Artists Rights Society (ARS), New York / ADAGP / Man Ray Trust, Paris; *29*, © 1997 Artists Rights Society (ARS), New York / ADAGP / Man Ray Trust, Paris; *30*, courtesy of the Metropolitan Museum of Art, all rights reserved. © 1997 Artists Rights Society (ARS), New York / ADAGP / Man Ray Trust, Paris; *32–35*, © 1996 The Museum of Modern Art, New York. ©Gilberte Brassaï; *36*, top, photo by Ellen Labenski; *36*, bottom, © 1996 Museum Associates, Los Angeles County Museum of Art. All Rights Reserved; *37*, courtesy of Galerie Berggruen, Paris; *38*, courtesy of Sotheby's London; *39*, © Mr. Tom Hustler; *40–44*, courtesy of Sotheby's London; *45–49*, © Yevonde Portrait Archive, England; *50*, courtesy of Musée National d'Art Moderne, Centre Georges Pompidou, Paris; *52*, courtesy of The Metropolitan Museum of Art, All rights reserved; *54*, *55*, © Staten Island Historical Society; *56*, © 1928 Man Ray Trust; *57*, © Centre Georges Pompidou, Paris. Photo by Jean-Claude Planchet. © 1997 Artists Rights Society (ARS), New York / ADAGP / Man Ray Trust, Paris; *58*, photo by A.G. Ville de Nantes; *60*, © 1997 Artists Rights Society (ARS), New York / ADAGP / Man Ray Trust, Paris; *61*, courtesy of the artist and Metro Pictures; *62*, courtesy of Musée National d'Art Moderne, Centre Georges Pompidou, Paris; *63*, left, photo by Bill Orcutt; *64*, photo by Bill Orcutt; *66*, © Katharina Sieverding. Photo by Ms. Seitz-Gray; *68–69*, © Galerie Bugdahn und Kaimer; *71*, © 1997 Andy Warhol Foundation for the Visual Arts / ARS, New York; *73*, © 1996 Whitney Museum of American Art. © 1997 Andy Warhol Foundation for the Visual Arts / ARS, New York; *74–75*, © 1997 The Museum of Modern Art, New York. © Lucas Samaras; *77*, © Lynn Hershman Leeson; *80*, *82–85*, courtesy of the artist and Metro Pictures; *87*, courtesy of Luhring Augustine Gallery, New York; *88*, *89*, photo by Michael James O'Brien, courtesy of Barbara Gladstone Gallery, New York; *92*, © Christian Marclay; *93*, photo by Ellen Labenski; *94*, *95*, © Inez van Lamsweerde; *97–101*, © Nan Goldin, courtesy of Matthew Marks Gallery, New York; *102*, *103*, © 1980 The Estate of Robert Mapplethorpe; *104–05*, © Catherine Opie; *106*, © Catherine Opie, Courtesy Regen Projects, Los Angeles; *108*, *109*, *110*, © Lyle Ashton Harris; *112–13*, © Janine Antoni; *120*, Sulkin Winters Partnership; *123*, © 1988 The Estate of Robert Mapplethorpe; *126*, *131*, photo by Zindman/Fremont; *134*, S.A.D.E. Archives, Milan; *136*, top, courtesy of William A. Ewing; *137*, right, courtesy of Courtauld Institute of Art Witt Library; *141*, photo by Ellen Labenski; *142*, left, courtesy Courtauld Institute of Art Witt Library; *143*, top left, © Estate of Eileen Agar; *143*, top right, courtesy of Courtauld Institute of Art Witt Library; *143*, bottom, courtesy of Courtauld Institute of Art Witt Library, *View* photos by Roger Schall and Francis Lee; *144*, photo by Laurent Condominas; *146*, photo by Sandra Lousada; *147*, © Lyle Ashton Harris; *148*, photo by Freda Leinwand, 1981; *149*, photo by Teri Slotkin, 1995; *151*, © Nicholas Sinclair. Outfit by E. Garbs; *156*, courtesy of Sotheby's London; *158*, photo by Ellen Labenski, © 1997 Artists Rights Society (ARS), New York / ADAGP / Man Ray Trust, Paris; *169*, photo by Adam Reich; *170*, © Katharina Sieverding, photo by Ms. Seitz-Gray; *182*, © 1990 Phyllis Christopher; *185*, *187*, © Catherine Opie.

drag racing credits:

Designer, Jody Zellen; Production manager, Alexander Gil; Production facilities courtesy of the Banff Centre for the Arts; opening text, Lyle Ashton Harris in collaboration with B. E. Myers, pages *7–8*, courtesy of Black Care (Community AIDS Research and Education Project) University of Southern California, page *9*, photo by Maggie Hopp, pages *13–14*, Video still from *Sites of Beauty* (1994), a collaborative work by Lyle Ashton Harris and Iké Udé.